REINTERPRETING SOUTHERN HISTORIES

WINNER OF THE JULES AND FRANCES LANDRY AWARD FOR 2020

REINTERPRETING SOUTHERN HISTORIES

ESSAYS IN HISTORIOGRAPHY

Edited by Craig Thompson Friend *&* Lorri Glover

LOUISIANA STATE UNIVERSITY PRESS BATON ROUGE

Published with the assistance of the V. Ray Cardozier Fund

Published by Louisiana State University Press

Manufactured in the United States of America
First printing

Designer: Barbara Neely Bourgoyne
Typeface: Arno Pro
Printer and binder: Sheridan Books

Names: Friend, Craig Thompson, editor. | Glover, Lorri, editor.
Title: Reinterpreting Southern histories : essays in historiography / edited by Craig Thompson Friend and Lorri Glover.
Description: Baton Rouge : Louisiana State University Press, [2020] | Includes bibliographical references and index.
Identifiers: LCCN 2019036673 | ISBN 978-0-8071-7256-8 (cloth) | ISBN 978-0-8071-7346-6 (paperback)
Subjects: LCSH: Southern States—Historiography.
Classification: LCC F208.2 .R45 2020 | DDC 975.0072—dc23
LC record available at https://lccn.loc.gov/2019036673

The paper in this book meets the guidelines for permanence and durability of the Committee on Production Guidelines for Book Longevity of the Council on Library Resources. ♾

CONTENTS

PREFACE

The two predecessors to this volume—*Writing Southern History* (1965) and *Interpreting Southern History* (1987)—were dedicated to scholars who exerted substantial influence over the field of southern history. We continue that tradition, and expand on it, by dedicating this book to three scholars who not only notably contributed to the field but also profoundly shaped our careers and lives: Lawrence J. Nelson, David L. Smiley, and Theda Perdue.

Lawrence J. Nelson (1944–2014) was born in Joliet, Illinois, and earned his PhD in 1972 from the University of Missouri. After brief appointments at Evangel College in Springfield, Missouri, and the University of South Alabama, he made his distinguished career at the University of North Alabama. For thirty years, he captivated, edified, and enriched the lives of UNA students. A specialist in modern American history, he published *King Cotton's Advocate: Oscar G. Johnston and the New Deal* (1999) and *Rumors of Indiscretion: The University of Missouri "Sex Questionnaire" Scandal in the Jazz Age* (2003). He was working on his third book at the time of his untimely death. One of his former students and colleagues, UNA Professor Matthew Schoenbachler, completed the manuscript: *Nikita Khrushchev's Journey into America* (2019).[1]

To say that Nelson's classes were rigorous does not do them justice. The syllabus for the first class that Lorri took, "Interpreting and Understanding the Civil War and Reconstruction," ran twelve single-space pages, besides the schedule

1. Lawrence J. Nelson, *King Cotton's Advocate: Oscar G. Johnston and the New Deal* (Knoxville: University of Tennessee Press, 1999); Nelson, *Rumors of Indiscretion: The University of Missouri "Sex Questionnaire" Scandal in the Jazz Age* (Columbia: University of Missouri Press, 2003); Nelson and Matthew G. Schoenbachler, *Nikita Khrushchev's Journey into America* (Lawrence: University Press of Kansas, 2019).

of classes, and included a glossary, which she—and nearly every student who took Nelson's classes—needed. She knew little, but enough to underline in red on page one: "History 476 is a course in substance and significance, not an exercise in trivia." That was the Nelson way. He was an exemplary intellectual with uncompromising standards and an infectious love for studying history. In class, he mesmerized. He strode into each session and filled every blackboard in the room with book and article citations. As he lectured in his booming voice, using wry asides and words his students did not yet know, he directed them toward a world of ideas, awaiting them at the library. Students adored him, trailed behind him on the way back to his office, honored him with teaching awards. Besides introducing undergraduates to academic history, he taught lessons for a lifetime, including, he always pressed, being a good steward of one's time and talents and opportunities. Every Nelson syllabus contained some variation of this language: "Learn not to recite isolated facts with no meaning; instead learn interpretation, edify and strengthen your mind, and see that history has meaning. The discipline of history (as well as the other disciplines you study) must make a difference in your life. It simply must. All of this will not happen overnight, of course, and it may never happen without considerable study and effort, but we must begin." Dr. Nelson remained Lorri's mentor as long as he lived.

David L. Smiley (1921–2005) taught at Wake Forest University from 1950 until his retirement in 1991. Born in Clarksville, Mississippi, and educated at Baylor University (BA, MA) and the University of Wisconsin (PhD), Smiley was an eccentric but endearing man, wearing a beret on his way to class every day whether by bicycle or on foot, shaking hands with students as he passed by, and challenging them to be critical of the world around them. He was an esteemed teacher, and his course, "History of the Old South," was a campus hallmark, with the lecture hall overflowing on the last session each fall as he sat in a rocking chair and told tales of Christmas on the plantation. Pete Daniel eulogized Smiley for his commitment to "cultivating fallow brains," a dedication for which he won the university's Joe Reinhardt Award for Distinguished Teaching. Smiley wrote *Lion of White Hall: The Life of Cassius M. Clay* (1962), *The South in American History* (1966; coauthored with William B. Hesseltine), and an article on "The Quest for the Central Theme in Southern History" (1972) that was a staple of southern history courses for decades.[2]

From 1979 through 1983, Smiley also taught and advised Craig's fallow brain. Smiley passed on his joy of history: an empathetic reading of the past, a passion for storytelling, the importance of making historical knowledge relevant to contemporary problems, and a playful classroom in which wit and emotion were as critical to learning as deep readings and pensive analysis. In the 1950s, Smiley had led efforts to integrate WFU's student body, challenging students' "Lost Cause and segregationist baggage," as Daniel related. During Craig's undergraduate years, Smiley took on a fraternity's decision to fly the Confederate flag. David Smiley embodied the activist historian, a model from which Craig drew his own interests in public history. Most importantly, however, Smiley taught that it is okay when the study of history touches the soul. A tear would occasionally appear in his eye when he related the tragedies of human enslavement and the disaster of civil war.

Theda Perdue was born in 1949 in McRae, Georgia. She attended Mercer University (AB) and the University of Georgia (MA, PhD), specializing in the history of Native peoples of the Southeast, particularly the Cherokees. She authored eight books on Native southern history, including *Slavery and the Evolution of Cherokee Society, 1540–1865* (1979); *Cherokee Women: Gender and Culture Change, 1700–1835* (1998), which won the Julia Cherry Spruill Award for the best book in southern women's history and the James Mooney Prize for the best book in the anthropology of the South; *"Mixed Blood" Indians: Racial Construction in the Early South* (2003); and *Race and the Atlanta Cotton States Exposition of 1895* (2010). She coauthored or coedited seven other books, including two with her husband, Michael D. Green (1941–2013): *The Cherokee Removal: A Brief History with Documents* (1995) and *The Cherokee Nation and the Trail of Tears* (2007).

2. Pete Daniel, obituary for David L. Smiley, *Journal of Southern History* 71 (May 2005): 527–28; David L. Smiley, *Lion of White Hall: The Life of Cassius M. Clay* (Madison: University of Wisconsin Press, 1960); Smiley, "The Quest for the Central Theme in Southern History," *South Atlantic Quarterly* 71 (Summer 1972): 307–25; Smiley and William B. Hesseltine, *The South in American History*, 2nd ed. (Englewood Cliffs, NJ: Prentice-Hall, 1960).

With Mike, she also coedited a book series with the University of Nebraska Press titled Indians of the Southeast which, according to Christina Snyder, "has been instrumental in creating the thriving field of native southern studies, an intellectual community that has bridged the gap between archaeology and history; profoundly altered the historiographies of Native American and southern history; and influenced other disciplines, including literary studies." Perdue served as president of the Southern Association for Women Historians in 1985–86, the American Society for Ethnohistory in 2001, and the Southern Historical Association in 2011.[3]

But we know her as Theda, and although she finished her career as the Atlanta Distinguished Professor of Southern Studies at the University of North Carolina at Chapel Hill, she was our doctoral advisor and mentor at the University of Kentucky. Well-known as a scholar of the Native South, Theda also served as the Old South historian, demonstrating her breadth of expertise. During her decade at UK (1988–1998), Theda supervised theses and dissertations in southern history, ranging topically from mules in the transformation of southern agriculture to Moravian missionaries to sibling relations among the colonial South Carolina elite and family relations among mid-nineteenth-century Kentucky planters. Beyond her own students, she influenced dozens more historians-in-training, setting a high bar of professional mentoring and inspiring toward excellence every student she encountered. She educated us all with her characteristic forthrightness and generosity. We left the most bruising of meetings—and there were many when writing under her direction—with a smile at her good humor, certainty that she was in our corner, confidence that we would succeed with more hard work and dedication, and knowledge that she would continue to be there for us long after we graduated.

3. Christina Snyder, obituary for Michael David Green, *Journal of Southern History* 80 (February 2014): 250–51; Theda Perdue, *Slavery and the Evolution of Cherokee Society, 1540–1865* (Knoxville: University of Tennessee Press, 1979); Perdue, *Cherokee Women: Gender and Culture Change, 1700–1835* (Lincoln: University of Nebraska Press, 1998); Perdue, *"Mixed Blood" Indians: Racial Construction in the Early South* (Athens: University of Georgia Press, 2003); Perdue, *Race and the Atlanta Cotton States Exposition of 1895* (Athens: University of Georgia Press, 2010); Perdue and Michael D. Green, *The Cherokee Removal: A Brief History with Documents* (New York: Bedford/St. Martin's, 1995); Perdue and Green, *The Cherokee Nation and the Trail of Tears* (New York: Penguin Books, 2007); Indians of the Southeast series, University of Nebraska Press, https://www.nebraskapress.unl.edu/series/indians-of-the-southeast/ (accessed 18 January 2019).

Preface

For their roles in advancing southern historiography and to honor the imprint they left on the lives of their students, us included, this book is dedicated to Lawrence J. Nelson, David L. Smiley, and Theda Perdue.

REINTERPRETING

SOUTHERN

HISTORIES

INTRODUCTION

The State of Southern Historiography

Craig Thompson Friend and Lorri Glover

"The time is coming, if indeed it has not already arrived, when the Southerner will begin to ask himself whether there is really any longer very much point in calling himself a Southerner." With that, C. Vann Woodward opened *The Burden of Southern History* in 1960. It was the American Century: the United States had proven victorious in a "morally impeccable" crusade (as Woodward put it) against fascism, with military, diplomatic, technological, economic, and political successes unparalleled in the country's history. Nationalism seemed to sweep aside regional loyalties and identities, and "the regional historian is likely to be oppressed by a sense of his unimportance." Within two decades, however, Woodward announced the resurrection of regionalism as nationalism wavered. Southern history seemed more relevant than ever as the United States fractured over the Vietnam War and the civil rights movement. In his final revision to his classic study in 1993, Woodward concluded that "Americans might still have something to learn, if they would, from the un-American and ironic experience of the South with history."[1]

From the Progressive-era historians of the early twentieth century to the consensus scholars of the 1940s and 1950s to Woodward and other progressives of the 1950s and 1960s, historians worked to address the simplicity of Victorian historiography's grand narratives and generalities, demonstrating how humans were

1. C. Vann Woodward, *The Burden of Southern History,* 3rd ed. (Baton Rouge: Louisiana State University Press, 1993), 3, 187, 213. The authors thank Douglas R. Egerton and Melissa Walker for their suggestions on the introduction and Sam Klee and Molly Lackey for their assistance in proofreading the collection.

not simply subjects of historical processes. Rather, they viewed the past through a modernist lens which, as philosopher Marshall Berman explained, sought to understand how people could "change the world that is changing them . . . and make it their own." Shaken by the tragedies of two world wars and the Great Depression, historians studied the past to determine what held humans back: the negative effects of traditionalism, urbanism, industrialism, and modernity itself.[2]

Southern history benefited tremendously from the arguments that arose as historians debated why the region seemed so misaligned with modern America. Most importantly, the debates situated scholars such as Woodward to argue that the South, with its unique racial and poverty problems, offered the best opportunity to break free from the grand narratives, or "legends" as he called them, of American "prosperity, progress, invincibility, righteousness, and innocence." Scholars produced so much work on the South that, as Arthur S. Link and Rembert W. Patrick, the editors of *Writing Southern History,* explained in 1965, "Southerners who lament that they are misunderstood or maligned must admit that in any event their region has not been ignored."[3]

Much of the scholarship was reactive to changes within the South. Over the century since the end of the Civil War, southern identity had been evolving and, perhaps, eroding. The Americanization of the South and the southernization of America had been simultaneous processes unfolding since at least the 1912 election of Woodrow Wilson and a Democratic Party–controlled Congress that marked the reemergence of southern political influence on the national level. The language of exceptionalism that accompanied the American Century demonized the South "as an aberrant, inscrutable region: a permanently available and discredited 'other,'" as historian Brian Ward explained in 2014. So, aided by federal programs, southerners worked to make it less aberrant. And scholars sought to

2. Marshall Berman, *All That is Solid Melts into Air: The Experience of Modernity* (New York: Simon & Schuster, 1982), 16.

3. Michael O'Brien, *The Idea of the American South, 1920–1941* (Baltimore: Johns Hopkins University Press, 1979); C. Vann Woodward, *The Strange Career of Jim Crow* (New York: Oxford University Press, 1955); John Hope Franklin, *Racial Equality in America* (Chicago: University of Chicago Press, 1976); C. Vann Woodward, *Thinking Back: The Perils of Writing History* (Baton Rouge: Louisiana State University Press, 1986), 107–8; Arthur S. Link and Rembert W. Patrick, "Preface," in *Writing Southern History: Essays in Historiography in Honor of Fletcher M. Green,* ed. Arthur S. Link and Rembert W. Patrick (Baton Rouge: Louisiana State University Press, 1965), vii.

identify the many ways in which the twentieth-century South was less "southern" and more modern.[4]

In the decade after the publication of *Writing Southern History,* no field underwent more radical reconceptualization and spawned more contentious debates than the study of the seemingly most southern and aberrant of institutions: racial slavery. From Stanley M. Elkins's *Slavery* (1959) to Winthrop D. Jordan's *White Over Black* (1968) to John W. Blassingame's *The Slave Community* (1972), Eugene D. Genovese's *Roll, Jordan, Roll* (1974), Edmund S. Morgan's *American Slavery, American Freedom* (1975), and Herbert G. Gutman's *The Black Family in Slavery and Freedom* (1976), historians debated the origins, character, and consequences of the South's system of enslavement.[5] The stakes seemed so high, in part, because scholars believed their findings informed larger discussions about civil rights and, more generally, the rancorous contests about American society that divided the country in the 1960s and 1970s. But even as these historians wrote their field-defining studies, historiography was changing, challenged by ideas about *how* and *why* historians should work.

Mid-twentieth-century scholars generally saw themselves as making discoveries, following the evidence to a historical reality hidden in the sources. But despite their occasional questioning of American legends of prosperity, progress, invincibility, righteousness, and innocence, most still worked within the grand

4. John Egerton, *The Americanization of Dixie: The Southernization of America* (New York: Harper's Magazine Press, 1974); James C. Cobb, *The South and America since World War II* (New York: Oxford University Press, 2010); Cobb, *Away Down South: A History of Southern Identity* (New York: Oxford University Press, 2005); Brian Ward, ed., "Forum: What's New in Southern Studies—And Why Should We Care?" *Journal of American Studies* 48 (August 2014): 691–733, quote on 692; Mel van Elteren, *Americanism and Americanization: A Critical History of Domestic and Global Influence* (Jefferson, NC: McFarland, 2006), 97–100; Ted Ownby, "'Does a South Still Exist?' A Historian's Critique of the Question," *Crossroads* 5 (Spring 1998): 3–12; Benjamin Schwarz, "The Idea of the South," *The Atlantic,* December 1997, www.theatlantic.com/magazine/archive/1997/12/the-idea-of-the-south/377028/ (accessed 18 January 2019).

5. Stanley M. Elkins, *Slavery: A Problem in American Institutional and Intellectual Life* (Chicago: University of Chicago Press, 1959); Winthrop D. Jordan, *White Over Black: American Attitudes toward the Negro, 1550–1812* (Chapel Hill: University of North Carolina Press, 1968); John W. Blassingame, *The Slave Community: Plantation Life in the Antebellum South* (New York: Oxford University Press, 1972); Eugene D. Genovese, *Roll, Jordan, Roll: The World the Slaves Made* (New York: Pantheon, 1974); Herbert G. Gutman, *The Black Family in Slavery and Freedom, 1750–1925* (New York: Pantheon, 1976); Edmund S. Morgan, *American Slavery, American Freedom: The Ordeal of Colonial Virginia* (New York: W. W. Norton, 1975).

narratives of their Victorian predecessors, drawing the ire of the novelist Ralph Ellison in 1968, for example, when he warned an audience at the Southern Historical Association of their complicity in perpetuating the white patriarchal past. Historiography had lost its credibility, he continued, leaving the American public, particularly black Americans, with "a high sensitivity to the ironies of historical writing and . . . a profound skepticism concerning the validity of most reports about what the past was like."[6]

A new generation of social historians who took seriously Ellison's meaning emerged in the 1970s and 1980s to rewrite entire fields of southern historiography—and not only the history of slavery. Their scholarship became the subject of John B. Boles and Evelyn Thomas Nolen's *Interpreting Southern History* in 1987, a revision and expansion of *Writing Southern History* and the intellectual predecessor to this volume. Boles and Nolen opened: "Probably no field of American history has been more transformed by recent scholarship than the study of the South." In the interim between *Writing Southern History* and *Interpreting Southern History,* the editors explained, "the new research on blacks in particular has created a 'new' Old South that bears little resemblance to the historical portrayals offered only a generation ago." Southern history also "begins earlier and is far more inclusive—free blacks, women, skilled slaves, sharecroppers, factory workers, and urban dwellers—than would have been imaginable only twenty-five years ago." This scholarly blossoming raised an important question: if historical scholarship was simply the historian following a line of reasoning in the evidence to a historical reality, why did so many different realities emerge in the scholarship?[7]

Interpreting Southern History marked a critical moment in southern historiography, even more so than *Writing Southern History.* The 1965 volume had surveyed the scholarly landscape. In 1987, the authors in *Interpreting Southern History* raised difficult questions about the direction of the discipline, including challenging grand narratives created or perpetuated by prominent historians. Harold D. Woodman critiqued the interpretive narrative of continuity and discontinuity of which C. Vann Woodward had become so fond. Drew Gilpin Faust took on

6. James L. W. West III, ed., *Conversations with William Styron* (Jackson: University Press of Mississippi, 1985), 114–44, quote on 126. See also Jason Phillips, "Introduction: The Liars at the Jung Hotel," in *Storytelling, History, and the Postmodern South,* ed. Jason Phillips (Baton Rouge: Louisiana State University Press, 2013), 1–11.

7. John B. Boles and Evelyn Thomas Nolen, eds., *Interpreting Southern History: Historiographical Essays in Honor of Sanford W. Higginbotham* (Baton Rouge: Louisiana State University Press, 1987), vii–viii.

the precapitalist, hierarchical vision that Eugene D. Genovese so successfully imposed on the study of enslavement. And Dan T. Carter questioned the liberal ideological commitment of historians studying Jim Crow because it pushed out of sight the embittered segregationists who lost.[8]

Interpreting Southern History also signaled scholars' return to regionalism as a meaningful influence in American politics, society, and culture. By the 1980s, the power of the southern Bible Belt had given rise to a conservative revolution. From *The Dukes of Hazzard* (1979–1985) to *Designing Women* (1986–1993) to the miniseries *North and South* (1985), television elevated southern history and culture as different from the rest of the nation—but delightfully American, nonetheless. In 1992 Arkansan William Jefferson "Bill" Clinton was elected president. The following year, C. Vann Woodward declared that Americans could indeed learn something from the South.

This new appreciation for regionalism did not last long. As industries moved overseas and the internet expanded, Americans became more aware of the technologies, commerce, and flows in investment, people, and information integrating them into a larger multicultural, global community. The 9/11 attacks on the United States brought home the negative consequences of such globalization. Regionalism seemed naively parochial in such contexts.

After the turn of the twenty-first century, historiography again shifted away from regionalism and pushed beyond parochialism to pursue transnational and global contexts.[9] For the seventeenth and eighteenth centuries, historians, particularly those who embraced the Atlantic turn, chipped away at lingering notions of southern uniqueness or even regional coherence as they buried the teleology of the "thirteen original" colonies. Besides emphasizing deep connections tying the South Carolina Lowcountry to the Caribbean, scholars documented profound differences between the Chesapeake and Lower South for Indigenous, enslaved,

8. Harold D. Woodman, "Economic Reconstruction and the Rise of the New South, 1865–1900," in Boles and Nolen, eds., *Interpreting Southern History*, 254–307; Drew Gilpin Faust, "The Peculiar South Revisited: White Society, Culture, and Politics in the Antebellum Period, 1800–1860," in Boles and Nolen, eds., *Interpreting Southern History*, 78–119; Dan T. Carter, "From Segregation to Integration," in Boles and Nolen, eds., *Interpreting Southern History*, 408–33.

9. To evidence how quickly and dramatically the historiography expanded, only one of twenty-nine essays in John B. Boles, ed., *A Companion to the American South* (Malden, MA: Blackwell Publishing, 2002) mentioned a broader geographical context for study of the region, and that reference was in passing: Randy J. Sparks, "Religion in the Pre–Civil War South" (156–75).

and colonizing peoples. Analyses of global trafficking of "southern" commodities, including cotton, added to new understandings of the southern provinces as immersed in Atlantic and worldwide commercial networks.[10] Ethnohistorians further propelled the move toward #VastEarlyAmerica (a mid-2010s historiographical concept that, according to Karin Wulf, "expresses the capaciousness of early America—the geographically expansive, multi-disciplinary study of the early modern world, Atlantic and beyond") by charting the persistent and sometimes overwhelming power of Native nations and empires in the southwestern interior and the Ohio Valley, merging southern history with that of the American West.[11]

Historians of slavery adopted the Atlantic turn and pursued interdisciplinarity, using diaspora studies, Africana studies, and new technology-based resources such as slave trade databases to uncover rich and complex histories that transcended the eastern seaboard of North America and old questions about southern enslavement. Scholars working on the nineteenth and twentieth centuries incorporated global, oceanic, and hemispheric approaches to studies of immigration, politics, religion, and even the Civil War—a series of transnational interventions that subsumed the South into ever larger contexts.[12]

By the early twenty-first century, such sweeping reconsiderations of the where and the when of the South led historians to openly question whether there was

10. See, for example, Matthew Mulcahy, *Hubs of Empire: The Southeastern Lowcountry and British Caribbean* (Baltimore: Johns Hopkins University Press, 2014); Marisa J. Fuentes, *Dispossessed Lives: Enslaved Women, Violence, and the Archive* (Philadelphia: University of Pennsylvania Press, 2016); Philip D. Morgan, *Slave Counterpoint: Black Culture in the Eighteenth-Century Chesapeake and Lowcountry* (Chapel Hill: University of North Carolina Press, 1998); Sven Beckert, *Empire of Cotton: A Global History* (New York: Alfred A. Knopf, 2014). For analysis on this framework, see Peter A. Coclanis, "Atlantic World or Atlantic/World?" *William and Mary Quarterly* 63 (October 2006): 725–42.

11. Karin Wulf, "The Past is Always Urgent," Vast Early America, http://karinwulf.com/about-vast-early-america/ (accessed 15 June 2019). For examples of the expansion of southern geographies and methods, see Juliana Barr, *Peace Came in the Form of a Woman: Indians and Spaniards in the Texas Borderlands* (Chapel Hill: University of North Carolina Press, 2007); Elizabeth A. Fenn, *Encounters at the Heart of the World: A History of the Mandan People* (New York: Hill and Wang, 2014); Christina Snyder, *Slavery in Indian Country: The Changing Face of Captivity in Early America* (Cambridge: Harvard University Press, 2010); Claudio Saunt, "Go West: Mapping Early American Historiography," *William and Mary Quarterly* 65 (October 2008): 745–78.

12. Exemplary works include Jennifer L. Morgan, *Laboring Women: Reproduction and Gender in New World Slavery* (Philadelphia: University of Pennsylvania Press, 2004); Sowande' M. Mustakeem, *Slavery at Sea: Terror, Sex, and Sickness in the Middle Passage* (Urbana: University of Illinois Press, 2016); John Thornton, *Africa and Africans in the Making of the Atlantic World, 1400–1800* (New York: Cambridge University Press, 1992). The Trans-Atlantic Slave Trade Database can be accessed at www.slavevoyages.org

any such thing as "southern" history beyond the anomaly of the mid-nineteenth century. Perusals of programs from the annual meetings of the Southern Historical Association and the tables of contents and book review listings from the *Journal of Southern History* evidence the centrifugal acceleration of the field, with topics spinning around an unasked but implicit question: exactly what is southern history in the twenty-first century?[13]

Our conclusion that the present state of southern history is decidedly postmodern will not be well received by those historians who imagine that postmodernism exerted a greater impact on literature and the social sciences than on history. But make no mistake: postmodernism arrived in southern historiography, early and clearly. By the late 1980s, southern historiography had already begun to shift toward a postmodern perspective that posited that evidence cannot relate the past but only interpretations of the past. As Drew Gilpin Faust concluded in her essay in *Interpreting Southern History,* "The choice between alternative interpretations of a body of data is often a theoretical rather than an empirical problem," and the inability to find a common "framework of analysis" impeded historians' ability "to assess the real meaning of the facts we have been so assiduously collecting."[14]

Of course, southern historians did not reject objective facts as the basis for critical analysis. But other veins of postmodern thought reshaped the field. A New Southern studies emerged that pursued postmodern, interdisciplinary methodologies, finding a home at the University of Georgia Press. Even among works that fell outside the New Southern studies, postmodern influences abounded: a questioning of narratives (including a general breakdown in narrative linearity, particularly the unquestioned assumption of liberal progress about which Dan T. Carter complained in 1987), a heavy and often Marxist critique of capitalism, diversification of voices and perspectives, self-reflexive analyses of the structures

(accessed 18 January 2019). Wendy Warren offered a powerful reminder of the scope of slavery in colonial North America in *New England Bound: Slavery and Colonization in Early America* (New York: Liveright, 2016). For the broadening of analysis of the Civil War, see Don H. Doyle, *The Cause of All Nations: An International History of the American Civil War* (New York: Basic Books, 2014); Patrick J. Kelly, "The European Revolutions of 1848 and the Transnational Turn in Civil War History," *Journal of the Civil War Era* 4 (September 2014): 431–43.

13. For the evolution of the *Journal of Southern History,* see John B. Boles, "My Life with the *Journal,*" *Journal of Southern History* 84 (February 2018): 7–38. See also "Forum: Commemorating Seventy-Five Years of the *Journal of Southern History,*" *Journal of Southern History* 75 (August 2009): 531–766.

14. Faust, "The Peculiar South Revisited," 119.

and elements of the discipline as much as factual content, and an emphasis on orality as found in podcasts, digital media, television, and film.[15]

The questioning of narratives, in particular, reshaped southern historiography. In 1997, Joel Williamson asked whether "It might be that we in America will decide that race, after all, is not very important." If race, the central story of the South, could be questioned as a narrative framework, what else might fall? Political and cultural reactions to the presidency of Barack Obama laid to rest any imagining of a postracial America. A new generation of African American scholars began dismantling the narrative of southern race relations constructed by (mostly white) twentieth-century historians, undertaking more complex and nuanced explorations of intersectionality and uncovering how ideas about race operated with constructs of gender, sexuality, class, and disability to create systems of power and oppression. Race itself has been complicated by the inclusion of Native southerners, long lost in southern historians' myopic focus on whiteness and blackness. In her 2012 presidential address to the Southern Historical Association, Theda Perdue called on scholars to stop overlooking Indians in southern history and pointed out how "Indians provide us with an opportunity to examine different experiences and perspectives in the history of the South, ones that do not follow the standard narrative but instead promise both to challenge and to enrich it."[16]

In fact, the deconstruction of previously unquestioned binaries—white/black,

15. See, for example, Phillips, ed., *Storytelling, History, and the Postmodern South*; Jon Smith, "What the New Southern Studies Does Now," *Journal of American Studies* 49 (November 2015): 861–70; The New Southern Studies, University of Georgia Press, www.ugapress.org/index.php/series/TNSS (accessed 18 January 2019). Edward L. Ayers has been at the forefront of digital history in Virginia from the beginning of the digital age, starting with The Valley of the Shadow project (www.valley.lib.uva.edu) and including the Digital Scholarship Lab (www.dsl.richmond.edu) and the web series Backstory (www.backstoryradio.org), all accessed 18 January 2019. Anya Jabour served as a historical advisor for the PBS series *Mercy Street* and blogged for the series at www.pbs.org/mercy-street/blogs/mercy-street-revealed/category/anya-jabour/ (accessed 18 January 2019). Southern historians have even seen their work turned into films. STX Entertainment acquired Victoria E. Bynum's *The Free State of Jones: Mississippi's Longest Civil War* (Chapel Hill: University of North Carolina Press, 2001) for *Free State of Jones,* directed by Gary Ross, screenplay by Gary Ross (STX Entertainment, 2016). For analysis and teaching approaches to film, see Brenda E. Stevenson, "Filming Black Voices and Stories: Slavery on America's Screens," *Journal of the Civil War Era* 8 (September 2018): 488–520. For television, see Lisa Hinrichsen, Gina Caison, and Stephanie Rountree, eds., *Small-Screen Souths: Region, Identity, and the Cultural Politics of Television* (Baton Rouge: Louisiana State University Press, 2017).

16. Joel Williamson, "Wounds Not Scars: Lynching, the National Consciousness, and the American Historian," *Journal of American History* 83 (March 1997): 1221–53, quote on 1252; Theda Perdue, "The Legacy of Indian Removal," *Journal of Southern History* 78 (February 2012): 3–36, quote on 36. See also

male/female, heterosexual/homosexual—became part of postmodern southern historiography. Feminist scholars led the way, illuminating not only the patriarchal structure of the southern past but also the persistence of patriarchy within the academy. Interplay between the historical past and the historical profession propelled the creation of the Southern Association for Women Historians in 1970. In 1984 the Julia Cherry Spruill Prize became the first book award designated for southern women's scholarship. Four years later, the SAWH held its first conference, designed to "reflect the diversity of women's experiences and to document the history of women from a wide variety of racial, class, and ethnic backgrounds."[17]

Along with African American history, women's and gender history stood at the vanguard of postmodern shifts in southern historiography. Three decades after she published *The Southern Lady* (1970), Anne Firor Scott praised the theoretical sophistication that emerged in postmodern gender studies, emphasizing that "how historians define history and what they choose to write about are also in part a function of their cultural milieu and the concepts and language available to them."[18] Social historians laid the foundation for uncovering southern women's

---

Andrew K. Frank and Kristofer Ray, "Guest Editors' Introduction: Indians as Southerners; Southerners as Indians: Rethinking the History of a Region," *Native South* 10 (2017): vi–xiv.

17. Catherine Clinton, "The Southern Social Network," *Journal of Southern History* 83 (February 2017): 7–36; Anne Firor Scott, "Introduction to the Norton Paperback Edition," in Julia Cherry Spruill, *Women's Life and Work in the Southern Colonies* (New York: W. W. Norton, 1998), xii; The First Southern Conference on Women's History conference program, Southern Association for Women Historians, Converse College, 10–11 June 1988, 3, SAWH Archives, http://thesawh.org/sawh-archives/ (accessed 18 January 2019). The American Historical Association has a long-standing record of publishing studies about gender in the academic workplace, including Robert B. Townsend, "Gender and Success in Academia: More from the Historians' Career Paths Survey," *Perspectives on History* 51 (January 2013): 15–18. Regarding sexual harassment, see "Results of the 2018 AHA Survey on Sexual Harassment," *Perspectives on History,* 27 September 2018, https://www.historians.org/publications-and-directories/perspectives-on-history/october-2018/results-of-the-2018-aha-survey-on-sexual-harassment (accessed 18 January 2019). For the gender gap in faculty salaries across disciplines, see Joshua Hatch, "Gender Pay Gap Persists Across Faculty Ranks," *Chronicle of Higher Education,* 22 March 2017, https://www.chronicle.com/article/Gender-Pay-Gap-Persists-Across/239553 (accessed 18 January 2019). See also "Diversity in Academe: The Gender Issue," *Chronicle of Higher Education,* 29 October 2012, https://www.chronicle.com/specialreport/Diversity-in-Academe-The/110 (accessed 18 January 2019).

18. Anne Firor Scott, *The Southern Lady: From Pedestal to Politics, 1830–1930* (Chicago: University of Chicago Press, 1970); Scott, "Unfinished Business," in Michele Gillespie and Catherine Clinton, eds., *Taking Off the White Gloves: Southern Women and Women Historians* (Columbia: University of Missouri Press, 1998), 111–22, quote on 111.

lives with explorations of material conditions, community and family structures, relationships between men and women, and intersections with southern race relations and class dynamics. The relationship between feminist activism and women's history focused attention on social constructions of gender, pushing against assumptions of essential and universal gender roles. Masculinity studies developed, too, exposing how all gender differences were constructed in specific historical contexts.[19]

Drawing from these historiographical developments, postmodern scholars began to ask about representation, symbolism, and the self, opening new inquiries into the body, sexual activity and fluidity, emotions, historical memory, and intersectionality in gendered identities. Like the feminist scholars who drove the expansion of women's history in the 1970s and 1980s, scholars of the Queer South began uncovering histories buried by nineteenth- and twentieth-century scholars and archivists. As with much postmodern work, distinctions between scholarship and activism blurred. Queer scholars appropriated many of the advances in women's and gender history, especially the idea that queer voices should not be considered historically invisible but be viewed instead as sites of contest and possibility. They demand recognition of a Queer South and dismantling of cis-sexist heteropatriarchal structures of historiographical oppression that have worked to hide that history.[20]

The expansion of archives, specifically the digitization of sources, aided reexamination of categories and incorporation of more voices. Ulrich B. Phillips recognized in 1903 that the future of southern history lay in the availability of primary sources, but he never imagined the accessibility that would come with computers, the internet, and digital archives. Technology transformed—and in

19. Influential works include Laura F. Edwards, *Gendered Strife and Confusion: The Political Culture of Reconstruction* (Urbana: University of Illinois Press, 1997); Thavolia Glymph, *Out of the House of Bondage: The Transformation of the Plantation Household* (New York: Cambridge University Press, 2008); Stephanie McCurry, *Masters of Small Worlds: Yeoman Households, Gender Relations, and the Political Culture of the Antebellum South Carolina Low Country* (New York: Oxford University Press, 1995); Nina Silber, *The Romance of Reunion: Northerners and the South, 1865–1900* (Chapel Hill: University of North Carolina Press, 1993); Bertram Wyatt-Brown, *Southern Honor: Ethics and Behavior in the Old South* (New York: Oxford University Press, 1982); Wyatt-Brown, *The Shaping of Southern Culture: Honor, Grace, and War, 1760s–1880s* (Chapel Hill: University of North Carolina Press, 2001).

20. For examples of postmodernism's influence on women's and gender history, see Riché Richardson, *Black Masculinity and the U.S. South: From Uncle Tom to Gangsta* (Athens: University of Georgia Press, 2007); Sasha Turner, *Contested Bodies: Pregnancy, Childrearing, and Slavery in Jamaica* (Philadelphia: University of Pennsylvania Press, 2017). For queer history, see Michael P. Bibler, *Cotton's Queer*

some ways democratized—research and teaching. Long trips to distant archives became increasingly replaced with interrogations of digitized and born-digital primary source collections. Scholars could conduct in minutes quantitative analyses that used to take weeks or months. Cellphone cameras and screen-grabs allowed researchers to capture hundreds of documents an hour.[21] Collaborative work became quicker and easier—not to say, quick and easy—for writing teams, including the partners who cowrote the essays in this collection.

As historians diversified the voices from the past, many embedded social justice work into their intellectual pursuits. In itself, reevaluation of the southern economy and its labor forces might appear to have been just another scholarly exercise. But employing the concept of "racial capitalism," the latest critique became part of a scholarly activism concerned with legacies of enslavement at colleges and universities, exploitation of incarcerated labor, human trafficking in the twenty-first century, the rights of laboring immigrants, debates about reparations for the descendants of enslaved people, and other social justice issues. In locating southern history's lingering appeal, Ted Ownby concluded that students want to study the South "so they can fix problems," and the region provides them a microcosm of social and economic problems that face the nation and world. The New Southern studies, probably the most politically charged field in southern historiography, positions the South as central to unpacking the idea of American exceptionalism by, as Ownby explained, "challenging past questions and assumptions, exploring through multiple perspectives, and taking seriously global interconnectedness," all of which carry contemporary political meanings.[22]

Relations: Same-Sex Intimacy and the Literature of the Southern Plantation, 1936–1968 (Charlottesville: University of Virginia Press, 2009); Benjamin E. Wise, *William Alexander Percy: The Curious Life of a Mississippi Planter and Sexual Freethinker* (Chapel Hill: University of North Carolina Press, 2012); E. Patrick Johnson, "Southern (Dis)Comfort: Creating and Crafting Homosex in the Black South," in *Creating and Consuming the American South,* ed. Martyn Bone, Brian Ward, and William A. Link (Gainesville: University Press of Florida, 2015), 97–116; Charles E. Morris III, "Introduction: 'Travelin' Thru' the Queer South," *Southern Communication Journal* 74 (July–September 2009): 233–42.

21. John David Smith, "The Historian as Archival Advocate: Ulrich Bonnell Phillips and the Records of Georgia and the South," *American Archivist* 52 (Summer 1989): 320–31. For a recent example of digitization and democratization, see the crowd-source database on fugitives from slavery, "Freedom on the Move," at www.freedomonthemove.org (accessed 25 February 2019).

22. Cedric J. Robinson, *Black Marxism: The Making of the Black Radical Tradition* (1983; repr., Chapel Hill, 2000), 2–3; Robin D. G. Kelley, "Foreword," in Robinson, *Black Marxism,* xiii; Jacquelyn Dowd Hall, "Mobilizing Memory: Broadening Our View of the Civil Rights Movement," *Chronicle of Higher Education,* 27 July 2001, https://www.chronicle.com/article/Broadening-Our-View-of-the/1847 (accessed

Although a rough consensus that rejects southern and American exceptionalism emerged in the twenty-first century, historians cannot ignore the fact that southerners and northerners, Americans and non-Americans argued about southern distinctiveness, and those fights (the Civil War being the most evident and bloody) shaped national politics and marked people's lives. Those arguments drove historiography, too, as many twentieth-century historians obsessed over finding the South's "central theme"—the singular qualifier of "southern" identity.[23]

Postmodernism, then, with its suspicion of narratives, provided another way to think about southern distinctiveness by placing memory at the heart of southern identity: that is, the incessant construction of the southern self through often poorly recalled or even purposefully distorted remembrance—mythologizing. Mythologies surround the region's Indigenous peoples, its religiosity, and even its civil rights icons. But the most persistent mythology has always centered on the Confederate South and the political deployment and often violent defensiveness of Confederate symbols, from the battle flags raised in response to *Brown v. Board of Education* to the 2017 Unite the Right rally in Charlottesville and its deadly aftermath.[24] Upon dismantling the Confederate monuments in New Orleans in 2017, Mayor Mitchell Landrieu concluded that the statues were "not just innocent remembrances of a benign history. These monuments purposefully celebrate a fictional, sanitized Confederacy; ignoring the death, ignoring the enslavement,

---

18 January 2019); Ted Ownby, "The New Southern Studies and Rethinking the Question, 'Is There Still a South?'" *Journal of American Studies* 49 (November 2015): 871–78, quotes on 874–76. For examples of historians employing the past to address contemporary social problems, see Historians against Slavery, http://www.historiansagainstslavery.org/main/ (accessed 18 January 2019); and the Unpaid Labor Project, https://www.unpaidlabor.com/ (accessed 18 January 2019).

23. Ulrich B. Phillips, "The Central Theme of Southern History," *American Historical Review* 34 (October 1928): 30–43; W. J. Cash, *The Mind of the South* (New York: Alfred A. Knopf, 1941); Frank E. Vandiver, ed., *The Idea of the South: Pursuit of a Central Theme* (Chicago: University of Chicago Press, 1964); David L. Smiley, "The Quest for the Central Theme in Southern History," *South Atlantic Quarterly* 71 (Summer 1972): 307–25; George A. Levesque, "Biracialism, the 'Central Theme' Thesis, and the Emergence of Southern Sectionalism," *Journal of Black Studies* 6 (December 1975): 158–74; John Shelton Reed, "The Central Theme," *Southern Cultures* 5 (Winter 1999): 96–99.

24. Transformational studies of commemoration and memory include Gaines M. Foster, *Ghosts of the Confederacy: Defeat, the Lost Cause, and the Emergence of the New South, 1865–1913* (New York: Oxford University Press, 1987); David W. Blight, *Race and Reunion: The Civil War in American Memory* (Cambridge: Harvard University Press, 2001); Karen L. Cox, *Dixie's Daughters: The United Daughters of the Confederacy and the Preservation of Confederate Culture* (Gainesville: University Press of Florida, 2003); Bruce E. Baker, *What Reconstruction Meant: Historical Memory in the American South* (Charlottesville: University of Virginia Press, 2007).

and the terror that it actually stood for." Destruction of and debates over Confederate monuments became the most public of postmodernism's impact on southern history and historiography. This civic reconsideration of statues honoring the Confederacy was informed by scholarship that interrogated the intersection of history and memory, advanced social justice activism, questioned narratives, and diversified voices. Within and outside the academy, we thus see a new appreciation of how history, once considered in opposition to memory, can be viewed as a system that forgets, distorts, and suppresses the past.[25]

Southern historiography since the publication of *Interpreting Southern History* in 1987 has been driven by disruption and disquietude, with scholars upending long-held narratives and, in some cases, creating such cacophony that it is difficult to draw thematic coherence from the diversity of voices, perspectives, and memories. The contributors to this collection experienced the challenge of discerning historiographical themes for familiar topics, a difficulty arising partially from the postmodern resistance to overarching synthesis. As scholars use new methodologies and technologies, incorporate diverse viewpoints and voices, and ask fresh questions to reinvigorate and expand southern historiography, they contest the idea of a coherent southern history.

Today we live in another era of intense and tension-producing nationalism. The United States remains engaged in a crusade against terrorism, sold to the public as morally impeccable but rife with moral quandaries. Symbols of nationalism—the American flag and the national anthem—are fiercely contested sites of patriotism. Regionalism, particularly southern regionalism, seems to have faded under the forces of consumerism, popular culture, and social media. The central geographical divide in America today is not regional but urban versus rural. And so, to echo Woodward, some scholars question if the time is coming when the southern historian must ask if there is any point in identifying as a historian of the South. Some conclude the time has already arrived. Perhaps.[26]

25. W. Fitzhugh Brundage, "Contentious and Collected: Memory's Future in Southern History," *Journal of Southern History* 75 (August 2009): 751–66; Tara McPherson, *Reconstructing Dixie: Race, Gender, and Nostalgia in the Imagined South* (Durham: Duke University Press, 2003); Jacquelyn Dowd Hall, "The Long Civil Rights Movement and the Political Uses of the Past," *Journal of American History* 91 (March 2005): 1233–63; Mitchell Landrieu, "We Can't Walk Away from This Truth," *The Atlantic,* 23 May 2017, www.theatlantic.com/politics/archive/2017/05/we-cant-walk-away-from-this-truth/527721/ (accessed 18 January 2019).

26. Laura F. Edwards suggested that the South was never distinctive in "Southern History as U.S. History," *Journal of Southern History* 75 (August 2009): 533–64. See also Numan V. Bartley, *A History*

Collectively, the essayists in this volume point out a myriad of ways in which the South was distinctive across more than four hundred years of history, but just as significant are the interconnections and immersions with the Atlantic World, the Western Hemisphere, the nation, and global markets, ideologies, and human experiences. One thing is abundantly clear: it is no longer viable to reflexively portray the South—at any time in its complicated history—as separate from the nation or the world. The literature on the histories of the many Souths is far richer for the questions asked in recent decades about the parameters, the essence, and even the existence of southern history. The narratives of social history—race, gender, and class—remain but are energized with a new dynamism as postmodern scholars interrogate the premises of those narratives, diversified voices, expanded archives, and enlarged geographical contexts.

In addition to studies that transformed academic history, writ large, historians of the South also produced scholarship that contributed to public use of history at rallies and protests, on social media, in political activism, and through popular culture. The first two decades of the twenty-first century served up forceful reminders of how memories of the southern past were and still are often deeply distorted and fiercely contested, sometimes with deadly results. As historian Julian Maxwell Hayter explained, the violent eruption in Charlottesville in August 2017 "reshaped the conversation about history, exposing the disparity among historical truth, historical interpretation and mythology." As scholars of the South, we need to continue to work to separate truth from interpretation from myth. Fortunately for historians, memory is the raw material we use to pursue our craft: the written memories of archival sources, the personal memories of oral histories, the physical memories of monuments and material culture, and the memories of memories related in historiography. And, thank goodness, much work remains to reinterpret the many histories of the American South.[27]

---

of the South. Vol. 11, *The New South, 1945–1980* (Baton Rouge: Louisiana State University Press, 1995), 450, which argued that the post–World War II South lost much of its distinctive character and regional identity due to Americanization.

27. Julian Maxwell Hayter, "Charlottesville Was About Memory, Not Monuments," *Washingtonpost.com*, 10 August 2018, https://www.washingtonpost.com/news/made-by-history/wp/2018/08/10/charlottesville-was-about-memory-not-monuments/?utm_term=.b4d74e18e5cf (accessed 18 January 2019). See also Hawes Spencer, *Summer of Hate: Charlottesville, USA* (Charlottesville: University of Virginia Press, 2018); Louis P. Nelson and Claudrena N. Harold, eds., *Charlottesville 2017: The Legacy of Race and Inequity* (Charlottesville: University of Virginia Press, 2018).

NATIVE HOMELANDS, IMPERIAL RIVALRIES, AND CONTESTED LEGACIES OF THE EARLY SOUTH

Alejandra Dubcovsky and Daniel H. Usner

In the 2010s, statues commemorating the Confederacy and its defenders galvanized a national conversation about southern history. The fervor, violence, and intensity with which the Civil War and its memory have been debated bring to mind William Faulkner's all-too-famous line about life in Mississippi: "The past is never dead. It is not even past." Southern history remains very much alive in how America and Americans imagine themselves—in the stories they long to tell and in those they wish to forget. But in this past that is also present, southern history is often conflated with the Confederacy and its legacy. Laura F. Edwards powerfully argued that: "Confederate statues present a simplified view of both Southern history and United States history. Southern history cannot be represented through Confederate soldiers, and neither the South nor the nation was ever as unified as many like to think."[1]

Encompassing a chronology that lasted far longer than the years from the Civil War to the present, the centuries before South Carolina seceded should not and, in fact, do not collapse neatly into the background. The early South and its borderlands offer a different framework from which to think about a region and time too often bound by a nationalist chronology and geography. Examining the vast temporal and physical parameters of southern history is not simply about adding

1. William Faulkner, *Requiem for a Nun* (1951; repr., New York: Random House, 1994), 77; Laura F. Edwards, "Why Confederate Statues Fail To Represent Southern History," *The Hill*, 23 August 2017, http://thehill.com/blogs/pundits-blog/civil-rights/347630-why-confederate-statues-fail-to-represent-southern-history (accessed 18 January 2019).

breadth and diversity to an already booming field. It requires reckoning with the past in ways that break the teleology of the Civil War and the Confederacy. In other words, the early South and its borderlands introduce much-needed contingency into a crucible for the American past, its meaning, and memorialization.

When did southern history start? Since the 1990s, the answers to that seemingly innocuous question have shifted and multiplied. The founding of Jamestown in 1607 remains an important anchor in the field. But starting in 1607 increasingly seems predicated on, at the very least, understanding the deeper roots of English colonial projects. In *The Jamestown Project* (2007), Karen Ordahl Kupperman discussed English experiences in the Ottoman Empire and in Africa before venturing across the Atlantic.[2] She showed how Jamestown was far from the only or earliest English colonial project; Jamestown, she argued, is best understood as part of a larger series of colonial ventures that included Ireland, the West Indies, Guiana, and Newfoundland. April Lee Hatfield's 2004 *Atlantic Virginia* also extended the history of the Virginia colony, emphasizing both its local and imperial connections, situating the colony in the larger Atlantic World.[3]

The impulse to expand the geographical and temporal extent of English colonization also became evident in Peter C. Mancall's *Hakluyt's Promise* (2007). This masterful work examined the careful and attentive ways English promoters, such as Richard Hakluyt, envisioned and argued for English colonization of North America.[4] Like Kupperman and Hatfield, Mancall situated Jamestown as part of a larger English imperial project that began earlier than 1607 and included more than just Virginia.

Historians have long recognized that the English were latecomers to the Americas, playing catch-up to the Spanish and French empires that had explored and attempted to colonize the region at least a century prior. What shifted in early twenty-first-century historiography is not the awareness of this multi-imperial competition for the early South, but the importance afforded to those earlier,

2. Karen Ordahl Kupperman, *The Jamestown Project* (Cambridge: Harvard University Press, 2007). See also Robert Appelbaum and John Wood Sweet, eds., *Envisioning an English Empire: Jamestown and the Making of the North Atlantic World* (Philadelphia: University of Pennsylvania Press, 2005); Jean B. Russo and J. Elliott Russo, *Planting an Empire: The Early Chesapeake in British North America* (Baltimore: Johns Hopkins University Press, 2012).

3. April Lee Hatfield, *Atlantic Virginia: Intercolonial Relations in the Seventeenth Century* (Philadelphia: University of Pennsylvania Press, 2004).

4. Peter C. Mancall, *Hakluyt's Promise: An Elizabethan's Obsession for an English America* (New Haven: Yale University Press, 2007).

non-Anglo colonial ventures. Spanish and French colonies were not merely featured in brief introductory remarks, only to be quickly brushed aside to explain the truly important—meaning English—colonization. Scholars such as Paul E. Hoffman, Amy Turner Bushnell, Jane G. Landers, Daniel H. Usner, Jennifer M. Spear, and Gwendolyn Midlo Hall revolutionized the study of the early South by centering the history of French and Spanish colonies. Mining Spanish and French archives in both Europe and North America, authors uncovered colonial projects that took shape long before English settlement and deeply informed how English colonization unfolded.[5]

Their early South began not in 1607 but in the sixteenth century with Spanish exploration of La Florida. Hoffman, Bushnell, and Landers helped reconstruct a colonial project rooted as much in the local intricacies of the region as it was connected to earlier Spanish imperial projects in the Caribbean, Catholic missionization endeavors, and the Atlantic slave trade. Formally founded in 1565, La Florida reshaped regional geopolitics through alliances, trade, and disease. Paul Kelton's 2007 work on epidemics showed the devastating impact of European germs and illnesses on Native communities. He argued that the rapid demographic decline in the region should not be studied in isolation. Disease and the forces of colonialism such as enslavement, violence, and displacement were concomitants: "Epidemics should be seen not as the inevitable consequence of biological force but instead as contingent on the type of colonial system."[6] In short, understanding basic demographic change in the early South required the inclusion of Spanish colonialism.

Twenty-first-century scholarship brought these intricate Spanish stories out of the confines of the archive and into the classroom. In a joint effort, J. Michael

5. Paul E. Hoffman, *A New Andalucia and a Way to the Orient: The American Southeast during the Sixteenth Century* (Baton Rouge: Louisiana State University Press, 1990); Hoffman, *Florida's Frontiers* (Bloomington: Indiana University Press, 2002); Amy Turner Bushnell, *Situado and Sabana: Spain's Support System for the Presidio and Mission Provinces of Florida* (New York: American Museum of Natural History, 1994); Jane G. Landers, *Black Society in Spanish Florida* (Urbana: University of Illinois Press, 1999); Gwendolyn Midlo Hall, *Africans in Colonial Louisiana: The Development of Afro-Creole Culture in the Eighteenth Century* (Baton Rouge: Louisiana State University Press, 1992); Daniel H. Usner Jr., *Indians, Settlers, and Slaves in a Frontier Exchange Economy: The Lower Mississippi Valley before 1783* (Chapel Hill: University of North Carolina Press, 1992); Jennifer M. Spear, *Race, Sex, and Social Order in Early New Orleans* (Baltimore: Johns Hopkins University Press, 2009).

6. Paul Kelton, *Epidemics and Enslavement: Biological Catastrophe in the Native Southeast, 1492–1715* (Lincoln: University of Nebraska Press, 2007), xxii.

Francis and Kathleen M. Kole translated and transcribed an excellent anthology of documents relating to the 1597 Guale Rebellion in Florida.[7] J. Michael Francis launched a collaborative and multinational digital project, La Florida: The Interactive Digital Archive of the Americas, which attempts to document the lives of all colonists in La Florida. Scholars created a flurry of new editions and translations of both canonical and unusual Spanish and French sources describing early southern colonization. For every individually curated account, such as Joseph M. Hall Jr.'s testimony of a Spanish soldier in 1611, there are also larger digital initiatives.[8] For example, Documenting the American South which is hosted and supported by the University of North Carolina at Chapel Hill and the Slave Societies Digital Archive directed by Jane G. Landers and hosted by Vanderbilt University (which curates and maintains documents related to Africans and African-descendant people all over the world, including Spanish Florida) are representative efforts that provide free access to colonial deeds, records, maps, wills, and narratives. Interdisciplinary scholarship, including Anna Brickhouse's *The Unsettlement of America* (2014), Michele Currie Navakas's *Liquid Landscapes* (2017), and Nancy O. Gallman's 2017 dissertation, "Blood & Property," centered these diverse sources, such as literary texts, maps, and laws.[9] Their works unsettled traditional paradigms for framing colonial history, enabling diverse, not exclusively Anglo, voices to shape the study, research, and teaching of the early South.

7. J. Michael Francis and Kathleen M. Kole, *Murder and Martyrdom in Spanish Florida: Don Juan and the Guale Uprising of 1597*, Anthropological Paper No. 95 (New York: American Museum of Natural History, 2011).

8. J. Michael Francis, La Florida: The Interactive Digital Archive of the Americas, http://laflorida.org/ (accessed 18 January 2019). For some examples of other documentary projects, see Luís Jerónimo de Oré, *Account of the Martyrs in the Provinces of La Florida*, ed. Raquel Chang-Rodríguez and Nancy Vogeley (Albuquerque: University of New Mexico Press, 2017); Joseph M. Hall Jr., "Glimpses of Roanoke, Visions of New Mexico, and Dreams of Empire in the Mixed-Up Memories of Gerónimo de la Cruz," *William and Mary Quarterly* 72 (April 2015): 323–50; Rolena Adorno and Patrick Charles Pautz, *Alvar Núñez Cabeza De Vaca: His Account, His Life, and the Expedition of Pánfilo De Narváez*. 3 vols. (Lincoln: University of Nebraska Press, 1999); Charles Bennett, *Laudonnière & Fort Caroline: History and Documents* (Tuscaloosa: University of Alabama Press, 2001).

9. Documenting the American South, https://docsouth.unc.edu/ (accessed 18 January 2019); Slave Societies Digital Archives, https://www.vanderbilt.edu/esss/ (accessed 18 January 2019); Anna Brickhouse, *The Unsettlement of America: Translation, Interpretation, and the Story of Don Luis de Velasco, 1560–1945* (New York: Oxford University Press, 2014); Michele Currie Navakas, *Liquid Landscape: Geography and Settlement at the Edge of Early America* (Philadelphia: University of Pennsylvania Press, 2017); Nancy O. Gallman, "Blood & Property: Spanish Law and Native Justice in the Florida-Georgia Borderlands, 1784–1821" (PhD diss., University of California, Davis, 2017).

French sources and accounts have also played a prominent role in diversifying the region's history. From Daniel H. Usner's and Gwendolyn Midlo Hall's 1992 groundbreaking works on the Lower Mississippi to Jennifer M. Spear's 2008 careful analysis of Louisiana's racial formations, and from Shannon Lee Dawdy's *Building the Devil's Empire* (2008) to Cécile Vidal's edited collection, *Louisiana* (2013), colonial experiences in and near present-day Louisiana encompassed the variety and asymmetrical struggles comprising the early South. John T. McGrath inserted French colonization into the Southeast. Like Mancall's work on English colonization and Hoffman's descriptions of Spanish Florida, McGrath's *The French in Early Florida* (2000) showed the long, transatlantic history of this French colonial project.[10]

Spanish, French, and English colonization efforts in the early South were interconnected ventures. Far from isolated projects, they built and fed off each other. In his overview of early America, Daniel K. Richter described a layered world where "earlier strata of society, culture, and politics" came to "mold the nation's current contours."[11] His analogy works nicely for the early, multi-imperial South where English, French, and Spanish waves of colonization and settlement crashed and ebbed against each other.

If the Spanish Crown rushed to expel French Huguenots, and English Carolinians wrestled with their Catholic neighbors, it was the region's Indigenous inhabitants and settlers who expertly manipulated competing European powers. In his excellent study of sixteenth-century Florida, Jonathan DeCoster showed how the Timucuas, a powerful Native group, employed French and Spanish presences for their own purposes. Similarly, Alejandra Dubcovsky argued that Native paths and alliances in the early South shaped the extent and success of European colonial projects. In *Informed Power* (2016), she showed how even the most basic European initiatives in the region, like finding food, traveling, and opening lines

10. Usner, *Indians, Settlers, and Slaves in a Frontier Exchange Economy;* Hall, *Africans in Colonial Louisiana;* Spear, *Race, Sex, and Social Order;* Shannon Lee Dawdy, *Building the Devil's Empire: French Colonial New Orleans* (Chicago: University of Chicago Press, 2008); Cécile Vidal, ed., *Louisiana: Crossroads of the Atlantic World* (Philadelphia: University of Pennsylvania Press, 2013); John T. McGrath, *The French in Early Florida: In the Eye of the Hurricane* (Gainesville: University Press of Florida, 2000). For other works on the region, see Bradley G. Bond, ed., *French Colonial Louisiana and the Atlantic World* (Baton Rouge: Louisiana State University Press, 2005); Kenneth J. Banks, *Chasing Empire across the Sea: Communications and the State in the French Atlantic, 1713–1763* (Montreal: McGill-Queen's University Press, 2002).

11. Daniel K. Richter, *Before the Revolution: America's Ancient Pasts* (Cambridge: Harvard University Press, 2011), 4.

of communication, depended on the support of Native peoples. Dubcovsky's work, like much of the scholarship on Natives and the early South, relied on Kathleen DuVal's groundbreaking *The Native Ground* (2006) which argued that "Indians were more often able to determine the form and content of intercultural relations than were their European would-be colonizers. As a whole, Indians outnumbered non-Indians. . . . Besides their numbers, Indians took advantage of Europeans' lack of information about the region and its people to shape their understandings and actions."[12] Simply put, the early South was not merely a multi-imperial world. It was controlled by a variety of different Indigenous actors.

The centrality of Native peoples in the history of the early South forces a reexamination of the essay's initial question: when does the history of the region begin? In "There's No Such Thing as 'Prehistory'" (2017), Juliana Barr urged scholars to "contend with the depth and the entirety of that timescale of the Native past." Examining the *longue durée* of Caddo and Pueblo pasts, she pushed southern history back to a much earlier start date, arguing that "the older and open-ended plotlines of the Native past subsume not only colonial America but also the U.S. nation-state, with beginnings in a time long before 1492 and endings we have not yet reached."[13] Her brilliant article emphasized the longevity of Native presence and power in the region, building upon an established practice in the early South: connecting the fields of history and archaeology.

The illustrious career and field-defining works of Charles Hudson exemplify that connection. After decades of anthropological work on Native peoples in the American South, he wrote a masterful book, *Knights of Spain, Warriors of the Sun* (1997), which attempted to follow some of the possible routes that Hernando de Soto traveled between 1539 and 1541. Building on earlier collaborations with Marvin T. Smith and Chester DePratter, Hudson recreated a complex Native world that existed at the eve of European colonization. Combining archaeology with history, Hudson provided a new way to approach the early sixteenth century. His methodology and painstaking findings inspired a generation of influential

12. Jonathan DeCoster, "Entangled Borderlands: Europeans and Timucuans in Sixteenth-Century Florida," *Florida Historical Quarterly* 91 (Winter 2013): 375–400; Alejandra Dubcovsky, *Informed Power: Communication in the Early American South* (Cambridge: Harvard University Press, 2016); Kathleen DuVal, *The Native Ground: Indians and Colonists in the Heart of the Continent* (Philadelphia: University of Philadelphia Press, 2006), 4.

13. Juliana Barr, "There's No Such Thing as 'Prehistory': What the Longue Durée of Caddo and Pueblo History Tells Us About Colonial America," *William and Mary Quarterly* 74 (April 2017): 203–40, quote on 240.

scholars, including Theda Perdue, Patricia Galloway, Robbie Ethridge, John E. Worth, and Eric E. Browne.[14] In their scholarship, the early South began long before Christopher Columbus sailed across the Atlantic. Their interdisciplinary approaches began to uncover the region's Indigenous geopolitics.

Anthropological sources expand the chronology, geography, and cast of actors in early southern history, but also emphasize the importance of that expanded chronology, geography, and set of actors. In her work on the Chickasaws, Ethridge placed Native-produced and manipulated artifacts in dialogue with European texts. She thus detailed a complex, hierarchical, and most importantly, ever-changing Native world that existed before and after European arrival. Like Patricia Galloway's superb work on the Choctaws and Theda Perdue's foundational research on the Cherokees, Ethridge argued that Native people had a dynamic past. Native peoples such as the Chickasaws, Choctaws, and Cherokees had a long history of adapting, growing, and working through change—they were not static peoples, doomed to collapse and fail.[15]

Archaeological work illuminated the experiences and significance of Native groups barely present in colonial archival sources. In 2015, John E. Worth and a team from the University of West Florida located the Tristán de Luna settlement. Worth's excavations and findings of this large but short-lived colonial project (1559–1561) provided incredible insight into the Native communities who lived near present-day Pensacola. Anthropological work in South Florida, for example the works of Peter Ferdinando, Alan Brech, and J. F. Lanham, fostered a more robust understanding of Indigenous life and experiences where European

14. Charles M. Hudson, *The Southeastern Indian* (Knoxville: University of Tennessee Press, 1976); Hudson, *Knights of Spain, Warriors of the Sun: Hernando De Soto and the South's Ancient Chiefdoms* (Athens: University of Georgia Press, 1997); Theda Perdue, *Slavery and the Evolution of Cherokee Society, 1540–1866* (Knoxville: University of Tennessee Press, 1979); Patricia Galloway, *Choctaw Genesis, 1500–1700* (Lincoln: University of Nebraska Press, 1995); Robbie Ethridge, *Creek Country: The Creek Indians and their World* (Chapel Hill: University of North Carolina Press, 2003); John E. Worth, *The Timucuan Chiefdoms of Spanish Florida.* Vol. 1, *Assimilation* (Gainesville: University Press of Florida, 1998); Worth, *The Timucuan Chiefdoms of Spanish Florida.* Vol. 2, *Resistance and Destruction* (Gainesville: University Press of Florida, 1998); Eric E. Browne, *The Westo Indians, Slave Traders of the Early Colonial South* (Tuscaloosa: University of Alabama Press, 2005). See also Robbie Ethridge, "Remembering Charles Hudson," *Native South* 7 (2014): 146–49.

15. Robbie Ethridge, *From Chicaza to Chickasaw: The European Invasion and the Transformation of the Mississippian World, 1540–1715* (Chapel Hill: University of North Carolina Press, 2010), 5; Galloway, *Choctaw Genesis;* Perdue, *Slavery and the Evolution of Cherokee;* Perdue, *Cherokee Women: Gender and Culture Change, 1700–1835* (Lincoln: University of Nebraska Press, 1998).

sources remain scant to say the least.[16] Even in places for which documents exist, anthropological findings greatly augmented understanding of Native choices, ideas, and decisions. Patrick Lee Johnson's work on the Apalachee Indians used material culture, including ceramics, to offer "insight into how individuals balanced traditions and regulations with frontier realities to create and maintain communities."[17] Elliot Blair's research on the Guale Indians in coastal Georgia employed social network analysis to plot the spread of glass beads, and through that painstaking work, he uncovered the internal socio-material relationships and interactions of Native communities living within Spanish missions.[18]

After the turn of the twenty-first century, exploration of European-Indigenous relations in the early South, already a cornerstone of the region's scholarship, became an increasingly populated subfield. Numerous projects focused on distinct Native nations. From Joshua Piker's study of an individual Upper Creek town to Steven C. Hahn's analysis of the emergence of their national identity, Creek became prominent players in the historiography of the eighteenth-century South.[19]

16. Peter John Ferdinando, "Atlantic Ais in the Sixteenth and Seventeenth Centuries: Maritime Adaptation, Indigenous Wrecking, and Buccaneer Raids on Florida's Central East Coast" (PhD diss., Florida International University, 2015); Alan Brech and J. F. Lanham, "The Location of the Paramount Town of the Ais Indians and the General Location of the Indians of Santa Lucia," *Florida Anthropologist* 63 (September–December 2010): 115–48.

17. Patrick Lee Johnson, "Apalachee Identity on the Gulf Coast Frontier," *Native South* 6 (2013): 110–41, quote on 111. See also Michelle Marie Pigott, "The Apalachee after San Luis: Exploring Cultural Hybridization through Ceramic Practice" (MA thesis, University of Central Florida, 2015).

18. Elliot H. Blair, "Glass Beads and Constellations of Practice," in *Knowledge in Motion: Constellations of Learning across Time and Place,* ed. Andrew P. Roddick and Ann B. Stahl (Tucson: University of Arizona Press, 2016), 97–125. See also Kathleen Deagan and David Hurst Thomas, eds., *From Santa Elena to St. Augustine: Indigenous Ceramic Variability (A.D. 1400–1700),* Anthropological Paper No. 90 (New York: American Museum of Natural History, 2009).

19. Joshua Piker, *Okfuskee: A Creek Indian Town in Colonial America* (Cambridge: Harvard University Press, 2004); Steven C. Hahn, *The Invention of the Creek Nation, 1670–1763* (Lincoln: University of Nebraska Press, 2004). For more work on the Creek, see Kathryn E. Holland Braund, *Deerskins and Duffels: Creek Indian Trade with Anglo-America, 1685–1815* (Lincoln: University of Nebraska Press, 1993); Claudio Saunt, *A New Order of Things: Property, Power, and the Transformation of the Creek Indians, 1733–1816* (New York: Cambridge University Press, 1999); Julie Anne Sweet, *Negotiating for Georgia: British-Creek Relations in the Trustee Era, 1733–1752* (Athens: University of Georgia Press, 2005); Andrew K. Frank, *Creeks and Southerners: Biculturalism on the Early American Frontier* (Lincoln: University of Nebraska Press, 2005); John T. Juricek, *Colonial Georgia and the Creeks: Anglo-Indian Diplomacy on the Southern Frontier, 1733–1763* (Gainesville: University Press of Florida, 2010); Steven J. Peach, "Creek Indian Globetrotter: Tomochichi's Trans-Atlantic Quest for Traditional Power in the Colonial Southeast," *Ethnohistory* 60 (Fall 2013): 605–35.

Similarly, there are a handful of works on the Cherokees, Chickasaws, Choctaws, Timucuas, Yamasees, and Natchez. Though many scholars devoted attention to the period after 1750, a growing number of monographs focused on developments of these prominent nations prior to 1750.[20]

Less populous Native groups also received recognition. Elizabeth N. Ellis wrote vividly about the Petites Nations in the Lower Mississippi Valley, showing how their small size and malleability proved key to their survival. John E. Worth detailed the experiences of the Guale Indians.[21] Ethnohistorical questions about who Native peoples were, where they lived, and how their communities, experiences, and structures changed over time guide many of these studies, expanding the chronology as well as the lists of *who* mattered and *where* the story unfolded in the early South.

Ethnohistory for ethnohistory's sake is not the goal of most of this scholarship. European-Indigenous relations have become a lens through which to consider bigger questions, such as the inner workings and development of empires or the reach and limitations of colonial authority.[22] In 2002 Alan Gallay wrote the

20. Three important annotated collections are Robbie Ethridge and Charles Hudson, eds., *The Transformation of the Southeastern Indians, 1540–1760* (Jackson: University Press of Mississippi, 2002); Richard F. Townsend, ed., *Hero, Hawk, and Open Hand: American Indian Art of the Ancient Midwest and South* (Chicago: Art Institute of Chicago, in Association with Yale University Press, 2004); Thomas J. Pluckhahn and Robbie Ethridge, eds., *Light on the Path: The Anthropology of the Southeastern Indians* (Tuscaloosa: University of Alabama Press, 2006). See also Kristofer Ray, "Cherokees and Franco-British Confrontation in the Tennessee Corridor, 1730–1760," *Native South* 7 (2014): 33–67; Miles P. Grier, "Staging the Cherokee Othello: An Imperial Economy of Indian Watching," *William and Mary Quarterly* 73 (January 2016): 73–106; Edward J. Cashin, *Guardians of the Valley: Chickasaws in Colonial South Carolina and Georgia* (Columbia: University of South Carolina Press, 2009); Ethridge, *From Chicaza to Chickasaw;* Wendy St. Jean, "Trading Paths: Mapping Chickasaw History in the Eighteenth Century," *American Indian Quarterly* 27 (Summer/Fall 2003): 758–80; Patricia Galloway, "A Storied Land: Choctaw Place-Names and the Emplotment of Land Use," in *Practicing Ethnohistory: Mining Archives, Hearing Testimony, Constructing Narrative* (Lincoln: University of Nebraska Press, 2006), 175–201; Alejandra Dubcovsky and George Aaron Broadwell, "Writing Timucua: Recovering and Interrogating Indigenous Authorship," *Early American Studies* 15 (Summer 2017): 409–41; DeCoster, "Entangled Borderlands."

21. Elizabeth N. Ellis, "The Many Ties of the Petites Nations: Relationships, Power, and Diplomacy in the Lower Mississippi Valley, 1685–1785" (PhD diss., University of North Carolina at Chapel Hill, 2015); John E. Worth, *The Struggle for the Georgia Coast: An 18th-Century Spanish Retrospective on Guale and Mocama* (New York: American Museum of Natural History, 1995).

22. For empire, see Robert Paulett, *An Empire of Small Places: Mapping the Southeastern Anglo-Indian Trade, 1732–1795* (Athens: University of Georgia Press, 2012). For limitations, see Joshua Piker, *The Four Deaths of Acorn Whistler: Telling Stories in Colonial America* (Cambridge: Harvard University Press, 2013).

field-changing *The Indian Slave Trade*.[23] He chronicled the development of an extensive trade network in which English South Carolinians traded weapons to their Native neighbors and expected to be paid back in Indian slaves. Gallay showed the massive extent of this trade: over fifty thousand people captured and sold, permanently altering the region's geopolitics. The Indian slave trade destabilized and destroyed many Native communities, especially those in Spanish Florida. It also enabled certain Native groups including the Westos, Yamasees, Cherokees, and Creeks to secure (at least for some time) more influence. Gallay demonstrated how the Indian slave trade, far from a peripheral endeavor, proved instrumental to expanding English power in the region.

James F. Brooks also published his widely influential *Captives and Cousins* in 2002. Like Gallay, Brooks argued that, between the 1540s and the 1880s, the capture and trade of enslaved Indians and livestock became a central force in shaping borderland political economies. He explored power relations among different Native groups and Euro-American settlers, showing how women and children become both kin who needed protection and commodities to be traded. In her transformational *Peace Came in the Form of a Woman* (2007), Juliana Barr employed a gendered lens to examine Indian-Spanish relations in the Texas borderlands from 1680 to 1790. In a world torn by Indian slavery, Barr argued that Native categories of gender provided the core political structure by shaping people's roles, identities, and status.[24]

Beginning in 2002, historians produced a flurry of scholarship on Indian slavery within and beyond the South. Some of the most notable studies include Eric E. Browne's work on the Westos and Christina Snyder's sweeping survey of the development and transformation of Indian slavery from pre-Columbian times to the Second Seminole War in 1842. Browne discussed the first Indian group armed and empowered by South Carolina traders to raid for Indian slaves. At first tenuous and ad hoc, English relations with the Westos created a pattern of violence and abuse. Snyder's 2010 *Slavery in Indian Country* showed that this pattern did not originate with the English. She used the enduring practice of captive-taking to reconceptualize the early South, arguing that "too narrow a

23. Alan Gallay, *The Indian Slave Trade: The Rise of the English Empire in the American South 1670–1717* (New Haven: Yale University Press, 2002).

24. James F. Brooks, *Captives and Cousins: Slavery, Kinship, and Community in the Southwest Borderlands* (Chapel Hill: University of North Carolina Press, 2002); Juliana Barr, *Peace Came in the Form of a Woman: Indians and Spaniards in the Texas Borderlands* (Chapel Hill: University of North Carolina Press, 2007).

focus on the region as the inevitable cotton kingdom obscures the complexity of the region's past and the diversity of its people."[25] Furthermore, Snyder interrogated the intersections of Indigenous and African slavery, highlighting Native people's roles in the development of racial slavery.

Violence and enslavement went hand in hand. Robbie Ethridge developed the concept of the "shatter zone" to describe the massive instability that characterized the South during the era of the Indian slave trade. Matthew Jennings appropriated that concept in his *longue durée* study, tracing the centrality, evolution, and meaning of violence in the early Southeast. Denise Ileana Bossy, Stephen Warren, and David La Vere focused less on the violence of slaving and more on the movement of people across a devastated landscape.[26] Each showed how mobility and migration, sometimes willingly and other times by force, accompanied and often expanded the violence of Indian slavery. They argued that Native mobility was a calculated strategy, enabling many groups such as the Yamasees, Shawnees, and Tuscaroras to resist and survive the powerful forces of slaving. The booming literature on Indian slavery has shown the centrality, pervasiveness, and power of the institution, but individual experiences of Indian slaves and slavers—which foreground different concerns such as gender, family, and community life—remain relatively underexamined. Exceptions include Denise Ileana Bossy's impressive study of the trading companies of South Carolina, Steven C. Hahn's exploration of the life of Mary Musgrove (a trade and slave agent), and Scott Cave's article on the life of an enslaved Floridian woman.[27]

25. Browne, *The Westo Indians;* Christina Snyder, *Slavery in Indian Country: The Changing Face of Captivity in Early America* (Cambridge: Harvard University Press, 2010), 8.

26. Robbie Ethridge, "Creating the Shatter Zone: Indian Slave Traders and the Collapse of the Southeastern Chiefdoms," in Pluckhahn and Ethridge, eds., *Light on the Path,* 207–18; Ethridge and Sheri M. Shuck-Hall, eds., *Mapping the Mississippian Shatter Zone: The Colonial Indian Slave Trade and the Regional Transformation in the American South* (Lincoln: University of Nebraska Press, 2009); Matthew Jennings, *New Worlds of Violence: Cultures and Conquests in the Early American Southeast* (Knoxville: University of Tennessee Press, 2011); Denise Ileana Bossy, "Shattering Together, Merging Apart: Colonialism, Violence, and the Remaking of the Native South," *William and Mary Quarterly* 71 (October 2014): 611–31; Stephen Warren, *The Worlds the Shawnees Made: Migration and Violence in Early America* (Chapel Hill: University of North Carolina Press, 2014); David La Vere, *The Tuscarora War: Indians, Settlers, and the Fight for the Carolina Colonies* (Chapel Hill: University of North Carolina Press, 2013).

27. Denise Ileana Bossy, "Godin & Co.: Charleston Merchants and the Indian Trade, 1674–1715," *South Carolina Historical Magazine* 114 (April 2013): 96–131; Steven C. Hahn, *The Life and Times of Mary Musgrove* (Gainesville: University Press of Florida, 2012); Scott Cave, "Madalena: The Entangled History of One Indigenous Floridian Woman in the Atlantic World," *The Americas* 74 (April 2017): 171–200.

Though vast and diverse, the scholarship on the early South to 1715 has a common thread: change. At their core, interdisciplinary and multiarchival works seek to explain a dynamic world that was not just messy or complicated, though at times it certainly was. Change was a structuring force that surely confounded some of the historical actors and continues to perplex the historians who study them.

In 1715 the Yamasee War threatened the expansive Indian slave trade. William L. Ramsey conducted the only book-length study of the conflict that pitted Yamasees and Lower Creeks against South Carolina. Steven J. Oatis, Steven C. Hahn, Joseph M. Hall Jr., Alejandra Dubcovsky, and other scholars interpreted the war as a pivotal turning point in the Indian slave trade.[28] Though enslavement and sale of Native peoples continued throughout the war, the lucrative and destabilizing trade networks began to erode. In turn, South Carolina shifted attention more directly to a rising plantation economy and the importation of enslaved Africans. After the Yamasee War, new concerns on the ground and in the literature shifted the conversation towards the expansion of African slavery, the early South's growing role in a complex world trade economy, and the expansion of imperial and state power, not just among the English but also in the French colonies. The Yamasee War thus became both a historical and historiographical turning point.

The older historiography that had relegated the sixteenth- and seventeenth-century South to obscurity had also reduced the eighteenth-century South to a story about nation-making and the region's inevitable occupation by the United States. Historians finally loosened the grip of that narrative by recovering the breadth, diversity, ambiguity, and contingency of a world that was far more vibrant and porous than previously thought. Well into the second half of the eighteenth century, most of what would become the American South remained a vast area still inhabited and possessed by American Indian nations. While studies of earlier Spanish and French efforts displayed the relative lateness of English colonization, works on the eighteenth century exposed the limits of Great Britain's eventual reach into the interior. Along with the persistence and centrality of American Indians across borderlands contested by Spain, France, and England, fundamental questions regarding the inner workings of empire and the limita-

28. William L. Ramsey, *The Yamasee War: A Study of Culture, Economy, and Conflict in the Colonial South* (Lincoln: University of Nebraska Press, 2008); Steven J. Oatis, *A Colonial Complex: South Carolina's Frontiers in the Era of the Yamasee War, 1680–1730* (Lincoln: University of Nebraska Press, 2004); Hahn, *Invention of the Creek Nation;* Joseph M. Hall Jr., *Zamumo's Gifts: Indian-European Exchange in the Colonial Southeast* (Philadelphia: University of Pennsylvania Press, 2009); Dubcovsky, *Informed Power.*

tions of imperial authority have come to the foreground. Who controlled the South? What did that control mean? How was it enforced?

To answer those questions, scholars have explored carefully the lives, conditions, and relations on the ground. Since Verner W. Crane's now classic text, *The Southern Frontier, 1670–1732* (1928), the region appears less like a colonial project shaped and defined from abroad, and more like a complex and diverse Native homeland negotiated and contested by many local actors and interests. Much of the scholarship discussed here supports Eliga Gould's claim that "the metropolitan capacity for shaping events on the periphery was never as great as historians once believed, and that the exercise of power at the center was intertwined in deep and profound ways with the exercise of power at the margins."[29] The weakness of imperial and state power in the early South further undermines any lingering assertion that the national and sectional future of what we now call "the South" can be foreseen in decades preceding the American Revolution.

After its original publication, Crane's *The Southern Frontier* stood alone as a study that ambitiously encompassed the vast area extending from the Virginia Backcountry across the Tennessee Valley to the Gulf of Mexico and Mississippi River. Crane remained concerned with Anglo-American origins and influences, but as Peter H. Wood observed in a timely resurrection of the book in 1981, Crane nonetheless carefully marked out the "winding pathways of the early South." And if *The Southern Frontier* was "far ahead of its time or too far off the beaten path," one can now confidently say that a growing number of scholars have effectively pursued those pathways.[30]

Essays solicited by Wood and coeditors Gregory A. Waselkov and Thomas Hatley for *Powhatan's Mantle* (1989) took Crane's call for a vast and multi-imperial southern history to heart. Multidisciplinary work by established authorities like Helen Hornbeck Tanner and Vernon James Knight, and by emerging scholars including Waselkov and Martha W. McCartney, displayed the wide range of directions that they and others were undertaking. Among the chapters written for

29. Eliga H. Gould, "Entangled Atlantic Histories: A Response from the Anglo-American Periphery," *American Historical Review* 112 (December 2007): 1415–22, quote on 1416. See, for example, Piker, *The Four Deaths of Acorn Whistler*; Barr, *Peace Came in the Form of a Woman*; Hoffman, *Florida's Frontiers*; Usner, *Indians, Settlers, and Slaves in a Frontier Exchange Economy*; Spear, *Race, Sex, and Social Order in Early New Orleans.*

30. Verner W. Crane, *The Southern Frontier, 1670–1732*, with a new preface by Peter H. Wood (1928; repr., New York: W. W. Norton, 1981), ix–x, xvii.

Powhatan's Mantle, Wood's "The Changing Population of the Colonial South" laid particularly valuable groundwork for appreciating changes in size and location of the region's Indigenous population. James H. Merrell's *The Indians' New World,* published the same year as *Powhatan's Mantle,* raised the highest standard for all future studies of Indian-colonial relations. Merrell closely examined Catawba history from Mississippian times into the nineteenth century, but his nuanced treatment of intercultural exchange during the eighteenth century, with heavy emphasis on Native resilience in the face of sequential threats and challenges, exerted a particularly robust influence on historians of the post–Yamasee War period.[31]

Once historians began integrating all colonial and Native spaces more fully in their views of the eighteenth-century Southeast, the region could be seen as a kaleidoscope of interests and interactions with interior Indian nations, facing all directions rather than simply facing eastward toward the English colonies.[32] Tracing trade, alliance, and movement across imperial frontiers and Indigenous homelands demands research across different colonial archives in order to explore stronger evidence of intercultural relations (communication, negotiation, conflict) and achieve a firmer grasp on Indigenous perspectives and purposes.

The emerging geographical breadth of Americanists' attention to the eighteenth-century South was prominently displayed in David J. Weber's *The Spanish Frontier in North America* (1992). In a sweeping survey of all Spanish colonial regions north of New Spain, Weber detailed the provinces of Florida, Louisiana, Texas, New Mexico, and California with a particular message for historians of the South. "Buried in historical memory, several levels below magnolias, juleps, and the War Between the States" lies the region's complex Hispanic past—a history that cannot be reduced to hyperbolic contrast with British North America or to romantic background for the United States' territorial expansion. Studying more fully Spain's commerce and diplomacy among Indian nations, as well as its policies and practices regarding slavery, is essential for a comprehensive history of the early South.[33]

31. Gregory A. Waselkov, Peter H. Wood, and Thomas Hatley, eds., *Powhatan's Mantle: Indians in the Colonial Southeast* (Lincoln: University of Nebraska Press, 1989), specifically Peter H. Wood's "The Changing Population of the Colonial South: An Overview of Race and Region, 1685–1790" (57–132); James H. Merrell, *The Indians' New World: Catawbas and Their Neighbors from European Contact through the Era of Removal* (Chapel Hill: University of North Carolina Press, 1989).

32. Daniel K. Richter, *Facing East from Indian Country: A Native History of Early America* (Cambridge: Harvard University Press, 2001).

33. David J. Weber, *The Spanish Frontier in North America* (New Haven: Yale University Press, 1992), 5.

Thanks to studies of the sixteenth and seventeenth centuries, the notion that Spanish Florida was a static and sparsely inhabited colony can no longer be supported. Scholarship on the decades following destruction of Florida's Indian missions and enslavement of their residents by South Carolinians and their Indian allies (although less voluminous than that written about earlier times) has shown that this Spanish colony continued to be a complex and volatile place. By the 1720s, Florida was inhabited by heterogenous Native and colonial groups, including former slaves from Carolina who found freedom across the borderland. Yamasees and other Indian refugees from the north joined Apalachees and other remaining mission Indians to form a string of communities near St. Augustine, a town of a few thousand military and civilian inhabitants. Forts along the Gulf Coast at St. Marks and Pensacola drew a fluid mix of neighbors. All of this movement and settlement has been explored in Jerald T. Milanich's *Laboring in the Fields of the Lord* (1999), Bonnie G. McEwan's edited collection, *Indians of the Greater Southeast* (2000), and Matthew J. Clavin's *Aiming for Pensacola* (2015). The flight of slaves from South Carolina into Florida, further diversifying borderland interactions and interests, received close scrutiny from Jane G. Landers, initially in "Gracia Real de Santa Teresa de Mose" (1990), then in *Black Society in Spanish Florida* (1999) and *Atlantic Creoles in the Age of Revolution* (2010).[34] The foundational scholarship of Kathleen Deagan showed how, before and after the founding of the colony of Georgia, this was the most hotly contested area within a vast region of competing and overlapping imperial claims.[35] In addition to well-documented military campaigns waged by British and Spanish officials, American Indians and African Americans living in Florida sustained significant

34. Jerald T. Milanich, *Laboring in the Fields of the Lord: Spanish Missions and Southeastern Indians* (Washington: Smithsonian Institution Press, 1999); Bonnie G. McEwan, ed., *Indians of the Greater Southeast: Historical Archaeology and Ethnohistory* (Gainesville: University Press of Florida, 2000); Matthew J. Clavin, *Aiming for Pensacola: Fugitive Slaves on the Atlantic and Southern Frontiers* (Cambridge: Harvard University Press, 2015); Jane G. Landers, "Gracia Real de Santa Teresa de Mose: A Free Black Town in Spanish Colonial Florida," *American Historical Review* 95 (February 1990): 9–30; Landers, *Black Society in Spanish Florida;* Landers, *Atlantic Creoles in the Age of Revolution* (Cambridge: Harvard University Press, 2010).

35. Kathleen A. Deagan, "Mestizaje in Colonial St. Augustine," *Ethnohistory* 20 (Winter 1973): 55–65; Deagan, *Artifacts of the Spanish Colonies of Florida and the Caribbean, 1500–1800* (Washington: Smithsonian Institution Press, 1987); Deagan, *America's Ancient City: Spanish St. Augustine, 1565–1763* (New York: Garland Publishing, 1991). See also Barbara L. Voss, "Gender, Race, and Labor in the Archaeology of the Spanish Colonial Americas," *Current Anthropology* 49 (October 2008): 861–93.

resilience and resistance, as ongoing work by Denise Ileana Bossy and Alejandra Dubcovsky showed.[36]

To the west, attention to a confluence of colonial and Indian peoples in the borderland between French Louisiana and Spanish Texas detailed an important network of trade in deerskins, buffalo robes, livestock, and human captives. By the 1720s, Spain operated a few missions among the Caddos and a fort at Los Adaes (only twelve miles from Natchitoches). Though no more than a thousand colonists occupied Texas as late as the 1760s, a sizable and diverse Native population routinely shifted into and out of mission communities. F. Todd Smith's *Caddo Indians* (1995) and David La Vere's *Caddo Chiefdoms* (1998) focused on the pivotal role played by the region's largest sedentary population. H. Sophie Burton and F. Todd Smith's *Colonial Natchitoches* (2008) closely studied the social and ethnic complexity of Louisiana's westernmost colonial community.[37] Meanwhile, Barr's *Peace Came in the Form of a Woman* and Pekka Hämäläinen's *Comanche Empire* (2008) breathtakingly demonstrated how enslavement of American Indians, driven by Louisiana commerce, expanded into the southern plains. While back east the Yamasee War brought the Indian slave trade to a virtual close, farther west, Apaches were being captured by Caddo, Wichita, and Comanche raiders and sold to colonial slave buyers, as featured in Paul Timothy Conrad's dissertation, "Captive Fates" (2011).[38] Plenty of the latest scholarship on early Florida, Louisiana, and Texas was synthesized into a fluent narrative by F. Todd Smith in

36. Denise Ileana Bossy, "Negotiating Slavery and Empire: Yamasee Indians in the Early Southeast," in *European Empires in the American South: Colonial and Environmental Encounters,* ed. Joseph P. Ward (Jackson: University Press of Mississippi, 2017), 57–86; Alejandra Dubcovsky, "'The Confines and Boundaries of the Land': The Struggle for Fort King George and the Southern Frontiers, 1721–1725," in Ward, ed., *European Empires in the American South,* 37–56.

37. F. Todd Smith, *The Caddo Indians: Tribes at the Convergence of Empires, 1542–1854* (College Station: Texas A&M University Press, 1995); David La Vere, *The Caddo Chiefdoms: Caddo Economics and Politics, 700–1835* (Lincoln: University of Nebraska Press, 1998); H. Sophie Burton and F. Todd Smith, *Colonial Natchitoches: A Creole Community on the Louisiana-Texas Frontier, 1714–1803* (College Station: Texas A&M University Press, 2008).

38. Barr, *Peace Came in the Form of a Woman;* Pekka Hämäläinen, *The Comanche Empire* (New Haven: Yale University Press, 2008); Paul Timothy Conrad, "Captive Fates: Displaced American Indians in the Southwest Borderlands, Mexico, and Cuba, 1500-1800" (PhD diss., University of Texas, 2011). See also Juliana Barr, "From Captives to Slaves: Commodifying Indian Women in the Borderlands," *Journal of American History* 92 (June 2005): 19–46; Barr, "Geographies of Power: Mapping Indian Borders in the 'Borderlands' of the Early Southwest," *William and Mary Quarterly* 68 (January 2011): 5–46.

Louisiana and the Gulf South Frontier, 1500–1821 (2014), making a region marginalized for a long time in general surveys of the South much more accessible.[39]

Advances in our understanding of complex relations between and within Indigenous societies resulted from scrutiny of anticolonial wars that, like the Yamasee War, broke out during the early eighteenth century in the South. In the last chapter of Noeleen McIlvenna's book on the long, contested history of North Carolina, she traced causes of the Tuscarora War to intratribal division and to intertribal provocation as well as to trade abuses and land pressures committed by colonists. David La Vere's study followed the impacts that the costly conflict had upon remaining and relocating Native communities, while noting important, albeit different, lessons learned by American Indians and colonists for subsequent interactions. The Natchez War against Louisiana has also been analyzed through multiple layers of causation and consequence. In the first book-length study of the conflict, James F. Barnett Jr. shed light on the role played by factionalism that originated in the plural composition of Natchez society. Arnaud Balvay emphasized the "irreparable break" that occurred in an earlier confrontation between the Natchez and the French. In *Natchez Country* (2015), George E. Milne pursued an especially ambitious and innovative exploration, incorporating spatial analysis of Indian villages and colonial sites to show precisely how establishment of tobacco plantations undermined French-Natchez relations. As the French started tightening control over enslaved Africans in their midst, according to Milne, the Natchez escalated their own fear of enslavement.[40]

For the Natchez and other Indigenous peoples in the eighteenth-century lower Mississippi Valley, Daniel H. Usner explored multiple forms of interaction with colonists and slaves. Much closer study of particular groups was carried out by Morris S. Arnold, Patricia Galloway, and Kathleen DuVal. Galloway followed her cutting-edge *Choctaw Genesis* (1995) with a collection of equally interdisciplinary essays that probed a range of topics including Natchez kinship, the Mo-

39. F. Todd Smith, *Louisiana and the Gulf South Frontier, 1500–1821* (Baton Rouge: Louisiana State University Press, 2014).

40. Noeleen McIlvenna, *A Very Mutinous People: The Struggle for North Carolina, 1660–1713* (Chapel Hill: University of North Carolina Press, 2009); La Vere, *The Tuscarora War;* James F. Barnett Jr., *The Natchez Indians: A History to 1735* (Jackson: University Press of Mississippi, 2007); Arnaud Balvay, *La Révolte des Natchez* (Paris: Editions du Félin, 2008); George E. Milne, *Natchez Country: Indians, Colonists, and the Landscapes of Race in French Louisiana* (Athens: University of Georgia Press, 2015).

bilian trade language, the Choctaw Civil War, French and British diplomacy, and Choctaw chief Alibamon Mingo.[41] DuVal's *Native Ground* (2006) became a landmark study, demonstrating with keen insight how the Quapaws maintained dominance in the lower Arkansas Valley. Quapaws treated French newcomers as just another group of neighbors who could enhance their own power. Eventual dissatisfaction with Spanish authorities who replaced the French, DuVal further explained, motivated the Quapaws to shift alliance to the Chickasaws and the English. When it comes to advancing knowledge about smaller nations in the lower Mississippi Valley, especially the Tunicas, essays by Elizabeth N. Ellis have blazed promising new paths of research.[42]

Much of the sustained attention to Native agency in the early South has focused on how commerce with the Atlantic World shaped colonial relations and affected change inside Indian societies. After the Yamasee War, the deerskin trade replaced the slave trade as the most important commerce among colonies and tribes. By the late 1750s, nearly 200,000 deerskins were exported annually from all southeastern colonies combined (Maryland to Louisiana). Kathryn E. Holland Braund's *Deerskins and Duffels* (1993) was a breakthrough study for demonstrating the powerful influence the trade exerted on both Indian and colonial societies. Tracing change and continuity within Creek society, Braund richly detailed aspects of production, consumption, regulation, and diplomacy generated by expanding commerce in peltry. For a long time, the intricate relationship between plantation economies and Indian trade economies had gone hardly noticed, but Kristalyn Marie Shefveland's *Anglo-Native Virginia* (2016) showed in exemplary fashion not only how Indian trade provided original sources of capital for prominent Chesapeake Bay tobacco-plantation families but also how frontier exchange and plantation slavery remained interconnected into the eighteenth century. Native communities reduced to tributary status after earlier wars, for example,

41. Usner, *Indians, Settlers, and Slaves in a Frontier Exchange Economy*; Usner, *American Indians in the Lower Mississippi Valley: Social and Economic Histories* (Lincoln: University of Nebraska Press, 1998); Galloway, *Practicing Ethnohistory*.

42. Morris S. Arnold, *Colonial Arkansas, 1686–1804: A Social and Cultural History* (Fayetteville: University of Arkansas Press, 1991); Arnold, *The Rumble of a Distant Drum: The Quapaws and Old World Newcomers, 1673–1804* (Fayetteville: University of Arkansas Press, 2000); DuVal, *The Native Ground;* Elizabeth N. Ellis, "Dismantling the Dream of 'France's Peru': Indian and African Influence on the Development of Early Colonial Louisiana," in *The World of Colonial America: An Atlantic Handbook,* ed. Ignacio Gallup-Diaz (New York: Routledge, 2017), 355–72; Ellis, "Petite Nation with Powerful Networks: The Tunicas in the Eighteenth Century," *Louisiana History* 58 (Spring 2017): 133–78.

became a source of scouts, interpreters, and even traders for the expansion of Indian trade beyond the Tidewater and Piedmont areas. In South Carolina and Georgia, the deerskin trade remained an integral part of Atlantic commerce right up to the American Revolution. Illustrating what can be learned through quantitative study of government and business records, scholars proved that trade with American Indians comprised significant value and volume in South Carolina's economy. Whether looking at the trade's substantial portion of the colony's imports and exports—as Peter C. Mancall, Joshua L. Rosenbloom, and Thomas J. Weiss explored in one essay—or at the large number of people working at different positions within the trade—as found in Eirlys M. Barker's essay—it is no longer possible to underestimate the economic influence of Indian commerce upon both colonial and Native societies across the South.[43]

Whether focusing on material exchange or diplomatic protocol that accompanied the deerskin trade, scholars introduced innovative approaches to the study of geographical and spatial dimensions of Indian-colonial relations. Works by Edward J. Cashin contributed plenty to our knowledge, particularly about the career of trader Lachlan McGillivray, the gateway function of Augusta, and Chickasaw migration to the Savannah River. Joshua Piker brought fresh insight into the central importance of the southeastern Indian town in *Okfuskee* (2004). He captured more skillfully than ever both the comparative and connected aspects of community life, breaking down the historiographical wall that for so long separated analyses of colonial and Indigenous towns. Commerce between Creek and British people depended on securing community-to-community relationships. But as Piker also argued, familiar forms of exchange nurtured by the deerskin trade during the 1760s became increasingly circumscribed by the colonial Backcountry economy. In *An Empire of Small Places* (2012), Robert Paulett brought insightful attention to both physical and metaphysical spaces generated by the

43. Braund, *Deerskins and Duffels;* Kristalyn Marie Shefveland, *Anglo-Native Virginia: Trade, Conversion, and Indian Slavery in the Old Dominion, 1646–1722* (Athens: University of Georgia Press, 2016); Peter C. Mancall, Joshua L. Rosenbloom, and Thomas J. Weiss, "Indians and the Economy of Eighteenth-Century Carolina," in *The Atlantic Economy during the Seventeenth and Eighteenth Centuries: Organization, Operation, Practice, and Personnel,* ed. Peter A. Coclanis (Columbia: University of South Carolina Press, 2005), 297–322; Eirlys M. Barker, "Indian Traders, Charles Town and London's Vital Link to the Interior of North America, 1717–1755," in *Money, Trade, and Power: The Evolution of Colonial South Carolina's Plantation Society,* ed. Jack P. Greene, Rosemary Brana-Shute, and Randy J. Sparks (Columbia: University of South Carolina Press, 2001), 141–65. See also Steven J. Peach, "Creek Indian Globetrotter: Tomochichi's Trans-Atlantic Quest for Traditional Power in the Colonial Southeast," *Ethnohistory* 60 (Fall 2013): 605–35.

deerskin trade outside Indian villages. Constructing a composite picture of the trade route linking Charleston with Creek country, Paulett examined tension between an idea of space pursued by imperial authorities and contrary ideas of space practiced by enslaved African Americans as well as by Indian and European travelers. Although trade houses symbolized an orderly commerce imposed by the Atlantic system, they actually became contested spaces governed in large part by American Indians. Paralleling Piker's direction of analysis, however, Paulett concluded that the openness and fluidity of borderland interactions were eventually jeopardized by colonial settlers' encroaching uses of space.[44]

Another important dimension of Indian-colonial commerce that long-awaited serious study was the large number of British traders who formed intimate partnerships with American Indian women. In *Creeks and Southerners* (2005), Andrew K. Frank systematically explored the lives of the hundreds of Scotsmen and other Britons who fathered children with women in the Creek Confederacy. Only a few well-known traders like Lachlan McGillivray and William McIntosh Sr. had received this degree of attention, and Frank delved more deeply into how Creek society incorporated outsiders through kinship. The prominence of Native women in facilitating and maintaining intercultural relations, and both the benefits and risks experienced by children of dual identity were also featured in Frank's analysis. Southern history's most familiar daughter of a trader and a Creek woman, Mary Musgrove, played a pivotal and persistent role in early Georgia's relations with Indian people. In an imaginatively researched biography, Steven C. Hahn finally rescued Musgrove from a narrowly mythologized place in Georgia's origin story by situating her life within broader trends of colonial-Indian interaction. Musgrove's multicultural origins and early life confronted mounting pressure from both imperial and Indigenous authorities to choose a single cultural identity. She consequently sacrificed a "future never realized," as Hahn put it, for the life of an Anglican minister's wife and plantation mistress.[45]

A range of works focusing on women, kinship, and gender in Indian-colonial relations across the early South has been influenced by Kathleen M. Brown's *Good Wives, Nasty Wenches, and Anxious Patriarchs* (1996) and Theda Perdue's

44. Edward J. Cashin, ed., *Colonial Augusta: "Key of the Indian Countrey"* (Macon: Mercer University Press, 1986); Cashin, *Lachlan McGillivray, Indian Trader: The Shaping of the Southern Colonial Frontier* (Athens: University of Georgia Press, 1992); Cashin, *Guardians of the Valley*; Piker, *Okfuskee*; Paulett, *An Empire of Small Places.*

45. Frank, *Creeks and Southerners*; Hahn, *The Life and Times of Mary Musgrove*, 7.

Cherokee Women (1998). In a study concentrating mostly on African American slavery in colonial Virginia, Brown nonetheless considered the intricacies of early interaction with Native women. Perdue's pathbreaking book focused on women's lives inside Indian country and over a longer span of time. Cherokee women, as Perdue argued, channeled shifts and changes caused by European contact in traditional ways. Securing their autonomous sphere of power, however, became more difficult as trade, diplomacy, and war tended to enhance men's power. In a remarkable interdisciplinary study of Choctaw-French relations, *Choctaw Women in a Chaotic World* (2005), Michelene E. Pesantubbee emphasized even more strongly the deleterious effects of colonial commerce and conflict upon the status of American Indian women. Kirsten Fischer innovatively explained in *Suspect Relations* (2002) how alternative gender roles among American Indians threatened white men's efforts to police sexual behavior and impose racial hierarchy in early North Carolina. Alongside analysis of colonial representation of Indian women, she explored intercultural sexual liaisons and how they changed over time. In two very different studies of colonial Louisiana—Jennifer M. Spear's *Race, Sex, and Social Order in Early New Orleans* (2009) and Sophie White's *Wild Frenchmen and Frenchified Indians* (2012)—both historians further demonstrated why understanding sexualization and racialization in colonial societies must include consideration of the behavior and representation of all interacting groups: Native American as well as African and European women.[46]

Additional studies have significantly expanded our knowledge about various ways that gender and kinship affected change inside and around Indigenous homelands. In her 2018 dissertation, "Possessing Native Women and Children," Haley Negrin showed how the violent incorporation of Native women into English plantations across the early South disrupted matrilineal and matrifocal Indigenous kinship systems. Negrin argued that Native women and children were central to the development of planter patriarchy, emphasizing as well ways in which they adopted and adapted kinship practices in the English colonial world.

46. Kathleen M. Brown, *Good Wives, Nasty Wenches, and Anxious Patriarchs: Gender, Race, and Power in Colonial Virginia* (Chapel Hill: University of North Carolina Press, 1996); Perdue, *Cherokee Women;* Michelene E. Pesantubbee, *Choctaw Women in a Chaotic World: The Clash of Culture in the Colonial Southeast* (Albuquerque: University of New Mexico Press, 2005); Kirsten Fischer, *Suspect Relations: Sex, Race, and Resistance in Colonial North Carolina* (Ithaca: Cornell University Press, 2002); Spear, *Race, Sex, and Social Order in Early New Orleans;* Sophie White, *Wild Frenchmen and Frenchified Indians: Material Culture and Race in Colonial Louisiana* (Philadelphia: University of Pennsylvania Press, 2012).

In *Brothers Born of One Mother* (2012), Michelle LeMaster captured the wide variety of roles played by Native women in intercultural trade and diplomacy as translators, messengers, and providers of hospitality as well as wives giving white men access to kinship. She probed the rhetoric of gender, as articulated by both American Indians and Europeans, to demonstrate its direct influence on the formation and evolution of relationships. Knowledge of how Indigenous and colonial networks of kinship actually shaped political and economic developments in the eighteenth-century South was also advanced in Natalie R. Inman's *Brothers and Friends* (2017). Through compelling case studies of the Chickasaw Colbert family, the Anglo-American Donelson family, and the Cherokee families of Little Carpenter and Major Ridge, Inman sharpened our vision of the different effects that intermarriage and adoption had upon negotiation and conflict.[47]

In the 2000s and 2010s, some of the most notable scholarship devoted to the early South's Native homelands and imperial borderlands emphasized a range of creative initiatives and resourceful responses undertaken by American Indian people in pursuit of trade and alliance with European colonies. The early to middle decades of the eighteenth century saw some Indigenous groups coalescing and other groups splintering in the face of heightening tensions among British, Spanish, and French empires. Not one of the empires, however, achieved sufficient power to determine choices and outcomes, so Native forms of political improvisation and innovation included shifting allegiances among nations as well as tightening linkage among towns. Along the way, American Indian people sought ways to adapt colonial commerce to traditional purposes and unpredictable circumstances. In *Zamumo's Gifts* (2009), a multidisciplinary analysis of material exchange, Joseph M. Hall Jr. depicted how Creek leaders turned Atlantic World trade goods into ceremonial means of governing and managing networks of power. He thereby added insight into the intertribal coalescence that went into the formation of the Creek Confederacy. How objects circulated and how they were used also mattered a great deal, so Jessica Yirush Stern drew attention to the essential distinction between gifts and commodities. Native and British leaders alike attempted to use gift exchange to secure authority, making everything from

47. Hayley Negrin, "Possessing Native Women and Children: Slavery, Gender and English Colonialism in the Early American South, 1670–1772" (PhD diss., New York University, 2018); Michelle LeMaster, *Brothers Born of One Mother: British-Native American Relations in the Colonial Southeast* (Charlottesville: University of Virginia Press, 2012); Natalie R. Inman, *Brothers and Friends: Kinship in Early America* (Athens: University of Georgia Press, 2017).

participation in ritual to involvement in the trade vital and contested processes. But as Stern showed in *The Lives of Objects* (2017), ordinary Indians and settlers simultaneously pursued more freewheeling commercial exchange that challenged colonial and Indigenous control. Another valuable feature of Stern's work was her thoughtful consideration of how ideologies of manufacturing differed between trade partners, showing that American Indians valued their ceremonial communal use while Europeans prized the individualizing labor and ownership behind them.[48]

Even the circulation of stories can tell us something valuable about the contingent and fragile nature of power in the southeastern borderlands, as demonstrated in Joshua Piker's *The Four Deaths of Acorn Whistler* (2013). His finely crafted analysis explored divergent narratives about one Creek leader's alleged attack on a group of Cherokees and his subsequent execution, reflecting a swirl of local, national, colonial, and imperial agendas that affected everyday life as well as politics and diplomacy. Intertwining stories told about such an incident, as Piker also showed, actually influenced unfolding events and long-term processes.[49] In *Voices of Our Ancestors* (2009), Patricia Causey Nichols further explored the role of language in these Native-European exchanges. Linguists like George Aaron Broadwell, Janine Scancarelli, and Heather K. Hardy also produced important scholarship using historical sources to reconstruct and recenter communications and miscommunications.[50]

As empires competed aggressively for alliance and trade with interior Indian nations, Native societies encountered destabilizing forces on multiple levels.

48. Hall, *Zamumo's Gifts*; Jessica Yirush Stern, *The Lives of Objects: Native Americans, British Colonists, and Cultures of Labor and Exchange in the Southeast* (Chapel Hill: University of North Carolina Press, 2017).

49. Piker, *The Four Deaths of Acorn Whistler*. See also Piker, "Lying Together: The Imperial Implications of Cross-Cultural Untruths," *American Historical Review* 116 (October 2011): 964–86.

50. Patricia Causey Nichols, *Voices of Our Ancestors: Language Contact in Early South Carolina* (Columbia: University of South Carolina Press, 2009); Janine Scancarelli and Heather K. Hardy, eds., *Native Languages of the Southeastern United States* (Lincoln: University of Nebraska Press, 2005); Dubcovsky and Broadwell, "Writing Timucua," 409–41. For good overviews, see Edward G. Gray and Norman Fiering, eds., *The Language Encounter in the Americas, 1492–1800: A Collection of Essays* (New York: Berghahn Books, 2000); Nancy Shoemaker, *A Strange Likeness: Becoming Red and White in Eighteenth-Century North America* (New York: Oxford University Press, 2004); Philip H. Round, *Removable Type: Histories of the Book in Indian Country, 1663–1880* (Chapel Hill: University of North Carolina Press, 2010). Specifically focused on the South is Gregory Evans Dowd, "The Panic of 1751: The Significance of Rumors on the South Carolina-Cherokee Frontier," *William and Mary Quarterly* 53 (July 1996): 527–60.

Conflict within and among communities, in other words, accompanied the coalescence and realignment underway during the eighteenth century. Among the new generation of historians concentrating on Indian-colonial relations, Claudio Saunt stood apart for his emphasis on how the deerskin trade threatened social and political stability within Native society. In *A New Order of Things* (1999), he tracked a steady loosening of young men's attachment to traditional customs and institutions caused by colonial commerce and warfare. Saunt paid most of his attention, however, to even more serious threats arising during the 1760s. With mestizo sons of British traders and Creek mothers coming of age and the white-tail deer population declining around Creek towns, a divisive and damaging set of practices began to infiltrate Indigenous society—most notably slavery and class schism. In an essay published in 2007, Claudio Saunt issued an additional cautionary note in regard to impacts of European colonialism by throwing light on how Atlantic-World empires practiced a policy of proxy war. Being drawn into conflict between European nations, as he argued in "'Our Indians'" (2007), had damaging, even destructive, effects on American Indian people. The Choctaws' costly participation in France's attempts to destroy the Chickasaws and their even more costly civil war (eight hundred Choctaw lives lost) clearly illustrate the limits for some Indigenous societies of playing off one European empire against another.[51]

Other historians supplemented Saunt's line of inquiry with scrutiny of various sources of intratribal and intertribal conflict. In *A Colonial Complex* (2004), Steven J. Oatis explained the Creek-Cherokee and Choctaw-Chickasaw wars as intertwined struggles over trade alliance with European colonies. While European colonies—even those within the same empire—competed over Indian trade, tribes fractured and clashed over access to colonial trade partners. In *Negotiating for Georgia* (2005), Julie Anne Sweet focused on Lower Creek relations with coastal settlers where early collaborations faltered quickly because of encroachment on Indian territory and sovereignty. The crucial importance of land rights became the central subject of John T. Juricek's multivolume scholarship on the Creeks. His thorough investigation of treaty proceedings before 1763 in *Colonial Georgia and the Creeks* (2010) highlighted a gulf between English and Indian perceptions of land originating in different meanings of sovereignty. Neverthe-

51. Saunt, *A New Order of Things;* Saunt, "'Our Indians': European Empires and the History of the Native American South," in *The Atlantic in Global History, 1500–2000,* ed. Jorge Cañizares-Esguerra and Erik R. Seeman (Upper Saddle River, NJ: Pearson/Prentice Hall, 2007), 61–75.

less, as Juricek observed, across three eighteenth-century imperial wars among the British, Spanish, and French, the Creeks managed to carefully maintain a profitable neutrality.[52]

Plenty of sophisticated work on Cherokee relations with English colonies has been well underway. In *The Dividing Paths* (1993), Thomas Hatley captured the complexity of production, exchange, and consumption inside Cherokee towns, emphasizing gender and generational differences, the role of women, and environmental impacts. Hatley also drew attention to the Cherokees' gradual alienation from Charleston-centered commerce. The persistent importance of town landscapes and architecture in Cherokee life was explored closely by Christopher B. Rodning in *Center Places and Cherokee Towns* (2015). Sociopolitical organization and geographical division in Cherokee society became the focus of Tyler Boulware's *Deconstructing the Cherokee Nation* (2011) in which he explained how the deerskin trade as well as alliances and warfare generated a unity beyond local and regional identities. Shared threats and wartime experiences, especially conflict with Creek Indians, reduced tension among Cherokee towns. Boulware demonstrated that the outbreak of war against English colonies allowed the Cherokees "a greater degree of collective action than had been known in prior conflicts." Collective action, however, did not reduce the centrality of localism and regionalism among the Cherokee people. Kristofer Ray further interrogated the central role of the Cherokees in his 2014 article, "Cherokees and Franco-British Confrontation in the Tennessee Corridor, 1730–1760." Ray argued that the "Cherokees provided both a bulwark and a means of expanding via the Tennessee River" for both the English and French empires.[53]

John Oliphant closely examined the breakdown in Cherokee relations with Great Britain in *Peace and War on the Cherokee Frontier* (2001). He found

52. Oatis, *A Colonial Complex;* Sweet, *Negotiating for Georgia;* John T. Juricek, *Endgame for Empire: British-Creek Relations in Georgia and Vicinity, 1763–1776* (Gainesville: University Press of Florida, 2015); Juricek, *Colonial Georgia and the Creeks.*

53. Thomas Hatley, *The Dividing Paths: Cherokees and South Carolinians through the Revolutionary Era* (New York: Oxford University Press, 1993); Christopher B. Rodning, *Center Places and Cherokee Towns: Archaeological Perspectives on Native American Architecture and Landscape in the Southern Appalachians* (Tuscaloosa: University of Alabama Press, 2015); Tyler Boulware, *Deconstructing the Cherokee Nation: Town, Region, and Nation among Eighteenth-Century Cherokees* (Gainesville: University Press of Florida, 2011), 110; Ray, "Cherokees and Franco-British Confrontation in the Tennessee Corridor," 36. See also Hilary E. Wyss, *English Letters and Indian Literacies: Reading, Writing, and New England Missionary Schools, 1750–1830* (Philadelphia: University of Pennsylvania Press, 2012), chap. 4.

causation in the recklessness of English traders, intrigue of French rivals, and encroachment of white settlers. This highly consequential crisis coincided with the beginnings of royal intervention in the appointment of superintendents to manage and regulate Indian affairs, a dimension of the rising tension captured by J. Russell Snapp in *John Stuart and the Struggle for Empire on the Southern Frontier* (1996). In "The British and Indian War" (2012), Paul Kelton discovered additional significance for what caused and resulted from the collapse in the Cherokees' alliance with England. Through close analysis of Cherokee decision-making and mobilization, including the influence of women, he found that Cherokee fighters played a pivotal role in Britain's victory over Ohio Valley Indians during the Seven Years' War. The disrespect and violence suffered by returning Cherokee warriors at the hands of nervous Virginians led to the subsequent Cherokee-British war and also hid from view the important Cherokee influence on the outcome of the Seven Years' War.[54]

Those nervous Virginians clashing with Cherokee and other Native travelers on the Warrior's Path were mostly recent migrants to the colonial southern Backcountry. Their movement to Virginia's frontier was driven by imperial forces and interests, paralleling to some extent the circumstances facing Indian people. In *Nature and History in the Potomac Country* (2009), James D. Rice carefully delineated and explained the long-term process of migration and interaction, including the environmental factors, particularly along the pathway used regularly by Iroquois and other Indian war parties. Warren R. Hofstra showed with skillful precision how imperial authorities sought to create a zone of security within the highly contested and volatile borderland beyond the Blue Ridge Mountains. As he demonstrated in *The Planting of New Virginia* (2004), the Scots-Irish and German Palatines recruited to settle the Backcountry already possessed experience as occupants of lands caught in national and imperial conflicts. Their aggressive bounding of land in Britain's colonial Backcountry did not bode well for American Indians living farther west, particularly in the Tennessee and Ohio valleys, who would soon face movement of Backcountry settlers deeper into the southern

54. John Oliphant, *Peace and War on the Cherokee Frontier, 1756–1763* (Baton Rouge: Louisiana State University Press, 2001); J. Russell Snapp, *John Stuart and the Struggle for Empire on the Southern Frontier* (Baton Rouge: Louisiana State University Press, 1996); Paul Kelton, "The British and Indian War: Cherokee Power and the Fate of Empire in North America," *William and Mary Quarterly* 69 (October 2012): 763–92. See also Jeff W. Dennis, *Patriots and Indians: Shaping Identity in Eighteenth-Century South Carolina* (Columbia: University of South Carolina Press, 2017), ch. 2.

interior.[55] Meanwhile, elite speculators further complicated a struggle that, as Woody Holton insightfully detailed in *Forced Founders* (1999), contributed to the independence movement in Virginia. Cherokee and Shawnee apprehension over encroachment by both settlers and speculators warranted stronger imperial authority in the interior, which in turn fueled resentment among colonists.[56]

Perhaps the quintessential borderland people in all of eastern North America, the Shawnees, a name meaning "southerners" in Algonquian, received exceptionally skillful attention from Stephen Warren and Sami Lakomäki. Both authors showed how Shawnees made movement and dispersal—much of it occurring across a sizable area in the South—an integral element of their culture and identity. Like all other southeastern Indians, the Shawnees were a village-centered people, but by the end of the seventeenth century they relied upon alliance networks that radiated outward, forming towns on the Savannah and Tallapoosa rivers as well as on the Illinois and Susquehanna rivers. As a "transient townspeople," according to Stephen Warren in *The Worlds the Shawnees Made* (2014), the Shawnees "carried a historical consciousness of their homeland" through spaces contested by colonial and other Native peoples. Eventual aggregation in the Ohio Valley, which they viewed as their homeland predating European colonialism, secured continuing autonomy for Shawnee communities. But this migration nonetheless also situated them within the tightening squeeze of imperial conflict between France and England, and then in direct confrontation with American expansionism. Warren's work, not incidentally, provides a fine example of what can be achieved when historians seek knowledge from American Indian consultants. In *Gathering Together* (2014), Sami Lakomäki also sustained

55. James D. Rice, *Nature and History in the Potomac Country: From Hunter-Gatherers to the Age of Jefferson* (Baltimore: Johns Hopkins University Press, 2009); Warren R. Hofstra, *The Planting of New Virginia: Settlement and Landscape in the Shenandoah Valley* (Baltimore: Johns Hopkins University Press, 2004); Hofstra, "'The Extention of His Majesties Dominions': The Virginia Backcountry and the Reconfiguration of Imperial Frontiers," *Journal of American History* 84 (March 1998): 1281–312. The planning and formation of Winchester, Staunton, and other early towns in the Great Valley were systematically studied in Christopher E. Hendricks, *The Backcountry Towns of Colonial Virginia* (Knoxville: University of Tennessee Press, 2006).

56. Woody Holton, *Forced Founders: Indians, Debtors, Slaves, and the Making of the American Revolution in Virginia* (Chapel Hill: University of North Carolina Press, 1999). See also L. Scott Philyaw, *Virginia's Western Visions: Political and Cultural Expansion of an Early American Frontier* (Knoxville: University of Tennessee Press, 2004) for analysis of longer-term aspects. In *Unification of a Slave State: The Rise of the Planter Class in the South Carolina Backcountry, 1760–1808* (Chapel Hill: University of North Carolina Press, 1990), Rachel N. Klein captured some comparable tensions in the Carolina Backcountry.

a Shawnee-centered focus but further considered how their own debates and decisions regarding survival of distinct peoplehood in moments of such movement, transition, and change compared with, and even influenced, the formation of national borders and identities among European Americans as well as other Native Americans.[57]

The early South and its borderlands remains an expanding, dynamic, and rapidly growing area of research, producing innovative scholarship that mines multi-imperial and multilingual archives while actively engaging with interdisciplinary methodologies such as archaeology, literary studies, linguistics, ethnohistory, and Indigenous studies. At their most basic level of intervention, scholars in the field tell the stories of peoples and places long excluded from the national narrative. But beyond filling some rather large and important historical lacunae, these works pose critical questions about who gets to be included, in what terms, and why these histories matter to understanding the American South. Novelist and activist James Baldwin wrote that "American history is longer, larger, more various, more beautiful, and more terrible than anything anyone has ever said about it." That could not be truer of the early South and its borderlands.[58]

57. Warren, *The Worlds the Shawnees Made,* 59; Sami Lakomäki, *Gathering Together: The Shawnee People through Diaspora and Nationhood, 1600–1870* (New Haven: Yale University Press, 2014).

58. James Baldwin, "The Negro Child—His Self-Image," *Saturday Review,* 21 December 1963, reprinted as "A Talk to Teachers," in *The Price of the Ticket: Collected Nonfiction, 1948–1985* (New York: St. Martin's Press, 1985), 332.

ORIENTED TOWARDS THE OCEAN
The Colonial South

Noeleen McIlvenna and Justin Roberts

The historian's life has changed dramatically since John B. Boles and Evelyn Thomas Nolen asked George C. Rogers Jr. to write a chapter on the colonial South for *Interpreting Southern History* (1987). The digitization of many archives has turned what used to be a long and beautiful escape from campus and family demands into no more than a short visit in search of the last few land deeds not yet accessible through the internet. Our archivist colleagues and friends have democratized research, allowing those who might not have been able to find the time or money for travel to share their gifts with us. Although southern historians no longer need to travel far and wide as often for sources, their conceptual frameworks have pushed them to range beyond the South into the wider Atlantic World and to incorporate all southern inhabitants in their stories. The digitization of sources spurred the expansion of these frameworks, allowing southern historians to access and share a wider array of sources from across the South and around the world.[1]

The single biggest development in the historiography of the colonial South over the last three decades has been the new paradigm of the Atlantic World. Championed by Bernard Bailyn and sponsored through sixteen seasons of the International Seminar on the History of the Atlantic World, 1500–1825, which he hosted at Harvard University beginning in 1995, the transnational approach brought us a rich and inclusive social history. It allowed historians to place south-

1. George C. Rogers Jr., "The South before 1800," in *Interpreting Southern History: Historiographical Essays in Honor of Sanford W. Higginbotham,* ed. John B. Boles and Evelyn Thomas Nolen (Baton Rouge: Louisiana State University Press, 1987), 6–47.

ern colonial development in the broader contexts of the Creek and Dahomey empires as well as those of the British, French, Spanish, and Dutch. And the stories that historians found exposed the limits that European empires faced in bringing their powers to bear on settlers who, thousands of miles away, gradually built a southern world of rich, poor, and enslaved based on skin color to replace the class systems they had left behind. That the southern grandees won was not inevitable. We see the resistance now: the ways black, white, and Indigenous inhabitants fought for alternatives, and ways in which people on the margins sought multiracial community. Marcus Rediker's entire oeuvre of maritime history, of pirate and slave ships, is not particularly southern history, but it informs the Atlantic history of the region. Perhaps most importantly, an Atlantic World scope shows us how small and unimportant on a global scale the colonists in the southern provinces were, for they all lived on the margins of the sugar islands that occupied the fulcrum of the seventeenth- and early eighteenth-century economy.[2]

Despite the centrality of the sugar islands to the story of the early South in the Atlantic World framework, it is still far too easy for southern historians to forget that the southern colonies were not always slave societies. Ian K. Steele's "Empire of Migrants and Consumers" laid out the new Atlantic approach as it stood in 1991, contrasting the global turn with the work of the 1970s and early 1980s which had concentrated on local microhistories to cast light on processes of early settlement and development. He saw Bailyn's *Voyagers to the West* (1986) and David Hackett Fischer's *Albion's Seed* (1989) as bases for studies of migration—both voluntary and involuntary. Since then, scholars have built a composite picture of the South in this larger context. Detailed work by Alison Games brought a clearer picture of the Chesapeake settlers of 1635. April Lee Hatfield's *Atlantic Virginia* (2004) highlighted connections, especially those of trade. Peter C. Mancall's edited volume, *The Atlantic World and Virginia, 1550–1624* (2007), pushed the story back in time, setting the global scene for Jamestown and reminding us of the

2. Marcus Rediker, *Outlaws of the Atlantic: Sailors, Pirates, and Motley Crews in the Age of Sail* (Boston: Beacon Press, 2014); Rediker, *The Amistad Rebellion: An Atlantic Odyssey of Slavery and Freedom* (New York: Viking-Penguin, 2012); Rediker, *The Slave Ship: A Human History* (New York: Viking-Penguin, 2007); Rediker, *Villains of All Nations: Atlantic Pirates in the Golden Age* (Boston: Beacon Press, 2004); Rediker, *Between the Devil and the Deep Blue Sea: Merchant Seamen, Pirates, and the Anglo-American Maritime World, 1700–1750* (New York: Cambridge University Press, 1987). On the International Seminar on the History of the Atlantic World, 1500–1825, see https://sites.fas.harvard.edu/~atlantic/ (accessed 18 January 2019).

extraordinary diversity of peoples who played a role in the founding of the colonial South.[3]

Steele called for more work on the Atlantic beyond migration and trade. Some works on religion met his call, such as James B. Bell's *Empire, Religion, and Revolution in Early Virginia* (2013) which compares the work of the Anglican Church in Virginia with its outreach in Ireland. Yet even as historians came to realize that Steele was right to depict the Atlantic Ocean as "a waterway, not a moat," many scholars continued to delve into the local to show how each new experimental society developed internally, from the moments that the first few boatloads of immigrants arrived until the grandee planters firmly held the reins of power over both enslaved Africans and poor whites. Meticulous work by the Chesapeake group of Lorena S. Walsh, Lois Green Carr, Russell R. Menard, Jean B. Russo, and J. Elliott Russo had begun by 1987 when Rogers wrote his historiographical survey, but it continued through the 1990s and beyond. Central to that scholarship were colonists who came to the Chesapeake in the mid-seventeenth century and how the scale of tobacco cultivation and the racist character of southern culture grew in tandem.[4] The Chesapeake group looked at Maryland and Virginia as a region, joined by economic forces more formative than political and religious structures.

Not surprisingly, the 400th anniversary of the Jamestown settlement in 2007 produced a flurry of publications that looked anew at the earliest days of Virginia, contributing to a much more inclusive narrative that recognized the dilemma of

3. Ian K. Steele, "Empire of Migrants and Consumers: Some Current Atlantic Approaches to the History of Colonial Virginia," *Virginia Magazine of History and Biography* 99 (October 1991): 489–512; David Hackett Fischer, *Albion's Seed: Four British Folkways in America* (New York: Oxford University Press, 1989); Bernard Bailyn, *Voyagers to the West: A Passage in the Peopling of America on the Eve of the Revolution* (New York: Alfred A. Knopf, 1986); Alison Games, *Migration and the Origins of the English Atlantic World* (Cambridge: Harvard University Press, 1999); April Lee Hatfield, *Atlantic Virginia: Intercolonial Relations in the Seventeenth Century* (Philadelphia: University of Pennsylvania Press, 2004); Peter C. Mancall, ed., *The Atlantic World and Virginia, 1550–1624* (Chapel Hill: University of North Carolina Press, 2007).

4. James B. Bell, *Empire, Religion and Revolution in Early Virginia, 1607–1786* (New York: Palgrave Macmillan, 2013); Lois Green Carr, Philip D. Morgan, and Jean B. Russo, eds., *Colonial Chesapeake Society* (Chapel Hill: University of North Carolina Press, 1988); Lois Green Carr, Russell R. Menard, and Lorena S. Walsh, *Robert Cole's World: Agriculture and Society in Early Maryland* (Chapel Hill: University of North Carolina Press, 1991); James Horn, *Adapting to a New World: English Society in the Seventeenth-Century Chesapeake* (Chapel Hill: University of North Carolina Press, 1994); Lorena S. Walsh, *Motives of Honor, Pleasure, and Profit: Plantation Management in the Colonial Chesapeake, 1607–1763* (Chapel Hill: University of North Carolina Press, 2010); Jean B. Russo and J. Elliott Russo, *Planting an Empire: The Early Chesapeake in British North America* (Baltimore: Johns Hopkins University Press, 2012).

Powhatan as he pondered how warmly he should have welcomed the English who brought trade goods but also coveted his lands. Thanks to Karen Ordahl Kupperman, Helen C. Rountree, James Horn, William M. Kelso, and others, a fuller understanding of those first two decades of settlement came into focus, demonstrating how Virginia survived despite the ubiquity of death for both Indians and newcomers. Kupperman's work in particular provided a fine example of how Atlantic World history explains the local.[5]

Virginia politics, especially the rise and entrenchment of the planter class, continues to attract much attention. Warren M. Billings's biography of William Berkeley, along with his *A Little Parliament* (2004), portrayed how elites solidified power over indentured servants and small farmers in the decades before and after Bacon's Rebellion. Emory G. Evans's *A "Topping People"* (2009) and John Gilman Kolp's *Gentlemen and Freeholders* (1998) carried the story through the mid-eighteenth century, seeking to clarify how elites held power and why many gentry families became so mired in debt by the time of the American Revolution, despite owning large numbers of enslaved people and landed properties. Kolp argued that historians overstated the notion of deference, and that the grandees had to interact with small farmers and respond to local concerns. A culture of conspicuous consumption complicated the lives of the elites: in their pursuit of Anglo grandeur they spiraled into tremendous debt, as outlined in Woody Holton's *Forced Founders* (1999). Kevin Joel Berland annotated the histories of one such grandee, William Byrd, offering interdisciplinary insights on eighteenth-century texts to both historians and literary scholars. Alejandra Dubcovsky's *Informed Power* (2016) illuminated oral networks beyond those of white elites.[6]

5. James Horn, *A Land as God Made It: Jamestown and the Birth of America* (New York: Basic Books, 2005); Karen Ordahl Kupperman, *The Jamestown Project* (Cambridge: Harvard University Press, 2007); Helen C. Rountree, *Pocahontas, Powhatan, Opechancanough: Three Indian Lives Changed by Jamestown* (Charlottesville: University of Virginia Press, 2005); Rachel B. Herrmann, "The 'Tragical Historie': Cannibalism and Abundance in Colonial Jamestown," *William and Mary Quarterly* 68 (January 2011): 47–74; William M. Kelso, *Jamestown: The Buried Truth* (Charlottesville: University of Virginia Press, 2006); Lorri Glover and Daniel Blake Smith, *The Shipwreck that Saved Jamestown: The* Sea Venture *Castaways and the Fate of America* (New York: Henry Holt, 2008); Kieran Doherty, Sea Venture: *Shipwreck, Survival, and the Salvation of Jamestown* (New York: St. Martin's, 2007).

6. Warren M. Billings, *Sir William Berkeley and the Forging of Colonial Virginia* (Baton Rouge: Louisiana State University Press, 2004); Billings, *A Little Parliament: The Virginia General Assembly in the Seventeenth Century* (Richmond: Library of Virginia, 2004); Emory G. Evans, *A "Topping People": The Rise and Decline of Virginia's Old Political Elite, 1680–1790* (Charlottesville: University of Virginia Press, 2009); John Gilman Kolp, *Gentlemen and Freeholders: Electoral Politics in Colonial Virginia* (Baltimore:

The central story of Virginia's seventeenth century is, of course, Bacon's Rebellion. The debate on its causes, consequences, and significance continues. Important new contributions came from James D. Rice, whose *Tales from a Revolution* (2013) placed Indians in the center of the story, and from Brent Tarter and Peter Thompson, whose close readings of the county grievances emphasized the class struggle underlying the rebellion. Bacon's Rebellion had been central to Edmund S. Morgan's transformational *American Slavery, American Freedom* (1975), but Kathleen M. Brown revised Morgan's analysis to address with more nuance the intersections of race, class, and gender in *Good Wives, Nasty Wenches, and Anxious Patriarchs* (1996).[7]

Maryland's politics received less attention. David W. Jordan's *Foundations of Representative Government in Maryland* (1988) explained how the Assembly asserted its position over the course of the seventeenth century, while Trevor Burnard picked up the story (at least that of the planter elite) and took it through the eighteenth century. Archaeologist Timothy B. Riordan's *The Plundering Time* (2003) is a history of St. Mary's City, incorporating detailed archival work and asking us to reconsider Ingle's Rebellion. In *Loyal Protestants and Dangerous Papists* (2015), Antoinette Sutto brought an Atlantic World focus to colonial Maryland, resituating the centrality of religion to politics in the seventeenth century, even outside New England.[8]

Johns Hopkins University Press, 1998); Woody Holton, *Forced Founders: Indians, Debtors, Slaves, and the Making of the American Revolution in Virginia* (Chapel Hill: University of North Carolina Press, 1999); Kevin Joel Berland, *The Dividing Line: Histories of William Byrd II of Westover* (Chapel Hill: University of North Carolina Press, 2013); Alejandra Dubcovsky, *Informed Power: Communication in the Early American South* (Cambridge: Harvard University Press, 2016).

7. James D. Rice, *Tales from a Revolution: Bacon's Rebellion and the Transformation of Early America* (New York: Oxford University Press, 2013); Brent Tarter, "Bacon's Rebellion, the Grievances of the People, and the Political Culture of Seventeenth-Century Virginia," *Virginia Magazine of History and Biography* 119 (March 2011): 2–41; Peter Thompson, "The Thief, the Householder, and the Commons: Languages of Class in Seventeenth-Century Virginia," *William and Mary Quarterly* 63 (April 2006): 253–80; Edmund S. Morgan, *American Slavery, American Freedom: The Ordeal of Colonial Virginia* (New York: W. W. Norton, 1975); Kathleen M. Brown, *Good Wives, Nasty Wenches, and Anxious Patriarchs: Gender, Race and Power in Colonial Virginia* (Chapel Hill: University of North Carolina Press, 1996).

8. David W. Jordan, *Foundations of Representative Government in Maryland, 1632–1715* (New York: Cambridge University Press, 1988); Trevor Burnard, *Creole Gentlemen: The Maryland Elite, 1691–1776* (New York: Routledge, 2002); Timothy B. Riordan, *The Plundering Time: Maryland and the English Civil War, 1645–1646* (Baltimore: Johns Hopkins University Press, 2003); Antoinette Sutto, *Loyal Protestants and Dangerous Papists: Maryland and the Politics of Religion in the Early Atlantic, 1630–1690* (Charlottesville: University of Virginia Press, 2015).

Colonial North Carolina also remains understudied. Noeleen McIlvenna's *A Very Mutinous People* (2009) explained how the first two generations of settlers sought an alternative to the plantation world taking shape around them, and how the Albemarle region offered a safe space for Quakers during William Berkeley's reign. David La Vere's *Tuscarora War* (2013) provided a detailed and compelling narrative of the 1711–1715 conflict, examining the fight from both sides. The standard work on the Regulator rebellion remains Marjoleine Kars's excellent analysis, *Breaking Loose Together* (2002), which contrasted the Tidewater with the Piedmont as it took shape in the mid-eighteenth century.[9]

South Carolina has never lacked attention, of course. Thomas D. Wilson's fascinating *Ashley Cooper's Plan* (2016) traced modern politics back to the earliest days of the Goose Creek men, demonstrating how their vision contrasted with that of Lord Proprietor Ashley Cooper and John Locke, his collaborator on *The Fundamental Constitutions of Carolina*. Works on Indian history enlightened colonial economic history as well, as pre-rice cultivation and the lucrative deerskin trade became enmeshed with the trade in Indian prisoners of war. Alan Gallay's *The Indian Slave Trade* (2002) exposed the extent of Indigenous slavery. More work by Owen Stanwood, Robbie Ethridge, and Christina Snyder expanded our understanding of Native southerners' roles in emerging colonial economies and politics. Studies of the Yamasee War by Steven J. Oatis and William L. Ramsey set the scene for frontier South Carolina settlement, exposing the complexities of Indian trade politics between Yamasees, traders, planters, and proprietors. Thomas Hatley and Daniel J. Tortora provided guides to the Anglo-Cherokee War of 1759–1761.[10]

9. Noeleen McIlvenna, *A Very Mutinous People: The Struggle for North Carolina, 1660–1713* (Chapel Hill: University of North Carolina Press, 2009); David La Vere, *The Tuscarora War: Indians, Settlers, and the Fight for the Carolina Colonies* (Chapel Hill: University of North Carolina Press, 2013); Marjoleine Kars, *Breaking Loose Together: The Regulator Rebellion in Pre-Revolutionary North Carolina* (Chapel Hill: University of North Carolina Press, 2002).

10. Thomas D. Wilson, *The Ashley Cooper Plan: The Founding of Carolina and the Origins of Southern Political Culture* (Chapel Hill: University of North Carolina Press, 2016); Steven J. Oatis, *A Colonial Complex: South Carolina's Frontiers in the Era of the Yamasee War, 1680–1730* (Lincoln: University of Nebraska Press, 2004); William L. Ramsey, *The Yamasee War: A Study of Culture, Economy, and Conflict in the Colonial South* (Lincoln: University of Nebraska Press, 2008); Alan Gallay, *The Indian Slave Trade: The Rise of the English Empire in the American South, 1670–1717* (New Haven: Yale University Press, 2002); Owen Stanwood, "Captives and Slaves: Indian Labor, Cultural Conversion, and the Plantation Revolution in Virginia," *Virginia Magazine of History and Biography* 114 (2006): 434–63; Robbie Ethridge and Sheri M. Shuck-Hall, eds., *Mapping the Mississippian Shatter Zone: The Colonial Indian Slave Trade and Regional Instability in the American South* (Lincoln: University of Nebraska Press, 2009); Christina Snyder, *Slavery*

The social history of South Carolina's white immigrants, in particular their experiences of trying to create lives alongside the dominant planters who arrived from Barbados, were addressed by Arlin C. Migliazzo and Bertrand Van Ruymbeke, with the latter demonstrating how the Huguenots attempted to maintain their Calvinism even as they acculturated into a politically astute planter society. Huguenots confronted an era of lessening religious toleration, as establishment of the Anglican Church became tied to the slave society—a multidimensional construction of elite planter power over every facet of southern life by the turn of the eighteenth century.[11]

Georgia's colonial past was only half a century long and has often been interpreted as a mere extension of South Carolina, but some interesting work reminds us how fundamentally oppositional those colonies were in origin. Julie Anne Sweet's many publications form the basis of any exploration of the Trustee era. Anthony W. Parker's *Scottish Highlanders* (1997) offered a social history of the Trustee era through the Scots whose reputations as warriors made them ideal residents to place along the contested Florida boundary until King George's War finally settled the issue. Biographies appear to be especially popular as a means of telling Georgia's story: William Stevens, Jonathan Bryan, James Habersham, Lachlan MacGillivray, George Galphin, and Mary Musgrove each earned a book. Mostly planters and/or traders, these individuals played oversized roles in the making of the colony. Less powerful residents of colonial Georgia were highlighted in Noeleen McIlvenna's *Short Life of Free Georgia* (2015) which looked at the colony's first two decades from the perspective of poor English, Irish, and Germans, demonstrating the class chasm between them and the South Carolina planters who thirsted for the rice lands. Timothy James Lockley's *Lines in the Sand* (2001) treats the relationships between poor whites and enslaved people after the legalization of slavery.[12]

in Indian Country: The Changing Face of Captivity in Early America (Cambridge: Harvard University Press, 2010); Thomas Hatley, *The Dividing Paths: Cherokees and South Carolinians through the Era of Revolution* (New York: Oxford University Press, 1995); Daniel J. Tortora, *Carolina in Crisis: Cherokees, Colonists, and Slaves in the American Southeast, 1756–1763* (Chapel Hill: University of North Carolina Press, 2015).

11. Bertrand Van Ruymbeke, *From New Babylon to Eden: The Huguenots and Their Migration to Colonial South Carolina* (Columbia: University of South Carolina Press, 2006); Arlin C. Migliazzo, *To Make This Land Our Own: Community, Identity and Social Adaptation in Purrysburg Township, South Carolina, 1732–1865* (Columbia: University of South Carolina Press, 2007).

12. Julie Anne Sweet, *Negotiating for Georgia: British-Creek Relations in the Trustee-Era, 1733–1752* (Athens: University of Georgia Press, 2005); Sweet, *William Stephens: Georgia's Forgotten Founder* (Baton

In the late 1990s and early 2000s, some scholars pushed beyond the traditional five southern colonies to explore their remote backcountries. Robert Paulett's *Empire of Small Places* (2012) put the Augusta Indian trade and its concomitant diplomacy at the center of southeastern history, tracing the commerce all the way to Mississippi. Other studies looking at those living on the fringes of eighteenth-century white settlement include Craig Thompson Friend's *Kentucke's Frontiers* (2010) and Warren R. Hofstra's "The Extention of His Majesties Dominions" (1998).[13]

Religion remains a popular theme of the colonial era, and historians often explore the tension between the Anglican establishment and dissenters of many different stripes, but especially the evangelists who emerged out of the Great Awakening. Jon F. Sensbach's "Religion and the Early South in the Age of Atlantic Empire" (2007) opened with a description of South Carolina's 1704 assault on the Florida mission Indians, reminding readers that southern religious history included more than Southern Baptists. He argued that "the most significant change in early southern religious history, arguably, was not the rise of evangelicalism but the replacement of Native religions by Christianity and African religions and the corresponding desacralization of native landscapes." Sensbach provided a compelling overview of the state of the field, drawing attention to the centrality of religion to Native, European, and African worldviews and to their political,

---

Rouge: Louisiana State University Press, 2010); Anthony W. Parker, *Scottish Highlanders in Colonial Georgia: The Recruitment, Emigration, and Settlement at Darien, 1735–1748* (Athens: University of Georgia Press, 1997); Edward J. Cashin, *Lachlan McGillivray, Indian Trader: The Shaping of the Southern Colonial Frontier* (Athens: University of Georgia Press, 1992); Michael P. Morris, *George Galphin and the Transformation of the Georgia-South Carolina Backcountry* (Lanham, MD: Lexington Books, 2015); Alan Gallay, *The Formation of a Planter Elite: Jonathan Bryan and the Southern Colonial Frontier* (Athens: University of Georgia Press, 1989); Frank Lambert, *James Habersham: Loyalty, Politics and Commerce in Colonial Georgia* (Athens: University of Georgia Press, 2005); Steven C. Hahn, *The Life and Times of Mary Musgrove* (Gainesville: University Press of Florida, 2012); Noeleen McIlvenna, *The Short Life of Free Georgia: Class and Slavery in the Colonial South* (Chapel Hill: University of North Carolina Press, 2015); Timothy James Lockley, *Lines in the Sand: Race and Class in Lowcountry Georgia, 1750–1860* (Athens: University of Georgia Press, 2001).

13. Robert Paulett, *An Empire of Small Places: Mapping the Southeastern Anglo-Indian Trade, 1732–1795* (Athens: University of Georgia Press, 2012); Craig Thompson Friend, *Kentucke's Frontiers* (Bloomington: Indiana University Press, 2010); Warren R. Hofstra, "The Extention of His Majesties Dominions: The Virginia Backcountry and the Reconfiguration of Imperial Frontiers," *Journal of American History* 84 (March 1998): 1281–312.

cultural, and economic relationships. Douglas Bradburn argued for a religious motivation in the planning of the Virginia colony, and its Anglican Church received attention from Edward L. Bond, John K. Nelson, and Jacob M. Blosser. In *For God, King, and People* (2017), Alexander B. Haskell reconstructed how the colony's religion and politics meshed in the seventeenth century. Charles Lippy's "Chastized by Scorpions" (2010), Samuel C. Smith's *A Cautious Enthusiasm* (2013), and Thomas Little's *Origins of Southern Evangelicalism* (2013) collectively demonstrate how the Great Awakening penetrated the Lower South, locating the development of evangelism at least a generation earlier than previously thought. Fred E. Witzig's biography of Alexander Garden recounted the Anglican defense against evangelical development.[14]

Just as Rhys Isaac shone a light on religion through a study of architecture in *The Transformation of Virginia* (1982), Louis P. Nelson's *Beauty of Holiness* (2009) used material culture to examine eighteenth-century religion in South Carolina. Lauren F. Winner did the same for Virginia gentry households in *A Cheerful and Comfortable Faith* (2010). Building on Ronald Hoffman, Mechal Sobel, and Fredrika J. Teute's 1997 collection, *Through a Glass Darkly*, Jennifer Van Horn's *The Power of Objects in Eighteenth-Century British America* (2017) employed a fresh range of material and decorative items to rethink elite culture and communities, while Barbara Mooney used the architecture of Tidewater plantation houses as

14. Jon F. Sensbach, "Religion and the Early South in an Age of Atlantic Empire," *Journal of Southern History* 73 (August 2007): 631–42, quote on 637; Douglas Bradburn, "The Eschatological Origins of the English Empire," in *Early Modern Virginia: Reconsidering the Old Dominion,* ed. Douglas Bradburn and John C. Coombs (Charlottesville: University of Virginia Press, 2011), 15–56; Edward L. Bond, *Damned Souls in a Tobacco Colony: Religion in Seventeenth-Century Virginia* (Macon: Mercer University Press, 2001); John K. Nelson, *A Blessed Company: Parishes, Parsons, and Parishioners in Anglican Virginia, 1690–1776* (Chapel Hill: University of North Carolina Press, 2001); Jacob M. Blosser, "Pursuing Happiness in Colonial Virginia: Sacred Words, Cheap Print, and Popular Religion in the Eighteenth Century," *Virginia Magazine of History and Biography* 118 (2010): 209–45; Charles H. Lippy, "Chastized by Scorpions: Christianity and Culture in Colonial South Carolina, 1669–1740," *Church History* 79 (June 2010): 253–70; Samuel C. Smith, *A Cautious Enthusiasm: Mystical Piety and Evangelicalism in Colonial South Carolina* (Columbia: University of South Carolina Press, 2013); Thomas J. Little, *Origins of Southern Evangelicalism: Religious Revivalism in the South Carolina Lowcountry, 1670–1760* (Columbia: University of South Carolina Press, 2013); Alexander B. Haskell, *For God, King, and People: Forging Commonwealth Bonds in Renaissance Virginia* (Chapel Hill: University of North Carolina Press, 2017); Fred E. Witzig, *Sanctifying Slavery and Politics in South Carolina: The Life of the Reverend Alexander Garden, 1685–1756* (Columbia: University of South Carolina Press, 2018).

a vehicle to explore the men who craved elite status. Cary Carson's article, "Banqueting Houses and the 'Need Society' among Slave-Owning Planters in the Chesapeake Colonies" (2013), is also essential reading.[15]

In 2007, Cynthia A. Kierner updated the historiography on colonial southern women, and on gender more broadly in "Women, Gender, Families and Households." She praised the groundbreaking work by the Chesapeake group and by Catherine Clinton, Michele Gillespie, Kathleen M. Brown, Kirsten Fischer, Jennifer L. Morgan, and Theda Perdue. Scholars have reimagined the roles of southern colonial women. Lorri Glover repositioned them in the epistolary affairs of South Carolina's sibling and kin networks in *All Our Relations* (2000). Ben Marsh's *Georgia's Frontier Women* (2012) cast a light on ways in which women founded colonies. Terri L. Snyder's "'To Seeke for Justice'" (2011) used court records to describe servant women's experiences. The University of Georgia Press has taken the lead in promoting southern women's history, producing collections of essays on the women of each southern state, collectively delivering a portrait of women's lives in the colonial South. Among some of the most interesting articles in these collections are Kierner's "The Edenton Ladies" and Sensbach's "Sister Anna," both in volume one of *North Carolina Women* (2014); Kristalyn M. Shefveland's "Cockacoeske and Sarah Harris Stegge Grendon" in *Virginia Women* (2015); and Craig Thompson Friend's "Nonhelema Hokolesqua, Jemima Boone Callaway, and Matilda Lewis Threlkeld" in *Kentucky Women* (2015).[16]

15. Rhys Isaac, *The Transformation of Virginia, 1740–1790* (Chapel Hill: University of North Carolina Press, 1982); Louis P. Nelson, *The Beauty of Holiness: Anglicanism & Architecture in Colonial South Carolina* (Chapel Hill: University of North Carolina Press, 2009); Lauren F. Winner, *A Cheerful and Comfortable Faith: Anglican Religious Practice in the Elite Households of Eighteenth-Century Virginia* (New Haven: Yale University Press, 2010); Barbara Mooney, *Prodigy Houses of Virginia: Architecture and the Native Elite* (Charlottesville: University of Virginia Press, 2008); Ronald Hoffman, Mechal Sobel, and Frederika J. Teute, eds., *Through A Glass Darkly: Reflections on Personal Identity in Early America* (Chapel Hill: University of North Carolina Press, 1997); Jennifer Van Horn, *The Power of Objects in Eighteenth-Century British America* (Chapel Hill: University of North Carolina Press, 2017); Cary Carson, "Banqueting Houses and the 'Need of Society' among Slave-Owning Planters in the Chesapeake Colonies," *William and Mary Quarterly* 70 (October 2013): 725–80.

16. Cynthia A. Kierner, "Women, Gender, Families, and Households in the Southern Colonies," *Journal of Southern History* 73 (August 2007): 643–58; Lorri Glover, *All Our Relations: Blood Ties and Emotional Bonds Among the Early South Carolina Gentry* (Baltimore: Johns Hopkins University Press, 2000); Ben Marsh, *Georgia's Frontier Women: Female Fortunes in a Southern Colony* (Athens: University of Georgia Press, 2007); Terri L. Snyder, "'To Seeke for Justice': Gender, Servitude, and Household

In 1993, Snyder pleaded, "we need more of almost everything in the legal history of the colonial South," and when Warren M. Billings surveyed the field in 2007, he could only echo her call. Their combined footnotes constitute a full bibliography of the field. Noteworthy are several chapters in Christopher L. Tomlins and Bruce E. Mann's *The Many Legalities of Early America* (2001) while Billings's *A Little Parliament* remains the best on Virginia's courts. Holly Brewer's *By Birth or Consent* (2005) is not solely devoted to the South but provides a model for understanding the evolution of the law in the colonial era. Of course, the most important matters that southern courts considered were concepts of freedom and property. Thomas D. Morris's *Southern Slavery and the Law* (1996) traced the slave system in legislature and courtroom from the seventeenth century through the antebellum era, while Sally E. Hadden described enforcement. Still, a scholar looking for a neglected topic can start with the law, especially south of Virginia.[17]

The colonial South has been a fertile field for environmental historians, including Timothy Silver, Mart A. Stewart, and James D. Rice. Virginia DeJohn Anderson's *Creatures of Empire* (2004) looked at the role of domesticated livestock in the Chesapeake as well as New England. Donald Edward Davis made a wonderful contribution to southern Appalachian colonial history in *Where There*

Governance in the Early Modern Chesapeake," in Bradburn and Coombs, eds., *Early Modern Virginia,* 128–57; Cynthia Kierner, "The Edenton Ladies: Women, Tea, and Politics in Revolutionary North Carolina," in *North Carolina Women: Their Lives and Times—Volume 1,* ed. Michele Gillespie and Sally G. McMillen (Athens: University of Georgia Press, 2014), 12–33; Jon F. Sensbach, "Sister Anna: An African Woman in Early North Carolina," in Gillespie and McMillen, eds., *North Carolina Women,* 34–53; Kristalyn M. Shefveland, "Cockacoeske and Sarah Harris Stegge Grendon: Bacon's Rebellion and the Roles of Women," in *Virginia Women: Their Lives and Times—Volume 1,* ed. Cynthia A. Kierner and Sandra Treadway (Athens: University of Georgia Press, 2015), 33–54; Craig Thompson Friend, "Nonhelema Hokolesqua, Jemima Boone Callaway, and Matilda Lewis Threlkeld: Searching for Kentucky's Female Frontier," in *Kentucky Women: Their Lives and Times,* ed. Melissa A. McEuen and Thomas H. Appleton Jr. (Athens: University of Georgia Press, 2015), 8–32. See also Cara Anzilotti, *In the Affairs of the World: Women, Patriarchy, and Power in Colonial South Carolina* (Westport: Greenwood Press, 2002).

17. Terri L. Snyder, "Legal History of the Colonial South: Assessment and Suggestions," *William and Mary Quarterly* 50 (January 1993): 18–27, quote on 27; Warren M. Billings, "Law in the Colonial South," *Journal of Southern History* 73 (August 2007): 603–16; Christopher L. Tomlins and Bruce H. Mann, *The Many Legalities of Early America* (Chapel Hill: University of North Carolina Press, 2001); Billings, *A Little Parliament;* Holly Brewer, *By Birth or Consent: Children, Law, and the Anglo-American Revolution in Authority* (Chapel Hill: University of North Carolina Press, 2005); Thomas D. Morris, *Southern Slavery and the Law, 1619–1860* (Chapel Hill: University of North Carolina Press, 1996); Sally E. Hadden, *Slave Patrols: Law and Violence in Virginia and the Carolinas* (Cambridge: Harvard University Press, 2001).

Are Mountains (2000). Keith Pluymers's 2016 article set ecology in an Atlantic World frame to argue that "the political ecology of wood shaped colonial development" in the seventeenth century.[18]

Some work, however, is difficult to label as either "agricultural" or "environmental" or even "economic" history, and almost all of it could be subsumed under the history of slavery. After the 1980s, historians grew more interested in the origin debates about enslavement and racism in the southern colonies than previous generations of historians had demonstrated. Scholars in the origins debate tended to align themselves to two camps: the first argued that both black racism and slavery developed slowly and were contingent on a series of events. As Edmund S. Morgan argued, racism was cultivated and slavery was entrenched after Bacon's Rebellion because planters realized that "resentment of an alien race might be more powerful than resentment of an upper class." The second camp claimed that racism was present from the outset in Virginia. Slavery was, as Winthrop D. Jordan maintained, an "unthinking decision" or the inevitable extension of a deeply ingrained English prejudice towards black peoples.[19] Since 1987, Ira Berlin and Anthony S. Parent Jr. produced works that favored the first view while David Eltis, Alden T. Vaughan, Lorena S. Walsh, and John Coombs endorsed the second point of view. Berlin, for example, developed Morgan's thesis by stressing that the "charter generation" of Africans in the Chesapeake had opportunities for freedom and autonomy that later generations lacked.[20] Eltis, in contrast, built

18. Timothy Silver, *A New Face on the Countryside: Indians, Colonists, and Slaves in South Atlantic Forests, 1500–1800* (New York: Cambridge University Press, 1990); Mart A. Stewart, *"What Nature Suffers to Groe": Life, Labor, and Landscape on the Georgia Coast, 1680–1920* (Athens: University of Georgia Press, 2002); James D. Rice, *Nature and History in the Potomac Country: From Hunter-Gatherers to the Age of Jefferson* (Baltimore: Johns Hopkins University Press, 2009); Virginia DeJohn Anderson, *Creatures of Empire: How Domestic Animals Transformed Early America* (New York: Oxford University Press, 2004); Donald Edward Davis, *Where There Are Mountains: An Environmental History of the Southern Appalachians* (Athens: University of Georgia Press, 2000); Keith Pluymers, "Atlantic Iron: Wood Scarcity and the Political Ecology of Early English Expansion," *William and Mary Quarterly* 73 (July 2016): 389–426, quote on 392.

19. Morgan, *American Slavery, American Freedom*, 270. See also Oscar and Mary F. Handlin, "The Origins of the Southern Labor System," *William and Mary Quarterly* 7 (April 1950): 199–222; Winthrop D. Jordan, *White Over Black: American Attitudes toward the Negro, 1550–1812* (Chapel Hill: University of North Carolina Press, 1968), 44–98; Carl N. Degler, "Slavery and the Genesis of American Race Prejudice," *Comparative Studies in Society and History* 2 (October 1959): 49–66.

20. Ira Berlin, *Many Thousands Gone: The First Two Centuries of Slavery in North America* (Cambridge: Harvard University Press, 1998), esp. 15–46; Anthony S. Parent Jr., *Foul Means: The Formation of a Slave Society in Virginia, 1660–1740* (Chapel Hill: University of North Carolina Press, 2003); John C. Coombs,

upon Jordan's position, by arguing that Europeans never considered lifetime and inheritable slavery for vulnerable European groups; the status was always reserved for non-Europeans. A historiographical consensus seemed to take hold that slavery was the default status for Africans arriving in the early Chesapeake and that determinative racial prejudice in some form, albeit malleable, existed in Virginia and Maryland from the outset. Notably, discussions about the origins of race and slavery in the Americas have also broadened significantly in the last two decades to incorporate Indian slavery throughout North America, especially in the seventeenth century. Scholars of southeastern slavery cannot now neglect the works of Alan Gallay, James F. Brooks, Robbie Ethridge, Juliana Barr, and Christina Snyder.[21]

The Atlantic turn breathed new life into the origins debate, expanding the interpretive landscape beyond England's Chesapeake colonies. Drawing from the erudite and expansive studies of pathbreakers such as Philip D. Curtin, historians are now far more likely to explore the Iberian origins of both slavery and racism in the Americas.[22] Whereas scholars once questioned the level of ingrained racism by highlighting many free blacks who lived in the early Chesapeake, such as Anthony Johnson who escaped lifetime enslavement, historians expanded their visions to include the Caribbean, specifically the early sugar colonies, where they found indentured white servants temporarily living in conditions that seem closer

---

"Beyond the 'Origins Debate': Rethinking the Rise of Virginia Slavery," in Bradburn and Coombs, eds., *Early Modern Virginia,* 90–127; Coombs, "The Phases of Conversion: A New Chronology for the Rise of Slavery in Early Virginia," *William and Mary Quarterly* 68 (July 2011): 332–60; Walsh, *Motives of Honor, Pleasure & Profit;* David Eltis, *The Rise of African Slavery in the Americas* (New York: Cambridge University Press, 2000), 273–78; Alden T. Vaughan, "The Origins Debate: Slavery and Racism in Seventeenth-Century Virginia," *Virginia Magazine of History and Biography* 97 (July 1989): 311–54.

21. David Eltis, "Europeans and the Rise and Fall of African Slavery in the Americas: An Interpretation," *American Historical Review* 98 (December 1993): 1399–423; Rebecca Anne Goetz, "Rethinking the 'Unthinking Decision': Old Questions and New Problems in the History of Slavery and Race in the Colonial South," *Journal of Southern History* 75 (August 2009): 599–612; Alan Gallay, ed., *Indian Slavery in Colonial America* (Lincoln: University of Nebraska Press, 2009); James F. Brooks, *Captives and Cousins: Slavery, Kinship, and Community in the Southwest Borderlands* (Chapel Hill: University of North Carolina Press, 2002); Ethridge and Shuck-Hall, *Mapping the Mississippian Shatter Zone;* Juliana Barr, "How Do You Get from Jamestown to Santa Fe? A Colonial Sun Belt," *Journal of Southern History* 73 (August 2007): 553–66; Snyder, *Slavery in Indian Country.*

22. See, for example, James H. Sweet, "The Iberian Roots of American Racist Thought," *William and Mary Quarterly* 54 (January 1997): 143–66; Philip D. Curtin, *The Rise and Fall of the Plantation Complex: Essays in Atlantic History,* 2nd ed. (New York: Cambridge University Press, 1998).

to enslavement than freedom, raising questions about the determinative power of race, clearly with important sociopolitical implications.[23] Not surprisingly, some Caribbean scholars reacted strongly to the idea that slavery differed from indentured servitude by degree more than kind, arguing that we cannot conflate enslavement and servitude. Racialized slavery, as these scholars explained, was uniquely dehumanizing because it was permanent and inheritable, and millions of peoples of African descent became subject to slavery from the outset in the English Americas.[24] These politicized debates, in turn, reinvigorated discussions about the nature of seventeenth-century indentured servitude, placing the meaning of servitude in broader contexts.[25]

The Atlantic turn also forced historians of slavery to pay close attention to the literature of the early Caribbean. It is now very clear that slavery spread to the early South in a kind of ripple effect out of the Caribbean. The first southern colonies perched like parasitical pirates on the edge of vast Iberian empires, and they remained peripheral to the locus of English economic and imperial power in the sugar islands until late in the seventeenth century. The first "twenty and odd negroes" in the English colonies arrived in Virginia in 1619 before the col-

23. For an example of Anthony Johnson as key evidence in the origins debate, see J. Douglas Deal, *Race and Class in Colonial Virginia: Indians, Englishmen and Africans on the Eastern Shore of Virginia during the Seventeenth Century* (New York: Garland Publishing, 1993), 217–50. Hilary McD. Beckles argued that Irish servants in Barbados "were nearer slavery than freedom"; see "A Riotous and Unruly Lot: Irish Indentured Servants and Freemen in the English West Indies, 1644–1713," *William and Mary Quarterly* 47 (October 1990): 511. Simon P. Newman also described a virtual slavery for many white indentured servants in early Barbados; see Newman, *A New World of Labor: The Development of Plantation Slavery in the British Atlantic* (Philadelphia: University of Pennsylvania Press, 2013). For a more comprehensive and nuanced examination of the Irish experience in the Caribbean, see Jenny Shaw, *Everyday Life in the Early English Caribbean: Irish, Africans, and the Construction of Difference* (Athens: University of Georgia Press, 2013). Some popular histories have also maintained that whites were virtually slaves in the English colonies. See, for example, Don Jordan and Michael Walsh, *White Cargo: The Forgotten History of Britain's White Slaves in America* (New York: New York University Press, 2007). For a critique of the reductionism in the "white slaves" argument, see Liam Hogan, "Two Years of the 'Irish Slaves' Myth: Racism, Reductionism and the Tradition of Diminishing the Transatlantic Slave Trade," *Open Democracy*, 7 November 2016, https://www.opendemocracy.net/beyondslavery/liam-hogan/two-years-of-irish-slaves-myth-racism-reductionism-and-tradition-of-diminis (accessed 18 January 2019).

24. See, for example, Jerome S. Handler, "Custom and Law: The Status of Enslaved Africans in Seventeenth-Century Barbados," *Slavery & Abolition* 37 (2016): 233–55; Handler and Matthew C. Reilly, "Contesting 'White Slavery' in the Caribbean: Enslaved Africans and European Indentured Servants in Seventeenth-Century Barbados," *New West Indian Guide* 91 (Summer 2017): 30–55.

25. See, for example, John Wareing, *Indentured Migration and the Servant Trade from London to America, 1618–1718: "There Is Great Want of Servants"* (New York: Oxford University Press, 2017).

onization of Barbados or St. Kitts, but the enslaved peoples had been captured by Dutch privateers from Iberian slave traders farther south. Black populations in the Chesapeake remained less than 5 percent of the population for the first five decades of settlement because there was no regular supply of African slaves. In the broader historiographical frameworks, Chesapeake planters could not compete, given the prices in Atlantic slave markets. By the time Chesapeake and Carolina planters turned towards slavery, enslaved Africans had become the default choice for labor in the Caribbean.[26]

Works by John C. Coombs, Russell R. Menard, and Demitri D. Debe underscored the idea that the wealthiest Chesapeake planters turned very quickly—as early as the 1650s—to the form of race-based chattel slavery already entrenched in Barbados, and indeed, it may have been introduced by Barbadian planters. Coombs showed that Virginia's elite officeholders clearly decided on the advantages of an enslaved labor force by 1660, long before Bacon's Rebellion which Morgan marked as the turning point in Chesapeake slavery and race relations. The scholarship now suggests that the supply and price of slaves relative to the supply and price of servants stalled the smaller Chesapeake planters in transitioning to an African labor force. A gradual shift towards a predominantly African labor force occurred between 1670 and 1720. A sharp reduction in the supply of servants from the British Isles, beginning in the 1680s, was probably more significant a factor in the Chesapeake's transition to slavery than the consolidation of power that came after Bacon's Rebellion.[27]

Yet much more work remains to weave the story of the emergence of slavery in the South into more global histories. One of the best examinations of a broader context for the origins of English slavery is Michael Gusaco's *Slaves and Englishmen* (2014). Guasco devoted attention to both the English Caribbean and the Chesapeake, demonstrating that before its establishment in the plantation Americas, slavery was "often only loosely related to the need for labor." Consequently, both Africans and Europeans were subject to an enslavement that was not always permanent or inheritable.[28]

26. Michael Guasco, *Slaves and Englishmen: Human Bondage in the Early Modern Atlantic World* (Philadelphia: University of Pennsylvania Press, 2014); Berlin, *Many Thousands Gone.*

27. Coombs, "The Phases of Conversion"; Goetz, "Rethinking the 'Unthinking Decision'"; Demetri D. Debe and Russell R. Menard, "The Transition to African Slavery in Maryland: A Note on the Barbados Connection," *Slavery & Abolition* 32 (March 2011): 129–41. See also Kenneth Morgan, *Slavery and Servitude in Colonial North America: A Short History* (New York: New York University Press, 2001).

28. Guasco, *Slaves and Englishmen,* 7.

Scholars of colonial Carolina had been conscious of Caribbean connections and comparisons, particularly South Carolina's relationship to Barbados, long before the Atlantic turn. But scholarship since the 1990s has been marked by deeper and more nuanced appreciations of Atlantic contexts and of the Caribbean world. The colony of Barbados, densely populated and filled with plenty of capital from the lucrative sugar economy, expanded outwards in a "Barbadian diaspora" from the late 1640s through the late 1660s. But by the time Charles Town was founded in 1670, the Barbadian population had been drained by warfare, hurricanes, and a long series of both successful and failed settlement schemes in other colonies. The Barbadians likely sent more capital than settlers to South Carolina.[29] Importantly, as Kinloch Bull made clear in "Settlers in Early Carolina" (1995), people sailing from Barbados were not necessarily residents; many stopped there in transit. The consensus remains that the Barbadian model of plantation slavery migrated to the Carolinas, but some strands of that argument have been challenged or complicated. Edward B. Rugemer, for example, suggested that South Carolina's slave code drew from Jamaican innovations to the Barbadian slave code instead of directly adopting the Barbadian code.[30]

Matthew Mulcahy's *Hubs of Empire* (2014) showed how immersed the Lowcountry became in a greater Caribbean world—especially after the transition to a staple-crop economy—and how much South Carolina shared in common with Caribbean slave societies in terms of the proportion of Africans, the great wealth generated by plantation economies, and the threat of hurricanes and natural disasters. Mulcahy's research joined Paul M. Pressley's work on Georgia, *On the Rim of the Caribbean* (2013), which highlighted networks between the sugar islands and the Lower South. The terrific edited collection *Money, Trade*

29. Justin Roberts, "Surrendering Surinam: The Barbadian Diaspora and the Expansion of the English Sugar Frontier, 1650–1675," *William and Mary Quarterly* 73 (April 2016): 225–56; Roberts and Ian Beamish, "Venturing Out: The Barbadian Diaspora and the Carolina Colony, 1650–1685," in *Creating and Contesting Carolina: Proprietary Era Histories,* ed. Bradford J. Wood and Michelle LeMaster (Columbia: University of South Carolina Press, 2013), 49–72. For other studies that downplay the influence of Barbadians in South Carolina, see L. H. Roper, *Conceiving Carolina: Proprietors, Planters and Plots, 1662–1729* (New York: Palgrave Macmillan, 2004); Kinloch Bull, "Settlers in Early Carolina: Historiographical Notes," *South Carolina Historical Magazine* 96 (October 1995): 329–39.

30. Bull, "Settlers in Early Carolina"; Edward B. Rugemer, "The Development of Mastery and Race in the Comprehensive Slave Codes of the Greater Caribbean during the Seventeenth Century," *William and Mary Quarterly* 70 (July 2013): 429–58.

and Power (2000) brought together early-career scholars to examine various aspects of South Carolina's economy in an Atlantic context. Emma Hart's *Building Charleston* (2015) and Andrea Feeser's *Red, White, and Black Make Blue* (2013) highlighted how Atlantic World questions seeped into very local studies. Christa Dierksheide's *Amelioration and Empire* (2014), an intellectual history of the English Atlantic, contrasted the planters of the South and the Caribbean with their peers in England. Dierksheide argued that slaveholders saw themselves as modern men and that, amidst a growing critique of slavery, they made peace with their position at the heart of the Atlantic slave trade.[31]

Since the 1990s, scholarly interest in colonial enslavement, comparative slavery studies, and the diversity of slave-based forms of production and slave experiences in the South surged. Older generations of southern scholars had found it strikingly easy to make monolithic and transhistorical claims about slavery as they battled over the nature and legacy of racial slavery in the United States.[32] The nineteenth-century antebellum cotton plantation became the archetype of the slave plantation. Since the 1990s, however, one of the major scholarly endeavors in studies of colonial slavery has been to disaggregate those historiographical monoliths and challenge that archetype. Two field-defining studies led the way, both published in 1998. Grounded in more than two decades of deep archival research, Philip D. Morgan's *Slave Counterpoint* showed that the work regimes in

31. Matthew Mulcahy, *Hubs of Empire: The Southeastern Lowcountry and British Caribbean* (Baltimore: Johns Hopkins University Press, 2014); Paul M. Pressly, *On the Rim of the Caribbean: Colonial Georgia and the British Atlantic World* (Athens: University of Georgia Press, 2013); Jack P. Greene, Rosemary Brana-Shute, and Randy J. Sparks, eds., *Money, Trade, and Power: The Evolution of Colonial South Carolina's Plantation Society* (Columbia: University of South Carolina Press, 2000); Emma Hart, *Building Charleston: Town and Society in the Eighteenth-Century British Atlantic World* (Columbia: University of South Carolina Press, 2010); Andrea Feeser, *Red, White, and Black Make Blue: Indigo in the Fabric of Colonial South Carolina Life* (Athens: University of Georgia Press, 2013); Christa Dierksheide, *Amelioration and Empire: Progress and Slavery in the Plantation Americas* (Charlottesville: University of Virginia Press, 2014). See also the much older, but still resonant, Peter H. Wood, *Black Majority: Negroes in Colonial South Carolina from 1670 through the Stono Rebellion* (New York: W. W. Norton, 1974).

32. For examples, see Ulrich B. Phillips, *American Negro Slavery: A Survey of the Supply, Employment and Control of Negro Labor as Determined by the Plantation Regime* (1918; repr., New York: D. Appleton, 1940); Kenneth M. Stampp, *The Peculiar Institution: Slavery in the Ante-Bellum South* (New York: Vintage, 1956); Stanley M. Elkins, *Slavery: A Problem in American Institutional and Intellectual Life* (Chicago: University of Chicago Press, 1959); Eugene D. Genovese, *Roll, Jordan, Roll: The World the Slaves Made* (New York: Pantheon Books, 1974).

the Lowcountry were more violent and destructive to the health of the enslaved than in the Chesapeake, but also that the slaves in the Lowcountry were better able to form autonomous communities composed of more African-born slaves.[33]

Ira Berlin's *Many Thousands Gone* took an even broader—albeit more synthetic—view of the many forms of slavery that emerged across the North American colonies. One of Berlin's most important innovations in the literature on colonial slavery was his concept of Atlantic Creoles—peoples of African descent brought to the colonies before the plantation system matured and became entrenched. Berlin argued that Creole peoples understood the Atlantic World, its languages, and its emerging economic and social systems. They also had connections to the Iberian world where boundaries between slavery and freedom were more permeable. All of this gave them greater negotiating power with their enslavers. Berlin concluded that this helped explain the large population of free blacks in the early Chesapeake. Although he thought of Atlantic creolism as a seventeenth-century phenomenon that disappeared as the plantation system strengthened, other scholars adopted the concept and tried to push it into later periods. Jane G. Landers, for example, tracked individual peoples of African descent in places such as Cuba and Florida during the American Revolutionary era, and she argued that such people had significant knowledge of the Atlantic World that they could leverage for greater autonomy and opportunity. Atlantic Creoles garnered enough attention to merit their own bibliographic essay in *Oxford Bibliographies Online: Atlantic History.*[34]

Historians of early American slavery are in the vanguard of efforts within the discipline to collapse traditional chronological and geographic boundaries. Indeed, the fact that slavery continued in the Caribbean until 1833 forces scholars who engage both Caribbean and southern slavery to push beyond traditional chronological boundaries of the colonial South. The abolition of the slave trade becomes a more obvious chronological divide than the American Revolution. As early as 1992, Michael Mullin explored slave resistance and slave culture across the South and the British Caribbean, bridging the colonial and antebellum peri-

33. Philip D. Morgan, *Slave Counterpoint: Black Culture in the Eighteenth-Century Chesapeake and Lowcountry* (Chapel Hill: University of North Carolina Press, 1998).

34. Berlin, *Many Thousands Gone;* Jane G. Landers, *Atlantic Creoles in the Age of Revolutions* (Cambridge: Harvard University Press, 2010); Landers, "Atlantic Creoles," in *Oxford Bibliographies Online: Atlantic History,* ed. Trevor Burnard, http://www.oxfordbibliographies.com/view/document/obo-9780199730414/obo-9780199730414–0090.xml (accessed 18 January 2019).

ods of the United States. In *Slavery and the Enlightenment* (2013), Justin Roberts offered a triangulated comparison of plantation slavery in late Barbados, Jamaica, and Virginia that stretched from 1750 to 1807. He argued that in terms of the proportion of Africans, diversified agriculture, and slave reproduction rates, late eighteenth-century Barbados shared as much in common with Virginia as it did Jamaica.[35] In 2015 Trevor Burnard published an erudite survey of slavery across the Anglo-American world from 1650 to 1820. Richard S. Dunn's much anticipated *A Tale of Two Plantations* (2014)—based on four decades of research—provided an incredibly detailed and rich comparative study of enslaved life on plantations in Virginia and Jamaica that underscored the violence and destructiveness of work regimes on sugar plantations. He also showed the trauma that peoples of African descent suffered when they were torn from their families in the Chesapeake as enslaved populations began to grow by natural reproduction and planters sold away people they deemed as excess. One of Dunn's most significant contributions was to show the foolishness in trying to gauge whether brutal sugar work and brutal punishments were worse than the act of wrenching children from their mother's arms to sell them.[36]

Although the Atlantic turn dramatically reshaped the history of the colonial South, historians have also asked whether the Atlantic turn is broad enough in scope. Some scholars situated the colonial South in broader continental and global narratives. Jonathan Eacott's *Selling Empire* (2017), for example, opened the door to a truly global perspective and serves as a reminder that southern colonies were more peripheral than typically portrayed. The Omohundro Insti-

35. Michael Mullin, *Africa in America: Slave Acculturation and Resistance in the American South and the British Caribbean, 1736–1831* (Urbana: University of Illinois Press, 1992); Justin Roberts, *Slavery and the Enlightenment in the British Atlantic, 1750–1807* (New York: Cambridge University Press, 2013). For other examples of slavery and slave society studies that bridge the gap between colonial and early national histories, see Rachel N. Klein, *Unification of a Slave State: The Rise of the Planter Class in the South Carolina Backcountry, 1760–1808* (Chapel Hill: University of North Carolina Press, 1990); Michael A. Gomez, *Exchanging Our Country Marks: The Transformation of African Identities in the Colonial and Antebellum South* (Chapel Hill: University of North Carolina Press, 1998); Thomas N. Ingersoll, *Mammon and Manon in Early New Orleans: The First Slave Society in the Deep South, 1718–1819* (Knoxville: University of Tennessee Press, 1999).

36. Trevor Burnard, *Planters, Merchants, and Slaves: Plantation Societies in British America, 1650–1820* (Chicago: University of Chicago Press, 2015); Richard S. Dunn, *A Tale of Two Plantations: Slave Life and Labor in Jamaica and Virginia* (Cambridge: Harvard University Press, 2014). For an important book-length comparison of Jamaica and South Carolina, see Edward B. Rugemer, *Slave Law and the Politics of Resistance in the Early Atlantic World* (Cambridge: Harvard University Press, 2018).

tute of Early American History and Culture and its flagship journal for the study of early American history, the *William and Mary Quarterly,* have advanced the #VastEarlyAmerica framework.[37]

By the end of the twentieth century, the historiography of southern slavery was immersed in a resistance paradigm that began in the 1960s and peaked in the 1980s and 1990s. Scholars stressed the variety of ways in which enslaved peoples exercised agency and resisted the dehumanization of the institution, from breaking tools and slowing down work to outright rebellions. Some of this interpretation was born in reaction to Stanley M. Elkins's insistence that slavery destroyed the psyche of the enslaved, damaging black culture and leaving the enslaved infantilized. Nathan I. Huggins insisted that there were dangerously "racist" undertones in Elkins's "damage thesis" because it implied that blacks, while not naturally inferior to whites, had been made so by the degenerative effects of slavery. A generation of scholars, including John W. Blassingame, refuted Elkins's claims and their implications for the legacy of enslavement in African American culture by arguing that slaves successfully resisted enslavement and that they created autonomous communities unified in resistance to their masters.[38] In the 1980s and 1990s, many historians, such as Michael Mullin, took the resistance argument a step further, arguing that maintenance of African culture and the assertion of humanity or cultural autonomy under this totalizing system of dehumanization should be seen as signs of resistance. Mullin, for example, defined cultural resistance as simply "the refusal to abandon one's values" in the face of slavery. A. J. William-Myers, in "Slavery, Rebellion and Revolution" (1996), encouraged historians of slavery and African American culture to continue to support the insights of the

37. Jonathan Eacott, *Selling Empire: India in the Making of Britain and America, 1600–1830* (Chapel Hill: University of North Carolina Press, 2016). Also, Jack P. Greene and Philip D. Morgan, eds., *Atlantic History: A Critical Appraisal* (New York: Oxford University Press, 2008), specifically the essays by Peter H. Wood, "From Atlantic History to a Continental Approach" (279–98); Jack P. Greene, "Hemispheric History and Atlantic History" (299–316); Nicholas Canny, "Atlantic History and Global History" (317–36); and Peter A. Coclanis, "Beyond Atlantic History" (337–56). For more on the #VastEarlyAmerica framework, see Karin Wulf, "For 2016, Appreciating #VastEarlyAmerica," *Uncommon Sense—the Blog,* 4 January 2016, https://blog.oieahc.wm.edu/for-2016-appreciating-vastearlyamerica/ (accessed 18 January 2019).

38. Elkins, *Slavery;* Nathan I. Huggins, "Deforming Mirror of Truth: Slavery and the Master Narrative of American History," *Radical History Review* 49 (Winter 1991): 25–48, quote on 29. Robert L. Douglas agreed that Elkins's thesis was potentially racist; see "Myth or Truth: A White and Black View of Slavery," *Journal of Black Studies* 19 (March 1989): 343–60, quote on 349; John W. Blassingame, *The Slave Community: Plantation Life in the Antebellum South* (New York: Oxford University Press, 1972).

renowned activist and slavery historian Herbert Aptheker: "resistance" is the "motive force of history" and it "remains constant in the face of human oppression." As early as 1991, David W. Blight suggested that slavery studies might be entering a neo-Elkins phase in which historians downplayed resistance and emphasized damage to the enslaved once again.[39]

Critiques of the resistance paradigm grew steadily after the turn of the twenty-first century, but scholars remained uncertain which theoretical framework would take its place. Peter A. Coclanis, in an extended review of Ira Berlin's *Generations of Captivity* in 2003, summed up the emerging critique by countering what he thought was Berlin's all too rosy depiction of the agency of Atlantic Creoles. Coclanis stressed that the seventeenth-century Atlantic World was "a raw, brutal world," and insisted that the emphasis on resistance "over the last two decades of slavery/agency studies" was "imbalanced, partial . . . lacking in formal rigor" and in "historical empathy and imagination."[40]

Some slavery specialists—especially those who study the brutal world of Caribbean sugar production—suggested the best path lay in avoiding the resistance paradigm altogether. Instead, they focused on how work regimes and agricultural routines shaped the lives of the enslaved, or they explored how people not only battled their enslavers but also each other and the environment in a "politics of survival" amidst scarce resources.[41] Burnard's 2015 survey of slavery across the Anglo-American world, *Planters, Merchants, and Slaves,* offered little on slave resistance and agency. Instead, the study returned to an emphasis on what Burnard called "the destructive" rather than "the creative characteristics" of slavery. He

39. Mullin, *Africa in America,* 2; A. J. Williams-Myers, "Slavery, Rebellion and Revolution: A Historiographical Scenario on the Theses of Genovese and Others," *Journal of Black Studies* 26 (March 1996): 385; David W. Blight, "The World the Slave Traders Made: Is There a Postrevisionism in Slavery Historiography?" *Reviews in American History* 19 (March 1991): 37–42.

40. Peter A. Coclanis, "Review: The Captivity of a Generation," *William and Mary Quarterly* 61 (July 2004): 544–55, quotes on 549–50. See also Ira Berlin, *Generations of Captivity: A History of African American Slaves* (Cambridge: Harvard University Press, 2003).

41. Roberts, *Slavery and the Enlightenment in the British Atlantic;* Newman, *A New World of Labor;* Ira Berlin and Philip D. Morgan, "Introduction," in *Cultivation and Culture: Labor and the Shaping of Slave Life in the Americas,* ed. Berlin and Morgan (Charlottesville: University Press of Virginia, 1993), 1–48. For "politics of survival," see Randy M. Browne, *Surviving Slavery in the British Caribbean* (Philadelphia: University of Pennsylvania Press, 2017), 168. Likewise, Peter McCandless stressed the ways in which slaves struggled with the disease environments in the Lower South caused by rice cultivation; see *Slavery, Disease, and Suffering in the Southern Lowcountry* (New York: Cambridge University Press, 2011).

argued that we best understand the experience of the enslaved "through the lens of trauma."[42] Successful resistance is an emotive and inspiring theme, and scholars will undoubtedly continue to explore ways in which captive peoples fought for some semblance of autonomy within the confines of slavery. Nonetheless, it is clear that an emphasis on planter violence and on the remarkable asymmetrical power imbalance between masters and slaves became prominent once again in the literature on slavery.

In the early twenty-first century, as many scholars returned to emphasizing the destructiveness of slavery over the ability of enslaved people to resist, they also started describing discordant and fractured relationships and interpersonal violence within slave communities. Although this interpretive vein has guided scholars of the Caribbean and antebellum United States, more reinvestigation of enslaved communities in the southern mainland colonies is needed. Roberts addressed these issues to some extent in eighteenth-century Virginia and in the Caribbean. Randy M. Browne explored such themes in the British Guianas. William Dusinberre examined fractured communities and the struggle to maintain families in the South Carolina rice swamps in the nineteenth century. Meanwhile Jeff Forret's *Slave against Slave* (2015) uncovered intraracial violence among the enslaved but also showed ways in which such violence was employed to assert and defend community values.[43]

It will not be surprising if historians of the colonial South begin to find common themes with Caribbean and antebellum southern slave histories, although the sources for understanding colonial slave life will always be scarcer. Colonial slavery scholars have to be more creative. Some have pushed beyond disciplinary boundaries to use archaeological evidence and material culture, made more accessible by the Digital Archaeological Archive of Comparative Slavery, that will yield new insights into the lives of the enslaved.[44]

42. Burnard, *Planters, Merchants, and Slaves,* 272. An excellent example of this neo-Elkins approach in the antebellum slavery literature is William Dusinberre, *Them Dark Days: Slavery in the American Rice Swamps* (New York: Oxford University Press, 1996).

43. Roberts, *Slavery and the Enlightenment in the British Atlantic;* Roberts, "The 'Better Sort' and the 'Poorer Sort': Wealth Inequalities, Family Formation and the Economy of Energy on British Caribbean Sugar Plantations, 1750–1800," *Slavery & Abolition* 35 (September 2014): 458–73; Browne, *Surviving Slavery in the British Caribbean;* Dusinberre, *Them Dark Days;* Jeff Forret, *Slave against Slave: Plantation Violence in the Old South* (Baton Rouge: Louisiana State University Press, 2015).

44. Digital Archaeological Archive of Comparative Slavery (DAACS), https://www.daacs.org (accessed 18 January 2019). For key findings in the archaeology of slavery in the colonial South, see

Alongside a vast literature on slave resistance, scholars of southern colonial slavery engaged for generations in deep and multisided debates about the relationship between slavery and modernity, and slavery and economic development. From Eugene D. Genovese's Marxist-grounded interpretation of southern slavery as inefficient and incompatible with economic progress, to Robert William Fogel and Stanley L. Engerman's insistence in their controversial *Time on the Cross* (1974) that slavery was profitable, efficient, and compatible with economic progress, the debate about slavery and modernity has been vociferous.[45] For many decades it focused mainly on the nineteenth-century South, where ample primary sources invited deep and nuanced interrogation. In the 1990s, scholars of colonial slavery asked the same questions but had far fewer primary sources from which to draw answers. Through the second decade of the twenty-first century, most scholars of colonial slavery formed a consensus around the profitability of slavery and its compatibility with technological innovation and modernity, even as they asserted that slavery was morally reprehensible. Joyce E. Chaplin's deeply sophisticated study of plantation management and agriculture in South Carolina, *An Anxious Pursuit* (1993), was a key work in this historiography, as was Lorena S. Walsh's 2010 book on plantation management in the Chesapeake, grounded in decades of deep archival research.[46]

The global financial crisis of 2008 helped spark a sudden reemergence of interest in capitalism, and historians in the South turned even more fully to the relationship between slavery and modernity or, in this iteration, capitalism as modernity. New literature on slavery and modernity stressed ways in which slaves themselves were not just exploited laborers producing exceptional profits but commodities—people with values and prices. A series of older questions about slavery and the economy, slavery and innovation, and slavery and progress re-

---

Christopher C. Fennell, "Early African America: Archaeological Studies of Significance and Diversity," *Journal of Archaeological Research* 19 (March 2011): 1–49; Patricia Samford, "The Archaeology of African American Slavery and Material Culture," *William and Mary Quarterly* 53 (January 1996): 87–114; Theresa A. Singleton, "The Archaeology of Slavery in North America," *Annual Review of Anthropology* 24 (October 1995): 119–40.

45. Eugene D. Genovese, *The Political Economy of Slavery: Studies in the Economy and Society of the Slave South* (New York: Pantheon Books, 1965); Robert William Fogel and Stanley L. Engerman, *Time on the Cross: The Economics of American Negro Slavery* (New York: Little, Brown, 1974). Fogel built on this work in *Without Consent or Contract: The Rise and Fall of American Slavery* (New York: W. W. Norton, 1989).

46. Joyce E. Chaplin, *An Anxious Pursuit: Agricultural Innovation and Modernity in the Lower South, 1730–1815* (Chapel Hill: University of North Carolina Press, 1993); Walsh, *Motives of Honor, Pleasure and Profit.*

emerged. New history of capitalism scholars—who are, as Seth Rockman called them, "*Marxish*" in their critique of capitalism—agreed with Fogel and Engerman's contention that slavery was profitable and compatible with economic progress.[47] They also rejected Fogel and Engerman's disturbing claims that whipping could sometimes be "mildly applied," that there could be as few as "an average of 0.7 whippings per hand per year" on a plantation, and that the whip was less damaging to the slaves than the starvation or incarceration used to compel free workers to labor in capitalist systems. Rather, the whip in the new history of capitalism is the driving force, an instrument of "torture" essential to what Edward E. Baptist called "the pushing system," and it compelled increasing levels of profitability and production.[48]

Far fewer southern scholars have probed the development of capitalism backwards into the seventeenth and eighteenth centuries. It is a field open to further exploration.[49] Caribbean historians, inspired by the anticolonial work of Eric Williams's *Capitalism and Slavery* (1944), have a much more developed literature on the relationship between slavery and capitalism.[50] It seems certain that scholars will draw from these adjacent fields and turn more fully to the same questions, examining the primitive accumulation stage of capitalism in the colonial South.

47. For prominent works on slavery and the new history of capitalism, see Walter Johnson, *Soul by Soul: Life Inside the Antebellum Slave Market* (Cambridge: Harvard University Press, 1999); Johnson, *River of Dark Dreams: Slavery and Empire in the Cotton Kingdom* (Cambridge: Harvard University Press, 2013); Edward E. Baptist, *The Half Has Never Been Told: Slavery and the Making of American Capitalism* (New York: Basic Books, 2014); Sven Beckert and Seth Rockman, eds., *Slavery's Capitalism: A New History of American Economic Development* (Philadelphia: University of Pennsylvania Press, 2016). For Rockman's argument that these scholars are "Marxish," see "What Makes the History of Capitalism Newsworthy?" *Journal of the Early Republic* 34 (Fall 2014): 439–66, quote on 447.

48. Fogel and Engerman, *Time on the Cross,* 144–47. For more on the whip's role as a torture instrument for productivity increases, see Edward E. Baptist, "Toward a Political Economy of Slave Labor: Hands, Whipping Machines, and Modern Power," in Rockman and Beckert, eds., *Slavery's Capitalism,* 31–61, quote on 40.

49. Walsh, *Motives of Honor, Pleasure, and Profit;* John Bezís-Selfa, *Forging America: Ironworkers, Adventurers, and the Industrious Revolution* (Ithaca: Cornell University Press, 2003); Laura Croghan Kamoie, *Irons in the Fire: The Business History of the Tayloe Family and Virginia's Gentry* (Charlottesville: University of Virginia Press, 2007); Bonnie Martin, "Slavery's Invisible Engine: Mortgaging Human Property," *Journal of Southern History* 76 (November 2010): 817–66.

50. Eric Williams, *Capitalism and Slavery* (Chapel Hill: University of North Carolina Press, 1944). The literature on slavery and capitalism in the Caribbean context includes Barbara L. Solow and Stanley L. Engerman, eds., *British Capitalism and Caribbean Slavery: The Legacy of Eric Williams* (New York:

The literature on the structure of eighteenth-century plantation economies and work regimes in the South is richer and more fully developed. Scholars exposed the extent to which the essential elements of the archetypal southern plantation—so familiar to an older generation of antebellum slavery scholars—were in place by the early eighteenth century. They have also detailed how much the Lowcountry plantation system, with its massive individual estates, staple-crop production, and task labor system, differed from typically smaller plantations, gang labor, and the increasingly diversified production systems in the Chesapeake. Several scholars demonstrated how plantation work regimes and the seasonal rhythms and demands of agriculture were the most significant factors in determining the lives of the enslaved, as well as the lives of the planter elite.[51] Coclanis and others thoroughly mapped the economy of South Carolina. Meanwhile, scholars such as Bradford J. Wood methodically investigated the economic structure and slaveholding patterns of peripheral plantation economies such as North Carolina's Cape Fear.[52]

Cambridge University Press, 1987); Hilary McD. Beckles, "Capitalism and Slavery: The Debate over Eric Williams," *Social and Economic Studies* 33 (December 1984): 171–89; Heather Cateau and Selwyn H. H. Carrington, eds., *Capitalism and Slavery Fifty Years Later: Eric Eustace Williams—A Reassessment of the Man and His Work* (New York: Peter Lang, 2000).

51. Berlin, *Many Thousands Gone*, 93–216; Morgan, *Slave Counterpoint*, 27–37; Walsh, *Motives of Honor, Pleasure and Profit*; Roberts, *Slavery and the Enlightenment in the British Atlantic;* Lorna S. Walsh, "Slave Life, Slave Society, and Tobacco Production in the Tidewater Chesapeake, 1620–1820," in Berlin and Morgan, eds., *Cultivation and Culture*, 170–202; Carville Earle and Ronald Hoffman, "Genteel Erosion: The Ecological Consequences of Agrarian Reform in the Chesapeake," in *Discovering the Chesapeake: The History of an Ecosystem*, ed. Philip D. Curtin, Grace S. Brush, and George W. Fisher (Baltimore: Johns Hopkins University Press, 2001), 279–303; T. H. Breen, *Tobacco Culture: The Mentality of the Great Tidewater Planters on the Eve of the Revolution* (Princeton: Princeton University Press, 1985); Steven Sarson, *The Tobacco-Plantation South in the Early American Atlantic World* (New York: Palgrave Macmillan, 2013). For the definitive work on the differences between task and gang labor, see Philip D. Morgan, "Task and Gang Systems: The Organization of Labor on New World Plantations," in *Work and Labor in Early America*, ed. Stephen Innes (Chapel Hill: University of North Carolina Press, 1988), 189–220.

52. Peter A. Coclanis, *The Shadow of a Dream: Economic Life and Death in the South Carolina Low Country, 1670–1920* (New York: Oxford University Press, 1989). See also Joyce E. Chaplin, "Tidal Rice Cultivation and the Problem of Slavery in South Carolina and Georgia, 1760–1815," *William and Mary Quarterly* 49 (January 1992): 29–61; Russell R. Menard, "Financing the Lowcountry Export Boom: Capital and Growth in Early South Carolina," *William and Mary Quarterly* 51 (October 1994): 659–67; Kenneth Morgan, "The Organization of the Colonial American Rice Trade," *William and Mary Quarterly* 52 (July 1995): 433–52; Bradford J. Wood, *This Remote Part of the World: Regional Formation in Lower Cape Fear, North Carolina, 1725–1775* (Columbia: University of South Carolina Press, 2004).

The origin of the rice-based plantation system became a major topic of debate with the publication of Peter H. Wood's *Black Majority* in 1974. Research by Daniel C. Littlefield and Judith Ann Carney supported the conclusion that the development of South Carolina's and Georgia's economies depended upon the skills and knowledge of African rice farmers. This interpretation met a challenge from David Eltis, Philip D. Morgan, and David Richardson's 2007 "Agency and Diaspora in Atlantic History," and S. Max Edelson's fine scholarship on the South Carolina rice industry, which blended economic and agricultural history. Walter Hawthorne responded to these challenges in 2010, defending Carney's perspective and conclusions. Coclanis and Barbara Hahn pushed the topic further in *Plantation Kingdom* (2016), examining the early roots of rice and tobacco and their place in world markets.[53]

Since the 1980s, one of the most significant contributions to the study of slavery across the Americas has been the creation of the Trans-Atlantic Slave Trade Database. Now available through open access online, the database includes records of over 35,000 slaving voyages made from Africa to the Americas that allow historians to understand with much more precision the timing of the development of slavery in the colonial South and the cultural origins of newly arriving African peoples. The database quantified the percentage of African captives arriving in the North American mainland colonies as miniscule, a small stream compared to the numbers arriving in the Caribbean and Brazil. Less than 4 percent of all enslaved Africans disembarked in the American South. In 2016, Gregory E. O'Malley began developing an intercolonial slave trade database to

53. Chaplin, *An Anxious Pursuit;* Wood, *Black Majority;* Daniel C. Littlefield, *Rice and Slaves: Ethnicity and the Slave Trade in Colonial South Carolina* (Baton Rouge: Louisiana State University Press, 1981); Judith A. Carney, *Black Rice: The African Origins of Rice Cultivation in the Americas* (Cambridge: Harvard University Press, 2001); David Eltis, Philip D. Morgan, and David Richardson, "Agency and Diaspora in Atlantic History: Reassessing the African Contribution to Rice Cultivation in the Americas," *American Historical Review* 112 (December 2007): 1329–58; S. Max Edelson, *Plantation Enterprise in Colonial South Carolina* (Cambridge: Harvard University Press, 2006); Walter Hawthorne, "From 'Black Rice' to 'Brown': Rethinking the History of Risiculture in the Seventeenth- and Eighteenth-Century Atlantic," *American Historical Review* 115 (February 2010): 151–63; Richard Follett, ed., *Plantation Kingdom: The American South and Its Global Commodities* (Baltimore: Johns Hopkins University Press, 2016), specifically Peter A. Coclanis, "The Road to Commodity Hell: The Rise and Fall of the First American Rice Industry" (12–38), and Barbara Hahn, "Tobacco's Commodity Route" (91–118). For a study that extends the discussion of African agency to the cultivation of other crops in the Americas, see Frederick C. Knight, *Working the Diaspora: The Impact of African Labor on the Anglo-American World, 1650–1850* (New York: New York University Press, 2010).

supplement the Trans-Atlantic Slave Trade Database. O'Malley's *Final Passages* (2014) offered groundbreaking research that showed how, after arriving in the transatlantic slave trade, approximately 15 percent of enslaved people were reshipped to other colonies. Evidence of such remarkable mobility challenges the archetype of the master-slave relationship. Slaves were often captive to multiple masters over the course of their lives.[54]

Anthropological approaches strongly influenced the study of slavery in the colonial South since the early 1980s, producing some impressive works such as Rhys Isaac's *Transformation of Virginia* (1982) and *Landon Carter's Uneasy Kingdom* (2004), Mechal Sobel's *The World They Made Together* (1987), and Robert Olwell's *Masters, Slaves, and Subjects* (1998).[55] The turn to anthropological approaches also led to a growing interest in microhistory—not the community studies of the 1970s but studies of specific incidents or nonelite individuals as windows into culture. Historians drew from Clifford Geertz's concept of "thick description" to craft remarkable microhistories, such as John Ruston Pagan's *Ann Orthwood's Bastard* (2002) and Randy J. Sparks's *The Two Princes of Calabar* (2004).[56]

Along with the anthropological and microhistorical influences on the historiography came new attention to gender as a category of historical analysis. Since the 1990s, studies of gender shifted perspectives on slavery to such an extent that a scholar can no longer thoughtfully examine slavery without careful attention to gender. The historiography demands recognition that enslaved women were the

54. David Eltis and Allen Tullos, coinvestigators, Voyages: The Trans-Atlantic Slave Trade Database, www.slavevoyages.org (accessed 18 January 2019); Scott Rappaport, "History professor Greg O'Malley to Create New Public Database about the Slave Trade," UC Santa Cruz NewsCenter, 30 May 2016, https://news.ucsc.edu/2016/05/greg-omalley-slavetrade.html (accessed 18 January 2019); Gregory E. O'Malley, *Final Passages: The Intercolonial Slave Trade of British America, 1619–1807* (Chapel Hill: University of North Carolina Press, 2014).

55. Isaac, *The Transformation of Virginia;* Isaac, *Landon Carter's Uneasy Kingdom: Revolution and Rebellion on a Virginia Plantation* (New York: Oxford University Press, 2004); Mechal Sobal, *The World They Made Together: Black and White Values in Eighteenth-Century Virginia* (Princeton: Princeton University Press, 1987); Robert Olwell, *Masters, Slaves, and Subjects: The Culture of Power in the South Carolina Low Country, 1740–1790* (Ithaca: Cornell University Press, 1998).

56. Clifford Geertz, "Deep Play: Notes on the Balinese Cock Fights," *Daedalus* 101 (Winter 1972): 1–37; Geertz, "Thick Description: Toward an Interpretive Theory of Culture," in *The Interpretation of Cultures: Selected Essays* (New York: Basic Books, 1973), 3–30; John Ruston Pagan, *Anne Orthwood's Bastard: Sex and Law in Early Virginia* (New York: Oxford University Press, 2002); Randy J. Sparks, *The Two Princes of Calabar: An Eighteenth-Century Atlantic Odyssey* (Cambridge: Harvard University Press, 2004).

most vulnerable in most plantation societies, and that they formed the majority of workers in enslaved gangs in the fields. In 1996 Kathleen M. Brown's *Good Wives, Nasty Wenches, and Anxious Patriarchs,* a field-defining study of gender in the formation of early Virginia's patriarchal plantation society, showed how the origins debate can be enriched by attention to intersections between race, class, and gender. In 2004, Jennifer L. Morgan's *Laboring Women* offered a sophisticated and nuanced reading of European interpretations of African women's bodies, and she also considered the labor that women performed and ways in which planters manipulated women's reproductive capacities against their will. Marissa J. Fuentes's 2016 study of enslaved women in Barbados and her critique of ways in which the archives shape scholarly interpretations exerted an important impact on the study of colonial southern slavery as well.[57]

Seventeenth-century southern colonies were born on the periphery of emerging Atlantic empires. Oriented towards the ocean, they had deep trade connections with the Caribbean. Since the 1980s, the Atlantic turn has made it impossible to ignore these points. One of the most significant elements of the eastern-oriented and Atlantic-focused southern colonies was the role that slavery and the slave trade came to play in their development. Historians have traditionally used the American Revolution as a chronological break to divide the colonial South from other eras. But the end of the Atlantic slave trade—the quintessential story of forced Atlantic migration and cultural exchange—perhaps provides a more meaningful chronological divide for understanding the development of the slave societies of the South. Many slavery scholars have recognized this and bridged the gap between the colonial and early national South, extending their studies until the abolition of the slave trade in 1807. By the late eighteenth century, the Upper South and Lower South turned from East to West: the Atlantic World became less important; southerners diversified, developed domestic economies, and expanded along the seaboard and into the continent. No longer colonists perched on the periphery of the British Empire, they became southerners. The end of the slave trade and the end of forced African migration to the South marked one of the most important moments in the development of southern Creole cultures.

57. Brown, *Good Wives, Nasty Wenches, and Anxious Patriarchs;* Jennifer L. Morgan, *Laboring Women: Reproduction and Gender in New World Slavery* (Philadelphia: University of Pennsylvania Press, 2004); Marissa J. Fuentes, *Dispossessed Lives: Enslaved Women, Violence, and the Archive* (Philadelphia: University of Pennsylvania Press, 2016). See also Betty Wood, *Women's Work, Men's Work: The Informal Slave Economies of Lowcountry Georgia* (Athens: University of Georgia Press, 1995).

The shift from the Atlantic World to a more fully domestic orientation began in the older colonies of the Upper South even before the official end of the slave trade. Whereas 84,000 enslaved people arrived in the Chesapeake in the slave trade from 1701 to 1750, only 32,000 arrived in the second half of the century. The last slave ship came to the Chesapeake in 1801 but it arrived after a twenty-year stretch in which there had not been a single ship. In fact, a regular slave trade to the region effectively ended by the early 1770s. As enslaved peoples of the Upper South began to reproduce naturally, Upper South planters began looking westward for lands more than they looked eastward for labor. They diversified their economies and continued to turn away from tobacco and towards grains and mixed farming. In the Lower South, brutal work regimes in rice and indigo cultivation meant that planters continued to rely on the slave trade until it became illegal. In the last five years before the Atlantic slave trade ended—and after the last ship brought sixty-eight enslaved people to the Chesapeake in 1801—the planters in Georgia and the Carolinas stepped up the trade and imported 65,000 slaves. In just five years, more Africans arrived in the Lower South than had been taken to the Upper South in the prior sixty years.[58] After 1807, the planters of the Lower South started to look to the Chesapeake for a supply of slave labor, effectively diminishing the importance of Atlantic ties, reinforcing the economic connections between the Chesapeake and the rest of the southern colonies and inspiring the growth of the domestic slave trade. This, in turn, orchestrated massive forced internal migrations of enslaved people overland from the Upper South to the cotton fields of the Deep South—and opened the next chapter of American slavery and American history.

58. Voyages: The Trans-Atlantic Slave Trade Database, http://www.slavevoyages.org/ (accessed 18 January 2019).

THE SOUTH IN THE REVOLUTIONARY ERA AND EARLY REPUBLIC

Brian Steele and Peter S. Onuf

When Alexis de Tocqueville made his way down the Ohio River, the landscapes of slavery and freedom stood starkly opposed on the southern and northern banks. In Kentucky, slavery presented a semi-barbarous face: "the population is sparse" and "society seems to slumber. Man appears idle." The concentration of capital and enslaved labor in Kentucky's widely dispersed plantations left the lands in between in a degraded state, reversing the progress of civilization so conspicuous in the neatly cultivated fields and bustling villages of the "improved" (and increasingly deforested) Ohio shore, where "prosperity is apparent everywhere. Man appears rich and content: he is at work."[1]

Here was a vivid image of the way the slave South looked, signifying a deepening sectional cleavage that would in a few short decades culminate in a catastrophically destructive civil war. Tocqueville recognized that the South was distinctive, and for reasons that seemed obvious to contemporaries in the 1830s and commentators ever since. Invoking what we might call long-term "path dependency," the French visitor observed that the introduction of slavery and the plantation complex into colonial Virginia was "the capital fact" destined "to exert immense influence on the character, laws, and the future of the whole South."[2]

In his masterwork, *Democracy in America* (1835–1840), Tocqueville did not dwell on sectional differences as he brilliantly dissected the American national

1. Alexis de Tocqueville, *Democracy in America,* trans. Arthur Goldhammer, 2 vols. (New York: Library of America, 2004), 1:399.

2. Tocqueville, *Democracy in America,* 1:35.

character nor, surprisingly, did he expect that sectional differences would ever jeopardize America's democratic destiny. Race played a crucial role in Tocqueville's failure to focus on sectionalism. His famous meditation on the "three races" effected a kind of segregation, abstracting the "peculiar institution" and Indian removal from America. For Tocqueville, the inevitable erasure of enslaved blacks and "uncivilized" Indians was overdetermined, even tragic. Yet for all the sympathy he evoked for the victims of white supremacy, his imaginative removal of the other races bore a close resemblance to the conspiracy of silence of American politicians in the Second Party System.[3]

Democrats and their Whig opponents robustly and raucously disagreed about myriad policy issues, but they kept quiet about slavery (even as it undergirded the very economy that sustained their conflict).[4] Intersectional peace, enforced by the great parties, depended on suppressing divisive sectional issues. Party attachment, far from kindling "the animosity of one part" of the community "against another" as George Washington had feared, would—so Martin Van Buren later hoped—provide "a complete antidote for sectional prejudices by producing counteracting feelings."[5] For partisan nationalists, the perpetuation of the union and America's destiny as a great nation, however differently they might conceive it, were too precious to risk loose talk. Tocqueville's eyes may have been wide open when he traveled down the Ohio, but he too tended to look away from its suggestive scenery as he contemplated the implications of American democracy for the future of Western civilization.

Tocqueville looked to the long-term development of provincial institutions, legal regimes, and "manners" (or political culture) for sources of the new na-

3. Tocqueville, *Democracy in America,* 1:365–476. Tocqueville's discussion of race as an intractable problem was taken as a prophetic warning by abolition-minded northerners. See Olivier Zunz, "Tocqueville and the Americans," in *The Cambridge Companion to Tocqueville,* ed. Cheryl B. Welch (New York: Cambridge University Press, 2006), 359–96. Tocqueville thus described the great American parties: "When citizens differ about matters that interest all portions of the country equally, such as general principles of government, then what may truly be called parties come into being"; see *Democracy in America,* 1:198.

4. See Harry L. Watson, *Liberty and Power: The Politics of Jacksonian America* (New York: Hill and Wang, 1990).

5. George Washington Farewell Address, *American Daily Advertiser* (Philadelphia), 19 September 1796; Martin Van Buren to Thomas Ritchie, 13 January 1827, Papers of Martin Van Buren, Series 1 (1 January 1825–3 March 1829), Manuscript Division, Library of Congress.

tion's exceptional character. Taking the union of provincial Anglo-Americans for granted, he discounted the significance of the revolutionary break with Britain: he did not see that the very existence of the American people was the contingent product of political and military mobilization in the imperial crisis. Nor did he recognize that the institutions he prized were fragile, that the union contained the seeds of disunion, or that American political culture could lead to fragmentation as easily as to unity. For in the early American Republic, almost everything that theoretically united Americans, North and South, could also be a pivot point of contention and an instrument of division. Still, the South that Tocqueville saw but read as inevitably American would eventually become the distinctive section of the nation that would justify the existence of this book: anachronistic, out of step with "mainstream America," a problem to be comprehended, worked through, reconciled.[6] But as Tocqueville understood, "the South" in the Early Republic was not that of W. J. Cash and V. S. Naipaul: altogether "another land, sharply differentiated from the rest of the American nation." *That* South was not a predicate of the Early Republic but somehow rather its product. Whatever the South happened to be then was continually in the process of becoming, as Christopher Morris has so nicely put it, "something else."[7] And the southern states started out as constitutive components of the American union, joint heirs with the other states of the British imperial legacy.[8]

6. See the essays in Larry J. Griffin and Don H. Doyle, eds., *The South as an American Problem* (Athens: University of Georgia Press, 1995). The historiographical roots of this observation are explored in Jack P. Greene, *Pursuits of Happiness: The Social Development of Early Modern British Colonies and the Formation of American Culture* (Chapel Hill: University of North Carolina Press, 1988).

7. W. J. Cash, *The Mind of the South* (1941; repr., New York: Alfred A. Knopf, 1991), xlvii; V. S. Naipaul, *A Turn in the South* (New York: Alfred A. Knopf, 1989); Christopher Morris, *Becoming Southern: The Evolution of a Way of Life, Warren County and Vicksburg, Mississippi, 1770–1860* (New York: Oxford University Press, 1995), xiv. See also Andrew McMichael, *Atlantic Loyalties: Americans in Spanish West Florida, 1785–1810* (Athens: University of Georgia Press, 2008).

8. Martin Brückner argued that "the South" was initially in some literal sense a legacy of British cartographers of the colonial era, and made the interesting observation (from the *OED*) that the very term "American South" was first used by British intelligence officers in 1777 in an effort to characterize Sir Henry Clinton's campaign in South Carolina. The South, in this respect then, "is the product of imperial institutional convenience, and not the expression of a locally formulated idea of region and regional self-identification"; see "Mapping the 'American South': Image, Archive, and the Textual Construction of Regional Identity in the Age of Washington," in *George Washington's South,* ed. Tamara Harvey and Greg O'Brien (Gainesville: University Press of Florida, 2004), 42–68, quote on 54.

Empire

Independence and union, a practical necessity and aspiration, were inextricably linked in the American "national imaginary." The colonists resisted British authority in the 1760s and 1770s not because they longed for independence but because the imperial connection was so critically important to them. As historians John Philip Reid, Jack P. Greene, and Craig Yirush demonstrated, Anglo-American patriots mobilized to defend rights they claimed *as* Britons *within* the empire. The growing interdependence of the British metropolis and its distant colonies precipitated the constitutional crisis—a great debate about the character of the empire—that led reluctant revolutionaries to declare their independence. Planter-patriots in Virginia became republicans because of their radical disenchantment with the monarchical old regime, not because they rejected the empire that they claimed the king betrayed. The rights they most cherished were those that had enabled them to accumulate property in land and enslaved labor and to envision future generations colonizing the continent. Virginians identified with Britain's territorial ambitions in North America, and the sense of betrayal that animated resistance and rebellion reflected what they saw as a radical reorientation of imperial policy. After 1763, colonizing agents of imperial expansion were increasingly treated as if they were the colonized subjects, or "slaves," of a despotic king.[9]

9. Jack P. Greene, *Peripheries and Center: Constitutional Development in the Extended Polities in the British Empire and the United States, 1607–1788* (Athens: University of Georgia Press, 1986); Greene, *Constitutional Origins of the American Revolution* (New York: Cambridge University Press, 2011); Greene, "'*Virtus et Libertas*': Political Culture, Social Change, and the Origins of the American Revolution in Virginia, 1763–76," in Greene, *Understanding the American Revolution: Issues and Actors* (Charlottesville: University Press of Virginia, 1995), 164–208; John Philip Reid, *Constitutional History of the American Revolution: Abridged Edition* (Madison: University of Wisconsin Press, 1995); Aziz Rana, *The Two Faces of American Freedom* (Cambridge: Harvard University Press, 2010); Craig Yirush, *Settlers, Liberty, and Empire: The Roots of Early American Political Theory, 1675–1775* (New York: Cambridge University Press, 2011); Woody Holton, *Forced Founders: Indians, Debtors, Slaves, and the Making of the American Revolution in Virginia* (Chapel Hill: University of North Carolina Press, 1999); J. C. A. Stagg, *Borderlines in Borderlands: James Madison and the Spanish-American Frontier, 1776–1821* (New Haven: Yale University Press, 2009); Sylvia R. Frey, *Water from the Rock: Black Resistance in a Revolutionary Age* (Princeton: Princeton University Press, 1991). On the concept of a national imaginary, see Peter S. Onuf, *Jefferson's Empire: The Language of American Nationhood* (Charlottesville: University of Virginia Press, 2000); Onuf, *Jefferson and the Virginians: Democracy, Constitutions, and Empire* (Baton Rouge: Louisiana State University Press, 2018), 117–54. See also Charles Taylor, *A Secular Age* (Cambridge: Harvard University Press, 2007), chap. 9; Taylor, *Modern Social Imaginaries* (Durham: Duke University Press, 2003).

If Virginians, then, first resisted imperial authority in defense of their corporate rights *within* the empire, they eventually concluded that those rights were incompatible with continued colonial status. Indeed, Virginians later embraced the settlement of 1789—the union and the powerful central state outlined in the United States Constitution—precisely because they became convinced, as Lance Banning argued, that their original goals would be met best by a continued union and national government powerful enough to enforce commercial policy and preserve Virginia's western interests (as well as the position and continuing relevance of the powerful political elite that led Virginia to independence).[10]

Forging a union depended on transcending differences among the rebellious colonies that the common cause made dauntingly conspicuous. An idealized conception of the old empire provided the template for a new union that would secure the autonomy of its consenting constituent parts, the newly self-constituted states. Far from escaping empire, as Bethel Saler argued, revolutionary republicans embraced it.[11] In doing so, they created a federal political arena within which their distinctive, inevitably conflicting interests became increasingly salient; the promise of union was thus inextricably linked to the danger of disunion. If Americans looked forward to a glorious republican future, then, they also looked back to an idealized imperial past.

Ambitious and enterprising patriot-planters thus cultivated an imperial imaginary that harked back to an idealized memory of the pre-1763 British Empire, while envisioning a broad distribution of productive resources among citizens of the new republics. The conventional wisdom of the age was that republics had to be small and their self-sacrificing citizens virtuous. But independent Americans imagined a democratized version of empire on a vast continental scale with land enough, as Thomas Jefferson put it so memorably, for the "thousandth to the thousandth generation"—as well as a plentiful supply of labor to yield its boun-

10. Lance Banning, "Virginia: Sectionalism and the General Good," in *Ratifying the Constitution,* ed. Michael Lienesch and Michael Allen Gillespie (Lawrence: University Press of Kansas, 1989), 261–99; Lorri Glover, *The Fate of the Revolution: Virginians Debate the Constitution* (Baltimore: Johns Hopkins University Press, 2016). On Virginia's political elite, see Jack P. Greene, "Character, Persona, and Authority: A Study of Alternative Styles of Political Leadership in Revolutionary Virginia," in *The Revolutionary War in the South: Essays in Honor of John Richard Alden,* ed. W. Robert Higgins (Durham: Duke University Press, 1979), 3–42.

11. Bethel Saler, *The Settlers' Empire: Colonialism and State Formation in the Old Northwest* (Philadelphia: University of Pennsylvania Press, 2014). See also Allison L. LaCroix, *The Ideological Origins of American Federalism* (Cambridge: Harvard University Press, 2010).

tiful harvests. It was a broadly appealing conception of empire that celebrated the central role of the separate provinces and their successor states in promoting imperial (or national) expansion and the westward progress of civilization.[12] Popular political mobilization democratized Virginia and the other new states, transforming provinces dominated by self-dealing oligarchies into revolutionary republics that could command the loyalty of a broad range of citizens.[13] Collectively, these new state-republics assumed the role of the deposed sovereign, authorizing, promoting, and securing the imperial aspirations of successive generations of the American people as a whole.

The central role of new state formation as the vehicle of American westward expansion, Christopher L. Tomlins demonstrated, also drew on the British imperial history of colonization through the agency of provincial jurisdictions. Taking the place of the Crown, the new federal government promoted colonization by distributing public lands and organizing new states in frontier regions, remaining largely out of sight from the perspective of the citizenry, to borrow Brian Balogh's phrase (or "light and inconspicuous," as Max M. Edling wrote).[14] With so much territory available for development in a highly competitive land market, slave-owning planters and free farmers could find homes on the expanding western frontier, imagining an ultimate convergence of their conflicting interests. Commentators, anticipating Tocqueville, thus celebrated the early western settle-

12. Thomas Jefferson, First Inaugural Address, 4 March 1801, in *Thomas Jefferson: Writings,* ed. Merrill D. Peterson (New York: Library of America, 1984), 494–95; Thomas Jefferson to William Ludlow, 6 September 1824, in Peterson, ed., *Thomas Jefferson: Writings,* 1496–97.

13. On mobilization, see Michal Jan Rozbicki, *Culture and Liberty in the Age of the American Revolution* (Charlottesville: University of Virginia Press, 2011); Michael A. McDonnell, *The Politics of War: Race, Class, and Conflict in Revolutionary Virginia* (Chapel Hill: University of North Carolina Press, 2007); Holton, *Forced Founders;* Robert G. Parkinson, *The Common Cause: Creating Race and Nation in the American Revolution* (Chapel Hill: University of North Carolina Press, 2016).

14. Christopher L. Tomlins, *Freedom Bound: Law, Labor, and Civic Identity in Colonizing English America, 1580–1865* (New York: Cambridge University Press, 2010); Brian Balogh, *A Government Out of Sight: The Mystery of Authority in Nineteenth-Century America* (New York: Cambridge University Press, 2009); Peter S. Onuf, "Democracy, Empire, and the 1816 Indiana Constitution," *Indiana Magazine of History* 111 (March 2015): 5–29. See also Max M. Edling, *A Revolution in Favor of Government: Origins of the U.S. Constitution and the Making of the American State* (New York: Oxford University Press, 2003); Edling, *A Hercules in the Cradle: War, Money, and the American State, 1783–1867* (Chicago: University of Chicago Press, 2014); William J. Novak, "The Myth of the 'Weak' American State," *American Historical Review* 113 (June 2008): 752–72; John Lauritz Larson, *Internal Improvement: National Public Works and the Promise of Popular Government in the Early United States* (Chapel Hill: University of North Carolina Press, 2001).

ments, centered on the Ohio Valley and drawing streams of settlers from northern as well as southern states, as the crucible of an emerging national identity.[15]

The rising empire promised to fulfill patriot dreams, securing the expansive continental union that misguided British imperial reformers had betrayed and that quarreling and mistrustful Americans nearly forfeited in the first great crisis of the union in the post–Revolutionary War years. Under the Articles of Confederation (1781–1789), coalitions of states promoted—and blocked—divisive policy initiatives; without an independent revenue, Congress was politically impotent, or "imbecilic." Powerful centrifugal tendencies threatened to cast the states (described by George Washington as "wretched fragments of empire") into an anarchic state of nature.[16] In the critical period leading up to the drafting and ratification of the federal Constitution, the specter of disunion constituted the most compelling argument for strengthening or renewing union.[17] For Washington and his fellow reformers, a stronger union was imperative because of a growing sense that the Confederation itself had become a dangerous "tool for sectional aggrandizement," in George William Van Cleve's apt characterization. When one section's gain was seen as another's loss, the union's collapse appeared inevitable.[18]

If the union failed, commentators agreed, the most likely outcome would be the formation of two or more separate (sectional) confederacies. Scrambling for frontier territory and commercial advantage, these rump unions would forge alliances with foreign powers, and so forfeit the promise of continental empire

15. Peter S. Onuf, *Statehood and Union: A History of the Northwest Ordinance* (Bloomington: Indiana University Press, 1987); Patrick Griffin, *American Leviathan: Empire, Nation, and Revolutionary Frontier* (New York: Hill and Wang, 2007); Craig Thompson Friend, *Along the Maysville Road: The Early American Republic in the Trans-Appalachian West* (Knoxville: University of Tennessee Press, 2005).

16. George William Van Cleve, *We Have Not a Government: The Articles of Confederation and the Road to the Constitution* (Chicago: University of Chicago Press, 2017); Kevin T. Barksdale, *The Lost State of Franklin: America's First Secession* (Lexington: University of Kentucky Press, 2009); George Washington to the Marquis de Lafayette, 25 August 1786, in *The Writings of George Washington,* ed. Worthington Chauncey Ford, 14 vols. (New York: G. P. Putnam's Sons, 1891), 11:56–59.

17. Peter S. Onuf, "Anarchy and the Crisis of the Union," in *"To Form a More Perfect Union": The Critical Ideas of the Constitution,* ed. Herman Belz, Ronald Hoffman, and Peter J. Albert (Charlottesville: University Press of Virginia, 1992), 272–302.

18. See Van Cleve, *We Have Not a Government,* 161–87, quote on 161; Joseph L. Davis, *Sectionalism in American Politics, 1774–1787* (Madison: University of Wisconsin Press, 1977); Cathy D. Matson and Peter S. Onuf, *A Union of Interests: Political and Economic Thought in Revolutionary America* (Lawrence: University Press of Kansas, 1990), 60–66.

that had inspired Anglo-American patriots to break with Britain. Empire was the patriots' dream; the fragmentation of the union was their nightmare. Anticipating the series of sectional crises that punctuated the history of the early American federal republic, the creation of a more perfect union under the Constitution drafted by the Philadelphia Convention of 1787 marked the culmination of the first great sectional crisis, as David C. Hendrickson and many other scholars suggested.[19]

Federalists promised that their Constitution would save the states from the anarchy that disunion would inevitably entail while enabling enterprising Americans to fulfill imperial ambitions. By creating what Eliga H. Gould called a "treaty-worthy" federal state (in a world of states governed by the law of nations), the United States could, as J. C. A. Stagg put it, assume its rightful role as "successor . . . to the rival European empires of North America."[20] Americans could have it both ways: energetic union would simultaneously secure peace at home—preserving the jurisdictional autonomy of the separate state republics—and promote the new nation's respectability and commercial interests abroad.[21] The new federal Constitution, supplemented by the Bill of Rights, perpetuated—or constitutionalized—but also clarified the tensions between center and peripheries chronicled by Jack P. Greene, thus (paradoxically) creating a venue for the articulation of sectional interest and identity.[22]

19. Van Cleve, *We Have Not a Government;* David C. Hendrickson, *Peace Pact: The Lost World of the American Founding* (Lawrence: University Press of Kansas, 2003); Peter S. Onuf, *The Origins of the Federal Republic: Jurisdictional Controversies in the United States, 1775–1787* (Philadelphia: University of Pennsylvania Press, 1983); Alexander Hamilton, No. 2: "Concerning Dangers from Foreign Force & Influence," in *The Federalist: The Gideon Edition,* ed. George W. Carey and James McClellan (Indianapolis: Liberty Fund, 2001), 6–8.

20. Eliga H. Gould, *Among the Powers of the Earth: The American Revolution and the Making of a New World Empire* (Cambridge: Harvard University Press, 2012), 12–13; Stagg, *Borderlines in Borderlands,* 5–6; Leonard J. Sadosky, *Revolutionary Negotiations: Indians, Empires, and Diplomats in the Founding of America* (Charlottesville: University of Virginia Press, 2010).

21. Onuf, "Anarchy and the Crisis of the Union"; Gould, *Among the Powers of the Earth;* Brian Schoen, *The Fragile Fabric of Union: Cotton, Federal Politics, and the Global Origins of the Civil War* (Baltimore: Johns Hopkins University Press, 2009); Don E. Fehrenbacher, *The Slaveholding Republic: An Account of the United States Government's Relations to Slavery,* ed. Ward M. McAfee (New York: Oxford University Press, 2001); Matthew Karp, *This Vast Southern Empire: Slaveholders at the Helm of American Foreign Policy* (Cambridge: Harvard University Press, 2016).

22. Greene, *Peripheries and Center;* Peter S. Onuf, "Federalism, Republicanism, and the Origins of American Sectionalism," in *All Over the Map: Rethinking American Regions,* ed. Edward L. Ayers et al. (Baltimore: Johns Hopkins University Press, 1996), 11–37.

Slavery and the Constitution

The emergence of the South as a distinctive region and of southerners as a self-conscious people reflected the enduring legacies of empire. Provincial Virginians had long dreamed about—and speculated in—the colonization of the Mississippi watershed, the continent's heartland.[23] Their expansionist aspirations harked back to the British Empire, culminating in the Seven Years' War against France—the Great War for Empire—and the Peace of Paris in 1763. Southerners' conception of the new nation's imperial future took on a distinctive form because of their insatiable appetite for land and their commitment to the institution of slavery.[24] With prospects for expansion most promising on the dynamic southwestern frontier (for many contemporary observers the West was the frontier of the South, not a distinct region), the success of constitutional reform and the spread of plantation slavery were inextricably linked: Jefferson's "empire of liberty" would be an empire for slavery.[25]

This link predated the Revolution and had long shaped the imperial imaginary. In 1775, Edmund Burke noted that the "love of Freedom" was the "predominating feature" of American character.[26] But the meaning of freedom for Britons was not a transcendent, abstract idea. Rather, as Michal Jan Rozbicki convincingly argued, it was "a social relation between unequals" that accepted various hier-

23. John Seelye, *Beautiful Machine: Rivers and the Republican Plan, 1755–1825* (New York: Oxford University Press, 1991).

24. See John Craig Hammond, *Slavery, Freedom, and Expansion in the Early American West* (Charlottesville: University of Virginia Press, 2007); Eberhard L. Faber, *Building the Land of Dreams: New Orleans and the Transformation of Early America* (Princeton: Princeton University Press, 2015).

25. Adam Rothman, *Slave Country: American Expansion and the Origins of the Deep South* (Cambridge: Harvard University Press, 2005); Peter J. Kastor, *The Nation's Crucible: The Louisiana Purchase and the Creation of America* (New Haven: Yale University Press, 2004); Morris, *Becoming Southern.* But see also Peter S. Onuf and Leonard J. Sadosky, who noted an assumed "natural complementarity of interest between Virginia and the new states of the West that did *not* depend on the spread of slavery," which had been banned in the Old Northwest; see *Jeffersonian America* (Malden, MA: Blackwell, 2001), 61. See also Drew R. McCoy, "James Madison and Visions of American Nationality in the Confederation Period: A Regional Perspective," in *Beyond Confederation: Origins of the Constitution and American National Identity,* ed. Richard Beeman, Stephen Botein, and Edward C. Carter II (Chapel Hill: University of North Carolina Press, 1987), 228–58.

26. Edmund Burke, Speech on Conciliation with the Colonies, 22 March 1775, in *Select Works of Edmund Burke: A New Imprint of the Payne Edition,* 4 vols. (Indianapolis: Liberty Fund, 1999), 1:237. On the link between liberty and slavery, see Edmund S. Morgan, *American Slavery, American Freedom: The Ordeal of Colonial Virginia* (New York: W. W. Norton, 1975).

archies and included rule over dependents and dispossession of rivals. Burke went on to note that the southern colonies, which contained "a vast multitude of slaves," were (precisely for that reason) "much more strongly . . . attached to liberty, than those to the North-ward."[27] Following the American Revolution, David Ramsay of South Carolina, a transplanted Pennsylvanian, affirmed Burke's assessment. "In the southern colonies slavery nurtured a spirit of liberty," he insisted, "nothing could more effectively animate the opposition of a planter to the claims of Great-Britain, than a conviction that those claims . . . degraded him to a degree of dependence on his fellow subjects, equally humiliating with that which existed between his slaves and himself."[28] Empire thus entailed domination of those deemed inferior, even—perhaps especially—for Anglo-American patriots, who insisted on their civic equality with metropolitan Britons and among themselves.[29] As Sylvia R. Frey, Woody Holton, and Gerald Horne demonstrated, the fear that more effective imperial governance would challenge their right to rule their slaves led many patriot masters to embrace the cause of independence. Lord Dunmore, the last royal governor in Virginia, confirmed the threat to mastery with his November 1775 proclamation offering freedom to enslaved Virginians who would aid him in quashing the rebellion. Southern planters could preserve their mastery only by leaving the empire and creating a new continental government capable of protecting and perpetuating the "peculiar institution."[30]

Unsurprisingly, then, the most famous (or notorious) compromises forged at the Philadelphia convention of 1787 secured the legal regimes of the slave-based

27. Burke, Speech on Conciliation with the Colonies, 240–41. On these themes, see Rozbicki, *Culture and Liberty in the Age of the American Revolution;* Rana, *The Two Faces of American Freedom;* Jack P. Greene, ed., *Exclusionary Empire: English Liberty Overseas, 1600–1900* (New York: Cambridge University Press, 2010).

28. David Ramsay, *The History of the American Revolution,* ed. Lester Cohen, 2 vols. (1789; repr., Indianapolis: Liberty Press. 1990), 1:40.

29. See Rana, *The Two Faces of American Freedom.*

30. David Waldstreicher, *Slavery's Constitution: From Revolution to Ratification* (New York: Hill and Wang, 2009), 21–56; Gerald Horne, *The Counter-Revolution of 1776: Slave Resistance and the Origins of the United States* (New York: New York University Press, 2014); Frey, *Water from the Rock;* Holton, *Forced Founders.* Alan Taylor, in *The Internal Enemy: Slavery and War in Virginia, 1772–1832* (New York: W. W. Norton, 2013), noted that one unintended result of the American Revolution in Virginia was a more widespread ownership of slaves among ordinary whites. For a countersuggestion of sorts, see Rhys Isaac, *Landon Carter's Uneasy Kingdom: Revolution and Rebellion on a Virginia Plantation* (New York: Oxford, 2004), which demonstrated the challenge posed by the Revolution to the patriarchal order—the unsettlement that threatened mastery over subordinates, including slaves.

political economies of the southern states and their replication in an expanding western hinterland.[31] Slavery had been a vitally important *imperial* interest; given the central importance of agricultural exports to the prosperity—and the very existence—of the new United States, it became an even more important *national* interest. As George William Van Cleve and David Waldstreicher emphasized, the federal Constitution thus mobilized the power of the new central government to secure this vital national interest, while simultaneously (and very explicitly) limiting federal power *over* slavery.[32] Security (if not sanction) for the institution was baked into the constitutional cake. Slavery, Waldstreicher argued, "gained the protection of the federal union while being protected from that union's new powers."[33]

Southern slave-owners were prime movers in the federal constitutional project, recognizing that the new nation could survive and prosper only if their property rights (in land and enslaved people) were secured. To characterize those rights as merely local or sectional, and therefore not integral and indispensable to the national project, was to turn a "self-evident" political economic and constitutional truth on its head. In other words, there could be no American union—or nation—*without* slavery. In this era, Don E. Fehrenbacher explained, slavery was

31. For a compelling discussion of the protean meaning of "compromise" in the "lexicon of American politics" and with specific application to the compromises hammered out at the Constitutional Convention, see Jack N. Rakove, *Original Meanings: Politics and Ideas in the Making of the Constitution* (New York: Alfred A. Knopf, 1996), 57–93.

32. George William Van Cleve, *A Slaveholders' Union: Slavery, Politics, and the Constitution in the Early American Republic* (Chicago: University of Chicago Press, 2010). See also Paul Finkleman, "The Proslavery Origins of the Electoral College," *Cardozo Law Review* 23 (2002): 1145–57. François Furstenberg, *In the Name of the Father: Washington's Legacy, Slavery, and the Making of a Nation* (New York: Penguin, 2006), suggested ways in which the civic texts of American nationalism subtly reconciled Americans to slavery. William J. Cooper Jr., *Liberty and Slavery: Southern Politics to 1860* (New York: Alfred A. Knopf, 1983), argued that voting patterns in the Confederation Congress already revealed a distinct sectional consciousness that southerners brought into the Constitutional Convention as a collective sense of interest in slavery. Don E. Fehrenbacher argued that the question of slavery tended to be incidental to other conundrums, primarily that of representation, noting that many southerners assumed (hoped?) that slavery was in the process of disappearing, that there were as many antislavery as proslavery features of the document, and that the "proslavery" features in the Constitution depended almost exclusively on implementation by the new government; see *The Slaveholding Republic,* esp. 15–47. Cooper argued that southern Federalists made a strong case during the ratification debate that the Constitution secured the institution, whereas Fehrenbacher argued that slavery was a marginal issue during ratification.

33. Waldstreicher, *Slavery's Constitution,* 102. See also the discussion of John Rutledge's motivations for championing the "supremacy clause" at the Constitutional Convention in Rakove, *Original Meanings,* 173–74.

easily "assimilated to the national interest" because "it coincided again and again with the dynamic force of expansionism," appealing to national devotion to property rights as well as racial hostilities and fears never confined to the South alone.[34]

Astute northerners recognized and resented the protected status of the "peculiar institution" and its implications for the sectional balance of power. But the price was nonetheless worth paying. The United States came into being as a union of states, each signifying its consent by ratifying the proposed Constitution. For reasons of their own, the eastern (or northern) states embraced the federal system with fewer reservations than their southern counterparts. Another way of interpreting the Constitution's silences on slavery, then, is to understand it not as the first great sectional compromise but as an expression of a federalism that, in James Madison's words, sought to maintain "the proper line of partition, between the authority of the general, and that of the state governments." Placing slavery "completely outside the national political arena," Eric Foner suggested, was understood by the framers to be "the only basis on which a national politics could exist."[35] Northern as well as southern framers rejected John Dickinson's logic that the influence of slavery upon "national happiness" rendered its legality a question for the "national Govt. not to the States particularly interested." Connecticut's Oliver Ellsworth spelled out the agreed-upon arrangement at the Convention: "The morality and wisdom of slavery," he said, "are considerations belonging to the states themselves."[36] And, in fact, as Douglas Bradburn argued, northern states in the Early Republic were as determined as their southern coun-

34. Fehrenbacher, *The Slaveholding Republic,* 132–33. William W. Freehling reminded us that slavery was kept out of southern Illinois, just across the river from and just as favorable to slavery as Missouri, by force of federal law alone; see *Road to Disunion.* Vol. 1, *Secessionists at Bay, 1776–1854* (New York: Oxford University Press, 1990). In 1824, citizens in Illinois voted down a proposal for a constitutional convention to reopen the state to slavery—in direct contravention to the Northwest Ordinance—by only 6,640 to 4,972. Historian James E. Davis called this a resounding defeat for proslavery forces in the state, but it certainly does not speak in favor of the sharpest distinction between North and South, even on this question, and hints at ways that slavery came to be central to the working of the politics and economy of the union as well as to the eventual sectional rupture; see Davis, *Frontier Illinois* (Bloomington: Indiana University Press, 1998), 167.

35. James Madison, No. 37: "Concerning the difficulties which the convention must have experienced in the formation of a proper plan," in Carey and McClellan, eds., *The Federalist,* 179–85; Eric Foner, "Politics, Ideology, and the Origins of the American Civil War," in *Politics and Ideology in the Age of the Civil War* (New York: Oxford University Press, 1980), 37.

36. Not to mention Marylander Luther Martin's insistence that slavery was "inconsistent with the principles of the revolution and dishonorable to the American character"; see Max Farrand, ed., *Records of the Federal Convention,* 3 vols. (New Haven: Yale University Press, 1911), 2:364.

terparts to maintain "local control over the municipal arrangements of the citizenry." The national government would be as limited in its power over slavery in Virginia as it was over the rights of free blacks in Vermont or the status of religious establishment in Connecticut.[37] Not surprisingly, then, wary southerners in later decades interpreted any prospective or imagined interference with slavery as a violation of the original constitutional understanding.[38]

Geopolitics

Patriotic southerners sought to fulfill their imperial aspirations as Americans. They understood that a strong central government could serve the interests of slave-based plantation agriculture by negotiating and enforcing favorable terms of trade abroad, securing extended boundaries both for the United States and the individual states, and protecting vulnerable regions from slave insurrections and Native American incursions. Their southern and American identities were not mutually exclusive. As continentalists, they thought of national prosperity and security in terms of geographic expansion, imagining that the interests of particular states and regions would converge in the West and so resolve the chronic conflicts that had jeopardized the Confederation and that might continue to threaten the union.[39]

Yet if the federal union saved the early American empire, the compromises that made union possible wrote the script for the empire's ultimate collapse. Ac-

37. Douglas Bradburn, *The Citizenship Revolution: Politics and the Creation of the American Union, 1774–1804* (Charlottesville: University of Virginia Press, 2009), 271, 290. Massachusetts, Bradburn pointed out, was the first state to endorse the Eleventh Amendment. According to Henry Adams, states' rights were originally "as dear to New England as to Virginia"; see *John Randolph* (Boston: Houghton, Mifflin, 1882), 273. See also Akhil Reed Amar, *The Bill of Rights: Creation and Reconstruction* (New Haven: Yale University Press, 1998); Hammond, *Slavery, Freedom, and Expansion in the Early American West.*

38. William Gilmore Simms may have expressed the sense of an increasing percentage of white southerners when he insisted in 1850 that "the history of our relations with the Northern States is a precise counterpart of the case of the whole of the colonies of Great Britain, prior to 1776, with the mother country"; see "The Southern Convention," *Southern Quarterly Review* 2 (September 1850): 191–232, quote on 207. See generally, Peter S. Onuf, "Antebellum Southerners and the National Idea," in *The Old South's Modern Worlds: Slavery, Region, and Nation in the Age of Progress,* ed. L. Diane Barnes, Brian Schoen, and Frank Towers (New York: Oxford University Press, 2011), 25–46.

39. Stagg, *Borderlines in Borderlands;* Fred Anderson and Andrew R. L. Cayton, *The Dominion of War: Empire and Liberty in North America, 1500–2000* (New York: Penguin, 2005), notes that Americans, from the Revolution on, associated security of the frontier with expansion. See also John Lewis Gaddis, *Surprise, Security, and the American Experience* (Cambridge: Harvard University Press, 2004), chap. 2.

cording to the conventional historiographical wisdom, the spread of the southern plantation complex from its Virginia and Carolina-Georgia hearths subverted the promise of a free West. But the notion that the West was "lost" is predicated on the Turnerian assumption that democracy was the natural, spontaneous expression of Anglo-American frontier settlement.[40] To the contrary, scholarship suggests that the frontier Frederick Jackson Turner celebrated in 1893 resulted from systematic planning and the strong tutelary presence of federal officials and institutions in the formative stages of settlement in the Old Northwest.[41]

North of the Ohio River in the 1790s, Andrew R. L. Cayton argued, the federal government played an important, ongoing role in Indian wars and diplomacy, public land distribution, road-building, territorial governance, and new state formation.[42] In the South in the same years, the federal presence was relatively

40. See Roger G. Kennedy, *Mr. Jefferson's Lost Cause: Land, Farmers, Slavery, and the Louisiana Purchase* (New York: Oxford University Press, 2003). For more nuanced accounts of the early West, see Stephen Aron, *How the West Was Lost: The Transformation of Kentucky from Daniel Boone to Henry Clay* (Baltimore: Johns Hopkins University Press, 1996); Elizabeth A. Perkins, *Border Life: Experience and Memory in the Revolutionary Ohio Valley* (Chapel Hill: University of North Carolina Press, 1998); Ellen Eslinger, *Citizens of Zion: The Social Origins of Camp Meeting Revivalism* (Knoxville: University of Tennessee Press, 1999); Friend, *Along the Maysville Road;* Honor Sachs, *Home Rule: Households, Manhood, and National Expansion on the Eighteenth-Century Kentucky Frontier* (New Haven: Yale University Press, 2015); Christopher Waldrep, "Opportunity on the Frontier South of the Green," in *The Buzzel About Kentuck: Settling the Promised Land,* ed. Craig Thompson Friend (Lexington: University Press of Kentucky, 1999), 153–72; Cynthia Cumfer, *Separate Peoples, One Land: The Minds of Cherokees, Blacks, and Whites on the Tennessee Frontier* (Chapel Hill: University of North Carolina Press, 2012); Kristofer Ray, *Middle Tennessee, 1775–1825: Progress and Popular Democracy on the Southwestern Frontier* (Knoxville: University of Tennessee Press, 2007); John R. Finger, *Tennessee Frontiers: Three Regions in Transition* (Bloomington: University of Indiana Press, 2001).

41. See William H. Bergmann, *The American National State and the Early West* (New York: Cambridge University Press, 2012). The role of federal officials and institutions in expansion was masterfully explored by Malcolm J. Rohrbough in *Trans-Appalachian Frontier: Peoples, Societies, and Institutions, 1775–1850,* 3rd ed. (Bloomington: Indiana University Press, 2008). Inspired by the influence of Rohrbough's scholarship, Indiana University Press sponsored the History of the Trans-Appalachian Frontier series, publishing state-level studies that examine early national expansion and the relationships of those settlements to national identity. The southern volumes in the series include Finger, *Tennessee Frontiers;* Paul E. Hoffman, *Florida's Frontiers* (2002); Stephen Aron, *American Confluence: The Missouri Frontier from Borderland to Border State* (2009); Craig Thompson Friend, *Kentucke's Frontiers* (2010); and Daniel S. Dupre, *Alabama's Frontiers and the Rise of the Old South* (2017).

42. Andrew R. L. Cayton, "'Separate Interests' and the Nation-State: The Washington Administration and the Origins of Regionalism in the Trans-Appalachian West," *Journal of American History* 79 (June 1992): 39–67; Cayton, *The Frontier Republic: Ideology and Politics in the Ohio Country, 1780–1815* (Kent: Kent State University Press, 1986); Cayton, "Radicals in the 'Western World': The Federalist Conquest

limited, with Virginia and North Carolina taking the lead in—or enabling—the often chaotic process of settlement in what became the new states of Kentucky and Tennessee (and perhaps explaining ongoing hostility to federal authority).[43] In the vast domain of Georgia's western land cession (1802), the Louisiana Purchase (1803), and the acquisition of the Floridas (ceded by Spain in the Transcontinental Treaty of 1819), federal authorities had to cope with preexisting populations, title claims, legal systems, and geopolitical rivalries, and therefore could exercise little direct or effective control over settlement and state formation.[44]

As speculators and settlers drew on customary modes of promoting and securing land title, the northwestern frontier was anomalous, the southwestern more spontaneous. Colonizers sought to reproduce the structures of British colonization by constituting autonomous local jurisdictions under the protective aegis of an imperial power—American or otherwise. The genius of southwestern frontier settlement was to accommodate facts on the ground in a contested borderland. The ultimately successful, but by no means predestined incorporation of the southwestern frontier into the union guaranteed the rising prosperity and power of the United States in the Atlantic and global trading system; it also shaped the political geography of the South as a distinctive section within the new American empire.[45]

---

of Trans-Appalachian North America," in *Federalists Reconsidered,* ed. Doron Ben-Atar and Barbara B. Oberg (Charlottesville: University Press of Virginia, 1998), 77–97; Cayton, *Frontier Indiana* (Bloomington: Indiana University Press, 1996).

43. Alan Taylor argued that an alienation bred of perceived neglect and reinforced during the War of 1812 rendered southerners deeply suspicious of northerners and distrustful of the ability or willingness of the national government to protect slavery and the rights of states. The South, he contended, "began to become Virginia's nation during the War of 1812"; see *Internal Enemy,* 396. See also Hammond, *Slavery, Freedom, and Expansion in the Early American West.* For another view, emphasizing the role of federal courts in consolidating property rights on both sides of the Ohio, see Gregory Ablavsky, "The Rise of Federal Title," *California Law Review* 106 (June 2018): 631–95. Marion Nelson Winship wrote about the efforts of some Kentuckians to create and reinforce networks between the national government and Kentucky in "Kentucky in the New Republic: A Study of Distance and Connection," in Friend, ed., *The Buzzel About Kentuck,* 101–24. On internal improvements and republican equality, see Larson, *Internal Improvement.*

44. See Robert V. Haynes, "Territorial Mississippi, 1798–1817," *Journal of Mississippi History* 64 (December 2002): 283–315; Haynes, *The Mississippi Territory and the Southwest Frontier, 1795–1817* (Lexington: University Press of Kentucky, 2010); Kristofer Ray, "New Directions in Early Tennessee History, 1540–1815," *Tennessee Historical Quarterly* 69 (Fall 2010): 204–23.

45. Tomlins, *Freedom Bound;* Rana, *The Two Faces of American Freedom;* Barksdale, *The Lost State of Franklin;* McMichael, *Atlantic Loyalties.* On the importance of cotton cultivation to these developments, see Schoen, *The Fragile Fabric of Union.*

The continuing presence of foreign powers in the southern borderlands from Florida to Texas demanded that the federal government play a major role in defining and promoting southern interests, with control of New Orleans and the Mississippi River determining the fate of empires.[46] Kathleen DuVal emphasized the radical contingency of a protracted period of unsettlement in the "divided ground" of the southern borderlands.[47] As the United States secured its international borders to the west and south, the settlement frontier moved inward, encircling and displacing Chickasaws, Cherokees, and other Indian peoples with extraordinary and brutal rapidity. State formation, Indian removal, and land distribution thus took a distinctive form in the Southwest. While planters depended on a strong and active federal government to eliminate imperial rivals and gain access to foreign markets for their staple products, they turned to state governments in Georgia and new southwestern states to expedite settlement and Indian removal in the interior, often in defiance of federal authorities.[48] The emerging South reflected this characteristic ambivalence, as white southerners vigilantly defended their domestic institutions and state jurisdictions against outside interference while demanding a strong, protective federal presence in the larger world.[49] This was the idealized old empire adapted for new American imperial purposes.

46. Rothman, *Slave Country;* Jon Kukla, *A Wilderness So Immense: The Louisiana Purchase and the Destiny of America* (New York: Alfred A. Knopf, 2003); Kastor, *The Nation's Crucible;* Edward E. Baptist, *Creating an Old South: Middle Florida's Plantation Frontier before the Civil War* (Chapel Hill: University of North Carolina Press, 2002); James E. Lewis Jr., *The American Union and the Problem of Neighborhood: The United States and the Collapse of the Spanish Empire, 1783–1829* (Chapel Hill: University of North Carolina Press, 1998); Morris, *Becoming Southern;* Friend, *Kentucke's Frontiers;* Haynes, "Territorial Mississippi"; Stagg, *Borderlines in Borderlands.* All of this literature, in one form or another, challenges both the concept of the frontier as a place where American freedom was wrested from the wilderness by rugged democrats, and the assumption of a timeless, changeless "South."

47. Kathleen DuVal, *Independence Lost: Lives on the Edge of the American Revolution* (New York: Random House, 2015). See also Ray, "New Directions in Early Tennessee History."

48. Tim Alan Garrison, *The Legal Ideology of Removal: The Southern Judiciary and the Sovereignty of Native American Nations* (Athens: University of Georgia Press, 2002); Lindsay G. Robertson, *Conquest by Law: How the Discovery of America Dispossessed Indigenous Peoples of Their Lands* (New York: Oxford University Press, 2005); Stuart Banner, *How the Indians Lost Their Land: Law and Power on the Frontier* (Cambridge: Harvard University Press, 2005); Anthony F. C. Wallace, *The Long Bitter Trail: Andrew Jackson and the Indians* (New York: Hill and Wang, 1993).

49. Andrew Jackson's career illuminates the protean loyalties of southerners-in-the-making. See J. M. Opal, *Avenging the People: Andrew Jackson, the Rule of Law, and the American Nation* (New York: Oxford University Press, 2017); Mark R. Cheathem, *Andrew Jackson, Southerner* (Baton Rouge: Louisiana State University Press, 2013).

If forward-looking Americans saw union as the constitutional means to fulfill imperial aspirations, they looked to their states and to sectional coalitions of states as bulwarks against the competing designs of rivals within the union. The great fear was the potential consolidation of authority in a powerful central government dominated by hostile interests. James E. Lewis Jr. persuasively argued that devotion to the union (and even to the exercise of federal power) coexisted with disunionist tendencies that could be activated by perceived threats to American liberties. To take one example, Aaron Burr's "conspiracy" to break up the union in 1807—and perhaps establish a new western confederacy—brought this powerful dynamic to the surface. In the following decades, suspicion that imperial ambitions masked or served sectionalist interests would provoke sectional responses and thus threaten the union's survival.[50]

From 1789 onward, every policy move, domestic and international, within the federal political arena carried implications for the union's constituent parts, sometimes confirming and other times belying Henry Clay's vision of a "harmony of interests." The very existence of the union and national government fostered a sense of distinctive interests vis-à-vis the new center in Washington, DC, and lent latent sectional differences in political economy and culture new and potentially antagonistic meaning. The constitutional settlement placed a premium on compromise and mutual restraint for the sake of union.[51] But as the foreign policy establishment increasingly pursued what was in effect a proslavery agenda in international relations, the progress of continental expansion—to which all parties were theoretically committed—raised concerns about the good faith of exponents of conflicting political economies.[52] As John Lauritz Larson put it, "each concession in the name of Union produced consequences that candidates and voters somewhere could denounce as partial, corrupt, and pernicious." Devotion

50. James E. Lewis Jr., *The Burr Conspiracy: Uncovering the Story of an Early American Crisis* (Princeton: Princeton University Press, 2017), 116–47.

51. Maurice G. Baxter, *Henry Clay and the American System* (Lexington: University Press of Kentucky, 1995); Peter B. Knupfer, *The Union as It Is: Constitutional Unionism and Sectional Compromise, 1787–1861* (Chapel Hill: University of North Carolina Press, 1991).

52. See Fehrenbacher, *The Slaveholding Republic*, esp. chaps. 4–6; Karp, *This Vast Southern Empire.* See also Peter O'Connor, *American Sectionalism in the British Mind, 1832–1863* (Baton Rouge: Louisiana State University Press, 2017), which notes that, well into America's antebellum era, the British public continued to identify slavery as a national rather than an exclusively southern preoccupation, reminding us that sectionalism's salience—and in this case existence—depended always upon the position from which it was observed.

to the union thus fostered a culture of mutual concession and compromise even as it promoted consciousness of distinctive sectional interests in a political culture of suspicion. The great and growing fear of national statesmen in the Early Republic was that hostile interests would capture the central state in pursuit of their own partial ends. The founding fathers compromised to create union, but compromises reached in the early nineteenth century to preserve the union exacted an increasing price that sectional patriots were unwilling to pay. In his later years, before his death in March 1850, John C. Calhoun—once an ardent nationalist—gave up on the promise of mutual concession. Every compromise with the free states of the North, he charged, masked an insidious tightening of the noose around the vital interests and "civilization" of the embattled South. Calhoun ultimately rejected the founders' Constitution and their design for continental empire. Following his lead, southerners instead began to envision their own empire of slavery.[53]

Political Economy and Sectional Crises

The impressive growth and prosperity of the colonial economy made "independence thinkable by the 1770s," as John McCusker and Russell Menard argued. But this is not to say that independence was *inevitable,* for economic growth in the colonies was fueled by their growing participation in Atlantic and global commercial networks dominated by Britain. Economic interdependence set the stage for political independence. In similar fashion, the southern economy became increasingly integrated into the emerging national economy during the Early Republic. American elites who led the movement toward independence were animated, wrote McCusker and Menard, by a "vision of an American empire, of a republican polity responsive to the common good that would protect American commerce, encourage American agriculture, develop American industry, promote the settlement of western lands, and, eventually, take Great Britain's place at the center of the Atlantic economy." Americans living south of Pennsylvania shared this vision and participated fully in efforts to realize it.[54]

53. John Lauritz Larson, "The Art of Compromise and the Right of Self-Creation," *Reviews in American History* 21 (March 1993): 45–50, quote on 48; James H. Read, *Majority Rule Versus Consensus: The Political Thought of John C. Calhoun* (Lawrence: University Press of Kansas, 2009); Merrill D. Peterson, *The Great Triumvirate: Webster, Clay, and Calhoun* (New York: Oxford University Press, 1987).

54. John J. McCusker and Russell R. Menard, *The Economy of British America, 1607–1789* (Chapel Hill: University of North Carolina Press, 1985), 352, 357. For confirmation of this point for Georgia and

The interests of northern commercial states in the post–Revolutionary War years, as John Rutledge noted at the Constitutional Convention, were never fully extricable from the flourishing slave economy, and this interconnection continued well into the nineteenth century. "Whoever says Industrial Revolution says cotton," Eric J. Hobsbawm famously wrote in 1968, and historians like Sven Beckert and Walter Johnson, among others, continue to confirm and extend his assessment. The explosive growth of cotton production fueled the Market Revolution and the early stages of industrialization that began to transform the North and, in turn, stimulated ongoing expansion of the slavery-based Cotton Kingdom. Rising international demand for cotton encouraged a large domestic trade in slaves from the Upper South to the Southwest as early as the 1790s.[55] As cotton production became ever more essential to the convergence of economic interests envisioned by Henry Clay and other reformers, southerners recognized that their economic imperatives (including climate and soil as well as the cultural power and prestige associated with plantation agriculture and accumulation of slaves) inhibited industrialization, the growth of urban areas, and the integration of urban centers with their hinterlands. Some anxious southerners feared future marginalization as their region failed to keep pace with the North in population growth and political power. A "developmental strategy based on the indefinite expansion of the plantation system and racial slavery," Peter A. Coclanis wrote, rendered the southern political economy increasingly "anachronistic."[56] Reliance

South Carolina, see Joyce Chaplin, "Creating a Cotton South in Georgia and South Carolina, 1760–1815," *Journal of Southern History* 57 (May 1991): 171–200; Chaplin, *An Anxious Pursuit: Agricultural Innovation and Modernity in the Lower South, 1730–1815* (Chapel Hill: University of North Carolina Press, 1993).

55. Farrand, *Records of the Federal Convention,* 2:364; Eric J. Hobsbawm, *Industry and Empire: The Making of Modern English Society, 1750 to the Present Day* (New York: Pantheon Books, 1968), 56; Sven Beckert, *Empire of Cotton: A Global History* (New York: Alfred A. Knopf, 2014); Walter Johnson, *River of Dark Dreams: Slavery and Empire in the Cotton Kingdom* (Cambridge: Harvard University Press, 2013); Michael Tadman, *Speculators and Slaves: Masters, Traders, and Slaves in the Old South* (Madison: University of Wisconsin Press, 1989). As Stanley L. Engerman noted, of all the states, Virginia continued to have the largest number of slaves on the eve of the Civil War; see "Slavery and Its Consequences for the South in the Nineteenth Century," in *The Cambridge Economic History of the United States.* Vol. 2, *The Long Nineteenth Century,* ed. Stanley L. Engerman and Robert E. Gallman (New York: Cambridge University Press, 2000), 329–66, quote on 339.

56. Peter A. Coclanis, "Tracking the Economic Divergence of the North and the South," *Southern Cultures* 6 (Winter 2004): 82–103, quote on 95. See also William L. Barney, *The Passage of the Republic: An Interdisciplinary History of Nineteenth-Century America* (Lexington: D. C. Heath, 1987), 18–30, 45–48.

on enslaved labor, Harry L. Watson aptly concluded, "had a powerful, paradoxical influence in pushing the South toward ever-greater commercialization, yet also in slowing its progress toward that end."[57] National economic integration underscored the distinctiveness of the southern economy.

Economies oriented around the export of staple crops and with a high concentration of slave labor created significant wealth but gave little impetus to the balanced and integrated economic development that characterized the Northeast and Old Northwest. From the beginning, southern colonies had been oriented toward international markets, with Virginia's tobacco and South Carolina's rice leading the way. But by the late eighteenth century, Chesapeake tobacco planters were already complaining bitterly about "stagnant profits, eroded fields, collapsed land values, and declining private fortunes." By 1820, white Virginians, Marylanders, and Carolinians were leaving their states in droves for richer lands, as cotton surpassed tobacco as the nation's leading export.[58] Migration to the Old Southwest—stimulated by the push of depleted soil and the pull of international demand for cotton—spread plantation agriculture and cotton production by ambitious and entrepreneurial planters. It also inspired a "safety-first" agriculture among small farmers who prioritized security from the caprice of the market and a passionate commitment to independence.[59] This dual economy generated enormous wealth (albeit unevenly distributed) but paradoxically retarded development, stamping the Old Southwest with what was coming to be understood as a "southern" economic orientation rather than a "western" economy characterized

57. Harry L. Watson, "Slavery and Development in a Dual Economy: The South and the Market Revolution," in *The Market Revolution in America: Social, Political, and Religious Expressions, 1800–1880*, ed. Melvyn Stokes and Stephen Conway (Charlottesville: University Press of Virginia, 1996), 43–73, quote on 47.

58. Watson, "Slavery and Development in a Dual Economy," quote on 57; Daniel Walker Howe, *What Hath God Wrought: The Transformation of America, 1815–1848* (New York: Oxford University Press, 2007), 158; Douglass C. North, *The Economic Growth of the United States, 1790–1860* (New York: Prentice Hall, 1961), 283, App. 3: Table 4; Worthy Putnam Sterns, "The Foreign Trade of the United States from 1820 to 1840," *Journal of Political Economy* 8 (September 1900): 452–90.

59. Gavin Wright and Howard Kunreuther, "Cotton, Corn and Risk in the Nineteenth Century," *Journal of Economic History* 35 (September 1975): 526–51. On the extension of this approach into the post–Civil War period, see Steven Hahn, "The 'Unmaking' of the Southern Yeomanry: The Transformation of the Georgia Upcountry, 1860–1890," in *The Countryside in the Age of Capitalist Transformation: Essays in the Social History of Rural America*, ed. Steven Hahn and Jonathan Prude (Chapel Hill: University of North Carolina Press, 1985), 179–204.

by mechanization of agriculture, specialization, manufacturing, and a dynamic interaction between urban areas and their hinterlands.[60]

The day would come when southern nationalists would conclude, as Paul Quigley summarized their argument, that "slavery generated different economic and foreign policy needs for the South," making political union difficult.[61] The day would come when observers from the increasingly bourgeois North (however indirectly dependent their own livelihoods might be on the Cotton Kingdom) would describe the southern economy and society as backward, premodern, even barbaric and ultimately incompatible with their free-labor regime.[62] It is true that economic development in the North left the South lagging in urbanization, industrialization, education, literacy, and population growth, all of which led many white southerners into a rearguard defense of tradition against northern innovation. But the emergence of the South as a distinctive section—and the self-identification of people who lived there as southern—was never fixed but always dependent on context and perspective.

Consciousness of distinct interests did not necessarily drive Americans apart in the Early Republic. To the contrary, the transportation and communications networks that accompanied and enabled the development of a national, interregional economy diminished distances and expanded horizons, fostering increasingly robust nationalist sentiments between 1789 and 1846. Southerners who resisted the claims of fire-eaters in the 1850s continually argued, with reason, that the Constitution and union had hitherto offered the most security for slavery and the southern economy. Yet if optimists celebrated the harmonizing of interests in an expanding national economy, quarrels over commercial and foreign policy, taxation, and the administration of public lands exposed intersectional fault lines and fostered a sense of victimhood in the South.[63] As Benjamin Park suggested,

60. See Barney, *The Passage of the Republic,* 25; Charles Sellers, *The Market Revolution: Jacksonian America, 1815–1846* (New York: Oxford University Press, 1991); John Lauritz Larson, *The Market Revolution in America: Liberty, Ambition, and the Eclipse of the Common Good* (New York: Cambridge University Press, 2010).

61. Paul Quigley, *Shifting Grounds: Nationalism and the American South, 1848–1865* (New York: Oxford University Press, 2012), 53, 55; John McCardell, *The Idea of a Southern Nation: Southern Nationalists and Southern Nationalism, 1830–1860* (New York: W. W. Norton, 1979).

62. See Eric Foner, *Free Soil, Free Labor, Free Men: The Ideology of the Republican Party Before the Civil War* (New York: Oxford University Press, 1970), chap. 2; John Ashworth, *Slavery, Capitalism, and Politics in the Antebellum Republic,* 2 vols. (New York: Cambridge University Press, 1995).

63. James M. McPherson, "Antebellum Southern Exceptionalism: A New Look at an Old Question," *Civil War History* 29 (September 1983): 230–44; Quigley, *Shifting Grounds;* Eric H. Walther, *The Fire-*

nationalism in the Early Republic was inflected in sectionally distinctive ways: as a result, the distinction between claiming to be a nationalist (a good thing) and being accused of being a sectionalist (a bad thing) was situational, not self-evident.[64]

What would retroactively be identified as sectionalism emerged out of this dialectic, as the fault lines of the imperial imaginary and its national successor became increasingly conspicuous and, in Jefferson's stark formulation, a "geographical line, coinciding with a marked principle, moral and political" was inscribed on the American map. For Jefferson, the irony and potential tragedy of the Missouri Crisis of 1819–1820 was that he and (he liked to think) a growing number of enlightened slaveholders shared the vision of a slave-free, republican future. Antislavery "restrictionists" who sought to make Missouri free jeopardized that outcome by denying the republican rights of constitution-writers to decide for themselves on the future of slavery in their new state. This had been the great British mistake in the imperial crisis, when Parliament's claim to sovereignty destroyed the imperial union that American patriots cherished.[65] Now, in the minds of some southern leaders, a sectional bloc in Congress was following Parliament's disastrous example, threatening the federal union's survival by exercising its controversial authority to shape Missouri's "domestic" institutions.[66]

Eaters (Baton Rouge: Louisiana State University Press, 1992). William Lee Miller's *Arguing about Slavery: The Great Battle in the United States Congress* (New York: Alfred A. Knopf, 1996) reminds us that the sense of victimhood was not confined to the South as southern insistence on tabling abolitionist petitions to Congress threatened northern conceptions of freedom.

64. Benjamin E. Park, *Imagining Union in the Age of Revolutions, 1783–1833* (New York: Cambridge University Press, 2018). Susan-Mary Grant, *North over South: Northern Nationalism and American Identity in the Antebellum Era* (Lawrence: University Press of Kansas, 2000), argues that because it was understood at the time—and since—as normative, northern nationalism, unlike southern nationalism, has been a relatively neglected topic of scholarly research. The definitive statement on this problem remains David M. Potter, "The Historian's Use of Nationalism and Vice Versa," in *History and American Society: Essays of David M. Potter*, ed. Don E. Fehrenbacher (New York: Oxford University Press, 1973), 60–108.

65. Thomas Jefferson to John Holmes, 22 April 1820, in Peterson, ed., *Thomas Jefferson: Writings*, 1434; Hammond, *Slavery, Freedom, and Expansion*, 150–68; Greene, *Constitutional Origins of the American Revolution*.

66. Robert Pierce Forbes, *The Missouri Compromise and Its Aftermath: Slavery and the Meaning of America* (Chapel Hill: University of North Carolina Press. 2007); Onuf, *Jefferson's Empire*, 109–17; Freehling, *Road to Disunion*. Vol. 1, *Secessionists at Bay*, 144–61. Note, however, that Freehling was at pains to claim that the Missouri Crisis did not evoke the "alarmed consolidation of *a* South" (157). Northerners, for their part, had ample evidence that the "slave power" exploited the constitutional structure and party system to dominate the central government in order to ride roughshod over the rights of northern states. See Leonard L. Richards, *The Slave Power: The Free North and Southern Domination, 1780–1860* (Baton

John Quincy Adams, who as Secretary of State in the Monroe Administration was doing as much as anyone to promote the interests of slaveholders abroad, ominously read Missouri as "a question between the rights of human nature and the Constitution of the United States." The resulting tension, he thought, would become the "basis for a new organization of parties" along largely sectional lines. By the 1850s, many white southerners came to retroactively interpret Missouri as the opening salvo of a series of assaults on "southern rights" to equal access to the West.[67] In the 1820s and 1830s, patriotic compromisers still commanded the high ground, recognizing and celebrating the patriotism of erstwhile adversaries. Michael F. Holt reminded us that, in the aftermath of the crisis rightly seen as revealing sectional discord, "a majority of Southern Congressmen [nevertheless] *willingly* accepted Congressional prohibition of slavery from almost all of the western territories." It may be misleading to call the subsequent years an "era of good feelings," but they were characterized by widespread display of unionist sentiment in the face of multiple threats to union itself, not all of them by any means promulgated by white southerners, as Kevin M. Gannon demonstrated.[68] Northerners and southerners alike continued to cherish a union that guaranteed geopolitical security and protected their essential interests while postponing,

Rouge: Louisiana State University Press, 2000); Richard R. John, *Spreading the News: The American Postal System from Franklin to Morse* (Cambridge: Harvard University Press, 1995), chap. 7. See also Kelly M. Kennington, *In the Shadow of* Dred Scott: *St. Louis Freedom Suits and the Legal Culture of Slavery in Antebellum America* (Athens: University of Georgia Press, 2017).

67. Entry for 20 February 1820, in *Memoirs of John Quincy Adams,* ed. Charles Francis Adams, 12 vols. (Philadelphia: J. B. Lippincott, 1874–77), 4:529. Calhoun's late view of the compromise as southern capitulation is briefly described in his "Speech on the Admission of California—and the General State of the Union," 4 March 1850, in *Union and Liberty: The Political Philosophy of John C. Calhoun,* ed. Ross M. Lence (Indianapolis: Liberty Fund, 1992), 578–81.

68. Michael F. Holt, *The Fate of Their Country: Politicians, Slavery Extension, and the Coming of the Civil War* (New York: Hill and Wang, 2004), 6, 94; Kevin M. Gannon, "Calculating the Value of Union: States' Rights, Nullification, and Secession in the North, 1800–1848" (PhD diss., University of South Carolina, 2002); Gannon, "Escaping 'Mr. Jefferson's Plan of Destruction': New England Federalists and the Idea of a Northern Confederacy, 1803–1804," *Journal of the Early Republic* 21 (December 2001): 313–43; Schoen, *Fragile Fabric of the Union,* chap. 3. On unionist sentiment in these years, see Rogan Kersh, *Dreams of a More Perfect Union* (Ithaca: Cornell University Press, 2001), esp. chap. 3. On conflicting views of states' rights and continued manifestation of commitment to union and compromise during the South Carolina nullification controversy, see Richard E. Ellis, *The Union at Risk: Jacksonian Democracy, States' Rights, and the Nullification Crisis* (New York: Oxford University Press, 1989); Drew R. McCoy, *The Last of the Fathers: James Madison and the Republican Legacy* (New York: Cambridge University Press, 1989), 119–70.

through the ingenious device of party politics, the "portentously terrible" contest that Adams foretold.[69]

Democrats and Whigs, the great national political parties of the Second Party System, institutionalized intersectional compromise, protesting their fealty to their interpretation of the federal Constitution and enforcing discipline by distributing the loaves and fishes of patronage. But devotion to the Spirit of 1776 could not banish the specter of sectionalism altogether. Sectional feeling in the South grew steadily stronger while partisans maintained an intersectional peace in Washington, DC, that was intermittently disrupted by new crises of union—and new opportunities for statesmen to resolve them.[70] The distinctiveness of frontier development to the North and South became increasingly conspicuous and every successive crisis illuminated and clarified—and over time, validated and affirmed—what it might mean to be southern (or northern or western) in a union of increasingly hostile interests. The cumulative effect of congressional divisions over the admission of new states was to draw Jefferson's "geographical line of distinction" between North and South, freedom and slavery. The West faded from view while the "many Souths" identified by William W. Freehling coalesced into an increasingly monolithic section. The South was still not precisely defined and would not be so until the secession winter of 1860–1861, but white southerners' commitment to slavery and alienation from fellow Americans in the North led them to forge political and economic ties that, in Brian Schoen's words, "united individuals otherwise separated by distance, class, gender, religious belief or party affiliation."[71]

Still, we cannot begin with these sectional divisions as if they were simply there to be revealed rather than products of historical development. The history of sectional conflict in the Early Republic confirms David M. Potter's hypothesis

69. Merrill D. Peterson, *Olive Branch and Sword: The Compromise of 1833* (Baton Rouge: Louisiana State University Press, 1982). Benjamin L. Carp described how Jefferson's embargo, which had to be enforced locally and thus stoked "regional anger," went some distance toward "sectionalizing" the parties (at least temporarily) as northern Republicans turned against the policy; see "Jefferson's Embargo: National Intent, Sectional Effects," in *Jeffersonians in Power: Ideas in Practice,* ed. Joanne B. Freeman and Johann Neem (Charlottesville: University of Virginia Press, 2019), chap. 6.

70. On the collapse of intersectional peace in Congress, see Joanne B. Freeman, *The Field of Blood: Violence in Congress and the Road to Civil War* (New York: Farrar, Straus and Giroux, 2018).

71. Freehling, *Road to Disunion.* Vol. 1, *Secessionists at Bay;* Schoen, *Fragile Fabric of Union,* 7; Mark V. Tushnet, *Slave Law in the American South:* State v. Mann *in History and Literature* (Lawrence: University Press of Kansas, 2003).

that cultural or economic "diversity will generate friction only when it has been translated into opposing policies for dealing with a particular question" and that "the disruptive potentials inherent in cultural diversity remain latent until conflicts of interest bring them into play." The various "crises of union" that provide American history textbooks with the building blocks of a narrative culminating in the Civil War appear almost preordained in retrospect. But North and South only *became* "a threat to each other's national ideal," as Susan-Mary Grant suggested, because they shared a common past of bloodshed in the Revolution and a shared commitment to nationhood and union born in the Early Republic. It was against this exalted standard that they questioned their adversaries' good faith and patriotism.[72]

In some fundamental sense, then, southerners eventually left the union, Peter S. Onuf argued, "*because* they had so fully embraced the democratic, egalitarian ideals of modern American nationhood." The South was not isolated or backward but was deeply integrated in the emerging national market. Wealth generated by slavery enabled white southerners to participate in an expanding domain of consumer culture as well as dynamic networks of communication, capital, and exchange. White southerners manifested ostensibly American character traits: mobility, enterprise, and commitment to democratic egalitarianism, however inflected with their commitment to white supremacy and slavery as a "positive good." Yet the crises that plagued the union in the Early Republic nonetheless led southerners to "conceive of their interests in regional ways" and created "regionally-defined historical memories" that would be reinforced in crisis after crisis to come. As distinctive as southern "nationalists" claimed the South to be, southerners affirmed their American identity when they finally seceded from the union by invoking the legacy of the American Revolution and drafting a new constitution modeled on its federal predecessor.[73]

72. Potter, "The Historian's Use of Nationalism," 105; Grant, *North over South,* 28–29; Charles Royster, "Founding a Nation in Blood: Military Conflict and American Nationality," in *Arms and Independence: The Military Character of the American Revolution,* ed. Ronald Hoffman and Peter J. Albert (Charlottesville: University Press of Virginia, 1984), 25–49.

73. Onuf, "Antebellum Southerners and the National Idea," 41; Quigley, *Shifting Grounds,* esp. 16–49; Brian Schoen, "Calculating the Price of Union: Republican Economic Nationalism and the Origins of Southern Sectionalism, 1790–1828," *Journal of the Early Republic* 23 (Summer 2003): 173–206, quote on 195; George C. Rable, *The Confederate Republic: A Revolution Against Politics* (Chapel Hill: University of North Carolina Press, 1994).

Dreams of southern nationhood faltered time and again on the shoals of states' rights and a profound orientation—shared by northerners—toward locality. Dreams of (and frantic efforts to manufacture) a unique southern civilization that would justify separation ran up against the history that southerners shared with all Americans and the fact that union secured southern interests more effectively than any plausible alternative. If, as Michael O'Brien noted, "animosity between Southern States was not small during the antebellum years," and if tensions emerged even at the intrastate and subregional level, there was little reason to expect a unified South. On the eve of the Civil War, the South was, in historian Clement Eaton's words, a "federalism of cultures." The South, after all, was not a nation apart but a fluid combination of the national, postcolonial, imperial, federal, and local: its culture "invented in the tense encounters among these conditions."[74]

Early in 1820, in the midst of the Missouri Crisis, Secretary of State John Quincy Adams recorded a conversation he had with John C. Calhoun, then Secretary of War. Calhoun, Adams wrote, did not think "the slave question pending in Congress . . . would produce a dissolution of the Union, but, if it should, the South would be from necessity compelled to form an alliance, offensive and defensive, with Great Britain." Adams wrote that "I said that would be returning to the colonial state." Calhoun "said, yes, pretty much, but it would be forced upon them."

Adams then asked whether Calhoun "thought, if by the effect of this alliance, offensive and defensive, the population of the North should be cut off from its natural outlet upon the ocean, it would fall back upon its rocks bound hand and foot, to starve, or whether it would not retain its powers of locomotion to move southward by land." "Then," Calhoun replied, "they would find it necessary to make their communities all military." Adams "pressed the conversation no further" but confided to his diary his prediction that "if the dissolution of the Union should result from the slave question, it is as obvious as anything that can be foreseen of futurity, that it must shortly afterwards be followed by the universal emancipation of the slaves." Adams went on to reflect on the likely outcomes:

74. Quigley, *Shifting Grounds*, chap. 2; Michael O'Brien, *Conjectures of Order: Intellectual Life and the American South, 1810–1860*, 2 vols. (Chapel Hill: University of North Carolina Press, 2004), 1:2, see also 336, 353–59; Clement Eaton, *The Growth of Southern Civilization, 1790–1860* (New York: Harper & Brothers, 1961).

anticipating Tocqueville's imaginative removal of race, he envisioned the "extirpation of the African race on this continent, by the gradual . . . bleaching process of intermixture." During the "momentous train of reflection" that Calhoun had stimulated, Adams also imagined that "the Union might then be reorganized on the fundamental principle of emancipation." However "awful in its prospects," such an event would be "sublime and beautiful. . . . A life devoted to it would be nobly spent or sacrificed."[75]

Adams's anticipation of some of Abraham Lincoln's private reflections during the Civil War is worth noting, as is his hint that the meaning of freedom in the North was gradually evolving from that originally embraced by American patriots. But the lines from Adams are significant here less for their predictions than for what they suggest about the architects of southern civilization who would, when they envisioned the threat to slavery and their perceived equality in the union to be beyond compromise, prefer to abandon the imperial promise of American nationhood, reembrace the colonial state cast off during the American Revolution, and militarize their communities to preserve the original freedom to mastery and mobility once promised by the British Empire and seemingly no longer secure in a union with northerners newly hostile to that kind of liberty.[76]

For the moment, Adams noted a few days later, "popular sentiment against slavery to the North" was not deep or widespread, the question being "merely speculative" where people "do not feel it in their persons or their purses." But in the South, already, Adams was quick to add, the question "comes home to the feelings and interests of every man in the community." Northerners, he predicted, would "immediately acquiesce" in the southern insistence on slavery in Missouri, and "it will be impossible to keep the controversy alive"—for the time being.[77]

75. Entry for 24 February 1820, in Adams, ed., *Memoirs of John Quincy Adams,* 4:530–31.

76. See J. Mills Thornton III, "The Ethic of Subsistence and the Origins of Southern Secession," *Tennessee Historical Quarterly* 48 (Summer 1989): 67–85. As Akhil Reed Amar suggested: "The fabric of the original Bill of Rights, interweaving freedom and federalism, was unraveling under the strain of slavery"; see *The Bill of Rights,* 162.

77. Entry for 27 February 1820, in Adams, ed., *Memoirs of John Quincy Adams,* 4:533.

NINETEENTH-CENTURY ENSLAVEMENT OF AFRICANS AND AFRICAN AMERICANS IN THE UNITED STATES

Vanessa M. Holden and Edward E. Baptist

In 1987, when Charles B. Dew published the chapter equivalent to this one in *Interpreting Southern History,* scholars of slavery in the nineteenth-century South could look back at their collective accomplishments with some degree of pride.[1] Over the three decades before 1987, enormous shifts had transformed the field, driving out much (if not all) of the planter apologia and open racism that characterized a significant portion of previous generations' scholarship—in particular, much of that carried out at historically white colleges and universities. It would not have been surprising if productivity, innovation, and debate slowed over the ensuing decades, after scholars fought great battles about resistance, community, hegemony, the role of African identity and culture, the nature and use of sources generated by enslavers and the formerly enslaved, the profitability of slavery, the comparative nature of various New World slave societies, and many other questions.

We are happy to report, however, that the study of slavery and enslavement in the pre–Civil War South has been thriving. In fact, no single scholar can keep up

1. Charles B. Dew, "The Slavery Experience," in *Interpreting Southern History: Essays in Honor of Sanford W. Higginbotham,* ed. John B. Boles and Evelyn Thomas Nolen (Baton Rouge: Louisiana State University Press, 1987), 120–61. The authors chose to capitalize "Black" and lowercase "white," equating Black to African American as an ethnicity, but also as a political response to white supremacist literature that regularly capitalizes "White" but not "black." See Lori L. Tharps, "The Case for Black with a Capital B," *New York Times,* 18 November 2014; Frances Robles, "Dylann Roof Photos and a Manifesto Are Posted on Website," *New York Times,* 20 June 2015; P. Gabrielle Foreman et al., "Writing about Slavery/Teaching about Slavery: This Might Help," https://bit.ly/2sxmQE2 (accessed 18 January 2019).

with the flood of research and analysis. The most important new direction has been the emergence of the history of Black women, which took root before 1987 with pioneers such as Deborah Gray White, Darlene Clark Hine, Brenda E. Stevenson, Wilma King, Angela Davis, Jacqueline Jones, Suzanne Lebsock, Hortense Spillers, and Paula Giddings, all of whose works transformed the study of antebellum slavery and Black life. The emergence of women's history democratized scholarship on nineteenth-century slavery. More and more of the scholarship and teaching is done by women, specifically women of color. Work on women's history in enslavement is reshaping virtually all questions that scholars ask about nineteenth-century slavery.[2]

Democratization simultaneously occurred in scholarly discussion and publication, and in research. The internet, unknown and unimaginable to most humanities scholars in 1987, opened new venues, from discussion boards through social media on Web 2.0 to ever-flowing liquid publication online, shifting the tempo and power balances of scholarship. For instance, the African American Intellectual History Society blog, founded in 2014 by Chris Cameron and relaunched by Keisha Blain as *Black Perspectives* in 2017, became a vibrant locus for African American studies. There, on Twitter, and at other sites like #ADPhD (a Tumblr account curated by Jessica Marie Johnson and others), graduate students and junior professors stand on more equal footing with tenured and institutionally privileged professors. Meanwhile, microfilm and digital reproduction of sources made research into nineteenth-century slavery exponentially more accessible. The Records of Antebellum Southern Plantations microfilm series began this process in the 1990s. The University of North Carolina's Documenting the American South online collection of nineteenth-century freedom narratives was the next step.[3] Digitization of historic newspapers, in projects such as those carried

2. Deborah Gray White, *Ar'n't I a Woman? Female Slaves in the Plantation South* (New York: W. W. Norton, 1985); Paula J. Giddings, *When and Where I Enter: The Impact of Black Women on Race and Sex in America* (New York: William Morrow, 1984); Darlene Clark Hine, ed., *Black Women in America: An Historical Encyclopedia,* 3 vols. (New York: Oxford University Press, 2005); Hine, Wilma King, and Linda Reed, eds., *We Specialize in the Wholly Impossible: A Reader in Black Women's History* (Brooklyn: Carlson Publishing 1995); Jacqueline Jones, *Labor of Love, Labor of Sorrow: Black Women, Work, and the Family, from Slavery to the Present,* 2nd ed. (New York: Basic Books, 2009); Suzanne Lebsock, *The Free Women of Petersburg: Status and Culture in a Southern Town, 1784–1860,* rev. ed. (New York: W. W. Norton, 1985).

3. In 2015, Keisha Blain became the AAIHS Blog's first senior editor. In 2017, with then associate editor Ibram Kendi, Blain relaunched the blog as *Black Perspectives;* see https://www.aaihs.org/black-perspectives/ (accessed 18 January 2019). For examples of the democratization of scholarly conversations,

out under the auspices of the Library of Congress, plus wider availability of books via Google Books, HathiTrust, and other online collections, increased and transformed access. None of these projects were as free as wide-eyed proclaimers of the internet circa 1994 had promised. Still, new resources generated more vibrant and democratic scholarship.

As primary sources became more accessible and scholarly conversation more democratic, tensions emerged between histories of slavery and histories of the enslaved.[4] Some scholars wrote about slavery as a system, focusing on institutions, the politics of enslavers who derived power from the system, and so on. Such scholarship does not necessarily adopt the views of enslavers, but it often draws primarily from sources written by whites, making whites almost necessarily the subjects of the story, and enslaved Blacks the objects of the institution.[5] Other scholars placed enslaved people at the center of the narrative, recognizing how documents were created by enslavers specifically for the purpose of tightening down the chains. Such scholarship painted the history of the enslaved in more complex hues, amplifying personal and familial concerns, internal conflicts, and individual and collective strategies of survival and resistance.[6]

---

see the Southern Historical Association's two Twitter accounts: @JourSouHist to complement the *Journal of Southern History* and @TheSouthernSHA for conference-related content. For examples of the digitization of primary sources, see Documenting the American South, University of North Carolina at Chapel Hill, docsouth.unc.edu; Virginia Memory, The Library of Virginia, Richmond, http://www.virginia memory.com; Legacy of Slavery in Maryland, Maryland State Archives, Annapolis, http://slavery.msa .maryland.gov/; Unknown No Longer: A Database of Virginia Slave Names, Library of Virginia, Richmond, https://www.virginiahistory.org/collections/unknown-no-longer-database-virginia-slave-names (all accessed 20 December 2018).

4. The debate over use of "slave" versus "enslaved" or "enslaved Africans" (or similar terms) is one that divides scholars. For instance, see the 2017 reflection on the terminological debate at the *Chronicle of Higher Education*'s blog *Lingua Franca:* https://www.chronicle.com/blogs/linguafranca/2017/10/12/the-language-of-enslavement/ (accessed 18 January 2019).

5. Stanley M. Elkins, *Slavery: A Problem in American Institutional and Intellectual Life,* 3rd ed. (Chicago: University of Chicago Press, 1976); David Eltis, *The Rise of African Slavery in the Americas* (New York: Cambridge University Press, 1999); Robert William Fogel and Stanley L. Engerman, *Time on the Cross: The Economics of American Slavery,* reissue ed. (New York: W. W. Norton, 1995); Ulrich B. Phillips, *American Negro Slavery: A Survey of the Supply, Employment and Control of Negro Labor as Determined by the Plantation Regime* (Baton Rouge: Louisiana State University Press, 1966).

6. For example, post-1968 "community studies" asserted that studying enslaved people by foregrounding their experiences, actions, and lives should shape our understanding of American slavery. See John W. Blassingame, *The Slave Community: Plantation Life in the Antebellum South,* rev. ed. (New York: Oxford University Press, 1979); Eugene D. Genovese, *Roll, Jordan, Roll: The World the Slaves Made* (New York:

Wider geographical and chronological contexts for southern slavery also complicate the historiography, making long-standing periodizations and geographies almost anachronistic. Almost, but not quite: the policies and dynamics of the postcolonial state-which-became-an-empire remains in tension with the specific dynamics of North American slavery. Joseph Miller's annual project in *Slavery & Abolition*—the collection and collation of a bibliography of the previous year's published books and essays on slavery—offers a systematic introduction to this amazing and expanding wealth of scholarship.[7]

Women's and Gender History

Deborah Gray White began "Mining the Forgotten" (1987) by stating plainly: "Ten years ago an article in a major historical journal on manuscript collections on black women would have been unlikely. Not only was interest in doing black women's history minimal, but some collections that exist today did not even exist then."[8] One could hardly overestimate the impact of women's and gender history on the study of American slavery: the field has enriched our understanding of how slavery changed over time and across regions, plantation sizes, and economies; exposed spectrums of femininities and masculinities in the antebellum South; introduced important methods for bridging the history of slavery as a social and economic system to the histories of the enslaved themselves; and provided compelling analyses of how race worked as a social construction with often deadly consequences.

The mid-1980s saw the publication of field-defining works that moved southern women's historical scholarship away from white elite women and towards significant investigation of the lives of women, white and Black, who labored both in and out of bondage.[9] Suzanne Lebsock's *The Free Women of Petersburg*

Vintage, 1976); Herbert G. Gutman, *The Black Family in Slavery and Freedom, 1750–1925* (New York: Vintage, 1970); White, *Ar'n't I a Woman?*

7. The annual supplements to Miller's bibliography appear in the journal *Slavery & Abolition,* and one can search the accumulated bibliography at http://www2.vcdh.virginia.edu/bib/about.php (accessed 18 January 2019).

8. Deborah Gray White, "Mining the Forgotten: Manuscript Sources for Black Women's History," *Journal of American History* 74 (June 1987): 237.

9. Earlier works had done much to show the necessity of histories that centered enslaved women. For example, Catherine Clinton's *The Plantation Mistress: Women's World in the Old South* (New York:

(1984) and Jaqueline Jones's *Labor of Love, Labor of Sorrow* (1985) argued for women's centrality to southern economy and culture, challenging tendencies to flatten women's history into one monolithic gendered experience or "women's culture." Elizabeth Fox-Genovese's *Within the Plantation Household* (1988) wed the question of women's labor on both sides of the color line by highlighting the fraught nature of antebellum southern households, challenging the idea of women's culture as monolithic by exposing fissures among women across class and racial lines, and painting a picture of women's place in the South's power structure. Even so, enslaved women often received historical treatment only in relation to white women, and not as subjects in their own right. In their landmark Black feminist collection, *All the Women Are White, All the Blacks Are Men, but Some of Us Are Brave* (1982), Akasha Gloria T. Hull, Patricia Bell-Scott, and Barbara Smith called for scholarship that attended to Black women as subjects.[10]

No one exerted more far-reaching influence in interrogating the lives of enslaved women without comparisons to white women than Deborah Gray White. In *Ar'n't I a Woman?* (1985), the first full-length treatment of enslaved women's lives in the nineteenth-century South, White excavated "a different kind of womanhood" by examining the racist archetypes that whites constructed about Black women's labor, sexuality, and temperament: Mammy, Jezebel, and Sapphire. Her landmark book became a beacon that guided other Black women's historians over the next decades. Darlene Clark Hine's "Rape and the Inner Lives of Black Women in the Middle West" (1989) and Evelyn Brooks Higginbotham's "African American Women's History and the Metalanguage of Race" (1992) introduced canonical vocabulary as well: Hine's discussion of "dissemblance" and Higginbotham's "politics of respectability" remain important concepts. In addition, le-

---

Pantheon Books, 1982) focused on the role that elite women played in defining the institution, but made it clear that a full history would require investigations in which African American women were subjects and not objects. Clinton's work, of course, followed Anne Firor Scott's field-defining *The Southern Lady: From Pedestal to Politics, 1830–1930* (Chicago: University of Chicago Press, 1970).

10. Jones, *Labor of Love, Labor of Sorrow*; Lebsock, *The Free Women of Petersburg*; Elizabeth Fox-Genovese, *Within the Plantation Household: Black and White Women of the Old South* (Chapel Hill: University of North Carolina Press, 1988); Akasha Gloria T. Hull, Patricia Bell-Scott, and Barbara Smith, eds., *All the Women Are White, All the Blacks Are Men, but Some of Us Are Brave: Black Women's Studies* (Old Westbury, NY: Feminist Press, 1982), specifically Brittney C. Cooper's "Afterword," in the second edition: Hall, Bell-Scott, and Smith, ed., *All the Women Are White, All the Blacks Are Men, but Some of Us Are Brave*, 2nd ed. (New York: Feminist Press, 2015), 379–86.

gal scholar Kimberlé Crenshaw coined the term "intersectionality" in analyzing subjects that occupy more than one social identity at once.[11] What Deborah Gray White had termed "a different kind of womanhood" became a historical, intersectional identity.

Brenda Stevenson's *Life in Black and White* (1997) took up the mantle of mid-twentieth-century community studies by providing a close reading of Loudoun County, Virginia. Juxtaposing white and Black society, Stevenson looked at marriage, family, labor, and the tension between white and Black communities, interrogating ways that power worked in antebellum slave societies and how individuals lived under, within, and around those systems. Dylan Penningroth's *The Claims of Kinfolk* (2003) and Anthony E. Kaye's *Joining Places* (2009) continued in the vein that Stevenson pioneered: attentive to the complex antagonisms and alliances within and between enslaved people.[12]

Labor anchored women's and gender histories of enslavement, including scholarship that interrogated gender-specific labor (reproductive, sexual, and domestic) alongside labor performed with men (field work, community-building, and resistance). Historians uncovered ways in which gender made American racial ideology and race made gendered labor experiences. Geographer Judith Ann Carney's *Black Rice* (2002) detailed African women's specialized agricultural knowledge and contributions to South Carolina's rice culture, revealing roles as key actors and not merely laborers. Daina Ramey Berry's *"Swing the Sickle for the Harvest Is Ripe"* (2010) demonstrated the importance of women's field work as skilled labor on antebellum Georgia plantations. Victoria E. Bynum's *Unruly Women* (1992) exposed ways in which women on the margins of antebellum southern society subsisted and resisted. Kathleen M. Brown's *Good Wives, Nasty Wenches, and Anxious Patriarchs* (1996), although focusing on the colonial era, provided a model of intersectional analysis. Her discussion of race, gender, class, and sexual norms positioned the competition over women's bodies, their auton-

11. White, *Ar'n't I a Woman?*, 176; Kimberlé Crenshaw, "Mapping the Margins: Intersectionality, Identity Politics, and Violence against Women of Color," *Stanford Law Review* 43 (July 1991): 1241–99.

12. Brenda E. Stevenson, *Life in Black and White: Family and Community in the Slave South* (New York: Oxford University Press, 1996); Anthony E. Kaye, *Joining Places: Slave Neighborhoods in the Old South* (Chapel Hill: University of North Carolina Press, 2009); Dylan C. Penningroth, *The Claims of Kinfolk: African American Property and Community in the Nineteenth-Century South* (Chapel Hill: University of North Carolina Press, 2003).

omy, and the racist project of building a plantation economy all as central, not marginal, concerns for male colonial authorities.[13]

By the early 2000s, scholars charted new ways to consider enslaved women's lives and labor. Jennifer L. Morgan's *Laboring Women* (2004) engaged the question of reproductive labor and chattel slavery, tying the deeply intimate labor of childbearing with the cold calculus of appreciating value to enslaved people in the Atlantic slave market. Morgan's work on the Atlantic World provided a linguistic and methodological model for antebellum scholars interested in reproductive labor.[14]

By the mid-2000s, scholars increasingly engaged the intersection of sex, sexuality, and the queer in antebellum slavery as well. Scholars also recognized that abusive sexual exploitation of enslaved women was an important but not the only entry point into histories of sexuality and slavery. In 2011 Daina Ramey Berry and Leslie M. Harris organized "Sexuality and Slavery: Exposing the History of Enslaved People in the Americas," a conference that called for a range of engagements with African American sexuality. Their edited volume, *Sexuality and Slavery* (2018), featured work by slavery scholars that engaged consensual sexual relationships, sex across the color line, and sex and sexuality as tools of control and oppression.[15]

13. Judith Ann Carney, *Black Rice: The African Origins of Rice Cultivation in the Americas* (Cambridge: Harvard University Press, 2002); Daina Ramey Berry, *"Swing the Sickle for the Harvest Is Ripe": Gender and Slavery in Antebellum Georgia* (Urbana: University of Illinois Press, 2010); Victoria E. Bynum, *Unruly Women: The Politics of Social and Sexual Control in the Old South* (Chapel Hill: University of North Carolina Press, 1992); Kathleen M. Brown, *Good Wives, Nasty Wenches, and Anxious Patriarchs: Gender, Race, and Power in Colonial Virginia* (Chapel Hill: University of North Carolina Press, 1996). See also Edda Fields-Black, *Deep Roots: Rice Farmers in West Africa and the African Diaspora* (Bloomington: Indiana University Press, 2008), a work of great breadth and creativity. Both Brown and Bynum also engaged sex and sexuality as important categories of analysis, as did Laura F. Edwards, *The People and Their Peace: Legal Culture and the Transformation of Inequality in the Post-Revolutionary South* (Chapel Hill: University of North Carolina Press, 2009).

14. Jennifer L. Morgan, "'Some Could Suckle over Their Shoulder': Male Travelers, Female Bodies, and the Gendering of Racial Ideology, 1500–1770," *William and Mary Quarterly* 54 (January 1997): 167–92; Morgan, *Laboring Women: Reproduction and Gender in New World Slavery* (Philadelphia: University of Pennsylvania Press, 2004).

15. Treva B. Lindsey and Jessica Marie Johnson, "Searching for Climax: Black Erotic Lives in Slavery and Freedom." *Meridians* 12 (2014): 169–95; Daina Ramey Berry and Leslie M. Harris, eds., *Sexuality and Slavery: Reclaiming Intimate Histories in the Americas* (Athens: University of Georgia Press, 2018). One significant contribution to furthering inquiry into sexual abuse engages age and generation as significant

Historians also moved away from engaging Black kinship structures as always and necessarily one type of family formation: *the* Black heterosexual couple with children. Historians writing in the 2000s and 2010s expanded the definition of family, investigating slave marriage as one of many types of couplings, and carefully parsing out the legal and political dimension of marriage for Black people in slavery and freedom.[16] Expanding the definition of kinship opened a new and needed historiographical direction in queering the history of slavery.[17] Just as with histories of heterosexuality, queering slavery requires engagement with parallel histories of sexual abuse and consensual sexual behavior. Works by Vincent Woodard, C. Riley Snorton, Aliyyah Abdur-Rahman, and Omise'eke Tinsley explored the possibility of queering and tracing African American history and histories of slavery.[18] Although historians had explored queer life in the eighteenth and nineteenth centuries, they often left out slavery in the narrative of LGBTQ history.[19] Twenty-first-century scholars are beginning to appreciate how study

categories. See Wilma King, "'Prematurely Knowing of Evil Things': The Sexual Abuse of African American Girls and Young Women in Slavery and Freedom," *Journal of African American History* 99 (July 2014): 173–96.

16. Tera W. Hunter, *Bound in Wedlock: Slave and Free Black Marriage in the Nineteenth Century* (Cambridge: Harvard University Press, 2017).

17. The Queering Slavery Working Group, co-organized by Vanessa M. Holden and Jessica Marie Johnson, fosters, supports, and organizes scholarship around the question: What would it mean to queer slavery? In a 2018 essay, Clare Sears maintained: "Queer historical studies of slavery are not only academically viable but also politically necessary to foreground the specificities of black queer histories and center slavery's constitutive role in modern sexualities." See "Centering Slavery in Nineteenth-Century Queer History (1800s–1890s)," in *The Routledge History of Queer America*, ed. Don Romesburg (New York: Routledge, 2018), 39.

18. Aliyyah Abdur-Rahman, *Against the Closet: Black Political Longing and the Erotics of Race* (Durham: Duke University Press, 2012); Aliyyah I. Abdur-Rahman, "'The Strangest Freaks of Despotism': Queer Sexuality in Antebellum African American Slave Narratives," *African American Review* 40 (June 2006): 223–37; C. Riley Snorton, *Black on Both Sides: A Racial History of Trans Identity* (Minneapolis: University of Minnesota Press, 2017); Vincent Woodard and Dwight McBride, *The Delectable Negro: Human Consumption and Homoeroticism within US Slave Culture* (New York: New York University Press, 2014); Omise'eke Natasha Tinsley, "Black Atlantic, Queer Atlantic: Queer Imaginings of the Middle Passage," *GLQ: A Journal of Lesbian and Gay Studies* 14 (June 2008): 191–215; Tinsley, "Femmes of Color, 'Femmes de Couleur': Theorizing Black Queer Femininity through Chauvet's 'La Danse Sur Le Volcan,'" *Yale French Studies* 128 (2015): 131–45; Tinsley, *Thiefing Sugar: Eroticism between Women in Caribbean Literature* (Durham: Duke University Press, 2010); Thomas A. Foster, "The Sexual Abuse of Black Men under American Slavery," *Journal of the History of Sexuality* 20 (September 2011): 445–64.

19. Excellent work by Rachel Hope Cleves and Thomas A. Foster provided important methodological models. See Rachel Hope Cleves, *Charity and Sylvia: A Same-Sex Marriage in Early America* (New York:

of the Queer South can lead to important interventions in the history of slavery, the histories of queer enslaved peoples, and investigations into the queerness of slavery.[20]

Slave Resistance and Rebellion

Stephanie M. H. Camp's *Closer to Freedom* (2004) galvanized a generation of scholars by broadening concepts of resistance and rebellion to include enslaved women and their experiences. Camp challenged historians to attend to the "subtler forms" of rebellion to better understand how enslaved people created a culture of resistance in the antebellum South. Her field-changing work built upon that of Angela Davis, Brenda Stevenson, and James Scott, but her contribution was bracing and original. In particular, Camp insisted that women reclaimed their bodies through dress and dance, through rebuke of enslavers and other oppressors, through joyous, forbidden movement through the dark night to parties: they became instruments of their own specific resistance. Despite Camp's intervention, the subfield of slave resistance and rebellion has yet to commit to her provocative lead: studies of slave rebellion have faced persistent accusations that they focus on "great man" history. Although in *American Negro Slave Revolts* (1943), Herbert Aptheker tried to distinguish between resistance, revolt, rebellion, truancy, insurrection, and uprising, by the mid-twentieth century, resistance scholarship often seemed obsessed with only a single possibility: armed enslaved men with one central leader who attempted to use violence to liberate other slaves.[21]

Oxford University Press, 2014); Thomas A. Foster, ed., *Long Before Stonewall: Histories of Same-Sex Sexuality in Early America* (New York: New York University Press, 2007); Foster, *Rethinking Rufus: Sexual Violations of Enslaved Men* (Athens: University of Georgia Press, 2019).

20. There is a literature in Black Queer Studies and history, but scholars in that field overwhelmingly work on the late nineteenth and twentieth centuries. See Roderick A. Ferguson, *Aberrations in Black: Toward A Queer of Color Critique* (Minneapolis: University of Minnesota Press, 2003); Farah Jasmine Griffin, ed., *Beloved Sisters and Loving Friends: Letters from Rebecca Primus of Royal Oak, Maryland, and Addie Brown of Hartford, Connecticut, 1854–1868* (New York: Ballantine, 2001); E. Patrick Johnson, *Black Queer Studies* (Durham: Duke University Press, 2005); Johnson, ed., *No Tea, No Shade: New Writings in Black Queer Studies* (Durham: Duke University Press, 2016); Omise'eke Natasha Tinsley, *Ezili's Mirrors: Imagining Black Queer Genders* (Durham: Duke University Press, 2018).

21. Stephanie M. H. Camp, *Closer to Freedom: Enslaved Women and Everyday Resistance in the Plantation South* (Chapel Hill: University of North Carolina Press, 2004); Herbert Aptheker, *American Negro Slave Revolts*, 3rd ed. (New York: Columbia University Press, 1945); Aptheker, *Nat Turner's Slave Rebellion: Including the 1831 "Confessions"* (Mineola, NY: Dover Publications, 2006); Stephen B. Oates, *The*

Historians have begun to provide greater nuance to the study of slave rebellion by better understanding context and highlighting the broader implications, grafting the history of slave rebellion and resistance into the history of the institution. In *Gabriel's Rebellion* (1993), Douglas R. Egerton narrated a slave rebellion's plot and demise in early republican Virginia. Gabriel, a blacksmith and community leader, emerged as a savvy strategist with a distinct political identity. Gabriel, the craftsman citizen, was not Nat Turner, the prophet preacher. Similarly, James Sidbury's *Ploughshares into Swords* (1997) pieced together the world of early republican Afro-Virginians, concluding that Richmond's people, faith communities, and politics produced the conspiracy as much as did Gabriel's tactical prowess.[22] Both scholars positioned slave resistance as a way to understand the institution of slavery and Black voices in the Early Republic.

By moving beyond the "great man" histories of the past and focusing instead on Black communities, historians transformed the narrative of America's most famous slave uprising: the Southampton Rebellion. Kenneth S. Greenberg's edited collection, *Nat Turner* (2004), accompanied the release of the documentary film, *Nat Turner: A Troublesome Property* (2003). In the Greenberg volume, Patrick H. Breen questioned Turner's place in Southampton's slave community while Mary Kempe Davis called for a women's history of the Southampton Rebellion. In a 2007 article, Anthony E. Kaye foregrounded community and neighborhood dynamics to better understand the rebellion's outcome.[23] The impact of this scholarship became evident in David F. Allmendinger 's *Nat Turner and the Rising in*

Fires of Jubilee: Nat Turner's Fierce Rebellion (1975; repr., New York: Harper Perennial, 2016); Henry Irving Tragle, *The Southampton Slave Revolt of 1831: A Compilation of Source Material, Including the Full Text of The Confessions of Nat Turner* (New York: Vintage, 1973). For music and dance, see Katrina Doyanne Thompson, *Ring Shout, Wheel About: The Racial Politics of Music and Dance in North American Slavery* (Urbana: University of Illinois Press, 2014).

22. Douglas R. Egerton, *Gabriel's Rebellion: The Virginia Slave Conspiracies of 1800 and 1802* (Chapel Hill: University of North Carolina Press, 1993); James Sidbury, *Ploughshares into Swords: Race, Rebellion, and Identity in Gabriel's Virginia, 1730–1810* (New York: Cambridge University Press, 1997).

23. Kenneth S. Greenberg, ed., *Nat Turner: A Slave Rebellion in History and Memory* (New York: Oxford University Press, 2004); *Nat Turner: A Troublesome Property,* directed by Charles Burnett, screenplay by Charles Burnett, Frank Christopher, and Kenneth S. Greenberg (California Newsreel, 2012); Patrick H. Breen, "A Prophet in His Own Land: Support for Nat Turner and His Rebellion within Southampton's Black Community" in Greenberg, ed., *Nat Turner,* 103–18; Mary Kemp Davis, "'What Happened in This Place?' In Search of the Female Slave in the Nat Turner Slave Insurrection," in Greenberg, ed., *Nat Turner,* 162–78. See also Anthony E. Kaye, "Neighborhoods and Nat Turner: The Making of a Slave Rebellion and the Unmaking of a Slave Rebellion," *Journal of the Early Republic* 27 (December 2007): 705–20.

Southampton County (2014) which presented a full community study of white Southampton County during the time of the rebellion.[24]

Still, in many cases, the sources available for studying Black rebellion actually chronicle white responses, giving only glimpses of Black brilliance, ingenuity, and freedom dreams. White views and imagination received full examination in Scot French's *The Rebellious Slave* (2003).[25] French returned to the historical figure Nat Turner, the 1831 rebellion that came to take his name, and what Turner inspired: white nightmares of retributive consequence on the one hand, and Black dreams of deliverance on the other. Importantly, French found that attending to cultural history should not negate or call into question the agency and rebellion of Black subjects.

The difference between a slave plot, discovered by whites before enslaved people could fulfill their plans, and a slave rebellion, a plot made manifest, exposed a crucial set of questions about interpretation and narrative. Torturers and executioners generated most of the documents in the wake of both plots and rebellions, raising the question: Could historians even move beyond the story of the suppression of the enslaved to tell the story of enslaved rebels? Such a vexed set of issues exploded in controversy in 2001 when Michael Johnson questioned the reality of the 1822 Charleston rebellion plot. He cast Denmark Vesey as the victim of white anxiety in his savaging review of Edward Pearson's *Designs against Charleston* (1999).[26] In the ensuing debate, Douglas R. Egerton rebutted Johnson's review by arguing for the existence of a real plot propagated by Denmark Vesey. In 2005, Walter Rucker published a sweeping history of Black

24. David F. Allmendinger Jr., *Nat Turner and the Rising in Southampton County* (Baltimore: Johns Hopkins University Press, 2014). Patrick H. Breen dissected the courtroom dynamics that produced the most heavily consulted archive related to the Southampton Rebellion, the county court minute books. See Patrick H. Breen, *The Land Shall Be Deluged in Blood: A New History of the Nat Turner Revolt* (New York: Oxford University Press, 2016).

25. Winthrop D. Jordan, *Tumult and Silence at Second Creek: An Inquiry into a Civil War Slave Conspiracy* (Baton Rouge: Louisiana State University Press, 1993); Scot French, *The Rebellious Slave: Nat Turner in American Memory* (Boston: Houghton Mifflin Harcourt, 2003).

26. Ultimately, the University of North Carolina Press withdrew Pearson's book from publication because of the number of errors in Pearson's transcription of the trial record. See Jon Wiener, "The Denmark Vesey 'Trial Record': A New Verdict," in *Historians in Trouble: Plagiarism, Fraud, and Politics in the Ivory Tower* (New York: New Press, 2005), 119–35. Also, Michael P. Johnson, "Denmark Vesey and His Co-Conspirators," *William and Mary Quarterly* 58 (October 2001): 915–76; Edward A. Pearson, ed., *Designs against Charleston: The Trial Record of the Denmark Slave Conspiracy of 1822* (Chapel Hill: University of North Carolina Press, 1999).

rebellion that, among other things, highlighted Vesey as a rebel and not as a case of mistaken identity.[27]

In that vein, historians have also sought to recover rebellions from America's past that do not have ready-made eponymous male leaders. Inspired in part by work on the wider Atlantic World, including Julius S. Scott's influential 1986 dissertation, "The Common Wind," scholars looked to recover not just the rebellious resistance, but also the complex experience and political wills of the enslaved, which brewed days of fire and blood.[28] Other scholars recovered forgotten rebellions. An 1811 slave revolt in Louisiana involved between two hundred and five hundred armed rebels, the biggest slave rebellion in United States history. The revolt reentered the historiographical imagination largely through the tireless efforts of slavery scholar Robert Paquette and New Orleans–based public historian Albert Thrasher.[29]

27. "Front Matter," *William and Mary Quarterly* 59 (January 2002): 1–2; Robert A. Gross, "Introduction," *William and Mary Quarterly* 59 (January 2002): 135–36; Edward A. Pearson, "Trials and Errors: Denmark Vesey and His Historians," *William and Mary Quarterly* 59 (January 2002): 137–42; Douglas R. Egerton, "Forgetting Denmark Vesey; Or, Oliver Stone Meets Richard Wade," *William and Mary Quarterly* 59 (January 2002): 143–52; David Robertson, "Inconsistent Contextualism: The Hermeneutics of Michael Johnson," *William and Mary Quarterly* 59 (January 2002): 153–58; Thomas J. Davis, "Conspiracy and Credibility: Look Who's Talking, about What: Law Talk and Loose Talk," *William and Mary Quarterly* 59 (January 2002): 167–74; Winthrop D. Jordan, "The Charleston Hurricane of 1822; Or, the Law's Rampage," *William and Mary Quarterly* 59 (January 2002): 175–78; James Sidbury, "Plausible Stories and Varnished Truths," *William and Mary Quarterly* 59 (January 2002): 179–84; Robert L. Paquette, "Jacobins of the Lowcountry: The Vesey Plot on Trial," *William and Mary Quarterly* 59 (January 2002): 185–92; Michael P. Johnson, "Reading Evidence," *William and Mary Quarterly* 59 (January 2002): 193–202. In 2004, Rowman & Littlefield reissued a revised edition of Douglas R. Egerton's *He Shall Go Out Free: The Lives of Denmark Vesey* (Lanham, MD: Rowman & Littlefield, 1999) that included a new chapter addressing the controversy with a full historiographical treatment of the conspiracy. See also Walter C. Rucker, *The River Flows On: Black Resistance, Culture, and Identity Formation in Early America* (Baton Rouge: Louisiana State University Press, 2006); Michael Gomez, *Exchanging Our Country Marks: The Transformation of African Identities in the Colonial and Antebellum South* (Chapel Hill: University of North Carolina Press, 1998).

28. Julius S. Scott, "The Common Wind: Currents of Afro-American Communication in the Era of the Haitian Revolution" (PhD diss., Duke University, 1986), published in book form as *The Common Wind: Afro-American Currents in the Age of the Haitian Revolution* (New York: Verso, 2018); Emília Viotti da Costa, *Crowns of Glory, Tears of Blood: The Demerara Slave Rebellion of 1823* (New York: Oxford University Press, 1994); Matt D. Childs, *The 1812 Aponte Rebellion and the Struggle against Atlantic Slavery* (Chapel Hill: University of North Carolina Press, 2006); Aisha K. Finch, *Rethinking Slave Rebellion in Cuba: La Escalera and the Insurgencies of 1841–1844* (Chapel Hill: University of North Carolina Press, 2015).

29. Albert Thrasher, *On to New Orleans: Louisiana's Heroic 1811 Slave Revolt* (New Orleans: Cypress Press, 1996); Robert L. Paquette, "'A Horde of Brigands?' The Great Louisiana Slave Revolt of 1811 Recon-

Focus on slave revolts, rebellions, and their central male leaders has drawn criticism, however, because such histories are often intertwined with masculinist understandings of politics and agency. Fugitivity was far more common as a form of everyday resistance, and John Hope Franklin and Loren Schweninger's *Runaway Slaves* (1999) offered a sweeping account of freedom-seeking people.[30] Other historians took seriously Stephanie M. H. Camp's argument for including enslaved women, their experiences, and their actions in histories of resistance as a starting point rather than a peripheral concern. Likewise, Sally Hadden's *Slave Patrols* (2003) helped decenter epic rebellion as the archetypal way to understand resistance. Raising questions about Black agency, rebellion, and white anxiety, Hadden noted differences between professional slave catchers and local patrols, and she dispelled the myth that slave patrols were comprised only of poor whites.[31]

Meanwhile, published slave narratives, the WPA collection of ex-slave narratives, and the papers of famous fugitives such as Frederick Douglass remain important primary sources for historians of American slavery. As scholars of

---

sidered," *Historical Reflections/Réflexions Historiques* 35 (Spring 2009): 72–96. See also Adam Rothman, *Slave Country: American Expansion and the Origins of the Deep South* (Cambridge: Harvard University Press, 2005); Daniel Rasmussen, *American Uprising: The Untold Story of America's Largest Slave Revolt* (New York: HarperCollins, 2011); David J. Libby, *Slavery and Frontier Mississippi, 1720–1835* (Jackson: University Press of Mississippi, 2004); Joshua D. Rothman, *Flush Times and Fever Dreams: A Story of Capitalism and Slavery in the Age of Jackson* (Athens: University of Georgia Press, 2012); Jordan, *Tumult and Silence at Second Creek;* Michael Wayne, *Death of an Overseer: Reopening a Murder Investigation from the Plantation South* (New York: Oxford University Press, 2001). See the increasing number of histories of Gulf Coast slavery and slave societies, including Gwendolyn Midlo Hall, *Africans in Colonial Louisiana: The Development of Afro-Creole Culture in the Eighteenth Century* (Baton Rouge: Louisiana State University Press, 1992); Richard J. Follett, *The Sugar Masters: Planters and Slaves in Louisiana's Cane World, 1820–1860* (Baton Rouge: Louisiana State University Press, 2005); Matthew Pratt Guterl, *American Mediterranean: Southern Slaveholders in the Age of Emancipation* (Cambridge: Harvard University Press, 2008).

30. John Hope Franklin and Loren Schweninger, *Runaway Slaves: Rebels on the Plantation* (New York: Oxford University Press, 1999). The work inspired creation of the North Carolina Runaway Slave Advertisements database at the University of North Carolina at Greensboro, http://libcdm1.uncg.edu/cdm/landingpage/collection/RAS (accessed 18 January 2019). See also the Freedom on the Move database, housed at Cornell's Institute of Social and Economic Research, and curated by Edward E. Baptist, Vanessa M. Holden, Hasan Kwame Jeffries, Mary Niall Mitchell, and Joshua Rothman, https://app.freedomonthemove.org/ (accessed 18 January 2019).

31. Maggie Montesinos Sale, *The Slumbering Volcano: American Slave Ship Revolts and the Production of Rebellious Masculinity* (Durham: Duke University Press, 1997); Sally E. Hadden, *Slave Patrols: Law and Violence in Virginia and the Carolinas* (Cambridge: Harvard University Press, 2003).

American literature worked doggedly to incorporate fugitive autobiographies into the literary canon, historians toiled to historicize these narratives. One of the earliest and most important biographical explorations of a formerly enslaved narrator is Jean Fagan Yellin's edition of Harriet Jacobs's narrative, *Incidents in the Life of a Slave Girl* (1987). Yellin not only confirmed the validity of the narrative that Jacobs wrote, but she also made available a valuable source on the life of an enslaved woman. Yellin's biography, *Harriet Jacobs* (2004), further solidified Jacobs's place in the canon of primary sources. In the years since, other works—for instance, Barbara McCaskill's *Love, Liberation, and Escaping Slavery* (2015)—further historicized published slave narratives.[32]

Earlier generations of white scholars often minimized the roles of the enslaved (and the formerly enslaved) in directing their own stories of escape from slavery. Indeed, narratives of the Underground Railroad that center white activism remain powerful in American historical memory and public spaces—although this is changing. Beginning in the 1980s and 1990s, the Black history of the abolitionist movement and the integral participation of enslaved resistors, former slaves, and free people of color garnered increasing scholarly attention. Gary Nash's *Forging Freedom* (1988) asserted the place of free people of color and fugitives in the history of abolition and the founding of Philadelphia's free Black community. In *Black Women Abolitionists* (1992), Shirley J. Yee explored the activism of women—both those born free, and those manumitted. Alongside Benjamin Quarles's seminal text, *Black Abolitionists* (1968; reprint, 1992), Yee's work brought new emphasis to African Americans' labor in the abolition struggle, emphasizing how the movement was neither solely a benevolent white enterprise nor an exclusively male prerogative. Further explorations of free people of color who pioneered and bolstered abolitionism, including Martha S. Jones's *All Bound Up Together* (2007), Erica Armstrong Dunbar's *A Fragile Freedom* (2008), and Britt

32. Harriet Ann Jacobs, *Incidents in the Life of a Slave Girl: Written by Herself*, ed. Jean Fagan Yellin (Cambridge: Harvard University Press, 1987); Jean Fagan Yellin, *Harriet Jacobs: A Life* (New York: Basic Civitas Books, 2004); Barbara McCaskill, *Love, Liberation, and Escaping Slavery: William and Ellen Craft in Cultural Memory* (Athens: University of Georgia Press, 2015). On the place of formal narratives in the American literary tradition, see William L. Andrews, *To Tell a Free Story: The First Century of Afro-American Autobiography, 1760–1865* (Urbana: University of Illinois Press, 1986); Andrews, *Slavery and Class in the American South: A Generation of Slave Narrative Testimony, 1840–1865* (New York: Oxford University Press, 2019). Historical photography, too, has provided important primary sources; see Matthew Fox-Amato, *Exposing Slavery: Photography, Human Bondage, and the Birth of Modern Visual Politics in America* (New York: Oxford University Press, 2019).

Rusert's *Fugitive Science* (2017), denoted the central role of African Americans in defining American freedom, cultivating free communities, and shoring up antislavery movements.[33]

Such work illuminated the tenuous lines between the North and South when it came to Black freedom struggles. When we grapple with the question of which free Blacks were "in the South," we realize that in a sense, all of them were. Self-liberators opened emancipation processes in the North only to find that slavery's many legacies continued to constrain their lives and kept them linked to their sisters and brothers in the South.[34] Ties of family often meant that free or becoming-free African American people in the North remained deeply involved in the South.[35] "Northern" African Americans shaped southern history to an extent disproportionate to their numbers, a pattern apparent in the post-1980s scholarship that sought to correct the white-focused narrative of abolitionism. This new wave recentered studies of abolitionism on the movement's Black ma-

33. Martha S. Jones, *All Bound Up Together: The Woman Question in African American Public Culture, 1830–1900* (Chapel Hill: University of North Carolina Press, 2007); Erica Armstrong Dunbar, *A Fragile Freedom: African American Women and Emancipation in the Antebellum City* (New Haven: Yale University Press, 2011); Britt Rusert, *Fugitive Science: Empiricism and Freedom in Early American Culture* (New York: New York University Press, 2017); Darryl Scriven, *A Dealer of Old Clothes: Philosophical Conversations with David Walker* (Lanham, MD: Lexington Books, 2007); Beverly C. Tomek, *Colonization and Its Discontents: Emancipation, Emigration, and Antislavery in Antebellum Pennsylvania* (New York: New York University Press, 2011); Leslie M. Alexander, *African or American? Black Identity and Political Activism in New York City, 1784–1861* (Urbana: University of Illinois Press, 2008).

34. Stanley Harrold, *Border War: Fighting over Slavery before the Civil War* (Chapel Hill: University of North Carolina Press, 2010); T. Stephen Whitman, *Challenging Slavery in the Chesapeake: Black and White Resistance to Human Bondage, 1775–1865* (Baltimore: Maryland Historical Society, 2007); Carol Wilson, *Freedom at Risk: The Kidnapping of Free Blacks in America, 1780–1865* (Lexington: University Press of Kentucky, 1994); James Oliver Horton and Lois E. Horton, *In Hope of Liberty: Culture, Community, and Protest among Northern Free Blacks, 1700–1860* (New York: Oxford University Press, 1997); Julie Winch, *Between Slavery and Freedom: Free People of Color in America from Settlement to the Civil War* (Lanham, MD: Rowman & Littlefield, 2014); Carter Godwin Woodson, *Free Negro Heads of Families in the United States in 1830: Together with a Brief Treatment of the Free Negro* (Washington: Association for the Study of Negro Life and History, 1925).

35. Sydney Nathans, *To Free a Family: The Journey of Mary Walker* (Cambridge: Harvard University Press, 2012); James H. Johnston, *From Slave Ship to Harvard: Yarrow Mamout and the History of an African American Family* (New York: Fordham University Press, 2012); Mary Frances Berry, *"We Are Who We Say We Are": A Black Family's Search for Home across the Atlantic World* (New York: Oxford University Press, 2015); Steven Hahn, *The Political Worlds of Slavery and Freedom* (Cambridge: Harvard University Press, 2009).

jority.[36] Many focused on how "northern" African American women defined freedom in their own lives and in their own activism.[37] Others attended to networks that transcended region and enabled escape and freedom. Cheryl Janifer LaRoche's *Free Black Communities and the Underground Railroad* (2013) explored the networks of resistance that free and enslaved Black people maintained to thwart white efforts to recover people who fled. Eric Foner took up the story of the Underground Railroad and fugitivity in New York City in *Gateway to Freedom* (2016), tracing the narrative from the Midwest to Manhattan, Brooklyn, and Upstate New York. Manisha Sinha's *The Slave's Cause* (2016) moved the history of American abolition away from white benevolence and situated African Americans at its center. Kelly Carter Jackson attended to political violence and force in her study of Black abolitionist activism in *Force and Freedom* (2019).[38]

36. Manisha Sinha, *The Slave's Cause: A History of Abolition* (New Haven: Yale University Press, 2016); Patrick Rael, *Black Identity and Black Protest in the Antebellum North* (Chapel Hill: University of North Carolina Press, 2002); Richard S. Newman and James Mueller, eds., *Antislavery and Abolition in Philadelphia: Emancipation and the Long Struggle for Racial Justice in the City of Brotherly Love* (Baton Rouge: Louisiana State University Press, 2011); Jasmine Nichole Cobb, *Picture Freedom: Remaking Black Visuality in the Early Nineteenth Century* (New York: New York University Press, 2015); Nell Irvin Painter, *Sojourner Truth: A Life, A Symbol* (New York: W. W. Norton, 1996); Margaret Washington, *Sojourner Truth's America* (Urbana: University of Illinois Press, 2009); Graham Russell Gao Hodges, *David Ruggles: A Radical Black Abolitionist and the Underground Railroad in New York City* (Chapel Hill: University of North Carolina Press, 2010). Much of this work builds on the foundational work of Benjamin Quarles, *Black Abolitionists* (New York: Oxford University Press, 1969).

37. Dunbar, *A Fragile Freedom*; Wilma King, *The Essence of Liberty: Free Black Women during the Slave Era* (Columbia: University of Missouri Press, 2006); Erica Ball, *To Live an Antislavery Life: Personal Politics and the Antebellum Black Middle Class* (Athens: University of Georgia Press, 2012); Rita Roberts, *Evangelicalism and the Politics of Reform in Northern Black Thought, 1776–1863* (Baton Rouge: Louisiana State University Press, 2010).

38. Cheryl Janifer LaRoche, *Free Black Communities and the Underground Railroad: The Geography of Resistance* (Urbana: University of Illinois Press, 2013); Eric Foner, *Gateway to Freedom: The Hidden History of the Underground Railroad* (New York: W. W. Norton, 2016); Kelly Carter Jackson, *Force and Freedom: Black Abolitionists and the Politics of Violence* (Philadelphia: University of Pennsylvania Press, 2019); Sinha, *The Slave's Cause.* The 2010s saw a flurry of microhistories on fugitive and free Blacks, including Sydney Nathans, *To Free a Family: The Journey of Mary Walker* (Cambridge: Harvard University Press, 2013); Nikki Marie Taylor, *Driven toward Madness: The Fugitive Slave Margaret Garner and Tragedy on the Ohio* (Athens: Ohio University Press, 2016); Erica Armstrong Dunbar, *Never Caught: The Washingtons' Relentless Pursuit of their Runaway Slave, Ona Judge* (New York: Atria, 2017); Karl Jacoby, *The Strange Career of William Ellis: The Texas Slaver Who Became a Mexican Millionaire* (New York: W. W. Norton, 2017); Caleb McDaniel, *Sweet Taste of Liberty: A True Story of Slavery and Restitution in America* (New York: Oxford University Press, 2019).

Free Blacks in the nineteenth-century South have always challenged historians. Were they "free" or were they actually "slaves without masters?" Since the 1990s, much scholarship focused on how free Black people often discovered how fleeting freedom could be: in the legal struggle between French and Anglo-American cultural regimes of slavery that followed US acquisition of Louisiana, for instance; or as free people across the slave South lost status, rights, property, and what little safety and security they had after state legislatures reacted to plots and rebellions, and as the sectional conflict grew more intense.[39]

Although many historians writing since the 1990s argued that poor and working-class whites in both the South and the North chose whiteness over class solidarity with free Blacks, scholarship on antebellum southern working classes opened new avenues into understanding the Black working class, particularly for free Black women.[40] Women who lived in cities such as Charleston, Balti-

39. Ira Berlin, *Slaves Without Masters* (New York: Pantheon Books, 1974); John Hope Franklin, *The Free Negro in North Carolina, 1790–1865* (Chapel Hill: University of North Carolina Press, 1943); Judith Kelleher Schafer, *Becoming Free, Remaining Free: Manumission and Enslavement in New Orleans, 1846–1862* (Baton Rouge: Louisiana State University Press, 2003). On rebellion scares, see Egerton, *He Shall Go Out Free.* On property, Penningroth, *The Claims of Kinfolk;* Loren Schweninger, *Black Property Owners in the South, 1790–1915* (Urbana: University of Illinois Press, 1990). On the constraints upon free Black people in the rural South, see Melvin Patrick Ely, *Israel on the Appomattox: A Southern Experiment in Black Freedom from the 1790s through the Civil War* (New York: Alfred A. Knopf, 2004); Edwards, *The People and Their Peace;* Kirt Von Daacke, *Freedom Has a Face: Race, Identity, and Community in Jefferson's Virginia* (Charlottesville: University of Virginia Press, 2012); Ted Maris-Wolf, *Family Bonds: Free Blacks and Re-Enslavement Law in Antebellum Virginia* (Chapel Hill: University of North Carolina Press, 2015); Joshua Rothman, *Notorious in the Neighborhood: Sex and Families across the Color Line in Virginia, 1787–1861* (Chapel Hill: University of North Carolina Press, 2003); Marie Tyler-McGraw, *An African Republic: Black and White Virginians in the Making of Liberia* (Chapel Hill: University of North Carolina Press, 2007); Claude Andrew Clegg, *The Price of Liberty: African Americans and the Making of Liberia* (Chapel Hill: University of North Carolina Press, 2004); Glenn McNair, *Criminal Injustice: Slaves and Free Blacks in Georgia's Criminal Justice System* (Charlottesville: University of Virginia Press, 2009).

40. Jennifer Hull Dorsey, *Hirelings: African American Workers and Free Labor in Early Maryland* (Ithaca: Cornell University Press, 2011); Seth Rockman, *Scraping by: Wage Labor, Slavery, and Survival in Early Baltimore* (Baltimore: Johns Hopkins University Press, 2009); Bynum, *Unruly Women;* Charles C. Bolton, *Poor Whites of the Antebellum South: Tenants and Laborers in Central North Carolina and Northeast Mississippi* (Durham: Duke University Press, 1994); Keri Leigh Merritt, *Masterless Men: Poor Whites and Slavery in the Antebellum South* (New York: Cambridge University Press, 2017). See also David R. Roediger, *The Wages of Whiteness: Race and the Making of the American Working Class* (New York: Verso, 1991), which explicates Du Bois's concept of "the psychological wage," from *Black Reconstruction: An Essay Toward a History of the Part Which Black Folk Played in the Attempt to Reconstruct Democracy in America, 1860–1880* (New York: Harcourt Brace, 1935).

more, and New Orleans have been subjects of groundbreaking research.[41] Long-obscured and long-ignored documents generated by free southern women reveal that urbanization in the early nineteenth century stimulated complex market economies which, in turn, led to Black women's wage labor, new kinds of sexual labor, narrow but real entrepreneurial opportunities, and property ownership. Court cases in which women petitioned for formal manumission, rejected sexual violence, sued to establish claims to property, or sought to revoke the apprenticeship of their children to whites evidence free Black women's incessant activity. Amrita Chakrabarti Myers, for example, concluded that free Black women in Charleston became "shrewd political actors who understood that manumission did not grant them unfettered access to equality."[42] In addition to exploring ways in which free people of African descent navigated urban spaces within the United States, scholars have also interrogated the lives of free Black women in the larger, transnational context of settler-colonial slave societies.[43]

Historians studying fugitivity expanded their vision as well, moving beyond the mythologized Underground Railroad and pushing the story back into the eighteenth century. Woody Holton's *Indians, Debtors, Slaves, and the Making of*

41. Amrita Chakrabarti Myers, *Forging Freedom: Black Women and the Pursuit of Liberty in Antebellum Charleston* (Chapel Hill: University of North Carolina Press, 2011); Emily Bingham, *Mordecai: An Early American Family* (New York: Hill and Wang, 2003). On Norfolk, see Tommy Bogger, *Free Blacks in Norfolk, Virginia, 1790–1860: The Darker Side of Freedom* (Charlottesville: University Press of Virginia, 1997). For New Orleans, see Kimberly S. Hanger, *Bounded Lives, Bounded Places: Free Black Society in Colonial New Orleans, 1769–1803* (Durham: Duke University Press, 1997); Schafer, *Becoming Free, Remaining Free;* Emily Clark and Virginia Meacham Gould, "The Feminine Face of Afro-Catholicism in New Orleans, 1727–1852," *William and Mary Quarterly* 59 (April 2002): 409–48; Emily Owens, "Promises: Sexual Labor in the Space Between Slavery and Freedom," *Louisiana History* 58 (Spring 2017): 179–216. For women in Maryland, see Jessica Millward, *Finding Charity's Folk: Enslaved and Free Black Women in Maryland* (Athens: University of Georgia Press, 2015). For free people of color in Baltimore (and Maryland) in general, see Christopher Phillips, *Freedom's Port: the African American Community of Baltimore, 1790–1860* (Urbana: University of Illinois Press, 1997). See also Virginia Meacham Gould, ed., *Chained to the Rock of Adversity: To Be Free, Black and Female in the Old South* (Athens: University of Georgia Press, 1998).

42. Myers, *Forging Freedom,* 115; Cynthia M. Kennedy, review of Amrita Chakrabarti Myers, *Black Women and the Pursuit of Liberty in Antebellum Charleston,* in *Journal of American History* 99 (December 2012): 905–6.

43. Important works include Jane G. Landers, ed., *Against the Odds: Free Blacks in the Slave Societies of the Americas* (London: Frank Cass, 1996); Marisa J. Fuentes, *Dispossessed Lives: Enslaved Women, Violence, and the Archive* (Philadelphia: University of Pennsylvania Press, 2016); Lisa Ze Winters, *The Mulatta Concubine: Terror, Intimacy, Freedom, and Desire in the Black Transatlantic* (Athens: University of Georgia Press, 2016); Childs, *The 1812 Aponte Rebellion in Cuba and the Struggle against Atlantic Slavery.*

the American Revolution in Virginia (1999), Cassandra Pybus's *Epic Journeys of Freedom* (2007), and Alan Taylor's *The Internal Enemy* (2014) demonstrated how fugitive slaves and white fears of slave rebellion shaped white Americans' participation in the Revolutionary War and the War of 1812. Black resistance shaped not only local communities but also national and global politics. More importantly, each historian noted how, despite the peril most runaways faced, African Americans built free lives for themselves.[44]

Scholars also began to contest the timeworn claim that *maronnage*—permanent flight away from enslavement through creation of viable, self-sufficient communities within the South—proved either impossible or so rare as to be unimportant.[45] Sylviane A. Diouf's *Slavery's Exiles* (2014) presented a much more common form of flight that constituted a brief rather than permanent absence from one's enslaver. By naming the truants and runaways who formed communities within the slave South as "maroons," Diouf and other historians allowed readers to understand that the South had its own form of *maronnage*. Such resistance, and the networks needed to sustain maroons as they continued to "lie out," became part of the larger investigation of how enslaved and free people maintained their own definitions of freedom. Consequently, because many runaways viewed their lives in the North as transitory, Steven Hahn argued that free Black communities in the antebellum North could be understood as maroon settlements.[46]

Although Hahn's thesis generated criticism, historians continue to broaden understandings of resistance and rebellion. For example, Sowande' M. Musta-

44. Woody Holton, *Forced Founders: Indians, Debtors, Slaves, and the Making of the American Revolution in Virginia* (Chapel Hill: University of North Carolina Press, 1999); Cassandra Pybus, *Epic Journeys of Freedom: Runaway Slaves of the American Revolution and Their Global Quest for Liberty* (Boston: Beacon Press, 2007); Alan Taylor, *The Internal Enemy: Slavery and War in Virginia, 1772–1832* (New York: W. W. Norton, 2014); Robert G. Parkinson, *The Common Cause: Creating Race and Nation in the American Revolution* (Chapel Hill: University of North Carolina Press, 2016); Emily Blanck, *Tyrannicide: Forging an American Law of Slavery in Revolutionary South Carolina and Massachusetts* (Athens: University of Georgia Press, 2014).

45. Nathaniel Millett, *The Maroons of Prospect Bluff and Their Quest for Freedom in the Atlantic World* (Gainesville: University Press of Florida, 2013); Timothy James Lockley, ed., *Maroon Communities in South Carolina: A Documentary Record* (Columbia: University of South Carolina Press, 2009). More controversial is Hugo Prosper Leaming, *Hidden Americans: Maroons of Virginia and the Carolinas* (New York: Garland Publishing, 1995).

46. Sylviane A. Diouf, *Slavery's Exiles: The Story of the American Maroons* (New York: New York University Press, 2014); Hahn, *The Political Worlds of Slavery and Freedom.*

keem's *Slavery at Sea* (2016) uncovered resistance that does not fit neatly into heroic narratives of perseverance and sacrifice. Nikki Marie Taylor's *Driven toward Madness* (2016) investigates the case of an enslaved mother who murdered her own children rather than relinquish them to slave catchers. Experiences of slaves during the middle passage and their acts of resistance that included shipboard rebellion, suicide, infanticide, and a litany of other violences rarely resulted in liberation, forcing scholars to reckon with "agency" and "resistance"—two terms that are woefully inadequate in the context of the transatlantic trade.[47]

Slavery and Capitalism

As scholars of slave rebellion and resistance drifted closer to writing histories of enslaved people and their lives in relation to the slave system, others turned to the workings of slavery as an economic system. In particular, in the 2000s and 2010s, a number of southern historians reframed their work as histories of slavery and capitalism, offering fresh insights into a topic that traces back to the era of slavery.

Nineteenth-century white abolitionists in the United States tended to believe in the efficiency and efficacy of free-labor economies and that slavery retarded growth.[48] Classical-liberal assumptions about economics and freedom denied

47. Sowande' M. Mustakeem, *Slavery at Sea: Terror, Sex, and Sickness in the Middle Passage* (Urbana: University of Illinois Press, 2016); Taylor, *Driven toward Madness;* Mary E. Frederickson and Delores M. Walters, eds., *Gendered Resistance: Women, Slavery, and the Legacy of Margaret Garner* (Urbana: University of Illinois Press, 2013); Steven Weisenburger, *Modern Medea: A Family Story of Slavery and Child-Murder from the Old South* (New York: Hill and Wang, 1998). On the legacies of such violence, see Vincent Brown, *The Reaper's Garden: Death and Power in the World of Atlantic Slavery* (Cambridge: Harvard University Press, 2008); Craig Thompson Friend, "Mutilated Bodies, Living Specters: Scalpings and Beheadings in the Early South," in *Death and the American South,* ed. Craig Thompson Friend and Lorri Glover (New York: Cambridge University Press, 2015), 15–34.

48. As Thomas C. Holt argued in his book about emancipation and race in Britain's Anglo-Atlantic empire, the claim that wage labor led to greater economic growth than slavery was, in the 1830s, commonly made by slavery's liberal critics. When Britain's 1834 emancipation seemed to lead, instead, to the collapse of Jamaica's sugar-plantation sector, some intellectuals blamed freedpeople's "race," carving "scientific" racist thought even deeper into emancipation policy in the West; see *The Problem of Freedom: Race, Labor, and Politics in Jamaica and Britain, 1832–1938* (Baltimore: Johns Hopkins University Press, 1992). For a classic investigation of the various expectations of northern whites on the one hand—shaped by their understanding of British emancipation—and formerly enslaved African Americans on the other, see Willie Lee Rose, *Rehearsal for Reconstruction: The Port Royal Experiment* (New York: Oxford University Press, 1976).

any causal link between cotton production and the emergence of industrial capitalism. Indeed, the northern white liberal critique of slavery, especially after the Missouri Crisis, derided slavery as an economic failure—even as the textile factories hummed away.[49] Enslaved people, and those who escaped, were more skeptical about claims that slavery was neither profitable nor truly capitalist. "I'll put you in my pocket!" said many an enslaver, in the memories of slavery's survivors. Such a terrifying moment inevitably reminded each man, woman, or child that they were a commodity. Enslaved people and survivors of enslavement did not doubt that their stolen labor made the United States and white Americans wealthy. They understood their centrality to a system of wealth-generation that linked the nineteenth-century South to a broader and fully complicit northern society. This understanding lay behind the long advocacy for reparations.[50]

Beginning in the 1960s, increasing numbers of scholars raised doubts about the assertions of both white abolitionists and plantation-mythologizing scholars such as Ulrich B. Phillips that slavery was economically static and unprofitable for individual enslavers. By the 1980s, that doubt led to a kind of historiographical amnesia, one generated by the continued influence of the myth about the antebellum southern plantation as a place unto itself, outside of time. Not much new work, and certainly none that received wide acclaim, focused on the relationship between the forced laborer and forced labor, or the way that expanding global capitalism fueled the expansion of antebellum southern slavery.[51]

49. Karl Marx concurred, though with the caveat that Atlantic slavery had been an immense process of primitive accumulation that helped make industrial capitalism possible; see *Capital: A Critique of Political Economy*. Vol. 1, *The Process of Capitalist Production* (1867; repr., New York: Penguin, 1992), chap. 26. See also Walter Johnson, "The Pedestal and the Veil: Rethinking the Capitalism/Slavery Question," *Journal of the Early Republic* 24 (Summer 2004): 299–308; Nikhil Pal Singh, "On Race, Violence, and So-Called Primitive Accumulation," *Social Text* 128 (September 2016): 27–50. See also the Brenner debate about primitive accumulation and the agrarian origins of capitalism: T. H. Aston and C. H. E. Philpin, eds., *The Brenner Debate: Agrarian Class Structure and Economic Development in Pre-Industrial Europe* (New York: Cambridge University Press, 1985).

50. For instance, see Mary Frances Berry, *My Face Is Black Is True: Callie House and the Struggle for Ex-slave Reparations* (New York: Alfred A. Knopf, 2005). For the diaspora-wide history of reparations movements, see Ana Lucia Araujo, *Reparations for Slavery and the Slave Trade: A Transnational and Comparative History* (New York: Bloomsbury, 2017).

51. Robert William Fogel and Stanley L. Engerman, *Time on the Cross: The Economics of American Negro Slavery* (Boston: Little, Brown, 1974). For critiques of Fogel and Engerman, see Paul A. David et al., eds., *Reckoning with Slavery: A Critical Study in the Quantitative History of American Negro Slavery* (New York: Oxford University Press, 1976); Herbert G. Gutman, *Slavery and the Numbers Game: A Critique*

After a flurry of debate surrounding the publication of Robert William Fogel and Stanley L. Engerman's *Time on the Cross* (1974), the field settled into a tacit acceptance of Eugene D. Genovese and Elizabeth Fox-Genovese's position on the nature of the "Old South" and its relationship to capitalism. The southern planter class, they wrote, was in, but not of, capitalism. The massive flow of cotton into the industrial economies of Britain and the northern United States made the planters' fortunes, but that relationship did not shape the planter class. Slaveholding and class hegemony did.[52]

Interpretations began to change in the late 1990s, however. Influences from other fields of history, other disciplines, and a growing critique of neoliberal globalization redirected scholars' attention. From within the broader field in the early 1990s, historians of the Early Republic began arguing about the nature and character of the Market Revolution.[53] Equally important was renewed attention by southern historians to longstanding arguments in African American and Afro-Caribbean scholarship about the relationship between whites' historical exploita-

---

of Time on the Cross (Urbana: University of Illinois Press, 1975). See also Fogel's counterresponse in *The Slavery Debates, 1952–1990: A Retrospective* (Baton Rouge: Louisiana State University Press, 2003); and Fogel, *Without Consent or Contract: The Rise and Fall of American Slavery* (New York: W. W. Norton, 1989). There was also a tradition of institutionalist scholarship of the cotton trade, banking, industry, and business in the Old South. See Harold D. Woodman, *King Cotton and His Retainers: Financing and Marketing the Cotton Crop of the South, 1800–1925* (Lexington: University of Kentucky Press, 1968).

52. Eugene D. Genovese, *In Red and Black: Marxian Explorations in Southern and Afro-American History* (Knoxville: University of Tennessee Press, 1971); Genovese, *The World the Slaveholders Made: Two Essays in Interpretation* (New York: Pantheon Books, 1969); Genovese and Elizabeth Fox-Genovese, *The Fruits of Merchant Capital: Slavery and Bourgeois Property in the Rise and Expansion of Capitalism* (New York: Oxford University Press, 1989). There were dissenters to this trend, including James Oakes, *Slavery and Freedom: An Interpretation of the Old South* (New York: Alfred A. Knopf, 1990); Oakes, *The Ruling Race: A History of American Slaveholders* (New York: Vintage, 1983).

53. Charles Sellers, *The Market Revolution: Jacksonian America, 1815–1846* (New York: Oxford University Press, 1991); Harry L. Watson, "'The Common Rights of Mankind': Subsistence, Shad, and Commerce in the Early Republican South," *Journal of American History* 83 (June 1996): 13–43. Some scholars argued that slavery was not really part of the Market Revolution; see, for example, Douglas R. Egerton, "Markets without a Market Revolution: Southern Planters and Capitalism," *Journal of the Early Republic* 16 (Summer 1996): 207–21. Others, using a more traditional first-world Marxist analysis, argued that if part of a Market Revolution, southern slavery remained fundamentally distinctive from the rest of emerging Anglo-Atlantic capitalism. See Scott P. Marler, *The Merchants' Capital: New Orleans and the Political Economy of the Nineteenth-Century South* (New York: Cambridge University Press, 2013); Scott Reynolds Nelson, *A Nation of Deadbeats: An Uncommon History of America's Financial Disasters* (New York: Alfred A. Knopf, 2012).

tion of enslaved and colonized people and the rise of the industrial capitalist West to global dominance.[54]

The change in historiographical direction manifested in new work about the domestic slave trade, beginning with Michael Tadman's *Speculators and Slaves* (1989). Tadman's study revealed that enslavers forcibly moved more than one million enslaved people into new territories and states, undermining accounts of the plantation community offered by a previous generation.[55] In reminding readers that the pre-Emancipation South was, in essence, an expansionist entity that ripped land from Native peoples and tore enslaved Blacks out of their Chesapeake and Carolina families, no work was more influential than Walter Johnson's stunning *Soul by Soul* (1999). His investigation of life inside the antebellum slave market drew from close readings of formerly enslaved people's memoirs and from New Orleans court documents. His analysis demonstrated how enslaved people,

54. Eric Williams, *Capitalism and Slavery* (Chapel Hill: University of North Carolina Press, 1944); C. L. R. James, *The Black Jacobins: Toussaint L'Ouverture and the San Domingo Revolution,* 2nd ed. (New York: Vintage, 1963); Walter Rodney, *How Europe Underdeveloped Africa* (1972; repr., Washington, DC: Howard University Press, 1981).

55. In a sense, Michael Tadman, *Speculators and Slaves: Masters, Traders, and Slaves in the Old South* (Madison: University of Wisconsin Press, 1989), revived the work of Frederic Bancroft and rejected the Phillips to Genovese lineage. While Genovese barely mentioned the domestic slave trade in *Roll, Jordan, Roll,* almost every slavery survivor's account did. The new scholarship on the disruptive role of the "domestic" trade built upon Gutman, *The Black Family in Slavery and Freedom,* but took a much less sanguine view. An array of work emerging between 1995 and 2005 insisted that territorial expansion, market revolutions, the expulsion of Native peoples from their lands, and forced migrations of enslaved Africans all reshaped the character and experience of enslavement: see Ira Berlin, *Many Thousands Gone: The First Two Centuries of Slavery in North America* (Cambridge: Harvard University Press, 1998); Joan E. Cashin, *A Family Venture: Men and Women on the Southern Frontier* (New York: Oxford University Press, 1991); Daniel S. Dupre, *Transforming the Cotton Frontier: Madison County, Alabama, 1800–1840* (Baton Rouge: Louisiana State University Press, 1997); Steven F. Miller, "Plantation Labor Organization and Slave Life on the Cotton Frontier: The Alabama-Mississippi Black Belt, 1815–1840," in *Cultivation and Culture: Labor and the Shaping of Slave Life in the Americas,* ed. Ira Berlin and Philip D. Morgan (Charlottesville: University Press of Virginia, 1993), 155–69; John Campbell, "As 'A Kind of Freeman'?: Slaves' Market-Related Activities in the South Carolina Up Country, 1800–1860," in Berlin and Morgan, eds., *Cultivation and Culture,* 243–74; Follett, *The Sugar Masters;* Sarah Paradise Russell, "Cultural Conflicts and Common Interests: The Making of the Sugar Planter Class in Louisiana, 1795–1853" (PhD diss., University of Maryland, 2000); Edward E. Baptist, *Creating an Old South: Middle Florida's Plantation Frontier Before the Civil War* (Chapel Hill: University of North Carolina Press, 2002); Rothman, *Slave Country.* Some of these works were more histories of slavery systems and enslavers than they were histories of the enslaved, and as such they represented bridges forward from the studies of planter culture and politics that were so prominent from the 1970s through the 1990s.

their lives destabilized by being wrenched from family and friends, had no choice but to survive by their wits and by whatever community they could create "between the trades." By this phrase, Johnson meant the time between when they were sold to the trader and when the trader resold them, a period during which the enslaved calculated and acted, trying to put a rudder in the flood carrying them westward and southward. Enslavers, meanwhile, were also calculating—but in their case, to fulfill their megalomaniac dreams of commodifying enslaved people for their own power and comfort. Johnson's portrait of the enslaver echoed the postmodern consumer making her or his world out of the commodities they consumed. It was a chilling but compellingly resonant note.[56]

Soul by Soul helped reinvigorate the methodology of following the money: mapping ways in which "the market" in enslaved bodies shaped white economic opportunities, white wealth, and white life. After Johnson's book appeared, additional works about the domestic slave trade further shifted the focus of nineteenth-century slavery scholarship, both among those who considered themselves southern historians and many who did not.[57]

56. Walter Johnson, *Soul by Soul: Life Inside the Antebellum Slave Market* (Cambridge: Harvard University Press, 1999). On the influence of scholarship from other disciplines, see Sidney Mintz, *Sweetness and Power: The Place of Sugar in Modern History* (New York: Viking, 1985); Arjun Appadurai, ed., *The Social Life of Things: Commodities in Cultural Perspective* (New York: Cambridge University Press, 1986); Sadiya V. Hartman, *Scenes of Subjection: Terror, Slavery, and Self-Making in Nineteenth-Century America* (New York: Oxford University Press, 1997); Eric Lott, *Love and Theft: Blackface Minstrelsy and the American Working Class* (New York: Oxford University Press, 1995); Ian Baucom, *Specters of the Atlantic: Finance Capital, Slavery, and the Philosophy of History* (Durham: Duke University Press, 2005). While some might set up a competition between historians of capitalism and cultural historians, it is the influence of the latter that really distinguishes the new history of capitalism from "old" histories. Along with Walter Johnson's work, one can see this clearly and powerfully in Stephanie E. Smallwood, *Saltwater Slavery: A Middle Passage from Africa to American Diaspora* (Cambridge: Harvard University Press, 2007).

57. Walter Johnson, ed., *The Chattel Principle: Internal Slave Trades in the Americas* (New Haven: Yale University Press, 2004); Steven Deyle, *Carry Me Back: The Domestic Slave Trade in American Life* (New York: Oxford University Press, 2005); Ariela Julie Gross, *Double Character: Slavery and Mastery in the Antebellum Southern Courtroom* (Princeton: Princeton University Press, 2000); David L. Lightner, *Slavery and the Commerce Power: How the Struggle against the Interstate Slave Trade Led to the Civil War* (New Haven: Yale University Press, 2006); Calvin Schermerhorn, *Money over Mastery, Family over Freedom: Slavery in the Antebellum Upper South* (Baltimore: Johns Hopkins University Press, 2011); Schermerhorn, *The Business of Slavery and the Rise of American Capitalism, 1815–1860* (New Haven: Yale University Press, 2015). On the continued "illegal" trade from Africa, see Sylviane A. Diouf, *Dreams of Africa in Alabama: The Slave Ship* Clotilda *and the Story of the Last Africans Brought to America* (New York: Oxford University Press, 2007); Sharla M. Fett, *Recaptured Africans: Surviving Slave Ships, Detention, and Dislocation in the*

Conventional wisdom holds that the turn to the new history of capitalism began because of the 2008 market crash and the ensuing Great Recession. Scholars certainly found an audience skeptical of the claims of market-fundamentalist neoliberal capitalism: that this system of structuring economies was natural and inevitable; that it was historically innocent of the Western past's horrors (slavery, genocide, theft); that the substitution of market relationships and econometric thinking brought greater freedom through economic efficiency.[58] But most of the histories categorized as part of the new history of capitalism, at least those published in the first half of the 2010s, were begun long before 2008. (Historians work slowly.) Their studies doubted the claims of triumphant neoliberals. Some had been steeped in traditions of anticolonial Marxism, African American critique of the enslaved origins of American wealth, postcolonial critique, or all three. Others could just as easily see that the prosperity promised by neoliberalism was tissue-paper thin. Eyes to see, ears to hear, it wasn't that complicated.[59]

And so historians of slavery kept following the money in many different types of sources: the "freedom narratives" composed by slavery's survivors, enslavers' records, bank archives, private letters about failed business ventures, and public speeches defending or attacking slavery as an economic system. They tried to map the impact of cotton, reconstruct the financial networks that sustained the domestic slave trade and the export of cotton, and trace the brutal extraction of

---

Final Years of the Slave Trade (Chapel Hill: University of North Carolina Press, 2017). For United States slaveholders' involvement in the expansion of other slave systems, see Matthew Karp, *This Vast Southern Empire: Slaveholders at the Helm of American Foreign Policy* (Cambridge: Harvard University Press, 2016); Gerald Horne, *The Deepest South: The United States, Brazil, and the African Slave Trade* (New York: New York University Press, 2007); Stephen M. Chambers, *No God but Gain: The Untold Story of Cuban Slavery, the Monroe Doctrine, and the Making of the United States* (New York: Verso, 2015); Márcia Regina Berbel, Rafael de Bivar Marquese, and Tâmis Parron, *Slavery and Politics: Brazil and Cuba, 1790–1850*, trans. Leonardo Marques (Albuquerque: University of New Mexico Press, 2016).

58. Critics and cartographers of neoliberalism include Wendy Brown, *Undoing the Demos: Neoliberalism's Stealth Revolution* (Brooklyn: Zone Books, 2015); Nancy Fraser, "Behind Marx's Hidden Abode," *New Left Review* 86 (March–April 2014): 55–72; Thomas Piketty, *Capital in the Twenty-First Century* (Cambridge: Harvard University Press, 2013).

59. See the website for the British Legacies of Slavery Project: https://www.ucl.ac.uk/lbs/ (accessed 18 January 2019), which presents data revealing the interweaving of wealth and slavery in the British Empire and elsewhere. See also Catherine Hall, *Legacies of British Slave-Ownership: Colonial Slavery and the Formation of Victorian Britain* (New York: Cambridge University Press, 2014); Nicholas Draper, *The Price of Emancipation: Slave-Ownership, Compensation and British Society at the End of Slavery* (New York: Cambridge University Press, 2010).

labor in the cotton fields that made it possible for factory wheels to turn in the revolutionary industrialization of Britain, the United States, and Western Europe. Historians showed how enslavers carefully measured labor and drove enslaved laborers with astounding violence. Scholars also revealed how white American popular-historical understanding had been disposed to attribute such violence to individual or even collective pathology, unwilling to consider that perhaps each drop of blood drawn with the lash allowed—still allows—white people to accumulate wealth.[60]

The economic development of the West, historians of capitalism implied, was contingent, not inevitable. One of the contingencies was the enslavement of millions of Africans in a plantation complex that produced commodities essential to the rise of capitalism—and did so in ways far more "modern" than nineteenth-century critics of slavery and boosters of free-market capitalism had been willing to acknowledge.[61] Some of these scholars produced histories of slavery and of its influence as a system: Sven Beckert, Caitlin Rosenthal, and Matthew Karp, for

60. Johnson, "The Pedestal and the Veil"; Johnson, *River of Dark Dreams: Slavery and Empire in the Cotton Kingdom* (Cambridge: Harvard University Press, 2013); Rothman, *Flush Times and Fever Dreams;* Edward E. Baptist, *The Half Has Never Been Told: Slavery and the Making of American Capitalism* (New York: Basic Books, 2014); Sven Beckert, *Empire of Cotton: A Global History* (New York: Alfred A. Knopf, 2014); Caitlin Rosenthal, *Accounting for Slavery: Master and Management* (Cambridge: Harvard University Press, 2019); Stephanie Jones-Rogers, *They Were Her Property: White Women as Slave Owners in the American South* (New Haven: Yale University Press, 2019); Daina Ramey Berry, *The Price for Their Pound of Flesh: The Value of the Enslaved, from Womb to Grave, in the Building of a Nation* (Boston: Beacon Press, 2017); Sven Beckert, ed., *Slavery's Capitalism: A New History of American Economic Development* (Philadelphia: University of Pennsylvania Press, 2016); Calvin Schermerhorn, *The Business of Slavery and the Rise of American Capitalism, 1815–1860* (New Haven: Yale University Press, 2015); Bonnie Martin, "Slavery's Invisible Engine: Mortgaging Human Property," *Journal of Southern History* 76 (November 2010): 817–66; Sharon Ann Murphy, *Other People's Money: How Banking Worked in the Early American Republic* (Baltimore: Johns Hopkins University Press, 2017); the essays in Jeff Forret and Christine E. Sears, eds., *New Directions in Slavery Studies: Commodification, Community, and Comparison* (Baton Rouge: Louisiana State University Press, 2015), esp. Karen Ryder, "To Realize Money Facilities: Slave Insurance, the Slave Trade, and Credit in the Old South" (53–61).

61. Often left out of these accounts are Kenneth Pomeranz, *The Great Divergence: Europe, China, and the Making of the Modern World Economy* (Princeton: Princeton University Press, 2000); Robin Blackburn, *The American Crucible: Slavery, Emancipation and Human Rights* (New York: Verso, 2011); Blackburn, *The Making of New World Slavery: From the Baroque to the Modern, 1492–1800* (New York: Verso, 1997); Dale W. Tomich, *Through the Prism of Slavery: Labor, Capital, and World Economy* (Lanham, MD: Rowman & Littlefield, 2004).

instance. Others, including Edward E. Baptist, Daina Ramey Berry, and Walter Johnson, attempted to write histories that were accounts both of systems and of the lives of the enslaved. Meanwhile, linking their work to this turn in studies of slavery and enslavement, other nineteenth-century historians reshaped their explorations of state market-making, finance, and changing cultural ideas about debt, production, consumption, and gender.[62]

Some historical economists pushed back with particular vigor, defending their turf against the claims made by historians of slavery. They insisted that the apparent efficiency of cotton production came not from violent exploitation of the enslaved but from the genius of cottonseed-selecting planters. Evidence for the latter was speculative, at best—as some fellow economists noted in critiques of their colleagues.[63] Economist critics also insisted that claims about the supposed contribution of enslaved people's labor, the financialization of bodies and lives, and the role of slavery in enabling United States national expansion were inconclusive. They dismissed historians' arguments about causality as inferential and conditional, hard to either prove or disprove.

No historian's argument had been harder to prove or disprove than that of Eric Williams, whose eponymous thesis launched much of this scholarship on slavery and capitalism. Williams argued that profits of the Atlantic slave trade and British Caribbean sugar helped finance the emergence of modern industry in Great Britain, and that abolition only developed when a rising source of industrial profits replaced the declining profits of plantation slavery. Indeed, another line of critique of the new scholarship was that it gave insufficient credit to Williams

62. Seth Rockman, "What Makes the History of Capitalism Newsworthy?" *Journal of the Early Republic* 34 (Fall 2014): 439–66; Rockman, "The Unfree Origins of American Capitalism," in *The Economy of Early America: Historical Perspectives and New Directions*, ed. Cathy Matson (State College: Pennsylvania State University Press, 2006); Jennifer Schuessler, "In History Classes, Capitalism Sees Its Stock Soar," *New York Times*, 7 April 2013; Sven Beckert, "History of Capitalism," in *American History Now*, ed. Eric Foner and Lisa McGirr (Philadelphia: Temple University Press, 2011), 314–35; Julia Cathleen Ott, "Slaves: The Capital That Made Capitalism," *Public Seminar*, 9 April 2014, http://www.publicseminar.org/2014/04/slavery-the-capital-that-made-capitalism/ (accessed 18 January 2019).

63. Scott Reynolds Nelson, "Who Put Their Capitalism in My Slavery?" *Journal of the Civil War Era* 5 (June 2015): 289–310; Alan L. Olmstead, Trevon D. Logan, et al., review of *The Half Has Never Been Told* by Edward E. Baptist, *Journal of Economic History* 75 (September 2015): 919–31; Eric Hilt, "Economic History, Historical Analysis, and the 'New History of Capitalism,'" *Journal of Economic History* 77 (June 2017): 511–36; Mark Stelzner and Enzo Cerrutti, "Workers and Technological Change in the United States," *Labor History* 59 (November 2018): 657–91.

and other, particularly Afro-Caribbean, scholars.[64] Of course, the argument that the rise of plantation slavery shaped the rise of Western capitalism ran back not only to Williams, but also to W. E. B. Du Bois and generations of scholars of African American history. Much had been synthesized by Cedric Robinson in his articulation of the concept of "racial capitalism," explicated by scholars including Robin D. G. Kelley, and deeply woven into Johnson's *River of Dark Dreams* (2013). By 2016, "racial capitalism" became the term of art for many who sought to understand the continuities of creation-by-exploitation that shaped American and global history before and after Emancipation.[65]

Meanwhile, work by scholars of the French and Spanish Caribbean, Brazil, and elsewhere had focused on capitalism for decades, including work that historical sociologist Dale W. Tomich termed "Second Slavery" scholarship, combining social history with world systems and Marxist analysis to argue that slavery was an integral part of (and not an exception to) the nineteenth-century Euro-Atlantic World. Scholars focused especially on Brazil, Cuba, and the southern United States, where slavery persisted and even expanded exponentially after the Haitian Revolution. In such states and colonies, one could find slaveries that were both "modern" and "modernizing."[66]

64. Williams, *Capitalism and Slavery;* James, *The Black Jacobins;* Rodney, *How Europe Underdeveloped Africa.* For works that incorporated the Caribbean intellectual tradition in a broader history of anticolonial ideologies, see Barbara L. Solow and Stanley L. Engerman, eds., *British Capitalism and Caribbean Slavery: The Legacy of Eric Williams* (New York: Cambridge University Press, 1987); Horace Campbell, *Rasta and Resistance: From Marcus Garvey to Walter Rodney* (Trenton: African World Press, 1987); William A. Darity Jr., "British Industry and the West Indies Plantations," *Social Science History* 14 (Spring 1990): 117–49.

65. Du Bois, *Black Reconstruction;* Du Bois, *Souls of Black Folk: Essays and Sketches,* 2nd ed. (Chicago: A. C. McClurg., 1903); William A. Darity Jr., "Eric Williams and Slavery: A West Indian Viewpoint?" *Callaloo* 20 (Fall 1997): 801–16; Oliver Cromwell Cox, *Race, Caste, and Class* (New York: Monthly Review Press, 1948); Cedric Robinson, "Oliver Cox and the Historiography of the West," *Cultural Critique* 17 (Winter 1990–91): 5–20; Cedric J. Robinson, *Black Marxism: The Making of the Black Radical Tradition* (London: Zed, 1983); Robin D. G. Kelley, "What Did Cedric Robinson Mean by Racial Capitalism," *Boston Review,* 12 January 2017, http://bostonreview.net/race/robin-d-g-kelley-what-did-cedric-robinson-mean-racial-capitalism (accessed 18 January 2019).

66. Rafael de Bivar Marquese, *Feitores Do Corpo, Missionários Da Mente: Senhores, Letrados e o Controle Dos Escravos Nas Américas, 1660–1860* (São Paulo: Companhia das Letras, 2004); Robin Blackburn, *The American Crucible: Slavery, Emancipation, Human Rights* (New York: Verso, 2011); Dale W. Tomich, ed., *Slavery and Historical Capitalism during the Nineteenth Century* (Lanham, MD: Lexington Books, 2017); Daniel Rood, *The Reinvention of Atlantic Slavery: Technology, Labor, Race, and Capitalism in the Greater Caribbean* (New York: Oxford University Press, 2017). See also Erik Mathisen, "The Second Slavery, Capitalism, and Emancipation in Civil War America," *Journal of the Civil War Era* 8 (December 2018): 677–99.

Meanwhile, another not unrelated critique pushed back against the dominance of white historians in replicating existing structures of scholarly control: an old story, too. This counterpoint followed a line of scholarship from Angela Davis forward through Deborah Gray White and Brenda Stevenson to Jennifer L. Morgan. Beyond a system of production for profit, slavery was equally a system of reproduction of the capacity for production, for wealth and accumulation, for power and exploitation and citizenship in the newborn modern world. The labor of Black families, the lives, the deaths, the bodies, the love, the care, the eating and the dying and the giving birth, all of which women did the most, sustained the system. For instance, Jennifer L. Morgan, in both her influential article "'Some Could Suckle over Their Shoulder'" (1997) and her ensuing book, *Laboring Women* (2004), asked readers to consider the consequences of European travel narratives' project of "othering." European assumptions, derived from the "difference" they perceived in African women's bodies, sexuality, and reproductive capacity, helped enable European slavers to understand and assess reproduction as labor. The consequence of reproduction, alienated by law and power, thus became capital.[67]

Daina Ramey Berry's *The Price for Their Pound of Flesh* (2017) used a life-cycle approach to explain two parallel systems of value: white Americans' assessments of the monetary value of human property, and African Americans' investment of "soul value" in themselves. "Ghost value," another concept Berry introduced, recovered the ambiguous grief and empty space left in the wake of those who disappeared in the internal slave trade and whose bodies were desecrated postmortem in medical colleges across the nation.[68] Historians, economists, political theorists have understood capitalism and its rise as a process that defines the economy as separate from the household, as something that replaced social relations with economic relations. Yet a fuller understanding of the history of reproductive labor within slavery undermines that set of assumptions, which was generated by those who sought to implement free-market capitalism as government policy in the first place. The Davis-to-Morgan and onward line of inquiry can unite the often separate accounts of slavery-as-system and slavery as the history of the enslaved.

67. Morgan, *Laboring Women;* Morgan, "'Some Could Suckle over Their Shoulder.'" See also Dorothy Roberts, *Killing the Black Body: Race, Reproduction, and the Meaning of Liberty* (New York: Vintage, 1998), which foregrounded enslaved women's reproductive lives in provocative and helpful ways that bridge economic history, histories of slavery as an institution, medical history, and African American women's history.

68. Berry, *The Price for Their Pound of Flesh.*

In doing so it could transform what we think about capitalism's rise, the significance of slavery's system of production, and ultimately, the history of capitalism.

Medicine and the Body

Between the 1980s and the 2010s, historians of the body fostered deeper understanding of the experience of commodification from the point of view of the enslaved. Intersecting with histories of gender, sexuality, and reproductive labor, scholars who focused on the history of enslaved people's bodies made valuable interventions in the history of antebellum science and medicine. They brought into contact histories of slavery and histories of the enslaved in provocative ways. In *Medicine and Slavery* (1978), Todd L. Savitt chronicled "medical conditions as they existed at the time, and a history of the relationship between black health and white society." He influenced a generation of historians who focused initially on white perceptions of Black health as well as terms like "fitness" and "soundness" for work, but the field also expanded to take up Black experiences. The edited collection, *Medicine, Nutrition, Demography, Slavery* (1990), for example, included essays on a range of topics relating to the medical care and health of enslaved populations.[69]

Some scholars turned to recovering African American medical practices during slavery. Wonda Fontenot and Katherine Bankole-Medina looked at enslaved people in Louisiana, for example. Fontenot explored the history of "secret doctoring" among Afro-Louisianans, and then continued with a study of ethnomedicine in Black southern Louisiana in *Secret Doctors* (1994). Bankole-Medina's *Slavery and Medicine* (1998) embodied the historiographical transition from white medical practices to African Americans and antebellum medical theories, and finally to African medical theories and practice as well as white perceptions of African American vernacular medicine.[70]

Central to the scholarship on medicine and the body is the effort to understand enslaved people on their own terms rather than through the eyes of whites.

69. Todd L. Savitt, *Medicine and Slavery: The Diseases and Health Care of Blacks in Antebellum Virginia* (Urbana: University of Illinois Press, 1981), 2; Paul Finkelman, *Medicine, Nutrition, Demography, Slavery* (New York: Routledge, 1990).

70. Wonda L. Fontenot, *Secret Doctors: Ethnomedicine of African Americans* (Westport: Praeger, 1994); Katherine Bankole-Medina, *Slavery and Medicine: Enslavement and Medical Practices in Antebellum Louisiana* (New York: Garland Publishing, 1998).

Sharla Fett's important *Working Cures* (2002) acknowledged the history of abuse by medical practitioners and the exploitative interests of slaveholders, and then pivoted to African American vernacular healing practices. Highlighting the work and experiences of female slaves to cultivate a "broader relational vision of health," Fett concluded that, "At each historical juncture, enslaved communities cultivated their own practitioners and therapies, and they influenced southern rural health practices in the process." Similarly, analysis of Black religious practices, often related to medicine and physical wholeness, escaped white contexts. Yvonne P. Chireau's *Black Magic* (2006) and Herbert C. Covey's *African American Slave Medicine* (2008) explored scientific and spiritual dimensions of African American healing traditions. Stephanie Mitchem's *African American Folk Healing* (2007) bridged centuries of Black medical practices, providing an interdisciplinary look at Black healing traditions, African American medical theories, and beliefs around health. And Daina Ramey Berry told the story of enslaved women's laboring lives and their own definitions of soundness in *"Swing the Sickle for the Harvest Is Ripe"* (2010).[71] Berry's discussion of hiring practices and the self-assessment of enslaved laborers anticipated other ways of defining health and wellness from the point of view of the enslaved.

Marli F. Weiner's *Sex, Sickness, and Slavery* (2012) delved into parallel intellectual, medical, and social histories to better understand antebellum racial science. At the heart of her work was an exploration of how antebellum Americans answered questions of intersecting classifications. In other words: what was more important to human taxonomy—sex or race? Similarly, Rana A. Hogarth's *Medicalizing Blackness* (2017) explored white doctors' preoccupation with reaching a definitive taxonomy of the races. Comparing the lives and health of enslaved peoples in Jamaica and the antebellum American South, Hogarth's study linked the lives and health of enslaved people in each plantation regime to unravel the race-making practices of physicians across contexts.[72]

71. Sharla M. Fett, *Working Cures: Healing, Health, and Power on Southern Slave Plantations* (Chapel Hill: University of North Carolina Press, 2002), quotes on 2, 35; Yvonne P. Chireau, *Black Magic: Religion and the African American Conjuring Tradition* (Berkeley: University of California Press, 2006); Herbert C. Covey, *African American Slave Medicine: Herbal and Non-Herbal Treatments* (Lanham, MD: Lexington Books, 2008); Stephanie Mitchem, *African American Folk Healing* (New York: New York University Press, 2007); Berry, *"Swing the Sickle for the Harvest Is Ripe."*

72. Marli F. Weiner with Mazie Hough, *Sex, Sickness, and Slavery: Illness in the Antebellum South* (Urbana: University of Illinois Press, 2014); Rana A. Hogarth, *Medicalizing Blackness: Making Racial Difference in the Atlantic World, 1780–1840* (Chapel Hill: University of North Carolina Press, 2017). See

The study of histories of medicine and the body during antebellum American slavery necessarily include explorations of maternity, the advent of gynecology, and reproductive labor. Deborah Kuhn McGregor's *From Midwives to Medicine* (1998) foregrounded the role of Black women and Black women's bodies in pioneering medical knowledge and treatment by white doctors anxious to establish medical authority. In *Birthing a Slave* (2006), Marie Jenkins Schwartz analyzed the complex social dynamics between enslaved people, slave-owners, doctors, and lay healers, juxtaposing the life cycle of enslaved women with the profit-motivated prerogatives of slave-owners and the doctors they hired. Other historians also took up the economic considerations of planters in examining enslaved women's reproductive lives. Gregory D. Smithers in *Slave Breeding* (2012) and Ned Sublette and Constance Sublette in *The American Slave Coast* (2017) investigated slave breeding, tracing the cultural history of the concept from abolitionist rhetoric to late twentieth-century literature and media. Smithers expressed concern with slave breeding as an idea and a memory, while Ned Sublette and Constance Sublette asserted that, after the close of the Atlantic slave trade in 1808, American slaveholders became reliant on the natural increase of enslaved populations.[73]

Historians of slavery have undertaken other promising explorations into the history of science, medicine, and the body. Britt Rusert recovered African Americans' scientific work in *Fugitive Science* (2017), demonstrating ways that free Blacks engaged with their contemporary discourse on racial science. Dia H. Boster centered the social construction of disability in *African American Slavery and Disability* (2012). In a series of articles, Jenifer L. Barclay explored different aspects of how slaveholders defined disability and how enslaved mothers coped with their children's disabilities. Using the 1850 and 1860 census records for Virginia and South Carolina, Jeff Forret's "'Deaf & Dumb, Blind, Insane, or Idiotic'" (2016) looked at how authorities documented disability.[74]

---

also Londa Schiebinger, *Secret Cures of Slaves: People, Plants, and Medicine in the Eighteenth-Century Atlantic World* (Stanford: Stanford University Press, 2017).

73. Deborah Kuhn McGregor, *From Midwives to Medicine: The Birth of American Gynecology* (New Brunswick: Rutgers University Press, 1998); Marie Jenkins Schwartz, *Birthing a Slave: Motherhood and Medicine in the Antebellum South* (Cambridge: Harvard University Press, 2006); Gregory D. Smithers, *Slave Breeding: Sex, Violence, and Memory in African American History* (Gainesville: University Press of Florida, 2012); Ned Sublette and Constance Sublette, *The American Slave Coast: A History of the Slave-Breeding Industry* (Chicago: Chicago Review Press, 2017).

74. Rusert, *Fugitive Science;* Jenifer L. Barclay, "Mothering the 'Useless': Black Motherhood, Disability, and Slavery," *Women, Gender, and Families of Color* 2 (Fall 2014): 115–40; Barclay, "'The Greatest

Finally, Deirdre Cooper Owens made two significant contributions in *Medical Bondage* (2017), intervening in histories of science, racial science, medicine, and the body by uncovering, first, the centrality of Black women's reproductive labor to the success of the slave economy and, second, how doctors used Black bodies as well as Black medical practices to solidify their professional claims to legitimacy. Women, the female body, and racialized medical practice were, she demonstrated, at the center and not the margins of American medical history.[75] Owens's work echoed beyond the academy, too.

Public Interpretations of Slavery and Enslavement

On 17 April 2018, the city of New York removed a statue of J. Marion Sims, which stood for decades on 5th Avenue next to Central Park. Sims, a gynecologist studied by Deirdre Cooper Owens and other historians of medicine and race, had been celebrated for more than a century as a father of modern medicine. But historians' critiques of his exploitation of enslaved women's bodies equipped activists, who organized repeated protests at the statue. These protestors numbered among many who critiqued public memorials of enslavers, arguing that statues, plaques, names on buildings, Confederate flags, and other such symbols were hardly neutral representations. Instead, such commemorations amounted to a public history that accommodated and even praised the institution of slavery, while simultaneously burying the experiences of enslaved people like Anarcha, the woman on whom Sims performed dozens of experimental surgeries to create techniques from which white women benefited.[76]

The Sims protests were part of a longer history of public debates about history and race. In the early 1990s, controversies arose over monuments, flags, and institutions that memorialized the Civil War. They continued apace into the

---

Degree of Perfection': Disability and the Construction of Race in American Slave Law," *South Carolina Review* 46 (Spring 2014): 27–43; Barclay, "Bad Breeders and Monstrosities: Racializing Childlessness and Congenital Disabilities in Slavery and Freedom," *Slavery & Abolition* 38 (April 2017): 287–302; Jeff Forret, "'Deaf & Dumb, Blind, Insane, or Idiotic': The Census, Slaves, and Disability in the Late Antebellum South," *Journal of Southern History* 82 (August 2016): 503–48.

75. Deirdre Cooper Owens, *Medical Bondage: Race, Gender, and the Origins of American Gynecology* (Athens: University of Georgia Press, 2017).

76. Owens, *Medical Bondage,* 1–41. On the Sims statue removal, see Meagan Flynn, "Statue of 'father of gynecology,' who experimented on enslaved women, removed from Central Park," *Washington Post,* 18 April 2018.

twenty-first century. Scholars kept reminding the larger public—at least people willing to listen—that such idols had been erected in the late nineteenth and early twentieth centuries in conjunction with a wave of disfranchisement and racist terror, or in the 1950s in response to the civil rights movement.[77]

On a more intimate scale, genealogical techniques and technological innovations revolutionized how the Black public investigated, encountered, and publicized the history of slavery. The upsurge in interest in Black family history began with Alex Haley's *Roots* (1976), inspiring many African Americans to study their enslaved ancestors. Remarkably, many succeeded, producing new information and bringing slavery research into the public sphere.[78] By the 2000s, a thriving Black genealogical community linked virtually on the internet and focused heavily on the discovery and identification of enslaved ancestors. It was emphatically a grassroots history of the enslaved, and not of the system of slavery. Henry Louis Gates Jr. drew enormous publicity to DNA analysis, enabling more people to learn about enslaved ancestors and to reclaim their relatives as complex individuals, not as one-dimensional victims or the nameless objects of white-written histories.[79]

77. Gaines M. Foster, *Ghosts of the Confederacy: Defeat, the Lost Cause, and the Emergence of the New South, 1865 to 1913* (New York: Oxford University Press, 1987); John M. Coski, *The Confederate Battle Flag: America's Most Embattled Emblem* (Cambridge: Harvard University Press, 2005); Robert E. Bonner, *Colors and Blood: Flag Passions of the Confederate South* (Princeton: Princeton University Press, 2002); J. Michael Martinez, William D. Richardson, and Ron McNinch-Su, eds., *Confederate Symbols in the Contemporary South* (Gainesville: University Press of Florida, 2000). Benedict Anderson's *Imagined Communities: Reflections on the Origins and Spread of Nationalism* (New York: Verso, 1983) influenced the wave of scholarship on the memorialization mania at the turn of the twentieth century, which had helped to create the white national state that was the New South. See James Oliver Horton and Amanda Kleintop, eds., *Race, Slavery and the Civil War: The Tough Stuff of American History and Memory* (Richmond: Virginia Sesquicentennial of the American Civil War Commission, 2011); Ana Lucia Araujo, *Shadows of the Slave Past: Memory, Heritage, and Slavery* (New York: Routledge, 2014).

78. Dorothy Spruill Redford and Michael D'Orso, *Somerset Homecoming: Recovering a Lost Heritage* (New York: Doubleday, 1988); Rachel L. Swarns, *American Tapestry: The Story of the Black, White, and Multiracial Ancestors of Michelle Obama* (New York: Amistad, 2012). Numerous genealogical guidebooks appeared, such as Donna Beasley, *Family Pride: The Complete Guide to Tracing African-American Genealogy* (New York: Macmillan, 1997). Genealogical communities formed on the internet as well, such as the Afrigeneas network at http://www.afrigeneas.com/ (accessed 18 January 2019).

79. Alondra Nelson, *The Social Life of DNA: Race, Reparations, and Reconciliation after the Genome* (Boston: Beacon Press, 2016); Keith Wailoo, Alondra Nelson, and Catherine Lee, eds., *Genetics and the Unsettled Past: The Collision of DNA, Race, and History* (New Brunswick: Rutgers University Press, 2012); Henry Louis Gates Jr., *In Search of Our Roots: How 19 Extraordinary African Americans Reclaimed Their Past* (New York: Crown, 2009); Michael Twitty, *The Cooking Gene: A Journey through African American Culinary History in the Old South* (New York: Amistad, 2017). One creative manifestation of the new

DNA also became the tool for overturning, or at least shaking, one of the longstanding public idols of (white) American history. Annette Gordon-Reed's meticulous research systematically refuted the many counterclaims that Thomas Jefferson's defenders mounted against the charge that he fathered multiple children with Sally Hemings. In 1998, Y-chromosome data evidenced that the third president and author of the Declaration of Independence repeatedly had fathered children with an enslaved woman, beginning when she was sixteen years old.[80] The revelations were part of a shift away from reflexive apologia for enslavers in the public history of slavery, symbolizing a greater willingness to confront the possibility that slavery was not a mere contradiction but a foundational feature of the American Republic.

Meanwhile, another history-writing phenomenon emerged: white retellings of family histories to incorporate (at least some) of the enslaved people's descendants. At best, such works revealed whites trying to make sense of once-revered ancestors who continuously committed acts of enormous violence and exploitation, and reconciling with descendants of the victims who had their own versions of that history.[81]

The early 2000s also saw revival of long-standing debates about reparations for enslavement. Especially after publication of Craig Steven Wilder's *Ebony and Ivy* (2013), new revelations of the deep histories of slave-ownership at and by historically white colleges and universities spilled over into public debates. Most dramatic, perhaps, was the (re)discovery of the fact that Georgetown University

---

interest in Black genealogy was Edda Fields-Black's "Casop: A Requiem for Rice," which incorporated the voices of enslaved ancestors in an orchestral arrangement that debuted in February 2019; see http://www.requiemforrice.com/ (accessed 18 January 2019).

80. Annette Gordon-Reed, *Thomas Jefferson and Sally Hemings: An American Controversy* (Charlottesville: University Press of Virginia, 1997); Joseph J. Ellis, "Jefferson: Post-DNA," *William and Mary Quarterly* 57 (January 2000): 125–38; Jan Lewis and Peter S. Onuf, eds., *Sally Hemings and Thomas Jefferson: History, Memory, and Civic Culture* (Charlottesville: University Press of Virginia, 1999); Gordon-Reed, *The Hemingses of Monticello: An American Family* (New York: W. W. Norton, 2008); Lucia C. Stanton, *"Those Who Labor for My Happiness": Slavery at Thomas Jefferson's Monticello* (Charlottesville: University of Virginia Press, 2012). Forrest McDonald and others who formed the Scholars Commission on the Jefferson-Hemings Matter continued to mount a rearguard action. See *The Jefferson-Hemings Controversy: Report of the Scholars Commission,* ed. Robert F. Turner (Durham: Carolina Academic Press, 2011).

81. Edward Ball, *Slaves in the Family* (New York: Farrar, Straus and Giroux, 1998); Henry Wiencek, *The Hairstons: An American Family in Black and White* (New York: St. Martin's Press, 1999). For a Black history that considers the white family, see Thulani Davis, *My Confederate Kinfolk: A Twenty-First Century Freedwoman Confronts Her Roots* (New York: Basic Civitas Books, 2006).

only staved off bankruptcy in the midst of the panics of 1837 and 1839 by selling 272 people enslaved by the Society of Jesus (the Jesuits). Still, as with other cases that uncovered institutional complicity in enslavement, reparative justice was more symbolic than actual: plaques were created, existing financial aid packages acquired new names.[82]

Each new call for reparations for slavery, whether by specific institutions or by the nation-state itself, sparked new discussions about slavery and its legacies.[83] The most well-known argument came from journalist Ta-Nehisi Coates in 2014, but historian John Hope Franklin had made a case during President Bill Clinton's Initiative on Race in the 1990s. Conservative gadfly David Horowitz generated debate about reparations for slavery on college campuses as an agent-provocateur in early 2001. And throughout the 2000s and 2010s, Black economists like William A. Darity Jr. and Darrick Hamilton championed the idea of reparations in both academic and public contexts.[84]

More Americans doubtless get their history from museums and historical sites than from scholarship or activism. And too many museums and historic sites remain out of date and distortive when it comes to the history of slavery. A study conducted in the late 1990s of almost two hundred southern "plantation historic sites" revealed that almost none substantively engaged with the extraction of slave labor. Enslaved people remained invisible, presented in racist contexts, or interpreted through apologetic language that indirectly or directly defended the enslavers.[85]

82. Craig Steven Wilder, *Ebony and Ivy: Race, Slavery, and the Troubled History of America's Universities* (New York: Bloomsbury Press, 2013); Rachel Swarns, "272 Slaves Were Sold to Save Georgetown: What Does it Owe Their Descendants," *New York Times*, 7 April 2016.

83. Berry, *My Face Is Black Is True;* Araujo, *Reparations for Slavery and the Slave Trade;* Martha Biondi, "The Rise of the Reparations Movement," *Radical History Review* 87 (October 2003): 5–18; Michael T. Martin and Marilyn Yaquinto, eds., *Redress for Historical Injustices in the United States: On Reparations for Slavery, Jim Crow, and Their Legacies* (Durham: Duke University Press, 2007); Ronald W. Walters, *The Price of Racial Reconciliation* (Ann Arbor: University of Michigan Press, 2008); Nelson, *The Social Life of DNA.*

84. Ta-Nehisi Coates, "The Case for Reparations," *The Atlantic,* 12 June 2014, https://www.theatlantic.com/magazine/archive/2014/06/the-case-for-reparations/361631/; William A. Darity Jr. and Dania Frank, "The Economics of Reparations," *American Economic Review* 93 (May 2003): 326–29; John Hope Franklin, *Mirror to America: The Autobiography of John Hope Franklin* (New York: Farrar, Straus and Giroux, 2005); Darrick Hamilton and William A. Darity Jr., "Can 'Baby Bonds' Eliminate the Racial Wealth Gap in Putative Post-Racial America?" *Review of Black Political Economy* 37 (2010): 207–16.

85. On public history interpretations of enslavement, see Jennifer L. Eichstedt and Stephen Small, *Representations of Slavery: Race and Ideology in Southern Plantation Museums* (Washington: Smithsonian

With growing success in the 2000s and 2010s, scholars, museum professionals, and Black visitors to historic sites challenged the standard model of slavery's public history, particularly the grip held by plantation romanticism. Workers at historic sites took to social media to inform a wider public of the everyday arguments over meaning and interpretation that pitted critical Black docents against defensive white visitors, or defensive white docents against critical Black visitors.[86] Parents pushed back against textbooks assigned to their children when slavery appeared veiled in sanitized terms. For instance, a mother went online to call out the racism of a middle-school textbook assigned in Texas public schools that referred to enslaved Africans as "immigrants."[87] Big-budget films like *12 Years A Slave* (2013) and short-form projects like Azie Mira Dungey's internet-based "Ask A Slave" series (2013–) refuted older white nationalist accounts.[88]

Institution Press, 2002); James Oliver Horton and Lois E. Horton, eds., *Slavery and Public History: The Tough Stuff of American Memory* (New York: New Press, 2006); Barbara Chase-Riboud, "Slavery as a Problem in Public History: Or Sally Hemmings and the 'One Drop Rule' of Public History," *Callaloo* 32 (Summer 2009): 826–31; Antoinette T. Jackson, *Speaking for the Enslaved: Heritage Interpretation at Antebellum Plantation Sites* (Walnut Creek, CA: Left Coast Press, 2012), 135–68; Kristin L. Gallas and James DeWolf Perry, eds., *Interpreting Slavery at Museums and Historic Sites* (Lanham, MD: Rowman & Littlefield, 2014); Max Van Balgooy, ed., *Interpreting African American History and Culture at Museums and Historic Sites* (Lanham, MD: Rowman & Littlefield, 2014); Julia Rose, *Interpreting Difficult History at Museums and Historical Sites* (Lanham, MD: Rowman & Littlefield, 2016); Ana Lucia Araujo, ed., *Politics of Memory: Making Slavery Visible in the Public Space* (New York: Routledge, 2012).

86. See some of the incidents reported at the Twitter feed @AfAmHistoryFail, or the controversies of reenactment at Colonial Williamsburg in which people tried to intervene and stop reenacted slave auctions. See also Gallas and Perry, *Interpreting Slavery at Museums and Historic Sites;* Horton and Horton, eds., *Slavery and Public History.*

87. Michael Shaub, "Texas Textbook Calling Slaves 'Immigrants' to be Changed, After Mom's Complaint," *Los Angeles Times,* 5 October 2015. A widely cited 2018 study commissioned by the Southern Poverty Law Center and advised by multiple historians, including Hasan Kwame Jeffries and David W. Blight, concluded: "Schools are not adequately teaching the history of American slavery. Educators are not sufficiently prepared to teach it. Textbooks do not have enough material about it." See Teaching the Hard History of American Slavery, https://www.splcenter.org/teaching-hard-history-american-slavery (accessed 18 January 2019).

88. Michael Rogin, "'The Sword Became a Flashing Vision': D. W. Griffith's *The Birth of a Nation,*" *Representations* 9 (Winter 1985): 150–95; *12 Years a Slave,* directed by Steve McQueen, screenplay by John Ridley (Twentieth-Century Fox, 2014); Azie Mira Dungey, "Ask A Slave," https://web.archive.org/web/20130911210333/http://dcist.com/2013/09/ask_an_actor_ask_a_slaves_azie_mira.php (accessed 18 January 2019). Dungey had worked for years as a docent at Mt. Vernon and drew in part on the often-bizarre questions asked by visitors.

In 2014, the Whitney Plantation slavery museum, an hour's drive west of New Orleans, opened to widespread publicity. Funded by a white real estate lawyer and directed by historian Ibrahima Seck, the site received acclaim as the first historic plantation to center on the experience of enslaved people. Other museums and sites moved in a similar direction. Not coincidentally, African American visitors to such sites increased. Heritage tourism—especially in Natchez, New Orleans, Mobile, Savannah, and the South Carolina Lowcountry (where Gullah and Geechee communities face both rampant cultural exploitation and the conversion of ancestral lands into golf courses)—remained deeply problematic. And yet something was undoubtedly shifting, a reality underlined at the core of the nation-state: after more than a decade of planning, the National Museum of African American History and Culture opened in September 2016 in Washington, DC, and did not shy away from describing the brutal violence and labor extractions of slavery in the United States. Attendance was unprecedented in the history of the Smithsonian.[89]

Despite the physical implantation of a Black historical narrative of slavery in the middle of the National Mall, debates about the history of slavery remained bitterly contested, accelerated as the #BlackLivesMatter movement amplified longstanding African American critiques of incarceration, policing, political disfranchisement, wealth distribution, and segregation: systems of power that grew out of slavery. By 2015, the struggle over meaning was fraught with the accelerating violence in American politics. When white terrorist Dylann Roof murdered eight members of Charleston's Emanuel African Methodist Episcopal Church (often called Mother Emanuel) on 17 June 2015, he was in part acting out a version of history in which Black people (such as Denmark Vesey, a founder of Mother Emanuel who was executed in 1822 for plotting a rebellion against slavery) were criminals who could only be contained by systems of violent repression.[90]

89. David Amsdem, "Building the First Slavery Museum in America," *New York Times Magazine,* 25 February 2015; Ibrahima Seck, *Bouki Fait Gombo: A History of the Slave Community of Haydel Habitation (Whitney Plantation), Louisiana, 1750–1860* (New Orleans: University of New Orleans Press, 2014); Melissa L. Cooper, *Making Gullah: A History of Sapelo Islanders, Race, and the American Imagination* (Chapel Hill: University of North Carolina Press, 2017); Joanne Pope Melish, Marcia Chatelain, and Hasan Kwame Jeffries, review of Smithsonian National Museum of African American History and Culture, Washington, DC, *Journal of American History* 104 (June 2017): 145–61.

90. W. Fitzhugh Brundage, *The Southern Past: A Clash of Race and Memory* (Cambridge: Harvard University Press, 2005); Rachel Kaadzi Ghansah, "Dylann Roof: The Making of An American Terrorist,"

In the days after Roof committed mass murder, Black activist Bree Newsome climbed the "compromise" flagpole at the South Carolina State House and tore down the Confederate battle flag. Around the South and the United States more broadly, an offensive against the public altars of the slavery regime grew. After a bruising public battle, the New Orleans city government took down the city's monument to Confederate General Robert E. Lee, while Baltimore removed its proslavery statues after most residents had gone to bed. In Lexington, Kentucky, two statues were removed to a local cemetery in the middle of the night after months of agitation by a local activist group named Take Back Cheapside. Lexington's mayor also oversaw the restoration of a plaque commemorating Cheapside as the city's once bustling slave market, just steps from where the statues once stood. But when Memphis attempted to tear down its statue of slave trader, war criminal, traitor, KKK founder and murderer Nathan Bedford Forrest, the Tennessee state government passed a law preventing the removal. North Carolina did the same thing. In Charlottesville, Virginia, in August 2017, white supremacists marched—equipped with tiki torches and shouting fascist "Blood and Soil" chants—in a Unite the Right rally to "protect" a statue of Lee. The next day, they touched off battles all over the city, and rally participant James Fields murdered counter-protester Heather Heyer, injuring nine additional people by plowing his car through a crowd of people.[91]

Dominant American cultural formations once presented an anodyne account of the enslavement of four million African Americans, an account wrapped up in (but hardly hidden by) the worshipful public idolatry of the Confederacy. Scholars who critique the distorted view of the past in both the historiography and in public spaces work in hopes of dispelling slavery's many long shadows. Activists, meanwhile, use that revised historiography to make history: to shape the present and the future. One such gathering of activists—students of slavery's

---

GQ, 21 August 2017. For a response to the Emanuel AME shootings, see Chad Williams, Kidada E. Williams, and Keisha N. Blain, *Charleston Syllabus: Readings of Race, Racism, and Racial Violence* (Athens: University of Georgia Press, 2016).

91. "Lexington Council Unanimous in Wanting Confederate Statues Relocated," *Lexington Herald-Leader*, 15 August 2017; Morgan Eads and Karla Ward, "In a Surprise Move, Lexington Removes Controversial Confederate Statues," *Lexington Herald-Leader*, 17 October 2017; Jonathan M. Katz and Farah Stockman, "James Fields Guilty of First-Degree Murder in Death of Heather Heyer," *New York Times*, 8 December 2018. See also Hawes Spencer, *Summer of Hate: Charlottesville, USA* (Charlottesville: University of Virginia Press, 2018); Louis P. Nelson and Claudrena N. Harold, eds., *Charlottesville 2017: The Legacy of Race and Inequity* (Charlottesville: University of Virginia Press, 2018).

long shadow on the southern past and present—gathered outside the courthouse in Durham, North Carolina, a few days after the white supremacists had run wild in Charlottesville. The crowd—students from North Carolina Central University, local community members, and students at local historically white colleges and universities—surrounded a statue of a Confederate soldier, the base of which was inscribed with the words "In Memory of the Boys Who Wore the Gray." They scratched "Death to the Klan" over the inscription. The people then attached tow straps to the statue and pulled it to the ground. As the crowd cheered and danced in joy, some took pictures of the fallen idol: a once-proud shrine of historical interpretations that sanitized theft, rape, and murder. The soldier's surprisingly thin metal twisted and crumpled. The statue, the whole world could now see, was hollow.[92]

92. "Commemorative Landscapes of North Carolina," 19 March 2010, https://docsouth.unc.edu/commland/monument/118/ (accessed 18 January 2019); David Graham, "How the Activists Who Tore Down Durham's Confederate Statue Got Away with It," *The Atlantic,* 21 February 2018, https://www.theatlantic.com/politics/archive/2018/02/durham-confederate-monument-charges-dismissed/553808/.

GENDER AND SEXUALITY IN THE OLD SOUTH

Catherine Clinton and Emily West

Perhaps no field in southern history has been more fluid and dynamic than that of gender studies, and scholarship on women, masculinity, and sexuality in the antebellum South continues to expand exponentially and intersect in revealing ways. Since the publication of *Interpreting Southern History* in 1985, southern women's historiography benefited greatly from field-defining books such as Sally G. McMillen's *Southern Women* (1992), Margaret Ripley Wolfe's *Daughters of Canaan* (1995), and Jacqueline Jones's *Labor of Love, Labor of Sorrow* (1985). The University of Georgia Press has published nearly twenty indispensable volumes in its ongoing Southern Women series.[1] In the 2000s and 2010s, innovative collections such as Susanna Delfino and Michele Gillespie's *Neither Lady nor Slave* (2002), Jennifer Brier, Jim Downs, and Jennifer L. Morgan's *Connexions* (2016), and Daina Ramey Berry and Leslie M. Harris's *Sexuality and Slavery* (2018) illuminated the intersectionality of gender, class, race, and sexuality.[2]

1. Sally G. McMillen, *Southern Women: Black and White in the Old South* (Arlington Heights, IL: Harlan Davidson, 1992); Margaret Ripley Wolfe, *Daughters of Canaan: A Saga of Southern Women* (Lexington: University Press of Kentucky, 1995); Jacqueline Jones, *Labor of Love, Labor of Sorrow: Black Women, Work and the Family, from Slavery to the Present* (New York: Basic Books, 1985). For details of the Southern Women series, see https://ugapress.org/series/southern-women-their-lives-and-times/ (accessed 18 January 2019).

2. Susanna Delfino and Michele Gillespie, eds., *Neither Lady nor Slave: Working Women of the Old South* (Chapel Hill: University of North Carolina Press, 2002); Jennifer Brier, Jim Downs, and Jennifer L. Morgan, eds., *Connexions: Histories of Race and Sex in North America* (Urbana: University of Illinois Press, 2016); Daina Ramey Berry and Leslie M. Harris, eds., *Sexuality and Slavery: Reclaiming Intimate Histories in the Americas* (Athens: University of Georgia Press, 2018).

Southern masculinities as well as examinations of same-sex desire moved southern sexuality studies by leaps and bounds.[3]

Treatment of southern women within American history, southern history, or women's history is no longer divided simply by binary categorization: black or white, enslaved or free, urban or rural. The trinitarian principle of "sex, race, and class" morphed over time into a framing which also considered "gender, color, and status." But these trends began with the revolutionizing intervention of feminist scholarship in women's history and in southern history in particular. Scholars then developed depth and nuance, making intersectionality a driving force within the twenty-first-century academy.[4]

Despite these impressive strides, much work remains to be done on understudied aspects of southern gender history. Scholars have only begun to explore gender and sexuality in the Native South. Valuable early work, including James Axtell's *The Indian People of Eastern America* (1981) and Nancy Shoemaker's *Negotiators of Change* (1995), laid the foundation for important developments since the 1980s and 1990s.[5] Theda Perdue produced a body of work that seeded and cultivated American Indian women's history in the South, including *Cherokee Women* (1998) and *Sifters* (2001). Perdue's portfolio in the field of Native American studies is vast, but her impact in southern women's history is significant as a mentor and champion for those who followed.[6] Some scholars undertook the heavy lifting to reveal gendered intersections between Indians and African Amer-

3. See Craig Thompson Friend and Lorri Glover, eds., *Southern Manhood: Perspectives on Masculinity in the Old South* (Athens: University of Georgia Press, 2004); David Stefan Doddington, *Contesting Slave Masculinity in the American South* (New York: Cambridge University Press, 2018); Jim Downs, "With Only a Trace: Same-Sex Sexual Desire and Violence on Slave Plantations, 1607–1865," in Brier, Downs, and Morgan, eds., *Connexions*, 15–37; Aliyyah Abdur-Rahman, "'The Strangest Freaks of Despotism': Queer Sexuality in Antebellum African American Slave Narratives," *African American Review* 40 (Summer 2006): 223–37.

4. Kimberle Crenshaw coined the term "intersectionality" in the 1980s; see "Demarginalizing the Intersection of Race and Sex: A Black Feminist Critique of Antidiscrimination Doctrine, Feminist Theory and Antiracist Politics," *University of Chicago Legal Forum* 140 (1989): 139–67.

5. James Axtell, ed., *The Indian People of Eastern America: A Documentary History of the Sexes* (New York: Oxford University Press, 1981); Nancy Shoemaker, ed., *Negotiators of Change: Historical Perspectives on Native American Women* (New York: Routledge, 1995). See also Juliana Barr, "From Captives to Slaves: Commodifying Indian Women in the Borderlands," *Journal of American History* 92 (June 2005): 19–46.

6. Theda Perdue, *Cherokee Women: Gender and Cultural Change, 1700–1835* (Lincoln: University of Nebraska Press, 1998); Perdue, *Sifters: Native American Women's Lives* (New York: Oxford University Press, 2001). See also Carolyn Ross Johnston, *Cherokee Women in Crisis: Trail of Tears, Civil War, and Allotment, 1838–1907* (Tuscaloosa: University of Alabama Press, 2003); Rose Stremlau, *Sustaining the*

icans, enslaved and free, including Barbara Krauthamer in *Black Slaves, Indian Masters* (2013). Tiya Miles also explored these complex questions in *Ties That Bind* (2005) and *The House on Diamond Hill* (2010).[7]

The gendered influence of French and Spanish culture on southern settlements, though also understudied, has been evident in signal works including Jane G. Landers's *Black Society in Spanish Florida* (1999), Juliana Barr's *Peace Came in the Form of a Woman* (2007), Jennifer M. Spear's *Race, Sex, and Social Order in Early New Orleans* (2009), and Emily Clark's *The Strange History of the American Quadroon* (2013).[8] Each of these scholars pushed early southern women's history to be more inclusive and more diverse. A new generation of innovative scholars, including Emily Clark and Marise Bachand, blurred and reconfigured the boundaries of gender, ethnicity, and culture.[9]

Historians studying the Native, French, and Spanish Souths offer a collective reminder of the need to interrogate chronological and geographical frameworks. Approaching southern women's history from the sixteenth and seventeenth centuries looking forward and/or from the West looking eastward, these scholars reorient perceptions of the early South. Old South historians owe other interpretive and methodological debts to early Americanists. For example, during

Cherokee Family: Kinship and the Allotment of an Indigenous Nation (Chapel Hill: University of North Carolina Press, 2011); Julie L. Reed, *Serving the Nation: Cherokee Sovereignty and Social Welfare, 1800–1907* (Norman: University of Oklahoma Press, 2016).

7. Barbara Krauthamer, *Black Slaves, Indian Masters: Slavery, Emancipation, and Citizenship in the Native American South* (Chapel Hill: University of North Carolina Press, 2013); Tiya Miles, *The House on Diamond Hill: A Cherokee Plantation Story* (Chapel Hill: University of North Carolina Press, 2010); Miles, *Ties That Bind: The Story of an Afro-Cherokee Family in Slavery and Freedom* (Berkeley: University of California Press, 2005). See also Kenneth Wiggins Porter, *Black Seminoles: History of a Freedom Seeking People,* rev. and ed. Alicone M. Amos and Thomas P. Senter (Gainesville: University Press of Florida, 2013); Shirley Boteler Mock, *Dreaming with the Ancestors: Black Seminole Women in Texas and Mexico* (Norman: University of Oklahoma Press, 2010).

8. Jane G. Landers, *Black Society in Spanish Florida* (Urbana: University of Illinois Press, 1999); Juliana Barr, *Peace Came in the Form of a Woman: Indians and Spaniards in the Texas Borderlands* (Chapel Hill: University of North Carolina Press, 2007); Jennifer M. Spear, *Race, Sex, and Social Order in Early New Orleans* (Baltimore: Johns Hopkins University Press, 2009); Emily Clark, *The Strange History of the American Quadroon: Free Women of Color in the Revolutionary Atlantic World* (Chapel Hill: University of North Carolina Press, 2013).

9. Marise Bachand, "Disunited Daughters of the Confederations: Creoles and Canadians at the Intersection of Nations, States, and Empires," *Journal of the Civil War Era* 7 (December 2017): 541–69; Emily Clark, *Masterless Mistresses: The New Orleans Ursulines and the Development of a New World Society, 1727–1834* (Chapel Hill: University of North Carolina Press, 2007).

the 1970s, a cohort of Chesapeake scholars, particularly Lorena Walsh and Lois Green Carr, made women count both literally and figuratively. In the 1990s and early 2000s, Jennifer L. Morgan and other Atlantic-focused historians generated original perspectives and posed new methodological questions about gendered and racial dynamics of Anglo-American settlements. Other scholars interrogated gender within the transition of southern colonies into states.[10]

All of this is to say that southern women's history is dynamic and well represented in southern historiography. The greatest transformation in southern gender history, however, has been the dramatic expansion of work on women of color, primarily enslaved and free black women of African descent, a turn in the literature that resulted in a fresh and enthusiastic burst of interest in both slavery studies and emancipationist frameworks to examine how gender and enslavement shaped southerners during the decades leading up to the Civil War.

Scholars used to conclude that insufficient evidence survived from the era of slavery to recover black women's lives. To be certain, archival silences bind gender history across eras and geographies. Such silences have become topics of consideration themselves, including Saidiya V. Hartman's *Scenes of Subjection* (1997) and Marissa J. Fuentes's *Dispossessed Lives* (2016). Still, despite the obstacles to researching their lives in the southern colonies and the larger Atlantic World,

10. Lois Green Carr and Lorena S. Walsh, "The Planter's Wife: The Experience of White Women in Seventeenth-Century Maryland," *William and Mary Quarterly* 34 (October 1977): 542–71; Jennifer L. Morgan, *Laboring Women: Reproduction and Gender in New World Slavery* (Philadelphia: University of Pennsylvania Press, 2004). Other influential works include Kathleen M. Brown, *Good Wives, Nasty Wenches, and Anxious Patriarchs: Gender, Race and Power in Colonial Virginia* (Chapel Hill: University of North Carolina Press, 1996); Catherine Clinton and Michele Gillespie, eds., *The Devil's Lane: Sex and Race in the Early South* (New York: Oxford University Press, 1997); Kirsten Fischer, *Suspect Relations: Sex, Race, and Resistance in Colonial North Carolina* (Ithaca: Cornell University Press, 2002); Laura F. Edwards, *The People and Their Peace: Legal Culture and the Transformation of Inequality in the Post-Revolutionary South* (Chapel Hill: University of North Carolina Press, 2009); Cynthia A. Kierner, *Scandal at Bizarre: Rumor and Reputation in Jefferson's America* (New York: Palgrave Macmillan, 2004); Kierner, *Beyond the Household: Women's Place in the Early South, 1700–1835* (Ithaca: Cornell University Press, 1998); Catherine Kerrison, *Claiming the Pen: Women and Intellectual Life in the Early American South* (Ithaca: Cornell University Press, 2006); Jon Kukla, *Mr. Jefferson's Women* (New York: Alfred A. Knopf, 2007); Ben Marsh, *Georgia's Frontier Women: Female Fortunes in a Southern Colony* (Athens: University of Georgia Press, 2007); John F. Sensbach, *Rebecca's Revival: Creating Black Christianity in the Atlantic World* (Cambridge: Harvard University Press, 2005); Terri L. Snyder, *Brabbling Women: Disorderly Speech and the Law in Early Virginia* (Ithaca: Cornell University Press, 2003). See also Cynthia A. Kierner's historiographical overview, "Women, Gender, Families, and Households in the Southern Colonies," *Journal of Southern History* 73 (August 2007): 643–58.

enslaved and free black women became more visible between the 1980s and the 2010s through richly textured, deep, and nuanced analyses. Scholars explored a creative range of primary evidence, including published autobiographies written by enslaved and formerly enslaved women, and Works Progress Administration (WPA) interviews that took place in the 1930s. Historians read sources against the grain and sometimes, as advocated by Stephanie M. H. Camp, introduced a bit of speculation, empathy, and imagination to shed light on the multiplicity of experiences, especially those of enslaved southern women.[11] A group of scholars undertook, and overcame, the challenge of writing biographies of black women, highlighted by Jean Fagan Yellin's *Harriet Jacobs* (2004) and Erica Armstrong Dunbar's *Never Caught* (2017).[12]

The flourishing of enslaved African American women's history originated in the 1970s and 1980s. Angela Davis penned her key article, "Reflections on the Black Woman's Role in the Community of Slaves" (1971), from a prison cell, and she systematically demolished the conventional narrative of enslaved women as domineering matriarchs independent of emasculated men. The "myth of matriarchy," she wrote, negated the multiple burdens placed upon enslaved women as women, as blacks, and as slaves. Davis also inspired historians to think differently about the sexual abuse inflicted upon enslaved women. Instead of being isolated incidents, sexual violence was used by white men as "institutional terrorism" to

11. Saidiya V. Hartman, *Scenes of Subjection: Terror, Slavery and Self-Making in Nineteenth Century America* (New York: Oxford University Press, 1997); Marisa J. Fuentes, *Dispossessed Lives: Enslaved Women, Violence and the Archive* (Philadelphia: University of Pennsylvania Press, 2016); Stephanie M. H. Camp, *Closer to Freedom: Enslaved Women and Everyday Resistance in the Plantation South* (Chapel Hill: University of North Carolina Press, 2004).

12. Interest in black women's biography flourished between the 1990s and the 2010s. Jean Fagan Yellin, *Harriet Jacobs: A Life* (New York: Basic Books, 2004); Erica Armstrong Dunbar, *Never Caught: The Washingtons' Relentless Pursuit of Their Runaway Slave, Ona Judge* (New York: Atria, 2017); Melton McLaurin, *Celia: A Slave* (Athens: University of Georgia Press, 1991); Sydney Nathans, *To Free a Family: The Journey of Mary Walker* (Cambridge: Harvard University Press, 2012); Catherine Clinton, *Harriet Tubman: The Road to Freedom* (New York: Little, Brown, 2004); Kate Clifford Larson, *Bound for the Promised Land: Harriet Tubman: Portrait of an American Hero* (New York: Ballantine Books, 2004); Jean M. Humez, *Harriet Tubman: The Life and the Life Stories* (Madison: University of Wisconsin Press, 2004); Beverly Lowry, *Harriet Tubman: Imagining a Life* (New York: Doubleday, 2007); Milton C. Sernett, *Harriet Tubman: Myth, Memory and History* (Durham: Duke University Press, 2007); Lois E. Horton, *Harriet Tubman and the Fight for Freedom: A Brief History with Documents* (New York: Bedford Books, 2013); Jacqueline Bernard, *Journey Toward Freedom: The Story of Sojourner Truth* (New York: W. W. Norton, 1996); Nell Irvin Painter, *Sojourner Truth: A Life, a Symbol* (New York: W. W. Norton, 1996); Margaret Washington, *Sojourner Truth's America* (Urbana: University of Illinois Press, 2009).

subjugate women. Deborah Gray White later picked up on this theme of sexual violence in her book, *Ar'n't I a Woman?* (1985), the first monograph to explore the lives of enslaved women in the Old South. Along with Elizabeth Fox-Genovese, White exposed how slaveholding men and women created and internalized sexualized stereotypes of enslaved women and men (including Jezebel, Sambo, Mammy, and Buck) to justify sexual violence specifically and slaveholding generally.[13]

Systematic sexual abuse of enslaved women by white men has been well documented by historians even though the topic can be methodologically challenging. For example, in the 1980s, Darlene Clark Hine persuasively argued women's "culture of dissemblance" understandably prevented them from being totally candid when discussing men's sexual violence towards them. Nell Irvin Painter powerfully described the psychological impact of such prevalent violence as "soul murder." And historians worked to expand the evidence and the analysis. By the 2010s, Wilma King and Brenda E. Stevenson each successfully highlighted the fact that younger girls, too, faced soul murder as victims of sexual violence, mostly at the hands of white men but occasionally from enslaved men as well.[14]

Public discussions about white men possessing black women's bodies flared with particular ferocity in the 1970s when Fawn M. Brodie wrote about Thomas Jefferson and Sally Hemings, and again in the 1990s when Annette Gordon-Reed returned the topic to scholarly prominence. The controversy over the nature of Jefferson and Hemings's relationship produced an outpouring of scholarly debate that culminated with Gordon-Reed's *The Hemingses of Monticello* (2008).[15]

13. Angela Davis, "Reflections on the Black Woman's Role in the Community of Slaves," *Massachusetts Review* 13 (Winter/Spring 1972): 81–100; Deborah Gray White, *Ar'n't I a Woman? Female Slaves in the Plantation South* (New York: W. W. Norton, 1985); Elizabeth Fox-Genovese, *Within the Plantation Household: Black and White Women of the Old South* (Chapel Hill: University of North Carolina Press, 1988).

14. Nell Irvin Painter, *Soul Murder and Slavery* (Waco: Baylor University Press, 1995); Darlene Clark Hine, "Rape and the Inner Lives of Black Women in the Middle West: Preliminary Thoughts on the Culture of Dissemblance," *Signs* 14 (Summer 1989): 912–20; Wilma King, "'Prematurely Knowing of Evil Things': The Sexual Abuse of African American Girls and Young Women in Slavery and Freedom," *Journal of African American History* 99 (Summer 2014): 173–96; Brenda E. Stevenson, "What's Love Got to Do with It? Concubinage and Enslaved Black Women and Girls in the Antebellum South," *Journal of African American History* 98 (Winter 2013): 99–125.

15. Fawn M. Brodie, *Thomas Jefferson: An Intimate History* (New York: W. W. Norton, 1974); Annette Gordon-Reed, *Thomas Jefferson and Sally Hemings: An American Controversy* (Charlottesville: University Press of Virginia, 1997); Gordon-Reed, *The Hemingses of Monticello: An American Family* (New York: W. W. Norton, 2008). See also Douglass Adair, "The Jefferson Scandals," in *Fame and the Founding Fathers,*

The flurry of scholarship on enslaved women's bodies inspired scholars, including Martha Hodes, to reconsider how white women's bodies might be recast within the Old South's patriarchal chess game. Black women forced into interracial sex often were placed upon the auction block; white women discovered in interracial relationships teetered on the pedestal. Often misperceived as "queens," white women occasionally engaged in interracial liaisons with black men, relationships purposefully hidden in records from the era and largely avoided by the white male historians of the mid- to late twentieth century. Diane Miller Sommerville's work on sexual violence, *Rape and Race in the Nineteenth-Century South* (2004), tackled many of the myths associated with white women and black men, examining 250 slave rape cases primarily from Virginia and North Carolina. Her work charted conflicts from the antebellum era through the end of the nineteenth century generated by patriarchal priorities.[16]

Historians understand that forced sex was more than sexual and more than violent: white men sexually assaulted enslaved women as an expression of patriarchal power *and* because they often saw enslaved women as mere possessions who

---

ed. Trevor Colbourn (New York: W. W. Norton, 1974), 160–91; Dumas Malone and Steven H. Hochman, "A Note on Evidence: The Personal History of Madison Hemings," *Journal of Southern History* 41 (November 1975): 523–28; Virginius Dabney and Jon Kukla, "The Monticello Scandals: History and Fiction," *Virginia Cavalcade* 29 (Autumn 1979): 52–61; Scot A. French and Edward L. Ayers, "The Strange Career of Thomas Jefferson: Race and Slavery in American Memory, 1943–1993," in *Jeffersonian Legacies*, ed. Peter S. Onuf (Charlottesville: University Press of Virginia, 1993), 418–56; Roger W. Wilkins, *Jefferson's Pillow: The Founding Fathers and the Dilemma of Black Patriotism* (Boston: Beacon Press, 2001); Jan Ellen Lewis and Peter S. Onuf, eds., *Sally Hemings and Thomas Jefferson: History, Memory, and Civic Culture* (Charlottesville: University Press of Virginia, 1999). For the descendants of Jefferson, see also Cynthia A. Kierner, *Martha Jefferson Randolph, Daughter of Monticello: Her Life and Times* (Chapel Hill: University of North Carolina Press, 2012); Catherine Kerrison, *Jefferson's Daughters: Three Sisters, White and Black, in a Young America* (New York: Ballentine Books, 2018).

16. Martha Elizabeth Hodes, *White Women, Black Men: Illicit Sex in the Nineteenth-Century South* (New Haven: Yale University Press, 1997); Victoria E. Bynum: *Unruly Women: The Politics of Social and Sexual Control in the Old South* (Chapel Hill: University of North Carolina Press, 1992); Joshua D. Rothman, *Notorious in the Neighborhood: Sex and Families across the Color Line in Virginia, 1787–1861* (Chapel Hill: University of North Carolina Press, 2003); Sharon Block, *Rape and Sexual Power in Early America* (Chapel Hill: University of North Carolina Press, 2006); Diane Miller Sommerville, *Rape and Race in the Nineteenth-Century South* (Chapel Hill: University of North Carolina Press, 2004). See also Catherine Clinton, "'With a Whip in His Hand': Rape, Memory and African American Women," in *History and Memory in African American Culture*, ed. Genevieve Fabre and Robert O'Meally (New York: Oxford University Press, 1994), 205–18; Crystal N. Feimster, *Southern Horrors: Women and the Politics of Rape and Lynching* (Cambridge: Harvard University Press, 2009).

might also bear them more valuable children if they became pregnant. The idea that enslaved women embodied value as laborers and as reproducers underlay Jennifer L. Morgan's pathbreaking *Laboring Women* (2004), and her article on the evolution of the law of *partus sequitur ventrem* (which rendered the offspring of enslaved women as enslaved themselves). The closing of the international slave trade in 1808 burdened enslaved women further as it cut off the importation of slave labor, leaving natural increase and a growing domestic trade as the main ways in which enslavers made money through selling humans.[17]

Antebellum slaveholders wanted—after 1808, needed—the women whom they enslaved to bear a maximum number of children at minimal cost, and they encouraged procreation in various ways. Some permitted flexible marriages. Others manipulated or forced enslaved women to bear children with men selected by the enslavers. Although Gregory D. Smithers showed how the alleged existence of systematic "stud farms" in the Old South was an abolitionist trope, slaveholders certainly sought to influence the "breeding" of their chattel through enticements and/or punishments. Indeed, the birthrate within enslaved communities boomed during the antebellum era, creating an expanding slave population (and profits) through natural increase.[18]

Historians have grown increasingly attentive to ways in which geography also shaped black women's lives in the domestic slave trade that gained momentum after 1808. Enforced separation, whether local in scope or as part of the westward movement of slavery (and the United States), separated wives from husbands and parents from children. Michael Tadman estimated the long-distance domestic trade broke up one in three enslaved marriages and separated one-fifth of children from their parents, while Emily West described the consequences of separations upon enslaved people in cross-plantation marriages. On a more personal level, Heather Andrea Williams explored the desperate attempts of formerly enslaved people to find family members after the Civil War. Edward E. Baptist showed how the exploitation of people within the domestic slave trade was both

17. Morgan, *Laboring Women;* Morgan, "*Partus sequitur ventrem:* Law, Race, and Reproduction in Colonial Slavery," *Small Axe* 22 (March 2018): 1–17; Diana Paton and Pamela Scully, eds., *Gender and Slave Emancipation in the Atlantic World* (Durham: Duke University Press, 2005).

18. Morgan, "*Partus sequitur ventrem*"; Gregory D. Smithers, *Slave Breeding: Sex, Violence and Memory in African American History* (Gainesville: University Press of Florida, 2012); Emily West, "Reflections on the History and Historians of the Black Woman's Role in the Community of Slaves: Enslaved Women and Intimate Partner Violence," *American Nineteenth-Century History* 19 (January 2018): 1–21.

gendered and multifaceted (for example, when women were frequently sold as "fetishized commodities" for the sexual whims of white men).[19]

The commodification of enslaved people's bodies foregrounds innovative works by Daina Ramey Berry and Stephanie Jones-Rogers. In *The Price for Their Pound of Flesh* (2017), Berry tracked ways in which slaveholders maximized profits from enslaved people, from the womb through death (for example, by trading in cadavers). More narrowly focused, Jones-Rogers described the creation of informal markets for enslaved women's breast milk across the South, milk that was often denied to their own infants.[20]

Historians also explored the intersection of labor and gender to better understand day-to-day experiences of enslaved women. Even when they had to "work like a man," according to Daina Ramey Berry, most women preferred the boring and repetitive labor of the fields to laboring in enslavers' residences. As Jean Fagan Yellin elaborated, in the plantation houses, black girls and women risked sexual assault at the hands of white men. Field labor situated women to form relationships with each other. Larry Hudson elaborated that in the South Carolina and Georgia Lowcountry, where slaveholders tended to use a task system, women undertook other chores after completing their assigned work, spending a considerable amount of time with each other in systems of mutual support. Stephanie M. H. Camp used the idea of "rival geographies" to show how enslaved women creatively used plantation spaces in ways at odds with the ambitions of slave-owners. Women's roles made them less likely than men to leave plantations, so their resistance to enslavement operated at a day-to-day level, often through temporarily absconding rather than seeking to run away.[21]

19. Michael Tadman, *Speculators and Slaves: Masters, Traders and Slaves in the Old South* (Madison: University of Wisconsin Press, 1989); Emily West, "Masters and Marriages, Profits and Paternalism: Slave Owners' Perspectives on Cross-Plantation Unions in Antebellum South Carolina," *Slavery & Abolition* 21 (April 2000): 56–72; Heather Andrea Williams, *Help Me to Find My People: The African American Search for Family Lost in Slavery* (Chapel Hill: University of North Carolina Press, 2012); Edward E. Baptist, *The Half Has Never Been Told: Slavery and the Making of American Capitalism* (New York: Basic Books, 2014).

20. Daina Ramey Berry, *The Price for Their Pound of Flesh: The Value of The Enslaved, from Womb to Grave, in the Building of A Nation* (Boston: Beacon Press, 2017); Stephanie Jones-Rogers, "'[S]he could . . . spare one ample breast for the profit of her owner': White Mothers and Enslaved Wet Nurses' Invisible Labor in American Slave Markets," *Slavery & Abolition* 38 (June 2017): 337–55.

21. Yellin, *Harriet Jacobs;* Daina Ramey Berry, *"Swing the Sickle for the Harvest Is Ripe": Gender and Slavery in Antebellum Georgia* (Urbana: University of Illinois Press, 2007); Larry E. Hudson, *To Have and to Hold: Slave Work and Family Life in Antebellum South Carolina* (Athens: University of Georgia Press, 1997); White, *Ar'n't I a Woman?;* Camp, *Closer to Freedom.* See also Emily West and Erin Shearer,

Other scholars used histories of science and medicine to enrich understanding of enslaved women's lives, particularly motherhood. Liese Perrin studied enslaved women's "scientific" attempts to control their fertility. By chewing cotton roots, she argued, women consumed gossypol (a toxic, crystalline compound) that they believed provided a potentially effective contraception. In this manner, black women resisted white men's power. Still, sustained high birth rates also suggest that the practice was unsuccessful or sporadically used. More commonly, enslaved women tried to avoid situations where sexual violence might occur, although fighting off sexual attackers was often futile. Andrea Livesey argued that, although it would not have been surprising to have seen both mothers and enslaved communities ostracize children conceived through rape, the children were fully loved and supported.[22]

Some historians explored ways in which white men described and used enslaved motherhood. Jenifer L. Barclay showed how women who did not have children and those who bore children with congenital disabilities often faced racist stereotypes about black women's lasciviousness and immorality. In *Medical Bondage* (2017), Deirdre Cooper Owens uncovered how white men often exploited enslaved women's reproductive capacities through medical experiments conducted by ambitious and self-styled "scientific" gynecologists. Nora Doyle's *Maternal Bodies* (2018) highlighted the disjuncture between the lived experience of motherhood, especially for enslaved women, and society's increasing veneration of mothers' emotional and spiritual roles. More broadly, Sarah Knott examined the labor of motherhood in multiple contexts across time and space, including enslaved, Native American, and white women in the Old South.[23]

"Fertility Control, Shared Nurturing, and Dual Exploitation: The Lives of Enslaved Mothers in the Antebellum United States," *Women's History Review* 27 (September 2018): 1006–20; Leslie A. Schwalm, *A Hard Fight for We: Women's Transition from Slavery to Freedom in South Carolina* (Urbana: University of Illinois Press, 1997). For the emergence and cultural differences of the task versus the gang labor system in the eighteenth century, see Philip D. Morgan, *Slave Counterpoint: Black Culture in the Eighteenth-Century Chesapeake and Lowcountry* (Chapel Hill: University of North Carolina Press, 1998).

22. Liese Perrin, "Resisting Reproduction: Reconsidering Contraception in the Old South," *Journal of American Studies* 35 (August 2001): 255–74; Andrea Livesey, "Conceived in Violence: Enslaved Mothers and Children Born of Rape in Nineteenth-Century Louisiana," *Slavery & Abolition* 38 (April 2017): 373–91.

23. Jenifer L. Barclay, "Bad Breeders and Monstrosities: Racializing Childlessness and Congenital Disabilities in Slavery and Freedom," *Slavery & Abolition* 38 (April 2017): 287–302; Deirdre Cooper Owens, *Medical Bondage: Race, Gender and the Origins of American Gynecology* (Athens: University of Georgia Press, 2017); Nora Doyle, *Maternal Bodies: Redefining Motherhood in Early America* (Chapel Hill:

Other scholars, including Wilma King and Marie Jenkins Schwartz, adopted a life-cycle analysis to understand enslaved women and their families. King's *Stolen Childhood* (1995) argued that childhood, at least with its modern connotations of nurture, play, and innocence, did not exist under slavery, but enslaved parents still tried to make childhood a special time. In *Born in Bondage* (2000), Schwartz traced the lives of enslaved children from birth through marriage. In her follow-up *Birthing a Slave* (2006), Schwartz focused on the struggles of enslaved women to fend off interference from medical doctors. Like Schwartz, Sharla M. Fett highlighted tensions between enslaved women's views of health and healing and those of enslavers. Richard Follett's work on enslaved women exposed how the arduous labor of Louisiana's sugar regime actually resulted in a natural decrease of children born into enslavement. Women struggled to conceive, maintain their pregnancies, bear children, and ensure their survival. In a wonderfully conceptualized collection of primary sources, Steven Mintz employed the concept of a life cycle to depict the collective lives of enslaved people from capture in Africa through the middle passage, enslavement, war, and emancipation.[24]

All of these works speak to the centrality of family to understanding black women's experiences in the antebellum South. Herbert G. Gutman's pioneering work in the 1970s emphasized consolidated families where husbands and wives lived together in nuclear households. Between the 1990s and the 2010s, a new generation of scholars challenged Gutman and other earlier historians of slave family life. Ann Patton Malone's analysis of rural Louisiana revealed that less than half of enslaved people lived in two-parent nuclear households. In *Life in Black and White* (1996), Brenda E. Stevenson likewise stressed the significance of single parent and "abroad" families in Loudoun County, Virginia. Emily West's work on South Carolina emphasized how attempts to initiate and maintain their own personal relationships demonstrated African Americans' resilience and strength in

University of North Carolina Press, 2018); Sarah Knott, *Mother Is a Verb: An Unconventional History* (New York: Farrar, Straus and Giroux, 2019).

24. Wilma King, *Stolen Childhood: Slave Youth in Nineteenth-Century America* (Bloomington: Indiana University Press, 1995); Marie Jenkins Schwartz, *Born in Bondage: Growing up Enslaved in the Antebellum South* (Cambridge: Harvard University Press, 2000); Schwartz, *Birthing a Slave: Motherhood and Medicine in the Antebellum South* (Cambridge: Harvard University Press, 2006); Sharla M. Fett, *Working Cures: Healing, Health and Power on Southern Slave Plantations* (Chapel Hill: University of North Carolina Press, 2002); Richard Follett, "Heat, Sex, and Sugar: Pregnancy and Childbearing in the Slave Quarters," *Journal of Family History* 28 (October 2003): 510–39; Steven Mintz, ed., *African-American Voices: The Life Cycle of Slavery*, 4th ed. (New York: Wiley-Blackwell Press, 2009).

the face of white oppression. Rebecca J. Fraser uncovered ways in which enslaved people fought to engage in courtship on their own terms in North Carolina. Wedding ceremonies themselves, where couples often jumped over a broom, also served as moments of resistance, according to research by Thomas E. Will and Tyler D. Parry.[25]

Rich insights into family histories expanded as scholars looked beyond the plantation model. Wilma A. Dunaway focused on Appalachia, where smaller slaveholding households predominated, emphasizing the difficulties that enslaved families faced as they tried to maintain connections in the face of sales, separations, sexual violence, and overwork. Around two-thirds of the couples Dunaway studied had abroad marriages. Her conclusions about the devastating impact of slavery upon enslaved families echoed the findings of William Dusinberre in his study of slavery in the South Carolina and Georgia Lowcountry rice swamps, where, conversely, large plantations were the norm. In *On Slavery's Border* (2010), Diane Mutti Burke, like Dunaway, examined smaller-scale slave-ownership in the border state of Missouri. Due to more hiring out and living in closer proximity to slaveholders, enslaved people's family lives differed significantly from those on plantations. In the coastal areas of the Upper South, Calvin Schermerhorn charted enslaved peoples' attempts to preserve families in an increasingly commercialized economic landscape. Crops formed the basis of Damian Allan Pargas's investigation into enslaved family life beyond the cotton-growing South. His comparative perspective, drawing on the earlier work of Philip D. Morgan, showed the centrality of crops in shaping enslaved people's labor and consequently, their family structures.[26] Considered collectively, these

25. Herbert G. Gutman, *The Black Family in Slavery and Freedom, 1750–1925* (New York: Pantheon Books, 1976); Ann Patton Malone, *Sweet Chariot: Slave Family and Household Structure in Nineteenth-Century Louisiana* (Chapel Hill: University of North Carolina Press, 1992); Brenda E. Stevenson, *Life in Black and White: Family and Community in the Slave South* (New York: Oxford University Press, 1996); Rebecca J. Fraser, *Courtship and Love among the Enslaved in North Carolina* (Jackson: University Press of Mississippi, 2007); Emily West, *Chains of Love: Slave Couples in Antebellum South Carolina* (Urbana: University of Illinois Press, 2004); Thomas E. Will, "Weddings on Contested Grounds: Slave Marriage in the Antebellum South," *The Historian* 62 (Fall 1999): 99–117; Tyler D. Parry, "Married in Slavery Time: Jumping the Broom in Atlantic Perspective," *Journal of Southern History* 81 (May 2015): 273–312.

26. Wilma A. Dunaway, *The African American Family in Slavery and Emancipation* (New York: Cambridge University Press, 2003); Dunaway, *Women, Work, and Family in the Antebellum Mountain South* (New York: Cambridge University Press, 2008); William Dusinberre, *Them Dark Days: Slavery in the American Rice Swamps* (New York: Oxford University Press, 1996); Diane Mutti Burke, *On Slavery's Border: Missouri's*

works draw attention to a diversity of experiences even as they add depth and texture to our understandings of gender and familial structures.

In 2017, Tera W. Hunter reimagined the synthesis of family life under enslavement in her sweeping work, *Bound in Wedlock*. Hunter traced African American marital trends from slavery through emancipation, revealing how couples entered into different kinds of intimate relationships, including more casual "taking up" and trial marriages. Some lived with their spouses; others lived in abroad marriages, residing on different plantations and visiting back and forth with their spouse. Custom, rather than law, governed slave marriage, since white society denied legal citizenship to free and enslaved people of color. Slaveholders permitted a variety of flexible marital forms to encourage pregnancies, but enslaved people ultimately sought to make their own decisions about their intimate partners, coming into conflict with enslavers who separated couples, sexually violated enslaved women, and occasionally forced intimate relationships between enslaved people.[27]

Historians have been less productive in examining free women and men of color. Their lives did not fit easily into the "plantation paradigm," and they left relatively few historical records. Yet approximately 250,000 free people of color lived in the United States on the eve of the Civil War. Some were born free to free black mothers. Others acquired their freedom through manumissions, an act that became progressively more difficult in the antebellum era. Free black women's lives differed from those of enslaved women in many ways, but the fact of freedom itself did not change everything. Free blacks, women and men, were also subject to legal restrictions (for example, laws about residency, occupations, and citizenship often restricted their autonomy and ambitions).[28]

Small-Slaveholding Households, 1815–1865 (Athens: University of Georgia Press, 2010); Calvin Schermerhorn, *Money over Mastery, Family over Freedom: Slavery in the Antebellum Upper South* (Baltimore: Johns Hopkins University Press, 2011); Damian Alan Pargas, *The Quarters and the Fields: Slave Families in the Non-Cotton South* (Gainesville: University Press of Florida, 2010); Morgan, *Slave Counterpoint.*

27. Tera W. Hunter, *Bound in Wedlock: Slave and Free Black Marriage in the Nineteenth Century* (Cambridge: Harvard University Press, 2017).

28. On citizenship, see Martha S. Jones, *Birthright Citizens: A History of Race and Rights in Antebellum America* (New York: Cambridge University Press, 2018); William A. Link et al., eds., *Creating Citizenship in the Nineteenth-Century South* (Gainesville: University Press of Florida, 2013). Laura F. Edwards demonstrated how blacks, women, and the poor were more successful in realizing rights before the 1830s, when political leaders began to consolidate protections for patriarchal inequalities into state laws; see *The People and Their Peace.*

Some early groundbreaking work on free women of color concentrated on residents of major cities and towns of the South. For example, Suzanne Lebsock's pioneering study, *The Free Women of Petersburg* (1985), celebrated free black women's ability to lead independent lives by avoiding marriage (admittedly in an environment where they outnumbered free black men). As scholarly investigations grew, studies emphasized the multiplicity of free black women's experiences. In *Chained to the Rock of Adversity* (1998), Virginia Meacham Gould focused on the precariousness of free black women in Louisiana. Jessica Millward noted the fluidity between slavery and freedom for women in Maryland. Amrita Chakrabati Myers highlighted attempts to gain upward mobility and eventually freedom in *Forging Freedom* (2011). Myers focused on Charleston to provide a case study of urban black women's lives, as did Cynthia M. Kennedy in her nuanced study of black and white, free and enslaved. Similar to Lebsock's study decades earlier, Kennedy's work on Charleston demonstrated ways in which space and class, courts and status intersected and complicated lives within urban slave centers. Judith Kelleher Schafer likewise used the context of another urban port city, New Orleans, to explore black women's aspirations to become free (and, for free black women, to fight enslavement) in *Becoming Free, Remaining Free* (2003).[29]

In contrast, Wilma King's *Essence of Liberty* (2006) used a wider lens to provide a more comprehensive overview of free black women's lives across the North and the South. King stressed the negative impact of both economic deprivation and restrictive legislation upon women's liberty. Kit Candlin and Cassandra Pybus pieced together the lives of free black women entrepreneurs in the colonial Caribbean in *Enterprising Women* (2015), using microbiographies to show how, instead of being dependent on men, free black women used familial and economic connections to achieve economic and social mobility. But not all free black women realized such success. Emily West's *Family or Freedom* (2012) conveyed how southern state legislatures worked to reduce, even eliminate, free blacks

29. Suzanne Lebsock, *The Free Women of Petersburg: Status and Culture in a Southern Town, 1784–1860* (New York: W. W. Norton, 1984); Virginia Meacham Gould, ed., *Chained to the Rock of Adversity: To Be Free, Black and Female in the Old South* (Athens: University of Georgia Press, 1998); Jessica Millward, *Finding Charity's Folk: Enslaved and Free Black Women in Maryland* (Athens: University of Georgia Press, 2015); Amrita Chakrabarti Myers, *Forging Freedom: Black Women and the Pursuit of Liberty in Antebellum Charleston* (Chapel Hill: University of North Carolina Press, 2011); Cynthia M. Kennedy, *Braided Relations, Entwined Lives: The Women of Charleston's Urban Slave Society* (Bloomington: University of Indiana Press, 2005); Judith Kelleher Schafer, *Becoming Free, Remaining Free: Manumission and Enslavement in New Orleans, 1846–1962* (Baton Rouge: Louisiana State University Press, 2003).

in their societies in order to create a biracial system of free whites and enslaved blacks. To protect their autonomy, some free black women sought to enslave themselves through petitioning state legislatures or local county courts. The abilities of black women (whether enslaved or free) to use the legal system spoke more broadly to the role of gender within an evolving legal landscape.[30]

Transformative works by Laura F. Edwards and Ariela J. Gross conveyed how, at local levels, southern black women frequently assumed their inclusion in the legal system, even though states denied citizenship to both enslaved and free black women. Gross noted how black women (and men) appealed to white lawmakers to improve their quality of life. Other historians shifted the focus toward women's lives along borderlands. Important books broadening the definition of the South also illuminate the legal culture of slavery: Kelly M. Kennington's research into freedom suits in St. Louis; Kimberly Welch's explorations into black litigants in the Natchez district; Anne Twitty's analysis of slavery and legal culture in the American confluence (where the Ohio, Mississippi, and Missouri rivers converge); and, at a more micro-level, Eva Sheppard Wolf's *Almost Free* (2012), which considered a free black man's attempts to liberate his family in Virginia.[31]

The proliferated historiography on southern black women has been enriching and transformative, and it deserves the space and attention given thus far. Works exploring the lives of women of color are very influential in the historiography, extending to and enhancing our appreciation for the role of white women in the antebellum South. In contrast to black women whose lives are often hidden in the archives, white women are sometimes hidden in plain sight, frequently shrouded in myth and stereotypes. From Anne Firor Scott's landmark study, *The*

30. Wilma King, *The Essence of Liberty: Free Black Women during the Slave Era* (Columbia: University of Missouri Press, 2006); Kit Candlin and Cassandra Pybus, *Enterprising Women: Gender, Race and Power in the Revolutionary Atlantic* (Athens: University of Georgia Press, 2014). See also David Barry Gaspar and Darlene Clark Hine, eds., *More Than Chattel: Black Women and Slavery in the Americas* (Bloomington: Indiana University Press, 1996); Emily West, *Family or Freedom: People of Color in the Antebellum South* (Lexington: University Press of Kentucky, 2012).

31. Edwards, *The People and Their Peace;* Ariela J. Gross, *Double Character: Slavery and Mastery in the Antebellum Southern Courtroom* (Athens: University of Georgia Press, 2000); Kelly M. Kennington, *In the Shadow of* Dred Scott: *St. Louis Freedom Suits and the Legal Culture of Slavery in Antebellum America* (Athens: University of Georgia Press, 2017); Kimberly Welch, *Black Litigants in the Antebellum American South* (Chapel Hill: University of North Carolina Press, 2018); Anne Twitty, *Before* Dred Scott: *Slavery and Legal Culture in the American Confluence, 1787–1857* (New York: Cambridge University Press, 2016); Eva Sheppard Wolf, *Almost Free: A Story about Family and Race in Antebellum Virginia* (Athens: University of Georgia Press, 2012).

Southern Lady (1970), well into the twenty-first century, the focus on mistresses monopolized southern gender studies, until the counterrevolution of books and articles reexamining the enslaved and the enslavers emerged. A bounteous crop of edited nineteenth-century letters and diaries flourished beginning with Robert Manson Myers's magisterial *Children of Pride* (1972), which stimulated a number of exciting reprints and new documentary volumes. From Catherine Clinton's *The Plantation Mistress* (1982) through Elizabeth Fox-Genovese's *Within the Plantation Household* (1988) and Marli F. Weiner's *Mistresses and Slaves* (1998), scholars pulled real women from the shadows and from behind white columns, and their voices emerged.[32]

Since the 1970s, planter wives, mothers, and daughters rose up from the footnotes, taking more prominent roles in books redefining the antebellum South, including Bertram Wyatt-Brown's instant classic *Southern Honor* (1982). Wyatt-Brown numbered among the first leading southern male historians to incorporate women's voices into his research. His influential study highlighted the way in which masculinity, race, and sexual relations created a distinctive regional mentalité among whites, despite class and status lines. Since the 1980s, more and more leading scholars moved toward topics centered on or including gender analysis and the complex and varied roles of white women.[33]

32. Anne Firor Scott, *The Southern Lady: From Pedestal to Politics, 1830–1930* (Chicago: University of Chicago Press, 1970); Robert Manson Myers, ed., *The Children of Pride: A True Story of Georgia and the Civil War* (New Haven: Yale University Press, 1972); Catherine Clinton, *The Plantation Mistress: Woman's World in the Old South* (New York: Pantheon Books, 1982); Fox-Genovese, *Within the Plantation Household;* Marli F. Weiner, *Mistresses and Slaves: Plantation Women in South Carolina, 1830–80* (Urbana: University of Illinois Press, 1998). See also Laura F. Edwards, *Scarlett Doesn't Live Here Anymore: Southern Women in the Civil War Era* (Urbana: University of Illinois Press, 2000); Elizabeth R. Varon, *We Mean to Be Counted: White Women and Politics in Antebellum Virginia* (Chapel Hill: University of North Carolina Press, 1998). Carol K. Bleser established a series with the University of South Carolina Press titled Women's Diaries and Letters of the South, which, under her editorship, published twenty-seven documentary volumes of mainly nineteenth-century material; see "Publisher Series: Women's Diaries and Letters of the Nineteenth Century South," University of South Carolina Press, https://www.sc.edu/uscpress/wdls.html (accessed 18 January 2019).

33. Bertram Wyatt-Brown, *Southern Honor: Ethics and Behavior in the Old South* (New York: Oxford University Press, 1982). See also Stephanie McCurry, *Masters of Small Worlds: Yeoman Households, Gender Relations, and the Political Culture of the Antebellum South Carolina Low Country* (New York: Oxford University Press, 1995); Gary W. Gallagher, *The Confederate War* (Cambridge: Harvard University Press, 1997); Christine Leigh Heyrman, *Southern Cross: The Beginnings of the Bible Belt* (New York: Alfred A. Knopf, 1997).

Scholars disagreed about how to interpret antebellum southern white women, but nearly all agreed to challenge the conventional wisdom that these women were mere decorative objects. Clinton and Weiner suggested that even the wealthiest planter-class women found themselves in challenging circumstances, trapped within confines not of their own design, charged with supervising their own families, and expected to minister to the people their husbands enslaved. All mistresses were expected to provide food, clothing, and medical care for the enslaved, and some were to address the spiritual and family needs of all those living on their estates as well. White women tasked with such duties often resented their charges rather than the system that imposed such work roles.

The patriarchal structure of the plantation South lay at the heart of *The Plantation Mistress,* in which Clinton argued that slavery entrapped all blacks and all white women within its hierarchical matrix, with most white women believing themselves to be victims. Marli F. Weiner claimed further that some women pursued sisterhood across the racial divide, suggesting humanitarian bonds developed within the forced intimacy of plantation life. Elizabeth Fox-Genovese, meanwhile, emphasized plantation mistresses' strong investment in maintaining patriarchy and their efforts to cement status within the slaveholders' empire. She argued that the intimacies between black and white women led to abuses—something to which Thavolia Glymph testified in her powerful, original study, *Out of the House of Bondage* (2008). Still, Glymph was not in accord with Fox-Genovese. She deconstructed and effectively destroyed notions that slaveholding women played humanitarian roles within slavery. Even if individuals transcended class conflict, she concluded, the ties that bound were kinship and race, with gender left at the wayside. Likewise, in *They Were Her Property* (2019), Stephanie Jones-Rogers demonstrated how white women were economic beneficiaries of slavery, exploiting enslaved women in particular for their own ends.[34]

Other scholars pointed out ways in which religion framed the lives of southern white women. Jean E. Friedman's *The Enclosed Garden* (1986) highlighted the powerful influence of kin networks and church communities, which curtailed white women's autonomy and imposed limitations on the development of southern feminism. Cynthia Lynn Lyerly's *Methodism and the Southern Mind* (2006)

34. Clinton, *Plantation Mistress;* Weiner, *Mistresses and Slaves;* Fox-Genovese, *Within the Plantation Household;* Thavolia Glymph, *Out of the House of Bondage: The Transformation of the Plantation Household* (New York: Cambridge University Press, 2008); Stephanie Jones-Rogers, *They Were Her Property: White Women as Slave Owners in the American South* (New Haven: Yale University Press, 2019).

underscored the feminine aspects of Methodism, excavating women's spirituality and identity. Because southern women embraced the Second Great Awakening before most men in their families, the Awakening disrupted planter-patriarchs' domination by unleashing women's spiritual energies and leveling direct assaults on racial and gendered hierarchies. Such challenges were short-lived, however. Christine Leigh Heyrman's momentous study of the post-Revolutionary South, *Southern Cross* (1997), emphasized the transformation that evangelicals, in their quest to court patriarchs, made from challenging to embracing southern hierarchies and from disrupting to upholding traditional family dynamics. Heyrman revealed how ministers aligned their messages with southern patriarchal values and charted the consequences for white women and enslaved people.[35]

As in studies of enslaved women and families, historians of white women attended to region as a defining characteristic of individual lives. Jane Turner Censer's *North Carolina Planters and Their Children, 1800-1860* (1984) looked closely at issues involving family, migration, community values, and regional identities; and Orville Vernon Burton's meticulous *In My Father's House Are Many Mansions* (1985) demonstrated how, in Edgefield District of South Carolina, the patriarchal model of family exemplified on the largest slaveholding estates not only became the pattern of family life among other whites but became emulated by black residents as well. Other state and regional studies followed. Joan E. Cashin's pioneering *A Family Venture* (1991) traced the migration of families to the southwestern frontier, emphasizing the gendered choices and experiences in those relocations. Men relished adventuring westward, seeing in migration economic opportunities and revivification of their independence and manhood. Women often suffered from leaving behind networks of kin and friends. Cashin's findings highlighted profound gender differences in more scarcely populated interior settlements.[36]

35. Jean E. Friedman, *The Enclosed Garden: Women and Community in the Evangelical South, 1830–1900* (Chapel Hill: University of North Carolina Press, 1985); Cynthia Lynn Lyerly, *Methodism and the Southern Mind, 1770–1810* (New York: Oxford University Press, 1998); Heyrman, *Southern Cross.*

36. Jane Turner Censer, *North Carolina Planters and their Children, 1800–1860* (Baton Rouge: Louisiana State University Press, 1984); Orville Vernon Burton, *In My Father's House Are Many Mansions: Family and Community in Edgefield, South Carolina* (Chapel Hill: University of North Carolina Press, 1985); Joan E. Cashin, *A Family Venture: Men and Women on the Southern Frontier* (New York: Oxford University Press, 1991). See also David R. Roediger, "The Pursuit of Whiteness: Property, Terror, and Expansion, 1790–1860," *Journal of the Early Republic* 19 (Winter 1999): 579–600; Laurel Clark Shire, "Turning Sufferers into Settlers: Gender, Welfare, and National Expansion in Frontier Florida," *Journal of the Early Republic* 33 (Fall 2013): 489–521; Dunaway, *Women, Work, and Family in the Antebellum Mountain South.*

Between the 1990s and the 2010s, historians studying white southern women undertook a diversity of projects, from sweeping overviews to revealing case studies. The best synthesis of women in the early South was Cynthia A. Kierner's *Beyond the Household* (1998). Other scholars focused on important life experiences that empowered white women: Christie Anne Farnham focused on the creation of white women's colleges and seminaries before the Civil War in *The Education of the Southern Belle* (1994); Charlene Boyer Lewis examined the role of display among elite white women; Kirsten E. Wood traced the evolution of slaveholding widows' power between the American Revolution and the Civil War in her *Masterful Women* (2004); and Anya Jabour considered stage of life as an important category of analysis in *Scarlett's Sisters* (2007).[37]

Motherhood was an early subject in southern white women's historiography. Becoming a mother, after all, provided commonly shared experiences for the great majority of white women, as it did for black women. By the nineteenth century, modern ideas that deemed mothers (of the white middling ranks and elites) exclusively responsible for their children's development became commonplace, and in 1980, Linda K. Kerber coined the term "republican motherhood" to denote the civic virtues of white mothers' moral roles as caretakers and nurturers in educating their husbands and sons for a more public life.[38]

Sally McMillen's 1980s research into elite white motherhood stressed the physical and emotional strains that childbearing and childrearing placed upon white women. Subsequent research by Thavolia Glymph and Kimberly Wallace-Sanders showed how wealthy white slaveholding women maintained privilege through farming out the role of mothering to enslaved females, especially "plantation mammies." Other scholars probed the distinctiveness of southern motherhood through comparative studies. V. Lynn Kennedy explored motherhood

37. Kierner, *Beyond the Household;* Christie Anne Farnham, *The Education of the Southern Belle: Higher Education and Student Socialization in the Antebellum South* (New York: New York University Press, 1994); Charlene Boyer Lewis, *Ladies and Gentlemen on Display: Planter Society at the Virginia Springs, 1790–1860* (Charlottesville: University Press of Virginia, 2002); Kirsten E. Wood, *Masterful Women: Slaveholding Widows from the American Revolution through the Civil War* (Chapel Hill: University of North Carolina Press, 2004); Anya Jabour, *Scarlett's Sisters: Young Women in the Old South* (Chapel Hill: University of North Carolina Press, 2007). For life-cycle studies of white women, see also Victoria E. Ott, *Confederate Daughters: Coming of Age during the Civil War* (Carbondale: Southern Illinois University Press, 2008).

38. Linda K. Kerber, *Women of the Republic: Intellect and Ideology in Revolutionary America* (Chapel Hill: University of North Carolina Press, 1980).

within both enslaved and slaveholding families in *Born Southern* (2012), while Katie Simpson Smith included Native American motherhood in *We Have Raised All of You* (2013). Both authors regarded motherhood as a site of empowerment for women.[39]

Of course, not all white women became mothers or even married. Christine Jacobson Carter, in *Southern Single Blessedness* (2009), wrote optimistically about the lives of unmarried southern urban women who valued their roles as sisters, aunts, and friends, and devoted themselves to their families and to community service. Marie Molloy's *Single, White, Slave-Holding Women in the Nineteenth-Century American South* (2018) explored singleness among those who never married alongside widowed, separated, or divorced white women. Like Carter, Molloy found being single increased white women's autonomy and independence. Loren Schweninger's work on divorce in the Old South provided a bleaker narrative. He concluded that poorer white women rarely had recourse to the law, and that men's violence against women and adultery with other women formed the basis of the great majority of divorce petitions.[40]

Although the history of the Old South traditionally centered on the actions and experiences of men, southern historians were slow to probe the complex meanings of masculinity. Early historians of slavery wrote about the lives of slaveholders and enslaved people from the perspective of men but most—wittingly or unwittingly—failed to consider ways in which gender shaped men's experiences in antebellum southern communities.[41]

39. Sally G. McMillen, *Motherhood in the Old South: Pregnancy, Childbirth and Infant Rearing* (Baton Rouge: Louisiana State University Press, 1990); Glymph, *Out of the House of Bondage*; Kimberly Wallace-Sanders, *Mammy: A Century of Race, Gender and Southern Memory* (Ann Arbor: University of Michigan Press, 2008); V. Lynn Kennedy, *Born Southern: Childbirth, Motherhood, and Social Networks in the Old South* (Baltimore: Johns Hopkins University Press, 2010); Katy Simpson Smith, *We Have Raised All of You: Motherhood in the South, 1750–1835* (Baton Rouge: Louisiana State University Press, 2013).

40. Christine Jacobson Carter, *Southern Single Blessedness: Unmarried Women in the Urban South, 1800–1865* (Urbana: University of Illinois Press, 2006); Marie S. Molloy, *Single, White, Slave-Holding Women in the Nineteenth-Century American South* (Columbia: University of South Carolina Press, 2018); Loren Schweninger, *Families in Crisis in the Old South: Divorce, Slavery, and the Law* (Chapel Hill: University of North Carolina Press, 2012).

41. One exception within the field of slavery studies was the debate about emasculation of black men and matriarchy within enslaved communities. See Kenneth M. Stampp, *The Peculiar Institution: Slavery in the Ante-Bellum South* (New York: Alfred A. Knopf, 1956); Herbert G. Gutman, *The Black Family in Slavery and Freedom, 1750–1925* (New York: Pantheon Books, 1976); Deborah Gray White, "Female Slaves: Sex Roles and Status in the Antebellum Plantation South," *Journal of Family History* 8 (Fall 1983): 248–61.

By 2007, however, in the preface to his edited collection of four southern white men's diaries, Stephen Berry contemplated how "gender history is at a crossroads. Either it will pursue men's history with all the rigor it has displayed in pursuing women's history or it will expire." As the field expanded, no consensus emerged on how to analyze southern masculinity. In the 1990s and 2000s, scholars had focused on conceptualizing manhood and masculinity within white communities in the Old South, drawing heavily from Wyatt-Brown's pioneering study of honor (regardless of one's class or status as enslaved or free). For example, Stephanie McCurry's groundbreaking work on yeoman households in the South Carolina Lowcountry showed how yeomen adhered to the ideal of "mastery" within their households, controlling the labor of the women, children, and slaves who worked for them.[42]

Scholars began to rigorously interrogate how enslaved men faced unique pressures and exploitations as victims of the slave regime, some of which related directly to the abuses endured by women in their families and communities and by slaveholders' racist stereotyping. Earl Ofari Hutchinson connected antebellum stereotyping to more contemporary contexts in *The Assassination of the Black Male Image* (1994). Sarah Roth considered portrayals of masculinity within fugitive slave autobiographies. Inspired by women scholars' research into the nature of sexual assaults upon enslaved females, Thomas A. Foster questioned the extent to which slave men were themselves victims of slaveholder sexual exploitation, as well as being forced to witness sexual violence directed against the women they loved as wives, mothers, and daughters. Sergio A. Lussana took Deborah Gray White's research of female slaves' camaraderie as a starting point in his thought-provoking analysis of the homosocial worlds of enslaved men and their friendships in *My Brother Slaves* (2016). David Stefan Doddington pointed out how ideas about manhood and individual status were highly contested within enslaved communities in *Contesting Slave Masculinity in the American South* (2018).[43]

42. Stephen Berry, ed., *Princes of Cotton: Four Diaries of Young Men in the South, 1848–1860* (Athens: University of Georgia Press, 2007), ix; McCurry, *Masters of Small Worlds;* Bertram Wyatt-Brown, *The Shaping of Southern Culture: Honor, Grace, and War, 1760s–1880s* (Chapel Hill: University of North Carolina Press, 2001), xii. See also Wyatt-Brown, "The Mask of Obedience: Male Slave Psychology in the Old South," *American Historical Review* 93 (December 1988): 1228–52.

43. Earl Ofari Hutchinson, *The Assassination of the Black Male Image* (Los Angeles: Middle Passage Press, 1994); Sarah N. Roth, "'How a Slave Was Made a Man': Negotiating Black Violence and Masculinity in Antebellum Slave Narratives," *Slavery & Abolition* 28 (August 2007): 255–75; Thomas A. Foster, "The Sexual Abuse of Black Men under American Slavery," *Journal of the History of Sexuality* 20 (September

Historians have thus moved away from notions of honorable white men and submissive white women, instead stressing diversity in men's lives in the Old South. Differing notions of masculinity and manly experiences were expressed well in Craig Thompson Friend and Lorri Glover's edited volume, *Southern Manhood* (2004). Their collection brought together studies of black, white, and Native American masculinities. Importantly, Friend and Glover noted how honor and mastery were indeed both dominant and idealized traits among southern white men, but others sought to transform, co-opt, and sometimes even reject both ideals. For example, Edward E. Baptist's essay on enslaved men swept up in the process of forced migration to the Southwest suggests manhood could be found in mere survival, in ordinary virtues that did not necessarily conform to archetypes of masculinity. For Baptist, masculinity did not have to be based on the tropes of "white domineering honor" or "black heroic resistance."[44]

Young white men also struggled within ideals of mastery and honor, as Lorri Glover revealed in *Southern Sons* (2007). She persuasively argued that notions of manhood, rather than honor, framed the lives of young men coming of age in the new nation. Ultimately, in a range of contexts, manhood existed as a point of contrast to womanhood, with oppositional duties. While more narrowly focused than the work of Friend and Glover, Sergio A. Lussana and Lydia Plath's 2009 edited collection on black and white masculinity in the South also moved away from the paradigm of mastery and honor as the defining features of southern manhood, especially in relation to poorer white men and the enslaved, for whom group solidarity provided an important feature of masculine expression. In that collection, Rebecca Fraser's essay revealed how enslaved men strove to be "protectors and providers" and that such roles fostered group solidarity.[45]

2011): 445–64; Foster, *Rethinking Rufus: Sexual Violations of Enslaved Men* (Athens: University of Georgia Press, 2019); Sergio A. Lussana, *My Brother Slaves: Friendship, Masculinity, and Resistance in the Antebellum South* (Lexington: University Press of Kentucky, 2016); Doddington, *Contesting Slave Masculinity in the American South.*

44. Friend and Glover, eds., *Southern Manhood,* vii–xvii; Edward E. Baptist, "The Absent Subject: African American Masculinity and Forced Migration to the Antebellum Plantation Frontier," in Friend and Glover, eds., *Southern Manhood,* 136–73, quote on 158. See also Friend, "'The Crushing of Southern Manhood': War, Masculinity, and the Confederate Nation-State, 1861–1865," in *Masculinities and the Nation in the Modern World,* ed. Pablo Dominguez Andersen and Simon Wendt (New York: Palgrave Macmillan, 2015), 19–38.

45. Lorri Glover, *Southern Sons: Becoming Men in the New Nation* (Baltimore: Johns Hopkins University Press, 2007); Rebecca Fraser, "Negotiating Their Manhood: Masculinity Amongst the Enslaved

Masculinity studies have therefore moved well beyond a narrowly defined paradigm of mastery and honor. In thinking more broadly about class and power, historians highlighted the diversity of male lives in the Old South. Ami Pflugrad-Jackisch examined secret fraternal orders in *Brothers of a Vow* (2010), discovering masculine ideals of self-discipline and civic brotherhood, at once challenging planter ethics while also reinforcing gender and racial hierarchies. Timothy J. Williams's research on white men who studied at the University of North Carolina conveyed how intellectualism linked middle-class masculinity to that of the southern planter class, complicating our understanding of the role of college education in the development of proslavery thought and secession. Jennifer R. Green revisited military education with an emphasis on gender analysis. Lorri Glover explored the intimacy of fatherhood in *Founders as Fathers* (2014). In *Citizens More than Soldiers* (2007), Harry S. Laver examined Kentucky militias as manly institutions that facilitated republican citizenship. Similarly, in *Home Rule* (2015) Honor Sachs found Kentucky fertile ground for studying the role of the state in structuring and empowering manhood for model citizenry. Importantly, both Sachs and Laver noted how early westward expansion meant an expansion of southern masculine identities, a point made even more powerfully by Amy S. Greenberg in *Manifest Manhood* (2005). Greenberg categorized gendered interpretations of manifest destiny in the 1840s and 1850s as either "aggressive" or "restrained," competing ideals that propelled territorial expansion.[46]

---

in the Upper South, 1830–1861," in *Black and White Masculinity in the American South, 1800–2000*, ed. Lydia Plath and Sergio A. Lussana (Newcastle upon Tyne: Cambridge Scholars, 2009), 76–94. See also Matthew G. Schoenbachler's portrayal of Jereboam O. Beachamp as more than honor-driven and his wife's Anna's motives as more than virtue-driven in their assassination of Solomon P. Sharp in *Murder and Madness: The Myth of the Kentucky Tragedy* (Lexington: University of Kentucky Press, 2011).

46. Ami Pflugrad-Jackisch, *Brothers of a Vow: Secret Fraternal Orders and The Transformation of White Male Culture in Antebellum Virginia* (Athens: University of Georgia Press, 2010); Timothy J. Williams, *Intellectual Manhood: University, Self, and Society in the Antebellum South* (Chapel Hill: University of North Carolina Press, 2015); Jennifer R. Green, *Military Education and the Emerging Middle Class in the Old South* (New York: Cambridge University Press, 2008); Lorri Glover, *Founders as Fathers: The Private Lives and Politics of the American Revolutionaries* (New Haven: Yale University Press, 2016); Harry S. Laver, *Citizens More than Soldiers: The Kentucky Militia and Society in the Early Republic* (Lincoln: University of Nebraska Press, 2007); Honor Sachs, *Home Rule: Households, Manhood, and National Expansion on the Eighteenth-Century Kentucky Frontier* (New Haven: Yale University Press, 2015); Amy S. Greenberg, *Manifest Manhood and the Antebellum American Empire* (New York: Cambridge University Press, 2005). See also Berry, ed., *Princes of Cotton;* John Mayfield, *Counterfeit Gentlemen: Manhood and Humor in the Old South* (Gainesville: University Press of Florida, 2009); Charity R. Carney, *Ministers and Masters:*

No scholar has done more to advance early American masculinity studies than Thomas A. Foster, whose impressive body of work crosses in and out of the South. Although demonstrating the necessity of interrogating gender in the study of men's lives, Foster specifically called into question the distinctiveness of southern experiences through examining the sexual activities of two of the most stereotyped of southern men: the Virginia elite such as George Washington and Thomas Jefferson, and enslaved black men. Not surprisingly, in both cases, Foster found intersections of sexuality, manhood, and power.[47] In fact, as noted earlier in reference to black women's sexual experiences, historians face great difficulty separating patriarchal power from southern sexualities, and most studies have centered on sexual violence and exploitation.[48]

Methodism, Manhood, and Honor in the Old South (Baton Rouge: Louisiana State University Press, 2011); Peter S. Carmichael, *The Last Generation: Young Virginians in Peace, War and Reunion* (Chapel Hill: University of North Carolina Press, 2005); Robert F. Pace, *Halls of Honor: College Men in the Old South* (Baton Rouge: Louisiana State University Press, 2004); Elizabeth B. Eubanks, "Benevolent Patriarchs: Gender and Charity in Early America" (PhD diss., University of Tennessee, 2019).

47. Thomas A. Foster's many works include *Sex and the Eighteenth-Century Man: Massachusetts and the History of Sexuality in America* (Boston: Beacon Press, 2006); *Sex and the Founding Fathers: The American Quest for a Relatable Past* (Philadelphia: Temple University Press, 2014); "The Sexual Abuse of Black Men under Slavery"; *Rethinking Rufus;* and the edited volumes, *Long Before Stonewall: Histories of Same-Sex Sexuality in Early America* (New York: New York University Press, 2007), and *New Men: Manliness in Early America* (New York: New York University Press, 2011).

48. On the colonial South, see Richard Godbeer, *Sexual Revolution in Early America* (Baltimore: Johns Hopkins University Press, 2004); Godbeer, "William Byrd's 'Flourish': The Sexual Cosmos of a Southern Planter," in *Sex and Sexuality in Early America,* ed. Merril D. Smith (New York: New York University Press, 1998), 135–62; Kenneth A. Lockridge, "Colonial Self-Fashioning: Paradoxes and Pathologies in the Creation of Genteel Identity in Eighteenth-Century America," in *Through a Glass Darkly: Reflections on Personal Identity in Early America,* ed. Ronald Hoffman, Mechal Sobel, and Frederika J. Teute (Chapel Hill: University of North Carolina Press, 1997), 274–339; Paul Finkelman, "Crimes of Love, Misdemeanors of Passion: The Regulation of Race and Sex in the Colonial South," in Clinton and Gillespie, ed., *The Devil's Lane,* 124–38; A. Leon Higginbotham and Barbara Kopytoff, "Racial Purity and Interracial Sex in the Law of Colonial and Antebellum Virginia," *Georgetown Law Journal* 77 (August 1989): 1967–2029. On the antebellum South, see James Hugo Johnston, *Race Relations in Virginia and Miscegenation in the South* (Amherst: University of Massachusetts Press, 1970); Joel Williamson, *New People: Miscegenation and Mulattoes in the United States* (New York: Free Press, 1980); Sabine Sielke, *Reading Rape: The Rhetoric of Sexual Violence in American Literature and Culture, 1790–1990* (Princeton: Princeton University Press, 2002); Craig Thompson Friend, "Sex, Self, and the Performance of Patriarchal Manhood," in *The Old South's Modern Worlds: Slavery, Region, and Nation in the Age of Progress,* ed. L. Diane Barnes, Brian Schoen, and Frank Towers (New York: Oxford University Press, 2011), 246–67; Karen Getman, "Sexual Control in the Slaveholding South: The Implementation and Maintenance of a Racial Caste System," *Harvard Women's*

Nevertheless, a few historians have tried to deconstruct the heteronormative assumptions that continue to frame much of the scholarship on gender and sexuality. Jim Downs has suggested new ways to explore same-sex desire among the enslaved. Marli F. Weiner offered a provocative notion of "ambiguous bodies" that originally applied to how white southern physicians viewed mixed race individuals and individuals with physical deformities. The idea applied as well to those who did not neatly fit antebellum ideals of heteronormative sexuality. As scholars of LGBTQ history expanded their vision southward in the 1990s, they inspired others to examine the sparse but intriguing evidence of sexually ambiguous bodies within antebellum southern culture: cross-dressers, transsexuals, and hermaphrodites.[49]

Queering southern sexuality has been most evident in studies of enslaved peoples. In *The Delectable Negro* (2014), Vincent Woodard read canonical texts such as Harriet Jacobs's and Frederick Douglass's narratives with a "queer eye." He took seriously the idea of black bodies as consumable, attending to ways in which homoerotic pleasure, subjugation, and consumption framed white mastery over black men. Similarly employing works by African American authors, Aliyyah Abdur-Rahman showed how literary representations of transgressive sexuality

---

Law Journal 7 (Spring 1984): 114–52; Catherine Clinton, "Southern Dishonor: Flesh, Blood, Race and Bondage," in *In Joy and In Sorrow: Women, Family and Marriage in the Victorian South,* ed. Carol K. Bleser (New York: Oxford University Press, 1991), 52–68; King, "'Prematurely Knowing of Evil Things'"; and essays in Berry and Harris, eds., *Sexuality & Slavery,* specifically Stephanie Jones-Rogers, "Rethinking Sexual Violence and the Marketplace of Slavery: White Women, the Slave Market, and Enslaved People's Sexualized Bodies in the Nineteenth-Century South" (109–23); David Stefan Doddington, "Manhood, Sex, and Power in Antebellum Slave Communities" (145–58); and Brenda E. Stevenson, "What's Love Got to Do with It? Concubinage and Enslaved Women and Girls in the Antebellum South" (159–88).

49. Treva B. Lindsey and Jessica Marie Johnson, "Searching for Climax: Black Erotic Lives in Slavery and Freedom," *Meridians* 12 (Fall 2014): 169–95; Martin B. Duberman, "'Writhing Bedfellows' in Antebellum South Carolina: Historical Interpretations and the Politics of Evidence," in *Carryin' On in the Lesbian and Gay South,* ed. John Howard (New York: New York University Press, 1997), 15–34; Elizabeth W. Knowlton, "'Only a Woman Like Yourself'—Rebecca Alice Baldy: Dutiful Daughter, Stalwart Sister, and Lesbian Lover of Nineteenth-Century Georgia," in Howard, ed., *Carryin' On in the Lesbian and Gay South,* 34–53. For same-sex desires, see Downs, "With Only a Trace." For "ambiguous bodies," see Marli F. Weiner with Mayzie Hough, *Sex, Sickness, and Slavery: Illness in the Antebellum South* (Urbana: University of Illinois Press, 2012), chap. 4. For studies on ambiguous sexual identities, see Mary Beth Norton, "Communal Definitions of Gendered Identity in Seventeenth-Century English America," in Hoffman, Sobel, and Teute, eds., *Through a Glass Darkly,* 40–66; Brown, *Good Wives, Nasty Wenches, and Anxious Patriarchs,* 75–80; Jonathan W. White, "A Civil War Hermaphrodite," *Civil War History* 62 (September 2016): 321–28.

expressed longings for individual and collective freedom. Vanessa M. Holden and Jessica Marie Johnson organized the Queering Slavery Working Group (#QSWG) as a way to organize and inspire scholarship around the concept of queering analyses of enslavement. In her contribution to *The Routledge History of Queer America* (2018), Clare Sears concluded that "queer historical studies of slavery are not only academically viable but also politically necessary to foreground the specificities of black queer histories and center slavery's constitutive role in modern sexualities." Such work promises not only to expand on LGBTQ history but to bring new insights into the sexualities of all early southerners.[50]

Still, as historians pursue more nuanced analyses of women, gender, and sexuality in the early South, popular perceptions of the region remain all too often locked in mythology. Persistent popular myths about gender and sexuality in the Old South have, in fact, created an entire subculture. For example, the Southern—a film genre like the Western—presents little more than nostalgia. From *Birth of a Nation* (1915) to *Gone with the Wind* (1939), powerful myths have reigned; from *Mandingo* (1975) to *Django Unchained* (2012), filmmakers have exploited stereotypes. The rise of the televised miniseries late in the twentieth century created a wave of portraits of the antebellum South including *Roots* (1977), *Freedom Road* (1979), and *North and South* (1985). From ghost tours to plantation "pilgrimages," a thriving cottage industry portrays a very idealized, partisan, and decidedly racialized image of an iconic South in broadcasting, media, and online culture (for example, Pinterest). Southern historians are thoughtfully interrogating that, too.[51]

50. Vincent Woodard, *The Delectable Negro: Human Consumption and Homoeroticism within U.S. Slave Culture,* ed. Justin A. Joyce and Dwight A. McBride (New York: New York University Press, 2014); Aliyyah I. Abdur-Rahman, *Against the Closet: Black Political Longing and the Erotics of Race* (Durham: Duke University Press, 2012); Abdur-Rahman, "'The Strangest Freaks of Despotism': Queer Sexuality in Antebellum African American Slave Narratives," *African American Review* 40 (Summer 2006): 223–37; C. Riley Snorton, *Black on Both Sides: A Racial History of Trans Identity* (Minneapolis: University of Minnesota Press, 2017); Omise'eke Natasha Tinsley, "Black Atlantic, Queer Atlantic: Queer Imaginings of the Middle Passage," *GLQ: A Journal of Lesbian and Gay Studies* 14 (June 2008): 191–215; Clare Sears, "Centering Slavery in Nineteenth-Century Queer History (1800s–1890s)," in *The Routledge History of Queer America,* ed. Don Romesburg (New York: Routledge, 2018), 39. For information on the Queering Slavery Working Group, see https://qswg.wordpress.com/about/ (accessed 18 January 2019).

51. *Birth of a Nation,* directed by D. W. Griffith, screenplay by Thomas Dixon Jr. (D. W. Griffith Corp., 1915); *Gone with the Wind,* directed by Victor Fleming, screenplay by Sidney Howard (Warner Bros., 1939); *Mandingo,* directed by Richard Fleischer, screenplay by Norman Wexler (Dino De Laurentiis Co., 1975); *Django Unchained,* directed by Quentin Tarantino, screenplay by Quentin Tarantino (Wienstein Co.,

Once understood and defined only as women's history, a marginal field attracting minority interest and either tagged onto the end of books or relegated to footnotes, writing history through the prism of gender has completely transformed the history of the Old South. Gender analysis, broadly defined, is challenging both the scope and methodology of the field. Such approaches to the southern past can require difficult reading and writing, especially when confronting racialized sexual violence and sexualized oppression. And scholars face an uphill battle in moving popular perceptions of southern gender and sexuality past the romanticized vision of Tara in *Gone with the Wind*. Yet this innovative and imbricated history is praiseworthy, providing an evolving historiography well worth emulating.

2012); *Roots,* eight episodes, directed by Marvin J. Chomsky et al., aired 23–30 January 1977 on ABC (David L. Wolper Prod., 1977); *Freedom Road,* directed by Jan Kadar, aired 29–30 October 1979 on NBC (Braun Entertainment Group, 1979); *North and South,* directed by Richard T. Heffron, aired 3–10 November 1985 on ABC (David L. Wolper Prod., 1985); Tara McPherson, *Reconstructing Dixie: Race, Gender and Nostalgia in the Imagined South* (Durham: Duke University Press, 2003); Karen L. Cox, *Dreaming of Dixie: How the South Was Created in American Popular Culture* (Chapel Hill: University of North Carolina Press, 2011); Edward D. C. Campbell Jr., *The Celluloid South: Hollywood and the Southern Myth* (Knoxville: University of Tennessee Press, 1981); David Ebner and Larry Langman, *Hollywood's Image of the South: A Century of Southern Film* (Westport: Greenwood Press, 2001); Rudyard Alcocer, Kristen Block, and Dawn Duke, eds., *Celluloid Chains: Slavery in the Americas Through Film* (Knoxville: University of Tennessee Press, 2018). See also Brenda E. Stevenson, "Filming Black Voices and Stories: Slavery on America's Screens," *Journal of the Civil War Era* 8 (September 2018): 488–520; Catherine Clinton, "Foucault Meets Mandingo," in *The Plantation Mistress,* 223–31; Clinton, "The Road to Tara," in *Tara Revisited: Women, War and the Plantation Legend* (New York: Abbeville Press, 1995), 191–213. On plantation tours, see, for example, the Natchez Pilgrimage Tour industry, https://natchezpilgrimage.com/ (accessed 18 January 2019).

ON THE BANKS OF THE JAMES OR THE CONGAREE

Antebellum Political Economy

Harry L. Watson and John D. Majewski

In his entry on "History" for Denis Diderot's great *Encyclopédie,* Voltaire posed to aspiring historians his own version of the "so what?" question. "If you have nothing to tell us," he asked, "other than that one Barbarian has replaced another Barbarian on the banks of the Oxus and the Jaxartes, in what way are you useful to the public?" Historians who wish to write about the barbarians who succeeded one another on the banks of the James, the Congaree, and other rivers of the antebellum South confront a similar question. Our dilemma is sharpened by a famously dismissive remark by Charles S. Sydnor, who charged that "party conflict south of the Potomac . . . had the hollow sound of a stage duel with tin swords." In Sydnor's view, Jacksonian party competition grew out of clashes between northern industrialists and free laborers, so "the agrarian South felt little interest." For Sydnor, the major issues and institutions of Jacksonian politics were disconnected from southern society, devised outside the region for the benefit of others and fundamentally imposed on voters whose real attentions lay elsewhere. "One must remember," he concluded, "that major southern hopes and fears found no champion in either [national] party."[1]

1. François-Marie Arouet de Voltaire, "Histoire," in Denis Diderot, ed., *Encyclopédie ou Dictionnaire raisonné des sciences, des arts et des métiers,* 28 vols. (Paris: Briasson, David, Le Breton, and Durand, 1765), 8: 220–25, in *The Encyclopedia of Diderot & d'Alembert Collaborative Translation Project,* trans. Jeremy Caradonna, 2006, http://hdl.handle.net/2027/spo.did2222.0000.088 (accessed 21 May 2019); Charles S. Sydnor, *The Development of Southern Sectionalism, 1819–1848* (Baton Rouge: Louisiana State University Press, 1948), 316. The Oxus and Jaxartes are rivers in Central Asia. The authors are grateful for the help of our research assistant, Luke Cullifer.

Taken literally, Voltaire's and Sydnor's dicta might give political historians little reason to study antebellum southern politics at all, at least outside the secession movement. If the party battles of Whigs and Democrats had little connection to southern society, why study them? But what if the dicta were wrong, especially Sydnor's? What if public affairs by the James and the Congaree were indeed deeply imbued with Sydnor's "major southern hopes and fears"? What would such contests and struggles concern? How should we look for them or interpret them? Since the 1970s, historians of antebellum southern politics have tried to look past the alleged stage duel. The questions they have asked point well beyond routine contests for public office to the broader topic of political economy and the viability of the South's slave-based society. How did southerners use state power to support their immediate economic ambitions and activities, and how did political debates reflect ways in which different groups imagined the long-term future of their slave society?

The result has been a series of lively debates over the character of the slaveholding economy and a new appreciation of contemporary efforts to control it through the exercise of state power. Much contention has revolved around a classic taxonomic question: was slavery a form of capitalism? The stakes for this seemingly abstract question are high, for scholars have generally assumed that if slavery was not capitalism, it must have been inefficient, backward, and doomed to collapse. It might have fallen on its own, or perhaps its fundamental differences with the northern economy made sectional conflict (and the South's defeat) inevitable.

Historians have approached these big questions through a series of smaller ones. Was the slave South truly backward economically, as northern observers long believed? Or was its slave-based economy—for all its moral horrors—nevertheless prosperous and dynamic, at least for the whites it was designed to serve? Were planters indifferent to progress or did they want to "modernize" slavery? And would they use state power to do so? Most fundamentally, did disputes over political economy have important consequences for southerners' readiness and disposition for sectional conflict? If so, the succession of leaders on the banks of the James and the Congaree (and elsewhere among the South's capitals) had important implications for the social, economic, and political stability of slave-based society. In short, the debate over capitalism takes us beyond the stage duel and allows us to analyze serious conflicts over the future of the nineteenth-century South.

Slavery as Anti-Capitalism

The capitalism debate is deeply rooted in a traditional view that free labor is always more efficient than enslaved labor and thus more profitable and progressive. Articulated most famously by Adam Smith, this critique of slavery became part of conventional wisdom.[2] Smith's contemporaries, such as Scottish gentlewoman Janet Schaw, saw that logic at work in the southern colonies. "Every instrument of husbandry [is] unknown here," she complained from North Carolina. "The only instrument used is a hoe, with which they at once till and plant the corn," a practice she called an "absurd method" for "it will take twenty [enslaved people] at least to do as much work as two horses with a man and a boy would perform" in Scotland. The Reverend Jedediah Morse added more detail in his *American Geography,* first published in 1784. Virginians, he found, were "indolent, easy, and good-natured; extremely fond of society, and much given to convivial pleasures" but "seldom show any spirit of enterprize, or expose themselves willingly to fatigue." Like countless other New Englanders, Morse blamed slavery, racism, and the weather. "Their authority over their slaves renders them vain and imperious," he decided, instilling "many errors and prejudices, especially in regard to Indians and Negroes," and leaving Virginians far behind in "literary, mechanical, nautical, agricultural, and manufactural improvements." Half a century later, future Republican giant William F. Seward was even more vivid: "It was necessary that I should travel in Virginia to have any idea of a slave State. . . . An exhausted soil, old and decaying towns, wretchedly-neglected roads, and, in every respect, an absence of enterprise and improvement, distinguish the region through which we have come, in contrast to that in which we live. Such has been the effect of slavery." Nineteenth-century southern novelists and political spokesmen often conveyed a similar impression with a different spin. In their view, slavery dampened the southern economy but softened greed and materialism, encouraged kindly relations between masters and the enslaved, and gave its inhabitants an easy, gracious, and refined lifestyle.[3]

2. Adam Smith, *An Inquiry into the Nature and Causes of the Wealth of Nations,* in *The Glasgow Edition of the Works and Correspondence of Adam Smith,* ed. William B. Todd, 2 vols. (New York: Oxford University Press, 2014), 2:387–88.

3. Janet Schaw, *Journal of a Lady of Quality; Being the Narrative of a Journey from Scotland to the West Indies, North Carolina, and Portugal, in the Years 1774 to 1776,* ed. Evangeline Walker Andrews and Charles McLean Andrews (New Haven: Yale University Press, 1921), 163–64; Jedidiah Morse, *The American Geography; or, A View of the Present Situation of the United States of America* (Elizabethtown, NJ: Shepard

Based on such apparently unanimous testimony, it was small wonder that early generations of professional historians accepted the story of a backward, premodern South. The more sophisticated statement of this view appeared in 1961 with the publication of Eugene D. Genovese's *The Political Economy of Slavery*, which was later buttressed by works he coauthored with Elizabeth Fox-Genovese. Grounded in a firm but nuanced Marxism, Genovese described enslavers as a ruling class devoted to self-preservation and whose entire culture and way of life depended upon slavery. Plagued by the institution's inefficiencies and their slaves' recalcitrance, however, Genovese's slaveholders found modernized agriculture and industrial adaptations both impossible and unthinkable, since adopting them would destroy the planter class. The result was recurrent soil exhaustion, feeding endless demands for more slave territory and resulting in irresolvable conflicts with the free states. Genovese thus neatly tied slavery's deficiencies and incompatibility with free labor to a theory of southern decline and Civil War causation. "From the moment slavery passed from being one of several labor systems into being the basis of the Southern social order," he concluded, "material and ideological conflict with the North came into being and had to grow worse."[4]

A similar perspective informed Genovese's and Fox-Genovese's rejection of slavery as a form of capitalism. Like Marx, they saw true capitalism as a progressive system, normally evolving continuously into something at once more developed, productive, exploitative, and unstable. Capitalists depended on the power to hire and fire workers freely and to move their capital nimbly as better opportunities appeared. Nominally free, wage workers who could not control what or how they produced were thus fundamental to the capitalist mode of production. An economy dependent upon slavery could never be true capitalism because owned workers tied up capital, constrained investment choices, hobbled the reallocation of labor, and thus discouraged industrialization. As the northern economy demonstrated, moreover, capitalism needed free workers who could de-

Kollock, 1789), 388; William R. Taylor, *Cavalier and Yankee: The Old South and American National Character* (New York: George Braziller, 1961), 145–65; Frederick W. Seward, *Autobiography of William H. Seward, from 1801 to 1834: With a Memoir of His Life, and Selections from His Letters from 1831 to 1846* (New York: D. Appleton, 1877), 268. Still more prominent critiques of the economic effects of slavery appeared in Hinton Rowan Helper, *The Impending Crisis of the South: How to Meet It* (New York: Burdick Bros., 1857); Frederick Law Olmsted, *The Cotton Kingdom: A Traveller's Observations on Cotton and Slavery in the American Slave States* (New York: Mason Brothers, 1861).

4. Eugene D. Genovese, *The Political Economy of Slavery: Studies in the Economy and Society of the Slave South* (New York: Pantheon Books, 1965), 8.

mand higher wages, seek better jobs, buy consumer goods, gain education, work for their own advancement, and stimulate the economy in ever-more complex directions. Though slaveholders freely conducted market-based exchanges with suppliers, factors, banks, slave traders, and each other, their productive system rested on captivity and force. Genovese and Fox-Genovese thus insisted that, without the defining freedoms of true capitalism, the Old South was "in but not of the capitalist world."[5]

As elaborated in his magnum opus, *Roll, Jordan, Roll* (1974), Genovese believed that violence alone could not have controlled enslaved people entirely, for it provoked resistance, outraged outsiders, and undermined the masters' self-regard. Instead, he argued, the planters preferred to rule by "paternalism," which was certainly not kindness, but a series of personal negotiations (evolving into customary rights) under which enslaved laborers more or less submitted to plantation discipline in exchange for concessions and some room for lives of their own. When these failed, the whip was always available. Genovese and Fox-Genovese stressed that planters praised their system, despite its underlying brutality, for the organic ties that supposedly bound masters to slaves, allowing kinder and gentler patriarchs to fondly refer to their dependents as "our family black and white."[6]

Genovese and Fox-Genovese thus called slavery "premodern," precapitalist," and "quasi-seigneurial."[7] The South exported commodities to an emerging capitalist world and brought riches and social and political power to its master class,

5. Elizabeth Fox-Genovese and Eugene D. Genovese, *Fruits of Merchant Capital: Slavery and Bourgeois Property in the Rise and Expansion of Capitalism* (New York: Oxford University Press, 1983), 16. A useful, contemporaneous survey that demonstrated how historians perpetuated the notion of a premodern, backward South is James C. Bonner, "Plantation and Farm: The Agricultural South," in *Writing Southern History: Essays in Historiography in Honor of Fletcher M. Green*, ed. Arthur S. Link and Rembert W. Patrick (Baton Rouge: Louisiana State University Press, 1965), 147–74.

6. Eugene D. Genovese, *Roll, Jordan, Roll: The World the Slaves Made* (New York: Pantheon Books, 1974), 25–97, esp. 75–77. See also Genovese and Elizabeth Fox-Genovese, *Fatal Self-Deception: Slaveholding Paternalism in the Old South* (New York: Cambridge University Press, 2011). Contrary to some readings, the planters' usage of "family" was archaic but not aberrant. From 1388, the oldest definition of "family" in *The Oxford English Dictionary* is "the servants of a particular household or establishment, considered collectively." By 1452, "family" also meant "a group of people living as a household, traditionally consisting of parents and their children, and also (chiefly in early use) any servants, boarders, etc."

7. Fox-Genovese and Genovese, *Fruits of Merchant Capital*, 59; Genovese, *The Political Economy of Slavery*, 3, 19.

but it could not sustain its own advanced capitalist society. It could therefore *grow* economically, but it could not *develop.*

Genovese and Fox-Genovese won widespread recognition and even acclaim, but as J. William Harris aptly observed in his thorough and sensitive 2014 retrospective of Eugene D. Genovese's work, "acclaim . . . did not equate to agreement." Many scholars recoiled at the word "paternalist," for example, and confused it with "benevolent," an interpretation Genovese always rejected. "No matter how much an historian may seek to use the word [paternalist] in a value-free sense," noted William Dusinberre in his study of major Lowcountry rice planters, "popular understanding of the term makes it almost impossible to do so." Others seemed impatient with abstract contrasts between waged and coerced labor, saw the planters' obvious profit motives, and applied the label "capitalist" as a common-sense distinction between plantations and subsistence agriculture. Also drawing on Marx, Charles Sellers linked "capitalist slavery" to the growth of capitalism per se and its cult of property rights, including the right to human property. According to Laurence Shore, proslavery ideologues put capitalist arguments at the core of slavery's defense and used them to prove the economic superiority of their system.[8]

The Liberal Critique of Slavery

A much different challenge to Genovese arose from economists such as Robert William Fogel and Stanley L. Engerman, who in *Time on the Cross* (1974) used econometric or "cliometric" analyses that treated the plantation like any other capitalist enterprise and attacked the notion of southern backwardness. Notwithstanding the arguments of Adam Smith, they relied heavily on cliometrics to find that slave labor was significantly more efficient than its northern counterpart, meaning that slaves produced more value per unit of labor, land, and capital

8. J. William Harris, "Eugene D. Genovese's Old South: A Review Essay," *Journal of Southern History* 80 (May 2014): 327–72, quote on 340; William Dusinberre, *Them Dark Days: Slavery in the American Rice Swamps* (New York: Oxford University Press, 1996), 202–6; Charles Sellers, *The Market Revolution: Jacksonian America, 1815–1846* (New York: Oxford University Press, 1991), 396–97; Laurence Shore, *Southern Capitalists: The Ideological Leadership of an Elite, 1832–1885* (Chapel Hill: University of North Carolina Press, 1986), 16–41. For a rebuttal, see Eugene D. Genovese, review of *Them Dark Days* by William Dusinberre, *African American Review* 32 (Spring 1998): 159–61.

than free laborers. Their work sparked a furious debate among cliometric and conventional historians and ultimately led Fogel to modify some of his earlier conclusions. He continued to maintain, however, that the appearance of southern backwardness had more to do the extraordinary wealth of the Northeast than any intrinsic weakness. In *Without Consent or Contract* (1989), he reiterated that the South, measured separately from the North, stood "as the fourth most prosperous nation of the world in 1860."[9]

The work of Fogel and Engerman cast a long shadow over southern economic history, but most economists rejected the notion of a highly successful slave economy. Gavin Wright ranked among the most persistent critics of Fogel and Engerman. In 1978, Wright made a useful distinction between the behavior of planters and that of yeoman farmers of the Cotton Belt. Both grew cotton, but unlike planters, yeomen tried to shun debt, avoid insolvency, and safeguard their small landholdings by growing proportionately more corn for family consumption. What Wright called "safety-first" farming brought yeoman farmers greater security but lower incomes and created two Souths—a prosperous plantation sector and a hardscrabble yeomanry who depended on barter for much of what they could not make themselves. The plantation sector *seemed* more efficient because yeomen grew their own food (which did not show up in sales figures), while planters took advantage of high prices and earned conspicuous profits by forcing their slaves to grow cotton for the market.[10] Roger L. Ransom and Richard Sutch agreed that "the South was indeed stagnating with respect to the North and that the only recourse left to white southerners who wished to better their positions was to move westward."[11]

9. Robert William Fogel and Stanley L. Engerman, *Time on the Cross: The Economics of American Negro Slavery* (Boston: Little, Brown, 1974), 191–96; Fogel, *Without Consent or Contract: The Rise and Fall of American Slavery* (New York: W. W. Norton, 1989), 87.

10. Gavin Wright, *The Political Economy of the Cotton South: Households, Markets, and Wealth in the Nineteenth Century* (New York: W. W. Norton, 1978), 87–88. For an analysis that builds on Wright to describe the Old South as a "dual economy," see Harry L. Watson, "Slavery and Development in a Dual Economy: The South and the Market Revolution," in *The Market Revolution in America: Social, Political, and Religious Expressions, 1800–1880*, ed. Melvyn Stokes and Stephen Conway (Charlottesville: University Press of Virginia, 1996), 43–73.

11. Roger L. Ransom, *Conflict and Compromise: The Political Economy of Slavery, Emancipation, and the American Civil War* (New York: Cambridge University Press, 1989), 51–53; Roger L. Ransom and Richard Sutch, *One Kind of Freedom: The Economic Consequences of Emancipation* (New York: Cambridge University Press, 1977), 268. See also Robert E. Wright, *The Poverty of Slavery: How Unfree Labor Pollutes the Economy* (New York: Palgrave Macmillan, 2017).

In *Slavery and Economic Development* (2006), Wright built on these ideas to ask why slavery apparently inhibited industrialization, technological growth, and other forms of economic improvement. He answered that slaves were most valuable as a form of property, which could be bought and sold. Mobility dissuaded ambitious slave-owners from improving their neighborhoods, investing in transportation to boost land values, or fostering education to upgrade local skills. Without large, profit-making plantations in which to invest their money, northern farmers provided a livelier market for consumer products, and a labor force to make them. The resulting economic variety led to more diversification, more nonfarm jobs, larger cities, and a higher volume of immigration. At first glance, slavery appeared so valuable that the region's wealth (including the value of enslaved people) per each free person was 80 percent higher than the North's, but the North was 64 percent richer than the South if the slaves were counted as persons rather than property. Planters could become very well off and the South seemed rich by some measures, but most of its capital consisted of enslaved bodies, and such wealth would not survive the Civil War.[12]

The critique offered by Wright and other economists resembled the accounts of eighteenth- and nineteenth-century liberals such as Smith and Seward. Indeed, one might classify the work of Wright and other economists as a continuation of the long-standing liberal critique of slavery. An important strand of economics literature has focused on the importance of democratic governance and the rule of law for achieving economic development. The inequality and privilege embedded in slavery thus created a political regime that worked against long-term development. Slaveholders resisted investments in public education, for example, so southern literacy and school attendance levels fell dramatically behind northern rates. Deficient education inhibited innovation before the Civil War: free southerners accounted for approximately 30 percent of the nation's free population, for example, yet patented less than 6 percent of its inventions.[13]

12. Gavin Wright, *Slavery and American Economic Development* (Baton Rouge: Louisiana State University Press, 2006), 57.

13. Stanley L. Engerman and Kenneth L. Sokoloff, "Factor Endowments, Inequality, and Paths of Development among New World Economies: A View from Economic Historians of the United States," in *How Latin America Fell Behind: Essays on the Economic Histories of Brazil and Mexico, 1800–1914*, ed. Stephen Haber (Stanford: Stanford University Press, 1997), 260–304; Sun Go and Peter Lindert, "The Uneven Rise of American Public Schools to 1850," *Journal of Economic History* 70 (March 2010): 1–26; Claudia Goldin and Lawrence F Katz, *The Race Between Education and Technology* (Cambridge: Harvard University Press, 2008), 129–62; B. Zorina Khan, *The Democratization of Invention: Patents and Copyrights*

The liberal critique of slavery extended well beyond economists. In *Slavery and Freedom* (1990), historian James Oakes offered an interpretation of the Old South that stressed the tight bonds between slavery and liberal capitalism, so much so that he and Genovese seemed at polar opposites. On closer examination, however, Oakes treated slavery and capitalism as connected but not identical, much as Genovese had situated slavery in the capitalist world but not of it. "A highly developed market economy was a precondition to the emergence of any slave society," Oakes wrote, "yet master and slave formed what was, at bottom, a nonmarket relationship." Genovese stressed soil exhaustion as a major factor in slavery's expansion, and Oakes linked planter migration to the economic ambitions and westward movement of American farmers, but both understood the importance of an ever-growing Cotton Belt. For Oakes, a common concern for landed property and white men's rights tied planters and yeomen together but left them far enough apart on issues of economic development to fuel ferocious party combat.[14]

The liberal critique of slavery acknowledged the modernizing impulses of profit-minded slaveholders, but it stressed how these efforts usually fell short, especially in comparison to northern efforts. Railroads offer a case in point. In 1860, the slave states contained 10,865 miles of railroad track to the free states' 19,770. The two regions differed in population and population density, of course, but the contrast in railroad infrastructure still seemed glaring. It appears, moreover, that planters hesitated to finance railroads themselves, preferring to concentrate their resources in land and slaves, or possibly that their system did not generate the capital required for infrastructural investments. Either way, southern railroads drew some 57 percent of their funding from various governments, especially the states, compared to 25 or 30 percent nationwide. Moreover, the South's transportation system mostly existed to carry imports and exports; it did not provide a network for diversified internal trade that could lead to future development. In fact, the South's railroad network was fragmented and incomplete, with railroad companies in states such as Virginia more interested in serving the local interests

---

in American Economic Development, 1790–1920 (New York: Cambridge University Press, 2005), 189. Keri Leigh Merrit highlights the lack of education for southern poor whites in *Masterless Men: Poor Whites and Slavery in the Antebellum South* (New York: Alfred A. Knopf, 2017), 143–78.

14. James Oakes, *Slavery and Freedom: An Interpretation of the Old South* (New York: Alfred A. Knopf, 1990), 54, 80–136. See also Oakes, *The Ruling Race: A History of American Slaveholders* (New York: Alfred A. Knopf, 1982).

of planters than in building an interregional network to spur industrialization and urbanization. The South's industrial development lagged, contributing only 11 percent of the nation's manufactured goods in 1860. To be sure, the South may have compared well with many other countries and with the western states, but as Douglas R. Egerton remarked, "southern whites compared their situation to the capitalist North, not to Colombia or Venezuela, and when they did so they found their own region sadly lacking."[15]

The South was not entirely bereft of factories. From 1845 until his death in 1867, William Gregg operated a large and productive cotton mill at Graniteville, South Carolina, and Daniel Pratt's Alabama factory became the world's largest producer of cotton gins. Richmond's Tredegar Iron Works flourished from 1837 until 1877 and became a major supplier of Confederate weaponry. Gregg employed white workers only; Pratt and Tredegar paid whites to work alongside enslaved blacks; and other southern factories relied entirely on enslaved operatives. Tom Downey found that the area of South Carolina surrounding William Gregg's Graniteville cotton mill became a hive of commercial and industrial activity by the 1850s, though the area's businessmen never broke the hold of agrarian and proslavery ideology among the region's planters. In his widely-praised *Bond of Iron* (1994), Charles B. Dew traced a very successful example from the Shenandoah Valley's Buffalo Forge, where an extensive ironmaking operation endured over multiple generations. Skilled enslaved workers who dominated its labor force were clearly key to its operations and earned wages for their work. But could slavery have survived if most slaves—like some at Buffalo Forge—held substantial bank accounts?[16]

15. George Rogers Taylor, *The Transportation Revolution, 1815–1860* (New York: Rinehart, 1951), 79; James A. Ward, "A New Look at Antebellum Southern Railroad Development," *Journal of Southern History* 39 (August 1973): 413; Sean Patrick Adams, *Old Dominion, Industrial Commonwealth: Coal, Politics, and Economy in Antebellum America* (Baltimore: Johns Hopkins University Press, 2004); John Majewski, *A House Dividing: Economic Development in Pennsylvania and Virginia before the Civil War* (New York: Cambridge University Press, 2000); Fox-Genovese and Genovese, *Fruits of Merchant Capital,* 59; Fred Bateman and Thomas Weiss, *A Deplorable Scarcity: The Failure of Industrialization in the Slave Economy* (Chapel Hill: University of North Carolina Press, 1981), 6; Douglas R. Egerton, "Markets without a Market Revolution: Southern Planters and Capitalism," *Journal of the Early Republic* 16 (Summer 1996): 215.

16. Genovese, *The Political Economy of Slavery,* 180–220; Tom Downey, *Planting a Capitalist South: Masters, Merchants, and Manufacturers in the Southern Interior, 1790–1860* (Baton Rouge: Louisiana State University Press, 2006); Charles B. Dew, *Bond of Iron: Master and Slave at Buffalo Forge* (New York: W. W. Norton, 1994). See also Bess Beatty, *Alamance: The Holt Family and Industrialization in a North Carolina County, 1837–1900* (Baton Rouge: Louisiana State University Press, 1999); Laura Croghan Kamoie,

Indeed, other examples of southern industry proved far less successful. Michael J. Gagnon's careful study of Athens, Georgia, suggests that material, cultural, and political barriers plagued the South's industrialists. As early as the 1820s, town boosters and local planters organized textile mills to stimulate and transform the local economy, successfully pushing for supportive rail connections. The early mills enjoyed some success making coarse cottons and woolens to clothe both enslaved laborers and yeoman farmers and their families. Northern mills enjoyed a head start, however, and used Athens's railroad to penetrate its markets and undersell local producers, badly damaging its local textile industry. If undisturbed, the town's industrialists might have ignited a self-starting economic transformation of the Georgia Upcountry. Or maybe not. Without a public education system comparable to that in New England, literacy rates lagged badly and robbed Georgians of the cultural capital to support a more developed economy.[17]

Slavery as a Form of Economic Modernity

Even as the liberal critique of slavery flourished, a series of books about the slave trade began depicting the institution as a thoroughly modern and successful system for southern planters. In 1989, Michael Tadman led with *Speculators and Slaves,* the first full-scale examination of the interstate slave trade since Frederic Bancroft's pioneering *Slave Trading in the Old South* (1931). The domestic slave trade hinged on the massive expansion of cotton culture that began in the 1790s and accelerated after 1815, prompted by the rise of the textile industry, the perfection of the cotton gin, the Louisiana Purchase, and the expulsion of the southwestern Indians. Tadman showed that as many as one million enslaved people were taken from the Upper to the Lower South following the end of legal

---

Irons in the Fire: The Business History of the Tayloe Family and Virginia's Gentry, 1700–1860 (Charlottesville: University of Virginia Press, 2007); Mark Cooper Pope III with J. Donald McKee, *Mark Anthony Cooper: The Iron Man of Georgia, A Biography* (Atlanta: Graphic Publishing, 2000). See also three excellent collections of essays sponsored by the Southern Industrial Project: Susanna Delfino and Michele Gillespie, eds., *Neither Lady nor Slave: Working Women of the Old South* (Chapel Hill: University of North Carolina Press, 2002); Delfino and Gillespie, eds., *Technology, Innovation, and Southern Industrialization: From the Antebellum Era to the Computer Age* (Columbia: University of Missouri Press, 2008); Delfino, Gillespie, and Louis M. Kyriakoudes, eds., *Southern Society and Its Transformations, 1790–1860* (Columbia: University of Missouri Press, 2011).

17. Michael J. Gagnon, *Transition to an Industrial South: Athens, Georgia, 1830–1870* (Baton Rouge: Louisiana State University Press, 2012).

importations from Africa in 1808, at least 60 percent of them by professional traders. The average Upper South slave, Tadman calculated, had a 30 percent chance of interregional sale before the age of forty. In addition, buyers and sellers made no serious effort to avoid family separations; the slave trade tore more than half of all enslaved African Americans in the Upper South from a spouse or a parent.[18]

Walter Johnson's *Soul by Soul* (1999) built on Tadman's grim statistics with a cultural analysis of the meaning of the slave market for buyers, sellers, and the sold. Focusing on New Orleans, the nation's largest slave market, Johnson found the essence of slavery in the "chattel principle," a term first coined by black abolitionist James W. C. Pennington, because it pinpointed the slave's status as property, as a "person with a price."[19] Johnson showed how slave sales penetrated virtually every corner of the South's society and culture, underpinning its economy, shaping individual and collective wealth, igniting dreams of riches, and pervading the consciousness of those who might be sold. In this environment, enslaved men and women, understanding their own skills and status, actively used their knowledge to manipulate the process of sale. Johnson thus pointed to the sale itself, not the brutality of fieldwork, as the defining moment of enslavement and the site of its victims' most effective resistance. The chattel principle was so central, he concluded, that "the history of the Antebellum South is the history of two million slave sales." Important works by historians Robert H. Gudmestad and Steven Deyle joined Johnson in pinpointing the centrality of the slave trade to southern society.[20]

Johnson's identification of the slave trade as the defining feature of southern society did not contradict Wright's analysis that slave mobility led to southern

18. Michael Tadman, *Speculators and Slaves: Masters, Traders, and Slaves in the Old South* (Madison: University of Wisconsin Press, 1989), 31, 45, 147; Frederic Bancroft, *Slave Trading in the Old South* (Baltimore: J. H. Furst, 1931). By comparison, one estimate reported just over 400,000 enslaved people arrived in North America over the centuries of the African slave trade. See Appendix 2 in Patrick Manning, Yun Zhang, and Bowen Yi, "Volume and Direction of the Atlantic Slave Trade, 1650–1870: Estimates by Markov Chain Carlo Analysis," *Journal of World Historical Information* 2–3 (2014–2015): 147.

19. Walter Johnson, *Soul by Soul: Life Inside the Antebellum Slave Market* (Cambridge: Harvard University Press, 1999), 1–44. New and republished essays by over a dozen leading historians of the slave trade appeared in Walter Johnson, ed., *The Chattel Principle: Internal Slave Trades in the Americas* (New Haven: Yale University Press, 2004).

20. Johnson, *Soul by Soul,* 17; Robert H. Gudmestad, *A Troublesome Commerce: The Transformation of the Interstate Slave Trade* (Baton Rouge: Louisiana State University Press, 2003); Steven Deyle, *Carry Me Back: The Domestic Slave Trade in American Life* (New York: Oxford University Press, 2005), 59–63.

underdevelopment, but a new focus on the modernity of the slave trade tied bondage to the birth of modern capitalism. Scholars began to view the southwestern expansion of slavery as part of a transnational movement that Dale W. Tomich has called the "Second Slavery," to distinguish it from its colonial-era predecessor. Far from constraining slavery, Tomich pointed out, the Haitian Revolution and the legal end of the transatlantic slave trade coincided with a dramatic expansion of slavery in the United States, Cuba, and Brazil, sparked by the spread of cotton factories and cotton plantations to supply them, as well as the growth of mass markets for cotton, sugar, and coffee among the new class of industrial workers. "After 1790," wrote Anthony E. Kaye, in summarizing the concept, "slavery expanded onto new ground, slaves tended new crops and new machinery, and the planter classes gained dominance in rising world markets and acquired new powers from reconstituted states in Cuba, Brazil, and the South."[21]

The trigger for Tomich's Second Slavery was the same dramatic expansion of technology and intensified power of transnational market relations that historians have called the Market Revolution and associated with a wide variety of economic, social, and political changes within the United States. Depending on definitions, the Market Revolution may or may not have qualified as a new phase in the development of capitalism, but it certainly had an important impact on slavery. "In the new techniques and increased scale of production and the sheer mobility and adaptability of slave labor," Kaye continued, "the second slavery was, in a word, modern."[22]

21. Dale W. Tomich, "The Second Slavery: Bonded Labor and the Transformation of the Nineteenth-Century World Economy," in *Through the Prism of Slavery: Labor, Capital, and World Economy* (Lanham, MD: Rowman & Littlefield, 2004), 56–71; Anthony E. Kaye, "The Second Slavery: Modernity in the Nineteenth Century South and the Atlantic World," *Journal of Southern History* 75 (August 2009): 627. See also Andrew J. Torget, *Seeds of Empire: Cotton, Slavery, and the Transformation of the Texas Borderlands, 1800–1850* (Chapel Hill: University of North Carolina Press, 2015).

22. Kaye, "The Second Slavery," 628. For important discussions of the concept of the Market Revolution, see Sellers, *The Market Revolution;* Stokes and Conway, eds., *The Market Revolution in America;* John Lauritz Larson, *The Market Revolution in America: Liberty, Ambition, and the Eclipse of the Common Good* (New York: Cambridge University Press, 2009). Harry L. Watson applied the concept to antebellum politics in his *Liberty and Power: The Politics of Jacksonian America,* rev. ed. (New York: Hill & Wang, 1990), while Daniel Walker Howe challenged it in "Charles Sellers, the Market Revolution, and the Shaping of Identity in Whig-Jacksonian America," in *God and Mammon: Protestants, Money, and the Market: 1790–1860,* ed. Mark A. Noll (New York: Oxford University Press, 2001), 54–74. See also Howe, *What Hath God Wrought: The Transformation of America, 1815–1848* (New York: Oxford University Press, 2007).

In 2011, L. Diane Barnes, Frank Towers, and Brian Schoen followed Kaye's striking invocation of slavery's modernity with *The Old South's Modern Worlds,* a provocative collection that made a sweeping case for the modernity of slavery and the southern civilization it supported. Agreeing that the Old South was highly diverse, the editors nonetheless insisted that "each of the 'many Souths' was inextricably shaped by modern experience." To reach this conclusion, Barnes, Towers, and Schoen reimagined the South at the center of US history instead of at the periphery, thereby placing the South in a global context from which its economy, culture, and labor system no longer seemed exceptional or out-of-step. They rejected the contention that the northern states (and their British role model) were the best or only versions of nineteenth-century modernity. Abandoning teleological expectations, the editors preferred a definition of modernity that stressed both "cultural outlook" (the desire to be "up-with-the-times") and "material achievement" (the drive for economic rationality and productivity), and found the slave South modern on both counts.[23] Though American slaveholders knew and feared that their sphere was contracting both domestically and hemispherically, *The Old South's Modern Worlds* made a strong case for their deep connections to an evolving contemporary world.

As if to punctuate the argument that the Second Slavery relied heavily on advanced technology, a large literature reinterpreted the South's railroad system, finding it extensive and effective. In *Southwest Virginia's Railroad* (1994), for example, Kenneth W. Noe found that the Virginia & Tennessee Railroad brought an isolated portion of the Old Dominion much closer to Richmond and the economic heart of the state. The result was a surge in tobacco production and other forms of commercial agriculture, as well as the spread of slavery, the expansion of mining and industry, and closer ties to secessionist politics. Aaron W. Marrs found slavery and railroad technology well suited to each other. Northern and southern rail companies drew on a common pool of construction and operating talent, he reported, and southerners were not befuddled by romantic pastoral ideals. Southern shippers cheerfully embraced the advantages of rail technol-

23. L. Diane Barnes, Brian Schoen, and Frank Towers, eds., *The Old South's Modern Worlds: Slavery, Region, and Nation in the Age of Progress* (New York: Oxford University Press, 2011), 4, 10. For a multifaceted critique of the analysis of capitalism and modernity mounted by Barnes, Schoen, Towers, and several others that deploys perspectives from Marxist, modernization, world systems, and staple theory, see Scott Reynolds Nelson, "Who Put Their Capitalism in My Slavery?" *Journal of the Civil War Era* 5 (June 2015): 289–310.

ogy, and enslaved laborers worked smoothly in virtually all aspects of railroad operations.[24]

William G. Thomas agreed, showing that enslaved workers toiled extensively and efficiently on southern railroads, while enduring the same brutality they faced elsewhere. "Every hour in the day we could hear the whip going," one bound construction worker remembered. "There was hardly any day that some of the slaves did not get crippled or killed." The South joined the rest of the United States in a major railroad construction boom in the 1850s, building 8,300 out of a total of 22,000 new miles of US track in that decade, and reaching a total mileage of more than 10,000 in the region by 1860. Focusing on "modernity"—a matter of culture and outlook as much as material infrastructure—Thomas found that late antebellum southerners saw slavery as "the central principle of their society's modern development."[25]

A modern slaveholding economy necessarily fostered a small but significant middle class. Jonathan Daniel Wells documented a growing stratum of lawyers, doctors, merchants, and other professionals in the South's towns and cities in *The Origins of the Southern Middle Class* (2004). Heavily indebted to northern bourgeois culture, these families firmly defended their own respectability against planter pretensions and a roughhewn, white working class. They refused to embrace antislavery, however, and appeared to pin their future hopes on slave-based industrialization. Similar findings appeared in case studies published in *The Southern Middle Class in the Long Nineteenth Century,* a 2011 collection of essays that Wells edited with Jennifer R. Green. In his study of southern merchants and their families, Frank J. Byrne reinforced Wells's conclusions from the perspective

24. Kenneth W. Noe, *Southwest Virginia's Railroad: Modernization and the Sectional Crisis* (Urbana: University of Illinois Press, 1994). Phillip Shaw Paludan's earlier study came to similar conclusions; see *Victims: A True Story of the Civil War* (Knoxville: University of Tennessee Press, 1981). See also Aaron W. Marrs, *Railroads in the Old South: Pursuing Progress in a Slave Society* (Baltimore: Johns Hopkins University Press, 2009).

25. William G. Thomas, *The Iron Way: Railroads, the Civil War, and the Making of Modern America* (New Haven: Yale University Press, 2011), 3, also 21–22, 26–27, 36. Economists Mark A. Yanochik, Mark Thornton, and Bradley T. Ewing maintained that, in the 1850s, the demand of southern railroads for slave labor was so high that it powered the 1850s spike in slave prices, though others call this claim exaggerated; see "Railroad Construction and Antebellum Slave Prices," *Social Science Quarterly* 84 (September 2003): 723–37; Peter A. Coclanis, "Off Track: The Railroading of Antebellum Southern Economic History," *Social Science Quarterly* 84 (September 2003): 738–42; Mark A. Yanochik, Mark Thornton, and Bradley T. Ewing, "Railroad Construction and Slave Prices: Rejoinder and Extension," *Social Science Quarterly* 84 (September 2003): 744–49.

of cultural history. He too found that southern merchants shared many "northern" ideals, cherishing progress, liberal capitalism, and evangelical Christianity, and standing apart from other groups in the social spectrum. Though loyal to the Confederacy, they bounced back from defeat and played a crucial role in the credit-based rural economy of the New South.[26]

Other authors extended and elaborated on Byrne's emphasis on middle-class values. Examining commercial culture in Spartanburg, South Carolina, Bruce W. Eelman found a community of antebellum merchants who deployed an early booster culture to press for factory development, including an iron industry. Spartanburg suffered from a lack of common schools, but Jennifer R. Green and Timothy J. Williams have shown just how significant education was in ambitious middle-class families. While earlier writers argued that southern colleges taught little besides drinking, dueling, and honor, Green demonstrated how military schools offered scientific training and rigorous personal discipline to upwardly mobile students. Williams likewise found that the University of North Carolina instilled a passionate desire for "intellectual manhood"—refined personal maturity along with devotion to Victorian bourgeois virtues—in its mixed elite and middle-class student body. Somehow, the antebellum South fostered within itself a culture of striving and respectability that contradicted the aristocratic braggadocio for which its planters became famous.[27]

How far did this acceptance of bourgeois values extend beyond the South's nascent middle class? If the southern economy was capitalist, liberal, progressive, or simply "modern," how did that affect its ideology, identity, and self-conception, especially among its dominant master class? By the early twenty-first century, intellectual historians began to see extensive connections.

Surprisingly, it was Eugene D. Genovese who began to see the connections

26. Jonathan Daniel Wells, *The Origins of the Southern Middle Class, 1800–1861* (Chapel Hill: University of North Carolina Press, 2004); Wells and Jennifer R. Green, eds., *The Southern Middle Class in the Long Nineteenth Century* (Baton Rouge: Louisiana State University Press, 2011); Frank J. Byrne, *Becoming Bourgeois: Merchant Culture in the South, 1820–1865* (Lexington: University Press of Kentucky, 2006).

27. Bruce W. Eelman, *Entrepreneurs in the Southern Upcountry: Commercial Culture in Spartanburg, South Carolina, 1845–1880* (Athens: University of Georgia Press, 2008); Jennifer R. Green, *Military Education and the Emerging Middle Class in the Old South* (New York: Cambridge University Press, 2008); Timothy J. Williams, *Intellectual Manhood: University, Self, and Society in the Antebellum South* (Chapel Hill: University of North Carolina Press, 2015). See also James A. Ramage and Andrea S. Watkins, *Kentucky Rising: Democracy, Slavery, and Culture from the Early Republic to the Civil War* (Lexington: University Press of Kentucky, 2011).

between slaveholders and modernity. Early in his career, Genovese shaped a generation of debate by firmly declaring that the South's intellectual climate had been as premodern, precapitalist, and prebourgeois as its economy and society. Over time, however, as other scholars attacked his analysis, Genovese retreated, and he addressed the problem squarely in *The Slaveholders' Dilemma* (1992), acknowledging that leading southern intellectuals deeply admired the world of nineteenth-century material progress and recognized it as the product of economic and political freedom. They insisted, however, that unfettered capitalist progress had brought misery to millions, who might strike back with violent revolution. Only slavery could provide the order, discipline, and reciprocal obligations needed to soften capitalism's sharp edges. Slavery did not exclude modernity, Genovese claimed, but modified it to balance freedom with just enough restriction (for just the right people) to control its worst possibilities. A pithy observation by Chad Morgan summarized their attitude neatly: "Planters did not want to suppress industrialization, they wanted to control it."[28]

Genovese and Fox-Genovese later elaborated their thesis in a massive examination of antebellum southern thought, *The Mind of the Master Class* (2005), which appeared shortly after an equally massive survey by Michael O'Brien, *Conjectures of Order* (2004).[29] The two surveys agreed on very little. O'Brien forcefully affirmed the intellectual modernity of slaveholders whereas Genovese and Fox-Genovese did so hesitantly. Though he crafted no grand structure to organize and direct southern antebellum thinking, O'Brien's southerners were deeply informed and reflective, and thoughtfully wrote about a wide variety of subjects, not all of them related to slavery. He concluded, however, that southern intellectuals followed a similar path as their counterparts around the Atlantic: beginning in the nineteenth century with Enlightenment rationalism, they turned to Romanticism before edging toward literary modernism and realism. Without the ambivalence of Genovese and Fox-Genovese's slaveholders, they embraced modernity while carving out an exception for their "peculiar institution." Like

28. Eugene D. Genovese, *The Slaveholders' Dilemma: Freedom and Progress in Southern Conservative Thought, 1820–1860* (Columbia: University of South Carolina Press, 1992); Chad Morgan, "Progressive Slaveholders: Planters, Intellectuals, and Georgia's Antebellum Economic Development," *Georgia Historical Quarterly* 86 (Fall 2002): 400.

29. Elizabeth Fox-Genovese and Eugene D. Genovese, *The Mind of the Master Class: History and Faith in the Southern Slaveholders' Worldview* (New York: Cambridge University Press, 2005); Michael O'Brien, *Conjectures of Order: Intellectual Life and the American South, 1810–1860*, 2 vols. (Chapel Hill: University of North Carolina Press, 2004).

the rational planters and slaveholding industrialists who surrounded them, they demanded their own version of progress, not its antithesis.

The New Historians of Capitalism

Focus on slavery's apparent modernity raised a question that turned the liberal consensus on its head: what if slavery was not simply consistent with economic modernization but *essential* for the rise of capitalism? The question motivated a 2011 conference at Brown University entitled "Slavery's Capitalism," whose proceedings Sven Beckert and Seth Rockman edited and published in 2016. The contributors did not tie themselves to a particular definition of capitalism; Rockman had already warned against the dead ends built into that puzzle. Instead, they took the Justice Potter Stewart approach ("I know it when I see it") and identified capitalism by such characteristic features as scientific management, advanced accounting practices, innovative technology, and sophisticated financial instruments. Their ultimate goal was clearly not to praise slavery's efficiency, but to assert the institution's role in creating modernity (especially in the United States) and to implicate capitalism in its brutality. The editors made this perspective clear in their introduction, calling slavery "*the* foundational American institution, organizing the nation's politics, legal structures, and cultural practices," and "indispensable to the economic development of the United States."[30] If this were true, could we ever call slavery the South's "peculiar institution" again?

These early papers helped set the stage for three important monographs that anchored discussion of slavery within the new history of capitalism: Sven Beckert's *Empire of Cotton* (2014), Walter Johnson's *River of Dark Dreams* (2013), and Edward E. Baptist's *The Half Has Never Been Told* (2014).[31] Of the three, Beckert's volume stretched widest, as it ranged from the earliest cultivation of *Gossypium hirsutum* in ancient Meso-America, across the bloody eras of European empire-building in the Americas, India, and Africa, through the factory growth

30. Sven Beckert and Seth Rockman, eds., *Slavery's Capitalism: A New History of American Economic Development* (Philadelphia: University of Pennsylvania Press, 2016), 1, italics added; Seth Rockman, "Slavery and Capitalism," in "Forum: The Future of Civil War Era Studies," *Journal of the Civil War Era* 2 (March 2012): 3. See also Walter Johnson, "The Pedestal and the Veil: Rethinking the Capitalism/Slavery Question," *Journal of the Early Republic* 24 (Summer 2004): 299–308.

31. Sven Beckert, *Empire of Cotton: A Global History* (New York: Alfred A. Knopf, 2014); Walter Johnson, *River of Dark Dreams: Slavery and Empire in the Cotton Kingdom* (Cambridge: Harvard University Press, 2013); Edward E. Baptist, *The Half Has Never Been Told: Slavery and the Making of American*

of the Industrial Revolution, and on to cotton's fate in the twentieth century. The South's Cotton Kingdom played a crucial role throughout, first as a source of slave-grown fiber and later as the center of twentieth-century spinning and weaving. For Beckert, the key factor in these centuries of growth and change—especially in the opening phases—was "war capitalism," by which states used all the violence they needed to seize foreign lands, enslave vulnerable peoples, discipline others to the rigors of machine-tending, overwhelm competitors, and force-feed a global cotton industry whose profits powered the transformation of virtually everything else. The Second Slavery played a crucial role, as demand for cotton lands drove American seizure of the Old Southwest, then Indian removal, the wrenching domestic slave trade, and the obsessive quest for more cotton lands that did not end until Emancipation. Thereafter, southern cotton planters replaced enslavement with a system of quasi-peonage that swept up black and white alike: American cotton production in 1890 was more than twice as high as in 1861. The capitalist logic that created the southern empire also destroyed it, however, as a shifting structure of costs eventually forced cotton's empire away from the United States and back to its birthplaces in China and India.

In *River of Dark Dreams* (2013), Walter Johnson told a more localized story that centered on the lower Mississippi Valley in the antebellum decades. Less a sustained narrative than a series of provocative vignettes, Johnson's account began with the Louisiana Purchase and Thomas Jefferson's exalted vision of an "Empire for Liberty" for America's yeoman farmers. Jefferson's empire became the Cotton Kingdom instead, and the center of American slavery. Johnson captured this irony deftly with quick portraits of the German Coast slave revolt of 1811 and the orgy of lynching that erupted when panicky Mississippians lashed out against John Murrell's imagined rebellion of 1835. Johnson addressed a variety of topics, from the experience of enslavement to steamboat technology to capitalist slavery itself, concluding with a suggestive set of chapters about late antebellum efforts to expand the reach of slavery, perhaps by filibustering in Latin America or by reopening the African slave trade. Both steps might have bolstered support for the system by offering master status to yeomen farmers increasingly priced out

Capitalism (New York: Basic Books, 2014). See also Caitlin Rosenthal's important addition to this literature, *Accounting for Slavery: Masters and Management* (Cambridge: Harvard University Press, 2018). For an earlier book that foreshadowed some of the themes of the new historians of capitalism, see Brian Schoen, *The Fragile Fabric of Union: Cotton, Federal Politics, and the Global Origins of the Civil War* (Baltimore: Johns Hopkins University Press, 2009).

of slave ownership, and by countering the threats of free labor and free soil with an "imperial vision of the future of slavery, patriarchy, and white supremacy."[32] As its title implies, *River of Dark Dreams* is not a cold economic analysis of slave capitalism but an effort to explore the cultural fantasies of capitalist slaveholders and their longing for a world that honored their values.

Edward E. Baptist's *The Half Has Never Been Told* (2014) also focused on the lower Mississippi Valley, particularly on cotton production in the Second Slavery. Using stark language, Baptist insisted that historians had vastly underestimated the pain and suffering inflicted on enslaved workers in the region's "forced labor camps." During the cotton boom of the early nineteenth century, he explained, professional slave traders drove thousands of enslaved workers from the Upper South to purchasers "down the river," destroying their families and communities in the process. Feverish to make their fortunes, enslavers discovered that the greatest bottleneck in cotton production was the need to pick the crop quickly in the short interval between ripening and damage by foul weather. Overcoming this barrier depended on a combination of "right-handed power," or force applied by planters and overseers, and "left-handed power," or the skills of the enslaved, who taught themselves how to pick ever faster to avoid the master's whip and meet a daily quota. Meeting one quota led to a higher one, but failure brought a whipping, until masters had exactly determined the maximum amount of work they could extract from each bound laborer. Baptist called this practice the "pushing system," and its steady use of lashes the "whipping machine." In his view, African American slavery was fully "in" and "of" the capitalist world, because "the measurement, surveillance, and violent coercion of enslaved people's labor were key components of the massive improvements in efficiency that made the Industrial Revolution possible."[33]

Empire of Cotton, River of Dark Dreams, and *The Half Has Never Been Told* all won enthusiastic praise from American historians.[34] All three also attracted sharp

32. Johnson, *River of Dark Dreams,* 418.

33. Edward E. Baptist, "Toward a Political Economy of Slave Labor: Hands, Whipping-Machines, and Modern Power," in Beckert and Rockman, eds., *Slavery's Capitalism,* 31–61; Baptist, *The Half Has Never Been Told,* 114, 125.

34. *Empire of Cotton* won the Bancroft Prize for 2014 and was a finalist for the Pulitzer Prize. *River of Dark Dreams* received the book prize from the Society for Historians of the Early American Republic, and Choice named it Outstanding Academic Title of the Year. *The Half Has Never Been Told* won the Avery Craven Prize of the Organization of American Historians in 2015, while *River of Dark Dreams* got Honorable Mention for it in 2013.

criticism. An anonymous reviewer for *The Economist* drew widespread condemnation for complaining that *The Half Has Never Been Told* was not "an objective history of slavery" because "almost all the blacks in the book are victims and almost all the whites villains."[35] Technically trained specialists in economic history leveled better informed and more specific criticisms. A review essay by Alan L. Olmstead and Paul W. Rhode faulted Baptist for misinterpreting their own research on more "pickable" cotton varieties, exaggerating the role of whipping, and lacking evidence for the "pushing system." They accused Beckert of misunderstanding the financing of the Louisiana Purchase, the South's alleged need for territorial expansion, and British policy toward slavery and cotton production in India. They charged Johnson with misunderstanding the tools of cotton planting and the source of the plantations' food supply. Addressing the overall treatment of slavery in the new history of capitalism, Olmstead and Rhode denied that "it was economically *essential* for the Industrial Revolution, for American prosperity, or even to produce cotton in the United States." They insisted instead that slavery inhibited economic progress in the South. Emphatically rejecting claims made by the new historians of capitalism, Olmstead and Rhode concluded that "the slave South did not build the institutions—educational, civic, and financial—to promote innovation and diversify away from the cotton staple. . . . The South therefore lacked the dynamic potential for modern economic growth that existed in the North."[36]

Olmstead and Rhode's pointed criticism suggested that the liberal critique of slavery was alive and well, at least within economics departments. Other leading economic historians echoed the criticisms, most agreeing with Eric Hilt that "each of these books would have been more compelling and better works of history if they had engaged with the economic history literature more fully."[37] The

35. "Blood Cotton," *The Economist,* 4 September 2014, 81. See also Matthew Pratt Guterl, "Slavery and Capitalism: A Review Essay," *Journal of Southern History* 86 (May 2015): 405–19; Joshua D. Rothman, review of *Empire of Cotton: A Global History* by Sven Beckert, *Journal of Southern History* 82 (February 2016): 127–30.

36. Alan L. Olmstead and Paul W. Rhode, "Cotton, Slavery, and the New History of Capitalism," *Explorations in Economic History* 67 (January 2018): 1–17, quote on 12. See also Alan L. Olmstead and Paul W. Rhode, "Biological Innovation and Productivity Growth in the Antebellum Cotton Economy," *Journal of Economic History* 68 (December 2008): 1123–71.

37. Eric Hilt, "Economic History, Historical Analysis, and the 'New History of Capitalism,'" *Journal of Economic History* 77 (June 2017): 519. See also John E. Murray, Alan L. Olmstead, Trevon D. Logan, Jonathan B. Pritchett, and Peter L. Rousseau, review of *The Half Has Never Been Told* by Edward E. Baptist, *Journal of Economic History* 75 (September 2015): 919–31.

economic historians did not dispute the underlying assertion that slavery was a highly significant part of the capitalist economy. As Gavin Wright said of *Slavery's Capitalism,* "The book's broad characterization of slave-owners as calculating, acquisitive, financially sophisticated and linked to international networks, is not one that economic historians will be inclined to object to, in large part because we have been arguing along similar lines for decades." Even so, Wright saw more value to concrete studies of northern and southern differences than in acrimony over how to classify them. "Calling one region or the other 'capitalist,'" he noted dryly, "will not contribute much to historical understanding."[38]

Political Economy and Party Politics

The debates over capitalism and modernization suggest that a range of views clearly existed within the antebellum South that laid the basis for significant political dispute. What then was the relationship between economic questions and antebellum politics and public policy? Did southern governments take sides in favor of economic change or stability? As sectional tensions rose, was it safe to push a slave-based agricultural system in new directions? And if governments intervened by fostering banks or funding programs of railroad construction, who should cover the cost? When historians shift their attention from purely economic developments to political economy, it seems increasingly clear that barbarous solons on the James and the Congaree considered these questions very closely.

Contrary to Sydnor's account, for example, it is now obvious that significant policy differences distinguished the Old South's political parties. Like their counterparts throughout the union, southern politicians split sharply over the administration of Andrew Jackson, particularly over his war on the Bank of the United States, and the Whig and Democratic parties emerged from this fracas. Both were coalitions of diverse elements, but most Democrats followed Jackson in supporting states' rights, limited government, and western expansion, but opposed using government subsidies for economic change. Whigs were more sympathetic to activist government at the state and federal government, entertained doubts over territorial growth, sympathized with reform projects such as public schools,

38. Gavin Wright, review of *Slavery's Capitalism: A New History of American Economic Development,* ed. Sven Beckert and Seth Rockman, *EH.Net,* http://eh.net/book_reviews/slaverys-capitalism-a-new-history-of-american-economic-development/ (accessed 18 January 2019).

penitentiaries, and mental hospitals, and supported economic development with railroad subsidies and even protective tariffs. A third group, the followers of Senator John C. Calhoun, held aloof from both parties, sympathized with South Carolina's effort to nullify protectionism, and cherished radical states' rights principles. In the South, all three groups supported slavery, but southern Whigs and Democrats believed that slavery was safest within the union, while nullifiers, with varying degrees of enthusiasm, dreamed of a separate slaveholding republic. The parties were more evenly matched in the Upper South, where social and economic diversity stoked political disagreement. Upcountry voters leaned Whig while lowland districts favored the Democrats. In the Cotton Belt, greater social and economic uniformity led to broader political consensus. Democrats thus led across the Lower South, though Whigs found a modest following in the wealthiest plantation districts. Homeland of the Nullifiers, South Carolina renounced party divisions and insisted that protecting slavery demanded sectional unity.

Considered in broad outlines, above the fray of annual elections and patronage quarrels, the southern parties conducted a serious debate over the future of the region. Determined to preserve white liberty and black bondage, they feared that both were fragile and menaced by outside forces. Democrats worried about local "aristocrats," but even more about the powers of an invasive federal government, wielded by a growing antislavery majority in the North. Their solution stressed agrarian principles, laissez-faire government, endless expansion of the plantation system, and white male solidarity, anchored in fierce racism and nominal political equality. In Upper South states such as Virginia, North Carolina, and Tennessee, lowland planters worried that hill country yeomen would raise taxes on land and slaves to pay for internal improvements. They accordingly leaned Democratic and opposed reapportionment and other electoral reforms that gave more power to westerners and nonlandowners. By the same token, their Upcountry rivals leaned Whig. The reverse was true in the Deep South, where steamboats did the work of costly railroads, but Delta and Black Belt planters supported Whigs' financial policies and hill country Democrats fought planter pretensions.

In comparison to the North, the political economy of southern Democrats would almost inevitably produce the appearance of economic stagnation and backwardness. By contrast, Whigs feared the debilitating effects of regional poverty and favored moderate reforms to protect slavery by making it more modern, more profitable, and more visibly progressive. Instead of exclusive reliance on agriculture, Whigs introduced banks and railroads, expanded commerce, and limited industrialization. If their changes brought class or racial instability, Whigs would take the risk. Others were more cautious. In 1848, for example, on the eve of the South's great railroad boom, South Carolinian James Henry Hammond admitted that public funding of railroads "on a small scale may be pardoned or commended as an elegant amusement or curious experiment," but "when applied on a wide surface, involving vast expenditures and affecting important interests [it] becomes unwise, dangerous, and destructive." Over time, Hammond's small government convictions combined with Democrats' white male egalitarianism and states' rights principles to win more elections, but the appeal of Whig-sponsored progress grew as well. Even during the 1850s, as the southern Whig Party faced collapse, Democrats increasingly adopted Whig programs of economic development.[39]

Beginning with J. Mills Thornton III's *Politics and Power in a Slave Society* (1978), a spate of books explored the South's party battles across individual states.[40] Concurring with Thornton, most found that white southerners of the 1830s clashed sharply over the state's role in economic development. Given the reluctance of southern investors to risk their own funds on costly development projects, these debates turned on the question of government subsidies of internal improvements. In most states, early railroads disappointed their supporters in the depression-scarred 1830s, but the 1850s saw greater prosperity, booming railroads,

39. Anti-Debt (James Henry Hammond), *The Railroad Mania: And Review of the Bank of the State of South-Carolina: A Series of Essays* (Charleston: Burges, James & Paxton, 1848), 13; Michael F. Holt, *The Political Crisis of the 1850s* (New York: John Wiley & Sons, 1978), 101–38; Michael Perman, *Pursuit of Unity: A Political History of the American South* (Chapel Hill: University of North Carolina Press, 2009), 30; Harry L. Watson, "Slavery and Development in a Dual Economy: The South in the Market Revolution," in Stokes and Conway, eds., *The Market Revolution in America*, 43–73.

40. J. Mills Thornton III, *Politics and Power in a Slave Society: Alabama, 1800–1860* (Baton Rouge: Louisiana State University Press, 1978); Marc W. Kruman, *Parties and Politics in North Carolina, 1836–1865* (Baton Rouge: Louisiana State University Press, 1983); William G. Shade, *Democratizing the Old Dominion: Virginia and the Second Party System, 1824–1861* (Charlottesville: University Press of Virginia, 1996); Jonathan M. Atkins, *Parties, Politics, and the Sectional Conflict in Tennessee, 1832–1861* (Knoxville: University of Tennessee Press, 1997); Anthony Gene Carey, *Parties, Slavery, and the Union in Antebellum Georgia* (Athens: University of Georgia Press, 1997); William A. Link, *Roots of Secession: Slavery and Politics in Antebellum Virginia* (Chapel Hill: University of North Carolina Press, 2003); Harry L. Watson, *Jacksonian Politics and Community Conflict: The Emergence of the Second American Party System in Cumberland County, North Carolina* (Baton Rouge: Louisiana State University Press, 1981). Regarding North Carolina, Thomas E. Jeffrey demurred from the prevailing view and found that intrastate sectional conflict paralyzed state development strategy and magnified the importance of national issues; see *State Parties and National Politics: North Carolina, 1815–1861* (Athens: University of Georgia Press, 1989).

and growing party consensus in favor of economic development at state expense, even as state aid waned nationally. William G. Thomas found that southern states covered $128 million in rail construction costs in the 1850s, raising 57 percent with state bonds. Scott Reynolds Nelson also concluded that southern railroads relied more heavily on state government-supported financing rather than private capital. As Michael F. Holt observed, however, Whig and Democratic agreement over economic development opened an unanticipated door for sectional extremism, as ambitious politicians cast about for new ways to distinguish themselves from competitors.[41]

The Jacksonian party system was mostly weaker in the Deep South, where widespread slave ownership and softer geographical contrasts alleviated the social and economic divisions that fed party conflict in the older states. The party systems of Alabama and Georgia flared in the 1840s but veered toward Democratic hegemony when sectional tensions rose in the 1850s. In Mississippi, Christopher Olsen found that parties were always weak and rested more on personal conflicts and masculine swagger than policy differences. By contrast, social and geographic diversity fostered a lively party system in antebellum Louisiana.[42]

South Carolina stood out as the major exception to most generalizations about Jacksonian party development and political culture, prompting much scholarly attention to "the problem of South Carolina."[43] With the nation's highest concentrations of slaves and slaveholders, the Palmetto State granted universal white male suffrage in 1809, but its politics remained highly undemocratic in other respects. Few offices were elective, a tiny class of densely intermarried planters dominated public life, malapportionment concentrated power in their hands, and many Assembly members disdained to live in their districts. South Carolina stood aloof from the Second Party System and control of its public affairs by Whigs and Democrats. When other states focused on the Bank War,

41. Thomas, *The Iron Way,* 26; Scott Reynolds Nelson, *Iron Confederacies: Southern Railways, Klan Violence, and Reconstruction* (Chapel Hill: University of North Carolina Press, 1999), 11–26; Holt, *The Political Crisis of the 1850s,* 101–38.

42. Thornton, *Politics and Power in a Slave Society;* Carey, *Parties, Slavery, and the Union;* Christopher J. Olsen, *Political Culture and Secession in Mississippi: Masculinity, Honor, and the Antiparty Tradition, 1830–1860* (New York: Oxford University Press, 2000); John M. Sacher, *A Perfect War of Politics: Parties, Politicians, and Democracy in Louisiana, 1824–1861* (Baton Rouge: Louisiana State University Press, 2003); Henry O. Robertson, *"In the Habit of Acting Together": The Emergence of the Whig Party in Louisiana, 1828–1840* (Lafayette: University of Louisiana at Lafayette, 2007).

43. James Banner, "The Problem of South Carolina," in *The Hofstadter Aegis: A Memorial,* ed. Stanley Elkins and Eric McKitrick (New York: Alfred A. Knopf, 1974), 60–93.

South Carolina provoked the Nullification Crisis and went on to become the fountainhead of southern sectional extremism.

William W. Freehling's *Prelude to Civil War* (1966) remains the best single approach to the episode. As early as the 1820s, South Carolina's planter magnates feared that economic decline could threaten the security of slavery but blamed their plight on tariffs instead of soil exhaustion and southwestern competition. Freehling showed how, without a large population of nonslaveholders to contest their power or temper their fears, paranoia over slavery drove the state's planters into florid effusions of states' rights extremism. Though other states did not join South Carolina's efforts to "nullify" or abrogate federal tax laws, they later deployed its rhetoric and constitutional reasoning in secessionism. Alert to these ramifications, Richard E. Ellis followed Freehling in exploring how nullification reverberated across the South. In Ellis's view, southern Jacksonians felt far closer to Calhoun than to Jackson on many of the constitutional issues at stake and used the crisis to shape the potent fusion of states' rights and white supremacy that would figure so largely in subsequent southern politics.[44]

Lacy K. Ford challenged Freeling's analysis by emphasizing the power and independence of South Carolina's Upcountry yeomen. Widespread slave ownership gave them more in common with the planter gentry than with the plain folk of other states. Ford was surely correct to insist that planters and yeomen throughout the South benefited from a slave-based economy that protected household independence and distinguished them from hirelings and slaves. Treasuring this independence, a broad range of white Carolinians naturally joined in radical measures to protect it. Ford received his own challenge from Stephanie McCurry, who emphasized the inequality of South Carolina planters and plain folk. Fundamentally, however, McCurry bolstered a growing consensus by showing how gender inequality strengthened the power of slavery. Yeoman clearly drew independence from all their dependents, white women as well as enslaved people, giving them yet another point of solidarity with more powerful planters. In the work of these highly perceptive scholars, South Carolina emerged as the exception that proved the rule: slavery, racism, and patriarchy clearly drew white southern voters together, beneath more divisive issues of economic strategy.[45]

44. William W. Freehling, *Prelude to Civil War: The Nullification Controversy in South Carolina, 1816–1836* (New York: Harper & Row, 1966); Richard E. Ellis, *The Union at Risk: Jacksonian Democracy, States' Rights, and the Nullification Crisis* (New York: Oxford University Press, 1987).

45. Lacy K. Ford, *Origins of Southern Radicalism: The South Carolina Upcountry, 1800–1860* (New York: Oxford University Press, 1988); Stephanie McCurry, *Masters of Small Worlds: Yeoman Households,*

What else did slaveholders want from their governments? Quite obviously, they demanded unbending support for their rights to human property from every organ of state and local government including judges, executives, and lawmakers. This included unrestricted corporal punishment, strict police legislation, vigilant slave patrols, rigid controls on free people of color, favorable tax policies, legal enforcement of slave sales, rentals, mortgages, and inheritance, as well as bans on "incendiary" speech, aid to runaways, unsupervised slave gatherings, and a host of other subversive activities. At the federal level, slaveholders gained their reputation as the "slave power" by likewise demanding protection for the domestic slave trade by land and sea, closure of the mails to antislavery publications, Congressional gag rules to deny public hearings to antislavery voices, and a host of similar measures carefully documented and explored in important works by Leonard L. Richards, Don E. Fehrenbacher, and John Ashworth.[46]

Robin L. Einhorn pressed beyond the issues of nullification and federal tariffs to investigate slaveholders' tax aversion at the local level, tracing it to colonial masters' unwillingness to pay taxes on slaves, their most valuable property. She found the same objection beneath debates over a federal impost under the Articles of Confederation, and later, a federal tariff as well as the Constitution's seldom-used application of the three-fifths clause to direct taxation. Within states, Einhorn demonstrated, constitutional clauses required equal tax rates on all forms of property to ensure that yeoman majorities would not tax slaves at higher rates than their own small farms. Ironically, free states extended this principle to the taxation of personal property, including paper wealth, hoping to support economic equality but actually achieving the opposite. Throughout the 1850s, state-level battles over taxing schemes exposed the clash between planters' demands for low taxes and the high cost of publicly funded railroads.[47]

Gender Relations, and the Political Culture of the Antebellum South Carolina Low Country (New York: Oxford University Press, 1995).

46. Leonard L. Richards, *The Slave Power: The Free North and Southern Domination, 1780–1860* (Baton Rouge: Louisiana State University Press, 2000); Don E. Fehrenbacher, *The Slaveholding Republic: An Account of the United States Government's Relations to Slavery,* ed. Ward M. McAfee (New York: Oxford University Press, 2001); John Ashworth, *Slavery, Capitalism, and Politics in the Antebellum Republic,* 2 vols. (New York: Cambridge University Press, 1995, 2007).

47. Robin L. Einhorn, *American Taxation, American Slavery* (Chicago: University of Chicago Press, 2006), 202–4; Thornton, *Politics and Power in a Slave Society,* 101–7, 267–80; Link, *Roots of Secession,* 10–27; Kruman, *Parties and Politics in North Carolina,* 189–96; Paul D. Escott, *Many Excellent People: Power and Privilege in North Carolina, 1850–1900* (Chapel Hill: University of North Carolina Press, 1985), 27–31.

Vociferous demands for the territorial expansion of slavery were also well-known features of national antebellum politics and could be driven by the simple desire for more plantation territory, by resentment of the moral critique implied by slavery restrictions, by a longing for more proslavery congressmen, or even by the quest for a wedge issue in the next election. Robert Pierce Forbes wrote an exhaustive account of the expansion issue as it first appeared in the Missouri Crisis of 1819–1820, as did Don E. Fehrenbacher for *Dred Scott v. Sandford,* an analysis unlikely to be soon surpassed.[48] In an important work that broke with tradition and pursued the story of territorial expansion backward in time to the Early Republic, Adam Rothman linked America's acquisition and development of the Old Southwest to the Second Slavery and southerners' drive to build an ever-greater Cotton Kingdom.[49]

Historians who took the unusual step of linking proslavery politics to foreign policy found dramatic new evidence of a transnational history of slavery expansion. Robert E. May introduced the subject in 1973 with *The Southern Dream of a Caribbean Empire, 1854–1861,* and followed with volumes on filibusterer John A. Quitman and other crusaders for proslavery expansion. David C. Keehn added a close study of the Knights of the Golden Circle, a secessionist secret society that plotted for Latin American annexations in the 1850s, and Tom Chaffin contributed *Fatal Glory* (1996), his own study of filibusterer Narciso López.[50]

Quite apart from the shenanigans of private adventurers, however, proximity, plantations, and slavery had long drawn the gaze of southern leaders southward.

48. Robert Pierce Forbes, *The Missouri Compromise and Its Aftermath: Slavery and the Meaning of America* (Chapel Hill: University of North Carolina Press, 2007); Don E. Fehrenbacher, *The* Dred Scott *Case: Its Significance in American Law and Politics* (New York: Oxford University Press, 1978). For the Missouri Crisis, see also John R. Van Atta, *Wolf by the Ears: The Missouri Crisis, 1819–1821* (Baltimore: Johns Hopkins University Press, 2015). For the *Dred Scott* case, see also David Thomas Konig, Paul Finkelman, and Christopher Alan Bracey, eds., *The* Dred Scott *Case: Historical and Contemporary Perspectives on Race and Law* (Athens: Ohio University Press, 2010); David M. Potter, *The Impending Crisis, 1848–1861* (New York: Harper & Row, 1976), 267–96.

49. Adam Rothman, *Slave Country: American Expansion and the Origins of the Deep South* (Cambridge: Harvard University Press, 2005).

50. Robert E. May, *The Southern Dream of a Caribbean Empire, 1854–1861* (Baton Rouge: Louisiana State University Press, 1973); May, *Manifest Destiny's Underworld: Filibustering in Antebellum America* (Chapel Hill: University of North Carolina Press, 2002); May, *Slavery, Race, and Conquest in the Tropics: Lincoln, Douglas, and the Future of Latin America* (New York: Cambridge University Press, 2013); David C. Keehn, *Knights of the Golden Circle: Secret Empire, Southern Secession, Civil War* (Baton Rouge: Louisiana State University Press, 2013); Tom Chaffin, *Fatal Glory: Narciso López and the First Clandestine U.S. War against*

In 1976, Lester D. Langley opened modern study of United States diplomacy in the Gulf-Caribbean basin with his *Struggles for the American Mediterranean.* Langley demonstrated how American interests had long been possessive and colonialist in the broadest sense, making the important point that the United States launched its efforts by joining with European powers to contain the Haitian Revolution. Matthew Pratt Guterl returned to this theme in *American Mediterranean* (2008), exploring the crucial place of neighboring plantation societies in the thought and imagination of North America's slaveholders, particularly as they struggled to anticipate whether rebellious St. Domingue, booming Cuba, or "abolitionized" Jamaica represented the wave of the future. Also publishing in 2008, Edward B. Rugemer explored similar issues in his *The Problem of Emancipation,* with particular attention to slaveholders' fearful contemplations of slavery's potential demise.[51]

Matthew Karp built on this scholarship to investigate the proslavery activities of the last antebellum generation of US diplomats and other officials. In *This Vast Southern Empire* (2016), Karp showed how concern for international protection and expansion of slavery, more so than a simple desire for more slave territory, became a major concern of antebellum policy. Men such as Secretary of State John C. Calhoun and Secretary of the Navy (and briefly Secretary of State) Abel P. Upshur envisioned the United States, Cuba, and Brazil as anchors of a hemispheric community of interest that would counteract Great Britain's free-labor dreams. Karp thus joined with the new historians of capitalism to link the political economy of slavery to the course of empire, especially in the so-called "American Mediterranean."[52]

Cuba (Charlottesville: University Press of Virginia, 1996). See also Charles H. Brown, *Agents of Manifest Destiny: The Lives and Times of the Filibusters* (Chapel Hill: University of North Carolina Press, 1980).

51. Lester D. Langley, *Struggle for the American Mediterranean: United States-European Rivalry in the Gulf-Caribbean, 1776–1904* (Athens: University of Georgia Press, 1976); Matthew Pratt Guterl, *American Mediterranean: Southern Slaveholders in the Age of Emancipation* (Cambridge: Harvard University Press, 2008); Edward Bartlett Rugemer, *The Problem of Emancipation: The Caribbean Roots of the American Civil War* (Baton Rouge: Louisiana State University Press, 2008).

52. Matthew Karp, *This Vast Southern Empire: Slaveholders at the Helm of American Foreign Policy* (Cambridge: Harvard University Press, 2016). See also Gerald Horne, *The Deepest South: The United States, Brazil, and the African Slave Trade* (New York: New York University Press, 2007); Amy S. Greenberg, *Manifest Manhood and the Antebellum American Empire* (New York: Cambridge University Press, 2005); Charles H. Brown, *Agents of Manifest Destiny: The Lives and Times of the Filibusters* (Chapel Hill: University of North Carolina Press, 1980).

Elaborating on this theme, Walter Johnson concluded *River of Dark Dreams* by returning to the most famous filibuster of all, describing William Walker's adventures in Nicaragua as the capstone of slavery's expansion into the lower Mississippi Valley. Johnson joined Karp and others in making a strong case that the most ambitious of late antebellum southern nationalists longed for a sphere of influence spreading from the northern Gulf Coast across Central America and at least as far as Brazil. Led by a breakaway US South, a new empire would arise of annexed territories and satellite republics, embodying a new civilization based on compulsion rather than the supposed merits of universal liberty extolled elsewhere around the North Atlantic basin. Johnson projected this imagined new empire as the apotheosis of slave-based modernity.[53] If Johnson was correct, political battles along the James and the Congaree amounted to far more than mechanical responses to soil exhaustion. They pointed to a very different American future.

But civil war came, and that future did not. Perhaps the single most important political decision facing the South was whether to leave the union in 1860. Slaveholders' support for secession spoke to their confidence that King Cotton and a modern slave economy could protect a strong, powerful, and independent Confederacy. On the other hand, secessionists often forthrightly acknowledged the South's laggard development within the nation. Conceding that the lack of southern cities, industry, and finance left the South dependent on the North for essential goods and services, key southern leaders and intellectuals certainly favored the modernization of slave-based society, relying on the tools of state power rather than laissez-faire to make it happen. In other words, their ideal society would rest on compulsion rather than liberty. The need for compulsion—and the unambiguous control of the central government via the Confederate state—demonstrated slavery's failure to modernize itself. By 1861 the South remained behind, at least in comparison to its northern adversary, the only rival that mattered.[54]

Something about the slave South held it back, and scholars who insist that the South was fully modern long before the Civil War—even in its own way—

53. Johnson, *River of Dark Dreams*, 303–30.

54. John D. Majewski, *Modernizing a Slave Economy: The Economic Vision of the Confederate Nation* (Chapel Hill: University of North Carolina Press, 2009); Majewski, "Why Did Northerners Oppose the Expansion of Slavery? Economic Development and Education in the Limestone South," in Beckert and Rockman, eds., *Slavery's Capitalism*, 277–98.

are surely exaggerating or seeing a partial picture. The forces of states' rights, planter autonomy, and tax aversion were very powerful and often frustrated the modernizers' efforts, especially when it came to crucial issues such as internal improvements, industrialization, and public education. Sydnor's dismissal notwithstanding, the debates over secession and modernization were evidently enmeshed with "major southern hopes and fears." There is consequently much for historians to ponder about the politicians who reigned on the banks of the James and the Congaree. Stage duels are not among them.

FROM RECONCILIATION TO RECKONING
Historiography of the South and the Civil War

Lesley J. Gordon and Stephen Berry

In *Causes Won, Lost, and Forgotten* (2013), historian Gary W. Gallagher postulated that there have been four cultural strains among Americans' attempts to make meaning of their Civil War.[1] The "Lost Cause" tradition casts the Confederacy as an agrarian underdog nobly standing on the principle of states' rights against what Robert E. Lee himself called the "overwhelming numbers and resources" of modernity. The "Union Cause" (sometimes also called the "Won Cause") emphasizes the preservation of the nation as the primary motivation for most federal soldiers and the critical result of the conflict. The "Emancipation Cause" puts slavery at the heart of the coming of the war, its prosecution, and its meaning. And the "Reconciliation Cause" mediates between these traditions, emphasizing the common ideals that brought Americans to the battlefield and portraying the war itself as the kiln in which the nation was fired. From 1870 until the 1960s, the reconciliationist narrative dominated all regions while also ignoring African Americans in favor of portraying the conflict as a (white) "Brothers War." After the civil rights movement, a kind of neo-reconciliationist bargain seemed to emerge: there was greater accommodation in some quarters for black history, with white southerners gradually and grudgingly agreeing that slavery caused the war; meanwhile blanket condemnations of the slaveholding Confederacy were largely muted, and academics and buffs alike expressed sober admiration for the CSA's military power. It appeared, on the surface at least, like a national

1. Gary W. Gallagher, *Causes Won, Lost, and Forgotten: How Hollywood and Popular Art Shape What We Know about the Civil War* (Chapel Hill: University of North Carolina Press, 2013).

win-win-win: black southerners got their history back; white southerners got to preserve a (perverse) point of pride; and the country as a whole got to continue celebrating the war as a story of American redemption.

On 17 June 2015, Dylann Roof entered the Emanuel African Methodist Episcopal Church and blew a giant hole in the neo-reconciliationist narrative. An academic zero-tolerance policy for Confederate mollycoddling and whataboutism had long been in force (if not always enforced), erected on a scholarly foundation that stretched through the Freedmen and Southern Society Project, Eric Foner's *Reconstruction* (1988), and all the way back to the work of John Hope Franklin and W. E. B. Du Bois.[2] But Roof's actions put a period on the end of a sentence for a broader southern culture that was ready, finally, to discuss the flags, the monuments, and the building names. This essay reviews historiographical resistance to the neo-reconciliationist mode as historical scholarship drove and was driven by these larger cultural forces.

In 1974, as the United States remained enmeshed in the Vietnam War, Michael Shaara published *Killer Angels,* the epitome of the reconciliationist narrative. Shaara's book, a fictionalized account of the Battle of Gettysburg, highlighted familiar luminaries like Generals Lee, Pickett, Meade, and Stuart, but also helped to resurrect the reputation of General James Longstreet and introduced to a wide audience the alleged daring story of Colonel Joshua Chamberlin. Mixing several powerful martial myths including parts of the Lost Cause, *Killer Angels* remains popular among readers. Nonetheless, scholar Craig A. Warren convincingly argued in *Scars to Prove It* (2009) that the attraction of *Killer Angels* to modern readers (and many notable historians) is due in part to its depiction of Americans willingly sacrificing themselves for a "cause," for democracy (the new over the old), and for their comrades. Warren explained that Shaara carefully constructed his story to take advantage of modern readers' assumptions about the Civil War era as being somehow "simpler and more unaffected" than their own. The novel downplays divisive issues like slavery and race; instead, as historian Edward L.

2. Eric Foner, *Reconstruction: America's Unfinished Revolution, 1863–1877* (New York: Harper & Row, 1988); John Hope Franklin, *From Slavery to Freedom: A History of African Americans* (New York: Alfred A. Knopf, 1947); W. E. B. Du Bois, *Black Reconstruction in America* (New York: Harcourt Brace, 1935). The Freedmen & Southern Society Project is associated particularly with the amazing work of Ira Berlin, Barbara J. Fields, Thavolia Glymph, Steven F. Miller, Joseph P. Reidy, Susan E. O'Donovan, and Leslie S. Rowland. For a full list of associated publications, see http://www.freedmen.umd.edu/fssppubs.htm (accessed 18 January 2019).

Ayers discerned in 1998 in his own reflective take on the field, "Worrying about the Civil War," what triumphs in Shaara's novel is a reassuring celebration of shared American military courage, an idealization of the war's causes, and the presumption that the brutal suffering and killing achieved the higher purpose of "freedom"—without ever admitting that the Confederacy fought for the freedom to keep African Americans unfree.[3]

In 1982, in the historiographical review of the Civil War South for *Interpreting Southern History*—this volume's predecessor—Joe Gray Taylor marveled that the increased appetite for the Civil War in the neo-reconciliationist mode also somehow defied the antimilitarism of Vietnam: "The antiwar movement of the 1960s seems to have had no effect at all on the fascination this bloodiest of all American Wars has for Americans."[4] Academic and nonacademic historians, documentary producers such as Ken Burns (also profoundly influenced by *Killer Angels*), screenwriters and movie directors (*Gettysburg* [1993] put Shaara onscreen), reenactors, roundtables, and even National Battlefield Parks helped to perpetuate that interest. All stressed that the American Civil War was a conflict like no other, where honorable men, whether Union or Confederate, fought for something admirable. It was a triumphant and redemptive struggle that combined, in Charles P. Roland's words, "heroism and sacrifice" with "cruelty and horror" to change all of world history. In his 1991 history, *An American Iliad,* Roland contended: "Most Americans, North and South, perceive the conflict as a tragic but inevitable and heroic episode in the life of the country."[5]

In the second half of the twentieth century, Civil War history increasingly became a hobby or pastime: something for Americans to do on their weekends or vacations, largely for pleasure or escape. In 1998 journalist Tony Horwitz commented on this phenomenon in his engaging book *Confederates in the Attic.* Civil

3. Craig A. Warren, *Scars to Prove It: The Civil War Soldier and American Fiction* (Kent: Kent State University Press, 2009), 122; Edward L. Ayers, "Worrying About the Civil War," in *Moral Problems in American Life: New Perspectives on Cultural History,* ed. Karen Halttunen and Lewis Perry (Ithaca: Cornell University Press, 1998), 145–65. See also Drew Gilpin Faust, "'We Should Grow Too Fond of It': Why We Love the Civil War," *Civil War History* 50 (December 2004): 368–83.

4. Joe Gray Taylor, "The White South from Secession to Redemption," in *Interpreting Southern History: Historiographical Essays in Honor of Sanford W. Higginbotham,* ed. John B. Boles and Evelyn Thomas Nolen (Baton Rouge: Louisiana State University Press, 1987), 162–98. In the text of his essay, Gray dated its writing to 1982 though the collection was not published until 1987.

5. Charles P. Roland, *An American Iliad: The Story of the Civil War* (New York: McGraw-Hill, 1991), xi, 263.

War enthusiasts, mainly white males but some white women, read almost solely about battles and leaders, journeyed to battlefields, joined Civil War Round Tables, reenacted combat, and purchased paintings of battles and soldiers, all the while shying away from discussing the unpleasant and divisive aspects of this complex and brutal war. Few wanted to dwell openly on the festering political issues swirling around the war: not only slavery, but also the segregated racist system that followed in its wake and lasted well into the twentieth century and beyond.[6] As Horwitz wrote, reenactments "blandly" reconcile "North and South in a grand spectacle that glorified battlefield valor and the stoicism of civilians."[7] And yet, when questioned, amateur historians' nostalgia for the Confederacy seemed directly tied to late twentieth-century racial anxieties: they bemoaned what they saw as an increasingly multicultural America.

As Civil War history became an enjoyable pastime for some Americans, commercial and even academic presses churned out volume after volume effectively supporting the pageantry and romanticism of war. This is readily apparent in the steady stream of conventional military biographies, battle narratives, unit histories, and edited soldiers' diaries and letters published between the 1980s and 2010s. These include studies detailing each day of Gettysburg, hagiographies, and narrowly focused regimentals.[8] Few of these works offered nuanced historiographical insight or new methodologies, instead recounting and propounding dramatic tales of mostly white men "coping with extraordinary circumstances" and almost always doing so heroically. There were exceptions: George C. Rable's *Fredericksburg! Fredericksburg!* (2002) recounted this important campaign but also highlighted civilians affected by the battle's destruction and the wider political context. Lee biographers like Elizabeth Brown Pryor, Michael Fellman, and Emory M. Thomas helped to strip away the pervasive mythology that distorted

6. A 1990 history of the first Civil War Round Table (founded in Chicago in 1940) includes a listing of monthly "speakers and topics." The majority focused on famous battles and leaders, with a few notable exceptions, including a presentation on slavery in Alaska and "How to Enjoy War." See Barbara Hughett, *The Civil War Round Table: Fifty Years of Scholarship and Fellowship* (Chicago: Civil War Round Table, 1990), 171–87.

7. Tony Horwitz, *Confederates in the Attic: Dispatches from the Unfinished Civil War* (New York: Pantheon Books, 1998), 144.

8. Just a small sampling of such works includes Harry W. Pfanz, *Gettysburg: The First Day* (Chapel Hill: University of North Carolina Press, 2010); James I. Robertson Jr., *Stonewall Jackson* (New York: Macmillan, 1997); S. C. Gwynne, *Rebel Yell: The Violence, Passion, and Redemption of Stonewall Jackson* (New York: Scribner, 2014); Jack Hurst, *Nathan Bedford Forrest: A Biography* (New York: Alfred A. Knopf, 1993).

popular perceptions of the general.[9] Others sought to place Confederate commanders within the broader societal context of their times, paying more attention to their private as much as their public lives.[10] Susannah Ural's 2017 book, *Hood's Texas Brigade,* offered a rare example of applying social and cultural analysis to a famed Confederate unit.[11]

These studies and others signaled a discernable shift in military history that helped to shine a light through the fog of romanticism and mythology. And here emerged some of the more innovative and insightful scholarship of the past forty years, sometimes coexisting or even fueling, but more often directly challenging the more triumphant and nationalist forms of Civil War history.

Even so, the larger challenge to the triumphalist narrative came from outside traditional Civil War military history as scholars of race and gender, social, cultural, and transnational approaches renewed the study of the conflict while rejecting the primacy of a solely military framework. The scholarship of this "counter-movement," while taking many forms, can largely be grouped into four broad categories: first, the extremely rich field of common-soldier studies; second, multiple monographs that connected the war more directly to the home front and to the fate of slavery; third, a widening of geographical context, both beyond the traditional focus on the eastern theater, but also and perhaps more significantly, beyond the nation's borders; and notably, fourth, the burgeoning interest in Civil War memory.

9. Warren Wilkinson and Steven E. Woodworth, *A Scythe of Fire: A Civil War Story of the Eighth Georgia Infantry Regiment* (New York: HarperCollins, 2002), x; George C. Rable, *Fredericksburg! Fredericksburg!* (Chapel Hill: University of North Carolina Press, 2002); Elizabeth Brown Pryor, *Reading the Man: A Portrait of Robert E. Lee through His Private Letters* (New York: Viking Press, 2007); Michael Fellman, *The Making of Robert E. Lee* (New York: Random House, 2000); Emory M. Thomas, *Robert E. Lee* (New York: W. W. Norton, 1995).

10. See for example, Brian Steele Wills, *A Battle from the Start: The Life of Nathan Bedford Forrest* (New York: HarperCollins, 1992); Peter S. Carmichael, *Lee's Young Artillerist: William R. J. Pegram* (Charlottesville: University Press of Virginia, 1995); Lesley J. Gordon, *General George E. Pickett in Life and Legend* (Chapel Hill: University of North Carolina Press, 1998).

11. Susannah J. Ural, *Hoods Texas Brigade: The Soldiers and Families of the Confederacy's Most Celebrated Unit* (Baton Rouge: Louisiana State University Press, 2017). Two additional books that offer a more balanced analysis of a single unit are Terry L. Jones, *Lee's Tigers: The Louisiana Infantry in the Army of Northern Virginia* (Baton Rouge: Louisiana State University Press, 1987); G. Ward Hubbs, *Guarding Greensboro: A Confederate Company in the Making of a Southern Community* (Athens: University of Georgia Press, 2003). Lesley J. Gordon, *A Broken Regiment: The 16th Connecticut's Civil War* (Baton Rouge: Louisiana State University Press, 2014), also took an integrated approach in rebooting the regimental and focusing on men who largely failed.

Common Soldiers

The 1980s and 1990s brought a renewed interest in common folk, fueled by trends in social and cultural history, which introduced new methodologies, sources, and questions. Authors such as Michael L. Barton, Randall C. Jimerson, Reid Mitchell, and Gerald F. Linderman looked afresh at the men in the ranks, building on Bell Irvin Wiley's nearly encyclopedic studies of the common soldiers from the 1940s and 1950s.[12] Wiley concluded that "Johnny Reb," and his counterpart "Billy Yank," were everyman: humorous, profane, dependable, and quietly heroic. They volunteered and fought because they felt obliged to do so but were not really driven by ideology. In the South, Wiley famously declared, "Confederates were the best fighters and the worst soldiers."[13]

The perception that white southern men were aggressive, unruly, and natural fighters can be traced to antebellum assumptions and realities of the violent slave South, propagated by the Lost Cause well into the twentieth century.[14] Some historians have pushed back on this stereotype, notably Marcus Cunliffe's *Soldiers and Civilians* (1968) and Michael C. C. Adams's *Our Masters the Rebels* (1978), which argued that violence and martialism were American traits, not necessarily southern ones.[15] In 1991, Don Higginbotham observed in his Southern Historical Association presidential address, that white "southerners perceived themselves as militarily superior"; yet he discovered a lack "southern effusions" about martial superiority until the eve of secession and war. In 1982 Grady McWhiney and

12. Many of these studies focused on both sides. See Michael L. Barton, *Goodmen: The Character of Civil War Soldiers* (University Park: Pennsylvania State University Press, 1981); Randall C. Jimerson, *The Private Civil War: Popular Thought During the Sectional Conflict* (Baton Rouge: Louisiana State University Press, 1988); Gerald F. Linderman, *Embattled Courage: The Experience of Combat in the American Civil War* (New York: Free Press, 1989); Reid Mitchell, *Civil War Soldiers: Their Expectations and Their Experiences* (New York: Viking, 1988).

13. Bell Irvin Wiley, *The Life of Johnny Reb: The Common Soldier of the Confederacy* (Indianapolis: Bobbs Merrill, 1943), 235. David Herbert Donald echoed this sentiment when he claimed that a Confederate soldier was "an admirable fighting man but a poor soldier"; see "The Confederate as a Fighting Man," *Journal of Southern History* 25 (May 1959): 193.

14. This idea of the "militant South" is best encapsulated in John Hope Franklin's 1956 book of the same name. He argued that "Southern life and culture" had a "penchant for militancy"; *The Militant South, 1800–1861* (Cambridge: Harvard University Press, 1956), viii.

15. Marcus Cunliffe, *Soldiers and Civilians: The Martial Spirit in America, 1775–1865* (Boston: Little, Brown, 1968); Michael C. C. Adams, *Our Masters the Rebels: A Speculation on Union Military Failure in the East, 1861–1865* (Cambridge: Harvard University Press, 1978).

Perry D. Jamieson's *Attack and Die* went so far as to maintain that the assumed distinctive heritage and ethnicity of Confederate soldiers made them fierce yet ineffective fighters. McWhiney and Jamieson's provocative theory that Confederates mimicked their Celtic forebears in reckless advance assaults was not widely supported—it rang of too much determinism and ethnic essentialism. Their corollary argument about tactics, that the rifle and its improved efficiency against frontal assaults literally bled the South to death, has not held up to close scrutiny either.[16] Yet the assertion that Confederate soldiers fought more purely for a "cause" than Union soldiers endured, at least in popular imagination.

A more complex portrait of Confederate soldiers gradually emerged, notably in investigating what has been postulated as the more human side of war. Inspired by John Keegan's 1976 book, *The Face of Battle,* Civil War scholars sought to delve into individuals' experiences in combat, portraying them as often disjointed, confusing, and contrasting with conventional expectations of war. In 1982 Marvin Cain proposed that historians apply Keegan's methodology to Civil War soldiers. "In the end," he concluded, "it may be that a new revisionism will be a fuller understanding of the feelings, fears, beliefs, and hopes that were shared by individuals under great stress in a terrible moment of history."[17]

Perhaps the volume that best represents this renewed focus on common soldiers is James M. McPherson's *For Cause and Comrades* (1997). McPherson, who credited Keegan's *The Face of Battle* for inspiring his own study, rejected Linderman and others who suggested that soldiers became jaded and demoralized by war and alienated as veterans. McPherson countered that Civil War soldiers, North and South, fought primarily for high-toned ideological motivations and stayed true to these motivations throughout the trials and tribulations of combat.

16. Don Higginbotham, "The Martial Spirit in the Antebellum South: Some Further Speculation in a National Context," *Journal of Southern History* 58 (February 1992): 6, 15; Grady McWhiney and Perry D. Jamieson, *Attack and Die: Civil War Military Tactics and the Southern Heritage* (Tuscaloosa: University of Alabama Press, 1982). In his 1987 study, Paddy Griffith argued that despite the technological improvements in arms, Civil War volunteer troops were unevenly trained and ill prepared for combat. "Human factors such as training and doctrine—or lack of them," Griffith asserted, "exerted a much greater influence upon the outcome than did the precise specifications of the weaponry in use"; see *Battle Tactics of the Civil War* (New Haven: Yale University Press, 1989), 27.

17. John Keegan, *The Face of Battle* (New York: Viking, 1976); Marvin R. Cain, "A Face of Battle Needed: An Assessment of Motives and Men in Civil War Historiography," *Civil War History* 28 (March 1982): 27. Cain concentrated on Union soldiers. He did not explain this focus, but his conclusions are just as relevant to Confederate troops.

In his closing paragraph, McPherson praised the seemingly selfless sacrifices of all Civil War soldiers, many of whom died "for the principles they perceived to be at stake in the war." Four years before 9/11, McPherson felt compelled to wonder: "Whether Americans today would be willing to make similar wartime sacrifices is unanswerable. One hopes that it will remain unanswered."[18]

McPherson's sentiments underscored two questions that continue to bedevil scholars: first, were Civil War soldiers heroic and stalwart men who fought for their ideals, or were they hapless victims of this horrific war, scarred and embittered by its brutality? Steven E. Woodworth complained that scholars such as Linderman portrayed soldiers "not as heroes—even quiet unassuming heroes, but rather as victims, behavioral specimens tossed to and fro and driven by various social forces acting upon them." In 2008 Jason Phillips warned scholars that the hero-victim debate created a false dichotomy. "Civil War soldiers were more than heroes, victims, villains, race warriors, and citizens," he observed. "They were individuals from diverse places who formed enormous armies bursting with local colors and scents, myriad accents, and internal rivalries."[19]

The second and more persistent question that McPherson raised has been the precise place of race and proslavery sentiment in the rebel army. For McPherson, slavery was entirely the cause of the war, but just as soldiers were not consciously fighting for Coca-Cola in Vietnam or oil in Iraq, rebel soldiers elided material realities and repackaged their peculiar form of white supremacy as deeply held platitudes, resulting in a fundamentally "American" fight for home and honor even among those warring against the United States.

The gradual integration of scholarship on black soldiers complicated this picture; indeed, perhaps nothing has done more to defeat the notion of a Brothers War than the demand that black brothers (and sisters) get a seat at the family table. In 1970, the study of the United States Colored Troops was in its infancy: Dudley Taylor Cornish produced *The Sable Arm* in 1956 and James M. McPherson published *The Negro's Civil War* in 1965, but neither had yet been fully integrated into an understanding of precisely how the Civil War became a war for and

18. James M. McPherson, *For Cause and Comrades: Why Men Fought in the Civil War* (New York: Oxford University Press, 1997), 178, 184.

19. Steven E. Woodworth, ed., *The Loyal True and Brave: America's Civil War Soldiers* (Wilmington: Scholarly Resources, 2002); Jason Phillips, "Battling Stereotypes: A Taxonomy of Common Soldiers in Civil War History," *History Compass* 6 (November 2008): 14–16. A similar complex and balanced new view appeared in Peter S. Carmichael, *The War for the Common Soldier: How Men Thought, Fought, and Survived in Civil War Armies* (Chapel Hill: University of North Carolina Press, 2018).

against emancipation.[20] This was remedied in part by Joseph T. Glatthaar's *Forged in Battle* (1990) and Chandra Manning's *What This Cruel War Was Over* (2007).[21] Manning particularly sought to tie rebel soldiers more clearly and carefully to their identities before and after the war as men who demanded and depended to a large degree, on the subjugation of blacks for their self-definition.

Also important was Stephen V. Ash's *Firebrand of Liberty* (2008). Just as fugitive slaves such as Frederick Douglass and Henry Highland Garnett did much to nudge abolitionism in the 1840s and 1850s into a confrontation with the Slave Power, fugitive slaves, especially as soldiers, shaped what the results of that confrontation would mean. As Ash made clear, for instance, it was not the Fifty-Fourth Massachusetts (largely composed of northern-born free blacks) at Battery Wagner but the First South Carolina (largely composed of formerly enslaved men) at Jacksonville who finally convinced the Lincoln administration that their black allies in the Deep South were more valuable than their white ones in the border states.[22]

Black soldiers' service off the battlefield was critical, too. As Andrew F. Lang noted in *In the Wake of War* (2017), virtually all white Americans in 1860 believed that citizen armies should gather, shoot bad guys, and go home. There was virtually no appetite among white volunteers for garrison duty much less nation-building (which is what true Reconstruction would have required). Here is where Lang's book is at its most original, however. When Lincoln first conceived of black Union army service, he was thinking in terms of garrison duty, guarding roads and checkpoints, and serving as peacekeepers. Lincoln did not mean any of this as a compliment. In the end, however, this *was* the work of nation-building, and the gains achieved by blacks in Reconstruction were often made on the ground by black soldiers who remained behind the lines to help transform civil society. Steven Hahn's *A Nation under Our Feet* (2003), Thavolia Glymph's *Out of the House of Bondage* (2008), Glenn David Brasher's *The Peninsula Campaign and*

20. Dudley Taylor Cornish, *The Sable Arm: Negro Troops in the Union Army* (New York: Longmans, Green, 1956); James M. McPherson, *The Negro's Civil War: How American Blacks Felt and Acted during the War for the Union* (New York: Pantheon, 1965).

21. Joseph T. Glatthaar, *Forged in Battle: The Civil War Alliance of Black Soldiers and White Officers* (New York: Free Press, 1990); Chandra Manning, *What This Cruel War Was Over: Soldiers, Slavery, and the Civil War* (New York: Alfred A. Knopf, 2008). See also John David Smith, *Lincoln and the U. S. Colored Troops* (Carbondale: Southern Illinois University Press, 2013).

22. Stephen V. Ash, *Firebrand of Liberty: The Story of Two Black Regiments that Changed the Course of the Civil War* (New York: W. W. Norton, 2008).

the Necessity of Emancipation (2012), and James Oakes's *Freedom National* (2012) were all also critical in placing the actions and activism of black southerners at the center of the politics of emancipation.[23]

All of these developments—the debates over battle trauma, white soldiers' motivations, white supremacy, and the contributions of African American soldiers—have had the collective effect of making Civil War soldiers seem less exceptional, more typical, and more an extension of their home-front societies.

The War Comes Home

In 1990, just as the publication of new works on common soldiers began to pick up speed, Maris A. Vinovskis issued a clarion call to social historians, claiming that they had "lost" the Civil War, chastising them for allegedly missing rich opportunities to examine the far-reaching effects that war had on individuals and the life of the nation. Nor was he happy with military historians whom he felt did not pay serious attention to soldiers' lives and families. "The study of wars," Vinovskis asserted, "cannot be left only to military historians, but must be undertaken by other scholars, so we can better appreciate the costs and meanings of warfare as well as today." Vinovskis wondered if it would take the next generation of Civil War historians to write the social history of the conflict. To prove his point, he included in his book several examples of community studies written by junior historians.[24]

Vinovkis's call proved prescient. Since its publication there has been a massive rise in "home front" studies; works by Daniel E. Sutherland, Joan E. Cashin, Stephen V. Ash, James Marten, John C. Inscoe, Jonathan Dean Sarris, and Jac-

23. Andrew F. Lang, *In the Wake of War: Military Occupation, Emancipation, and Civil War America* (Baton Rouge: Louisiana State University Press, 2017); Steven Hahn, *A Nation under Our Feet: Black Political Struggles in the Rural South from Slavery to the Great Migration* (Cambridge: Harvard University Press, 2003); Thavolia Glymph, *Out of the House of Bondage: The Transformation of the Plantation Household* (New York: Cambridge University Press, 2008); Glenn David Brasher, *The Peninsula Campaign and the Necessity of Emancipation: African Americans and the Fight for Freedom* (Chapel Hill: University of North Carolina Press, 2012); James Oakes, *Freedom National: The Destruction of Slavery in the United States, 1861–1865* (New York: W. W. Norton, 2012). For a decimation of the opposite notion—that black southerners served willingly and in large numbers for the Confederacy—see Kevin M. Levin, *Searching for Black Confederate Soldiers: The Civil War's Most Persistent Myth* (Chapel Hill: University of North Carolina Press, 2019).

24. Maris A. Vinovskis, ed., *Toward A Social History of American History: Exploratory Essays* (New York: Cambridge University Press, 1990), xii, vii.

queline Glass Campbell, to name just a few, have highlighted southern regions, communities, towns, families, and personal relationships directly touched and often torn asunder by the war.[25] The works of Catherine Clinton and Nina Silber, including their edited volume *Divided Houses* (1992), led the way in creating a new social history of the conflict. In seeking to better understand what the war meant to civilians, including white women, children, and enslaved persons, not merely in the war's power centers but in "border" communities, historians came to document the war's impact on the home front, the home front's impact on the war, and the interpenetration of the two.[26] Such accounts are less traditionally heroic and awe-inspiring than Pickett's Charge, and for some critics these works question the very definition of "military history" and even threaten its supremacy as a field.[27]

And indeed, by 2000 the notion of a "home front" itself was beginning to collapse as scholars working on guerrilla warfare, contraband camps, occupation

25. Daniel E. Sutherland, *Seasons of War: The Ordeal of a Confederate Community, 1861–1865* (New York: Free Press, 1995); Joan E. Cashin, ed., *The War Was You and Me: Civilians in the American Civil War* (Princeton: Princeton University Press, 2002); Stephen V. Ash, *When the Yankees Came: Conflict and Chaos in the Occupied South, 1861–1865* (Chapel Hill: University of North Carolina Press, 1995); John C. Inscoe, *Mountain Masters: Slavery and the Sectional Crisis in Western North Carolina* (Knoxville: University of Tennessee Press, 1989); James Marten, *The Children's Civil War* (Chapel Hill: University of North Carolina Press, 1998); Jonathan Dean Sarris, *A Separate Civil War: Communities in Conflict in the Mountain South* (Charlottesville: University of Virginia Press, 2006); Jacqueline Glass Campbell, *When Sherman Marched North from the Sea: Resistance on the Confederate Home Front* (Chapel Hill: University of North Carolina Press, 2003).

26. Catherine Clinton and Nina Silber, eds., *Divided Houses: Gender and the Civil War* (New York: Oxford University Press, 1992). Examples include Victoria E. Bynum, *The Free State of Jones: Mississippi's Longest Civil War* (Chapel Hill: University of North Carolina Press, 2001); Scott Reynolds Nelson and Carol Sheriff, *A People at War: Civilians and Soldiers in America's Civil War, 1845–1877* (New York: Oxford University Press, 2007); Diane Mutti Burke, *On Slavery's Border: Missouri's Small-Slaveholding Households, 1815–1865* (Athens: University of Georgia Press, 2010); Mark W. Geiger, *Financial Fraud and Guerrilla Violence in Missouri's Civil War, 1861–1865* (New Haven: Yale University Press, 2010).

27. The debate about the role (and primacy) of military history in Civil War studies has proven bitterly divisive in print and at scholarly conferences. Mark Grimsley asked pointedly in 1996, "what can military historians tell other historians that they can't figure out on their own? Why exactly do we need experts in the subject?" See "Why Military History Sucked," http://warhistorian.blogspot.com/2016/06/why-military-history-sucked.html (accessed 18 January 2019). Nonetheless, for some, the perceived waning of traditional military history is cause for alarm. See Gary W. Gallagher and Katheryn Shively Meier, "Coming to Terms with Civil War Military History," *Journal of the Civil War Era* 4 (December 2014): 487–508; Earl J. Hess, "Where Do We Stand? A Critical Assessment of Civil War Studies in the Sesquicentennial Era," *Civil War History* 60 (December 2014): 371–403.

studies, and Civil War refugees demanded an end to the home-front/battlefront binary. Their work collectively forced historians to recognize something that was painfully obvious to the Union army—that the most important terrain it had to navigate as it penetrated and occupied the South was the human one. Placing white women, enslaved people, even children into the metanarrative of war meant recasting objects as subjects and reimagining the military conflict in broader social contexts. In the works of Stephanie McCurry, LeeAnn Whites, Elizabeth R. Varon, Leslie A. Schwalm, Thavolia Glymph, and Alecia P. Long, women white and black took center stage in a war fought in and by, through and on southern households in a historiography of intersectionality and interconnectedness.[28] David Silkenat's *Driven From Home* (2016), Lorien Foote's *The Yankee Plague* (2016), and Amy Murrell Taylor's *Embattled Freedom* (2018) all situate Civil War armies as critical actors but demand and demonstrate that they cannot be understood outside the social matrix they were composed of and moved through.[29] The military narrative, they insist, is inseparable from the political narrative, the refugee narrative, the guerrilla narrative, the emancipation narrative, and the story of the Civil War as a war of occupation—because even those without a musket on their shoulder exerted a profound influence on the war's course and consequences.[30]

28. Stephanie McCurry, *Confederate Reckoning: Power and Politics in the Civil War South* (Cambridge: Harvard University Press, 2010); LeeAnn Whites, *The Civil War as a Crisis in Gender: Augusta, Georgia, 1860–1890* (Athens: University of Georgia Press, 1995); Elizabeth R. Varon, *Southern Lady, Yankee Spy: The True Story of Elizabeth Van Lew, a Union Agent in the Heart of the Confederacy* (New York: Oxford University Press, 2003); Leslie A. Schwalm, *A Hard Fight for We: Women's Transition from Slavery to Freedom in South Carolina* (Urbana: University of Illinois Press, 1997); LeeAnn Whites and Alecia P. Long, eds., *Occupied Women: Gender, Military Occupation, and the American Civil War* (Baton Rouge: Louisiana State University Press, 2009); Glymph, *Out of the House of Bondage*. As McCurry wrote: "The challenge is to make women subjects of, as well as images in, the history we write"; see *Confederate Reckoning*, 30.

29. David Silkenat, *Driven from Home: North Carolina's Civil War Refugee Crisis* (Athens: University of Georgia Press, 2016); Lorien Foote, *The Yankee Plague: Escaped Prisoners and the Collapse of the Confederacy* (Chapel Hill: University of North Carolina Press, 2016); Amy Murrell Taylor, *Embattled Freedom: Journeys through the Civil War's Slave Refugee Camps* (Chapel Hill: University of North Carolina Press, 2018).

30. For similar approaches to guerrilla war, see Joseph M. Beilein Jr., *Bushwhackers: Guerrilla Warfare, Manhood, and the Household in Civil War Missouri* (Kent: Kent State University Press, 2016); Daniel E. Sutherland, *A Savage Conflict: The Decisive Role of Guerrillas in the American Civil War* (Chapel Hill: University of North Carolina Press, 2009). For a historiographical overview of the homefront/battlefront binary and its problems, see Lorien Foote, "Rethinking the Confederate Homefront," *Journal of the Civil War Era* 7 (September 2017): 446–65; Carol K. Bleser and Lesley J. Gordon, "Editors' Introduction," in

In *Troubled Refuge* (2016), to take a last example, Chandra Manning treated contraband camps as a critical theater of war. Beginning with Frederick Douglass, the bedrock of black citizenship has always been assumed to be military service. "Once let the black man get upon his person the brass letter, U.S.," wrote Douglass, "let him get an eagle on his button, and a musket on his shoulder and bullets in his pocket, there is no power on earth that can deny that he has earned the right to citizenship." Manning posited, however, that the Civil War and Emancipation inaugurated larger refugee and humanitarian crises leading to broader debates over the dispossessed. Scholars have traditionally seen the formerly enslaved in a sort of liminal status—temporarily, legally and literally, unmoored by emancipation—but eventually redefined as (practically) serfs under a peonage system. It was, in the words of one historian, "slavery by another name."[31] Manning offered another way forward, a sense that African American families—men, women, and children—hollowed out the space where they could make claims for themselves, not merely as soldiers or soldiers' wives, but simply as people, claims that would ultimately come to redefine citizenship for everyone, black and white.

In making these essentially intersectional claims about the need to simultaneously understand the Civil War as a crisis of armies, politics, capitalism, class, gender, race, and the household, Civil War historians had to push and interrogate the very archives that privileged the elite battlefront histories in the first place. James M. McPherson based much of *For Cause and Comrades* on exhaustive archival research. He pointedly criticized prior works on common soldiers, Linderman in particular, as overly reliant on published materials, which he found flawed for being "written for publication." In time, however, even McPherson's preferred sources came into question. Especially in the South, the traditional archive often remains a monument to elite white families that must be read "against the grain" to produce a history of the disadvantaged, white and black. Notwithstanding the fact that all written texts have limitations, a dramatic shift occurred in the availability of primary documents, both published and digitized, as presses and

Intimate Strategies of the Civil War: Military Commanders and Their Wives, ed. Carol K. Bleser and Lesley J. Gordon (New York: Oxford University Press, 2001), ix–xxiii.

31. Chandra Manning, *Troubled Refuge: Struggling for Freedom in the Civil War* (New York: Alfred A. Knopf, 2016); Frederick Douglass, "Negroes and the National War Effort: An Address Delivered in Philadelphia, Pennsylvania, on 6 July 1863," in *Frederick Douglass Papers: Speeches, Debates, and Interviews.* Vol 3, *1855–1863*, ed. John W. Blassingame (New Haven: Yale University Press, 1985), 596; Douglas A. Blackmon, *Slavery by Another Name: The Re-Enslavement of Black Americans from the Civil War to World War II* (New York: Doubleday, 2008).

digital humanities projects opened new avenues into understanding a broader cross-section of Americans caught up in the war. Edward L. Ayers led the way with The Valley of the Shadow project, but today many university presses publish dedicated series aimed at redrafting the Civil War archive, and a growing number of rich digital collections magnify the depth and range of resources open to Civil War scholars of every stripe.[32]

It is not yet clear how digitization and the attempt to remodel and interrogate the archive will affect the broader historiography of the Civil War, but promising signs emerged in early twenty-first-century scholarship. Gregory P. Downs, in *After Appomattox* (2015), mined conventional sources to generate an interactive website locating federal troops stationed throughout the former Confederacy.[33] Anne Sarah Rubin created an interactive digital map—highlighting the varying experiences of civilians and soldiers affected by Sherman's route through Georgia—to accompany her 2015 study of the march.[34] In treating the archive itself as a problem to be solved, Civil War scholars have begun building the foundation for the next generation of historians of the conflict.

Looking West and Abroad

The third major historiographical trend since the 1980s involves recentering (as much as decentering) the conflict within a wider national and international

32. McPherson, *For Cause and Comrades,* 11; The Valley of the Shadow, http://valley.lib.virginia.edu/ (accessed 18 January 2019). The University of Tennessee Press's Voices in the Civil War (http://utpress.org/voices-of-the-civil-war/) and the University of Virginia's Southern Texts Society (http://www.upress.virginia.edu/series/southern-texts-society) are two examples of series highlighting published primary texts (both accessed 30 September 2018). Other valuable digital collections are the Auburn University Civil War Diary and Letters Collection at http://diglib.auburn.edu/collections/civilwardiaries/ (accessed 18 January 2019); Virginia Military Institute's Civil War Letters, Diaries, and Manuscripts Collection at http://www.vmi.edu/archives/manuscripts/civil-war-manuscripts/ (accessed 18 January 2019); Virginia Tech's Virginia Center for Civil War Studies Gateway to Digitized Sources in Civil War Era at https://secure.hosting.vt.edu/www.sources.civilwar.vt.edu/ (accessed 18 January 2019); and University of Georgia's Private Voices at https://altchive.org/private-voices (accessed 18 January 2019).

33. Gregory P. Downs, *After Appomattox: Military Occupations and the Ends of War* (Cambridge: Harvard University Press, 2015). The digital site can be found at https://www.mappingoccupation.org/ (accessed 18 January 2019).

34. Anne Sarah Rubin, *Through the Heart of Dixie: Sherman's March and American Memory* (Chapel Hill: University of North Carolina Press, 2014). The digital site Mapping Memory can be found at http://shermansmarch.org/ (accessed 18 January 2019).

context. For many decades, both public and academic attention focused on the primacy of Lee's army and the eastern theater. Some continue to argue that the emphasis on Lee and his army is wholly justified. Joseph T. Glatthaar argued that by understanding the men in Lee's army, their motivations, hardships, triumphs, and ultimate defeat, "you understand fundamentally the war itself." In *The Confederate War* (1997), Gary W. Gallagher concluded that for a majority of white southerners, it was General Lee and his men who sustained their hopes for victory, despite increasing deprivations and military defeats. "Robert E. Lee and the Army of Northern Virginia," Gallagher maintained, "eventually became the most important national institution."[35]

And yet as early as 1965, John G. Barrett detected an increased interest in the West as a "neglected theater of the war" and predicted that eventually the imbalance would be corrected. For scholars such as Richard M. McMurray, the western front was "by far, the most important part of the struggle."[36] There have been a number of important studies about western battles, armies, and leaders published since 2000.[37] The Trans-Mississippi Theater, too, received renewed attention, and yet in 2017, Thomas Cutrer noted that this subject remains largely "unknown and understudied," languishing in the "backwaters of Civil War historiography."[38] Some scholars called for a deeper expansion of the war's geographical scope especially to include the Indian conflict. By doing so, Ari Kelman reasoned, the Civil

35. Joseph T. Glatthaar, *General Lee's Army: From Victory to Collapse* (New York: Free Press, 2008), xiii; Gary W. Gallagher, *The Confederate War* (Cambridge: Harvard University Press, 1997), 8.

36. John G. Barrett, "The Confederate States of America at War on Land and Sea," in *Writing Southern History: Essays in Historiography in Honor of Fletcher M. Green,* ed. Arthur S. Link and Rembert W. Patrick (Baton Rouge: Louisiana State University Press, 1965), 290; Richard M. McMurray, *Two Great Rebel Armies: An Essay in Confederate Military History* (Chapel Hill: University of North Carolina Press, 1989), x.

37. A sampling of studies about the western theater includes Earl J. Hess, *The Civil War in the West: Victory and Defeat from the Appalachians to the Mississippi* (Chapel Hill: University of North Carolina Press, 2012); Lawrence Lee Hewitt and Arthur W. Bergeron Jr., eds., *Confederate Generals in the Western Theater,* 3 vols. (Knoxville: University of Tennessee Press, 2010–2011); Steven E. Woodworth, *Nothing but Victory: The Army of the Tennessee, 1861–1865* (New York: Vintage Press, 2005).

38. Thomas W. Cutrer, *Theater of a Separate War: The Civil War West of the Mississippi River, 1861–1865* (Chapel Hill: University of North Carolina Press, 2017), xi. See also Jay Monaghan, *Civil War on the Western Border, 1854–1865* (Boston: Little, Brown, 1955); Richard Lowe, *Walker's Texas Division C. S. A.: Greyhounds of the Trans-Mississippi* (Baton Rouge: Louisiana State University Press, 2004); Jeffery S. Prushankin, *A Crisis in Confederate Command: Edmund Kirby Smith, Richard Taylor, and the Army of the Trans-Mississippi* (Baton Rouge: Louisiana State University Press, 2005).

War becomes redefined as a "war for empire, a contest to control expansion into the west, rather than a war for liberation."[39]

This urge to view the Civil War in broader contexts also animates the "internationalization" and "transnational" turn in Civil War studies. In *The Cause of All Nations* (2014), Don H. Doyle rightly quoted the late, great David M. Potter: "Some of our worst navel-gazing has occurred in connection with the Civil War," producing an illusion of "a conflict all our own, as American as apple pie." Arguably no aspect of Civil War history has been more harmful than this intellectual closed-border doctrine of American exceptionalism. Certainly the Americans who lived through the Civil War understood it in a global context, just as they understood their entire history in a global context. "More obviously than most nations," Edward L. Ayers argued, "the United States was the product of global history." C. A. Bayly concurred, suggesting that the Civil War must be understood as a "global event," produced from, and consequential for, a broad swath of the world.[40]

To be sure, the story of the Civil War as product and producer of larger global forces is age-old, beginning in 1860 with the idea that the Confederacy represented the last earthly gasp of organic agrarianism standing nobly if doomed before the threat of modernity. The Union war effort had its own, similarly overblown, notion of global significance: Lincoln and the Republicans fought to preserve the "last best hope of earth" and extinguish the last "relic of barbarism."[41]

39. Ari Kelman, *A Misplaced Massacre: Struggling Over the Memory of Sand Creek* (Cambridge: Harvard University Press, 2013), xi. Other works by historians who agreed with Kelman in challenging traditional chronological and geographical boundaries in interpreting the Civil War and Reconstruction Era writ large include Alvin M. Josephy Jr., *The Civil War in the American West* (New York: Alfred A. Knopf, 1991); Elliott West, *The Last Indian War: The Nez Perce Story* (New York: Oxford University Press, 2009); Megan Kate Nelson, "The Civil War from Apache Pass," *Journal of the Civil War Era* 6 (December 2016): 510–35. Such challenges have not gone unanswered. See, for example, Gary W. Gallagher, "Out West: The Importance, or Lack Thereof, of the Various Western Theaters of War," *Civil War Times Magazine*, August 2017, http://www.historynet.com/out-west.htm (accessed 18 January 2019).

40. Don H. Doyle, *The Cause of All Nations: An International History of the American Civil War* (New York: Basic Books, 2014); Edward L. Ayers, "The American Civil War, Emancipation, and Reconstruction on the World Stage," *OAH Magazine of History* 20 (January 2006): 54–61; C. A. Bayly, *The Birth of the Modern World, 1780–1914* (New York: Wiley-Blackwell, 2003), 162.

41. Lincoln referred to the United States as the "last best hope of earth" in his 1 December 1862 "Annual Message to Congress." Full text of his speech can be found in Roy P. Basler, ed., *Collected Works of Abraham Lincoln*, 8 vols. (New Brunswick: Rutgers University Press, 1953), 5:518–37. The 1856 Republican Party platform included the statement that "it is both the right and the imperative duty of Congress to prohibit in the Territories those twin relics of barbarism—Polygamy, and Slavery." See "Republican Party

These structural interpretations of the conflict continued under the influence of Charles A. Beard and Mary R. Beard and their students, who claimed, for instance, that united northern industrialists prosecuted the war to produce a Fourteenth Amendment whose real purpose was establishing the personhood of corporations that would go on to dominate the globe.[42]

These older structural interpretations, however, lacked theoretical sophistication and historical depth, and as late as 2012, W. Caleb McDaniel and Bethany L. Johnson could rightly complain that "there are more manifestoes for a 'new transnational history' than clear examples of it."[43] Civil War historians have gone to work, however, carefully considering how the conflict, and the South's role in it, related to and was consequential for a range of issues across the Atlantic World, including the development of commodity capitalism, liberal nationalism, public health movements, global food and energy systems, and the rise of the technocratic state. To take one exemplary work advancing this trend: Sven Beckert noted in *Empire of Cotton* (2014) that, in 1862, "fully 20 million people worldwide—one out of every 65 people alive—were involved in the cultivation of cotton or the production of cotton cloth." Given its superabundance of land, labor, and loose credit, the United States was a critical locus of this production but was in no sense the master of its own domain. Indeed, by 1860 "American slavery had begun to threaten the very prosperity it produced," unnerving global investors concerned that insurrection or antislavery agitation might disrupt capital flows. Cotton could still be king, the international community concluded, but slavery had reached the limits of its modernization and would have to yield to more subtle and sophisticated technologies for extracting labor value. From Beckert's perspective, global forces propelled the rise and fall of the Cotton Kingdom, and claims for the significance of the Civil War must be made at a similar scale—anything else would be too crabbed. To take another example: Scott Reynolds Nelson showed that, just as cheap cotton rewrote the global order in

---

Platform of 1856," The American Presidency Project, https://www.presidency.ucsb.edu/node/273293 (accessed 18 January 2019).

42. Charles A. Beard and Mary R. Beard, *The Rise of American Civilization* (New York: Macmillan, 1927).

43. W. Caleb McDaniel and Bethany L. Johnson, "New Approaches to Internationalizing the History of the Civil War Era: An Introduction," *Journal of the Civil War Era* 2 (June 2012): 145–50. See also Walter Johnson, *River of Dark Dreams: Slavery and Empire in the Cotton Kingdom* (Cambridge: Harvard University Press, 2013); Edward E. Baptist, *The Half Has Never Been Told: Slavery and the Making of American Capitalism* (New York: Basic Books, 2014).

the years immediately before the war, cheap food did the same during and immediately after, as the North shifted mechanized wheat production into overdrive, first to feed its soldiers and then to feed the world, all with deep implications for the outcome of the Civil War, the worldwide Panic of 1873, and, ultimately, the Russian Revolution.[44]

The transnational turn in Civil War studies treats American exceptionalism as a form of myopia, causing American Civil War scholars to simultaneously claim too little and too much in their assessment of the war's significance. The United States was, perhaps uniquely, the product of the first geopolitical economy, which included the colonization and depopulation of a continent, the mass importation of slaves, a redistribution of the planet's products and peoples, and the staggering rise of commodity capitalism.[45] If the Civil War represents the essence of America, it must be understood as essentially global, and students of that war should be as ready to explain the significance of its outcome for Canada and Mexico as they are to explain the second day of Gettysburg.

Memory and Commemoration

Perhaps no topic has gained greater prominence in Civil War history since the 1980s than the emergence of memory studies. The publication of David W. Blight's *Race and Reunion* (2001) marked a turning point in the scholarship, but many others contributed to this pivot in the historiography. Seminal works in the 1980s by Charles Reagan Wilson and Gaines M. Foster delved into the Lost Cause. Additional studies by Lesley J. Gordon, Nina Silber, Kirk Savage, Carol Reardon, Karen L. Cox, Ann Sarah Rubin, John R. Neff, William Blair, and Caroline E. Janney demonstrated how communal recollections of the war were perpetrated in rituals, statues, parks, parades, holidays, textbooks, and other parts of southern culture.[46] These historians stressed the political and cultural

44. Sven Beckert and Seth Rockman, eds., *Slavery's Capitalism: A New History of American Economic Development* (Philadelphia: University of Pennsylvania Press, 2016); Daniel Rood, *The Reinvention of Atlantic Slavery: Technology, Labor, Race, and Capitalism in the Greater Caribbean* (New York: Oxford University Press, 2017); Sven Beckert, *Empire of Cotton: A Global History* (New York: Alfred A. Knopf, 2014), quotes on 242–43, 245; Scott Reynolds Nelson, *A Nation of Deadbeats: An Uncommon History of America's Financial Disasters* (New York: Alfred A. Knopf, 2012).

45. Ayers, "The American Civil War, Emancipation, and Reconstruction on the World Stage," 54.

46. David W. Blight, *Race and Reunion: The Civil War in American Memory* (Cambridge: Harvard University Press, 2001); Charles Reagan Wilson, *Baptized in Blood: The Religion of the Lost Cause, 1865–1920*

constructions of popular memory, deliberately fashioned by a particular subset of ex-Confederate veterans and white southern women, and later by Americans and historians themselves. The scholarship since the 1980s has further shown how Confederate veterans, with varying memories of the war, wanted at times to forget, but found themselves driven to remember and eventually conform their individual, even mundane, memories to a more unified and decidedly militaristic celebration of the Lost Cause. The result was largely a sanitized story of a heroic soldier's war that remains settled into the fabric of American culture.[47] The southern memorial landscape fails not just black southerners who fought in the United States Colored Troops or white Unionists who fought against their Confederate neighbors; even the rough edges of Confederate memory were buffed out to support the Lost Cause. In *The Ghosts of Guerrilla Memory* (2016), Matthew Christopher Hulbert noted, for instance, that the eastern "Lost Cause" narrative

---

(Athens: University of Georgia Press, 1980); Gaines M. Foster, *Ghosts of the Confederacy: Defeat, the Lost Cause and the Emergence of the New South, 1865–1913* (New York: Oxford University Press, 1987); Lesley J. Gordon, *General George E. Pickett in Life and Legend* (Chapel Hill: University of North Carolina Press, 1998); Nina Silber, *The Romance of Reunion: Northerners and the South, 1865–1900* (Chapel Hill: University of North Carolina Press, 1993); Kirk Savage, *Standing Soldiers, Kneeling Slaves: Race, War, and Monument in Nineteenth-Century America* (Princeton: Princeton University Press, 1997); Carol Reardon, *Pickett's Charge in History and Memory* (Chapel Hill: University of North Carolina Press, 1997); Karen L. Cox, *Dixie's Daughters: The United Daughters of the Confederacy and the Preservation of Confederacy* (Gainesville: University Press of Florida, 2003); Ann Sarah Rubin, *A Shattered Nation: The Rise and Fall of the Confederacy, 1861–1868* (Chapel Hill, University of North Carolina Press, 2005); John R. Neff, *Honoring the Civil War Dead: Commemoration and the Problem of Reconciliation* (Lawrence: University Press of Kansas, 2005); William Blair, *Cities of the Dead: Contesting the Memory of the Civil War in the South, 1865–1914* (Chapel Hill: University of North Carolina Press, 2004); Caroline E. Janney, *Remembering the Civil War: Reunion and the Limits of Reconciliation* (Chapel Hill: University of North Carolina Press, 2013).

47. Important works on Confederate veterans include R. B. Rosenburg, *Living Monuments: Confederate Soldiers' Homes in the New South* (Chapel Hill: University of North Carolina Press, 1993); Jeffrey W. McClurken, *Take Care of the Living: Reconstructing Confederate Veteran Families in Virginia* (Charlottesville: University of Virginia Press, 2009); James Marten, *Sing Not War: The Lives of Union and Confederate Veterans in Gilded Age America* (Chapel Hill: University of North Carolina Press, 2011). For more on the endurance of the heroic image of the Confederate soldier (and most generals), see Thomas Lawrence Connelly, *The Marble Man, Robert E. Lee and His Image in American Society* (New York: Random House, 1977); William Garrett Piston, *Lee's Tarnished Lieutenant: James Longstreet and His Place in Southern History* (Athens: University of Georgia Press, 1988); Gary W. Gallagher and Alan T. Nolan, eds., *The Myth of the Lost Cause and Civil War History* (Bloomington: Indiana University Press, 2000); David R. Goldfield, *Still Fighting the Civil War: The American South and Southern History* (Baton Rouge: Louisiana State University Press, 2002).

sat uneasily in places such as Missouri and Kentucky, where the Civil War seemed less like a series of large, pitched battles and more like a sequence of home invasions and a general breakdown of law and order. These communities, he showed, created their own memorial culture of the war that could not be absorbed into the national memory of the conflict and so, in intellectual and cultural terms, was instead reinscribed as an aspect of the Old West, where lawlessness was permitted and even celebrated as fundamentally American.[48]

In *Looming Civil War* (2018), Jason Phillips offered another potentially foundational text in a related new field: the "history of the future." An inversion and companion to memory studies, future studies call on historians to focus with more sophistication on how historical actors anticipated, prophesied, and dreaded the events they collectively produced but individually experienced.[49] Events, he noted, do not unfold merely, or perhaps even primarily, within a matrix of farsighted calculation. Instead past actors, like present ones, wallow in a contingent stew of fantasy and apocalyptic vision that shaped not just how people experienced events but the trajectories of the events themselves.

The rise and proliferation of memory studies, like the maturing historiography on the common soldier, the home front, and the war's global context and significance, have had the effect of making the Civil War less triumphalist and less exceptional. And yet as we moved past the 150th anniversary of the conflict, much of the overtly jingoistic, militaristic, and aseptic portrait of the war endured in the popular culture at a time when the country remains enveloped in a "war on terror," confronting contentious questions of patriotism, including Confederate commemoration. Despite scholars such as Mark E. Neely Jr. who continued to stress the "limits" of the war's destruction, others such as Franny Nudelman, Harry S. Stout, Drew Gilpin Faust, Mark S. Schantz, and Diane Miller Sommerville turned to explore the reinforcing interconnections of violence, death, nationalism, militarism, and the American culture of war more broadly.[50] This is

48. Matthew Christopher Hulbert, *The Ghosts of Guerrilla Memory: How Civil War Bushwhackers Became Gunslingers in the American West* (Athens: University of Georgia Press, 2016).

49. Jason Phillips, *Looming Civil War: How Nineteenth-Century Americans Imagined the Future* (New York: Oxford University Press, 2018).

50. Mark E. Neely Jr., *The Civil War and the Limits of Destruction* (Cambridge: Harvard University Press, 2010); Franny Nudelman, *John Brown's Body: Slavery, Violence, and the Culture of War* (Chapel Hill: University of North Carolina Press, 2004); Harry S. Stout, *Upon the Altar of the Nation: A Moral History of the Civil War* (New York: Viking, 2006); Drew Gilpin Faust, *This Republic of Suffering: Death and the American Civil War* (New York: Alfred A. Knopf, 2008); Mark S. Schantz, *Awaiting the Heavenly*

where some of the most fruitful and timely questions about the Civil War history of the South rest. But the popular audience, which continues to seek entertainment and reassurance from its history, may not want to follow.

On 19 May 2017, New Orleans Mayor Mitchell Landrieu gave an eloquent speech about the controversial removal of four Confederate statues from his city. He asked why the Confederacy and its leaders deserved monuments and celebratory plaques when the deeper history of this diverse city, which included centuries of slavery, were largely omitted. "These monuments purposefully celebrate," Landrieu stated, "a fictional, sanitized Confederacy; ignoring the death, ignoring the enslavement, and the terror that it actually stood for." Removing the monuments, he insisted, did not mean silencing history. Instead, Landrieu sought to challenge the "false narrative of our history that I think weakens us."[51]

The challenging and reckoning of what in many ways was a false narrative of the Confederacy and the Civil War has been a long time coming. But as the twenty-first century unfolds, it appears, slowly but surely, that a more accurate albeit complicated narrative is taking its place.

Country: The Civil War and America's Culture of Death (Ithaca: Cornell University Press, 2008); Diane Miller Sommerville, *Aberration of Mind: Suicide and Suffering in the Civil War–Era South* (Chapel Hill: University of North Carolina Press, 2018).

51. Mitchell Landrieu, "We Can't Walk Away from This Truth," *The Atlantic,* 23 May 2017, https://www.theatlantic.com/politics/archive/2017/05/we-cant-walk-away-from-this-truth/527721/ (accessed 18 January 2019).

AGAINST SYNTHESIS

Diverse Approaches to the History of Reconstruction

Bruce E. Baker and Elaine S. Frantz

Though always lurking in the shadows of the Civil War, Reconstruction historiography came into its own between 1988 and 2018. These years saw a strikingly unified effort by historians to expand the narrative by making central the experiences and analysis of peoples previously marginalized or objectified in the historiography, particularly black Americans, women of all races, and non-elites. With the Cold War ended, the historical profession had unusual freedom to engage in introspection, critique, and reframing of our national history: historians of the Reconstruction era seized this opportunity. Some scholars objected to this critical orientation, feeling that marginalized groups were being emphasized at the expense of more influential, traditionally recognized figures. Still, incorporating previously excluded voices has been very much a collective project and the dominant focus of the scholarship, although historians have differed on how best, and to what extent, to write marginalized southerners into history. This shift in focus from center to periphery benefited the field of Reconstruction studies by drawing attention from the war to its aftermath, making this a particularly vigorous and generative moment in the historiography.

Historians in the decades after Reconstruction generally had embraced a white supremacist, male-focused, Social Darwinist orthodoxy. They blamed the failure of Reconstruction on black American men who, despite their alleged practical and moral incompetence to govern, had been granted power by victorious northerners. Through the mid-twentieth century, most historians writing about Reconstruction seemed to accept as inevitable that white southern men would have reclaimed their dominant political and social roles. This view always had faced opposition from scholars unwilling to concede the premise of black inferiority: most notably, in *Black Reconstruction* (1935), W. E. B. Du Bois proposed a powerful antiracist countermodel.[1]

Historians who rejected a white supremacist reading of the Reconstruction era found themselves greatly outnumbered until the rise of the civil rights movement. In its wake, two groups of scholars writing in the 1960s through 1980s fundamentally reconceived of the period in antiracist terms. The "revisionists" emphasized the competence of Reconstruction-era governments long disparaged by previous historians, though conceding that Reconstruction's opponents undermined their accomplishments. The "postrevisionists," who chronologically overlapped with the revisionists rather than followed them, emphasized the extent to which Reconstruction failed freedmen and freedwomen, leaving them economically exploited, subject to violence, and lacking meaningful civil rights. By the late 1980s, these interpretations had thoroughly displaced white supremacist readings of Reconstruction.[2]

In Reconstruction-era studies as in other historical subjects, many historians argued in the 1980s that the field needed a dominant narrative.[3] Eric Foner's *Reconstruction* (1988) sought to fill that role. Foner carefully incorporated the insights of the revisionists and postrevisionists, praising what Reconstruction-era governments achieved under adverse circumstances and taking seriously their failures and how those failures impacted black southerners. Reaching back to Du Bois for inspiration, Foner acknowledged black southerners' central position as interpreters of Reconstruction; their struggles reordered the social and economic

1. W. E. B. Du Bois, *Black Reconstruction in America: An Essay Toward a History of the Part Which Black Folk Played in the Attempt to Reconstruct Democracy in America 1860–1880* (New York: Harcourt, Brace, 1935).

2. On the revisionist school, see Lawanda Cox, "From Emancipation to Segregation: National Policy and Southern Blacks," in *Interpreting Southern History: Historiographical Essays in Honor of Sanford W. Higginbotham*, ed. John B. Boles and Evelyn Thomas Nolen (Baton Rouge: Louisiana State University Press, 1987), 199–253; Thomas J. Brown, ed., *Reconstructions: New Perspectives on the Postbellum United States* (New York: Oxford University Press, 2006), specifically Thomas J. Brown, "Introduction" (3–9), John C. Rodrigue, "Black Agency after Slavery" (40–65), and Michael W. Fitzgerald, "Reconstruction Politics and the Politics of Reconstruction" (91–116). On the postrevisionists, see Eric Foner, "Reconstruction Revisited," *Reviews in American History* 10 (December 1982): 82–100; Fitzgerald, "Reconstruction Politics and the Politics of Reconstruction."

3. In reaction to the new social history of the 1960s to 1980s, the mid-1980s saw many calls for historical synthesis in fields that had been radically expanded by new scholarship. See, for instance, Theodore K. Rabb, "Toward the Future: Coherence, Synthesis, and Quality in History," *Journal of Interdisciplinary*

character of southern society, transforming not only race but class relations. In introducing his work, Foner included a quote from Du Bois that the problem with "most recent writers toward Reconstruction" had been that "they cannot conceive of Negroes as men." Foner explored why the Republicans, given their radical positions, failed so strikingly to implement a "free labor" system in the South. He concluded that Reconstruction was heavily constrained, largely because the South was increasingly part of national political, social, and economic systems with antidemocratic tendencies. In his review of Foner's book, Michael Perman noted that it raised the "unsettling question" of "what is left to be done."[4] But this concern was misplaced: Foner simply provided a comprehensive platform and reference point for the field as it continued to undergo a radical transformation.

Foner's *Reconstruction* served its synthetic purpose. Yet even as he wrote, some historians, drawing upon theories which highlighted the importance of peripheral or liminal spaces to historical change, began to rethink how power worked in ways that would stand in some tension with it. Michel Foucault's concept of "capillary power," for instance, conceived of modern power structures as not exerted centrally within a society but instead embedded in local and regional institutions and informal relationships and practices. James C. Scott, in *Weapons of the Weak* (1985) and *Domination and the Arts of Resistance* (1990), powerfully articulated how marginalized groups, even those lacking any formal means of power, worked together to create a common discourse, developed parapolitical informal social structures, and effectively exercised certain political powers, a process Scott referred to as "infrapolitics." The new approach inspired by Foucault, Scott, and other scholars of the "cultural turn" encouraged historians to analyze how all

---

History 12 (Fall 1981): 315–32; Thomas Bender, "Wholes and Parts: The Need for Synthesis in American History," *Journal of American History* 73 (June 1986): 120–36; J. Carroll Moody and Alice Kessler-Harris, eds., *Perspectives on American Labor History: The Problems of Synthesis* (DeKalb: Northern Illinois University Press, 1989). Others were wary of synthesis: Eric H. Monkkonen, "The Dangers of Synthesis," *American Historical Review* 91 (December 1986): 1146–57; Nell Irvin Painter, "Bias and Synthesis in History," *Journal of American History* 74 (June 1987): 109–12. Dorothy Ross productively reframed the problem of synthesis perceived in this period as a problem of narrative in "Grand Narrative in American Historical Writing: From Romance to Uncertainty," *American Historical Review* 100 (June 1995): 666–67.

4. Eric Foner, *Reconstruction: America's Unfinished Revolution, 1863–1877* (New York: Harper & Row, 1988), xxi; Michael Perman, "Eric Foner's Reconstruction: A Finished Revolution," *Reviews in American History* 17 (March 1989): 78. See also David Montgomery, *Beyond Equality: Labor and the Radical Republicans, 1862–1872* (New York: Alfred A. Knopf, 1967).

historical subjects built relationships, used words, and told stories to one another, and called on scholars to understand this process as part of "the political."[5]

Several historians began to bring Scott's emphasis on the agency of the oppressed to Reconstruction-era scholarship: Julie Saville, for instance, influentially wrote in that vein in 1994, though without explicitly citing Scott. It was Steven Hahn's *A Nation under our Feet* (2003), however, which emerged as a new synthesis, more of a friendly amendment than a displacement of Foner. Rather than seeing freedom and political participation coming to black southerners through the spread of white ideas and institutions, Hahn traced the growth of democracy within "the institutions, customs, and relations of black life."[6] Hahn's broader definition of the political also enabled him to recognize women's roles within family and community as crucial historical forces.

The Foner and Hahn syntheses enjoyed remarkable influence and endurance, even in the face of widespread skepticism about the very idea of "framing" books, and the power of the (usually) white men who authored them. During the 1990s, battles raged in many disciplines over "the canon" and "cultural literacy": some argued, and others disputed, that to maintain a common culture, scholars needed to organize thoughts around a central set of facts and ideas. Similarly, in history, many late twentieth- and early twenty-first-century historians questioned the wisdom of seeking to impose a single national story. The same theoretical ap-

5. Michel Foucault, *"Society Must Be Defended": Lectures at the Collège de France, 1975–1976,* trans. David Macey (New York: Picador, 2003), 27–29; Foucault, *Discipline and Punish: The Birth of the Prison,* trans. Alan Sheridan (New York: Pantheon Books, 1977); James C. Scott, *Weapons of the Weak: Everyday Forms of Peasant Resistance* (New Haven: Yale University Press, 1985); Scott, *Domination and the Arts of Resistance: Hidden Transcripts* (New Haven: Yale University Press, 1990). See also William J. Novak, "The Myth of the 'Weak' American State," *American Historical Review* 113 (June 2008): 752–72; James W. Cook and Lawrence B. Glickman, "Twelve Propositions for a History of U.S. Cultural History," in *The Cultural Turn in U.S. History: Past, Present, and Future,* ed. James W. Cook, Lawrence B. Glickman, and Michaels O'Malley (Chicago: University of Chicago Press, 2008), 3–58.

6. Steven Hahn, *A Nation under Our Feet: Black Political Struggles in the Rural South from Slavery to the Great Migration* (Cambridge: Harvard University Press, 2003), 4, 483n3. Julie Saville's *The Work of Reconstruction: From Slave to Wage Labor in South Carolina 1860–1870* (New York: Cambridge University Press, 1994) provided a critical bridge in the historiography. See Peter A. Coclanis's scathing critique of Saville's (silent) use of Scott in "Slavery, African-American Agency, and the World We Have Lost," *Georgia Historical Quarterly* 79 (Winter 1995): 880. See also John C. Rodrigue, "Black Agency after Slavery," in *Reconstructions: New Perspectives on Postbellum United States,* ed. Thomas J. Brown (New York: Oxford University Press, 2006), 40–65.

proaches which focused on the power of narrative might imply that in an inherently diverse world, a grand narrative was necessarily "a coercive category."[7] Yet Hahn's and Foner's work proved tenacious. Perhaps ironically, the turn against grand narratives entrenched them by discouraging ambitious younger scholars from producing new synthetic works to displace them.

Structural changes in the profession mattered, too. The casualization of the profession with the decline of tenure and shrinking higher education budgets brought a substantial decline in professional historians' status, security, and access to resources. These trends created practical barriers to producing resource-intensive "big books." And while women and racial minorities brought fresh analyses with them as they succeeded in breaking barriers and establishing a larger foothold in the profession in the late twentieth and early twenty-first centuries, members of this dynamic new cohort, struggling against gender and racial discrimination, were perhaps less likely to have the influence to fundamentally challenge a hegemonic narrative.[8] Those few influential scholars who proposed innovative new syntheses, often supported by monumental research, failed to gain the momentum to supplant Foner and Hahn, perhaps reflecting dwindling investment on the part of their peers in the very project of a grand narrative. Eric Foner, considering the breadth of topics being explored by scholars of Re-

7. John Guillory, *Cultural Capital: The Problem of Literary Canon Formation* (Chicago: University of Chicago Press, 1983); Ross, "Grand Narrative in American Historical Writing," 673. Eric Foner reflected on the competing desires for a master narrative and substantial representation of previously neglected groups in his Organization of American Historians Presidential Address, "The Meaning of Freedom in the Age of Emancipation," *Journal of American History* 81 (September 1994): 435–60.

8. In 1988, around 18 percent of faculty in history departments in the United States were female. By 2007, this number had increased to 35 percent. Robert B. Townsend, "What the Data Tells Us About Women Historians," *Perspectives on History,* 12 April 2010, http://blog.historians.org/2010/04/what-the-data-tells-us-about-women-historians/ (accessed 18 January 2019). Scholarship on the Reconstruction-era South reflected this change. In the late 1980s and early 1990s, women comprised only one-tenth of the authors of Reconstruction-themed articles and of Reconstruction-themed books reviewed in the *Journal of American History.* By the 2010s, women made up one-third of such authors. Similarly, racial diversity in the profession increased: from 1995 to 2014, for instance, the percentage of history PhDs earned by members of traditionally underrepresented racial groups increased from 5.6 to 11 percent; see "Percentages of Doctoral Degrees in History Awarded to Members of Racial/Ethnic Minority Groups, 1995–2014," in "Racial/Ethnic Distribution of Degrees in History," Humanities Indicators, https://humanitiesindicators.org (accessed 18 January 2019). See also Table 22, "Subfield, Citizenship Status, Ethnicity, and Race," NCSES Survey of Earned Doctorates, FY 2016, National Science Foundation, https://www.nsf.gov/statistics/2018/nsf18304/data.cfm (accessed 18 January 2019).

construction, had his own explanation for his staying-power: asked in a 2015 *Civil War History* forum whether a new synthesis would be possible, he replied, "It would take quite an effort to integrate the dramatic and complex local story with national and international events. I wish anyone trying to accomplish this feat the best of luck."[9]

The cultural turn and the quest for a master narrative in studies of Reconstruction intersected as historians reflected on the profession and its civic purpose. In the 1990s and 2000s, historians became increasingly sensitive to the fact that institutions which funded, validated, and organized historians' work were themselves centralized, hierarchical, and network-driven. Historians also grew concerned about maintaining their public authority in the face of politically motivated accusations about the perils of "political correctness." Foner and Hahn, and a few other well-known and well-placed historians, held important roles within the profession, training and endorsing new scholars and ensuring that historians of Reconstruction would be in conversation with one another. They also, crucially, served as credible, authoritative public faces of a field—and a discipline—that felt under siege.[10]

Still, the discipline progressed. A digital revolution at the turn of the twenty-first century profoundly shaped Reconstruction-era studies as it did other fields of history and other disciplines in the humanities. This brought both new access to primary sources and new types of analytical tools. Genealogists drove one early phase of this process, with the launch of Ancestry.com in 1996 and the beginning of their digitized census schedules in 2000. Next, through improvements in digital imaging, data storage, and optical character recognition, libraries and archival

9. Mark Wahlgren Summers, *The Ordeal of the Reunion: A New History of Reconstruction* (Chapel Hill: University of North Carolina Press, 2014); Douglas R. Egerton, *The Wars of Reconstruction: The Brief, Violent History of America's Most Progressive Era* (New York: Bloomsbury Press, 2014); Michael W. Fitzgerald, *Splendid Failure: Postwar Reconstruction in the American South* (Chicago: Ivan R. Dee, 2007); "Historians' Forum: Reconstruction," *Civil War History* 61 (September 2015): 297. Arguably, Richard White's *The Republic for Which It Stands: The United States during Reconstruction and the Gilded Age, 1865-1896* (New York: Oxford University Press, 2017) made a bid for this space as well.

10. Moira Weigel, "Political correctness: how the right invented a phantom enemy," *The Guardian*, 30 November 2016, https://www.theguardian.com/us-news/2016/nov/30/political-correctness-how-the-right-invented-phantom-enemy-donald-trump (accessed 18 January 2019); Gary B. Nash, Charlotte Crabtree, and Ross E. Dunn, *History on Trial: Culture Wars and the Teaching of the Past* (New York: Alfred A. Knopf, 1997). See also "History and the Public: What Can We Handle? A Round Table about History after the Enola Gay Controversy," *Journal of American History* 82 (December 1995): 1029–135.

repositories and government agencies began to digitize massive amounts of text: newspapers, magazines, books, and pamphlets. Starting in the 1980s, the United States Newspaper Program, funded by the National Endowment for the Humanities and supported by the Library of Congress, began to systematically microfilm and catalog a wide range of local newspapers, and in 2003, the two institutions began the National Digital Newspaper Program to make newspapers through the 1920s available digitally through the Library of Congress's Chronicling America website. Each year more states' newspapers are incorporated into the project.[11]

After printed text came the digitization of manuscript materials. In 2007 the Southern Historical Collection at the University of North Carolina at Chapel Hill received funding from the Andrew W. Mellon Foundation for a project called "Extending the Reach of Southern Sources: Proceeding to Large-Scale Digitization of Manuscript Collection" which, in its first ten years, produced more than one million scans of archival material, including key Reconstruction collections: the diaries of Sea Islands missionary teacher Martha Schofield, the Heyward and Ferguson Family Papers, the Daniel R. Goodloe Papers, and many others. Other repositories undertook similar programs.[12] Simultaneously, new digital techniques enabled new forms of analysis and representation. Digital mapping allowed historians of Reconstruction to visualize Emancipation and military occupation.[13] Topic modeling has been used to automate the categorization of large amounts of texts, revealing significant patterns. Network analysis became

11. For an early overview and assessment, see Roy Rosenzweig, "The Road to Xanadu: Public and Private Pathways on the History Web," *Journal of American History* 88 (September 2001): 548–79; "Our Story: Ancestry Corporate," *Ancestry.com*, https://www.ancestry.com/corporate/about-ancestry/our-story (accessed 18 January 2019); "National Digital Newspaper Program: About the Program," Library of Congress, https://www.loc.gov/ndnp/about.html (accessed 18 January 2019).

12. Southern Historical Collection, "Extending the Reach of Southern Sources: Proceeding to Large-Scale Digitization of Manuscript Collection," June 2009, https://docsouth.unc.edu/watson/archival massdigitization/download/extending_the_reach.pdf (accessed 18 January 2019). Examples mentioned are the Martha Schofield Papers, 1865–1869 (https://finding-aids.lib.unc.edu/00999/), the Heyward and Ferguson Family Papers (https://finding-aids.lib.unc.edu/02754/), and the Daniel R. Goodloe Papers (https://finding-aids.lib.unc.edu/00278/).

13. John R. Logan, "Racial Segregation in Postbellum Southern Cities: The Case of Washington, D.C." *Demographic Research* 36 (January–June 2017): 1759–84. Examples of digital mapping in Reconstruction scholarship include Scott Nesbit and Edward L. Ayers, Visualizing Emancipation, http://dsl.richmond.edu/emancipation/ (accessed 18 January 2019); and Gregory P. Downs and Scott Nesbit, Mapping Occupation: Force, Freedom and the Army in Reconstruction, http://mappingoccupation.org/ (accessed 18 January 2019).

available to reconstruct and characterize social systems. The digital revolution, then, fundamentally changed how historians of Reconstruction conduct research and analysis, most notably by enabling historians to track down "needles in a haystack," and find and convey patterns in large bodies of data. Both are particularly useful in recovering events and lives outside of elite culture and discourse. That is, the digital revolution made it more feasible to write histories of a much broader portion of the population during the Reconstruction era.[14]

The cultural turn, culture wars, and digital revolution complicated efforts to propose a holistic replacement for Foner's and Hahn's frameworks. Many historians insisted on an irreducibility of difference that made such a project impossible. Most notably, women's historians were constructing very different narratives of the period. In the mid-1990s, foundational works in Reconstruction-era women's history appeared in rapid succession: Elsa Barkley Brown's "Negotiating and Transforming the Public Sphere" (1994), LeeAnn Whites's *The Civil War as a Crisis in Gender* (1995), Laura F. Edwards's *Gendered Strife and Confusion* (1997), Tera W. Hunter's *To 'Joy My Freedom* (1997), and Leslie A. Schwalm's *A Hard Fight for We* (1997) all used a cultural history approach to recover the lives, agency, and relationships of black and white women during Reconstruction. In 2003 Jane Turner Censer revisited elite white southern women, finding moments, however brief, when they pushed back against men's orthodoxies.[15] A wave of works followed, with authors shifting focus from households to women's defense of their bodily integrity: Lisa Cardyn's "Sexualized Racism/Gendered Violence" (2002), Diane Miller Sommerville's *Rape and Race in the Nineteenth-*

14. Daniel Taylor Young, "How Do You Measure a Constitutional Moment? Using Algorithmic Topic Modeling to Evaluate Bruce Ackerman's Theory of Constitutional Change," *Yale Law Journal* 122 (May 2013): 1990–2054; Elaine Frantz Parsons, *Ku-Klux: The Birth of the Klan During Reconstruction* (Chapel Hill: University of North Carolina Press, 2015), 215–63; Eric Foner, "Afterword," in *After Slavery: Race, Labor, and Citizenship in the Reconstruction South*, ed. Bruce E. Baker and Brian Kelly (Gainesville: University Press of Florida, 2013), 222.

15. Elsa Barkley Brown, "Negotiating and Transforming the Public Sphere: African American Political Life in the Transition from Slavery to Freedom," *Public Culture* 7 (Fall 1994): 107–46; LeeAnn Whites, *The Civil War as a Crisis in Gender: Augusta, Georgia, 1860–1890* (Athens: University of Georgia, 1995); Leslie A. Schwalm, *A Hard Fight for We: Women's Transition from Slavery to Freedom in South Carolina* (Urbana: University of Illinois Press, 1997); Tera W. Hunter, *To 'Joy My Freedom: Southern Black Women's Lives and Labor after the Civil War* (Cambridge: Harvard University Press, 1997); Laura F. Edwards, *Gendered Strife and Confusion: The Political Culture of Reconstruction* (Urbana: University of Illinois Press, 1997); Jane Turner Censer, *The Reconstruction of White Southern Womanhood, 1865–1895* (Baton Rouge: Louisiana State University Press, 2003).

Century South (2004), Hannah Rosen's *Terror in the Heart of Freedom* (2009), and Kidada E. Williams's *They Left Great Marks on Me* (2012).[16] These historians insisted that formal politics fundamentally began with, and remained intricately interwoven with, struggles around family roles and bodily control. While they generally saw their work as compatible with Foner and Hahn, they tended to understand these "master narratives" as not just flattening a diversity of experiences but neglecting crucial sites of historical change. Ultimately these scholars imagined their collective work as transformative rather than additive.

Arguments that developed primarily to demand recognition of the diversity of racial and gendered experience could also be applied to other communities under-represented by master narratives: poor whites; people who lived along the various borders of the South; people who did not fit into the reified categories of white or black, male or female; and urbanites. As traditional white-male-dominated spaces became less important to the literature of Reconstruction, some historians claimed that such relative neglect distorted how power actually worked. In a heavily debated 2014 article, Gary W. Gallagher and Kathryn Shively Meier argued that while cultural history approaches provided important contexts, accounts of the Civil War and Reconstruction eras needed to work outward from the battlefield. Gallagher and Meier welcomed accounts of people farther from or in resistance to formal power; they engaged in such work themselves. But they also insisted that any such studies needed to explain the subordinate nature of such individuals' roles and accurately credit and describe the sources of formal power. Formal power played "a decisive role" in directing the course of Reconstruction in the South. Therefore, phrases that downplayed the formal, such as "self-emancipation," were misleading.[17]

Another important innovation in the field came with the "dark history" debate. Inspired in part by whiteness and manhood studies of the 1990s that reinterpreted

16. Lisa Cardyn, "Sexualized Racism/Gendered Violence: Outraging the Body Politic in the Reconstruction South," *Michigan Law Review* 100 (February 2002): 675–867; Diane Miller Sommerville, *Rape and Race in the Nineteenth-Century South* (Chapel Hill: University of North Carolina Press, 2004); Hannah Rosen, *Terror in the Heart of Freedom: Citizenship, Sexual Violence, and the Meaning of Race in the Postemancipation South* (Chapel Hill: University of North Carolina Press, 2009); Kidada E. Williams, *They Left Great Marks on Me: African American Testimonies of Racial Violence from Emancipation to World War I* (New York: New York University Press, 2012).

17. Don H. Doyle, *New Men, New Cities, New South: Atlanta, Charleston, Nashville, Mobile, 1860–1910* (Chapel Hill: University of North Carolina Press, 1990); Eric Arnesen, *Waterfront Workers of New Orleans: Race, Class, and Politics, 1863–1923* (New York: Oxford University Press, 1991); Bernard E. Powers

male and white identities as always constructed, unstable, and fraught, some Reconstruction historians turned their focus back to the traditional white male subjects of history, refusing to represent them as healthy, empowered, and agentic.[18] As Diane Miller Sommerville wrote in her 2018 book on Civil War–era suicide, "Quite a few [Confederate soldiers] brought home with them the visible scars of war including missing limbs, disfigurement, and unhealed wounds. Mental scars, less visible, were just as debilitating." A collection, *Weirding the War* (2011), which included essays covering the Reconstruction era, most starkly represented this tendency. Historians who pushed back against dark history argued that such scholarship, with its focus on guerrilla fighting, mental illness, amputation, and terrorism, was motivated by a presentist political agenda and fundamentally misrepresented men's normal experiences in the Civil War and Reconstruction eras.[19]

Other historians suggested that the project of recovering the agency of the oppressed necessarily produced hyper-politicized caricatures of historical actors. In a 1995 review of books on black land ownership, Peter A. Coclanis derided "works overstuffed with agency . . . underdogs and overdogs, routinized acts of heroism, and clockwork villainy." More nuanced critiques continued to question the use of the concept of agency, suggesting that it needed to be understood in more complex terms.[20]

Jr., *Black Charlestonians: A Social History, 1822–1885* (Fayetteville: University of Arkansas Press, 1994); Mark V. Wetherington, *The New South Comes to Wiregrass Georgia, 1860–1910* (Knoxville: University of Tennessee Press, 1994); Gary W. Gallagher and Kathryn Shively Meyer, "Coming to Terms with Civil War Military History," *Journal of the Civil War Era* 4 (December 2014): 496.

18. Edwards, *Gendered Strife and Confusion;* Carole Emberton, *Beyond Redemption: Race, Violence, and the American South after the Civil War* (Chicago: University of Chicago Press, 2013); Parsons, *Ku-Klux;* Alexander Saxton, *The Rise and Fall of the White Republic: Class Politics and Mass Culture in Nineteenth-Century America* (New York: Verso, 2003); David R. Roediger, *The Wages of Whiteness: Race and the Making of the American Working Class* (New York: Verso, 1999).

19. Diane Miller Sommerville, *Aberration of Mind: Suicide and Suffering in the Civil War–Era South* (Chapel Hill: University of North Carolina Press, 2018), 4; Stephen Berry, ed., *Weirding the War: Stories from the Civil War's Ragged Edges* (Athens: University of Georgia Press, 2011); Gary W. Gallagher and Kathryn Shively Meier, "Coming to Terms with Civil War Military History," *Journal of the Civil War Era* 4 (December 2014): 493.

20. Peter A. Coclanis, "Slavery, African American Agency, and the World We Have Lost," *Georgia Historical Quarterly* 79 (Winter 1995): 879; Walter Johnson, "On Agency," *Journal of Social History* 37 (Autumn 2003): 113–24; Brian Kelly, review of *Nation under Our Feet: Black Political Struggles in the Rural South, from Slavery to the Great Migration* by Steven Hahn, *Labor* 1 (Fall 2004): 145–47. Ironically, in his attempt to use humor to delegitimize an increasingly hegemonic interpretation, Coclanis could be said to have been employing one of Scott's "weapons of the weak," much as his theory predicted.

Despite vigorous scholarly debates about inclusiveness, it nonetheless fundamentally changed how historians interpreted Reconstruction. To begin with, inclusiveness forced historians to rethink the chronology of Reconstruction. Richard Zuczek gave the conventional periodization when he defined Reconstruction for the *Encyclopedia of the Reconstruction Era* (2006) as generally encompassing "the period 1862–1877, during which the United States sought to bring order from the tremendous social, political, economic, physical, and constitutional changes wrought by secession and the Civil War."[21] As historians continued to move towards a model of inchoate collective agency, however, the formal events traditionally used to mark the beginnings and endings of periods—laws, elections, wars, even the Emancipation Proclamation—came to seem epiphenomenal.[22]

Scholars since the 1980s played with the traditional temporal boundaries of Reconstruction.[23] Steven Hahn began his account with life during slavery (rather than enfranchisement) and ended with the Great Migration (rather than disfranchisement). In his interpretation, the story of black political agency neither began nor ended with whites' decisions whether to bestow rights upon them. Susan Eva O'Donovan's more pessimistic narrative similarly began with the slavery period, explaining that when emancipated African Americans entered Reconstruction, they "voiced desires that emerged out of a past distinctly their own," drawing on a world of meanings and relationships they had created "right under their masters' (and mistresses') noses."[24] Gregory P. Downs's *After Appomattox* (2015) numbered among the books that brought this impulse to its logical conclusion

21. Richard Zuczek, "Introduction," in *Encyclopedia of the Reconstruction Era,* 2 vols. (Westport: Greenwood Press, 2006), 1:xxxi. See a discussion about inclusiveness and chronology in Thomas J. Brown, *Reconstructions: New Perspectives on the Postbellum United States* (New York: Oxford University Press, 2006), 3–7.

22. In their "Editors' Introduction" to Foner's *Reconstruction,* Henry Steele Commager and Richard B. Morris admitted that "Even the chronology is chaotic." See *Reconstruction,* xvii.

23. Many historical fields have seen similar changing chronologies, most notably the "long eighteenth century" and the "long civil rights movement." See J. C. D. Clark, *English Society, 1660–1832: Ideology, Social Structure, and Political Practice during the Ancien Regime* (New York: Cambridge University Press, 1985); Jacquelyn Dowd Hall, "The Long Civil Rights Movement and the Political Uses of the Past," *Journal of American History* 91 (March 2005): 1233–63.

24. Hahn, *A Nation under Our Feet,* 4; Susan Eva O'Donovan, *Becoming Free in the Cotton South* (Cambridge: Harvard University Press, 2007), 4, 6. Dylan C. Penningroth also argued that freedpeople's situation in Reconstruction was based on their experiences during slavery in *Claims of Kinfolk: African American Property and Community in the Nineteenth-Century South* (Chapel Hill: University of North Carolina Press, 2003).

by suggesting that the Civil War and Reconstruction were best seen as one continuous period. Rather than ending at a farmhouse in Virginia in April 1865, the Civil War continued, in other forms. Much of Reconstruction was merely what happened in the Civil War as the armies demobilized.[25]

If determining when Reconstruction began has proven contentious, its end has nearly disappeared in the works of leading scholars. Heather Cox Richardson argued that the national debate during Reconstruction "was not only about race but also about the clash between two concepts of political economy." This struggle played out "in the years between 1865 and 1901, [as] a new definition of what it meant to be an American developed from a heated debate over the proper relationship of the government to its citizens." Focusing on North Carolina, Gregory P. Downs traced the development of a "long reconstruction" of "American patronalism" that saw individuals make "claims of dependence" that were "innovative efforts to take advantage of new government powers," a shift that unfolded away from the negative antebellum attitude toward dependence across the last four decades of the nineteenth century. A 2017 volume in the Oxford History of the United States suggests another possible future for the periodization of Reconstruction. Richard White's *The Republic for Which It Stands* is subtitled *The United States during Reconstruction and the Gilded Age, 1865–1896,* formalizing some of these trends for a blurred ending of Reconstruction.[26] It is possible that we are seeing the end of Reconstruction as a distinctive period in American history.

As with chronology, geography has sparked vigorous debates among historians since the 1990s. Sensitive to the constructed nature of identities, historians recognized that the South itself was a construct, an imagined community com-

25. Gregory P. Downs, *After Appomattox: Military Occupation and the Ends of War* (Cambridge: Harvard University Press, 2015). See a similar suggestion in Ian Tyrrell's foreword to David Prior, ed., *Reconstruction in a Globalizing World* (New York: Fordham University Press, 2018), xi–xiv; James K. Hogue, *Uncivil War: Five New Orleans Street Battles and the Rise and Fall of Radical Reconstruction* (Baton Rouge: Louisiana State University Press, 2006).

26. Heather Cox Richardson, *The Death of Reconstruction: Race, Labor, and Politics in the Post–Civil War North, 1865–1901* (Cambridge: Harvard University Press, 2001), xii; Richardson, *West from Appomattox: The Reconstruction of America after the Civil War* (New Haven: Yale University Press, 2007), 1; Gregory P. Downs, *Declarations of Dependence: The Long Reconstruction of Popular Politics in the South, 1861–1908* (Chapel Hill: University of North Carolina Press, 2011), 7; Richard White, *The Republic for Which It Stands: The United States during Reconstruction and the Gilded Age, 1865–1896* (New York: Oxford University Press, 2017).

posed of many distinct regions. Some places fit better than others into the simplifications required by historical syntheses. Studies of western North Carolina and Alabama filled in some parts of the southern map whose narratives had not been rewritten since the revisionist movement. Local and regional scholarship proved particularly important when addressing areas on the edges of the South. A robust body of scholarship on Reconstruction-era Texas, Appalachia, and Florida, for instance, emphasized unique economies, cultures, and demographies.[27]

Community studies, a staple of the social history movement of the 1960s through 1980s, have been kept alive in regional history journals even when neglected by national gatekeepers. In the 1990s and 2000s, scholars returning to a community-centered focus spoke to key trends within the field of Reconstruction-era studies. In privileging the local and insisting on difference, these community studies—now labeled "microhistories"— called for a less centralized model of the Reconstruction-era South. Earlier generations of historians tended to emphasize the power of state governments and state-level politics. Community studies oriented around different modes of power: in some cases, a county as in T. R. C. Hutton's study of Breathitt County, Kentucky, or Martin Crawford's study of Ashe County, North Carolina; in other cases, a single city such as St. Louis, Mobile, New Orleans, or Washington, DC.[28] Some historians

27. Edward L. Ayers et al., *All Over the Map: Rethinking American Regions* (Baltimore: Johns Hopkins University Press, 1996); Ayers and John C. Willis, eds., *The Edge of the South: Life in Nineteenth-Century Virginia* (Charlottesville: University of Virginia Press, 1991); Carl H. Moneyhon, *The Impact of the Civil War and Reconstruction on Arkansas: Persistence in the Midst of Ruin* (Baton Rouge: Louisiana State University Press, 1994); Moneyhon, *Texas After the Civil War: The Struggle of Reconstruction* (College Station: Texas A&M University Press, 2004); Steven E. Nash, *Reconstruction's Ragged Edge: The Politics of Postwar Life in the Southern Mountains* (Chapel Hill: University of North Carolina Press, 2016); Michael W. Fitzgerald, *Reconstruction in Alabama: From Civil War to Redemption in the Cotton South* (Baton Rouge: Louisiana State University Press, 2017); Justin Behrend, *Reconstructing Democracy: Grassroots Black Politics in the Deep South in the Civil War* (Athens: University of Georgia Press, 2015); Aaron Astor, *Rebels on the Border: Civil War, Emancipation, and the Reconstruction of Kentucky and Missouri* (Baton Rouge: Louisiana State University Press, 2012); Paul Ortiz, *Emancipation Betrayed: The Hidden History of Black Organizing and White Violence in Florida From Reconstruction to the Bloody Election of 1920* (Berkeley: University of California Press, 2005); Daniel R. Weinfeld, *The Jackson County War: Reconstruction and Resistance in Post–Civil War Florida* (Tuscaloosa: University of Alabama Press, 2012).

28. Altina L. Waller, *Feud: Hatfields, McCoys, and Social Changes in Appalachia, 1860–1900* (Chapel Hill: University of North Carolina Press, 1988); T. R. C. Hutton, *Bloody Breathitt: Politics and Violence in the Appalachian South* (Lexington: University Press of Kentucky, 2013); Martin Crawford, *Ashe County's Civil War: Community and Society in the Appalachian South* (Charlottesville: University Press of Virginia, 2001); Mary Beth Pudup, Dwight B. Billings, and Altina L. Waller, eds., *Appalachia in the Making: The*

examined parts of a state, unified by settlement or economic patterns, paying increasing attention to local governments.[29] Microhistorical approaches situated scholars to show how specific people in specific communal relations experienced larger movements or transformations. Local differences and the choices and situations of individuals and small groups not only responded to but also sometimes altered the broader southern story.[30]

Increasingly aware of discontinuities within the South, historians also recognized the Reconstruction South as less "peculiar." Earlier historians constructed theories of regional cultures around particular regimes of racial exploitation: slavery lay at the root of the South and explained it, just as the West emerged out of a deadly combination of land theft from Native Americans and the labor exploitation of Mexican Americans and Asian Americans, while the Midwest and Northeast oppressed European immigrants. In the wake of the 1960s, however, some historians began seeing more continuity, interdependence, and even shared identity among these regional systems. Employing comparative research, they highlighted similarities and continuities between the Reconstruction unfolding in the South and events in other regions and nations. Works such as David Montgomery's *Beyond Equality* (1967) traced the influence of radical ideas about workers' rights on the emerging labor movement in the North. By the late 1990s, new

---

Mountain South in the Nineteenth Century (Chapel Hill: University of North Carolina Press, 1995); Kate Masur, *An Example for All the Land: Emancipation and the Struggle Over Equality in Washington, D.C.* (Chapel Hill: University of North Carolina Press, 2010); Robert Harrison, *Washington During Civil War and Reconstruction: Race and Radicalism* (New York: Cambridge University Press, 2011); Michael W. Fitzgerald, *Urban Emancipation: Popular Politics in Reconstruction Mobile, 1860–1890* (Baton Rouge: Louisiana State University Press, 2002); Justin A. Nystrom, *New Orleans after the Civil War: Race, Politics, and a New Birth of Freedom* (Baltimore: Johns Hopkins University Press, 2010); Michael A. Ross, *The Great New Orleans Kidnapping Case: Race, Law and Justice in the Reconstruction Era* (New York: Oxford University Press, 2014); Adam Arenson, *The Great Heart of the Republic: St. Louis and the Cultural Civil War* (Cambridge: Harvard University Press, 2011).

29. Christopher Waldrep, "Substituting Law for the Lash: Emancipation and Legal Formalism in a Mississippi County Court," *Journal of American History* 82 (March 1996): 1425–51; Waldrep and Donald G. Niemen, eds., *Local Matters: Race, Crime and Justice in the Nineteenth-Century South* (Athens: University of Georgia Press, 2001); T. R. C. Hutton, "The Irreducibility of the County in the South and America, Past and Present," *American Nineteenth Century History* 15 (Winter 2014): 1–13.

30. For example, Bruce E. Baker argued that Ku Klux Klan attacks in Union, York, Chester, and Fairfield counties in South Carolina in 1870 and 1871 tipped those counties to Democratic control in 1872, setting the stage for the state's crucial contested election in 1876; see *This Mob Will Surely Take My Life: Lynchings in the Carolinas, 1871–1947* (London: Continuum, 2008), 36–41.

scholarship developed this approach but also considered how lines of influence moved in both directions, with northern ideas about contract law and vagrancy shaping the work of the Freedmen's Bureau.[31] A raft of studies highlighted how Reconstruction in the South bled into other regions, which also had to reconcile with their own histories of forced labor and racial oppression.[32]

Transnational studies came late to Reconstruction-era historiography, but the approach gained steam in the early 2000s. Rebecca J. Scott's *Degrees of Freedom* (2005), for instance, demonstrated the remarkable similarities between the lives of people working in the sugar economies of Louisiana and Cuba, despite the very different political systems unfolding around them. Other scholars interrogated the process of emancipation in different countries, depicting slavery as less an exceptional original sin against American democracy and more a global economic and social system. The slave societies of the Caribbean offered an obvious initial point of comparison, and scholars also investigated Russian emancipation of the serfs. Reconstruction has come to be seen as part of a transnational process of civil war and state stabilization, with parallels in Mexico and other Latin America nations, as well as in Europe, Japan, and China.[33]

31. Ronald Takaki, *A Different Mirror: A History of Multicultural America* (Boston: Little, Brown, 1993); David Montgomery, *Beyond Equality: Labor and the Radical Republicans, 1862–1872* (New York: Alfred A. Knopf, 1967); James D. Schmidt, *Free to Work: Labor Law, Emancipation, and Reconstruction, 1815–1880* (Athens: University of Georgia Press, 1998).

32. Leslie A. Schwalm, *Emancipation's Diaspora: Race and Reconstruction in the Upper Midwest* (Chapel Hill: University of North Carolina Press, 2009); Stacey Smith, *Freedom's Frontier: California and the Struggle over Unfree Labor, Emancipation, and Reconstruction* (Chapel Hill: University of North Carolina Press, 2015); Brent M. S. Campney, *This is Not Dixie: Racist Violence in Kansas, 1861–1927* (Urbana: University of Illinois Press, 2015); Elliot West, "Reconstructing Race," *Western Historical Quarterly* 34 (Spring 2003): 6–26; Stephen Kantrowitz, *More than Freedom: Fighting for Black Citizenship in a White America, 1829-1889* (New York: Penguin, 2012); Andrew L. Slap, ed., *Reconstructing Appalachia: The Civil War's Aftermath* (Lexington: University Press of Kentucky, 2010); Gregory P. Downs and Kate Masur, *The World the Civil War Made* (Chapel Hill: University of North Carolina Press, 2015); Joshua Paddison, *American Heathens: Religion, Race, and Reconstruction in California* (Berkeley: University of California Press, 2012); Adam Arenson and Andrew R. Graybill, eds., *Civil War Wests: Testing the Limits of the United States* (Berkeley: University of California Press, 2015).

33. Peter Kolchin, "The South and the World," *Journal of Southern History* 75 (August 2009): 565–80; Frederick Cooper, Thomas C. Holt, and Rebecca J. Scott, eds., *Beyond Slavery: Explorations of Race, Labor, and Citizenship in Postemancipation Societies* (Chapel Hill: University of North Carolina Press, 2000); Rebecca J. Scott, *Degrees of Freedom: Louisiana and Cuba after Slavery* (Cambridge: Harvard University Press, 2005); Gregory P. Downs, "The Mexicanization of American Politics: The United States' Transnational Path from Civil War to Stabilization," *American Historical Review* 117 (April 2012): 387–409.

Even when they worked within areas that have canonically been at the core of southern history, and perhaps with more traditional historical subjects, historians have shifted their approach to these places and figures. Taking popular narrative seriously as a primary force driving historical change, they began paying close attention to places where southern people talked about important matters with one another. Churches and schools competed with newspapers and political organizations as the most influential of such spaces. In religious history, scholarly work has largely divided along lines of race, much as the religious lives of most Reconstruction southerners did. While some texts, most notably Daniel W. Stowell's *Rebuilding Zion* (1998) and Paul Harvey's *Redeeming the South* (1997), took a bird's-eye view of religious divergences and convergences as racial relations and regional and partisan lines shifted in the war's wake, most scholars chose a closer focus. Edward J. Blum, Luke E. Harlow, and Beth Barton Schweiger looked through the lens of white Christian churches that adjusted their theologies to reconcile with military defeat and the end of slavery, and to accommodate new regimes of racial oppression.[34] These scholars emphasized continuity between

David Prior began his essay on transnational studies in *Reconstruction in a Globalizing World* with the regret that "transnational history and Reconstruction scholarship have yet to develop a self-sustaining conversation." See "Introduction," 1–20.

34. Mark A. Noll, "Reconstructing Religion," in *Journal of the Civil War Era* 7 (March 2017): 11; Daniel W. Stowell, *Rebuilding Zion: The Religious Reconstruction of the South, 1863–1877* (New York: Oxford University Press, 1998); Edward J. Blum, *Reforging the White Republic: Race, Religion, and American Nationalism, 1865–1898* (Baton Rouge: Louisiana State University Press, 2005); Blum and W. Scott Poole, eds., *Vale of Tears: New Essays on Religion and Reconstruction* (Macon: Mercer University Press, 2005); Victor B. Howard, *Religion and the Radical Republican Movement, 1860–1870* (Lexington: University Press of Kentucky, 1990); William E. Montgomery, *Under Their Own Vine and Fig Tree: The African-American Church in the South, 1865–1900* (Baton Rouge: Louisiana State University Press, 1993); Eugene D. Genovese, *A Consuming Fire: The Fall of the Confederacy in the Mind of the White Christian South* (Athens: University of Georgia Press, 1998); Randall M. Miller, Harry S. Stout, and Charles Reagan Wilson, eds., *Religion and the American Civil War* (New York: Oxford University Press, 1998); Luke E. Harlow, *Religion, Race, and the Making of Confederate Kentucky, 1830–1880* (New York: Cambridge University Press, 2014); Paul Harvey, *Redeeming the South: Religious Cultures and Racial Identities Among Southern Baptists, 1865–1925* (Chapel Hill: University of North Carolina Press, 1997); Harvey, *Freedom's Coming: Religious Culture and the Shaping of the South from the Civil War through the Civil Rights Era* (Chapel Hill: University of North Carolina Press, 2005); John M. Giggie, *After Redemption: Jim Crow and the Transformation of African American Religion in the Delta, 1875–1915* (New York: Oxford University Press, 2008); George C. Rable, *God's Almost Chosen Peoples: A Religious History of the American Civil War* (Chapel Hill: University of North Carolina Press, 2010); Beth Barton Schweiger, *The Gospel Working Up: Progress and the Pulpit in Nineteenth-Century Virginia* (New York: Oxford University Press, 2000); Lawrence A. Q. Burnley, *The*

North and South and the centrality of the white church to the project of reimposing a new, more nationalized, form of white oppression. An even more vibrant body of scholarship focused on the church as an institutional backbone of black culture. William E. Montgomery's *Under Their Own Vine and Fig Tree* (1993) was the break-through in this field, and works such as Emily Suzanne Clark's *A Luminous Brotherhood* (2016) advanced understanding of African American religion beyond Baptist and Methodist denominations.[35]

In educational history, James D. Anderson's *The Education of Blacks in the South, 1860–1935* (1988) established the template for the field. He emphasized freedmen and freedwomen's roles in building their own educational structures.[36] Heather Andrea Williams's *Self-Taught* (2005) pushed the theme forward, focusing on the specific processes of teacher selection and training, and curriculum-building during Reconstruction. Others, including Ronald E. Butchart, considered the fundamentally imperialistic nature of the efforts of northern whites to establish educational systems for freedpeople.[37] Hilary Green and Kate Masur read educational policy in the urban South as a crucial area of black political investment and organization.[38]

For some scholars, renewed focus on northerners' roles in rebuilding the South provided opportunity to examine the "language" of Reconstruction. For

---

Cost of Unity: African-American Agency and Education in the Christian Church, 1865–1914 (Macon: Mercer University Press, 2008); Matthew Harper, *The End of Days: African American Religion and Politics in the Age of Emancipation* (Chapel Hill: University of North Carolina Press, 2016).

35. Ben Wright and Zachary W. Dresser, eds., *Apocalypse and the Millennium in the American Civil War Era* (Baton Rouge: Louisiana State University Press, 2013); Emily Suzanne Clark, *A Luminous Brotherhood: Afro-Creole Spiritualism in Nineteenth-Century New Orleans* (Chapel Hill: University of North Carolina Press, 2016).

36. James D. Anderson, *The Education of Blacks in the South, 1860–1935* (Chapel Hill: University of North Carolina Press, 1988); Heather Andrea Williams, *Self-Taught: African American Education in Slavery and Freedom* (Chapel Hill: University of North Carolina Press, 2007); Ward M. McAfee, *Religion, Race, and Reconstruction: The Public School in the Politics of the 1870s* (Albany: State University of New York Press, 1998); Christopher M. Span, *From Cotton Field to Schoolhouse: African American Education in Mississippi, 1862–1875* (Chapel Hill: University of North Carolina Press, 2009).

37. Ronald E. Butchart, *Schooling the Freed People: Teaching, Learning, and the Struggle for Black Freedom, 1861–1876* (Chapel Hill: University of North Carolina Press, 2010); William H. Watkins, *The White Architects of Black Education: Ideology and Power in America, 1865–1954* (New York: Teachers College Press, 2001).

38. Hilary Green, *Educational Reconstruction: African American Schools in the Urban South, 1865–1890* (New York: Fordham University Press, 2016); Masur, *An Example for All the Land.*

generations, historians used terms such as "carpetbagger" and "scalawag" in much the same way as the originators of those derogatory terms, even while historians' evaluation of these groups evolved. The linguistic turn inspired a step away from this reflexive acceptance of the traditional language of Reconstruction in the form of studies that examined in detail who the carpetbaggers and scalawags were and what they did.[39] Other historians investigated the origins of these terms, denaturalizing them and showing that the language of Reconstruction itself had a history that shaped how Reconstruction unfolded.[40]

Historiographical interest in churches, schools, and public discourse expanded into an understanding that even the state itself was necessarily responsive to, or even constituted by, the aggregated choices of "the people," elite and non-elite. Laura F. Edwards argued in 2015 that understanding the Reconstruction era required appreciating that the state constituted only one of many elements of "governance," which in the aftermath of the Civil War remained largely local and rooted in community relationships, traditions, and institutions. Her work more generally challenged the reified image of the nineteenth-century state, explaining that it could function only within and through personal and informal relationships and community norms. Though historians of Reconstruction largely rejected the older notion of the state as the sole or primary agent of change, most agreed that the Reconstruction period saw dramatic growth and consolidation of the state. In fact, political history enjoyed a rebirth in the 1990s and 2000s, albeit with a sociocultural approach. New institutionalism emphasized that individuals comprised each bureaucratic entity; that those people all had their own agency and operated in complex relationships with one another and the stated goals of the institution; and that institutions often behaved differently than intended.

39. Allen W. Trelease, "Who Were the Scalawags?" *Journal of Southern History* 29 (November 1963): 445–68; Peter Kolchin, "Scalawags, Carpetbaggers, and Reconstruction: A Quantitative Look at Southern Congressional Politics, 1868–1872," *Journal of Southern History* 45 (February 1979): 63–76; Richard Nelson Current, *Those Terrible Carpetbaggers* (New York: Oxford University Press, 1988); James Alex Baggett, *The Scalawags: Southern Dissenters in the Civil War and Reconstruction* (Baton Rouge: Louisiana State University Press, 2003).

40. Ted Tunnell, "Creating the 'Propaganda of History': Southern Editors and the Origins of 'Carpetbagger' and 'Scalawag,'" *Journal of Southern History* 72 (November 2006): 789–822; Adam Fairclough, "'Scalawags,' Southern Honor, and the Lost Cause: Explaining the Fatal Encounter of James H. Cosgrove and Edward L. Pierson," *Journal of Southern History* 77 (November 2011): 799–826; K. Stephen Prince, "Legitimacy and Interventionism: Northern Republicans, the 'Terrible Carpetbagger,' and the Retreat from Reconstruction," *Journal of the Civil War Era* 2 (December 2012): 538–63.

As Gary W. Gallagher and Rachel A. Shelden wrote of political history in the 2010s, "the institutions themselves become crucial actors in American political development."[41]

The fact remains that the state, however internally complex and embedded in a broader context, grew in size and capacity during the era of Reconstruction. Scholars in history and political science have come to understand how events in the Reconstruction-era South propelled the growth of government at the national and state levels. Heather Cox Richardson's *The Death of Reconstruction* (2001) uncovered widespread skepticism among whites across the political spectrum about the increase of federal power. Nevertheless, the war and immediate aftermath amplified the government's strength and capacity.[42] The widely studied Freedmen's Bureau exemplified the growth in governmental power, with scholars making extensive use of the Freedmen and Southern Society Project which, beginning in 1976, copied, indexed, organized, and made accessible relevant papers from the National Archives, many in edited collections. Although the editors expressed less interest in "purely administrative records" and sought documents which "convey . . . the experience of the liberated," the books ended up being enormously useful in constructing an understanding of the workings of the Bureau.[43] Still, some historians have concluded that the state's expansion

41. Laura F. Edwards, "Reconstruction and the History of Governance," in Downs and Masur, eds., *The World the Civil War Made*, 22–45; Meg Jacobs and Julian E. Zelizer, "The Democratic Experiment," in *The Democratic Experiment: New Directions in American Political History*, ed. Meg Jacobs, William J. Novak, and Julian E. Zelizer (Princeton: Princeton University Press, 2003), 1–19; Gary W. Gallagher and Rachel A. Shelden, *A Political Nation: New Directions in Mid-Nineteenth-Century American Political History* (Charlottesville: University of Virginia Press, 2012). "New Institutionalism" emerged from political science and sociology in the 1980s. Two key texts were James G. March and Johan P. Olsen, "The New Institutionalism: Organizational Factors in Political Life," *American Political Science Review* 78 (September 1984): 734–49; Walter W. Powell and Paul J. DiMaggio, *The New Institutionalism in Organizational Analysis* (Chicago: University of Chicago Press, 1991).

42. Richard Franklin Bensel, *Yankee Leviathan: The Origins of Central State Authority in America, 1859–1877* (New York: Cambridge University Press, 1990); Wilbur R. Miller, *Revenuers and Moonshiners: Enforcing Federal Liquor Law in the Mountain South, 1865–1900* (Chapel Hill: University of North Carolina Press, 1991); Stephen Cresswell, *Mormons and Cowboys, Moonshiners and Klansmen: Federal Law Enforcement in the South and West, 1870–1893* (Tuscaloosa: University of Alabama Press, 1991); Richardson, *The Death of Reconstruction*.

43. William Richter, *Overreached on All Sides: The Freedmen's Bureau Administrators in Texas, 1865–1868* (College Station: Texas A&M University Press, 1991); Barry A. Crouch, *The Freedmen's Bureau and Black Texans* (Austin: University of Texas Press, 1992); Paul A. Cimbala, *Under the Guardianship of the Nation:*

can be overstated: Gregory P. Downs and Kate Masur argued that the Civil War produced a "stockade state" in the South whose writ ran only as far as its soldiers could project force, an interpretation partly influenced by twenty-first-century comparisons with the aftermath of wars in Iraq and Afghanistan.[44]

Historians of Reconstruction have always recognized the era as rife with extreme violence, largely perpetrated by white southerners against black southerners and those few whites who allied with them. Some violence was formal and institutional: most obviously, federal troops were garrisoned in parts of the South during the early years. Between the 1990s and the 2010s, historians also focused on state-sanctioned use of violence as manifested in policing, incarceration, and executions. Police, sheriffs, and other formal law enforcement institutions often exerted significant powers throughout the South.[45] As the incarceration crisis of the 1990s, with its apparent connections to racial inequality, became more visible, historians gave renewed attention to the history of the incarceration system, and particularly the regimes of forced prison labor.[46] In the 2010s, important works

---

The Freedmen's Bureau and the Reconstruction of Georgia, 1865–1870 (Athens: University of Georgia Press, 1997); Ira Berlin, Barbara J. Fields, Joseph P. Reidy, and Leslie S. Rowland, "Writing Freedom's History," *Prologue: Journal of the National Archives* 14 (Fall 1982): 129–39.

44. Gregory P. Downs and Kate Masur, "Introduction," in Downs and Masur, eds., *The World the Civil War Made*, 6–11; Edward L. Ayers, "Exporting Reconstruction," in *What Caused the Civil War? Reflections on the South and Southern History* (New York: W. W. Norton, 2005), 145–66; Richard Zuczek, "The Last Campaign of the Civil War: South Carolina and the Revolution of 1876," *Civil War History* 42 (March 1996): 18–31.

45. Christopher Waldrep, *Roots of Disorder: Race and Criminal Justice in the American South, 1817–1880* (Urbana: University of Illinois Press, 1998); Dennis C. Rousey, *Policing the Southern City: New Orleans, 1805–1889* (Baton Rouge: Louisiana State University Press, 1996); Bryan Wagner, *Disturbing the Peace: Black Culture and the Police Power After Slavery* (Cambridge: Harvard University Press, 2009); Barry A. Crouch and Donaly E. Brice, *The Governor's Hounds: The Texas State Police, 1870–1873* (Austin: University of Texas Press, 2011); Adam Malka, *The Men of Mobtown: Policing Baltimore in the Age of Slavery and Emancipation* (Chapel Hill: University of North Carolina Press, 2018).

46. Donald R. Walker, *Penology for Profit: A History of the Texas Prison System, 1867–1912* (College Station: Texas A&M University Press, 1988); Alex Lichtenstein, *Twice the Work of Free Labor: The Political Economy of Convict Labor in the New South* (New York: Verso, 1996); Matthew J. Mancini, *One Dies, Get Another: Convict Leasing in the American South, 1866-1928* (Columbia: University of South Carolina Pres, 1996); David M. Oshinsky, *"Worse than Slavery": Parchman Farm and the Ordeal of Jim Crow Justice* (New York: Free Press, 1996); Milfred C. Fierce, *Slavery Revisited: Blacks and the Southern Convict Lease System, 1865–1933* (Brooklyn: African Studies Center, 1994); Karin A. Shapiro, *A New South Rebellion: The Battle Against Convict Labor in the Tennessee Coalfields, 1871–1896* (Chapel Hill: University of North Carolina Press, 1998).

on the distinct experiences of women prisoners and the importance of gender and sexuality to state regimes of incarceration followed.[47]

State violence was always closely interwoven with private violence, in ways that recent scholarship has more fully appreciated. Political institutions expressed decisions made by voters as filtered through layers of human institutional actors, and criminal justice was heavily influenced by entrenched informal systems of violent racial control. White southerners effectively used private violence, buttressed by state support or tolerance, to curtail black civil rights and prevent Republicans from governing successfully. Earlier historians could hardly ignore the pervasiveness of private violence, but they tended to interpret it as an exceptional response to an exceptional time—private white violence did the work of racial suppression that the state was temporarily unwilling to do. Although historians before the 1970s often explored private violence from the perspective of its perpetrators, revisionists and postrevisionists began more substantially to consider and condemn oppression by this violence. Still, they fundamentally understood private violence as a substitute for the political: the Klan, for instance, operated as the "military arm of the Democratic party."[48]

Since the 1990s, historical interpretations of violence have changed markedly, as historians approached acts of violence and suffering not only as part of a political program but as intense and revealing moments of struggle that expressed and attempted to impose certain cultural meanings. Seeing individual bodies as sites of the struggle for political power, some historians addressed how perpetrators, victims, and witnesses experienced violent acts and transformed in response. Such studies merge into both "dark history" and the history of gender,

47. Talitha L. LeFlouria, *Chained in Silence: Black Women and Convict Labor in the New South* (Chapel Hill: University of North Carolina Press, 2015); Sarah Haley, *No Mercy Here: Gender, Punishment, and the Making of Jim Crow Modernity* (Chapel Hill: University of North Carolina Press, 2016). Mary Ellen Curtin bridged the incarceration studies of the 1990s and the gender and incarceration studies of the 2010s with *Black Prisoners and Their World: Alabama, 1865–1900* (Charlottesville: University Press of Virginia, 2000), which included a pathbreaking chapter on women prisoners.

48. Victor B. Howard may have invented this widely used phrase to describe the Ku Klux Klan in "The Kentucky Press and the Black Suffrage Controversy, 1865–1872," *Filson Club Historical Quarterly* 47 (July 1973): 228, 233, though it was popularized by George C. Rable in *But There Was No Peace: The Role of Violence in the Politics of Reconstruction* (Athens: University of Georgia Press, 1984), 95, 132, 162. Other examples of the earlier approach to violence include Allen W. Trelease, *White Terror: The Ku Klux Klan Conspiracy and Southern Reconstruction* (New York: Harper & Row, 1971); LeeAnna Keith, *The Colfax Massacre: The Untold Story of Black Power, White Terror, and the Death of Reconstruction* (New York: Oxford University Press, 2008).

particularly since one of the first things that they revealed was the centrality of sexual assault to Reconstruction-era violence.[49] Perpetrators used violence to mark subservience on the bodies of their victims.

Large-scale and well-known episodes of violence have been subjected to detailed scrutiny, providing much more nuanced accounts of who was involved and what they were trying to accomplish.[50] Historians Scott Reynolds Nelson and Elaine Frantz Parsons demonstrated that the Ku Klux Klan, far from being an aberrant response to African American enfranchisement, was grounded in wartime and even antebellum culture and social networks.[51] In *They Left Great Marks on Me* (2012), Kidada E. Williams brought the idea of "trauma studies" to bear on Reconstruction violence to reveal the lasting effects of violence on individuals and families. In *Beyond Redemption* (2013), Carole Emberton examined how the cultural assumption that manhood, and therefore citizenship, was built upon the capacity for violence worked against black men, as they came to be seen as incapable of countering white violence.[52] Other studies blurred the boundaries between guerrilla warfare and Reconstruction violence, emphasizing the lasting social and political effects of wartime violence in local communities.[53]

49. Gilles Vandal, *Rethinking Southern Violence: Homicides in Post–Civil War Louisiana, 1866–1884* (Columbus: Ohio State University Press, 2000); Martha Hodes, "The Sexualization of Reconstruction Politics: White Women and Black Men in the South after the Civil War," *Journal of the History of Sexuality* 3 (January 1993): 402–17; Cardyn, "Sexualized Racism/Gendered Violence"; Rosen, *Terror in the Heart of Freedom.*

50. James G. Hollandsworth Jr., *An Absolute Massacre: The New Orleans Race Riot of July 30, 1866* (Baton Rouge: Louisiana State University Press, 2001); Rosen, *Terror in the Heart of Freedom;* Kevin R. Hardwick, "'Your Old Father Abe Lincoln Is Dead and Damned': Black Soldiers and the Memphis Race Riot of 1866," *Journal of Social History* 27 (Autumn 1993): 109–28; Keith, *The Colfax Massacre.*

51. Scott Reynolds Nelson, *Iron Confederacies: Southern Railways, Klan Violence, and Reconstruction* (Chapel Hill: University of North Carolina Press, 1999); Elaine Frantz Parsons, "Midnight Rangers: Costume and Performance in the Reconstruction-Era Ku Klux Klan," *Journal of American History* 92 (December 2005): 811–36; Parsons, *Ku-Klux;* Bradley Proctor, "'From the Cradle to the Grave': Jim Williams, Black Manhood, and Militia Activism in Reconstruction South Carolina," *American Nineteenth Century History* 19 (March 2018): 47–79.

52. Williams, *They Left Great Marks on Me;* Carole Emberton, *Beyond Redemption: Race, Violence, and the American South after the Civil War* (Chicago: University of Chicago Press, 2013).

53. Daniel E. Sutherland, *A Savage Conflict: The Decisive Role of Guerrillas in the American Civil War* (Chapel Hill: University of North Carolina Press, 2009); Noel C. Fisher, *War at Every Door: Partisan Politics and Guerrilla Violence in East Tennessee, 1860–1869* (Chapel Hill: University of North Carolina Press, 1997); Matthew C. Hulbert, *The Ghosts of Guerrilla Memory: How Civil War Bushwhackers Became Gunslingers in the American West* (Athens: University of Georgia Press, 2016).

Economic forces disrupted the lives of many southerners in the era of Reconstruction, giving rise to moments of violence. Historians of the early twenty-first century returned to a serious engagement with economic history. The winding down of the Cold War ended a certain kind of teleology that had affected economic history since the beginning of the discipline. Projects that fit the plantation and freedpeople into either neoclassical or Marxist interpretations of the South's economic structures faced revision by a new institutional economic history that blazed a more contingent, path-dependent model as a middle ground between the two poles. Was the postbellum South evolving toward industrial capitalism or was it hobbled by a lingering attachment to merchant capitalism? Were sharecroppers more like feudal tenants or modern wage earners? Were freedpeople proletarians or peasants? Questions such as these received thoughtful responses, but after the early 1990s, they no longer seemed to drive the field.[54]

Other changes in the historiography of Reconstruction influenced how historians approached the period's economic history. Periodization had always been particularly uncomfortable for economic history since it tended to cut off connections and continuities that developed slowly and did not necessarily align with sharply defined political transitions. The looser chronology of Reconstruction helped historians explain how the specific experience of enslavement and slave-based economies shaped how freedpeople would, in the words of Sharon Ann Holt's 2000 book title, make freedom pay.[55] Some scholars expanded on insights advanced by Steven Hahn about how transformations in the southern economy at the end of the war underlay the discontent of the Populists.[56] Others

54. Peter A. Coclanis and Scott Marler set up this basic framework (neoclassical versus Marxist, with new institutional economics in the middle) in "The Economics of Reconstruction," in *A Companion to the Civil War and Reconstruction,* ed. Lacy K. Ford (Oxford: Blackwell, 2005), 342–65. The best example of an economic history of Reconstruction influenced by new institutional economics remains Roger L. Ransom and Richard Sutch, *One Kind of Freedom: The Economic Consequences of Emancipation,* 2nd ed. (New York: Cambridge University Press, 2001).

55. Sharon Ann Holt, *Making Freedom Pay: North Carolina Freedpeople Working for Themselves, 1865–1900* (Athens: University of Georgia Press, 2000). See also John C. Rodrigue, *Reconstruction in the Cane Fields: From Slavery to Free Labor in Louisiana's Sugar Parishes, 1862–1880* (Baton Rouge: Louisiana State University Press, 2001).

56. Steven Hahn, *The Roots of Southern Populism: Yeoman Farmers and the Transformation of the Georgia Upcountry, 1850–1890* (New York: Oxford University Press, 1983); Stephen Kantrowitz, *Ben Tillman and the Reconstruction of White Supremacy* (Chapel Hill: University of North Carolina Press, 2000);

traced the multiple strategies southerners employed during Reconstruction to protect themselves—complex landholding schemes, illicit commerce, flouting internal revenue laws, and use of the commons.[57] None of these historians' findings fit neatly into early frameworks, nor did they cohere around a new framework. If anything, the 2008 financial crisis inspired a body of scholarship that emphasized crises rather than stability of economic structures.[58]

Scholarship on memory and Reconstruction is not as advanced as that on the Civil War, but historians have produced important, multilayered studies.[59] Historians of the Lost Cause have long understood that the phrase emerged at the beginning of Reconstruction, but not until the 1980s and 1990s did historians examining memory of the Civil War begin to explain how historical memory of the war affected Reconstruction. In the mid-1980s, Charles Reagan Wilson described the Lost Cause as the South's civil religion, and Gaines M. Foster argued that white southerners learned during Reconstruction to integrate the idea of defeat in the Civil War into their identity so that, by the 1870s, they confidently asserted the worth of their Lost Cause, building institutions, monuments, and cultural practices that dominated the region's culture for decades.[60] Caroline E. Janney's 2008 study of Ladies' Memorial Associations in Virginia illustrated the influence and scope for action of elite white women, while W. Scott Poole demonstrated

---

James C. Cobb, "Beyond Planters and Industrialists: A New Perspective on the New South," *Journal of Southern History* 54 (February 1988): 45–68.

57. Holt, *Making Freedom Pay;* Thad Sitton and James H. Conrad, *Freedom Colonies: Independent Black Texans in the Time of Jim Crow* (Austin: University of Texas Press, 2005); Mary Ellen Curtin, *Black Prisoners and Their World, Alabama, 1865–1900* (Charlottesville: University Press of Virginia, 2000), 43–54; Wilbur R. Miller, *Revenuers and Moonshiners: Enforcing Federal Liquor Law in the Mountain South, 1865–1900* (Chapel Hill: University of North Carolina Press, 1991); Scott E. Giltner, *Hunting and Fishing in the New South: Black Labor and White Leisure after the Civil War* (Baltimore: Johns Hopkins University Press, 2008).

58. See, for example, Scott Reynolds Nelson, *A Nation of Deadbeats: An Uncommon History of America's Financial Disasters* (New York: Alfred A. Knopf, 2012), 159–79.

59. Nina Silber, *The Romance of Reunion: Northerners and the South, 1865–1900* (Chapel Hill: University of North Carolina Press, 1993); Jane Turner Censer, "Mary Bayard Clarke's Plain-Folk Humor: Writing Women into the Literature and Politics of Reconstruction," *Journal of Southern History* 76 (May 2010): 241–74.

60. Charles Reagan Wilson, *Baptized in Blood: The Religion of the Lost Cause, 1865–1920* (Athens: University of Georgia Press, 1980); Gaines M. Foster, *Ghosts of the Confederacy: Defeat, the Lost Cause, and the Emergence of the New South, 1865 to 1913* (New York: Oxford University Press, 1987).

how irredentist claims that "South Carolinians never surrender" set the tone for political resistance to Republican governments in that state.[61] Most influential has been David W. Blight's *Race and Reunion* (2001), which traced the slow decline of an emancipationist vision of the Civil War as the price that white supremacists demanded for reunion.[62] In a larger study about the social memory of Reconstruction in the construction, maintenance, and contestation of Jim Crow, Bruce E. Baker argued that the struggles over what Reconstruction meant began with contending narratives during the era itself.[63]

Although the historiography came to be characterized by a strong emphasis on the collective, and a deliberate turn away from elite individuals who might have been key subjects of earlier historians, it is striking that the subfield of biography has thrived and arguably gained more relevance within academia. Biography had, of course, never gone away: it has always been the favorite form of history for educated nonspecialist readers, and thus a pathway to popular audiences. There are several ways to understand the renewed attention that academics paid to biography in the early twenty-first century: academic historians' interest in reaching a broader readership; biography's end-run around the problem of assigning agency; space left by the non-elite focus of most monographs. Biographies are powerful in part because they reconcile a strong sense of personal agency with vivid representations of swirling and compelling social forces. Hans L. Trefousse,

61. Caroline E. Janney, *Burying the Dead but Not the Past: Ladies' Memorial Associations and the Lost Cause* (Chapel Hill: University of North Carolina Press, 2008); W. Scott Poole, *Never Surrender: Confederate Memory and Conservatism in the South Carolina Upcountry* (Athens: University of Georgia Press, 2004). See also Anne E. Marshall, *Creating a Confederate Kentucky: The Lost Case and Civil War Memory in a Border State* (Chapel Hill: University of North Carolina Press, 2010); Kathleen Ann Clark, *Defining Moments: African American Commemoration and Political Culture in the South, 1863–1913* (Chapel Hill: University of North Carolina Press, 2005); William A. Blair, *Cities of the Dead: Contesting the Memory of the Civil War in the South, 1865–1914* (Chapel Hill: University of North Carolina Press, 2004).

62. David W. Blight, *Race and Reunion: The Civil War in American Memory* (Cambridge: Harvard University Press, 2001); W. Fitzhugh Brundage, "On *Race and Reunion,*" African-American Religion: A Documentary History Project, 27 October 2001, https://aardoc.sites.amherst.edu/Brundage.html (accessed 18 January 2019).

63. Bruce E. Baker, *What Reconstruction Meant: Historical Memory in the American South* (Charlottesville: University of Virginia Press, 2007), 13–20. On memory of Reconstruction, see also K. Stephen Prince, *Stories of the South: Race and the Reconstruction of Southern Identity, 1865–1915* (Chapel Hill: University of North Carolina Press, 2014); Carole Emberton and Bruce E. Baker, eds., *Remembering Reconstruction: Struggles Over the Meaning of America's Most Turbulent Era* (Baton Rouge: Louisiana State University Press, 2017).

for instance, wrote a number of well-received biographies of Reconstruction-era political leaders, including Andrew Johnson and Rutherford B. Hayes. And a spate of books on President Ulysses S. Grant came to press around the 150th year anniversary of the Reconstruction era.[64] Others, such as Ted Tunnell's treatment of Marshall Twitchell and Mark Elliott's study of Albion Tourgée, focused on less prominent figures important to the struggles for Reconstruction on the ground. T. J. Stiles's work on Jesse James has been particularly influential. Written for a popular audience but adhering closely to scholarly conventions of evidence and contextualization, and fully conversant with the relevant scholarly literature, Stiles presented a model of relevant and accessible scholarship. He argued convincingly that James should be seen as a southern, fundamentally Confederate figure who emerged from the bloody ground of the Missouri border. Stiles used the story of James's life and fame to trace the nation through the Civil War, the bloody years of Reconstruction, and to a new peace constructed on the basis of black repression. And David W. Blight's masterful treatment of Frederick Douglass's later years seems likely to profoundly influence the field.[65]

As the United States struggled over identity in the early twenty-first century, historians revised accounts of the post–Civil War South to reflect the lessons of the political moment: increased awareness of the political and cultural significance of middle America; sensitivity to the circulation of ideas and the significance of network relationships; the decisive importance of resistance from non-elites to the plans, policies, and institutions of policymakers; and the fact that historical forces within the United States are not only constrained or inspired

64. Hans L. Trefousse, *Andrew Johnson: A Biography* (New York: W. W. Norton, 1989); Trefousse, *Rutherford B. Hayes* (New York: Times Books, 2002); Ronald C. White, *American Ulysses: A Life of Ulysses S. Grant* (New York: Random House, 2016); Charles W. Calhoun, *The Presidency of Ulysses S. Grant* (Lawrence: University Press of Kansas, 2017); Ron Chernow, *Grant* (New York: Penguin, 2017); H. W. Brands, *The Man Who Saved the Union: Ulysses Grant in War and Peace* (New York: Doubleday, 2012); Joan Waugh, *U. S. Grant: American Hero, American Myth* (Chapel Hill: University of North Carolina Press, 2009); Geoffrey Perret, *Ulysses S. Grant: Soldier and President* (New York: Random House, 1997); Brooks D. Simpson, *Let Us Have Peace: Ulysses S. Grant and the Politics of War and Reconstruction, 1861–1868* (Chapel Hill: University of North Carolina Press, 1991).

65. Ted Tunnell, *Edge of the Sword: The Ordeal of Carpetbagger Marshall H. Twitchell in the Civil War and Reconstruction* (Baton Rouge: Louisiana State University Press, 2001); Mark Elliot, *Color-Blind Justice: Albion Tourgée and the Quest for Racial Equality from the Civil War to* Plessy v. Ferguson (New York: Oxford University Press, 2008); T. J. Stiles, *Jesse James: Last Rebel of the Civil War* (New York: Alfred A. Knopf, 2002): David W. Blight, *Frederick Douglass: Prophet of Freedom* (New York: Simon and Schuster, 2018).

by, but continuous with, broader global influences. While historians have become increasingly skeptical of simplistic, progressive narratives which imagine unidimensional disempowered people striving for and, inevitably, gradually achieving, liberation, our access to new methods and sources have allowed a more sophisticated reading of the centrality of non-elite, previously unnoticed southerners to the history of Reconstruction.

THE HISTORIOGRAPHY OF THE BLACK SOUTH

From Reconstruction to Jim Crow

Blair L M Kelley and Claudrena N. Harold

On the morning of 20 October 1946, the campus of Benedict College in Columbia, South Carolina, buzzed with excitement as nearly seven hundred young women and men crammed into Antisdel Chapel for the closing session of the Southern Youth Congress. After months of strategic planning, conference organizers had secured the country's most formidable scholar-activist, W. E. B. Du Bois, as the closing speaker. Not one to mince words, he opened with a simple yet powerful declaration: "The future of the American Negro is in the South." Without the slightest equivocation, Du Bois positioned black southerners as the revolutionary vanguard in the global struggle against white supremacy and capitalist exploitation. The South, he argued, was "the firing line not simply for the emancipation of the American Negro but for the emancipation of the African Negro and the Negroes of the West Indies, for the emancipation of the colored races, and for the emancipation of the white slaves of modern capitalistic monopoly."[1]

This was not the first time Du Bois invested revolutionary hope in the former states of the Confederacy. The South, as both a real and imagined place, had long loomed large in the scholar-activist's work and his political imagination. Du Bois's two most enduring works, *The Souls of Black Folk* (1903) and *Black Reconstruction* (1935), chronicled the South's shift from the revolutionary promises of

1. W. E. B. Du Bois, "Behold the Land," in *W. E. B. Du Bois Reader,* ed. David Levering Lewis (New York: Macmillan, 1995), 545.

Emancipation to the regressive politics of the Jim Crow era. The valiant efforts of African Americans to build a true democracy in the aftermath of the Civil War were epically detailed in *Souls of Black Folk* and *Black Reconstruction,* as were the violent aggressions of a southern oligarchy intent on maintaining political power and economic dominance in the region.[2] Du Bois's visionary work foreshadowed many of the dominant themes that preoccupied historians of the Emancipation and Jim Crow South for the next century and beyond. From *Souls*'s insistence that the problem of the twentieth century would be the problem of the color line and the powerful imagery of the veil, to *Black Reconstruction*'s groundbreaking General Strike thesis that powerfully countered the Dunning School scholars' insistence that the enslaved were docile and did not shape the outcome of the Civil War, Du Bois's profound influence echoes in scholarship on the African American experience in the South.

Invoking Du Bois's scholarship as a starting point, this essay highlights the centrality of the African American experience for any understanding of the American South. The historiography flourished despite the neglect of archivists who judged African American sources to be unworthy of preservation. The first generation of African American scholars of the southern black experience recognized the urgency; beginning with Du Bois and the scholarship and activism of Carter G. Woodson, Rayford Logan, Charles Spurgeon Johnson, Pauli Murray, and John Hope Franklin, they began chronicling the African American past.[3]

By the mid-twentieth century, C. Vann Woodward's *The Strange Career of Jim Crow* (1955) sparked a wave of new scholarship. The Woodward-driven debate and the aftereffect of the modern civil rights generation's activism produced a scholarly cohort seeking to revisit history with an eye toward the modern movement. Crafting local histories and chronicling the lives of black political leaders, historians laid much of the groundwork for contemporary scholars. August

2. Du Bois, *The Souls of Black Folk* (Chicago: A. C. McClurg, 1903); Du Bois, *Black Reconstruction* (New York: Harcourt, Brace, 1935).

3. For early roots of this field after Du Bois, see Carter G. Woodson, *The History of the Negro Church* (Washington: Associated Publishers, 1922); Woodson, *The Mis-Education of the Negro* (Washington: Associated Publishers, 1933); Rayford Logan, *The Negro in American Life and Thought: The Nadir, 1877–1901* (New York: Dial Press, 1954); Charles Spurgeon Johnson, *Patterns of Negro Segregation* (New York: Harper & Brothers, 1943); Pauli Murray, *States' Laws on Race and Color* (Cincinnati: Women's Division of Christian Service, The Methodist Church, 1951); John Hope Franklin, *From Slavery to Freedom: A History of African Americans* (New York: Alfred A. Knopf, 1947). See also Pero Gaglo Dagbovie, *The Early Black History Movement, Carter G. Woodson, and Lorenzo Johnston Greene* (Urbana: University of Illinois Press, 2007).

Meier, Elliott Rudwick, and Howard N. Rabinowitz did essential work to delineate a richer historiography.[4] At the same time, a new generation of archivists built important collections that preserved extant black newspapers, documents, and manuscripts, and recorded oral histories to build new collections in order to correct the neglect of earlier generations.[5] The study of black life during Jim Crow segregation became a vital area of study for southern historians, and indeed essential to understanding the mass movement for civil, labor, women's, and human rights that defined the mid-twentieth century.

Since the 1970s, historians built on this work, drawing on older archives, revising earlier decades of scholarship in increasingly creative ways, and conducting and drawing on the oral histories of African American informants who witnessed the violence of lynching, segregation, and disfranchisement. Scholars also turned their attention to the legacy of black resistance and the creation of institutions and cultures behind the veil. This essay explores ways in which the field has evolved since the rise of the new social history, both building on and challenging existing scholarship as well as taking on new archives and emerging theoretical frameworks to continue the process of rethinking scholarly understanding of the African American experience in the Jim Crow South.

4. For more on midcentury scholarship, see C. Vann Woodward, *The Strange Career of Jim Crow* (New York: Oxford University Press, 1955); August Meier, "Booker T. Washington and the Negro Press: With Special Reference to the Colored American Magazine," *Journal of Negro History* 38 (January 1953): 67–90; Meier, "Negro Class Structure and Ideology in the Age of Booker T. Washington," *Phylon* 23 (Fall 1962): 258–66; Meier and David Lewis, "History of the Negro Upper Class in Atlanta, Georgia, 1890–1958," *Journal of Negro Education* 28 (Spring 1959): 128–39; Meier and Elliott Rudwick, "The Boycott Movement against Jim Crow Streetcars in the South, 1900–1906," *Journal of American History* 55 (March 1969): 756–75; Meier and Rudwick, "The Origins of Nonviolent Direct Action in Afro-American Protest: A Note on Historical Discontinuities," *Along the Color Line* (Urbana: University of Illinois Press, 1976), 307–404; I. Garland Penn, *The Afro-American Press and Its Editors* (1891; repr., New York: Arno Press, 1969); Robert E. Perdue, *The Negro in Savannah, 1865–1900* (New York: Exposition Press, 1973); Howard N. Rabinowitz, *Race Relations in the Urban South, 1865–1890* (New York: Oxford University Press, 1978); Charles E. Wynes, "The Evolution of Jim Crow Laws in Twentieth Century Virginia," *Phylon* 28 (Winter 1967): 416–25.

5. There was a renewed drive to build the archives of black history in the late 1960s and 1970s. See the Civil Rights Documentation Project at the Moorland-Spingarn at Howard University, the National Archives for Black Women's History (commonly known as the Bethune Archives) in Washington, the Fisk University Black Oral History Project, and the Alabama Center for Higher Education Statewide Oral History Project. For a closer discussion of this archival movement, see Benjamin Quarles, "Black History Unbound," *Daedalus* 103 (Spring 1974):163–78; Deborah Gray White, "Mining the Forgotten: Manuscript Sources for Black Women's History," *Journal of American History* 74 (June 1987): 237–42.

The Black Experience in the Jim Crow South

Given the breadth of this history, few scholars have taken on the challenge of crafting a definitive history of the black experience in Jim Crow. Leon Litwack's *Trouble in Mind* (1998) stands out as one such important attempt. Author of several comprehensive works, Litwack wrote *Trouble in Mind* in his distinctive and compelling narrative style, and he provocatively moved away from a chronological accounting of change over time.[6] The most striking element of the narrative was an unflinching re-creation of Jim Crow's heavy price on black southerners. The horrors of lynching and the perils of living in a society where any sign of black success posed a threat to the ideology of white supremacy stood center stage in *Trouble in Mind,* making it a bleak but accurate detailing of the suppression that black southerners faced. Litwack's unflinching vision of the Jim Crow South was harrowing; it provided an important accounting of all the ways that freedom fell well short of the mark for thousands of black southerners in the first few decades after Reconstruction. However, with a focus primarily on the time that Rayford Logan called "the nadir"—the lowest point in the quest for African American citizenship since the Civil War—and drawing heavily from black autobiographies of literary luminaries to voice the black experience, *Trouble in Mind* left too little room for black agency, the crucial legacy of black resistance, and the particularities of black life in diverse places.

One important counterbalance to Litwack's assessment was *Remembering Jim Crow* (2001). Drawing on some of the most compelling interviews from Duke University's Behind the Veil Collection, a series of interviews spearheaded by editors William H. Chafe, Raymond Gavins, and Robert Korstad with over three thousand African American southerners recalling their experiences between the 1920s and 1950s, *Remembering Jim Crow* provided a close look at African Americans' lives. Following quickly on the heels of Litwack's work, the collection served as an important addendum to *Trouble in Mind,* highlighting cultural and political resistance and the strategies that black southerners developed to survive in spite of the barbs of white supremacy. *Remembering Jim Crow* reminded readers that life behind Du Bois's metaphorical veil was still life with a vibrancy that found

6. Leon Litwack, *Trouble in Mind: Black Southerners in the Age of Jim Crow* (New York: Alfred A. Knopf, 1998). Litwack made a career writing broad histories of the African American experience. See *North of Slavery: The Negro in the Free States* (Chicago: University of Chicago Press, 1961); and the Pulitzer Prize–winning *Been in the Storm So Long: The Aftermath of Slavery* (New York: Vintage Books, 1979).

a way to thrive within the black community. The oral histories detailed the harrowing costs of segregation, disfranchisement, and racial violence, but the heavy price of Jim Crow was coupled with insights into ways that black southerners organized in spite of it. Their resistance served as a bridge to the modern civil rights movement and the upbuilding of a people resistant to efforts to diminish their human capabilities. The narratives that make up *Remembering Jim Crow* captured often-neglected voices of everyday folks, allowing the history to be informed by women and men, working class and middle class, rural and urban residents.[7]

While not a strictly southern story, Patricia Sullivan's *Lift Every Voice* (2009) highlights the vital streams of resistance from activists and the work of the NAACP in its earliest decades.[8] An important corrective to contemporary readings of the oldest American civil rights organization, Sullivan's careful and detailed narrative traced the founding of the NAACP from its early interracial origins to the 1954 *Brown v. Board of Education* decision, emphasizing its organization and its leadership, both well-known and lesser-recognized. A particular strength of the text lay in Sullivan's analysis of local branches, field organizers, and lawyers. Local branches faced challenges from within and without, but the work of the organization's first full-time fieldworker, Katherine Johnson, and the brave and visionary Ella Baker laid the groundwork for the growth of a mass movement. Beginning in 1914, Johnson traveled the country, facing down the dangers of organizing in the Deep South, assisting local communities, and encouraging agitation in the bleak times. Disliked by moderates within the NAACP for her outspoken nature, she accurately predicted that active branches would be the lifeblood of the organization.

Sullivan also wrote a compelling account of the legal campaign waged by Charles Hamilton Houston, arguing that his work in the courts was directly tied to documenting inequities in the South. Houston's vision enabled the growth of a

7. William H. Chafe, Raymond Gavins, and Robert Korstad, eds., *Remembering Jim Crow: African Americans Tell about Life in the Segregated South* (New York: New Press, 2001). Behind the Veil: Documenting African American Life in the Jim Crow South, the oral history collection from which *Remembering Jim Crow* arose, exists as a digital collection at https://library.duke.edu/digitalcollections/behindtheveil/ (accessed 18 January 2019). Another instructive edited oral history of the black experience is Michael Keith Honey, *Black Workers Remember: An Oral History of Segregation, Unionism, and the Freedom Struggle* (Berkeley: University of California Press, 1999).

8. Patricia Sullivan, *Lift Every Voice: The NAACP and the Making of the Civil Rights Movement* (New York: New Press, 2009). For more on NAACP leadership, see Kenneth Robert Janken, *White: The Biography of Walter White, Mr. NAACP* (New York: New Press, 2003).

cadre of attorneys who mounted cases fed by the energized activism of southern black communities. Although *Lift Every Voice* could be described as a top-down organizational history, it highlighted the steady stream of agitation, litigation, and protest that fueled resistance in the era of Jim Crow. Sullivan's scholarship dovetailed nicely with Glenda Elizabeth Gilmore's skillful *Defying Dixie* (2008). Gilmore detailed the Left's role in the origins of the modern movement. Her work, particularly her compelling retelling of the work of Pauli Murray, pointed to other large thematic currents to explore in broadening the history of black experience in the age of Jim Crow.[9]

Trouble in Mind, Remembering Jim Crow, and *Lift Every Voice* outlined ways in which the historiography constantly ranged from detailing unimaginable repression and remarkable resistance. Jim Crow was a time when black southerners faced the unthinkable, but through their own resistance and institution-building behind the veil, they forged communities and provided pathways of resistance that became the modern civil rights movement. The back-and-forth between violent repression, activism, agitation, and resilience must be factored into any study that probes the meanings of Jim Crow.

The Moment of Freedom

Du Bois's *Black Reconstruction* remains tremendously influential; its reverberations can be seen in the building blocks of twenty-first-century scholarship. His General Strike thesis greatly informed such seminal works as Eric Foner's *Reconstruction* (1988), Julie Saville's *The Work of Reconstruction* (1994), Steven Hahn's *A Nation under Our Feet* (2003), Stephanie McCurry's *Confederate Reckoning* (2010), and Chandra Manning's *What This Cruel War Was Over* (2008).[10]

In the years between Emancipation and the solidification of de jure segregation, African Americans played a critical role in making and remaking US politics,

9. Glenda Elizabeth Gilmore, *Defying Dixie: The Radical Roots of Civil Rights, 1919–1950* (New York: W. W. Norton, 2008).

10. Eric Foner, *Reconstruction: America's Unfinished Revolution 1863–1877* (New York: Harper & Row, 1988); Julie Saville, *The Work of Reconstruction: From Slave to Wage Laborer in South Carolina, 1860–1870* (New York: Cambridge University Press, 1994); Steven Hahn, *A Nation under Our Feet: Black Political Struggles in the Rural South from Slavery to the Great Migration* (Cambridge: Harvard University Press, 2003); Chandra Manning, *What This Cruel War Was Over: Soldiers, Slavery, and the Civil War* (New York: Vintage, 2008); Stephanie McCurry, *Confederate Reckoning: Power and Politics in the Civil War South* (Cambridge: Harvard University Press, 2010).

society, and culture through the creation of democratically robust institutions that not only challenged legal, political, social, and cultural underpinnings of white supremacy but also provided the nation (and the larger world) with alternative visions of justice, freedom, and human possibility. As the scholarship of Tera W. Hunter, James D. Anderson, Heather Andrea Williams, Elsa Barkley Brown, Steven Hahn, and others demonstrated, newly freed blacks prioritized stabilizing families, securing education for their children, and gaining control over their economic lives.[11]

Urban centers such as Richmond, Jacksonville, and Atlanta became popular destinations for many who yearned for educational and economic opportunities and an escape from their enslaved pasts. Migrants, along with established residents, propelled social and political vibrancy of the urban South. In their efforts to realize their freedom dreams, African Americans encountered whites who also desired to carve out a more liberated existence for themselves.

These complex encounters took center stage in Eric Arnesen's *Waterfront Workers of New Orleans* (1994), a brilliant work that explored the strengths and limitations of interracial unionism. Like the Woodward thesis before it, Arnesen's study treated the emergence of the South's segregation order as contingent rather than inevitable.[12] Combining social, political, and labor history, Arnesen illuminated a post–Civil War nation in the throes of major political, social, and economic change. More than four million enslaved people secured their freedom, transformations in the political economy resulted in the emergence and consolidation of large-scale corporations, and wartime exigencies augmented the power of the federal government. Under these circumstances, he explained, Americans

11. Tera W. Hunter, *To 'Joy My Freedom: Southern Black Women's Lives and Labors After the Civil War* (Cambridge: Harvard University Press, 1997); James Anderson, *The Education of Blacks in the South, 1860–1935* (Chapel Hill: University of North Carolina Press, 1988); Elsa Barkley Brown, "Negotiating and Transforming the Public Sphere: African American Political Life in the Transition from Slavery to Freedom," *Public Culture* 7 (Fall 1994): 107–46; Heather Andrea Williams, *Self-Taught: African American Education in Slavery and Freedom* (Chapel Hill: University of North Carolina Press, 2005); Christopher M. Span, *From Cotton Field to Schoolhouse: African American Education in Mississippi, 1862–1875* (Chapel Hill: University of North Carolina Press, 2009); Corey D. B. Walker, *A Noble Fight: African American Freemasonry and the Struggle for Democracy in America* (Urbana: University of Illinois Press, 2008); Ronald E. Butchart, *Schooling the Freed People: Teaching, Learning, and the Struggle for Black Freedom, 1861–1876* (Chapel Hill: University of North Carolina Press, 2010); Clyde Woods, *Development Arrested: The Blues and Plantation Power in the Mississippi Delta* (New York: Verso, 1998).

12. Eric Arensen, *Waterfront Workers of New Orleans: Race, Class, and Politics* (Urbana: University of Illinois Press, 1994).

confronted complex questions about what form and shape the nation would take, who and which class would steer its course and direction, how it would relate to the growing number of American wage earners troubled by their declining power, and how it would respond to newly emancipated peoples seeking to define the terms of their freedom and, in the process, expand the possibilities and practices of American democracy. Whereas African Americans pledged allegiance to the Republican Party, labor-conscious whites supported the Workingmen's Party. With vivid detail, Arnesen highlighted how various biracial initiatives buckled under the weight of a labor movement unable to transcend the white supremacist ethos and dictates of the times.

Historians face a recurring challenge as they seek to illuminate the resiliency and pervasiveness of white supremacy in the South without denying the humanity and agency of African Americans. Few strike this balance with greater clarity and theoretical nuance than Tera W. Hunter who, in her influential study *To 'Joy My Freedom* (1997), explored the politics, labor, and culture of Atlanta's black domestic workers. *To 'Joy My Freedom* transformed the fields of African American, southern, women's, cultural, and labor histories. It detailed the myriad ways black women sought to recuperate their bodies from exploitation, reap the benefits of their labor, and define and defend the terms of their freedom. *To 'Joy My Freedom* emerged in a moment when a growing number of scholars were focusing on the experiences of black workers, their relationships with the white laboring class, and their efforts to improve their material condition through formal organizations and everyday acts of resistance. Building on the rich, groundbreaking theoretical work of James C. Scott's scholarship on resistance outlined in *Weapons of the Weak* (1985) and further synthesized in *Domination and the Arts of Resistance* (1990), and Robin D. G. Kelley's application of infrapolitics to black life during Jim Crow, Hunter attended to the intersection of race, gender, and resistance. Her work became a crucial guide for further scholarship. Without slighting the hardships endured by African Americans, Hunter illuminated moments of joy and pleasure when African Americans found cultural affirmation, fellowship, and a much-needed respite from the hardships of the Jim Crow South.[13] Hunter's interpretive

13. Hunter, *To 'Joy My Freedom*; James C. Scott, *Weapons of the Weak: Everyday Forms of Peasant Resistance* (New Haven: Yale University Press, 1985); Scott, *Domination and the Arts of Resistance: Hidden Transcripts* (New Haven: Yale University Press, 1990); Robin D. G. Kelley, "'We Are Not What We Seem': Rethinking Black Working-Class Opposition in the Jim Crow South," *Journal of American History* 80 (June 1993): 75–112.

and methodological innovations profoundly influenced scholars in the 2000s and 2010s, particularly those whose work engaged the fields of carceral studies and black women's studies. Her detailed attention to the lives of African American women, particularly the 1881 Washerwoman's Strike, provided an important counterpoint to the new labor history, which focused overwhelmingly on men.

Gender Studies

Taking on the challenge of considering what it meant for historians to have characterized the turn of the twentieth century as both the women's era and "the nadir" of African American history, Evelyn Brooks Higginbotham's *Righteous Discontent* (1993) forced a reconsideration of gender and black activism.[14] Reading racial uplift as resistance, Higginbotham framed the all-black Women's Convention of the National Baptist Convention as more than an auxiliary within the largest black church denomination. It was a black public sphere where women who held less status in the outside world shared ideas about the best possible means to contest white supremacy. This black women's public sphere became a space where they honed ideas about educational advancement and black institution-building. Tracing the development of black women's education, particularly Spelman College's early efforts, Higginbotham outlined the richness and complexity of black women's intellectual life despite the racial climate.

In a powerful theoretical turn, one she more closely outlined in the groundbreaking article "African-American Women's History and the Metalanguage of Race" (1992), Higginbotham redefined uplift—the black middle-class effort to assist the poor and uneducated—as much more than simple accommodation to white norms. Instead, Higginbotham saw uplift as a means by which black women of all class backgrounds could use middle-class behavioral norms as a means to perform racial equality, termed the "politics of respectability." Higginbotham's study, along with the groundbreaking work of other historians of black women, opened up space to richly theorize and explore women's resistance in a time once considered inherently conservative and largely defined by Booker T. Washington's narrow political outlook.[15]

14. Evelyn Brooks Higginbotham, *Righteous Discontent: The Women's Movement in the Black Baptist Church, 1880–1920* (Cambridge: Harvard University Press, 1993).

15. Higginbotham, "African-American Women's History and the Metalanguage of Race," *Signs* 17 (Winter 1992): 251–74. This was a rich period for scholars employing gender theory to reimagine the lives

Higginbotham modeled how scholars might use the intersection of race, gender, and segregation as fertile ground for theorizing ideological, political, and cultural richness during "the nadir." Glenda Elizabeth Gilmore's *Gender and Jim Crow* (1992) examined the white supremacist coup in Wilmington, North Carolina, and the statewide movement for black disfranchisement. In addition to this political narrative, Gilmore also included a close reading of black women's efforts to contest white supremacy through political alliances with white women in North Carolina. Gilmore brought black women's activism into closer conversation with the historiography of the South as a whole, making black women pivotal to southern politics writ large. Deborah Gray White's *Too Heavy a Load* (1999) further theorized and synthesized black women's political world. Two influential 2017 studies incorporated an explicitly black feminist analysis beyond black feminist movements. Brittney C. Cooper's *Beyond Respectability* utilized the politics of respectability as a departure point to delineate the wider political trajectory of black women thinkers, and Treva B. Lindsay's *Colored No More* provided a close reading of the complexity of New Negro black womanhood in the nation's capital.[16]

Carceral Studies

No small factor in southern history's continued vibrancy has been its engagement with the most cutting-edge scholarship in the interdisciplinary fields of African

---

of black women during Reconstruction and the Progressive era. In addition to Tera W. Hunter, see Elsa Barkley Brown's timeless articles: "Womanist Consciousness: Maggie Lena Walker and the Independent Order of Saint Luke," *Signs* 14 (Spring 1989): 610–33; and "'What Has Happened Here': The Politics of Difference in Women's History and Feminist Politics," *Feminist Studies* 18 (Summer 1992): 295–312; Rosalyn Terborg-Penn, "Discontented Black Feminists: Prelude and Postscript to the Passage of the Nineteenth Amendment," in *The Black Studies Reader*, ed. Jacqueline Bobo, Cynthia Hudley, and Claudine Michel (New York: Rutledge, 2004), 65–78; Stephanie J. Shaw, *What a Woman Ought to Be and to Do: Black Professional Women Workers during the Age of Jim Crow* (Chicago: University of Chicago Press, 1996).

16. Glenda Elizabeth Gilmore, *Gender and Jim Crow: Women and the Politics of White Supremacy in North Carolina, 1896–1920* (Chapel Hill: University of North Carolina Press, 1992); Deborah Gray White, *Too Heavy a Load: Black Women in Defense of Themselves, 1894–1994* (New York: W. W. Norton, 1999); Brittney C. Cooper, *Beyond Respectability: The Intellectual Thought of Race Women* (Urbana: University of Illinois Press, 2017); Treva B. Lindsey, *Colored No More: Reinventing Black Womanhood in Washington* (Urbana: University of Illinois Press, 2017).

American, cultural, gender, and carceral studies. Perhaps nowhere is that engagement more apparent than in literature on the problem of crime and punishment. Between the 1990s and the 2010s, historians of the post-Emancipation South combined archival research with the theoretical insights of critical race theory to facilitate a deeper understanding of the historical origins and genealogical roots of the nation's mass incarceration crisis, the punishment industry's historic role in ensuring the stability of the US political economy, and the penal system's political significance as not only a site of the most brutal forms of racial oppression but also a space in which African Americans exposed the hollowness of the American democratic experiment. Thanks to the works of Mary Ellen Curtin, Sarah Haley, David M. Oshinsky, Robert Perkins, Alex Lichtenstein, Talitha L. LeFlouria, and Douglas Blackmon, we have a better understanding of how and why African Americans became a permanent fixture in the South's penal system. In the aftermath of the Civil War, state and local governments passed a series of laws to criminalize African Americans who transgressed racial, class, and gender norms. These new laws resulted in the rapid expansion of the black prison population. Several studies, most notably Oshinsky's *"Worse Than Slavery"* (1996), deepened our understanding of how state-sanctioned forms of punishment created during the peak years of American slavery informed US penal policy well into the twentieth century.[17]

In the 2010s, scholars of the carceral regime devoted increased attention to the experiences of black women. Two studies, in particular, stand out for their attention to the experiences of black women inmates: Sarah Haley's *No Mercy Here* (2016) and Talitha L. LeFlouria's *Chained in Silence* (2015). LeFlouria's work made two major interventions in the field of carceral studies: it rescued African American women from the margins of the historical literature on the rise and fall of the convict lease system; and it demonstrated the centrality of black women

17. See David M. Oshinsky, *"Worse Than Slavery": Parchman Farm and the Ordeal of Jim Crow Justice* (New York: Free Press, 1996); Alex Lichtenstein, *Twice the Work of Free Labor: The Political Economy of Convict Labor in the New South* (New York: Verso, 1996); Mary Ellen Curtin, *Black Prisoners and Their World: Alabama, 1865–1900* (Charlottesville, University Press of Virginia, 2000); Kali Gross, *Colored Amazons: Crime, Violence, and Black Women in the City of Brotherly Love, 1880–1910* (Durham: Duke University Press, 2006); Douglas Blackmon, *Slavery by Another Name: The Re-Enslavement of Black Americans from the Civil War to World II* (New York: Anchor Press, 2008); Robert Perkinson, *Texas Tough: The Rise of America's Prison Empire* (New York: Henry Holt, 2010); Khalil Gibran Muhammad, *The Condemnation of Blackness: Race, Crime and the Making of Modern America* (Cambridge: Harvard University Press, 2010).

laborers, particularly those ensnared in the South's penal system, to the making of New South modernity. Through her innovative use of prison records, LeFlouria vividly chronicled how black female convicts who toiled in Georgia's railroad camps, coal mines, timber industry, and cotton fields contributed to the state's penal industrial labor market. Through her analysis of the various technologies of terror operating at private lease camps, the state penitentiary, and the chain gang, LeFlouria never allowed the reader to forget how much violence undergirded New South modernity. As she powerfully wrote, "The imprisoned black female body was a tableau of violence, accentuated with cuts, scrapes, scratches, broken bones, black eyes, bruises, and scabs left by the whip."[18]

Though attentive to ways in which white supremacists invoked the specter of black female criminality to rationalize the mass imprisonment of formerly enslaved women and men in the post–Civil War era, LeFlouria did not attempt to sanitize the lives of black women. With vivid clarity and great imagination, she reconstructed the lives of African American women who endured the violent realities of Georgia's convict lease system. She captured their complexity, detailing the broad range of impulses that drove black women to engage in criminal behavior, particularly larceny and "disorderly conduct." LeFlouria's study beautifully complemented the works of scholars such as Kali Gross and Cheryl Hicks, who studied the urban North, particularly New York and Philadelphia.[19]

LeFlouria exposed the limitations of prison reform though her analysis of Camp Heardmont, a prison farm created in response to social reformers' criticisms of Georgia's penal system, its brutal practices, and its failure to recognize and uphold men's and women's separate working roles. LeFlouria detailed the struggles of sixteen-year-old Carrie Massie and other black women. Three years after arriving at Camp Heardmont, Massie died after giving birth to her last child. The cause of death was listed as puerperal sepsis, a bacterial infection of the female reproductive organs usually caused by the insertion of contaminated forceps or other medical equipment into a woman's genital tract during childbirth. Throughout *Chained in Silence,* LeFlouria detailed the intersection of incarceration and medical abuse inflicted upon African American convict women. One

18. Talitha L. LeFlouria, *Chained in Silence: Black Women and Convict Labor in the New South* (Chapel Hill: University of North Carolina Press, 2015), 78; Sarah Haley, *No Mercy Here: Gender, Punishment, and the Making of Jim Crow Modernity* (Chapel Hill: University of North Carolina Press, 2016).

19. Gross, *Colored Amazons;* Cheryl Hicks, *Talk with You Like a Woman: African American Women, Justice and Reform in New York, 1890–1935* (Chapel Hill: University of North Carolina Press, 2010).

imagines other scholars will follow her lead in drawing more attention to the medical lives of the black female prisoners.

Additionally, LeFlouria gave voice to black female inmates who refused the orders of their guards, feigned sickness, engaged in arson, and challenged assaults on their femininity by rejecting prison-issued masculine uniforms. Coupled with these challenges from the convict women were strong critiques of the convict lease system emanating from respected social reformers and activists, most notably Ida B. Wells, W. E. B. Du Bois, Frances Kellor, Mary Church Terrell, Clarissa Keeler, and Rebecca Felton. LeFlouria explained how many reforms that emerged out of critiques of the convict lease system unintentionally laid the foundation for continued exploitation of African American prisoners.

Like LeFlouria's work, Sarah Haley's *No Mercy Here* made several critical interventions. It is a deeply researched, beautifully written, and cogently argued book that chronicled the experiences of black female convicts in Georgia between the post-Emancipation period and the 1920s. *No Mercy Here* illuminated the importance of African American women ensnared in the South's penal system to the making of New South modernity. The book also elucidated the centrality of the carceral regime in the production of gender categories in the New South; and it deepened our knowledge of the trajectory and genealogy of black intellectual work around the US prison regime through Haley's highly sophisticated readings of Mary Church Terrell, Selena Sloan Butler, Bessie Smith, and other African American women thinkers and artists. Groundbreaking and boundary-crossing, both Haley's and LeFlouria's masterful works, informed by scholarship at the intersection of race and gender, enriched this growing and crucial historiography.

Racial Violence

What made "the nadir" such a low point was certainly passage of new segregation laws that, beginning in the 1890s, regulated public transportation and then expanded to every aspect of public life. Segregation in the public sphere coupled with the passage of laws to disfranchise black voters with punitive poll taxes, literacy tests, and all-white primaries. New tides of racial violence made black resistance difficult and dangerous. Kidada E. Williams's excellent *They Left Great Marks on Me* (2012) reminded readers that lynchings and deadly race riots reached a high point at the turn of the twentieth century, terrorizing black populations and acting out the spectacles that sought to strengthen white supremacy.

Williams demonstrated the centrality of racial violence to understanding the post–Civil War South.[20]

They Left Great Marks on Me analyzed the testimonies of black survivors of racial violence. Centering black peoples' accounts of the everyday violence they suffered, Williams demonstrated that by telling their stories in black newspapers, in testimony to the Freedmen's Bureau and the United States Congress, in their own writings, and in the stories that they told one another, black witnesses passed on a consciousness of resistance to future generations. By elevating the practice of bearing witness, Williams created important new frameworks for considering the meanings of racial violence.[21]

Amy Louise Wood's *Lynching and Spectacle* (2009) provided a searing account of the mobs of killers and spectators driven by irrational fears about black criminality and drawn to witness and act out brutality on behalf of their race. Wood explored the modernity at play in these spectacles of torture and violence, specifically how the utilization of photography and moving images facilitated circulation of lynching imagery around the nation as souvenirs of these macabre killings. Key was her analysis of the photographs: postcards of the images told the story of controlled and orderly mobs enacting justice to resistant black criminals deserving of brutality. Wood demonstrated that images of killers posing with the dead bodies, like prey captured in the hunt, were meant to exhibit unity and common cause among white southerners standing in the shadows of black corpses. Wood turned her analysis towards the activism of antilynching advocates, particularly the NAACP's use of lynching photography in their 1930s campaign to pass

20. Kidada E. Williams, *They Left Great Marks on Me: African American Testimonies of Racial Violence from Emancipation to World War I* (New York: New York University Press, 2012). See also Fitzhugh W. Brundage, *Lynching in the New South: Georgia and Virginia, 1880–1930* (Urbana: University of Illinois Press, 1993); Robert L. Zangrando, *The NAACP Crusade against Lynching, 1909–1950* (Philadelphia: Temple University Press, 1980); Paul Finkelman, *Lynching, Racial Violence, and Law* (New York: Garland Publishing, 1992); Dominic Capeci, *The Lynching of Cleo Wright* (Lexington: University Press of Kentucky, 1998); Crystal N. Feimster, *Southern Horrors: Women and the Politics of Rape and Lynching* (Cambridge: Harvard University Press, 2009); Suzanne Lebsock, *A Murder in Virginia: Southern Justice on Trial* (New York: W. W. Norton, 2003); Claude A. Clegg III, *Troubled Ground: A Tale of Murder, Lynching, and Reckoning in the New South* (Urbana: University of Illinois Press, 2010); Stewart E. Tolnay and E. M. Beck, *A Festival of Violence: An Analysis of Southern Lynchings, 1882–1930* (Urbana: University of Illinois Press, 1995); Jonathan Markovitz, *Legacies of Lynching: Racial Violence and Memory* (Minneapolis: University of Minnesota Press, 2004).

21. Williams, *They Left Great Marks on Me.*

antilynching legislation. In the hands of antilynching advocates, the images that had once portrayed strength could provide clear evidence of white southerners' backwardness and barbarity. Although Wood focused predominately on the mob itself and not the black experience of lynching, she provided keen insight into the role of racial violence as a public performance of white supremacy.[22]

Several biographies of antilynching crusader and journalist Ida B. Wells published in the 2000s and 2010s provide key insight into the life of one of the most important individuals in the fight against lynching. Paula Giddings's *Ida* (2008) offered a broad and rich synthesis of the antilynching advocate's life and the challenges she confronted as an outspoken advocate. Wells's life and work are masterfully analyzed in Patricia Schechter's *Ida B. Wells-Barnett and American Reform, 1880–1930* (2001), which combines biography with theory to explore the complicated dynamics of gender and race that played into Wells's antilynching work.[23]

Crystal N. Feimster's *Southern Horrors* (2009) took on the challenge of contrasting Ida B. Wells with Rebecca Felton, women journalists and activists on opposite sides of the fight about the meanings of rape and lynching in the South. She complicated Felton as a white supremacist who exploited racial fears for her own political gain in the fight for suffrage, but who grew to see the limits of her racially exploitive bargain with white men. Putting Felton in conversation with the better-known Wells demonstrated the importance of reading race and gender in a wider context on both sides of the color line.[24]

Scholars studying racial violence during "the nadir" should also consider David Fort Godshalk's *Veiled Visions* (2005), a masterful account of the Atlanta Race Riot, and David S. Cecelski and Timothy B. Tyson's edited collection, *Democracy Betrayed* (1998), about the 1898 Wilmington Race Riot. Both books took rich advantage of historiographical advances to combine layers of crucial gender and

22. Amy Louise Wood, *Lynching and Spectacle: Witnessing Racial Violence in America, 1890 to 1940* (Chapel Hill: University of North Carolina Press, 2009). See also Kris Drocher, *Raising Racists: The Socialization of White Children in the Jim Crow South* (Lexington: University Press of Kentucky, 2011).

23. Paula Giddings, *Ida: A Sword among Lions: Ida B. Wells and the Campaign against Lynching* (New York: HarperCollins, 2008); Patricia Schechter, *Ida B. Wells-Barnett and American Reform 1880–1930* (Chapel Hill: University of North Carolina Press, 2001). See also Mia Bey, *To Tell the Truth Freely: The Life of Ida B. Wells* (New York: Hill and Wang, 2009). In addition to the works on Wells, Ann Field Alexander's *Race Man: The Rise and Fall of the Fighting Editor, John Mitchell, Jr.* (Charlottesville: University of Virginia Press, 2002) is a strong biography of a lesser known journalist and vocal antilynching advocate in Virginia.

24. Feimster, *Southern Horrors.*

class complexity with the peculiar, yet universal circumstances that fueled the mob and its rampage in progressive New South cities.[25]

Urban and Regional Studies

Much of the historiography of the black experience centers on urban and regional studies, and scholars often take a deep dive into individual cities or states.[26] Neil R. McMillen's powerful *Dark Journey* (1989) set a standard. His study reflected its times, countering some of the generalizations of the Woodward thesis and presenting Mississippi as a place where little to no fluidity about the meaning of race was possible for black or white residents.[27]

Instead, McMillen chronicled a state driven by white domination in every aspect of life: party politics, education, labor, rule over the land, and criminal justice. White Mississippians may have thought of domination as necessary to controlling the labor of such a large black population, but for African Americans, Mississippi became a bleak place that grew more horrific over time. *Dark Journey* notes how the structures of race grew so strong that segregation became de facto: white Mississippians did not even have to codify much of what became a terrible custom. However, white domination in Mississippi met with a constant

25. David Fort Godshalk, *Veiled Visions: The 1906 Atlanta Race Riot and the Reshaping of American Race Relations* (Chapel Hill: University of North Carolina Press, 2005); David S. Cecelski and Timothy B. Tyson, *Democracy Betrayed: The Wilmington Race Riot of 1898 and Its Legacy* (Chapel Hill: University of North Carolina Press, 1998). See also Willam Ivy Hair, *Carnival of Fury: Robert Charles and the New Orleans Race Riot of 1900* (Baton Rouge: Louisiana State University Press, 1976); Richard C. Cortner, *A Mob Intent on Death: The NAACP and the Arkansas Race Riot* (Middletown: Wesleyan University Press, 1988); Robert V. Haynes, *A Night of Violence: The Houston Riot of 1917* (Baton Rouge: Louisiana State University Press, 1976); James S. Hirsch, *Riot and Rememberance: The Tulsa Race War and Its Legacy* (Boston: Houghton Mifflin, 2002); Charles L. Lumpkins, *American Pogrom: The East St. Louis Race Riot and Black Politics* (Youngstown: Ohio University Press, 2008).

26. Given the breadth of scholarship on blacks' experiences in distinct locales, it is impossible to offer a comprehensive survey, or even a comprehensive footnote. For a few excellent examples of urban and regional studies, see Earl Lewis, *In Their Own Interests: Race, Class, and Power in Twentieth-Century Norfolk, Virginia* (Berkeley: University of California Press, 1991); Karen Ferguson, *Black Politics in New Deal Atlanta* (Chapel Hill: University of North Carolina Press, 2002); Paul Ortiz, *Emancipation Betrayed: The Hidden History of Black Organizing and White Violence in Florida from Reconstruction to the Bloody Election of 1920* (Berkeley: University of California Press, 2006).

27. Neil R. McMillen, *Dark Journey: Black Mississippians in the Age of Jim Crow* (Urbana: University of Illinois Press, 1989).

drumbeat of black resistance. By taking on the perspectives of black Mississippians, McMillen demonstrated that even behind the mask of cringing servility, African Americans bent in public so that they might create spaces behind the veil to contest white supremacy, protect their children from its nastiest lessons, and—when the Great Migration began in 1916—escape its clutches altogether.

Urban and regional scholars built on McMillen's foundation and took on the challenge of a complex reading of intersecting dynamics. In *Houston Bound* (2015), Tyina L. Steptoe thoughtfully examined historical experiences as polycultural rather than multicultural, and presented an analysis attentive to racial fluidity and cross-cultural conversations.[28] Situated at the intersection of various historical fields including migration studies, studies of the Jim Crow South, urban studies, and southern studies, *Houston Bound* found black, creole of color, and Mexican/Tejano voices in Houston's folklore and music. Steptoe created a new portrait of the American South, one where resistance against the impediments of racial segregation were shaped and sometimes misshapen by the particularities of various histories of enslavement, colonization, and migration. Generic assumptions about Jim Crow segregation did not account for the lived complexities of race. Beginning with the descendants of the freed slaves with roots all over the former Confederacy as her starting point, Steptoe chronicled the growth of a resistant and increasingly large and resilient black Houston that emerged in spite of white supremacy. She recounted the Houston Race Riot of 1917, tracking not only black resistance to police violence but also remaining attentive to the ways that cultural and economic expansion of black Houston in the era of the New Negro impacted their collective response. Steptoe read the riot as part of a larger critique of Houston that emerged through black journalism and music and a renewed push of economic independence. Although they faced violent policing, racialized limits in employment, and exclusion from white businesses, black Houstonians forged rich and increasingly prosperous communities behind the veil.

Steptoe then tracked the establishment of a distinctive creole of color community in Houston in the wake of the Great Mississippi Flood of 1927. Carefully mining documentary evidence from the WPA, oral histories, songs, folktales, and a growing body of secondary historical literature, she established the distinctive separations between creole of color migrants and the established black community, complicating the narrative further by tracing the arrival of Mexican and

28. Tyina L. Steptoe, *Houston Bound: Culture and Color in a Jim Crow City* (Berkeley: University of California Press, 2015).

then Italian and Jewish immigrants to the city. Her analysis carefully teased out many of the complexities of what it meant to be something other than "white" or "black" in the Jim Crow South. *Houston Bound* presented a city that was strikingly unique while also offering a model of how histories of race, space, and place could be examined in every southern, indeed every American, city.

In the effort to push beyond the boundaries created when historians write about a single place, growing numbers of twenty-first-century scholars took on questions unique to the years between Emancipation and "thc nadir." For example, Heather Andrea Williams's poignant *Help Me Find My People* (2012) traced the consequences of slavery-era family separations in a post-Emancipation society. Samuel Kelton Roberts Jr.'s masterful *Infectious Fear* (2009) investigated tuberculous, one of the leading causes of death among black urbanites. Reading the problem of public health through the lens of racial segregation, Roberts provided a historical look at the contemporary problem of racial health disparities. In *Right to Ride* (2010), Blair L M Kelley reexamined the history of segregated trains and streetcars before and after *Plessy v. Ferguson.* Tracing the history of the 1900–1907 streetcar boycott movement that took place in over twenty-five different southern cities, Kelley found that those protests characterized what had once simply been dismissed as the Washingtonian age of accommodation.[29]

Post-Reconstruction Black Leadership

Although Evelyn Brooks Higginbotham's *Righteous Discontent* opened up conversation about the political, theological, and social contributions of African American women in the National Baptist Convention, it also had a profound influence on future works in the subfields of intellectual, religious, gender, women, and African American history. With the hardening of Jim Crow segregation and the rise of political disfranchisement, African Americans employed new political

29. Heather Andrea Williams, *Help Me Find My People: The African American Search for Family Lost in Slavery* (Chapel Hill: University of North Carolina Press, 2012); Samuel Kelton Roberts Jr., *Infectious Fear: Politics, Disease, and the Health Effects of Segregation* (Chapel Hill: University of North Carolina Press, 2009); Blair L M Kelley, *Right to Ride: Streetcar Boycotts and African American Citizenship in the Era of* Plessy v. Ferguson (Chapel Hill: University of North Carolina Press, 2010). See also R. Volney Riser, *Defying Disfranchisement: Black Voting Rights Activism in the Jim Crow South, 1890–1908* (Baton Rouge: Louisiana State University Press, 2010); Robin D. G. Kelley, *Race Rebels: Culture, Politics, and the Black Working Class* (New York: Free Press, 1994); N. D. B. Connolly, *A World More Concrete: Real Estate and the Remaking of Jim Crow South Florida* (Chicago: University of Chicago Press, 2014).

strategies to advance their collective interests. Higginbotham addressed the effectiveness of these strategies, which further revealed deep class and gender fissures within the African American community. When combined with Kevin Gaines's *Uplifting the Race* (1996), *Righteous Discontent* ranks among the most influential books published in the 1990s.[30]

Like Higginbotham, Gaines moved the scholarly conversation of post-Reconstruction black leadership beyond the Washington–Du Bois debate with his nuanced analysis of black uplift strategies. Examining a diverse cast of political actors and intellectuals that included Anna Julia Cooper, W. E. B. Du Bois, and Alice Dunbar Nelson, Gaines detailed how black elites positioned themselves as bourgeois agents of civilization in order to achieve social mobility, moral authority, and status recognition. "Racial uplift ideals," he argued, "were offered as a form of cultural politics, in the hope that unsympathetic whites would relent and recognize the humanity of middle-class African Americans, and their potential for citizenship rights black men had possessed during Reconstruction." Far from racial egalitarians, the women and men examined in Gaines's text insisted that their cultural attributes (religious piety, frugality and thriftiness, chastity, adherence to heteronormative rules of patriarchal authority) entitled them to the fruits of citizenship. To his credit, Gaines paid close attention to ways in which advocates of uplift ideology adopted fluid and at times shifting positions on a variety of issues. Anna Julia Cooper, for example, railed against "the male prerogatives encoded within racial uplift ideology." And yet she held deeply conservative views on labor issues and trade union politics.[31]

Though not fully developed in *Uplifting the Race,* Gaines's analysis of Cooper's regressive labor views brought into focus an issue that other scholars discussed in great detail: the complex relationship of African American leaders to New South ideology. Echoing sentiments put forth by Du Bois in *Souls of Black Folk,* seminal works by James D. Anderson, Brian Kelly, and Adolph Reed examined the regressive politics of post–Reconstruction era black leaders and their roles in reconciling the black laboring class to its subordinate place in the South's political economy. New South boosters promoted industrial development and heralded the region's abundant supply of cheap labor as its greatest resource, preaching a harmony of interest between capital and labor, and they fiercely condemned any

30. Higginbotham, *Righteous Discontent;* Kevin K. Gaines, *Uplifting the Race: Black Leadership, Politics, and Culture in the Twentieth Century* (Chapel Hill: University of North Carolina Press, 1996).

31. Gaines, *Uplifting the Race,* 3.

assertion of political autonomy on the part of workers white or black.[32] Thus, in the opinion of Brian Kelly, the ascension of Booker T. Washington and his accommodationist politics resulted from "the compatibility of his formula for race progress with elite requirements for a tractable workforce." Here Washington mirrored other black conservatives who emphasized white-black elite collaboration, undermined the collective efforts of organized labor, and worked against the material interest of African American workers.[33]

The critical role of the South's educational institutions in the cultivation of such a class of race leaders received significant attention in James D. Anderson's pioneering study, *The Education of Blacks in the South, 1860–1935* (1988). Anderson demonstrated how the uplift vision and freedom dreams of African Americans clashed against the conservative agenda of New South elites, northern philanthropists, and racial accommodationists. Instead of viewing the New South's political order as inevitable, he recounted with vivid detail how leading industrialists sought to realize their political and economic vision through the control of black educational institutions. Anderson's analysis of the racial politics of Samuel Armstrong and the "Hampton-Tuskegee Ideal" is especially valuable. As Anderson pointed out, "Armstrong developed a pedagogy and ideology designed to avoid such confrontations and to maintain within the South a social consensus that did not challenge traditional inequities of wealth and power." The Hampton-Tuskegee philosophy advised black southerners to avoid electoral politics, remain tied to the plantation economy, and focus their attention on economic development. Such a philosophy, according to Anderson, was "the logical extension of an ideology that rejected black political power while recognizing that the South's agricultural economy rested on the backs of black agricultural workers." Not just in the South but throughout the nation, the white elite championed Hampton and Tuskegee as providing a solution to the Negro problem domestically and globally.[34]

32. James D. Anderson, *The Education of Blacks in the South, 1860–1935* (Chapel Hill: University of North Carolina Press, 1988); Brian Kelly, "Sentinels for New South Industry: Booker T. Washington, Industrial Accommodation and Black Workers in the Jim Crow South," *Labor History* 44 (August 2003): 337–58; Adolph Reed, *Stirrings in the Jug: Black Politics in the Post-Segregation Age* (Minneapolis: University of Minnesota Press, 1999).

33. Kelly, "Sentinels for New South Industry," 339. See also Robert J. Norrell, *Up from History: The Life of Booker T. Washington* (Cambridge: Harvard University Press, 2009).

34. Anderson, *The Education of Blacks in the South*, 34, 44.

Black Southern Politics in Transition

Just as scholars of Emancipation and the Jim Crow era acknowledged class differentiation and ideological diversity within southern black communities, they also noted how African Americans' social, cultural, and political lives changed over time. One of the more interesting historiographical developments since the 1990s has been the richly textured accounts of African American life in the period between World War I and the New Deal.[35] With the outbreak of World War I, the South experienced profound changes in its economic, political, and cultural life. A booming wartime economy, military enlistment, and massive demographic shifts altered everyday life for millions of southerners. Of the many wartime developments transforming the region, few received more public attention than the massive migration of southern blacks to the industrial North. Dramatic decline in the number of European laborers coming to the United States, along with the conscription of 2.7 million men and enlistment of hundreds of thousands more American workers into the armed forces, created an acute labor shortage in northern industries. To maintain production levels to meet the intense demand for American goods and maximize wartime profits, northern industrialists increasingly turned to southern black laborers. Swift-talking labor recruiters from Chicago, New York, Gary, Pittsburgh, and Cleveland blanketed the South, offering a consistent and persuasive sales pitch: Far away from Jim Crow's oppressive regime, black women and men could improve their economic standing, secure a quality education for their children, and escape the political restrictions and violent racism that marred their experiences in the South.

Thanks to the work of Isabel Wilkerson, James Grossman, Joe William Trotter Jr., and Peter Gottlieb, among others, we have a better grasp of the external and internal factors responsible for black southerners' move to the North. We also

35. See Robin D. G. Kelley, *Hammer and Hoe: Alabama Communism during the Great Depression* (Chapel Hill: University of North Carolina Press, 1990); Earl Lewis, *In Their Own Interests: Race, Class and Power in Twentieth-Century Norfolk, Virginia* (Berkeley: University of California Press, 1991); Karen Ferguson, *Black Politics in New Deal Atlanta* (Chapel Hill: University of North Carolina Press, 2003); Nan Elizabeth Woodruff, *American Congo: The African American Freedom Struggle in the Delta* (Cambridge: Harvard University Press, 2003); Paul Ortiz, *Emancipation Betrayed: The Hidden History of Black Organizing and White Violence in Florida from Reconstruction to the Bloody Election of 1920* (Berkeley: University of California Press, 2005); Jared Roll, *Spirit of Rebellion: Labor and Religion in the New Cotton South* (Urbana: University of Illinois Press, 2010; Claudrena N. Harold, *New Negro Politics in the Jim Crow South* (Athens: University of Georgia Press, 2016).

have a more nuanced understanding of how their movements altered the cultural and intellectual landscape of northern cities like Pittsburgh, New York, and Chicago. In *Passionately Human* (2005), Wallace Best detailed how black migrants from the South gave rise to black Chicago's new sacred order which, according to Best, "didn't so much topple an old religious establishment as it rendered that establishment's long-held institutional priorities ineffective in a rapidly changing religious climate. In contrast to the old religious establishment that was run by a coterie of well-educated, middle-class male ministers, the new sacred order was largely a female order, as black women constituted more than 70 percent of the membership in many churches."[36]

Though the Great Migration continues to occupy an important place in the historiography of the Jim Crow era, some of the most exciting literature since the 1980s focused on the political struggles and cultural lives of those who remained in the South during and after World War I. Emboldened by the egalitarian rhetoric of the war, as well as their own legacies of protest, black southern women and men put the nation's commitment to democracy to the ultimate test by protesting the racially stratified labor market, repressive federal and local "work-or-fight" ordinances, Jim Crow segregation in public accommodations, and their systematic exclusion from the electoral arena. Numerous works document their collective battles, including Paul Ortiz's *Emancipation Betrayed* (2005), Eric Arnesen's *Waterfront Workers of New Orleans* (1994), and Claudrena N. Harold's *New Negro Politics in the Jim Crow South* (2016).[37]

36. Wallace Best, *Passionately Human, No Less Divine: Religion and Black Culture in Chicago* (Princeton: Princeton University Press, 2005), 2. Detailed information on the Great Migration can be found in: Florette Henri, *Black Migration: Movement North, 1900–1920* (New York: Anchor Press, 1975); Peter Gottlieb, *Making Their Own Way: Southern Blacks' Migration to Pittsburgh, 1916–1930* (Urbana: University of Illinois Press, 1987); Carol Marks, *Farewell, We're Good and Gone* (Bloomington: Indiana University Press, 1989); James Grossman, *Land of Hope: Chicago, Black Southerners, and the Great Migration* (Chicago: University of Chicago Press, 1989); Joe William Trotter Jr., ed., *The Great Migration in Historical Perspective: New Dimensions of Race, Class, and Gender* (Bloomington: Indiana University Press, 1991); Earl Lewis, *In Their Own Interests: Race, Class, and Power in Twentieth-Century Norfolk* (Berkeley: University of California Press, 1991); Alferdteen Harrison, ed., *The Great Migration from the American South* (Jackson: University Press of Mississippi, 1992); Milton C. Sernett, *Bound for the Promised Land: African American Religion and the Great Migration* (Durham: Duke University Press, 1997); Kimberly L. Phillips, *Alabama North: African-American Migrants, Community, and Working-Class Activism in Cleveland, 1915–1945* (Urbana: University of Illinois Press, 1999); Isabel Wilkerson, *The Warmth of Other Suns: The Epic Story of America's Great Migration* (New York: Random House, 2010).

37. Ortiz, *Emancipation Betrayed;* Arsenen, *Waterfront Workers of New Orleans;* Harold, *New Negro Politics in the Jim Crow South.*

Earl Lewis's *In Their Own Interests* (1991) traced how blacks constantly modified their strategies, sometimes placing emphasis on development in the "home sphere" and, at other times, putting their collective energy primarily behind workplace advancement. His analysis of black Norfolk during World War I and the 1920s shed light on political actors largely ignored in most studies: rank-and-file trade unionists, organizing longshoremen, tobacco stemmers, domestic workers, devout Garveyites building vibrant divisions and chapters of the Marcus Garvey's Universal Negro Improvement Association, and mass culture consumers seeking to add joy and meaning to their lives. Without minimizing the harsh realities of Jim Crow, Lewis showcased a vibrant world in which African Americans, to paraphrase his language, turned segregation into congregation. By focusing on such important cultural institutions as the *Norfolk Journal and Guide* and the Attucks Theater, as well as the world of jazz and gospel music, Lewis positioned the South as an important site for black popular modernism. Put another way, *In Their Own Interests* provided an important reminder of how leisure became a critical site of both pleasure and politics for black southerners.[38]

Perhaps few studies better demonstrate the tremendous insights derived from exploring the leisure world of the Jim Crow South than Andrew Kahrl's *The Land Was Ours* (2012) and Cara Caddoo's *Envisioning Freedom* (2014). Kahrl drew from a rich collection of archival material, interweaving the largely untold history of the rise and fall of African American property ownership in the coastal and waterfront areas of the Atlantic Seaboard and Gulf Coast with an equally riveting narrative on the evolution of coastal capitalism, its devastating environmental and human costs, and its role in shaping the economic landscape of the Sunbelt South. Kahrl covered more than a century of African American history, recounting black Americans' protracted struggle for recreational rights and thereby enriching our understanding of what Jacquelyn Dowd Hall referred to as the "long civil rights movement."[39]

Several of the class tensions discussed in the works of Gaines and Higginbotham are detailed in Kahrl's examination of black resort communities, par-

38. Lewis, *In Their Own Interests.*

39. Cara Caddoo, *Envisioning Freedom: Cinema and the Building of Modern Black Life* (Cambridge: Harvard University Press, 2014); Andrew Kahrl, *The Land Was Ours: African American Beaches from Jim Crow to the Sunbelt South* (Cambridge: Harvard University Press, 2012); Jacquelyn Dowd Hall, "The Long Civil Rights Movement and the Political Uses of the Past," *Journal of American History* 91 (March 2005): 1233–63.

ticularly Gulfside. The story of Gulfside begins in the spring of 1923, when its founder, Bishop Robert E. Jones, acquired three hundred acres of coastal land near Waveland, Mississippi. The Methodist minister envisioned Gulfside as a Christian-centered sanctuary for race leaders, a reform for "wayward" African American youth, and a space of wholesome amusement and leisure for fatigued black laborers. Four years after acquiring the land, Jones opened Gulfside Chautauqua and Camp Meeting Grounds, which drew more than two thousand attendees to its dedication services. The resort received a great deal of attention and praise from the black press, but struggled to survive in the face of escalating property taxes and the shore erosion brought about by the completion of a nearby seawall. Notwithstanding these economic and environmental difficulties, Gulfside remained a permanent fixture in the black community well into the civil rights era, functioning as an organizing site for political groups like the Student Non-Violent Coordinating Committee.

To his credit, Kahrl did not examine African Americans' leisure pursuits in isolation from the South's major political and economic developments. His analysis of black workers' fight to enjoy existing and developing urban shorelines in Norfolk and New Orleans provides a powerful example of this approach. In painstaking detail, he outlined how coastal capitalism remapped the urban landscape, hardened de facto segregation, and further decreased the life chances and experiences of African Americans in the cities. In doing so, Kahrl forced his readers to view Jim Crow segregation as not a static system, but one constantly evolving in response to local, regional, and national changes. As cities reengineered urban shorelines for the benefit of commercial and residential developers, and access to urban leisure increasingly determined real estate markets, local officials expanded the contours of Jim Crow segregation to ensure "the total exclusion of persons of color from developed shorelines and safe, supervised places of play." This, according to Kahrl, contributed "in a direct and unambiguous manner to an increase in the exposure of urban black populations to environmental hazards and the deterioration of their overall health and safety during the summer months." Of course, one of the most direct results in African Americans' exclusion from safe, supervised spaces of leisure was the dramatic spike in black youth drowning deaths during the summer months. To remedy the situation, African Americans in Norfolk and New Orleans poured tremendous energy into establishing their own beaches. The mixed results of their efforts are examined in Kahrl's exploration of the rise (and fall) of Little Bay Beach and Ocean Beach in the Norfolk area and Lincoln Beach in New Orleans.[40]

The political and social dimensions of leisure are also examined in Cara Caddoo's important work, *Envisioning Freedom.* With significant focus on the South, Caddoo documented African Americans' relationship and contribution to early cinema, their evolving views concerning the representational power of the screen, and their deep commitment to visual self-determination. Caddoo established the cinema as a critical site for the formation of a national, black public sphere as well as a driving force in shaping African Americans' perception of themselves as constituting a nation within a nation. *Envisioning Freedom* also positioned the South as a site for the creation of a black popular modernism, framing ongoing debates about black representation in cinema and other black popular culture forms.

In many ways, Caddoo's emphasis on black southerners' cosmopolitanism reflected a larger trend in the historical literature. Not just in the cultural arena but in the political realm as well, black women and men living below the Mason-Dixon Line were at the center of larger developments in black political culture, both nationally and internationally. To elevate themselves, black southern women and men participated in a wide range of leftist and nationalist movements. Over the interwar years, they formed vibrant chapters of Marcus Garvey's Universal Negro Improvement Association (UNIA), as well as pledged allegiance to the Communist Party. Their embrace of the UNIA's pan-African agenda is documented in Mary G. Rolinson's *Grassroots Garveyism* (2007) and Claudrena N. Harold's *The Rise and Fall of the Garvey Movement in the Urban South* (2007), two studies that explored how working women and men balanced their commitments to Garvey's international agenda with their local political commitments.[41]

Like so much scholarship published since the 1980s, Rolinson's and Harold's works bear the imprint of the influence of Robin D. G. Kelley's highly influential study, *Hammer and Hoe* (1990). Employing an interdisciplinary approach that relied on the theoretical and methodological tools of social and gender history and cultural studies, Kelley explained how and why the Communist Party came

40. Kahrl, *The Land Was Ours,* quotes on 116.

41. Mary Rolinson, *Grassroots Garveyism: The Universal Negro Improvement Association in the Rural South, 1920–1927* (Chapel Hill: University of North Carolina Press, 2007); Claudrena N. Harold, *The Rise and Fall of Marcus Garvey and the Universal Negro Improvement Association in the Urban South, 1918–1942* (New York: Routledge, 2007).

to occupy such a central place in the political lives of thousands of African Americans living in Alabama between the onset of the Great Depression and the fall of the Popular Front. As the harsh realities of the Great Depression shifted black politics further to the left, the Communist Party established strong networks of support among African Americans not only in places like Chicago and New York but also in Birmingham, Alabama. According to Kelley, it was the Communist Party's strident critiques against the capitalist system, its call for state-supported relief for unemployed and underemployed workers, and its defense of the nine "Scottsboro Boys" wrongfully accused of raping two white women that garnered tremendous respect within many segments of black America.[42] Challenging the idea of black southern Communists as the pliant tools of outside agitators, Kelley demonstrated how black Alabamians embraced the socialist agenda of the Communist Party while advancing their own local and regional interests.

Hammer and Hoe bore the imprint of the social milieu in which it was written. "The book's genesis," Kelley admitted, reflected presentist concerns: "I felt an urging to study black working-class radicalism, not because the old Soviet states were crumbling in the face of revolt, but because the apartheid state of South Africa was succumbing to a massive multiracial movement—a movement in which Left trade unions and the South African Communist Party played leading roles." First appearing in 1990, the book also bore the imprint of the triumph of Reaganism and Thatcherism. In the United States, this was an era of "capital flight, the erosion of the welfare state, neoliberal privatization schemes, the weakening of anti-discrimination laws and policies." According to Kelley, he wrote the book during a time in which "a wave of police and vigilante killings . . . struck our communities with the force of a cluster bomb." By digging into the history of the Communist Party in Alabama and highlighting the organizing endeavors of working-class activists like Hosea Hudson and Lemon Johnson, Kelley provided a blueprint of how ordinary women and men challenged "racial capitalism" and state-sanctioned violence and worked to build a true democracy in one of the nation's most repressive states.[43]

And therein lies the strength of not just *Hammer and Hoe* but the corpus of

42. Kelley, *Hammer and Hoe.* For additional literature on the Scottsboro case, see Dan T. Carter, *Scottsboro: A Tragedy of the American South* (Baton Rouge: Louisiana State University Press, 1979); James Goodman, *Stories of Scottsboro* (New York: Vintage Press, 1994); Walter T. Howard, *Black Communists Speak on Scottsboro: A Documentary History* (Philadelphia: Temple University Press, 2008).

43. Kelley, *Hammer and Hoe,* xii.

black historiography that has emerged since the 1980s to explain the Jim Crow era. From examining the founding of black civil rights organizations to tracking the resistance of subversive activities of black workers to discussing women's activism against Jim Crow segregation to analyzing the critical role of imprisoned black women in the making of New South modernity, the most provocative historical research on the Jim Crow era has enriched our understanding of not just the past but our contemporary political terrain. In fact, the works of several scholars of the black experience during the Jim Crow era was crucial to understanding the historical forces and political transformations responsible for the election of Barack Obama as the nation's first African American president in 2008, Hurricane Katrina's devastating impact on blacks in the Gulf Coast, ongoing debates about Confederate monuments and memorialization, violent white supremacist marches in Charlottesville during the summer of 2017, and the pervasiveness of voter suppression tactics in the South, particularly Georgia, Florida, and North Carolina. Moving beyond the ivory tower, these scholars drew attention to the troubling parallels between the regressive politics of the late nineteenth and early twentieth centuries and those of the early twenty-first century.

In terms of its engagement with the larger public, especially intriguing and indicative of where the field may be headed has been the work of Carol Anderson, whose first book, *Eyes Off the Prize* (2003), situated African Americans' fight for racial equality and economic justice within a broader international context and human rights framework. In the aftermath of Donald Trump's presidential victory in 2016, Anderson turned her attention to two critical issues: white resentment and voter suppression. Using the lens of history, she rooted manifestations of white anger in a longer past: "White resentment," she explained in a 2017 *New York Times* essay, "has long thrived on the fantasy of being under siege and having to fight back, as the mass lynchings and destruction of thriving, politically active blacks communities in Colfax, La. (1873), Wilmington, N.C. (1898), Ocoee, Fla. (1920), and Tulsa, Okla. (1921) attest." Just as white resentment had deeper roots, so did the efforts of the Republican Party to safeguard whites' political power through a variety of disfranchisement measures targeted specifically at African Americans and other people of color. "The disappearing minority voter," Anderson argued in *One Person, No Vote* (2018) and in subsequent editorials, is "the campaign's most misunderstood story."[44]

44. Carol Anderson, *Eyes Off the Prize: The United Nations and the African American Struggle for Human Rights, 1944–1955* (New York: Cambridge University Press, 2003); Anderson, "The Politics of

Attentive to how the past continues to inform the present, Anderson enumerated the various tactics employed by the Republican Party to suppress the black vote and maintain political power, particularly after the Supreme Court's 2013 gutting of the Voting Rights Act. These tactics included the implementation of voter ID laws, the relocation and closure of polling stations, felony disfranchisement, redistricting, and the purging of voter rolls. "The U.S. has consistently been comfortable with the veneer of democracy—the performance of an election—rather than the actual substance," Anderson explained, "There is still no real process to reckon with the electoral consequences of and results of systematic efforts to keep black voters from the polls."[45] Throughout the midterm election campaign of 2018, she recounted the antidemocratic machinations of Secretary of State Brian Kemp of Georgia and Governor Rick Scott of Florida, detailing their adoption of tactics employed by the white southern oligarchy during the Reconstruction and Jim Crow eras.

Anderson's pithy yet theoretically sophisticated and historically informed editorials, which appeared in both the *New York Times* and *The Guardian,* were a testament to not only the many advances in the historical literature but also the new opportunities for public engagement. The appearance of such digital platforms as the *Washington Post*'s Made by History and the African American Intellectual History Society's *Black Perspectives* provided historians with even greater opportunities to share their expertise with the broader public.[46]

In their public endeavors, many historians do much more than shed light on the nation's dark past and present. They also move us forward, highlighting individuals, organizations, and movements seeking to transform their communities and the larger world. If we return to historian Carol Anderson, we see this in her coverage of the 2018 gubernatorial race in Georgia, which pitted Democrat Stacey Abrams against Republican Brian Kemp, then-Secretary of State. Even

White Resentment," *New York Times,* 5 August 2017, https://www.nytimes.com/2017/08/05/opinion/sunday/white-resentment-affirmative-action.html (accessed 18 January 2019); Anderson, *One Person, No Vote: How Voter Suppression Is Destroying Our Democracy* (New York: Bloomsbury, 2018), 1.

45. Anderson, "Why Is No One Talking About the Uncounted, Suppressed Votes in Florida?" *The Guardian,* 14 November 2018, https://www.theguardian.com/commentisfree/2018/nov/14/why-no-one-talking-uncounted-suppressed-votes-florida (accessed 18 January 2019).

46. "Made by History," *Washington Post,* https://www.washingtonpost.com/news/made-by-history/?noredirect=on&utm_term=.304c8dc5ee08 (accessed 18 January 2019); AAIHS, *Black Perspectives,* https://www.aaihs.org/black-perspectives/ (accessed 18 January 2019).

amid rampant electoral (not voter) corruption, Anderson discovered hope in the grassroots organizing work of the New Georgia Project (NGP), which Abrams founded in 2013. The NGP aimed to increase voter registration in the state and politicize marginalized groups in both rural and urban areas. Tera W. Hunter also turned her attention to Abrams's campaign with a particular focus on the organizing activities of Care in Action, a domestic workers union. Throughout metropolitan Atlanta, Care in Action members canvassed neighborhoods, knocked on doors, and shared Abrams's message with thousands of locals. As Hunter noted, "Despite their marginalized positions and the many obstacles in their way, they insist on making their voices heard."[47]

In ways both subtle and direct, Hunter and Anderson have built on one of W. E. B. Du Bois's most important lessons, which he communicated most forcefully during his tenure as editor of the NAACP's *Crisis* magazine: the protection and deepening of our democracy demands not just blistering critiques of white supremacy and economic exploitation, but also a commitment to documenting and advancing alternative visions of freedom and human possibility. They are lessons well explored by historians of "the nadir."

47. Tera W. Hunter, "Fighting for Stacey Abrams and Empowerment in Georgia," *New York Times*, 5 November 2018, https://www.nytimes.com/2018/11/05/opinion/atlanta-domestic-workers-vote-stacey-abrams.html (accessed 18 January 2019).

NEW STORIES FOR A "NEW SOUTH"

Race-Making, Ethnic Diversity, Urbanization, and Gendered Politics

Mikaëla M. Adams and Ted Ownby

Where should a historiographic essay on the New South begin? When they wrote their historical syntheses in the mid-twentieth century, C. Vann Woodward and George Brown Tindall knew how to start. While these two groundbreaking historians covered an impressive range of topics, they began with politics. Woodward opened *Origins of the New South* (1951) with "The Redeemers," a chapter detailing the leaders and policies of the Democratic Party. In *The Emergence of the New South* (1967), Tindall characterized the presidential election of Woodrow Wilson as "a kind of vindication of the South," and his first chapter raised questions about the Democratic Party and the meaning of Progressivism. Even when later historians turned to the economic and social frameworks of the New South—whether Paul M. Gaston's 1970 study of Henry Grady and the New South creed, or Edward L. Ayers's *The Promise of the New South* (1992), which emphasized the railroad as a force of change in economic and social life—they could not escape the political landscapes that Woodward and Tindall described.[1]

When surveying the past generation of scholarship on the history of the South from the 1870s to the 1920s, however, it actually becomes clear where to begin. Many of the most exciting developments in southern history involve race-making

1. C. Vann Woodward, *Origins of the New South, 1877–1913* (Baton Rouge: Louisiana State University Press, 1951); George Brown Tindall, *The Emergence of the New South, 1913–1945* (Baton Rouge: Louisiana State University Press, 1967), 2; Edward L. Ayers, *The Promise of the New South: Life after Reconstruction* (New York: Oxford University Press, 1992). On naming the region the "New South," see Paul M. Gaston, *The New South Creed: A Study in Southern Mythmaking* (New York: Alfred A. Knopf, 1970).

and challenges to that process. The historiographical currents have moved from race relations to race-making, from divisions between political and social history to a broad definition of politics that conceptualizes power in all topics, and to an intersectional approach to southern racial politics that includes issues of gender, bodies, and cultural identity. Law, government, and politics always matter, but they have faded as the primary subjects capturing scholars' attentions.

The single volume that best illustrates many of these historiographical developments is *Jumpin' Jim Crow* (2000), edited by Jane Dailey, Glenda Elizabeth Gilmore, and Bryant Simon. The volume's significance lay not just in the quality of its essays but in the attention to gender and households, violence, health, respectability, consumption, historical memory, and religion as manifestations of southern politics and power relations. The authors emphasized that race-making was a process: Jim Crow was "a precarious balancing act, pulled in all directions by class, gender, and racial tensions."[2]

Two works from the same moment in southern scholarship illustrate the significance of that balancing act. Grace Elizabeth Hale's *Making Whiteness* (1998) analyzed the development of "whiteness" as a concept that was always under challenge, most obviously from African Americans but also from technological and economic changes that destabilized both white identity and authority. Her volume was wide-ranging, but the chapters on consumption and lynching attracted the most significant scholarly attention. Hale argued that white southern legislators passed Jim Crow laws about streetcars and trains because travelers were strangers without clear identities. What was once a gendered division between ladies' cars (for polite people, including white women and children) and smoking cars (for smoking men, most of them lower-class) became a racialized division that rejected the idea that African Americans could be upper-class, polite, or fit to be among white women and children. Hale demonstrated that as consumer society offered the anonymity of mass culture, people who wanted to draw clear racial lines countered with racist advertising and new rules about segregated shopping. Twentieth-century spectacle lynchings with crowds, travel calendars, and souvenirs were significantly modern ways to make whiteness by dramatizing and commercializing the positions of blacks as victims and white as participants.[3]

2. Jane Dailey, Glenda Elizabeth Gilmore, and Bryant Simon, eds., *Jumpin' Jim Crow: Southern Politics from Civil War to Civil Rights* (Princeton: Princeton University Press, 2000), 4.

3. Grace Elizabeth Hale, *Making Whiteness: The Culture of Segregation in the South, 1890–1940* (New York: Pantheon Books, 1998).

Glenda Elizabeth Gilmore's *Gender and Jim Crow* (1996) likewise represented important new directions in scholarship about race, gender, and power. In an intriguing introduction, she summed up the volume as "a study of North Carolina politics with black women at its center," beginning a story of politics by studying people who were neither voting nor holding office.[4] Like Hale, Gilmore analyzed stories that blurred the boundaries that many white southerners constructed between race and class. Black and white men believed in leadership by the "best men," even as they disputed the meaning of that concept. Violence, as when whites used an 1898 riot in Wilmington to reject both African Americans' political participation and claims of respectability, had political consequences. In reaction to that masculinized interpretation of political power, African American women pursued uplift and respectability through education, temperance work, and demands for the vote.

Some of the most dramatic historiographical changes in the study of the New South have been in scholarship on prisons and prisoners. In the 1980s and 1990s, important works illuminated connections between convict labor, chain gangs, prisons, the goals of powerful landowners and employers, and prison reform. Scholars demonstrated how incarceration served as a tool to control and force labor from black prisoners.[5] The scholarship intersected with two larger historiographical trends: one emphasized women prisoners and issues of sexuality; the second studied the construction of identities as crucial to issues of power. Sarah Haley's *No Mercy Here* (2016) and Talitha L. LeFlouria's *Chained in Silence* (2015) analyzed the image of the bad black mother that accompanied African American women's experiences in prison. Depicting African American women as lascivious individuals and failed mothers not only reinforced that they belonged in prison but also validated policies that made imprisonment more likely and motherhood extremely difficult. Although children born to African American women in prison were often conceived through rape, authorities repeatedly identified the problem

4. Glenda Elizabeth Gilmore, *Gender and Jim Crow: Women and the Politics of White Supremacy in North Carolina, 1896–1920* (Chapel Hill: University of North Carolina Press, 1996), xvi.

5. Matthew J. Mancini, *One Dies, Get Another: Convict Leasing in the American South, 1866–1928* (Columbia: University of South Carolina Press, 1996); Alex Lichtenstein, *Twice the Work of Free Labor: The Political Economy of Convict Labor in the New South* (New York: Verso, 1996); Mary Ellen Curtin, *Black Prisoners and Their World, Alabama, 1865–1900* (Charlottesville: University Press of Virginia, 2000); David M. Oshinsky, *"Worse than Slavery": Parchman Farm and the Ordeal of Jim Crow Justice* (New York: Free Press, 1996).

as irresponsible women. Unlike white women, some of whom gained pardons or paroles to care for their children, black women left prison only in cases of mental illness or when influential white employers offered them domestic work.[6]

Scholarship on extralegal intimidation and violence also helped to illuminate the construction and enforcement of social and racial hierarchies in the New South. Although early twentieth-century antilynching activists and sociologists wrote about lynching, few historians studied mob violence in depth before the last decades of the twentieth century.[7] Since the late 1970s and 1980s, there has been an explosion of scholarship as historians seek to understand who perpetuated lynching violence, how it operated, its consequences, and what it relates about economic, gendered, religious, and racial tensions. As scholars have demonstrated, racism motivated much of this violence as whites reasserted their supremacy through institutionalized segregation. Lynching stemmed black political participation and retarded African American economic success.[8] In addition, as Jacquelyn Dowd Hall, Nancy MacLean, and Crystal N. Feimster argued, white

6. Sarah Haley, *No Mercy Here: Gender, Punishment, and the Making of Jim Crow Modernity* (Chapel Hill: University of North Carolina Press, 2016); Talitha L. LeFlouria, *Chained in Silence: Black Women and Convict Labor in the New South* (Chapel Hill: University of North Carolina Press, 2015).

7. For a notable exception to this early dearth of scholarship, see Arthur F. Raper, *The Tragedy of Lynching* (Chapel Hill: University of North Carolina Press, 1933). Beginning in the late 1970s and early 1980s, scholarship like Jacquelyn Dowd Hall's *Revolt Against Chivalry: Jessie Daniel Ames and the Women's Campaign against Lynching* (New York: Columbia University Press, 1979) and Robert L. Zangrando's *The NAACP Crusade Against Lynching, 1909–1950* (Philadelphia: Temple University Press, 1980) examined antilynching campaigns, while others, like James R. McGovern's *Anatomy of a Lynching: The Killing of Claude Neal* (Baton Rouge: Louisiana State University Press, 1982) and Robert Seitz Frey, Nancy Thompson-Frey, and John Seigenthaler's *The Silent and the Damned: The Murder of Mary Phagan and the Lynching of Leo Frank* (Lanham, MD: Madison Books, 1988), explored individual episodes of violence. Edward L. Ayers's *Vengeance and Justice: Crime and Punishment in the 19th-Century American South* (New York: Oxford University Press, 1984) considered lynching within the framework of southern criminal justice. In 1988, Robert P. Ingalls produced a regional study of mob violence in *Urban Vigilantes in the New South: Tampa, 1882–1936* (Knoxville: University of Tennessee Press, 1988). The first sweeping historical study of interracial violence, including lynching, appeared with Herbert Shapiro's *White Violence and Black Response: From Reconstruction to Montgomery* (Amherst: University of Massachusetts Press, 1988). Since then, more than forty historical monographs have examined extralegal violence and its consequences in the New South.

8. W. Fitzhugh Brundage, *Lynching in the New South: Georgia and Virginia, 1880–1930* (Urbana: University of Illinois Press, 1993); Shapiro, *White Violence and Black Response;* George C. Wright, *Racial Violence in Kentucky, 1865–1940: Lynchings, Mob Rule, and "Legal Lynchings"* (Baton Rouge: Louisiana State University Press, 1990).

men articulated the image of the "black rapist" not only to defend extralegal violence but to expand "their own sexual power over both black and white women."[9]

Some scholars framed mob violence as an outgrowth of southern agricultural production and premodern codes of behavior that eventually gave way to modernization.[10] In *A Festival of Violence* (1995), Stewart E. Tolnay and E. M. Beck argued that lynching served three main functions: "first, to maintain social control over the black population through terrorism; second, to suppress or eliminate black competitors for economic, political, or social rewards; and third, to stabilize the white class structure and preserve the privileged status of the white aristocracy." As economic conditions stabilized over the first few decades of the twentieth century, and as New South industrialists sought investors, lynching no longer seemed necessary to preserve the old order, and the practice declined.[11] Other scholars asserted, however, that modernization and its destabilizing effects on traditional social relations led to lynching in the South. As Nancy MacLean argued, "Economic development acted as a solvent on older relations of power and authority—between men and women and between parents and children as well as between workers and employers and blacks and whites." Anxious about social change, white southerners attacked individuals who seemed to threaten racial, class, gender, and generational norms. White participants, moreover, embraced modern technologies of communication and transportation to advertise

9. Hall, *Revolt Against Chivalry;* Nancy MacLean, "The Leo Frank Case Reconsidered: Gender and Sexual Politics in the Making of Reactionary Populism," *Journal of American History* 78 (December 1991): 917–48; Crystal N. Feimster, *Southern Horrors: Women and the Politics of Rape and Lynching* (Cambridge: Harvard University Press, 2009), 5. Also on issues of rape, see Joel Williamson, *The Crucible of Race: Black/White Relations in the American South since Emancipation* (New York: Oxford University Press, 1984); Lisa Lindquist Dorr, *White Women, Rape, and the Power of Race in Virginia, 1900–1960* (Chapel Hill: University of North Carolina Press, 2004); Kate Côte Gillin, *Shrill Hurrahs: Women, Gender, and Racial Violence in South Carolina, 1865–1900* (Columbia: University of South Carolina Press, 2013).

10. See Richard Maxwell Brown, *Strain of Violence: Historical Studies of American Violence and Vigilantism* (New York: Oxford University Press, 1975); Ayers, *Vengeance and Justice;* Ingalls, *Urban Vigilantes in the New South;* Michael J. Pfeifer, *The Roots of Rough Justice: Origins of American Lynching* (Urbana: University of Illinois Press, 2010); Michael J. Pfeifer, *Rough Justice: Lynching and American Society, 1874–1947* (Urbana: University of Illinois Press, 2004); William D. Carrigan, *The Making of a Lynching Culture: Violence and Vigilantism in Central Texas, 1836–1916* (Urbana: University of Illinois Press, 2004); John Hammond Moore, *Carnival of Blood: Dueling, Lynching, and Murder in South Carolina, 1880–1920* (Columbia: University of South Carolina Press, 2006).

11. Steward E. Tolnay and E. M. Beck, *A Festival of Violence: An Analysis of Southern Lynchings, 1882–1930* (Urbana: University of Illinois Press, 1995), 18–19; Pfeifer, *Rough Justice.*

and bring spectators to lynching sites. Rather than "barbaric relics of a bygone era," lynchings were in fact a "peculiarly modern ritual."[12]

African American men were the most frequent victims of lynch mobs, but neither the South nor the victims of southern lynchings were monolithic. As William D. Carrigan and Clive Webb demonstrated in *Forgotten Dead* (2013), Mexicans in the Southwest faced violence at rates equal to those of African Americans in the Deep South. In *Lynched* (2015), Amy Kate Bailey and Stewart E. Tolnay's data on lynch victims revealed personal characteristics that made certain individuals more likely targets than others. Lynch victims tended to be black men who stood out from the local African American population, like those born out of state who moved where interstate migrants were less concentrated, agricultural workers in communities that faced a labor shortage, or economically successful African Americans in regions where most black people were poor. Specific contexts mattered, rendering problematic scholars' ability to offer simple answers to questions surrounding lynching.[13]

In addition to analyzing the underlying causes and targets of lynching, scholars also deconstructed the forms of lynching violence. In *Lynching in the New South* (1993), W. Fitzhugh Brundage identified four main types of mobs: small "terrorist mobs" of less than fifty participants that made no pretense of upholding the law; equally small "private mobs" that exacted vengeance for a wide array of alleged crimes; "posses," which ranged in size from a few to hundreds of participants; and "mass mobs" of hundreds or even thousands of members, which punished supposed criminals with overwhelming brutality and, sometimes, great ceremony. Although not every lynching was "laden with symbolism," many included ritualized elements to provoke particular reactions from both participants

12. MacLean, "The Leo Frank Case Reconsidered"; Amy Louise Wood, *Lynching and Spectacle: Witnessing Racial Violence in America, 1890–1940* (Chapel Hill: University of North Carolina Press, 2009), 5–6. See also Feimster, *Southern Horrors;* Kimberly Harper, *White Man's Heaven: The Lynching and Expulsion of Blacks in the Southern Ozarks, 1894–1909* (Fayetteville: University of Arkansas Press, 2010); Jonathan Markovitz, *Legacies of Lynching: Racial Violence and Memory* (Minneapolis: University of Minnesota Press, 2004), xxvi.

13. William D. Carrigan and Clive Webb, *Forgotten Dead: Mob Violence against Mexicans in the United States, 1848–1928* (New York: Oxford University Press, 2013); Amy Kate Bailey and Steward E. Tolnay, *Lynched: The Victims of Southern Mob Violence* (Chapel Hill: University of North Carolina Press, 2015), 208–10. For other studies on regional variations of racial violence, see Brundage, *Lynching in the New South;* Terence Finnegan, *A Deed So Accursed: Lynching in Mississippi and South Carolina, 1881–1940* (Charlottesville: University of Virginia Press, 2013).

and observers. For many southern white evangelicals, as Donald G. Mathews argued, lynching was not simply punishment for a crime, but a sacrificial, religious act that seemingly affirmed the moral order, generated community solidarity, and restored balance to the cosmos. As Tolnay and Beck explained, lynching also sent messages to the black community: "first, aggression toward whites would not be tolerated and violators would be put to death; second, some kinds of deaths are truly more horrible and frightening than others."[14] Representations of violence in souvenir postcards, songs, news accounts, and other narratives reinforced these messages, ensuring that lynching terrorized even those blacks who did not witness it directly. As Amy Louise Wood contended in *Lynching and Spectacle* (2009), "It was the spectacle of lynching, rather than the violence itself, that wrought psychological damage, that enforced black acquiescence to white domination."[15]

Despite the fear inspired by mob violence, African Americans fought back by speaking and writing about their experiences, forming antilynching organizations, and appealing to politicians. Beginning in 1889, Ida B. Wells wrote passionately against mob violence, making the case that lynching victims were not, as defenders of lynching claimed, black men who raped white women.[16] Following the 1908 race riot in Springfield, Illinois, blacks and white allies united to form the National Association for the Advancement of Colored People (NAACP), which began to publicize cases of racial injustice.[17] Numerous black people testified about racial violence at forums sponsored by federal officials, journalists, and civil

14. Brundage, *Lynching in the New South,* 15, 18–19; Hale, *Making Whiteness;* Donald G. Mathews, "The Southern Rite of Human Sacrifice," *Journal of Southern Religion* 3 (2000), http://jsr.fsu.edu/mathews.htm (accessed 18 January 2019); Mathews, *At the Altar of Lynching: Burning Sam Hose in the American South* (New York: Cambridge University Press, 2017); Tolnay and Beck, *A Festival of Violence,* 23.

15. Wood, *Lynching and Spectacle,* 2; James Allen, *Without Sanctuary: Lynching Photography in America* (Santa Fe: Twin Palms Publishers, 2000); Dora Apel, *Imagery of Lynching: Black Men, White Women, and the Mob* (New Brunswick: Rutgers University Press, 2004); Apel and Shawn Michelle Smith, *Lynching Photographs* (Berkeley: University of California Press, 2007).

16. Tolnay and Beck, *A Festival of Violence.* For more on Ida B. Wells, see Patricia A. Schechter, *Ida B. Wells-Barnett and American Reform, 1880–1930* (Chapel Hill: University of North Carolina Press, 2001); James West Davidson, *"They Say": Ida B. Wells and the Reconstruction of Race* (New York: Oxford University Press, 2007); Rebecca N. Hill, *Men, Mobs, and Law: Anti-Lynching and Labor Defense in U.S. Radical History* (Durham: Duke University Press, 2008); Mia Bay, *To Tell the Truth Freely: The Life of Ida B. Wells* (New York: Hill and Wang, 2009); Feimster, *Southern Horrors;* Sarah L. Silkey, *Black Woman Reformer: Ida B. Wells, Lynching, and Transatlantic Activism* (Athens: University of Georgia Press, 2015).

17. Tolnay and Beck, *A Festival of Violence,* 28. For more on the NAACP, see Zangrando, *The NAACP Crusade Against Lynching;* Merline Pitre, *In Struggle against Jim Crow: Lulu B. White and the NAACP, 1900–1957* (College Station: Texas A&M University Press, 1999); Patricia Bernstein, *The First Waco Horror:*

rights organizations. According to Kidada E. Williams in *They Left Great Marks on Me* (2012), African Americans' efforts to share their stories "constitutes an underappreciated form of resistance to white supremacy." Antilynching campaigns eventually drew national and international attention to racial violence. Riots, such as the one that left more than two dozen black people dead in Atlanta in 1906, inspired many southern Progressives to denounce white mob violence.[18] Although southern Democrats in the United States Senate ensured that no antilynching law made it through Congress, state legislatures began passing antilynching laws. By the mid-1930s, lynching declined, although blacks continued to find themselves disproportionately targeted by legal justice systems.[19] The history of lynching reveals the extremes to which white southerners went to perpetuate hierarchies of race and power; the fact that they believed such violence was necessary demonstrates the ultimate instability of those hierarchies.

Although many historians have analyzed the New South through the lens of race, they have tended to view "race" as comprising only two categories. As George Brown Tindall argued in *Natives and Newcomers* (1995), "in the two centuries after the American Revolution, relatively few immigrants came south, the Indian population was largely expelled, and the South became that part of the country where the melting pot worked best. Out of the crucibles of the South, two new ethnic groups emerged: white and black." Yet, even as white southerners endeavored to reduce people into these deceptively simplistic categories, southern identities remained far more complex. Southern and eastern European immigrants, as well as Native Americans, Mexicans, and Asians all confounded the color line.[20]

Southern historians have increasingly recognized how other ethnicities con-

---

The Lynching of Jesse Washington and the Rise of the NAACP (College Station: Texas A&M University Press, 2005); Kevern Verney and Lee Sartain, eds., *Long Is the Way and Hard: One Hundred Years of the NAACP* (Fayetteville: University of Arkansas Press, 2009).

18. Kidada E. Williams, *They Left Great Marks on Me: African American Testimonies of Racial Violence from Emancipation to World War I* (New York: New York University Press, 2012), 3; Feimster, *Southern Horrors.* See also Tameka Bradley Hobbs, *Democracy Abroad, Lynching at Home: Racial Violence in Florida* (Gainesville: University Press of Florida, 2015); Bruce E. Baker, *This Mob Will Surely Take My Life: Lynchings in the Carolinas, 1871–1947* (New York: Continuum, 2008).

19. Feimster, *Southern Horrors;* Wright, *Racial Violence in Kentucky, 1865–1940.* See also Pfeifer, *The Roots of Rough Justice;* Bailey and Tolnay, *Lynched.*

20. George Brown Tindall, *Natives and Newcomers: Ethnic Southerners and Southern Ethnics* (Athens: University of Georgia Press, 1995), xii; Stephanie Cole and Alison M. Parker, eds., *Beyond Black and White: Race, Ethnicity, and Gender in the U.S. South and Southwest* (College Station: Texas A&M University Press, 2004).

tributed to the region's racial constructions and reconstructions. Some southern and eastern European immigrants, including Jewish individuals, pursued whiteness through assimilation. By changing their names, joining white fraternal organizations, participating in civic life, downplaying religious differences, succeeding economically, and joining in antiblack violence, they demonstrated their belonging to white southern societies.[21] As Cynthia Skove Nevels demonstrated in *Lynching to Belong* (2007), Italian, Irish, and Bohemian immigrants in Brazos County, Texas, actively participated in the lynching of black men in the 1890s to prove their "whiteness." Yet whiteness could be elusive. The 1915 slaying of Jewish factory manager Leo Frank in Marietta, Georgia, exposed how Jews could face persecutions similar to those of African Americans. Although many southern rabbis advocated for social justice and condemned the brutality of the Ku Klux Klan, their congregations often preferred more conservative stances that avoided unwanted attention. Black-Jewish relations thus remained in flux throughout the twentieth century.[22]

21. For more on these ethnic European immigrants in the South, see Bryan Albin Giemza, ed., *Rethinking the Irish in the American South: Beyond Rounders and Reelers* (Jackson: University Press of Mississippi, 2013); A. V. Margavio and Jerome J. Salomone, *Bread and Respect: The Italians of Louisiana* (Gretna, LA: Pelican Publishing, 2002); Paul V. Canonici, *The Delta Italians: Their Pursuit of "The Better Life" and Their Struggle Against Mosquitos, Floods, and Prejudice* (Madison, MS: Calo Creative Designs, 2003); Gary Ross Mormino, *Immigrants on the Hill: Italian-Americans in St. Louis, 1882–1982* (Urbana: University of Illinois Press, 1986); Lazar Odzak, *"Demetrios Is Now Jimmy": Greek Immigrants in the Southern United States, 1895–1965* (Durham: Monograph Publishers, 2006); Gary Ross Mormino and George E. Pozzetta, *The Immigrant World of Ybor City: Italians and Their Latin Neighbors in Tampa, 1885–1985* (Urbana: University of Illinois Press, 1987); Steven Hertzberg, *Strangers within the Gate City: The Jews of Atlanta, 1845–1915* (Philadelphia: Jewish Publication Society of America, 1978); Selma S. Lewis, *A Biblical People in the Bible Belt: The Jewish Community of Memphis, Tennessee, 1840s–1960s* (Macon: Mercer University Press, 1998); Wendy Lowe Besmann, *A Separate Circle: Jewish Life in Knoxville, Tennessee* (Knoxville: University of Tennessee Press, 2001); Leonard Rogoff, *Homelands: Southern Jewish Identity in Durham and Chapel Hill, North Carolina* (Tuscaloosa: University of Alabama Press, 2001); Deborah R. Weiner, *Coalfield Jews: An Appalachian History* (Urbana: University of Illinois Press, 2006); Lee Shai Weissbach, *Jewish Life in Small-Town America: A History* (New Haven: Yale University Press, 2005); Mark Cowett, *Birmingham's Rabbi: Morris Newfield and Alabama, 1895–1940* (Tuscaloosa: University of Alabama Press, 1986); Bobbie Malone, *Rabbi Max Heller: Reformer, Zionist, Southerner, 1860–1929* (Tuscaloosa: University of Alabama Press, 1997); Henry Cohen II, *Kindler of Souls: Rabbi Henry Cohen of Texas* (Austin: University of Texas Press, 2007); Louis D. Rubin Jr., *My Father's People: A Family of Southern Jews* (Baton Rouge: Louisiana State University Press, 2002); Eliza R. L. McGraw, *Two Covenants: Representations of Southern Jewishness* (Baton Rouge: Louisiana State University Press, 2005).

22. Cynthia Skove Nevels, *Lynching to Belong: Claiming Whiteness through Racial Violence* (College Station: Texas A&M University Press, 2007); Mark K. Bauman and Berkley Kalin, eds., *The Quiet Voices:*

Many ethnic Europeans eventually claimed whiteness, but other groups found it impossible—as well as undesirable—to conform to Jim Crow's black-white dichotomy. American Indians insisted not only on a separate racial identity but also on recognition of their political status as citizens of sovereign nations. Although most histories of the Native South end with the forced removals of the 1830s and 1840s, scholars increasingly have acknowledged that Indians did not disappear following the Trail of Tears. Remnant populations of removed nations as well as dozens of other, smaller groups stayed in the South where they rebuilt communities, resisted dispossession, and rejected efforts to classify them as "colored."[23] Indians battled racial reclassification in various ways. Some replicated white attitudes towards African Americans, refused to use "colored" amenities, and insisted upon the creation of their own segregated institutions. As Malinda Maynor Lowery demonstrated in *Lumbee Indians in the Jim Crow South* (2010), Indians in Robeson County, North Carolina, persuaded state legislators to recog-

---

Southern Rabbis and Black Civil Rights, 1880s to 1990s (Tuscaloosa: University of Alabama Press, 1997); Jeffrey Melnick, *Black-Jewish Relations on Trial: Leo Frank and Jim Conley in the New South* (Jackson: University Press of Mississippi, 2000); Micah D. Greenstein and Howard Greenstein, "'Then and Now': Southern Rabbis and Civil Rights," in Bauman and Kalin, eds., *The Quiet Voices*, 325–37.

23. For an overview of Indians in the postremoval South, see Theda Perdue, "The Legacy of Indian Removal," *Journal of Southern History* 78 (February 2012): 3–36. For more on southern Indian nations, see John R. Finger, *The Eastern Band of Cherokees, 1819–1900* (Knoxville: University of Tennessee Press, 1984); Harry A. Kersey Jr., *Pelts, Plumes, and Hides: White Traders among the Seminole Indians, 1870–1930* (Gainesville: University Presses of Florida, 1975); Kersey, *The Florida Seminoles and the New Deal, 1933–1942* (Boca Raton: Florida Atlantic University Press, 1989); Kersey, *An Assumption of Sovereignty: Social and Political Transformation among the Florida Seminoles, 1953–1979* (Lincoln: University of Nebraska Press, 1996); Mark Edwin Miller, *Claiming Tribal Identity: The Five Tribes and the Politics of Federal Acknowledgment* (Norman: University of Oklahoma Press, 2013); Katherine M. B. Osburn, *Choctaw Resurgence in Mississippi: Race, Class, and Nation Building in the Jim Crow South, 1830–1977* (Lincoln: University of Nebraska Press, 2014); Samuel J. Wells and Roseanna Tubby, eds., *After Removal: The Choctaw in Mississippi* (Jackson: University Press of Mississippi, 1986); Clara Sue Kidwell, *Choctaws and Missionaries in Mississippi, 1818–1918* (Norman: University of Oklahoma Press, 1995); Helen C. Rountree, *Pocahontas's People: The Powhatan Indians of Virginia Through Four Centuries* (Norman: University of Oklahoma Press, 1990); Gerald M. Sider, *Lumbee Indian Histories: Race, Ethnicity, and Indian Identity in the Southern United States* (New York: Cambridge University Press, 1993); Malinda Maynor Lowery, *Lumbee Indians in the Jim Crow South: Race, Identity, and the Making of a Nation* (Chapel Hill: University of North Carolina Press, 2010); Christopher Arris Oakley, *Keeping the Circle: American Indian Identity in Eastern North Carolina, 1885–2004* (Lincoln: University of Nebraska Press, 2005); Daniel H. Usner, *Weaving Alliances with Other Women: Chitimacha Indian Work in the New South* (Athens: University of Georgia Press, 2015); Jonathan B. Hook, *The Alabama-Coushatta Indians* (College Station: Texas A&M University Press, 1997).

nize them as a tribe with rights to separate schools and churches. Many southern Indians refused to marry black people since they feared that intermarriage would cast doubt on their own racial identity. Yet as Mikaëla M. Adams argued in *Who Belongs?* (2016), even though race influenced how southern Indians determined tribal citizenship, the ways that they constructed race depended on their own cultural conceptions of belonging.[24] In addition to devising solutions to the problem of race, some southern Indians forged alliances with friendly whites. As Daniel H. Usner demonstrated in *Weaving Alliances with Other Women* (2015), Chitimacha basket weavers in Louisiana deployed innovative networking strategies with white women not only to sell their wares but also to challenge white domination. At the heart of southern Indians' struggle during the early twentieth century was an effort to preserve their tribal sovereignty. As Katherine M. B. Osburn argued in *Choctaw Resurgence in Mississippi* (2014), Indians appealed to the federal government for legal recognition of their citizenship in tribal nations.[25] Their determination to maintain a separate identity in the New South challenged the region's biracial order.

Latinx Americans, especially those of Mexican descent, also complicated race-making. In addition to people of Spanish descent who had inhabited borderlands regions like Texas since colonial times, a new wave of Mexican migrants arrived in the South following the outbreak of the Mexican Revolution in 1910.[26] White employers eagerly exploited Mexican laborers, whom they believed easier to control than black workers. Whites were unwilling, however, to afford Mexicans racial parity, characterizing all Latinx Americans—even those born in the United States—as "Mexican," and thus "foreign." As Neil Foley argued in *The White Scourge* (1997), most white southerners "regarded Mexicans as a 'mongrelized' race of Indian, African, and Spanish ancestry." Mexicans responded by building

24. Lowery, *Lumbee Indians in the Jim Crow South;* Mikaëla M. Adams, *Who Belongs? Race, Resources, and Tribal Citizenship in the Native South* (New York: Oxford University Press, 2016).

25. Usner, *Weaving Alliances with Other Women;* Osburn, *Choctaw Resurgence in Mississippi.*

26. Arnoldo de León, *Ethnicity in the Sunbelt: A History of Mexican Americans in Houston* (Houston: University of Houston Mexican American Studies Program, 1989), 3. See also David Montejano, *Anglos and Mexicans in the Making of Texas, 1836–1896* (Austin: University of Texas Press, 1987); Neil Foley, *The White Scourge: Mexicans, Blacks, and Poor Whites in Texas Cotton Culture* (Berkeley: University of California Press, 1997); Roberto R. Calderón, *Mexican Coal Mining Labor in Texas and Coahuila, 1880–1930* (College Station: Texas A&M University Press, 2000); Emilio Zamora, *The World of the Mexican Worker in Texas* (College Station: Texas A&M University Press, 1993); Julie M. Weise, *Corazón de Dixie: Mexicanos in the U.S. South since 1910* (Chapel Hill: University of North Carolina Press, 2015).

their own schools, churches, and mutual aid and fraternal insurance companies. They also brought their own ideas of race to the South, including popular conceptions in Mexico that "focused on cultural traits far more than biological inheritance." As Julie M. Weise demonstrated in *Corazón de Dixie* (2015), some Mexican migrants also used the political power of the post-revolutionary Mexican state to pressure white schools in the American South to accept their children.[27]

People of Asian descent also challenged the emerging biracial order of the New South. As scholars such as James W. Loewen, Lucy M. Cohen, and Moon-Ho Jung demonstrated, Lower South planters actively recruited "coolie" workers to alleviate postbellum labor shortages. Many Chinese eventually abandoned agricultural work and became merchants and grocers.[28] By the 1880s, Bengali Muslim peddlers also made their way to the South where they took advantage of Americans' growing interest in "the Orient" to sell "exotic" goods. Although restrictive immigration laws kept Asian populations in the South low, scholars including Khyati Y. Joshi and Jigna Desai argued that "the *figure* of the Chinese and Indian coolie has been essential for the discourses of freedom and race." Americans debated, for example, whether the recruitment of "coolies" represented an illegal revival of the slave trade or whether Chinese workers were "voluntary immigrants."[29] The presence of Asian migrants vexed white southerners who, Leslie Bow argued in *Partly Colored* (2010), turned to "creative interpretations of Jim Crow etiquette" to make sense of these populations. Asians did their best to navigate segregation's black-white dichotomy, in some cases by rejecting associations with African Americans and emphasizing their cultural similarities to whites. Even so, in contrast to European immigrants who achieved "whiteness,"

27. Foley, *The White Scourge*, 5; De León, *Ethnicity in the Sunbelt*; Weise, *Corazón de Dixie*. See also Roberto R. Treviño, *The Church in the Barrio: Mexican American Ethno-Catholicism in Houston* (Chapel Hill: University of North Carolina Press, 2006); Benjamin Heber Johnson, *Revolution in Texas: How a Forgotten Rebellion and Its Bloody Suppression Turned Mexicans into Americans* (New Haven: Yale University Press, 2005).

28. James W. Loewen, *The Mississippi Chinese: Between Black and White* (Cambridge: Harvard University Press, 1971); Lucy M. Cohen, *Chinese in the Post–Civil War South: A People without a History* (Baton Rouge: Louisiana State University Press, 1984); Moon-Ho Jung, *Coolies and Cane: Race, Labor, and Sugar in the Age of Emancipation* (Baltimore: Johns Hopkins University Press, 2006).

29. Vivek Bald, *Bengali Harlem and the Lost Histories of South Asian America* (Cambridge: Harvard University Press, 2013); Khyati Y. Joshi and Jigna Desai, eds., *Asian Americans in Dixie: Race and Migration in the South* (Urbana: University of Illinois Press, 2013), 2; Jung, *Coolies and Cane*. See also Raymond A. Mohl, John E. Van Sant, and Chizuru Saeki, eds., *Far East, Down South: Asians in the American South* (Tuscaloosa: University of Alabama Press, 2016).

Asians could achieve just "near-whiteness." Whites defined them as distant from the dominant culture and therefore as inconsequential to the region's black-white paradigm. Like Mexicans, Asians became "foreigners," while Native Americans lived beyond "civilization." But Asians, Mexicans, and Native peoples were not beyond the South's social formations. Their presence complicated southern governance and cultural practices. As Bow contended, nonwhite/nonblack peoples highlighted the "contradictions and irrationalities at the heart of white supremacist thought."[30]

Questions of race-making also complicated histories of economics and labor. For some time, historians studying the southern economy in the late 1800s and early 1900s divided over the reasons for widespread poverty and dependence in the region. Some argued that the South took a "Prussian Road" to industrialization, in which planters, industrialists, and governments devised and enforced an economic and legal system to keep workers poorly paid and with few options. Others argued that sharecropping, tenancy, and poorly paying domestic and industrial labor emerged from market forces, even as people with power held most of the advantages.[31]

In an important change in scholarship since the 1980s, many historians turned away from a distinction between a form of economic history that explains power structures as part of economic forces and a form of labor history that details the labor and activism of working people. Instead, labor histories and economic histories are part of the same story and, significantly, many scholars incorporated issues of race and gender into scholarship on both workers and employers.

Who controlled the land and its use became a prominent historiographical question in 1986 when Gavin Wright distinguished between the *labor* lords of the antebellum period and the *land* lords of the postbellum South, arguing that wealthy southerners who had long invested in enslaved labor sought new ways to profit from the land. They turned to timbering, mining, and profit-generating cash crops. Large landowners relied on what Jeannie Whayne called "a fiction of

30. Leslie Bow, *Partly Colored: Asian Americans and Racial Anomaly in the Segregated South* (New York: New York University Press, 2010), 5; Jung, *Coolies and Cane.*

31. For discussions of this scholarship, see James C. Cobb, "Beyond Planters and Industrialists: A New Perspective on the New South," *Journal of Southern History* 54 (February 1988): 45–68; Harold D. Woodman, "Economic Reconstruction and the Rise of the New South, 1865–1900," in *Interpreting Southern History: Historiographical Essays in Honor of Sanford W. Higginbotham,* ed. John B. Boles and Evelyn Thomas Nolen (Baton Rouge: Louisiana State University Press, 1987), 254–307.

partnership" with workers clearing land for productive possibilities.[32] Cotton, memorialized in songs and movies as the crop of the antebellum South, became far more prominent in New South agriculture. It was the cash crop that bought goods and paid off debts, while corn and hogs declined in economic significance. Antebellum southerners had let branded livestock run wild and had assumed they could hunt and fish just about anywhere. By the late nineteenth century, however, southerners faced fenced-in properties, the diminishment of common lands, and laws that restricted access to good hunting and fishing. Southerners who once lived in relative self-sufficiency turned to cash crops, credit relations with local merchants, and dependence on market demand. In Appalachia, many landowners sold mineral rights to their land, often suffering dire, unexpected consequences.[33] The pursuit of greater production, whether in mining, farming, timber, or livestock, commanded the attention of southern governments and colleges by the early twentieth century. Welcoming investment, seeking markets, and increasing agricultural and industrial efficiency became central to virtually any discussions of state-sponsored New South progress.[34]

Sharecropping and tenancy became prominent forms of agricultural control over land and labor. Sharecropping developed as a way for landowners to secure a full year's crop from laborers, particularly African Americans but also whites who had little to offer other than field work. It soon forced workers into long-term dependency, sometimes through crop liens and peonage, sometimes by limiting other work opportunities. As James C. Cobb detailed in *The Most Southern Place on Earth* (1992), numerous African Americans who moved to the Mississippi Delta hoping to own land eventually became workers in a "New South Plantation Kingdom" owned by extremely wealthy white landowners. In *American Congo*

32. Gavin Wright, *Old South, New South: Revolutions in the Southern Economy since the Civil War* (New York: Basic Books, 1986); Jeannie M. Whayne, *A New Plantation South: Land, Labor, and Federal Favor in Twentieth-Century Arkansas* (Charlottesville: University Press of Virginia, 1996), 6.

33. Steven Hahn, *The Roots of Southern Populism: Yeoman Farmers and the Transformation of the Georgia Upcountry, 1850–1900* (New York: Oxford University Press, 1983); Charles L. Flynn Jr., *White Land, Black Labor: Caste and Class in Late Nineteenth-Century Georgia* (Baton Rouge: Louisiana State University Press, 1983); Scott E. Giltner, *Hunting and Fishing in the New South: Black Labor and White Leisure after the Civil War* (Baltimore: Johns Hopkins University Press, 2008); Ronald D. Eller, *Miners, Millhands, and Mountaineers: Industrialization of the Appalachian South, 1880–1930* (Knoxville: University of Tennessee Press, 1982).

34. Pete Daniel, *Breaking the Land: The Transformation of Cotton, Tobacco, and Rice Cultures since 1880* (Urbana: University of Illinois Press, 1985); Jack Temple Kirby, *Rural Worlds Lost: The American South, 1920–1960* (Baton Rouge: Louisiana State University Press, 1987).

(2003), Nan Elizabeth Woodruff told the stories of timber workers and agricultural workers in Mississippi and Arkansas who faced similar poor pay, limited options, and potential violence.[35]

Still, some African Americans managed to become landowners. As Loren Schweninger showed in *Black Property Owners in the South* (1990), the percentage of black households owning farmland increased from about 2 percent in 1870 to about 20 percent in 1910.[36] But large landowners benefited most, making the economic decisions, controlling state and local governments, and profiting from national and global markets.

Industrial development accompanied agricultural innovation in exploiting southern laborers, particularly African Americans. As David L. Carlton demonstrated, most construction, timber, mining, coal, and steel production relied on the backs of men in extractive industries, and textile mills required the hands of men, women, and children. Carlton portrayed tobacco processing and furniture industries as exceptional in that they offered opportunities for laborers to improve economic conditions in multiple ways, but most southern industries did little to help workers develop new skills or achieve middle-class jobs.[37] Historians have detailed the disheartening stories of those who worked in lumber, iron and steel, textiles, mines, and railroads with great sympathy for the workers and the everyday challenges they faced.[38] With so many poorly paid workers indebted

35. James C. Cobb, *The Most Southern Place on Earth: The Mississippi Delta and the Roots of Regional Identity* (New York: Oxford University Press, 1992), 98; Nan Elizabeth Woodruff, *American Congo: The African American Freedom Struggle in the Delta* (Cambridge: Harvard University Press, 2003). See also Gerald D. Jaynes, *Branches without Roots: Genesis of the Black Working Class in the American South, 1862–1882* (New York: Oxford University Press, 1986); Edward Cary Royce, *The Origins of Southern Sharecropping* (Philadelphia: Temple University Press, 1993); Daniel, *Breaking the Land;* J. William Harris, *Deep Souths: Delta, Piedmont, and Sea Island Society in the Age of Segregation* (Baltimore: Johns Hopkins University Press, 2001).

36. Loren Schweninger, *Black Property Owners in the South, 1790–1915* (Urbana: University of Illinois Press, 1990).

37. David L. Carlton, "The Revolution from Above: The National Market and the Beginnings of Industrialization in North Carolina," in *The South, the Nation, and the World: Perspectives on Economic Development,* ed. David L. Carlton and Peter A. Coclanis (Charlottesville: University of Virginia Press, 2003), 73–98.

38. William P. Jones, *The Tribe of Black Ulysses: African American Lumber Workers in the Jim Crow South* (Urbana: University of Illinois Press, 2005); Mark Fannin, *Labor's Promised Land: Radical Visions of Gender, Race, and Religion in the South* (Knoxville: University of Tennessee Press, 2003); Henry M. McKiven Jr., *Iron and Steel: Class, Race, and Community in Birmingham, Alabama, 1875–1920* (Chapel Hill: University of North Carolina Press, 1995); Jacquelyn Dowd Hall et al., *Like a Family: The Making of a Southern Cotton Mill World* (Chapel Hill: University of North Carolina Press, 1987); Bryant Simon,

at company stores or struggling to survive until the end of cottonpicking season, the southern economy did not encourage consumer pleasures that were popular in many parts of the country and contributed to social and racial intermingling. Instead, in the South, popular entertainments tended to reinforce and sometimes intensify social divisions.[39]

By far the most common paid employment for African American women was domestic labor, described by Rebecca Sharpless as "cooking in other women's kitchens." Domestic workers, as Tera W. Hunter explained in her 1997 study of Atlanta, "creatively maneuvered gainful labor patterns, demonstrating an acute awareness of the limits of continuous, grossly underpaid labor." In 1881, over three thousand Atlanta laundresses formed a trade union, the Washing Society of Atlanta, to seek higher pay and autonomy over their work. They boldly went on strike simultaneously with the great Cotton Exposition of 1881, both to publicize their grievances and to contest the exposition's claims that New South progress benefited all southerners.[40]

Studies of southern labor evidenced the discursive turn in southern historiography by shifting from discussions of tradition to analyses of discourse. For example, although previous historians concluded that southern white men avoided working for others because they aspired to economic independence, late twentieth-century historians increasingly turned to the discourse about independence to uncover claims for specific white male privileges. As Wayne Flynt

---

A Fabric of Defeat: The Politics of South Carolina Millhands, 1910–1948 (Chapel Hill: University of North Carolina Press, 1998); I. A. Newby, *Plain Folk in the New South: Social Change and Cultural Persistence, 1880–1915* (Baton Rouge: Louisiana State University Press, 1989); Eller, *Miners, Millhands, and Mountaineers;* Eric Arnesen, *Brotherhoods of Color: Black Railroad Workers and the Struggle for Equality* (Cambridge: Harvard University Press, 2001); Jack Santino, *Miles of Smiles, Years of Struggle: Stories of Black Pullman Porters* (Urbana: University of Illinois Press, 1989); Melinda Chateauvert, *Marching Together: Women of the Brotherhood of Sleeping Car Porters* (Urbana: University of Illinois Press, 1998).

39. Ted Ownby, *American Dreams in Mississippi: Consumers, Poverty, and Culture, 1830–1998* (Chapel Hill: University of North Carolina Press, 1999); Robert E. Weems Jr., *Desegregating the Dollar: African American Consumerism in the Twentieth Century* (New York: New York University Press, 1998); Hale, *Making Whiteness;* Gregory J. Renoff, *The Big Tent: The Traveling Circus in Georgia, 1820–1930* (Athens: University of Georgia Press, 2008).

40. Rebecca Sharpless, *Cooking in Other Women's Kitchens: Domestic Workers in the South, 1865–1960* (Chapel Hill: University of North Carolina Press, 2010); Tera W. Hunter, *To 'Joy My Freedom: Southern Black Women's Lives and Labors after the Civil War* (Cambridge: Harvard University Press, 1997), 28; Thavolia Glymph, *Out of the House of Bondage: The Transformation of the Plantation Household* (New York: Cambridge University Press, 2008).

wrote in *Poor but Proud* (1989), "above all else poor whites maintained a culture based on race" that connected them to wealthier and more powerful white men and separated them from all people, especially African Americans, whom they perceived as dependent workers. White male farmers in Texas feared that becoming poor and dependent made them comparable to Mexican workers who they assumed would always labor as agricultural employees. Ironically, as white men rejected such labor, their decisions forced white women into what had long been considered men's work. As a recurring theme in the discourse of economic independence, race became a central consideration in southern employment. Steel employers in Alabama claimed black men did not have industrial skills; Carolina textile mills offered jobs for whites only, in part to clarify that white women would not be working next to African Americans. When reformers sought to limit child labor in the textile mills, they made clear that their arguments related only to white children. The discourse about African American labor had its own set of assumptions. Black railroad porters enjoyed a great deal of mobility and relatively high wages, but they had to play roles that fit white customers' expectations of polite servility.[41]

Working people protested, organized, and found numerous creative forms of resistance. Sleeping car porters, laundresses, miners, timber workers, sharecroppers, steel workers, factory workers, and small farmers formed organizations, unions, and cooperatives and in many other ways struggled for respect. Tracy Campbell detailed how tobacco farmers' protests drew attention, not as labor activism but as manifestations of premodern feuding. Other laborers, appealing to what Jarod Roll called "the reciprocal cross-currents of Socialism and Pentecostalism," had their messages lost in the language of religion.[42] Many movements did not succeed. Political and military opposition crushed some. Scholars detailed violence against protesting cigar workers in Tampa, textile workers in Tennessee, and agricultural workers in Arkansas, Mississippi, and Texas. Some protests failed when potential coalitions did not form or persist. Working-class

41. Wayne Flynt, *Poor but Proud: Alabama's Poor Whites* (Tuscaloosa: University of Alabama Press, 1989), 212; Foley, *The White Scourge;* McKiven, *Iron and Steel;* Hall et al., *Like a Family;* Shelley Sallee, *The Whiteness of Child Labor Reform in the New South* (Athens: University of Georgia Press, 2004); Santino, *Miles of Smiles, Years of Struggle;* Chateauvert, *Marching Together.*

42. Tracy Campbell, *The Politics of Despair: Power and Resistance in the Tobacco Wars* (Lexington: University Press of Kentucky, 1993); Jarod Roll, *Spirit of Rebellion: Labor and Religion in the New Cotton South* (Urbana: University of Illinois Press, 2010), 29.

whites' use of race to define themselves and others inhibited opportunities to build broader labor coalitions, despite Communist efforts to call for a brotherhood of all working people that cut across racial lines.[43]

Scholars reached no grand conclusions about worker activism in the New South, but as a group they have shown the extraordinary amount of activism and the creative forms it often took. Some historians concentrated on what did *not* happen—a movement toward a class-based crusade that could have overcome divisions based on race. Others framed the era as background to major changes in worker organizing, economics, and government during the 1930s. Still, even without a synthesis, book by book and article by article, historians revealed the New South as marked by extraordinary worker ferment and experimentation.

As in economic history, scholars of southern politics moved beyond the traditional questions of who was and was not part of the political process, who was in charge, and what government did and failed to do.[44] On the whole, such scholarship detailed and evaluated the actions of white men. Notably, much of the best scholarship abandoned those questions, studying instead people who could not vote and political action that went far beyond electoral politics and legislation.

In *A Nation under Our Feet* (2003), Steven Hahn analyzed paramilitary politics, colonization efforts, the possibilities of voting and governing, the contemporaneous rise of populism and lynching, and the migrations of the late 1910s. In Hahn's view, all reflected southern political life. In *Emancipation Betrayed* (2005), Paul Ortiz demonstrated how black Floridians politicized their mutual aid societies to reestablish their voting rights. Although the story ended with the bloodiest election day in twentieth-century American history, Ortiz highlighted the many ways that African Americans expanded the idea of political freedom. Elsa Barkley Brown and Robin D. G. Kelley showed that studying resistance politics

43. Simon, *A Fabric of Defeat;* Glenda Elizabeth Gilmore, *Defying Dixie: The Radical Roots of Civil Rights, 1919–1950* (New York: W. W. Norton, 2008).

44. See Richard L. Watson, "From Populism Through the New Deal: Southern Political History," in Boles and Nolen, eds., *Interpreting Southern History,* 308–89. See also the essays in John B. Boles and Bethany L. Johnson, eds., *"Origins of the New South" Fifty Years Later: The Continuing Influence of a Historical Classic* (Baton Rouge: Louisiana State University Press, 2003), esp. Sheldon Hackney, "*Origins of the New South* in Retrospect" (25–49); Hackney, "*Origins of the New South* in Retrospect, Thirty Years Later" (50–58); Carl V. Harris, "Right Fork or Left Fork? The Section-Party Alignments of Southern Democrats in Congress, 1873–1897" (59–95); Harris, "Redeemers versus Agrarians?" (96–108); James Tice Moore, "Redeemers Reconsidered: Change and Continuity in the Democratic South, 1870–1900" (109–30); and Moore, "The Historical Context for 'Redeemers Reconsidered'" (131–43).

means studying countless ways, obvious and subtle, that working people resisted, undermined, and circumvented the problems of the New South.[45] One work in religious history that influenced scholars far beyond that field is Evelyn Brooks Higginbotham's *Righteous Discontent* (1993). In her final chapter, "The Politics of Respectability," Higginbotham coined a term for uplift, organizing, and personal behavior as both a critique of racist imagery and a strategy for leadership.[46]

Some historians continued to interpret southern political history through more traditional methods, to great effect. Michael Perman's *Struggle for Mastery* (2001) analyzed the political, legal, and constitutional processes of disfranchisement from 1888 to 1908. Demonstrating that black disfranchisement was the goal of multiple groups and came from many directions, Perman traced the intricacies of disfranchisement as southern state governments found ways to make it virtually impossible for African Americans to register to vote.[47]

The Populist movement long seemed crucial to scholarship on southern history, because of both the movement's language about Jeffersonian roots of farm life and the questions it raised about the potential for interracial coalitions. C. Vann Woodward's 1938 analysis of Tom Watson's transformation from profarmer politics that included interracial political coalition to white supremacy epitomized both the potential and failures of the era.[48] For many historians, however, Populism no longer seemed so central to southern history. In *The Populist Vision* (2007), Charles Postel minimized southern Populism, contextualizing it

45. Steven Hahn, *A Nation under Our Feet: Black Political Struggles in the Rural South from Slavery to the Great Migration* (Cambridge: Harvard University Press, 2003); Paul Ortiz, *Emancipation Betrayed: The Hidden History of Black Organizing and White Violence in Florida from Reconstruction to the Bloody Election of 1920* (Berkeley: University of California Press, 2005); Robin D. G. Kelley, *Race Rebels: Culture, Politics, and the Black Working Class* (New York: Free Press, 1994); Elsa Barkley Brown, "To Catch the Vision of Freedom: Reconstructing Southern Black Women's Political History, 1865–1885," in *African American Women and the Vote, 1837–1965*, ed. Ann D. Gordon and Bettye Collier-Thomas (Amherst: University of Massachusetts Press, 1997), 66–99.

46. Evelyn Brooks Higginbotham, *Righteous Discontent: The Women's Movement in the Black Baptist Church, 1880–1920* (Cambridge: Harvard University Press, 1993).

47. Michael Perman, *Struggle for Mastery: Disfranchisement in the South, 1888–1908* (Chapel Hill: University of North Carolina Press, 2001).

48. C. Vann Woodward, *Tom Watson, Agrarian Rebel* (New York: Macmillan, 1938); Lawrence Goodwyn, *The Populist Moment: A Short History of the Agrarian Revolt in America* (New York: Oxford University Press, 1978); Bruce Palmer, *"Man over Money": The Southern Populist Critique of American Capitalism* (Chapel Hill: University of North Carolina Press, 1980); Hahn, *Roots of Southern Populism.*

within a larger national movement in which farming men and women formed coalitions with labor organizers and urban bohemians. As Postel argued, although the Populist vision offered potential for shared political action among blacks and whites, many African Americans understood it as only one of many strategies for economic reform and political participation. They seldom thought of Populism as an opportunity to supersede issues of race with class unity.[49]

Rather than a singular moment of great opportunity, Populism emerged from scholarship as a complicated story of working people's idealism and of calls for white supremacy. Numerous works detailed extraordinary ferment and creativity, with studies on Populism developing among the Colored Farmers' Alliances, white farmers' groups working with the Knights of Labor, and hill country farmers rejecting planter-dominated Democratic Party policies about credit, taxes, and the purposes of government.[50] If there is an illustrative biography of a southern political figure who represented farmers, it is Stephen Kantrowitz's 2000 study of Ben Tillman. Rather than portraying Tillman as a study of failed possibilities, Kantrowitz tracked ways in which race and gender framed Tillman's ideology and, consequently, South Carolina's political landscape during the Populist era. Tillman, South Carolina governor from 1890 to 1894 and United States

49. Charles Postel, *The Populist Vision* (New York: Oxford University Press, 2007). Robert C. McMath Jr. likewise takes a national approach in *American Populism: A Social History, 1877–1898* (New York: Hill and Wang, 1993).

50. Omar H. Ali, *In the Lion's Mouth: Black Populism in the New South, 1886–1900* (Jackson: University Press of Mississippi, 2010); Matthew Hild, *Greenbackers, Knights of Labor, and Populists: Farmer-Labor Insurgency in the Late-Nineteenth-Century South* (Athens: University of Georgia Press, 2007); Deborah Beckel, *Radical Reform: Interracial Politics in Post-Emancipation North Carolina* (Charlottesville: University of Virginia Press, 2011); James M. Beeby, *Revolt of the Tar Heels: The North Carolina Populist Movement, 1890–1901* (Jackson: University Press of Mississippi, 2008); James M. Beeby, ed., *Populism in the South Revisited: New Interpretations and New Departures* (Jackson: University Press of Mississippi, 2012); Connie L. Lester, *Up from the Mudsills of Hell: The Farmers' Alliance, Populism, and Progressive Agriculture in Tennessee, 1870–1915* (Athens: University of Georgia Press, 2006); Michael R. Hyman, *The Anti-Redeemers: Hill-Country Political Dissenters in the Lower South from Redemption to Populism* (Baton Rouge: Louisiana State University Press, 1990); Samuel L. Webb, *Two-Party Politics in the One-Party South, Alabama's Hill Country, 1874–1920* (Tuscaloosa: University of Alabama Press, 1997); Gregg Cantrell, *Kenneth and John B. Rayner and the Limits of Southern Dissent* (Urbana: University of Illinois Press, 1993); Stephen A. West, *From Yeoman to Redneck in the South Carolina Upcountry, 1850–1915* (Charlottesville: University of Virginia Press, 2008); Glenn Feldman, *The Disfranchisement Myth: Poor Whites and Suffrage Restriction in Alabama* (Athens: University of Georgia Press, 2004).

Senator from 1895 to 1918, argued that meanings of whiteness and maleness excluded not just African American men but white merchants and, significantly, white men who formed political alliances with African Americans.[51]

Just as Populism no longer commands such a central place in southern scholarship, Progressivism seems to attract less excitement than in earlier generations. The big books by Woodward and Tindall emphasized, in Woodward's words, "progressivism—for whites only," an approach Jack Temple Kirby and Dewey W. Grantham generally followed in their works in 1972 and 1983.[52] Since the 1980s, scholars have not spent a great deal of time comparing Populism and Progressivism or debating whether to consider Progressivism as conservative, liberal, or radical, but they have significantly expanded the range of reformers to consider.

William A. Link's *The Paradox of Southern Progressivism* (1992) analyzed the evolution of Progressive reform efforts from locally based to nationally oriented. In trying to address issues of temperance and prohibition, education, health, family and child labor, violence, and women's access to the vote, reformers turned to professional leaders and organizations that rallied attention and focused issues on laws and government programs. A recurring "guerrilla warfare between centralizers and localists," Link argued, created a paradox in which Progressives sought to force their understanding of progress on resistant fellow southerners. In *The Problem South* (2012), Natalie J. Ring thought both nationally and globally about the concept of regional definition, attending more to the discourse of progress and backwardness that framed the South. She drew upon the works of social scientists, philanthropists, and government policy-makers who defined the South as a problem in economics, health, literacy, race, and violence. Ring concluded that "fascination with the 'southern problem' appeared during an era marked by an absolute faith in abundance, progress, and the value of scientific solutions."[53]

51. Stephen Kantrowitz, *Ben Tillman and the Reconstruction of White Supremacy* (Chapel Hill: University of North Carolina Press, 2000). Another important biography of a Populist is James L. Hunt, *Marion Butler and American Populism* (Chapel Hill: University of North Carolina Press, 2003).

52. Woodward, *Origins of the New South*, 369–95; Tindall, *The Emergence of the New South;* Jack Temple Kirby, *Darkness at the Dawning: Race and Reform in the Progressive South* (Philadelphia: Lippincott, 1972); Dewey W. Grantham, *Southern Progressivism: The Reconciliation of Progress and Tradition* (Knoxville: University of Tennessee Press, 1983).

53. William A. Link, *The Paradox of Southern Progressivism, 1880–1930* (Chapel Hill: University of North Carolina Press, 1992), 294; Natalie J. Ring, *The Problem South: Region, Empire, and the New Liberal State, 1880–1930* (Athens: University of Georgia Press, 2012), 8.

As a crucial part of the Progressive movement, women's suffrage exemplifies how the southern narrative complicates any easy notions of progress. Scholarship on women's suffrage in the South began with work by A. Elizabeth Taylor in 1951 and Anne Firor Scott's influential 1972 work, *The Southern Lady.* Scott showed how new authority over homes during the Civil War led to more work outside the home, then to clubs, church organizations, and temperance and prohibition work, culminating in successful demands for the vote. In her 2003 work, *The Reconstruction of White Southern Womanhood,* Jane Turner Censer pointed to the development of "a new domesticity" as an important component of those reforms.[54] In *New Women of the New South* (1993), Marjorie Spruill Wheeler studied eleven southern suffrage leaders, demonstrating how they united as feminists who were "profoundly unhappy with the traditional role of women in the South and impatient for change." In her study of black suffragists, Rosalyn Terborg-Penn similarly showed how African American women's demands for the vote emerged from dissatisfaction with their traditional roles and how they employed club work to address education, temperance, and antiviolence. Race still remained a potent variable, often keeping black and white women from finding common cause. Suffragists faced opposition because, as Anastatia Sims explained, "in the South ideas about gender were inextricably intertwined with ideas about race." Elna C. Green demonstrated that opposition came from different quarters, not only from the rural South but also from textile and railroad leaders who depicted suffragists as feminists challenging all sorts of social structures, from white supremacy to the patriarchal home.[55]

54. A. Elizabeth Taylor, "The Woman Suffrage Movement in Texas," *Journal of Southern History* 17 (May 1951): 194–215; Anne Firor Scott, *The Southern Lady: From Pedestal to Politics, 1830–1930* (Chicago: University of Chicago Press, 1970); Jane Turner Censer, *The Reconstruction of White Southern Womanhood, 1865–1920* (Baton Rouge: Louisiana State University Press, 2003).

55. Marjorie Spruill Wheeler, *New Women of the New South: The Leaders of the Woman Suffrage Movement in the Southern States* (New York: Oxford University Press, 1993), 73; Anastatia Sims, "Beyond the Ballot: The Radical Vision of the Antisuffragists," in *Votes for Women!: The Woman Suffrage Movement in Tennessee, the South, and the Nation,* ed. Marjorie Spruill Wheeler (Knoxville: University of Tennessee Press, 1995), 107; Sims, *The Power of Femininity in the New South: Women's Organizations and Politics in North Carolina, 1880–1930* (Columbia: University of South Carolina Press, 1997); Rosalyn Terborg-Penn, *African American Women in the Struggle for the Vote, 1850–1920* (Bloomington: Indiana University Press, 1998); Elna C. Green, *Southern Strategies: Southern Women and the Woman Suffrage Question* (Chapel Hill: University of North Carolina Press, 1997).

Many important studies of government expansion in the New South analyze specific issues rather than the general concept of progressivism. Education, for example, seems a clear story of progress, with dramatic expansions in literacy, increased school attendance (including those attending high schools and colleges), the movement for grade schools, the consolidation of rural schools into larger schools, increased bureaucracy and oversight, and women's movement into the teaching profession.[56] As scholars such as Heather Andrea Williams and Jennifer Ritterhouse showed, however, a great deal of education—some of it liberating, some of it supporting white supremacy—took place outside schools.[57] Work by Lu Ann Jones, Melissa Walker, and Elizabeth S. D. Engelhardt situated home extension workers as educators who delivered government instruction about women's work, gender, and race to individual homes. Extension workers could be patronizing, with experts idealizing separate spheres and extending new kitchen technologies to the less educated. Lessons were inconsistent between white and black audiences, yet many extension workers listened and learned as they taught, developing new ideas about redefining gender relations and moving off the farm.[58]

For much of the twentieth century, the debate initiated by W. E. B. Du Bois and Booker T. Washington about the objectives of African American schools dominated the historiography of New South education. Scholarship since the 1980s, however, has expanded into definitions of education and issues of school control. James D. Anderson and Adam Fairclough showed how advocates of black education persisted, creatively built schools, and taught in the face of recurring opposition from white political leaders who considered African American education as wasted money. Mary S. Hoffschwelle argued that new school buildings

56. James L. Leloudis, *Schooling the New South: Pedagogy, Self, and Society in North Carolina, 1880–1920* (Chapel Hill: University of North Carolina Press, 1996); William A. Link, *A Hard Country and a Lonely Place: Schooling, Society, and Reform in Rural Virginia, 1870–1920* (Chapel Hill: University of North Carolina Press, 1986); Katherine C. Reynolds and Susan L. Schramm, *A Separate Sisterhood: Women Who Shaped Southern Education in the Progressive Era* (New York: Peter Lang, 2002).

57. Heather Andrea Williams, *Self-Taught: African American Education in Slavery and Freedom* (Chapel Hill: University of North Carolina Press, 2005); Jennifer Ritterhouse, *Growing Up Jim Crow: How Black and White Southern Children Learned Race* (Chapel Hill: University of North Carolina Press, 2006); Kristina DuRocher, *Raising Racists: The Socialization of White Children in the Jim Crow South* (Lexington: University Press of Kentucky, 2011).

58. Lu Ann Jones, *Mama Learned Us to Work: Farm Women in the New South* (Chapel Hill: University of North Carolina Press, 2002); Melissa Walker, *All We Knew Was to Farm: Rural Women in the Upcountry South, 1919–1941* (Baltimore: Johns Hopkins University Press, 2000); Elizabeth S. D. Engelhardt, *A Mess of Greens: Southern Gender and Southern Food* (Athens: University of Georgia Press, 2011).

became crucial public spaces that helped to "subvert the material culture of Jim Crow."[59] Historians also traced the complex terrain of African American schools, ranging from missionary institutions to Tuskegee-style industrial schools to segregated public schools. In 1999, Eric Anderson and Alfred A. Moss Jr. analyzed the challenge facing well-meaning philanthropists who imagined their long-term support for public schools and universities would address the problems facing African Americans: Carnegie, Jeanes, and Rosenwald organizations poured millions of dollars into the South, especially into public schools and teachers' colleges. Although they hoped to alleviate the New South's racial inequalities, their money helped southern state and local governments to perpetuate Jim Crow segregation.[60]

Scholars of the temperance and prohibition movements likewise found it difficult to interpret their topics as signs of progress or embodiments of the Progressive movement. Many emphasized gender. For example, the Women's Christian Temperance Union attempted to minimize the "sinful" good times of the male sphere and aspired instead to a domestic harmony they idealized as part of home life. Other historians pointed to ways that prohibitionists identified their cause with honor and controlling white men's passions. Temperance studies emphasized race as well. Some scholars argued that white prohibitionists targeted African American men as the New South's most inebriated population; others stressed the movement's potential to bring together African American and white reformers. Finally, some scholars interpreted temperance more as a class issue, an attempt to fit new factory workers into industrial routines.[61]

Scholarship on prohibition, suffrage, and education suggests that progressivism continues to be a meaningful concept well into the twenty-first century, but

59. James D. Anderson, *The Education of Blacks in the South, 1860–1935* (Chapel Hill: University of North Carolina Press, 1988); Adam Fairclough, *A Class of Their Own: Black Teachers in the Segregated South* (Cambridge: Harvard University Press, 2007); Mary S. Hoffschwelle, *The Rosenwald Schools of the American South* (Gainesville: University Press of Florida, 2006), 5.

60. Eric Anderson and Alfred A. Moss Jr., *Dangerous Donations: Northern Philanthropy and Southern Black Education, 1902–1930* (Columbia: University of Missouri Press, 1999).

61. On controlling men's behavior, see Ted Ownby, *Subduing Satan: Religion, Recreation, and Manhood in the Rural South, 1865–1920* (Chapel Hill: University of North Carolina Press, 1990); Sims, *The Power of Femininity.* On honor, see James D. Ivy, *No Saloon in the Valley: The Southern Strategy of Texas Prohibitionists in the 1800s* (Waco: Baylor University Press, 2003); Joe L. Coker, *Liquor in the Land of the Lost Cause: Southern White Evangelicals and the Prohibition Movement* (Lexington: University Press of Kentucky, 2007). On interracial prohibition work, see Janette Thomas Greenwood, *Bittersweet Legacy: The Black and White "Better Classes" in Charlotte, 1850–1910* (Chapel Hill: University of North Carolina

only in reference to specific issues. Some reform efforts expanded freedoms for some people, and others created new limitations on individual freedoms. Thus, in an age when the historiography of New South politics has expanded beyond traditional definitions, southern progressivism seems to await a new synthesis.

One difficulty with synthesizing New South progressivism is that, for many years, historians contextualized progress in a region that they considered largely rural, neglecting the study of urban life where reform efforts typically focused.[62] Between the 1980s and 2010s, however, scholars made important inroads into constructing a history of the urban South, one which complicates our understandings of key themes such as progressive reform, as well as economic change, boosterism, modernization, tourism, migration, segregation, and race-making.[63] As Don H. Doyle demonstrated in *New Men, New Cities, New South* (1990), urban development through expanding networks of commerce and tourism helped to transform the New South's economy. Entrepreneurs and boosters forged a new commercial-civic culture in southern cities to attract northern investment, paving the way for the "modern" South.[64] Although elite white men played the

---

Press, 1994); Lee L. Willis, *Southern Prohibition: Race, Reform, and Public Life in Middle Florida, 1821–1920* (Athens: University of Georgia Press, 2011). On expanding the power of government, see Joseph L. Locke, *Making the Bible Belt: Texas Prohibitionists and the Politicization of Southern Religion* (New York: Oxford University Press, 2017).

62. According to the 1900 United States Census, only 17 percent of people living in the South Atlantic states (Delaware, Maryland, Virginia, West Virginia, North Carolina, South Carolina, Georgia, and Florida) and only 11.1 percent of people living in the South Central states (Kentucky, Tennessee, Alabama, Mississippi, Louisiana, Arkansas, Texas, Oklahoma, and "Indian Territory") resided in urban areas of 8,000 people or more. See John William Graves, *Town and Country: Race Relations in an Urban-Rural Context, Arkansas, 1865–1905* (Fayetteville: University of Arkansas Press, 1990), 1; David R. Goldfield, *Region, Race, and Cities: Interpreting the Urban South* (Baton Rouge: Louisiana State University Press, 1997), 1.

63. Among the earliest works to demonstrate the potential of southern urban history were Richard C. Wade's *Slavery in the Cities: The South, 1820–1860* (New York: Oxford University Press, 1964); Blaine A. Brownell's *The Urban Ethos in the South, 1920–1930* (Baton Rouge: Louisiana State University Press, 1975); and David R. Goldfield's *Urban Growth in the Age of Sectionalism: Virginia, 1847–1861* (Baton Rouge: Louisiana State University Press, 1977). Brownell and Goldfield's edited volume, *The City in Southern History: The Growth of Urban Civilization in the South* (Port Washington, NY: Kennikat Press, 1977), encouraged other historians to pursue themes in southern urban history.

64. Don H. Doyle, *New Men, New Cities, New South: Atlanta, Nashville, Charleston, Mobile, 1860–1910* (Chapel Hill: University of North Carolina Press, 1990). For more on urban development and the role of city boosters, see Harold L. Platt, *City Building in the New South: The Growth of Public Services in Houston, Texas, 1830–1910* (Philadelphia: Temple University Press, 1983); James Michael Russell, *Atlanta, 1847–1890: City Building in the Old South and the New* (Baton Rouge: Louisiana State University Press,

most visible roles in this transformation, white women contributed to urban development by forming associations and pushing for reforms that ultimately motivated municipal governments to assume greater social responsibilities.[65] Tourism also contributed to urban growth as business leaders in cities such as Atlanta partnered with local governments to promote the city "as a place to visit and to do business."[66]

In addition to exploring urban growth, scholars investigated the interplay between city and country, as well as the mass migration of rural southerners to the South's urban centers. David R. Goldfield argued in *Cotton Fields and Skyscrapers* (1982) that the context of the rural South shaped the regional distinctiveness of southern cities, including their conservative values, racism, and colonial economic dependence on the North. In contrast, Doyle contended that "cities were the nerve centers of a changing economy and culture that penetrated the rural hinterland and remade the South."[67] Taking a middle ground in *Town and Country* (1990), John William Graves agreed that "cities set the pace and tone," in particular when it came to race relations. "After all," Graves asserted, "many of the traditional objects of segregation—streetcars, hotels, saloons, restaurants, theaters, and public parks, to name a few—were largely nonexistent in rural settings." Yet the racial practices found in southern cities arose in relationship to the racial traditions of the rural South. In *Social Origins of the Urban South* (2003), Louis M. Kyriakoudes argued that the "southern great migration" of tens of millions of rural people to urban areas not only affected the character of southern cities such as Nashville, but that these cities also exerted a "powerful influence . . . over their rural hinterlands." Hard-pressed rural families took advantage of Nash-

---

1988); Robert B. Fairbanks, *For the City as a Whole: Planning, Politics, and the Public Interest in Dallas, Texas, 1900–1965* (Columbus: Ohio State University Press, 1998); Steven J. Hoffman, *Race, Class and Power in the Building of Richmond, 1870–1920* (Jefferson, NC: McFarland, 2004).

65. See Marsha Wedell, *Elite Women and the Reform Impulse in Memphis, 1875–1915* (Knoxville: University of Tennessee Press, 1991); Elizabeth York Enstam, *Women and the Creation of Urban Life: Dallas, Texas, 1843–1920* (College Station: Texas A&M University Press, 1998); Georgina Hickey, *Hope and Danger in the New South City: Working-Class Women and Urban Development in Atlanta, 1890–1940* (Athens: University of Georgia Press, 2003).

66. Harvey K. Newman, *Southern Hospitality: Tourism and the Growth of Atlanta* (Tuscaloosa: University of Alabama Press, 1999), 8; Anthony J. Stanonis, *Creating the Big Easy: New Orleans and the Emergence of Modern Tourism, 1918–1945* (Athens: University of Georgia Press, 2006).

67. David R. Goldfield, *Cotton Fields and Skyscrapers: Southern City and Region, 1607–1980* (Baton Rouge: Louisiana State University Press, 1982); Doyle, *New Men, New Cities, New South*, xiii.

ville's markets to pursue new economic activities in the countryside such as fruit-growing, livestock-raising, and logging. Thousands eventually extended seasonal and circular rural migration patterns to include relocation to Nashville.[68]

Race profoundly influenced urban development as white southerners searched for ways to bring order to urban spaces and to maintain white supremacy. In *Race Relations in the Urban South* (1978), Howard N. Rabinowitz challenged the Woodward thesis that the period from 1865 to 1890 was a time of testing in southern race relations. Rabinowitz documented widespread de facto racial separation in Nashville, Atlanta, Richmond, Montgomery, and Raleigh prior to 1890. According to Rabinowitz, exclusion, not integration, was the obvious "forgotten alternative" to segregation in the urban South. White Republicans initiated de facto segregation as a progressive alternative to racial exclusion and many blacks accepted it for this reason. The Redeemers then accepted and expanded the system once they came into power. In the 1890s, as southern blacks began resisting de facto segregation, southern whites looked for legal ways to enforce it, and de facto segregation became de jure segregation. Other scholars offered a less continuous narrative for racial segregation, interpreting how it developed in fits and starts in southern cities and varied significantly by locale. In *Sorting Out the New South City* (1998), Thomas W. Hanchett argued that "neither segregation by income nor segregation by race has been as constant as we might imagine." Instead, southern cities, including Charlotte, underwent a period of "sorting out" whereby urban spaces where people "of all types lived intermingled" gradually transformed "into a patchwork of well-defined neighborhoods, then into groups of neighborhoods arranged in sectors demarcated by color and class." Once in place, "separation begat separation" as people came to view these divisions as natural.[69]

Scholars of southern cities paid particular attention to how urban environments shaped African Americans' lived experiences. Studies of housing and residential patterns demonstrated ways that segregation created separate and unequal spaces that prevented black southerners from fully participating in urban

68. Graves, *Town and Country,* 2; Louis M. Kyriakoudes, *The Social Origins of the Urban South: Race, Gender, and Migration in Nashville and Middle Tennessee 1890–1930* (Chapel Hill: University of North Carolina Press, 2003), 2. For more on the segregation of restaurants and other eateries in the urban South, see Angela Jill Cooley, *To Live and Dine in Dixie: The Evolution of Urban Food Culture in the Jim Crow South* (Athens: University of Georgia Press, 2015).

69. Howard N. Rabinowitz, *Race Relations in the Urban South, 1865–1890* (New York: Oxford University Press, 1978), 331–33; Thomas W. Hanchett, *Sorting Out the New South City: Race, Class, and Urban Development in Charlotte, 1875–1975* (Chapel Hill: University of North Carolina Press, 1998), 8, 259–60.

economic development. In *Race and the Shaping of Twentieth-Century Atlanta* (1996), Ronald H. Bayor argued that race touched upon "all aspects of city life—politics, housing, street and highway patterns, neighborhood formation, annexation, employment, basic city services, park and recreational space, health care, mass transit development, and schooling." Black Atlantans "pushed, prodded, negotiated, and resisted" racialized urban policies, but as the city grew it became increasingly segregated with long-range and often debilitating consequences.[70]

The segregation of urban space is more complicated than a simple story of whites imposing their will on peoples of color. Scholars including Michael Phillips uncovered the insidious ways that Jim Crow required complicity by many of the very people it oppressed. In *White Metropolis* (2006), Phillips analyzed how, in Dallas, race, gender, and class created divisions between minorities that ultimately served the interests of the white elite. Mexican Americans and ethnic immigrants occupied "an uncomfortable middle ground in the city's racial hierarchy." To achieve even limited positions of power, some nonwhite communities adopted Anglo-American norms and rejected alliances with blacks and even with each other. In *A World More Concrete* (2014), N. D. B. Connolly argued that segregation in Miami "required repeated buy-in from people across the class and color spectrums, trade-off after trade-off, year upon year." White elites developed a profitable system of racially divided real estate through careful land regulation, but they also cultivated "a kind of indirect rule" by encouraging black elites to control black communities. Nonwhite property owners acquiesced out of economic self-interest: they saw property ownership "as a symbol of racial equality and a means for community uplift." Nonetheless, as they accepted the ideal of property ownership, nonwhites also began to view black people, and especially poor black people, as detrimental to property values.[71]

Historians detailed the numerous strategies that black southerners devised to push back against discrimination. In *In Their Own Interests* (1991), Earl Lewis showed not only how African Americans in Norfolk sought to improve materially but also how they "fought for equal treatment, sometimes quietly and sometimes visibly." By shifting focus between advances at work and advances at home, black

70. Ronald H. Bayor, *Race and the Shaping of Twentieth-Century Atlanta* (Chapel Hill: University of North Carolina Press, 1996), xiv, 255. An early example of this work is Robert D. Bullard's *Invisible Houston: The Black Experience in Boom and Bust* (College Station: Texas A&M University Press, 1987).

71. Michael Phillips, *White Metropolis: Race, Ethnicity, and Religion in Dallas, 1841–2001* (Austin: University of Texas Press, 2006), 1, 8; N. D. B. Connolly, *A World More Concrete: Real Estate and the Remaking of Jim Crow South Florida* (Chicago: University of Chicago Press, 2014), 7.

urbanites—both working-class and elite—transformed Norfolk to meet their needs. Similarly, in *A Sense of Place* (1999), Lynne B. Feldman argued that black elites in Birmingham formed their own segregated community in the suburb of Smithfield where they could "temporarily ignore the hostilities of the outside world" and create "an infrastructure of organizations designed to serve their needs and desires." Both Lewis and Feldman recognized that in some urban communities, the needs and goals of working-class and middle-class blacks diverged. Blair L M Kelley analyzed one such example: streetcar protests, especially in New Orleans, that evidenced "the collective nature of the struggle against the segregation of trains and streetcars and the tensions that existed within black communities."[72]

Some provocative scholarship arose around the intersection of gender and race in the urban South. As Michelle R. Scott demonstrated in *Blues Empress in Black Chattanooga* (2005), cities provided African American women, including blues singer Bessie Smith, with new recreational spaces including saloons, vaudeville houses, tent shows, juke joints, and even street corners where they could experiment with art forms and hone their crafts. Such spaces could be revolutionary: not only did African American women establish safe places to be black, but they also achieved entry into the public—and almost exclusively male—sphere. But southern cities also challenged black women's expansion of their freedoms. In efforts to clean up New Orleans, white reformers segregated sex work into the Storyville neighborhood, creating a district in which white men paid for sex with women of color and consequently dramatized fantasies about the beauty and sexual desirability of women characterized as quadroons and octoroons.[73]

Whether black women creating spaces for themselves or white reformers shaping a city's geography, much of the historiography centers upon the idea of constructing a New South. Many scholars have analyzed both the people who observed, studied, toured, and sometimes manipulated southern culture and the people being observed, studied, objectified, and sometimes manipulated. Even

72. Earl Lewis, *In Their Own Interests: Race, Class, and Power in Twentieth-Century Norfolk, Virginia* (Berkeley: University of California Press, 1991), 3; Lynne B. Feldman, *A Sense of Place: Birmingham's Black Middle-Class Community, 1890–1930* (Tuscaloosa: University of Alabama Press, 1999), 2, 3; Blair L M Kelley, *Right to Ride: Streetcar Boycotts and African American Citizenship in the Era of* Plessy v. Ferguson (Chapel Hill: University of North Carolina Press, 2010), 12.

73. Michelle R. Scott, *Blues Empress in Black Chattanooga: Bessie Smith and the Emerging Urban South* (Urbana: University of Illinois Press, 2008); Emily Epstein Landau, *Spectacular Wickedness: Sex, Race, and Memory in Storyville, New Orleans* (Baton Rouge: Louisiana State University Press, 2013).

the verbs in several book titles emphasize this process of "making," "creating," "designing," "dreaming," or "constructing." In *Designing Dixie* (2014), Reiko Hillyer contended that southern entrepreneurs and boosters "did not rely solely upon an agrarian landscape of aristocratic leisure or valiant war stories" to court northern tourists and investors. Instead, they discarded contentious memories and in some cases eschewed the plantation myth altogether.[74] In *Making Gullah* (2017), Melissa L. Cooper examined anthropologists and folklorists who converged on Sapelo Island in the 1920s and 1930s to determine how African traditions survived, layering their own theories about "African survivals" on their studies of voodoo, music, and residents' physical and economic separation from the rest of the South. In *Monuments to Absence* (2017), Andrew Denson demonstrated how early twentieth-century white southerners employed memories of Indian removal to ground their identities and legitimize their possession of the southern landscape.[75]

Literature, music, and film all show the intersection of southern cultural imagery and broader national fascinations. Sarah E. Gardner's *Reviewing the South* (2017) analyzed how book reviewers in national publications chose, constructed, and complicated conceptions of the South.[76] Scholars of southern music, sometimes building on David E. Whisnant's 1983 study of Appalachian music and culture, detailed how some of the most vivid images of southern cultural life formed in part from what people outside the region wanted to hear about the South. Karl Hagstrom Miller analyzed in *Segregating Sound* (2010) how academic folklorists and record companies turned the wide spectrum of southern music into more narrow, racialized categories such as "race music" and "hillbilly music." Scholars of the blues discussed how the idea of gritty, elemental authenticity became crucial to the earliest recorders, students, and fans as they defined "the blues."[77] And several scholars interested in race and regional construction analyzed how white audiences across the country in 1915 made *Birth of a Nation,* based on a white

74. Reiko Hillyer, *Designing Dixie: Tourism, Memory, and Urban Space in the New South* (Charlottesville: University of Virginia Press, 2014), 4. See also Karen L. Cox, *Dreaming of Dixie: How the South was Created in American Popular Culture* (Chapel Hill: University of North Carolina Press, 2011).

75. Melissa L. Cooper, *Making Gullah: A History of Sapelo Islanders, Race, and the American Imagination* (Chapel Hill: University of North Carolina Press, 2017); Andrew Denson, *Monuments to Absence: Cherokee Removal and the Contest over Southern Memory* (Chapel Hill: University of North Carolina Press, 2017).

76. Sarah E. Gardner, *Reviewing the South: The Literary Marketplace and the Southern Renaissance, 1920–1941* (New York: Cambridge University Press, 2017).

77. David E. Whisnant, *All That Is Native and Fine: The Politics of Culture in an American Region* (Chapel Hill: University of North Carolina Press, 1983); Karl Hagstrom Miller, *Segregating Sound: Inventing Folk and Pop Music in the Age of Jim Crow* (Durham: Duke University Press, 2010); Benjamin

southerner's novel about the heroic force of the Ku Klux Klan and directed by a white southerner, into the country's most popular movie.[78]

Since the rise of social history, the historiography of the New South has spread in many directions, telling multiple stories but leading to few big conclusions about the nature of the New South. Like all scholarship, the literature emerged from the questions of its own time. Modern concerns, such as the problem of mass incarceration, debates over immigration, police violence against African Americans, sexual harassment and assault of women, and gun violence have inspired new scholarship. Twenty-first-century historians recognized, perhaps more than ever, the centrality of image to elements of power, that laws and lawmakers constitute only a part of politics, and that human beings live and have long lived in a global community belying any attempts to create fixed binaries of any kind.

The effort to ask a lot of questions and to study multiple perspectives, however, has resulted in diminishing many past questions, especially past dichotomies, that dominated the literature well into the 1980s. *Continuity* or *change?* Change has won; things were always changing, often contentiously and occasionally with major analytical concepts assuming new shapes. *Modern* or *traditional?* Both have become constructions used for political agendas, but scholars have spent a great deal of time exploring modernity, including the modernity of practices once considered old and traditional. *Southern distinctiveness?* It was once a construction that people used for particular purposes, but globalization has raised questions as to the significance of the question. *Race* or *class?* Both, and more. Issues of power involved multiple and overlapping categories; gender and sexuality intersected with the experiences and meanings of both; and southern historians' rejection of the white-black dichotomy and attention to the many other peoples who inhabited the New South have become essential to the story of race-making. *Central themes of southern history?* Historians no longer seem interested in them and are not looking for them.

Filene, *Romancing the Folk: Public Memory and American Roots Music* (Chapel Hill: University of North Carolina Press, 2000); Marybeth Hamilton, *In Search of the Blues* (New York: Basic Books, 2008).

78. Robert Jackson, *Fade In, Crossroads: A History of the Southern Cinema* (New York: Oxford University Press, 2017); Gregory A. Waller, *Main Street Amusements: Movies and Commercial Entertainment in a Southern City, 1896–1930* (Washington: Smithsonian Institution Press, 1995); Deborah E. Barker and Kathryn McKee, ed., *American Cinema and the Southern Imaginary* (Athens: University of Georgia Press, 2011); Wood, *Lynching and Spectacle;* Hale, *Making Whiteness.*

"WE WHO BELIEVE IN FREEDOM CANNOT REST"

The Civil Rights Movement

Katherine Mellen Charron and Cherisse Jones-Branch

What is the civil rights movement? Most people would define it as the period in America's history when African Americans challenged their second-class citizenship in the alleged most democratic nation in the world. Southern black activists, the standard narrative holds, engaged in multiple protests against the injustices they confronted in daily life, and the United States Congress responded with a slew of civil rights laws that ended legalized discrimination and racism. Many Americans mark the movement's beginning with the Supreme Court's 1954 decision in *Brown v. Board of Education of Topeka,* which overturned legal segregation in public schools. Others locate it in 1955, when Rosa Parks refused to obey segregated public transportation laws in Montgomery, Alabama. Her subsequent arrest inaugurated a yearlong bus boycott and launched an unknown twenty-six-year-old minister, Dr. Martin Luther King Jr., into the national spotlight. King then led several campaigns that garnered national attention and persuaded the federal government to act. Meanwhile, youth and college students also protested and organized communities in ways that helped produce substantive change. With the passage of the 1964 Civil Rights Act and the 1965 Voting Rights Act, the movement seemed to accomplish its goals. Though African Americans continued to demand justice in the ensuing years, King's 1968 assassination in Memphis, Tennessee, signaled the end of this momentous era.

Civil rights historiography, however, offers a much more complex and nuanced evaluation than these iconic moments and temporal markers suggest and generates additional questions. Was the movement a legal one fought mostly in the courts? Was it a political movement in the form of a massive voter registration drive to enable southern African Americans to use the ballot to achieve full and equal citizenship? Was it an economic justice movement to secure better jobs and wages and access to federal benefits that other Americans enjoyed? Actually, the civil rights movement encompassed all of these things, and much more.

The first generation of scholarship has proven the most resilient when it comes to influencing popular conceptions of the civil rights movement and public school curricula. Initial studies in the 1970s and 1980s constructed accounts using a national, top-down perspective, typically emphasizing the interplay between presidential administrations, Congress, and Martin Luther King Jr.[1] Some historians argued that World War II represented the dawn of the movement because a struggle against fascism that the United States fought with a Jim Crow army exposed the nation's hypocrisy. They also examined African Americans' wartime engagement, looking to A. Phillip Randolph's March on Washington movement that yielded Executive Order 8802 in 1941, banning employment discrimination in defense industry firms with federal contracts. Additionally, scholars considered the role of the black press and activism on the home front, which included the "Double V" campaign calling for victory against fascism abroad and racism at home, and a surge in membership in extant civil rights organizations.[2]

A second trend in the scholarship in the late 1970s and 1980s focused attention on discrete communities and activists.[3] Reflecting the rise of social history and brimming with new insights, these works downplayed the intersections between local and national civil rights struggles. By the 1990s, scholars began to correct the disparity by charting grassroots efforts in relation to national developments. John Dittmer's and Charles M. Payne's seminal works on Mississippi assessed

1. Steven F. Lawson, "Freedom Then, Freedom Now: The Historiography of the Civil Rights Movement," *American Historical Review* 96 (April 1991): 456–71. See also Lawson, *Black Ballots: Voting Rights in the South, 1944–1969* (New York: Columbia University Press, 1976); Harvard Sitkoff, *The Struggle for Black Equality, 1954–1980* (New York: Hill and Wang, 1981); Robert Weisbrot, *Freedom Bound: A History of America's Civil Rights Movement* (New York: W. W. Norton, 1990).

2. Richard M. Dalfiume, "The Forgotten Years of the Negro Revolution," *Journal of American History* 55 (June 1968): 90–106; Harvard Sitkoff, "Racial Militancy and Interracial Violence in the Second World War," *Journal of American History* 58 (December 1971): 661–81; Steven F. Lawson, *Running for Freedom: Civil Rights and Black Politics in America Since 1941* (Philadelphia: Temple University Press, 1991).

3. Lawson, "Freedom Then, Freedom Now." Howell Raines's collection of oral histories complemented this trend; see *My Soul Is Rested: Movement Days in the Deep South Remembered* (New York: G. P. Putnam's Sons, 1977).

the political, economic, and social dynamics of indigenous African American activism, the assistance local people received from civil rights organizers and organizations, and their experiences on the national stage. Both Dittmer and Payne stressed the role of veterans as well, but their works provided little insight into how World War II radicalized African American women.[4] Nevertheless, they helped to establish a more balanced prototype that prevails among movement historians. Contributors to Emilye Crosby's edited collection, *Civil Rights History from the Ground Up* (2011), extended the emphasis beyond Mississippi to radical activists and activism across the South.[5]

Scholars now conceptualize the national civil rights struggle as an amalgam of many local freedom movements. Moreover, the dawn of the twenty-first century ushered in important reconsiderations of the movement's institutional foundations, mobilization strategies, leadership, generational distinctions, gender and class dynamics, cultural manifestations, and relationship to local, national, and international politics. Equally crucial is a body of work concerned with how the United States and its citizens remember and memorialize the movement.

The proliferation of studies led to diverse views about what kind of activism comprised the civil rights movement and when it occurred. The most significant change in the era's periodization arose in 2005, when Jacquelyn Dowd Hall published "The Long Civil Rights Movement and the Political Uses of the Past," in which she asked how memory and the mainstream national narrative intersected to temper contemporary understandings of the movement's radicalism. Hall argued that stories that celebrate a 1954–1968 movement as "a triumphal moment in a larger American progress narrative" had damaging consequences, and she pointed to the New Right's efforts to co-opt the movement's victories and invalidate its gains. Hall proposed a timeline spanning the 1930s to 1970s and placed the fight for economic justice at the center. Her model promised to reorient scholarly interpretations in vital ways. First, it allowed the critical role of labor, or interracial "civil rights unionism," of the New Deal and Popular Front eras—when the Communist Party USA's economic critiques attracted many Americans—to emerge more clearly into view. This, in turn, broadened the movement's geography beyond the South and underscored the changes that Cold

4. John Dittmer, *Local People: The Struggle for Civil Rights in Mississippi* (Urbana: University of Illinois Press, 1994); Charles M. Payne, *I've Got the Light of Freedom: The Organizing Tradition and the Mississippi Freedom Struggle* (Berkeley: University of California Press, 1995).

5. Emilye Crosby, ed., *Civil Rights History from the Ground Up: Local Struggles, A National Movement* (Athens: University of Georgia Press, 2011).

War anticommunism wrought in 1950s and 1960s civil rights radicalism. A "long" model also offered fresh readings of generational continuities, and activists' lived experiences over time. Extending investigations into the 1970s, Hall asserted, disrupts a narrative of declension and the arguments that buttress it. Finally, placing conservative resistance alongside movement developments illustrated how it evolved concurrently with activists' gains rather than as a delayed response.[6] Numerous scholars appropriated Hall's chronology, producing valuable studies on the long civil rights movement.[7]

Others vigorously contested that perspective, creating an ongoing debate that revolves around the premise that if everything in the black freedom struggle between the 1930s and 1970s counts as *the* civil rights movement, the activism of the mid-1950s and 1960s loses its uniqueness. Equally problematic, a "long" framework that includes interracial antecedents obscures African American agency in a black-led movement and the reliance on nonviolence as its distinguishing strategy. Collapsing temporal and geographical particularities also risks confusing the boundaries between the civil rights and Black Power movements, especially after 1965.[8] Parsing continues to occur over ways that larger structural changes influenced movement possibilities and the singular importance of King as the movement's spokesperson. Historians who argued against a long civil rights movement attempted to address the nationalized, gendered, top-down view of early works by insisting that unprecedented federal action and mass grassroots

6. Jacquelyn Dowd Hall, "The Long Civil Rights Movement and the Political Uses of the Past," *Journal of American History* 91 (March 2005): 1233–63, quote on 1234.

7. See, for example, Robert Korstad, *Civil Rights Unionism: Tobacco Workers and the Struggle for Democracy in the Mid-Twentieth-Century South* (Chapel Hill: University of North Carolina Press, 2003); Glenda Elizabeth Gilmore, *Defying Dixie: The Radical Roots of Civil Rights, 1919–1950* (New York: W. W. Norton, 2008); Thomas J. Sugrue, *Sweet Land of Liberty: The Forgotten Struggle for Civil Rights in the North* (New York: Random House, 2008). For views of a "long movement" among conservatives, see Stephanie R. Rolph, *Resisting Equality: The Citizens' Council, 1954–1989* (Baton Rouge: Louisiana State University Press, 2018); Elizabeth Gillespie McRae, *Mothers of Massive Resistance: White Women and the Politics of White Supremacy* (New York: Oxford University Press, 2018).

8. See, for example, Sundiata Keita Cha-Jua and Clarence Lang, "The 'Long Movement' as Vampire: Temporal and Spatial Fallacies in Recent Black Freedom Studies," *Journal of African American History* 92 (Spring 2007): 265–88; Steven F. Lawson, "Long Origins of the Short Civil Rights Movement, 1965–1968," in *Freedom Rights: New Perspectives on the Civil Rights Movement,* ed. Danielle L. McGuire and John Dittmer (Lexington: University Press of Kentucky, 2011), 9–37; Eric Arnesen, "Reconsidering the 'Long Civil Rights Movement,'" *Historically Speaking* 10 (April 2009): 31–34; Peniel E. Joseph, *Waiting 'til the Midnight Hour: A Narrative History of Black Power in America* (New York: Henry Holt, 2007); Joseph, ed., *The Black Power Movement: Re-thinking the Civil Rights–Black Power Era* (New York: Routledge, 2006).

participation differentiates the Cold War era from the earlier period. Scholarly consensus acknowledges the interplay between activist endeavors and budding federal support of civil rights from the 1930s to early 1950s, including Supreme Court decisions pertaining to segregated education and transportation and black voting rights as well as Cold War foreign policy changes.[9] However, where Hall sought continuity, other scholars privileged discontinuity. They contended that a constellation of factors between 1954 and 1968 produced a "short" civil rights movement and lent it an incomparable character.[10]

Regardless of one's position on the movement's chronology, it is important to stress that at no point in American history did African-descended people accept their inferior status. Many historians traced the struggle for full equality from the time of their earliest arrival in America.[11] Long before Rosa Parks's 1955 refusal to stand in Alabama, Frederick Douglass and Elizabeth Jennings Graham challenged segregated public transportation in the urban North. Focusing on gender and the working class, Blair L M Kelley's study of streetcar boycotts in the late nineteenth century adeptly unpacked black people's civil rights struggles prior to the *Plessy v. Ferguson* (1896) Supreme Court decision.[12] Activists in this era, and afterward, vacillated between assimilationist, black independence, and nationalist strategies as options to secure social, political, and economic freedom. Furthermore,

9. See Mary L. Dudziak, *Cold War Civil Rights: Race and the Image of American Democracy* (Princeton: Princeton University Press, 2000); Thomas Borstelmann, *The Cold War and the Color Line: American Race Relations in the Global Arena* (Cambridge: Harvard University Press, 2001); Brenda Gayle Plummer, *Rising Wind: Black Americans and U.S. Foreign Affairs, 1935–1960* (Chapel Hill: University of North Carolina Press, 1996). For legal studies, see Michael J. Klarman, *From Jim Crow to Civil Rights: The Supreme Court and the Struggle for Racial Equality* (New York: Oxford University Press, 2004); Risa L. Goluboff, *The Lost Promise of Civil Rights* (Cambridge: Harvard University Press, 2007). See also Patricia Sullivan, *Days of Hope: Race and Democracy in the New Deal Era* (Chapel Hill: University of North Carolina Press, 1996).

10. A certain irony remains, namely that a 1954–1968 chronology can subtly fortify the sense that the movement "began" when white people started paying attention to news reports brought to them by a white media and "ended" when they became disillusioned. Nor do Hall's critics usually address the questions she raised regarding "the political uses of the past."

11. Martha S. Jones, *Birthright Citizens: A History of Race and Rights and Antebellum America* (New York: Cambridge University Press, 2018); R. J. M. Blackett, *The Captive's Quest for Freedom: Fugitive Slaves, the 1850 Fugitive Slave Law, and the Politics of Slavery* (New York: Cambridge University Press, 2018); Manisha Sinha, *The Slave's Cause: A History of Abolition* (New Haven: Yale University Press, 2016); Elizabeth Stordeur Pryor, *Colored Travelers: Mobility and the Fight for Citizenship before the Civil War* (Chapel Hill: University of North Carolina Press, 2016).

12. Blair L M Kelley, *Right to Ride: Streetcar Boycotts and African American Citizenship in the Era of* Plessy v. Ferguson (Chapel Hill: University of North Carolina Press, 2010).

although historians of this earlier period often concentrated on black men, black women headed many efforts. Biographies of Ida B. Wells-Barnett, Mary Church Terrell, and Mary McLeod Bethune outlined their leadership and their laying the groundwork for what Americans define as the "modern civil rights movement."[13]

As the oldest national civil rights organization, the National Association for the Advancement of Colored People (NAACP) both molded and spearheaded many civil rights campaigns. Established in 1909 in the wake of racial violence in Springfield, Illinois, the NAACP attracted an integrated membership from its inception and primarily relied on litigation in pursuit of multipronged goals. Historians surveyed the NAACP's advocacy, including leading the antilynching fight, in its early years. For example, in *Lift Every Voice* (2010), Patricia Sullivan contextualized the NAACP's role in challenging racial injustice prior to 1954, and explicated how it chipped away at the legal and political edifice of American apartheid.[14]

Scholars especially concentrated on the NAACP and battles for African American suffrage. Manfred Berg observed that, from the early 1900s to 1970, black people struggled mightily for the right to vote, and he stressed the importance of activism that stemmed from NAACP branches. Kevern Verney and Lee Sartain's edited collection, *Long Is the Way and Hard* (2007), considered the NAACP's national impact but devoted more attention to state, city, and local NAACP activism in the southern, midwestern, and western United States from the World War I years through the civil rights era.[15]

13. See Paula J. Giddings, *Ida: A Sword among Lions: Ida B. Wells and the Campaign against Lynching* (New York: Amistad, 2008); Mia Bay, *To Tell the Truth Freely: The Life of Ida B. Wells* (New York: Hill and Wang, 2009); Sarah L. Silkey, *Black Woman Reformer: Ida B. Wells, Lynching and Transatlantic Activism* (Athens: University of Georgia Press, 2015); Joan Quigley, *Just Another Southern Town: Mary Church Terrell and the Struggle for Racial Justice in the Nation's Capital* (New York: Oxford University Press, 2016); Joyce A. Hanson, *Mary McLeod Bethune and Black Women's Political Activism* (Columbia: University of Missouri Press, 2003).

14. Patricia Sullivan, *Lift Every Voice: The NAACP and the Making of the Civil Rights Movement* (New York: New Press, 2010). See also Patricia Bernstein, *The First Waco Horror: The Lynching of Jesse Washington and the Rise of the NAACP* (College Station: Texas A&M University Press, 2005); Thomas L. Bynum, *NAACP Youth and the Fight for Black Freedom, 1936–1965* (Knoxville: University of Tennessee Press, 2013). For a view of the organization in an international context, see Carol Anderson, *Bourgeois Radicals: The NAACP and the Struggle for Colonial Liberation, 1941–1960* (New York: Cambridge University Press, 2015).

15. Manfred Berg, *The Ticket to Freedom: The NAACP and the Struggle for Black Political Integration* (Gainesville: University Press of Florida, 2005); Kevern Verney and Lee Sartain, eds., *Long Is the Way and Hard: One Hundred Years of the NAACP* (Fayetteville: University of Arkansas Press, 2009). See also Gloria J. Browne-Marshall, *The Voting Rights War: The NAACP and the Ongoing Struggle for Justice* (Lanham, MD: Rowman & Littlefield, 2016).

Most Americans automatically associate the NAACP with *Brown v. Board of Education.* Focusing on this single victory, however, obscures the difficult path to achieving it. Mark V. Tushnet clarified the organization's long assault on segregated schools, including a calculated shift from educational equalization as a way to enforce "separate but equal"—and thus literally bankrupting Jim Crow—to integration. More broadly, Tushnet argued that the NAACP emphasized the significance of "public interest law," whereby its attorneys viewed litigation as a social process that could be wielded to rectify racial injustice.[16]

Historians also raised the question of women's roles in the NAACP. Though many scholars credit W. E. B. Du Bois as one of the organization's founders, Ida B. Wells-Barnett and Mary Church Terrell were involved as well. Studies that center black women depicted their crucial labors in local chapters as grassroots organizers, public relations managers, and membership recruiters who employed their community connections and fundraising skills to maintain the NAACP's daily operations.[17]

African Americans and their allies specifically capitalized on World War II's antiracist rhetoric to establish the Congress of Racial Equality (CORE) in Chicago in 1942. August Meier and Elliott Rudwick chronicled prominent CORE members' pioneering nonviolent direct action as a tactical strategy.[18] In 1947, CORE launched its first national campaign, the Journey of Reconciliation, to test a Supreme Court decision banning segregation on interstate travel. In the South, CORE resurrected the 1947 Journey of Reconciliation in the form of the 1961 Freedom Rides, and had a notable presence in Florida, Kentucky, Louisiana, Mississippi, and South Carolina. Yet because CORE's beginnings lay in the urban North, additional studies focused on its members' activism in Brooklyn, Cleveland, and as far west as Seattle.[19]

16. Mark V. Tushnet, *The NAACP's Legal Strategy against Segregated Education, 1925–1950* (Chapel Hill: University of North Carolina Press, 1987).

17. Lee Sartain, *Invisible Activists: Women of the Louisiana NAACP and the Struggle for Civil Rights, 1915–1945* (Baton Rouge: Louisiana State University Press, 2007); Cherisse Jones-Branch, "African American Women and the South Carolina NAACP, 1930s and 1940s," in *The True Worth of a Race: African American Women and the Struggle for Freedom,* ed. Lopez D. Matthews Jr. and Kenvi C. Phillips (Washington: Association of Black Women Historians, 2013), 164–74.

18. August Meier and Elliott Rudwick, *CORE: A Study in the Civil Rights Movement, 1942–1968* (New York: Oxford University Press, 1973).

19. Brian Purnell, *Fighting Jim Crow in the County of Kings: The Congress of Racial Equality in Brooklyn* (Lexington: University Press of Kentucky, 2013); Joan Singler et al., *Seattle in Black and White: The Congress of Racial Equality and the Fight for Equal Opportunity* (Seattle: University of Washington Press, 2011);

Dr. King and the Southern Christian Leadership Conference (SCLC) understandably dominated the movement's initial organizational studies. Founded in 1957, SCLC dedicated itself to nonviolent direct action and civil disobedience, often orchestrating a powerful media drama to expose Jim Crow's injustices, appeal to supporters, and prompt meaningful action from the federal government. Sociologist Aldon Morris's *Origins of the Civil Rights Movement* (1984) utilized SCLC to offer an analysis of the roles that black churches played in the movement, particularly in urban areas, while historian David Garrow's *Bearing the Cross* (1986) detailed SCLC's strategic decisions and when, how, and why federal officials intervened. Taylor Branch's three-volume biography of King covered similar ground but incorporated a much wider array of characters—both local and national as well as religious and secular leaders and grassroots activists—to paint a fuller portrait.[20] Other scholars who focused on King's biography explored the movement in the context of international developments, especially the embrace of Gandhian philosophy and tactics as well as the influence of the Cold War and anticolonial struggles in Africa.[21]

King's national celebrity made SCLC synonymous with the movement's most famous moments: Birmingham in the spring of 1963, the March on Washington for Jobs and Freedom in August 1963, and Selma in 1965.[22] This, in turn, rein-

Nishani Frazier, *Harambee City: The Congress of Racial Equality in Cleveland and the Rise of Black Power Populism* (Fayetteville: University of Arkansas Press, 2017). On the Freedom Rides, see Raymond Arsenault, *Freedom Riders: 1961 and the Struggle for Racial Justice* (New York: Oxford University Press, 2006).

20. Aldon D. Morris, *Origins of the Civil Rights Movement: Black Communities Organizing for Change* (New York: Free Press, 1984); David J. Garrow, *Bearing the Cross: Martin Luther King Jr. and the Southern Christian Leadership Conference* (New York: William Morrow, 1986); Taylor Branch, *Parting the Waters: America in the King Years, 1954–63* (New York: Simon & Schuster, 1988); Branch, *Pillar of Fire: America in the King Years, 1963–65* (New York: Simon & Schuster, 1998); Branch, *At Canaan's Edge: America in the King Years, 1965–68* (New York: Simon & Schuster, 2006). See also Adam Fairclough, *To Redeem the Soul of America: The Southern Christian Leadership Conference and Martin Luther King Jr.* (Athens: University of Georgia Press, 1987).

21. See, for example, Lerone Bennett Jr., *What Manner of a Man: A Biography of Martin Luther King Jr.* (Chicago: Johnson Publishing, 1964); Michael Eric Dyson, *I May Not Get There with You: The True Martin Luther King Jr.* (New York: Free Press, 2000); David Levering Lewis, *King: A Biography* (Urbana: University of Illinois Press, 2013); Cornel West, ed., *The Radical King* (Boston: Beacon Press, 2015). See also Kevin M. Gaines, "The Civil Rights Movement in World Perspective," *OAH Magazine of History* 21 (January 2007): 57–64.

22. Garrow, *Bearing the Cross*; Glenn T. Eskew, *But for Birmingham: The Local and National Movements in the Civil Rights Struggle* (Chapel Hill: University of North Carolina Press, 1997); Diane McWhorter, *Carry Me Home: Birmingham, Alabama: The Climatic Battle of the Civil Rights Revolution* (New York:

forced the tendency to identify the 1964 Civil Rights Act and the 1965 Voting Rights Act as the movement's most consequential accomplishments. Yet scholars shed light on the evolutions in King's thinking by looking to SCLC's experience in Chicago in 1966, where it confronted less visible forms of institutional racism. Failure to achieve clear-cut victories in the urban North help to explain how King moved from an emphasis on civil rights and voting to a broader structural critique of American society, particularly the links between racism, economic injustice, and militarism evident in his public opposition to the Vietnam War in 1967.[23]

Histories of SCLC showed how it wrestled with external attacks and its own internal chaos. Rivalries with other groups flared constantly, and tensions increased in the mid-1960s as the Black Power movement emerged. Additional studies reassessed the cross-fertilization among organizations on the ground—particularly in Mississippi, where repression forced all to unite in the Council of Federated Organizations (COFO)—and how SCLC programs provided behind-the-scenes training for grassroots activists that made its more public successes possible.[24] A number of works also interrogated SCLC's gender politics. Barbara Ransby's 2003 biography of Ella Baker serves as the foremost example. Detailing Baker's brief tenure with SCLC, Ransby plumbed her resentment of men's refusal to accord her ideas equal weight and respect, specifically when it came to the importance of women's movement work and her belief in participatory democracy. Other women, such as Septima Clark, encountered similar problems but did not break with SCLC. Baker, by contrast, resigned shortly after the founding of the Student Nonviolent Coordinating Committee (SNCC).[25]

Simon & Schuster, 2001); William P. Jones, *The March on Washington: Jobs, Freedom, and the Forgotten History of Civil Rights* (New York: W. W. Norton, 2013); David J. Garrow, *Protest at Selma: Martin Luther King, Jr., and the Voting Rights Act of 1965* (New Haven: Yale University Press, 1978). For an assessment of shortcomings in an iconic civil rights campaign, see Karlyn Forner, *Why the Vote Wasn't Enough for Selma* (Durham: Duke University Press, 2017).

23. Michael K. Honey, *To the Promised Land: Martin Luther King and the Fight for Economic Justice* (New York: W. W. Norton, 2018); James R. Ralph Jr., *Northern Protest: Martin Luther King Jr., Chicago, and the Civil Rights Movement* (Cambridge: Harvard University Press, 1993); Mary Lou Finley et al., eds., *The Chicago Freedom Movement: Martin Luther King Jr. and Civil Rights Activism in the North* (Lexington: University Press of Kentucky, 2016).

24. Dorothy F. Cotton, *If Your Back's Not Bent: The Role of the Citizenship Education Program in the Civil Rights Movement* (New York: Atria Books, 2012); Katherine Mellen Charron, *Freedom's Teacher: The Life of Septima Clark* (Chapel Hill: University of North Carolina Press, 2009).

25. Barbara Ransby, *Ella Baker and the Black Freedom Movement: A Radical Democratic Vision* (Chapel Hill: University of North Carolina Press, 2003), esp. chap. 6; Septima Clark, *Ready from Within: Septima*

Having remained in SCLC's shadow for decades, SNCC assumed prominence in civil rights movement scholarship due to a marked increase of scholarly biographies, published firsthand accounts by SNCC veterans, and the SNCC Legacy Project, an online resource sponsored by the Center for Documentary Studies at Duke University.[26] The collective effect of SNCC studies yielded substantive reevaluations of the movement's geography, tactics, achievements, and shortcomings.[27] Scholarly writing about SNCC directed attention to the rural South, especially in Mississippi where it led COFO, but also to places like Cambridge, Maryland, where it had a significant presence.[28] Wesley C. Hogan's *Many Minds, One Heart* (2007) attributed SNCC's efficacy to its members' understanding of "freedom as an inside job," or the personal transformations that accompanied

---

Clark and the Civil Rights Movement, ed. Cynthia Stokes Brown (Navarro, CA: Wild Trees Press, 1986), esp. 77–83. See also J. Todd Moye, *Ella Baker: Community Organizer of the Civil Rights Movement* (Lanham, MD: Rowman & Littlefield, 2013); Joanne Grant, *Ella Baker: Freedom Bound* (New York: John Wiley and Sons, 1998).

26. For the SNCC Digital Gateway, see https://snccdigital.org/ (accessed 18 January 2019). A sampling of such autobiographies includes: James Farmer, *Lay Bare the Heart: An Autobiography of the Civil Rights Movement* (New York: Arbor House, 1985); Mary King, *Freedom Song: A Personal Story of the 1960s Civil Rights Movement* (New York: Morrow, 1987); John Lewis with Michael D'Orso, *Walking with the Wind: A Memoir of the Movement* (New York: Simon & Schuster, 1998); Stokely Carmichael with Ekwueme Michael Thewell, *Ready for Revolution: The Life and Struggles of Stokely Carmichael (Kwame Ture)* (New York: Scribner, 2003); Hollis Watkins with C. Leigh McInnis, *Brother Hollis: The Sankofa of a Movement Man* (Clinton, MS: Sankofa Southern Publishing, 2015); Faith S. Holsaert et al., eds., *Hands on the Freedom Plow: Personal Accounts by Women in SNCC* (Urbana: University of Illinois Press, 2010). Biographies of SNCC activists include: Kay Mills, *This Little Light of Mine: The Life of Fannie Lou Hamer* (New York: Dutton Books, 1993); Laura Visser-Maessen, *Robert Parris Moses: A Life in Civil Rights and Leadership at the Grassroots* (Chapel Hill: University of North Carolina Press, 2016); Cynthia Griggs Fleming, *Soon We Will Not Cry: The Liberation of Ruby Doris Smith Robinson* (Lanham, MD: Rowman & Littlefield, 1998); Chana Kai Lee, *For Freedom's Sake: The Life of Fannie Lou Hamer* (Urbana: University of Illinois Press, 1999); Peniel E. Joseph, *Stokely: A Life* (New York: Basic Books, 2014); Andrew B. Lewis, *The Shadows of Youth: The Remarkable Journey of the Civil Rights Generation* (New York: Hill and Wang, 2009). See also Vincent Harding, *Hope and History: Why We Must Share the Story of the Movement* (Maryknoll, NY: Orbis Books, 1990).

27. Clayborne Carson, *In Struggle: SNCC and the Black Awakening of the 1960s* (Cambridge: Harvard University Press, 1981); Dittmer, *Local People;* Payne, *I've Got the Light of Freedom.* See also Howard Zinn, *SNCC: The New Abolitionists* (Boston: Beacon Press, 1964).

28. Peter B. Levy, *Civil War on Race Street: The Civil Rights Movement in Cambridge, Maryland* (Gainesville: University Press of Florida, 2003); Jennifer Jensen Wallach and John A. Kirk, eds., *ARSNICK: The Student Nonviolent Coordinating Committee in Arkansas* (Fayetteville: University of Arkansas Press, 2011).

their advocacy and emboldened them. The group's democratic decision-making and organizing approach, which reflected Ella Baker's mentoring, also set it apart. With the sit-ins and their participation in the Freedom Rides, SNCC insurgents deployed direct action tactics on a scale that revolutionized both the movement and the decade of the 1960s. As Simon Hall and others pointed out, SNCC influenced an entire generation of white college-aged activists who later led the antiwar movement.[29]

Most crucially, scholarship on SNCC's work among the grass roots revealed ordinary poor and working-class people's power to create key transformations at local, state, and national levels. The Mississippi Freedom Democratic Party, which challenged the seating of the state's all-white delegation to the 1964 Democratic National Convention, offers a prominent example. Disappointment with white liberals in the aftermath of this episode marked a dramatic shift in direction for SNCC, which many historians read as the beginning of the group's decline.[30] In the realm of cultural and gender politics, Leigh Raiford and Tanisha C. Ford considered the group's use of photography and fashion, respectively, while Dan Berger examined how members' incarceration informed broader critiques and activism against a rising carceral state.[31] Taken together, these works point toward a more capacious civil rights and black empowerment agenda enabled by cross-regional alliances.

SNCC's centrality in the historiography, however, has certain limitations. For one, it consigns the movement's timeline to the single decade in which SNCC flourished. It also restricts the movement's geography to locations where SNCC made the most difference. Finally, aside from buttressing the problematic divide

29. Wesley C. Hogan, *Many Minds, One Heart: SNCC's Dream for a New America* (Chapel Hill: University of North Carolina Press, 2007); Simon Hall, *Peace and Freedom: The Civil Rights and Antiwar Movements in the 1960s* (Philadelphia: University of Pennsylvania Press, 2005).

30. On the Mississippi Freedom Democratic Party, see Dittmer, *Local People;* Lee, *For Freedom's Sake.* On 1964 as a turning point in SNCC strategy, see Carson, *In Struggle,* esp. parts 2 and 3; Payne, *I've Got the Light of Freedom,* esp. chaps. 12–13; Akinyele Umoja, "1964: The Beginning of the End of Nonviolence in the Mississippi Freedom Movement," *Radical History Review* 85 (Winter 2003): 201–26.

31. Tanisha C. Ford, "SNCC Women, Denim, and the Politics of Dress," *Journal of Southern History* 79 (August 2013): 625–58; Leigh Raiford, "Come Let Us Build a New World Together: SNCC and the Photography of the Civil Rights Movement," *American Quarterly* 59 (December 2007): 1129–57; Dan Berger, *Captive Nation: Black Prison Organizing in the Civil Rights Era* (Chapel Hill: University of North Carolina Press, 2014). See also Tanisha C. Ford, *Liberated Threads: Black Women, Style, and the Global Politics of Soul* (Chapel Hill: University of North Carolina Press, 2015).

between a "good" civil rights movement and a "bad" Black Power era, explanations for SNCC's demise eclipse the import of the local activists it inspired and their ongoing work in communities across the South.

Most participants in the civil rights movement undertook considerable training, and the Highlander Folk School (HFS), a radical adult education center in Tennessee established in 1932, served as another site of strategizing and leadership development. *Unearthing Seeds of Fire* (1975) by Frank Adams, *Highlander* (1988) by John M. Glenn, and *The Highlander Folk School* (1989) by Aimee Isgrig Horton reviewed HFS's unique approach to educating adults, namely that founder Myles Horton and staff had faith in poor and working-class people's ability to identify the sources of the oppressions they confronted. What they needed was a space to meet with others to share their ideas and build their confidence. During the civil rights era, HFS's weeklong interracial workshops brought activists of all ages from across the South together to discuss problems in their communities and to articulate concrete solutions.[32] Music played a crucial role during such sessions, fostering group cohesion and cultural exchange. HFS staff also traveled into the field to assist local campaigns, particularly in South Carolina and Mississippi. In the broadest sense, scholarly attention to Highlander accentuated the interaction between movement organizations and people as well as the deeds of those who accepted local leadership responsibilities.[33]

The Southern Conference Educational Fund (SCEF), founded in 1948 after the dissolution of the interracial Southern Conference for Human Welfare, used education to promote integration. Comprised of white southern radicals and led by Carl and Anne Braden in the mid-1960s, SCEF acted as an information clearinghouse that supported civil rights work and raised funds to assist activists. Scholars writing about SCEF noted that it was not a protest organization. Nevertheless, the networks it nurtured and the civil rights efforts it publicized in its

32. Frank Adams with Myles Horton, *Unearthing Seeds of Fire: The Idea of Highlander* (Winston-Salem: John F. Blair, 1975); John M. Glen, *Highlander: No Ordinary School* (Lexington: University Press of Kentucky, 1988); Aimee Isgrig Horton, *The Highlander Folk School: A History of Its Major Programs, 1932–1961* (New York: Carlson, 1989).

33. Donna Langston, "The Women of Highlander," in *Women in the Civil Rights Movement: Trailblazers and Torchbearers, 1941–1965*, ed. Vicki L. Crawford, Jacqueline Anne Rouse, and Barbara Woods (New York: Carlson, 1990), 145–67; Guy Carawan, Candie Carawan, and Robert Yellin, *Ain't You Got a Right to the Tree of Life? The People of Johns Island, South Carolina—Their Faces, Their Words, and Their Songs* (New York: Simon & Schuster, 1966); Morris, *Origins of the Civil Rights Movement*, esp. chap. 7; Charron, *Freedom's Teacher*, chaps. 7 and 8.

newspaper, *The Southern Patriot,* attracted support for the movement. SCEF also continued to bring attention to radical activism in the 1970s.[34]

Alongside scholarly consideration of varied campaigns and organizations, studies of distinct locations contributed to the recognition that there were many civil rights movements. Works on Greensboro, North Carolina, Tuskegee, Alabama, and St. Augustine, Florida, were actually among the first to appear in the 1980s, and focused on sites with strong institutional foundations, including historically black colleges and universities (HBCUs).[35] These early place studies demonstrated how the particularities of municipal and state politics shaped activist tactics and highlighted black middle-class leadership.

Scholarship on civil rights movements in the urban segregated South also revealed that African Americans living in cities had a greater chance to leverage new federal opportunity. After gaining access to the ballot through the Supreme Court's 1944 *Smith v. Allwright* decision, for example, activists in cities immediately organized voter registration drives. Though they still faced hurdles at the white registrar's office, simply attempting to register did not cost urban residents their life, as it did in rural areas. In South Carolina, civil rights advocates formed the Progressive Democratic Party (PDP) in 1944 and ran the first African American for the United States Congress since Reconstruction. Here and elsewhere, scholars showed that whether black candidates won or not, such efforts influenced local political balances of power and forced a recalibration in strategy for white leaders who were intent on maintaining Jim Crow.[36] Considering white responses

34. Irwin Klibaner, *Conscience of a Troubled South: The Southern Conference Educational Fund, 1946–1966* (Brooklyn: Carlson, 1989); Linda Reed, *Simple Decency and Common Sense: The Southern Conference Movement, 1938–1963* (Bloomington: Indiana University Press, 1991); Catherine Fosl, *Subversive Southerner: Anne Braden and the Struggle for Racial Justice in the Cold War South* (New York: Palgrave Macmillan, 2002); Frank T. Adams, *James A. Dombrowski: An American Heretic, 1897–1983* (Knoxville: University of Tennessee Press, 1992), esp. chaps. 12–16.

35. William H. Chafe, *Civilities and Civil Rights: Greensboro, North Carolina and the Black Struggle for Equality* (New York: Oxford University Press, 1980); Robert J. Norell, *Reaping the Whirlwind: The Civil Rights Movement in Tuskegee* (New York: Alfred A. Knopf, 1985); David R. Colburn, *Racial Change and Community in Crisis: St. Augustine, Florida, 1877–1980* (New York: Columbia University Press, 1985).

36. See Sullivan, *Days of Hope,* esp. chaps. 5 and 6; Cherisse Jones-Branch, *Crossing the Line: Women's Interracial Activism in South Carolina during and after World War II* (Gainesville: University Press of Florida, 2014), 6, 19–20, 39, 44, 49; Peter F. Lau, *Democracy Rising: South Carolina and the Fight For Black Equality since 1865* (Lexington: University Press of Kentucky, 2006); Lawson, *Black Ballots,* chap. 2; Miles S. Richards, "Osceola E. McKaine and the Struggle for Black Civil Rights, 1917–1946" (PhD diss., University of South Carolina, 1994).

to movement gains also enabled historians Kevin M. Kruse and Matthew D. Lassiter to rethink how southern space and the changes produced by the movement related to Sunbelt suburbanization and the region's rising economic prosperity.[37]

By the 2000s, an increased number of studies began to survey urban civil rights movements outside of the South, illuminating struggles for economic justice, equal employment, and school integration along with those against residential segregation. Authors typically evaluated both the public and private sectors to explain how "racial capitalism" and public policy intersected to perpetuate black inequality. Scholarship on the North, West, and Midwest more self-consciously considered the role of organized labor, including its discrimination against black workers, while dissecting the specifics of federal, state, and municipal decisions in relation to suburbanization and urban renewal. Because more activist opportunities existed earlier in the urban United States, many non-southern studies also located the movement's beginnings in the World War II and postwar years, and traced its extension into the Black Power era. Chronicling white resistance, these works critically interrogated southern exceptionalism and documented the endemic racism built into every aspect of American society.[38]

A full portrait of the civil rights movement requires a consideration of the rural South as well, where agricultural struggles assumed greater importance than residential segregation and school integration. Howard Kester's 1936 work situated rural southern radicalism squarely within the economic upheaval of the New Deal and the federal government's failure to ensure that its agricultural re-

37. Kevin M. Kruse, *White Flight: Atlanta and the Making of Modern Conservatism* (Princeton: Princeton University Press, 2005); Matthew D. Lassiter, *The Silent Majority: Suburban Politics in the Sunbelt South* (Princeton: Princeton University Press, 2006).

38. See Jeanne Theoharis and Komozi Woodward, eds., *Freedom North: Black Freedom Struggles Outside the South, 1940–1980* (New York: Palgrave Macmillan, 2003); Robert O. Self, *American Babylon: Race and the Struggle for Postwar Oakland* (Princeton: Princeton University Press, 2003); Martha Biondi, *To Stand and Fight: The Struggle for Civil Rights in Postwar New York City* (Cambridge: Harvard University Press, 2006); Stefan M. Bradley, *Upending the Ivory Tower: Civil Rights, Black Power, and the Ivy League* (New York: New York University Press, 2018); Matthew J. Countryman, *Up South: Civil Rights and Black Power in Philadelphia* (Philadelphia: University of Pennsylvania Press, 2006); Lisa Levenstein, *A Movement without Marches: African American Women and the Politics of Poverty in Postwar Philadelphia* (Chapel Hill: University of North Carolina Press, 2009); Patrick D. Jones, *The Selma of the North: Civil Rights Insurgency in Milwaukee* (Cambridge: Harvard University Press, 2009); Matthew C. Whitaker, *Race Work: The Rise of Civil Rights in the Urban West* (Lincoln: University of Nebraska Press, 2005). Sugrue's *Sweet Land of Liberty* provides a synthesis of non-southern civil rights movements. See also Matthew D. Lassiter and Joseph Crespino, eds., *The Myth of Southern Exceptionalism* (New York: Oxford University Press, 2010).

covery programs benefited all who lived and worked on the land. He also shed light on how rural black people upended oppressive racial and social structures in their efforts to realize political and economic justice.[39]

Other scholars chronicled rural black agricultural laborers' struggles against the exploitative sharecropping system. In *American Congo* (2012), Nan Elizabeth Woodruff explored how those in Arkansas and the Mississippi Delta challenged local law enforcement and white planters who kept them impoverished and disfranchised in order to retain economic and political control.[40] The extent of the violence that rural whites deployed demonstrates that their labor force was anything but compliant in the face of oppressive forces.

Rural African Americans engaged in political and economic activism through such organizations as the NAACP, the Universal Negro Improvement Association, the Popular Front–era Communist Party, and the interracial Southern Tenant Farmers Union (founded in Tyronza, Arkansas, in 1934).[41] James D. Ross Jr. emphasized the stories of black and white sharecroppers, small landowning farmers, and union members who recalled the horrors they endured at the hands of landowners, as well as how they resisted and survived the worst vestiges of racial terrorism.[42] Equally important, Jarod Roll addressed how sharecroppers incorporated grassroots religion into their agrarian protests, using Pentecostal revivals as spaces to organize around such issues as economic security, decent housing, and basic health care. Through their shared evangelical faith, rural blacks and whites forged a radical agenda based on concerns that mattered to rural people regardless of race.[43]

39. Howard Kester, *Revolt Among the Sharecroppers* (New York: Covici, 1936).

40. Nan Elizabeth Woodruff, *American Congo: The African American Freedom Struggle in the Delta* (Cambridge: Harvard University Press, 2003). See also Pete Daniel, *The Shadow of Slavery: Peonage in the South, 1901–1969* (Urbana: University of Illinois Press, 1972).

41. Mary G. Rolinson, *Grassroots Garveyism: The Universal Negro Improvement Association in the Rural South, 1920–1927* (Chapel Hill: University of North Carolina Press, 2007); Robin D. G. Kelley, *Hammer and Hoe: Alabama Communists during the Great Depression* (Chapel Hill: University of North Carolina Press, 1990); Gilmore, *Defying Dixie.*

42. James D. Ross Jr., *The Rise and Fall of the Southern Tenant Farmers Union in Arkansas* (Knoxville: University of Tennessee Press, 2018). One of the most violent episodes in this earlier period occurred in Elaine, Arkansas. See Guy Lancaster, *The Elaine Massacre and Arkansas: A Century of Atrocity and Resistance, 1819–1919* (Little Rock: Butler Center for Arkansas Studies, 2018); Robert Whitaker, *On the Laps of Gods: The Red Summer of 1919 and the Struggle for Justice That Remade a Nation* (New York: Crown, 2008).

43. Jarod Roll, *Spirit of Rebellion: Labor and Religion in the New Cotton South* (Urbana: University of Illinois Press, 2010).

The propagation of local studies that foreground the civil rights experience in rural places and small towns both broadened and enriched the field. For example, Françoise N. Hamlin's work on Clarksdale, Mississippi, affirmed that African Americans ran a strong and active NAACP chapter but lived in a fiercely controlled and unflinchingly brutal political, social, and economic regime. Hamlin also maintained that wider recognition of male leaders in Clarksdale overshadowed the "activist mothering" of community women. Taken as a whole, monographs pertaining to such indigenous civil rights struggles deepened the understanding of what the movement could and could not achieve. As local leaders attempted to dismantle segregation, new challenges—including structural changes in the agricultural economy—arose that thwarted their efforts.[44]

Scholarship that delved into questions of gender and women's leadership enhanced an appreciation of how the fight for justice involved tackling both internal and external gender and class fissures. In *How Long? How Long?* (1997), sociologist Belinda Robnett articulated a useful model of women as "bridge leaders" who linked civil rights organizations and the grassroots, and contended that a gendered division of labor enabled the movement's success.[45] Other scholars focused on ideologies of manhood to ask how these influenced activist approaches and movement organizations, and how gendered political, economic, and cultural assumptions shaped official responses to movement demands.[46] Aside from

44. Françoise N. Hamlin, *Crossroads at Clarksdale: The Black Freedom Struggle in the Mississippi Delta after World War II* (Chapel Hill: University of North Carolina Press, 2012). See also Chris Myers Asch, *The Senator and the Sharecropper: The Freedom Struggles of James O. Eastland and Fannie Lou Hamer* (Chapel Hill: University of North Carolina Press, 2011); J. Todd Moye, *Let the People Decide: Black Freedom and White Resistance Movements in Sunflower County, Mississippi, 1945–1986* (Chapel Hill: University of North Carolina Press, 2004).

45. Belinda Robnett, *How Long? How Long? African American Women in the Struggle for Civil Rights* (New York: Oxford University Press, 1997). For other works on women in the movement, see Christina Greene, *Our Separate Ways: Women and the Black Freedom Movement in Durham, North Carolina* (Chapel Hill: University of North Carolina Press, 2005); Shannon Frystak, *Our Minds on Freedom: Women and the Struggle for Black Equality in Louisiana, 1924–1967* (Baton Rouge: Louisiana State University Press, 2009); Crawford, Rouse, and Woods, eds., *Women in the Civil Rights Movement;* Bettye Collier-Thomas and V. P. Franklin, eds., *Sisters in the Struggle: African American Women in the Civil Rights–Black Power Movement* (New York: New York University Press, 2001).

46. Timothy B. Tyson, *Radio Free Dixie: Robert F. Williams and the Roots of Black Power* (Chapel Hill: University of North Carolina Press, 1999); Steve Estes, *I Am a Man!: Race, Manhood, and the Civil Rights Movement* (Chapel Hill: University of North Carolina Press, 2005); Peter L. Ling, "Gender and Generation: Manhood at the Southern Christian Leadership Conference," in *Gender and the Civil Rights Movement,* ed. Peter L. Ling and Sharon Monteith (New Brunswick: Rutgers University Press, 2004), 101–29.

acknowledging the associations between women's civil rights activism and their increased consciousness of gender inequality, feminist scholars interested in the origins of the women's liberation movement looked to the civil rights era and theorized distinct trajectories for African American women.[47]

Many historians underscored the importance of beauty shops, women's organizations, and other women-centered spaces to the movement because black women logically drew on their networks to strengthen civil rights efforts.[48] In this vein, Tiyi M. Morris offered a comprehensive examination of Womanpower Unlimited (WU), a middle-class group in Jackson, Mississippi, led by Clarie Collins Harvey. Founded in 1961, WU first aided those arrested and jailed for participating in the Freedom Rides. WU then promoted voter education drives and youth education and tackled food security issues. WU members also joined over fifty thousand women from across the country to protest above-ground testing of nuclear weapons.[49]

Sexual violence, including assault, rape, and the denial of bodily integrity, has always informed black women's activism. As early as 1892, Ida B. Wells-Barnett famously interrogated the lynching of black men for allegedly raping white women by redirecting attention to the long history of white men's assaults of black women.[50] Yet, as Darlene Clark Hine made clear in her 1989 essay "Rape and the Inner Lives of Black Women in the Middle West," white supremacist stereotypes of black women as sexually licentious left many reluctant to discuss sexuality publicly. Migration out of the South represented an option for black

47. See, for example, Sara Evans, *Personal Politics: The Roots of Women's Liberation in the Civil Rights Movement and the New Left* (New York: Alfred A. Knopf, 1979); Benita Roth, *Separate Roads to Feminism: Black, Chicana, and White Feminist Movements in America's Second Wave* (New York: Cambridge University Press, 2004); Nancy Hewett, ed., *No Permanent Waves: Recasting Histories of U.S. Feminism* (New Brunswick: Rutgers University Press, 2010).

48. See, for example, Tiffany M. Gill, *Beauty Shop Politics: African American Women's Activism in the Beauty Industry* (Urbana: University of Illinois Press, 2010), esp. chap. 5; Greene, *Our Separate Ways;* Charron, *Freedom's Teacher,* esp. chaps. 4, 8, and 9.

49. Tiyi M. Morris, *Womanpower Unlimited and the Black Freedom Struggle in Mississippi* (Athens: University of Georgia Press, 2015).

50. Ida B. Wells-Barnett, *Southern Horrors and Other Writings: The Anti-Lynching Campaign of Ida B. Wells, 1892–1900,* ed. Jacqueline Jones Royster (Boston: Bedford, 1996); Crystal N. Feimster, *Southern Horrors: Women and the Politics of Rape and Lynching* (Cambridge: Harvard University Press, 2009); Jacquelyn Dowd Hall, "The Mind That Burns in Each Body: Women, Rape, and Racial Violence," in *Powers of Desire: The Politics of Sexuality,* ed. Ann Snitow, Christine Stansell, and Sharon Thompson (New York: Monthly Review Press, 1983), 328–49.

women to escape racial and sexual terrorism, while groups like the National Association of Colored Women permitted them to link intimate personal issues to civil rights activism.[51]

Danielle L. McGuire's *At the Dark End of the Street* (2010) profoundly reoriented scholarly awareness of the extent to which fighting sexual violence motivated female and male activists of all ages. She demonstrated that Rosa Parks's work on this issue predated her more famous bus defiance. In 1944, a local NAACP branch sent Parks to Abbeville, Alabama, to investigate the rape of twenty-four-year-old mother and sharecropper Recy Taylor by six white men. In fact, Parks's activism and that of other women during the bus boycott—including Mary Fair Burks, founder of the Women's Political Council (WPC), and WPC chapter president Jo Ann Robinson—stemmed from opposition to verbal, physical, and sexual assaults they, and others, had experienced from bus drivers and local police. McGuire also covered the antirape activism of college students and carried her investigation into the 1970s by reviewing the North Carolina trial of Joan Little, who killed the white jailer who attempted to rape her.[52]

Other scholars also detailed the intimate traumas black female civil rights activists encountered from white male authorities. SNCC's Ruby Doris Smith (later Robinson) spent time at Mississippi's Parchman Penitentiary for participating in the Freedom Rides. When she refused to take off her clothes to shower, male guards stripped her and scrubbed her with a wire brush. Fannie Lou Hamer survived a savage and sexually tinged beating in a Winona, Mississippi, jail, and, like many black women, was sterilized without her consent.[53] During the 1965 Selma campaign, a movement doctor estimated that he treated twenty women a day, on average, "whose vaginas had been burned by cattle prod-wielding police." The United States Justice Department never acted on the affidavits he sent.[54]

51. Darlene Clark Hine, "Rape and the Inner Lives of Black Women in the Middle West: Thoughts on the Culture of Dissemblance," *Signs* 14 (Summer 1989): 912-20; Hine, *Hine Sight: Black Women and the Re-Construction of American History* (Brooklyn: Carlson Publishing, 1994); Deborah Gray White, *Too Heavy a Load: Black Women in Defense of Themselves, 1894–1994* (New York: W. W. Norton, 1999).

52. Danielle L. McGuire, *At the Dark End of the Street: Black Women, Rape, and Resistance—A New History of the Civil Rights Movement from Rosa Parks to the Rise of Black Power* (New York: Alfred A. Knopf, 2010).

53. See Rickie Solinger, *Pregnancy and Power: A Short History of Reproductive Politics in America* (New York: New York University Press, 2005), 187; Dorothy Roberts, *Killing the Black Body: Race, Reproduction, and the Meaning of Liberty* (New York: Pantheon Books, 1997), esp. 89–93, 98–103; Dittmer, *Local People*, 229.

54. Hogan, *Many Minds, One Heart*, 240.

Such incidents underscore the links between sexual violence and racial control that permeated life for black women in the segregated South.

More broadly, the everyday violence African Americans experienced led to the deaths of many, including fourteen-year-old Emmet Till, whose open-casket funeral in 1955 galvanized an entire generation of young civil rights activists.[55] At the start of Freedom Summer, white supremacists murdered three SNCC workers, black Mississippian James Cheney and white northerners Michael Schwerner and Andrew Goodman. As SNCC had predicted, the case drew national attention and prompted a massive search for the bodies by the federal government, because two white men had died. Speaking in Jackson, Mississippi, in August 1964, Ella Baker underscored the different value the nation placed on African American and white lives when she declared that, until the killing of "black mothers' sons" mattered as much as the killing of "white mothers' sons," "we who believe in freedom cannot rest."[56]

Though most Americans associate the movement with nonviolent resistance, black people knew their heightened antiracist activism would prompt a proportional increase in white terrorism and that they had to defend themselves. Timothy B. Tyson detailed how Robert F. Williams, a World War II veteran and president of the NAACP branch in Monroe, North Carolina, advocated "armed self-reliance" to parry Klan attacks. Disingenuously, and certainly hypocritically, national NAACP leaders considered Williams's armed response unacceptable. However, his story demonstrated most acutely that armed self-defense and nonviolent resistance were not mutually exclusive. No less than Rosa Parks counted herself an admirer of Williams and considered Malcolm X a personal hero.[57] Similarly, in *The Deacons of Defense* (2006), Lance Hill chronicled an armed self-defense group in Louisiana, while Akinyele Omowale Umoja's 2013 monograph, *We Will Shoot Back,* confirmed that self-defense was necessary to counter white intimidation and to dismantle segregation in Mississippi. SNCC veteran

55. Mamie Till-Mobley with Christopher Benson, *Death of Innocence: The Story of the Hate Crime that Changed America* (New York: Random House, 2003); Timothy B. Tyson, *The Blood of Emmett Till* (New York: Simon & Schuster, 2017).

56. Sweet Honey in the Rock, a group founded by SNCC Freedom Singer Bernice Johnson Reagon, later memorialized this quote; see "Ella's Song," *Sweet Honey in the Rock: Selections 1976–1988,* Flying Fish, 1997, compact disc. Reagon also compiled a collection of movement songs; see *Voices of the Civil Rights Movement: Black American Freedom Songs 1960–1966,* Smithsonian Folkways Recordings, 1997, compact disc.

57. Tyson, *Radio Free Dixie.* See also Jeanne Theoharis, *The Rebellious Life of Mrs. Rosa Parks* (Boston: Beacon Press, 2013).

Charles E. Cobb Jr. also accentuated the paradox inherent in movement activists' public support for nonviolence as a tactical strategy and their embrace of their constitutional right to protect themselves.[58] Collectively, this scholarship exposed a more complicated reality at the local level that activists at the time hid from the national media.

Like those on armed self-defense, the number of studies explicating the role of interracial activism and nonblack activists in the civil rights movement has increased. Scholars began with examinations of white volunteers who went to Mississippi in 1964 to participate in COFO's Freedom Summer.[59] SNCC veteran Constance Curry's edited collection, *Deep in Our Hearts* (2010), contained first-person accounts of white women who came of age in the 1960s and renewed their commitment to the freedom struggle through such organizations as SNCC and Students for a Democratic Society. Elsewhere, scholars addressed an older generation of white southerners who joined the movement.[60] Historians explored the capacity of interracial activism to bring change. Cherisse Jones-Branch's *Crossing the Line* (2014) chronicled black and white women who contested South Carolina's racial status quo through such organizations as the NAACP, the PDP, the YWCA, and Church Women United. While black and white women's interracial attempts often proved futile, both groups wanted to improve African Americans' political and educational access in the state.[61]

Southern whites who publicly opposed segregation incurred the wrath of

58. Lance Hill, *The Deacons for Defense: Armed Resistance and the Civil Rights Movement* (Chapel Hill: University of North Carolina Press, 2004); Akinyele Omowale Umoja, *We Will Shoot Back: Armed Resistance in the Mississippi Freedom Movement* (New York: New York University Press, 2013); Charles E. Cobb Jr., *This Nonviolent Stuff'll Get You Killed: How Guns Made the Civil Rights Movement Possible* (New York: Basic Books, 2014).

59. In addition to works on SNCC that cover this topic, see Doug McAdam, *Freedom Summer* (New York: Oxford University Press, 1988); Sally Belfrage, *Freedom Summer* (New York: Viking Press, 1965); Debbie Z. Harwell, *Wednesdays in Mississippi: Proper Ladies Working for Radical Change, Freedom Summer 1964* (Jackson: University Press of Mississippi, 2014).

60. Constance Curry et al., *Deep in Our Hearts: Nine White Women in the Freedom Movement* (Athens: University of Georgia Press, 2002). Other studies on interracial activism and white civil rights activists include Kathryn L. Nasstrom, *Everybody's Grandmother and Nobody's Fool: Frances Freeborn Pauley and the Struggle for Social Justice* (Ithaca: Cornell University Press, 2000); Tinsley E. Yarbrough, *A Passion for Justice: J. Waties Waring and Civil Rights* (New York: Oxford University Press, 1987); Patricia Sullivan, ed., *Freedom Writer: Virginia Foster Durr, Letters from the Civil Rights Years* (New York: Routledge, 2003); Fosl, *Subversive Southerner.*

61. Jones-Branch, *Crossing the Line.*

their families, friends, and communities. In some cases, they, too, paid for their activism with their lives. Mary Stanton recounted the experience of seventh-generation white southerner and third-generation Alabamian, Juliette Hampton Morgan, who challenged segregation on Montgomery busses before the famous boycott. After penning a scathing letter to the local newspaper questioning community wisdom about black inferiority and Jim Crow laws, Morgan faced near constant harassment and threats. On 15 July 1957, deeply traumatized by such incidents, she committed suicide. Northern whites gave their lives to the struggle as well. In addition to the brutal Klan murders of two white SNCC activists at the outset of Freedom Summer in Mississippi, during the 1965 march from Selma to Montgomery, the Reverend James Leeb died after white supremacists attacked him, and Klan members shot and killed Detroit homemaker Viola Liuzzo.[62]

In the twenty-first century, scholars began to illuminate the lives of people from more diverse racial backgrounds who embraced the movement. Mexican Americans Elizabeth "Betita" Martinez and Maria Varela worked with SNCC before turning their attention to the Chicano civil rights movement.[63] In 2005, Diane C. Fujino published a biography of Asian American civil rights activist Yuri Kochiyama. Her family's internment at a camp in Jerome, Arkansas, during World War II solidified Kochiyama's awareness of the nation's entrenched racism. In 1963, after moving to New York, she met Malcolm X and soon joined his Organization of Afro-American Unity. Two years later, she held him in her arms as he died in the Audubon Ballroom. Still relatively unknown, Yuri Kochiyama remained a dedicated activist until her death in 2014.[64]

Yet another notable evolution in civil rights historiography centers on the many forms in which education shaped liberation. The struggle to integrate public schools has always had a prominent place in the scholarship, and the centrality of *Brown v. Board of Education* remains indisputable. In addition to documenting

62. Mary Stanton, *Journey toward Justice: Juliette Hampton Morgan and the Montgomery Bus Boycott* (Athens: University of Georgia Press, 2006); Stanton, *From Selma to Sorrow: The Life and Death of Viola Liuzzo* (Athens: University of Georgia Press, 1998). Nearly all works on SNCC address the killings of Chaney, Goodman, and Schwerner.

63. See Gordon K. Mantler, *Power to the Poor: Black-Brown Coalition and the Fight for Economic Justice, 1960–1974* (Chapel Hill: University of North Carolina Press, 2013), 11. See also Brian D. Behnken, *Fighting Their Own Battles: Mexican Americans, African Americans, and the Struggle for Civil Rights in Texas* (Chapel Hill: University of North Carolina Press, 2011).

64. Diane C. Fujino, *Heartbeat of Struggle: The Revolutionary Life of Yuri Kochiyama* (Minneapolis: University of Minnesota Press, 2005).

the NAACP's legal strategy, scholars detailed the risks involved for black plaintiffs and called attention to the costs of integration, both in terms of the closing of schools that served as vital community institutions and the loss of jobs for African American teachers and principals.[65] More in-depth examinations of the effects on black youth who assumed the burdens of desegregation have supplemented participants' autobiographies.[66] Surveying earlier cases pertaining to desegregating higher education and teacher salary equalization, historians illustrated how NAACP legal victories in the years leading up to *Brown v. Board of Education* tutored segregationist legislators in tactics to avoid compliance with federal court orders, and how involvement in these campaigns could radicalize or mitigate black students' and educators' activism.[67]

Scholars also examined tensions between adults and youth at HBCUs. Foremost, the extent of civil rights activity on campus depended on whether an HBCU was public (and thereby dependent on state funding) or private. The positions adopted by administrators and individual faculty varied when it came to supporting or dampening protest. Indeed, civil rights histories that highlight the role of HBCUs mapped the movement's generational divide, especially in its nascent years, as cautious leaders of state institutions attempted to rein in student activists. Ironically, that often fed their students' determination.[68] Addi-

65. See Richard Kluger, *Simple Justice: The History of* Brown v. Board of Education *and Black America's Struggle for Equality* (New York: Alfred A. Knopf, 1976); David S. Cecelski, *Along Freedom Road: Hyde County, North Carolina, and the Fate of Black Schools in the South* (Chapel Hill: University of North Carolina Press, 1994); Sarah Caroline Thuesen, *Greater than Equal: African American Struggles for Schools and Citizenship in North Carolina, 1919–1965* (Chapel Hill: University of North Carolina Press, 2013).

66. See Melba Pattillo Beals, *Warriors Don't Cry: A Searing Memoir of the Battle to Integrate Little Rock's Central High* (New York: Pocket Books, 1994); Rachel Devlin, *A Girl Stands at the Schoolhouse Door: The Generation of Young Women Who Desegregated America's Schools* (New York: Basic Books, 2018); Jon N. Hale, "Future Foot Soldiers or Budding Criminals?: The Dynamics of High School Student Activism in the Southern Black Freedom Struggle," *Journal of Southern History* 84 (August 2018): 615–52.

67. Charron, *Freedom's Teacher,* chaps. 5–6; Tushnet, *The NAACP's Legal Strategy against Segregated Education.*

68. See Chafe, *Civilities and Civil Rights;* Norrell, *Reaping the Whirlwind;* Elizabeth A. Lundeen, "Brick and Mortar: Historically Black Colleges and the Struggle for Equality, 1930–1960" (PhD diss., University of North Carolina at Chapel Hill, 2018); Adam Fairclough, "The Black College Presidents Who Tried to Thwart the Racial Integration of Higher Education," *Journal of Blacks in Higher Education* 55 (Spring 2007): 71–75; Crystal R. Sanders, "Pursuing the Unfinished Business of Democracy: Willa B. Player and Liberal Arts Education in the Civil Rights Era," *North Carolina Historical Review* 96 (January 2019): 1–33. See also Martha Biondi, *The Black Revolution on Campus* (Berkeley: University of California Press, 2012).

tional works documented how HBCUs provided all-black spaces for training in nonviolence and other organizing strategies.[69]

Moreover, scholarship emphasized the fundamental links between grassroots education and grassroots activism. Katherine Mellen Charron's *Freedom's Teacher* (2009) charted the lifelong educational activism of Septima Clark, who developed the Citizenship Schools, an adult education program first sponsored by HFS and then SCLC. Works on this site of radical education illuminated the processes that prepared African Americans to register to vote and to take effective action in civil rights campaigns while also facilitating women's community leadership.[70] Where the Citizenship Schools targeted adults, SNCC addressed the needs of black youth when it established the Freedom Schools in Mississippi in the summer of 1964. Jon N. Hale and William Sturkey showed that beyond compensating for the separate and unequal education black children received in public school, Freedom Schools fostered their self-esteem by emphasizing black history, culture, and self-determination.[71]

Finally, Crystal S. Sanders's *A Chance for Change* (2016) documented grassroots participation in the Child Development Group of Mississippi (CDGM), a radical Head Start program. As an initiative connected to the War on Poverty, CDGM prepared impoverished black children to enter school and gave them access to social services. Sanders argued that it also created a pathway for working-class movement women to obtain relatively well-paid jobs with benefits, and trained them to manage their own programs and write grants. Segregationists eventually succeeded in defunding CDGM, but it functioned as a clear symbol of poor black people's resolve to improve conditions for their children and their communities despite considerable resistance from white people and some African Americans.[72]

69. This is especially apparent in the opening chapters of Hogan's *Many Minds, One Heart,* which covered nonviolent training at Fisk University in Nashville.

70. Charron, *Freedom's Teacher;* Deanna M. Gillespie, "'First Class' Citizenship Education in the Mississippi Delta, 1961–1965," *Journal of Southern History* 80 (February 2014): 109–42; Cotton, *If Your Back's Not Bent;* Payne, *I've Got the Light of Freedom,* esp. 68–76, 142–44.

71. Jon N. Hale, *The Freedom Schools: Student Activists in the Mississippi Civil Rights Movement* (New York: Columbia University Press, 2016); William Sturkey and Jon N. Hale, eds., *To Write in the Light of Freedom: The Newspapers of the 1964 Mississippi Freedom Schools* (Jackson: University Press of Mississippi, 2015). See also Robert P. Moses and Charles E. Cobb Jr., *Radical Equations: Civil Rights from Mississippi to the Algebra Project* (Boston: Beacon Press, 2001).

72. Crystal R. Sanders, *A Chance for Change: Head Start and Mississippi's Black Freedom Struggle* (Chapel Hill: University of North Carolina Press, 2016).

Studies that reviewed what movement activists did in the latter half of the 1960s build upon such insights. Susan Youngblood Ashmore, Kent B. Germany, and William S. Clayton detailed the War on Poverty in the urban and rural South and underscored the linkages between civil rights activism and attempts to capitalize on new forms of federal support.[73] Their works, too, revealed the limitations of that same support in terms of funding and oversight that necessitated navigating bureaucratic rules and regulations. Additionally, federal programs and their modes of delivery at the state level allowed the movement's foes to contain its radicalism and weaken its gains in the name of fiscal conservatism.

Civil rights warriors' continuing calls for full economic citizenship are evident in Michael K. Honey's *Going Down Jericho Road* (2008) and *Southern Labor and Black Civil Rights* (1993). Both accentuated how labor issues animated King's participation in the 1968 sanitation workers' strike in Memphis, where he died.[74] Demands for economic justice shaped the 1968 Poor People's Campaign (PPC) as well. Organized by SCLC, the PPC also represented an attempt for broader engagement with the many movements that civil rights insurgency spawned. As Gordon K. Mantler argued in *Power to the Poor* (2013), the PPC's shortcomings elucidate the difficulty of multiracial organizing and coalition building. At the same time, he challenged the idea that a fractious identity politics undermined the era's rights revolutions. SCLC also combined labor and civil rights struggles in its last national fight—the 1969 hospital workers' strike that black women led in Charleston, South Carolina.[75]

Scholarship pertaining to the quest for economic self-determination by the grass roots uncovered the importance of new black-controlled organizations

73. Susan Youngblood Ashmore, *Carry It On: The War on Poverty and the Civil Rights Movement in Alabama, 1964–1972* (Athens: University of Georgia Press, 2008); Kent Germany, *New Orleans after the Promises: Poverty, Citizenship, and the Search for the Great Society* (Athens: University of Georgia Press, 2007); William S. Clayson, *Freedom Is Not Enough: The War on Poverty and the Civil Rights Movement in Texas* (Austin: University of Texas Press, 2010).

74. Michael K. Honey, *Going Down Jericho Road: The Memphis Strike, Martin Luther King's Last Campaign* (New York: W. W. Norton, 2007); Honey, *Southern Labor and Black Civil Rights: Organizing Memphis Workers* (Urbana: University of Illinois Press, 1993). See also Thomas F. Jackson, *From Civil Rights to Human Rights: Martin Luther King Jr. and The Struggle for Economic Justice* (Philadelphia: University of Pennsylvania Press, 2007).

75. Mantler, *Power to the Poor.* See also Gerald D. McKnight, *The Last Crusade: Martin Luther King Jr., the FBI, and the Poor People's Campaign* (Boulder: Westview Press, 1998); Steve Estes, *Charleston in Black and White: Race and Power in the South after the Civil Rights Movement* (Chapel Hill: University of North Carolina Press, 2015).

formed by movement veterans. Utilizing an interdisciplinary approach, Monica M. White examined rural black radicalism with the 1967 establishment of the Freedom Farms Cooperative (FFC), a community-based economic development project. The FFC provided sharecroppers, tenant farmers, and domestic workers with access to health care and cultivated their political and economic independence. Similarly, in *You Can't Eat Freedom* (2016), Greta de Jong focused on the rural cooperatives that emerged in the Deep South in the last half of the 1960s. Such endeavors epitomized another way for black agriculturalists to apply the ideological and practical lessons they had learned from their involvement in the movement. Yet most cooperative goals for economic self-sufficiency remained unmet due to national political realignments and changing federal policies in the Nixon era.[76]

Following those who capitalized on their engagement with SNCC enabled historians to explore additional groups concerned with black empowerment. In *Bloody Lowndes* (2009), Hasan Kwame Jeffries chronicled the Lowndes County Freedom Organization in Alabama, and black farmers' efforts to gain representation on local agricultural committees and to win as candidates running for office. Meanwhile Pete Daniel's *Dispossession* (2013) documented ongoing discrimination by the United States Department of Agriculture that led to significant black land loss. Such works sharpen the appreciation of a problem the movement always confronted: even as one part of the federal government acquiesced to its demands—particularly with regard to equal treatment under the law, and voting rights—other agencies and departments preserved class- and race-based structural inequalities. Of necessity, this scholarship outlined the erosion of civil rights advances beyond the 1960s.[77] These studies provided evidence that prompted

76. Monica M. White, *Freedom Farmers: Agricultural Resistance and the Black Freedom Movement* (Chapel Hill: University of North Carolina Press, 2018); Greta de Jong, *You Can't Eat Freedom: Southerners and Social Justice after the Civil Rights Movement* (Chapel Hill: University of North Carolina Press, 2016). See also Lee, *For Freedom's Sake;* Dittmer, *Local People,* chap. 16. For a longer view of the cooperative movement, see Jessica Gordon Nembhard, *Collective Courage: A History of African American Cooperative Economic Thought and Practice* (University Park: Pennsylvania State University Press, 2014).

77. Hasan Kwame Jeffries, *Bloody Lowndes: Civil Rights and Black Power in Alabama's Black Belt* (New York: New York University Press, 2009); Pete Daniel, *Dispossession: Discrimination against African American Farmers in the Age of Civil Rights* (Chapel Hill: University of North Carolina Press, 2013). See also John Dittmer, *The Good Doctors: The Medical Committee for Human Rights and the Struggle for Justice in Health Care* (New York: Bloomsbury, 2009); Evan Faulkenbury, *Poll Power: The Voter Education Project and the Movement for the Ballot in the American South* (Chapel Hill: University of North Carolina Press, 2019).

some scholars to reappraise how the movement's energy endured in new forms; for other scholars, they served as a clear dividing line between the civil rights years and what followed.

One of the most difficult tasks historians face when writing about the civil rights movement involves how the nation and its citizens commemorate it. Works on ways that sundry actors appropriate movement memory point to patterns of sanitizing the era's radicalism while also distorting and dismissing the intricate realities that shaped activists' experiences and their labors. Contributors to Renee C. Romano and Leigh Raiford's edited collection, *The Civil Rights Movement in American Memory* (2006), probed the stakes of such struggles as evinced in museum exhibitions, cultural representations, legal trials, movement-related media coverage, and conservatives' adaptation of its rhetoric. Doing so, they concentrated on how civil rights memory diverges in efforts to institutionalize, visualize, and deploy it.[78] Jeanne Theoharis addressed the same problems in *A More Beautiful and Terrible History* (2018), and highlighted women's and young people's contributions in a much-needed corrective that outlined the depth and breadth of engagement by movement participants and in its organizing structures.[79]

Civil rights memory as expressed in autobiographies and memoirs penned by movement veterans represents another avenue of scholarly investigation. Kathryn L. Nasstrom argued that in such works activists chafed at mainstream interpretations of the movement, asserting the accuracy of their own voices and contesting the crystallization of a "grand narrative" that ends the civil rights era in 1968 with King's assassination and reduces the Black Power movement to a "tragic epilogue." Nasstrom demonstrated that such publications, even with the risks they pose as primary sources, allow historians to "understand the full spectrum of action, inaction, and reaction that constituted the movement and determined its outcomes."[80]

78. Renee C. Romano and Leigh Raiford, *The Civil Rights Movement in American Memory* (Athens: University of Georgia Press, 2006), xiii, also the bibliography on 367–69; Raiford, *Imprisoned in a Luminous Glare: Photography and the African American Freedom Struggle* (Chapel Hill: University of North Carolina Press, 2011); Romano, *Racial Reckoning: Prosecuting America's Civil Rights Murders* (Cambridge: Harvard University Press, 2014).

79. Jeanne Theoharis, *A More Beautiful and Terrible History: The Uses and Misuses of Civil Rights History* (Boston: Beacon Press, 2018).

80. Kathryn L. Nasstrom, "Between Memory and History: Autobiographies of the Civil Rights Movement and the Writing of Civil Rights History," *Journal of Southern History* 74 (May 2008): 325–64, quotes on 330 and 363.

Public history sites and spaces of commemoration exemplify significant locations of movement memory-making as well. Strewn across the country in the form of streets named after national and local civil rights leaders or statues dedicated to prominent activists, these memorials constitute important evidence of the increased inclusion of African Americans in southern and American public space, and in historical narratives. Indeed, the Martin Luther King Jr. Memorial occupies a prominent place near the National Mall in Washington, DC, and the National Museum of African American History opened in September 2016. Yet as geographers Owen J. Dwyer and Derrick H. Alderman observed, the majority of such tangible movement markers appear in socially and geographically marginalized spaces. By examining the processes that determine where such memorials predominate, scholars revealed much about what has changed as a result of the civil rights movement. At the same time, they remind us how much of America's racist past remains uninterpreted and unrepresented in the present.[81]

81. Owen J. Dwyer and Derek H. Alderman, *Civil Right Memorials and the Geography of Memory* (Athens: University of Georgia Press, 2008).

GENDER AND SEXUALITY IN THE TWENTIETH-CENTURY SOUTH

Blain Roberts and Megan Taylor Shockley

When Anne Firor Scott and Jacquelyn Dowd Hall wrote the historiographical entry on southern women's history in the 1987 volume, *Interpreting Southern History,* they noted that "in no way has the historical landscape changed more radically in the past two decades than in the emergence from the deep shadows of the other half of the population."[1] While they detailed the expansion of the field and the questions asked by historians about women's economic activities—as well as their roles in social justice, labor, and civil rights movements—Scott and Hall explained that more needed to be done to examine women in the twentieth-century South. Much of the chapter addressed the scholarship of the pre-twentieth century, a reflection of the state of the field. They identified a need especially for more studies of women in the rural South, in factory and industrial work, and in reform and progressive social efforts.

Much has changed: the historiographical landscape on southern women grew so much in the ensuing decades that it is appropriate that this volume includes one essay examining women's experiences before the Civil War and another examining them after. And women's history inspired studies on gender and sexuality that require historiographical contextualization as well. Indeed, when Hall and Scott summarized the literature on southern women's history, they rarely invoked the concept of gender. This is not to suggest that either they or the historians

1. Jacquelyn Dowd Hall and Anne Firor Scott, "Women in the South," in *Interpreting Southern History: Historiographical Essays in Honor of Sanford W. Higginbotham,* ed. John B. Boles and Evelyn Thomas Nolen (Baton Rouge: Louisiana State University Press, 1987), 455. The authors are grateful to Seth Kotch, Rose Stremlau, and Jennifer Ritterhouse for their bibliographic suggestions.

about whom they wrote were unaware of or uninterested in questions of gender. Rather, as Hall and Scott wrote, historians of southern women looked at what women were doing—or what "their particular part [was] in the phenomenon under consideration." Gendered analysis had not yet transformed the field; Joan W. Scott's pathbreaking "Gender: A Useful Category of Historical Analysis" had been published, after all, just one year earlier.[2]

Hall and Scott concluded their essay by predicting that southern historians would increasingly explore issues of gender. They were right. Historians of the South have been at the forefront of showing how constructs of gender and sexuality shaped the past, and the postbellum South provided fertile ground for this type of analysis. The Civil War, insisted LeeAnn Whites in 1995, represented a "crisis in gender," raising thorny questions about how white and black southerners understood their appropriate gender roles after the abolition of slavery.[3] As Laura F. Edwards, Glenda Elizabeth Gilmore, Jane Dailey, Bryant Simon, Stephen Kantrowitz, and others showed, the relationship between gender and this crisis and the many others that followed—Reconstruction, industrialization, segregation—was not peripheral to late nineteenth-century and early twentieth-century southern history. On the contrary, throughout these developments, gender determined political power.[4]

2. Hall and Scott, "Women in the South," 457, 509; Joan W. Scott, "Gender: A Useful Category of Historical Analysis," *American Historical Review* 91 (December 1986): 1053–75.

3. LeeAnn Whites, *The Civil War as a Crisis in Gender: Augusta, Georgia, 1860–1890* (Athens: University of Georgia Press, 1995); Whites, *Gender Matters: Race, Class, and Sexuality in the Nineteenth-Century South* (New York: Palgrave Macmillan, 2005).

4. Laura F. Edwards, *Gendered Strife and Confusion: The Political Culture of Reconstruction* (Urbana: University of Illinois Press, 1997); Glenda Elizabeth Gilmore, *Gender and Jim Crow: Women and the Politics of White Supremacy in North Carolina, 1896–1920* (Chapel Hill: University of North Carolina Press, 1996); Jane Dailey, *Before Jim Crow: The Politics of Race in Postemancipation Virginia* (Chapel Hill: University of North Carolina Press, 2000); Bryant Simon, *A Fabric of Defeat: The Politics of South Carolina Millhands, 1910–1948* (Chapel Hill: University of North Carolina Press, 1998); Stephen Kantrowitz, *Ben Tillman and the Reconstruction of White Supremacy* (Chapel Hill: University of North Carolina Press, 2000); Kantrowitz, "Ben Tillman and Hendrix McLane, Agrarian Rebels: White Manhood, 'The Farmers,' and the Limits of Southern Populism," *Journal of Southern History* 66 (August 2000): 497–524; Jane Dailey, Glenda Elizabeth Gilmore, Bryant Simon, eds., *Jumpin' Jim Crow: Southern Politics from Civil War to Civil Rights* (Princeton: Princeton University Press, 2000); Peter W. Bardaglio, *Reconstructing the Household: Families, Sex, and the Law in the Nineteenth-Century South* (Chapel Hill: University of North Carolina Press, 1995); Glenda Elizabeth Gilmore, "Gender and *Origins of the New South*," *Journal of Southern History* 67 (November 2001): 769–88.

Edwards, for example, centered the politics of Reconstruction within the household. With the institution of slavery gone, both white and black men rooted claims to public power in their roles as heads of households. But white men's eventual success at redefining manhood along racial and class lines—at removing manhood from within the reach of black men—brought the revolutionary promise of Reconstruction to an end. Gendered constructions, in other words, contributed to the failures of Reconstruction, in the same way, as Gilmore demonstrated, that they explained the success of white supremacy campaigns in the Progressive-era South. Collectively, scholars erased the line between private and public, between the home and the state, highlighting the inseparability of gender from politics as southerners battled to define the New South. Prescribed notions of masculinity and femininity could empower and constrain both women and men across color lines in their efforts to claim the full rights of citizenship, earn a living, establish better working environments, reform cities, and refashion culture in the twentieth century.[5]

In the late twentieth and early twenty-first centuries, historians built upon these insights as they filled several of the historiographical gaps that Hall and Scott identified. With a few notable exceptions—including Jacqueline Jones's *Labor of Love, Labor of Sorrow* (1985)—the history of women in the twentieth-century rural South, as they noted, was sadly lacking. Historians stepped in to examine the roles of rural women in perpetuating a non-urban economy, focusing on their work in the home, in the fields, and in the markets, and often using oral histories to better understand a population that left few written records. For example, Rebecca Sharpless's *Fertile Ground, Narrow Choices* (1999) analyzed women from different racial/ethnic backgrounds in the cotton fields of Texas's blackland prairie region. She found that women were often doubly burdened with agricultural and reproductive labor, but that they fought for independence by producing their own food to counter the crop-lien system, forming strong community networks for mutual support, and even choosing to leave their rural communities. Focusing on 1919–1941, Melissa Walker's *All We Knew Was to Farm* (2000) examined ways in which South Carolina, West Virginia, and Tennessee women strove to create agricultural businesses, keep their land in the face of federal encroachment from the Tennessee Valley Authority and the military, and maintain autonomy as independent farmers. Her analysis of a white-dominated region explored interracial tensions that emerged over federal job opportuni-

5. Edwards, *Gendered Strife and Confusion;* Gilmore, *Gender and Jim Crow.*

ties. Walker also uncovered the gradations of "class"—determined not always by income alone, but by behavior and social capital maintained by kinship ties. Sharpless and Walker, along with many other historians, highlighted the crucial labor done by women of all socioeconomic levels to support family farms.[6]

Walker's work addressed a serious hole in rural history: the labor of Appalachian women. In the late 1990s, Barbara Ellen Smith called for a feminist reinterpretation of a region dominated by narratives of masculinity and stereotypical views of individuals fighting against outside and corporate interests. Though earlier generations of historians challenged Appalachian stereotypes, they often underused women's roles in exploring how Appalachian peoples built kin networks, produced and sold agricultural goods, and took care of families in a place known for its isolation and poverty.[7] Correlating with greater opportunity to incorporate women's voices into analysis of Appalachian history has been an unearthing of greater resources about the role of women in Appalachian industries, reform and religious/educational mission movements, activist and cultural movements, and on farms (which remains curiously understudied given the rich oral history collections now housed at southern institutions).[8] Given the growing

6. Jacqueline Jones, *Labor of Love, Labor of Sorrow: Black Women, Work, and the Family from Slavery to the Present* (New York: Basic Books, 1985); Rebecca Sharpless, *Fertile Ground, Narrow Choices: Women on Texas Cotton Farms, 1900–1940* (Chapel Hill: University of North Carolina Press, 1999); Melissa Walker, *All We Knew Was to Farm: Rural Women in the Upcountry South, 1919–1941* (Baltimore: Johns Hopkins University Press, 2000). Other works that explore women's kinship networks and field work in the rural South include Evan P. Bennett, *When Tobacco Was King: Families, Farm Labor, and Federal Policy in the Piedmont* (Gainesville: University Press of Florida, 2014); and Rebecca Sharpless and Melissa Walker, eds., *Work, Family, and Faith: Rural Southern Women in the Twentieth Century* (Columbia: University of Missouri Press, 2006), whose contributors explore the lives of women in many different socioeconomic circles of the rural South, some professional home demonstration agents, some poor, some independent landowners, and some whose families left their rural homes to migrate to industries for better opportunities.

7. Barbara Ellen Smith, "'Beyond the Mountains': The Paradox of Women's Place in Appalachian History," *NWSA Journal* 11 (Fall 1999): 1–17. See also Connie Park Rice and Marie Tedesco, eds., *Women of the Mountain South: Identity, Work, and Activism* (Athens: Ohio University Press, 2015). There was an intermediary stage in the historiography during which historians admirably included women in studies of Appalachia but underutilized them analytically. See Altina L. Waller, *Feud: Hatfields, McCoys, and Social Change in Appalachia, 1860–1900* (Chapel Hill: University of North Carolina Press, 1988); Ronald D. Eller, *Miners, Millhands, and Mountaineers: Industrialization of the Appalachian South, 1880–1930* (Knoxville: University of Tennessee Press, 1982); Margaret Lynn Brown, *The Wild East: A Biography of the Great Smoky Mountains* (Gainesville: University Press of Florida, 2000).

8. While the collected oral histories are not without problems, particularly in their romanticization of the mountain South, the Foxfire Project documented women's myriad activities in the heart of the southern Appalachian region (as well as the lives of many male residents of the region). For a list of

interest in regional food networks and localism, the study of farm women in the twentieth- and twenty-first-century Appalachian South appears to be an area rich with opportunities for study.

Historians have worked, however, to uncover the economic power held by rural women in Appalachia and elsewhere throughout the South, often arguing that women's direct participation in the rural economy, whatever shape that took, made the difference between family success and failure. More importantly, scholars showed how women often took control of economic forces. Lu Ann Jones argued in *Mama Learned Us to Work* (2002) that North Carolina women essentially crafted the economy as consumers in a rural network, trading eggs and dairy products for goods. They also created a burgeoning egg industry that became a mainstay in the South after World War II. Evan P. Bennett posited the importance of women in setting up cooperatives and setting prices in "'A Responsibility on Women that Cannot Be Delegated to Father, Husband, or Son'" (2006), and Ann E. McCleary's "Seizing the Opportunity" (2006) argued that white women in Virginia became the proprietors of a successful curbside market movement that grew out of the efforts of home demonstration agents. Agricultural and domestic extension programs, as Lynne Rieff explained in "Revitalizing Southern Homes" (2006), provided assistance to rural women and created an avenue of professionalization for women who were hired as agents—to a point. As it became more specialized, this assistance often proved less useful to rural women. Carmen Harris's examination of black home demonstration agents in the collection *Rethinking Home Economics* (1997) argued that black home demonstration agents, fewer in number and paid less than white agents, helped black rural women work through segregated rural extension services to receive the support and assistance they deserved.[9]

Foxfire publications, as well as more information on the project, visit https://www.foxfire.org/ (accessed 18 January 2019). Appalachian oral histories can be found at several institutions, including the Southern Oral History Program at the University of North Carolina at Chapel Hill, https://sohp.org/ (accessed 18 January 2019); the Appalachia Oral History collection at the University of Kentucky, https://kentuckyoralhistory.org/catalog/xt71rn305d4z (accessed 18 January 2019); and the Marshall University Oral History collection, https://mds.marshall.edu/oral_history/ (accessed 18 January 2019).

9. Lu Ann Jones, *Mama Learned Us to Work: Farm Women in the New South* (Chapel Hill: University of North Carolina Press; 2002); Evan P. Bennett, "'A Responsibility on Women that Cannot Be Delegated to Father, Husband, or Son': Farm Women and Cooperation in the Tobacco South," in Sharpless and Walker, eds., *Work, Family, and Faith*, 67–96; Ann E. McCleary, "Seizing the Opportunity: Home Demonstration Curb Markets in Virginia," in Sharpless and Walker, eds., *Work, Family, and Faith*, 97–134;

Studies of rural women have avoided romanticizing rural work; in fact, struggles over family strategies, as well as the undermining of the importance of women's labor as men took on wage work and dealt in finances with crops, suggested women's lower status in the rural hierarchy. Women often gained more by leaving rural life and moving to cities where they could take advantage of modern conveniences and closer neighbors. Still, historians argued that rural women of the late nineteenth and early twentieth centuries could, and did, claim autonomy, albeit within prescribed boundaries set by racial, gendered, and class-based societal norms.

Agricultural women in the second half of the twentieth century garnered less scholarly attention than did farm women from earlier in the century. Still, historians are advancing the field of gender and rural life in the post–World War II South. For example, Melissa Walker's sweeping analysis in *Southern Farmers and Their Stories* (2006) examined how farmers dealt with dramatic change in the twentieth century, and discussed gendered labor and how women worked and formed communities. Evan P. Bennett also explored how families farmed tobacco in the Piedmont of North Carolina and Virginia from 1860 to 2004 in *When Tobacco Was King* (2014). He argued women were critical to important production processes related to tobacco curing, and that they negotiated networks of support to help with production. From the influx of Latinx migrants to the challenges of exurbanization paving over acres of farmland to pipelines and other industries threatening the landscapes of rural life, the twenty-first century brought new challenges to southern rural life, and women responded. As urbanites changed zoning laws to raise chickens, and farmers' markets arose in parking lots, at breweries, and on college campuses, small farmers aggressively participated in the local food movement. Many of these farmers were women, or women who participated actively in the business. We need more historians to explore the emergence of this twenty-first century phenomenon, perhaps tying it to the earlier economic networks built by women to support their families in the first half of the twentieth century.[10]

Lynn Rieff, "Revitalizing Rural Homes: Rural Women, the Professionalization of Home Demonstration Work, and the Limits of Reform, 1917–1945," in Sharpless and Walker, eds., *Work, Family, and Faith,* 135–65; Carmen Harris, "Grace Under Pressure: The Black Home Extension Service in South Carolina, 1919–1966," in *Rethinking Home Economics: Women and the History of a Profession,* ed. Sarah Stage and Virginia B. Vincenti (Ithaca: Cornell University Press, 1997), 203–28.

10. Melissa Walker, *Southern Farmers and Their Stories: Memory and Meaning in Oral History* (Lexington: University Press of Kentucky, 2006); Bennett, *When Tobacco Was King.* Other works include Cherisse Jones-Branch, "Empowering Families and Communities: African American Home Demon-

Since the 1980s, historians also worked to understand women's role in the wage labor economy. As small-scale farmers struggled to make ends meet in the early twentieth century, many families moved to newly established mill towns, or company towns, often in the very rural places inhabited by farm families. Perhaps nothing defined the New South more than the many textile mills and needlework/garment factories that sprang up throughout the region, and for decades, historians documented ways in which white women created community, challenged low wages and conditions, and survived as best they could in the face of industry decline in the paternalistic company towns. Through oral histories, Jacquelyn Dowd Hall and the other authors of *Like A Family* (1987) introduced us to mill women's lives, both in the factories and in the home, arguing that white women sought work in the mills to claim autonomy or to support their husbands who identified as farmers. The women often found themselves stuck in the lowest-paying jobs, subjected to sexual harassment, balancing the double duties of reproductive and wage labor, and struggling against the vagaries of the larger economy with no work protections. Because companies controlled so much of mill life, from the stores to workers' physicians, they could curtail protest strategies. In fact, Hall pointed out in "Disorderly Women" (1986) that the women who helped lead unionization efforts in the late 1920s and early 1930s found themselves fired—losing not just their jobs but their homes and their communities as well. Other scholars explored ways in which women tried to claim autonomy in a patriarchal system, even as women dominated the low-wage labor force.[11]

---

stration Agents in Arkansas, 1913–1965," in *Race and Ethnicity in Arkansas: New Perspectives,* ed. John Kirk (Fayetteville: University of Arkansas Press, 2015), 85–95; Leon Fink, *The Maya of Morganton: Work and Community in the Nuevo New South* (Chapel Hill: University of North Carolina Press, 2003).

11. Jacquelyn Dowd Hall et al., *Like a Family: The Making of a Southern Cotton Mill World* (Chapel Hill: University of North Carolina Press, 1987); Hall, "Disorderly Women: Gender and Labor Militancy in the Appalachian South," *Journal of American History* 73 (September 1986): 354–82. Kristina L. Horton, *Martyr of Loray Mill: Ella May and the 1929 Textile Workers' Strike in Gastonia, North Carolina* (Jefferson, NC: McFarland, 2015), examines one of the most notable women organizers, who was killed on the way to an organizational meeting. Other works exploring the lives, labors, and protests of women in textile mills include Patricia Evridge Hill, "Real Women and True Womanhood: Grassroots Organizing among Dallas Dressmakers in 1935," *Labor's Heritage* 5 (Spring 1994): 4–17; Cynthia A. Kierner, Jennifer R. Loux, and Megan Taylor Shockley, *Changing History: Virginia Women Through Four Centuries* (Richmond: Library of Virginia Press, 2013); Jacquelyn Dowd Hall, "O. Delight Smith's Progressive Era: Labor, Feminism, and Reform in the Urban South," in *Visible Women: New Essays on American Activism,* ed. Nancy A. Hewitt and Suzanne Lebsock (Urbana: University of Illinois Press, 1993), 166–98. And it was not just in work and village life that men were dominant. Simon's *A Fabric of Defeat* argued that politicians such

In the 1970s and 1980s, most works addressing women in the textile industry focused on the pre–World War II period. By the 1990s, in the wake of the decline of the South's textile industry, scholars began to explore the postwar period, too, focusing not only on textiles but on the needlework/garment industry. They examined ways that white women reacted to the hiring of women of color, how women often oversaw unionization efforts in the face of factory decline, and how women handled the closing of factories. For example, in her study of the Chicana women who led a strike at Farah Industries in El Paso in 1972, Emily Honig found that the event empowered strike leaders in other areas of their lives long after they had left the industry. Michelle Haberland's *Striking Beauties* (2015) examined how African American women entered the needlework industry and broke down barriers set by Jim Crow policies, and how unions facilitated—or ignored or thwarted—their inclusion. She also explored the unionization movement of the 1970s, which ultimately failed in the wake of international competition. As more scholars focused on the post–World War II decades, their studies emphasized a more diversified workforce and gains made by women. However, the relatively rapid closing of these industries in the South by the 1990s meant that women who worked to claim space in the factories did not enjoy any long-term benefits.[12]

Textile and garment industries may have dominated the South, but women's historians explored many other aspects of female wage labor in factory settings. Dolores E. Janiewski's *Sisterhood Denied* (1992), a community study of Durham, North Carolina, included analysis of women in early twentieth-century textile and tobacco industries. She found that segregation in all aspects of life—both inside and outside of factories—hampered unionization efforts and prevented

---

as Ben Tillman built a base of support among poor white male millworkers, calling upon their racial and gendered privilege to wrest control from lowcountry South Carolina elites in the first half of the twentieth century.

12. Emily Honig, "Women at Farah Revisited: Political Mobilization and Its Aftermath among Chicana Workers in El Paso, Texas, 1972–1992," *Feminist Studies* 22 (Summer 1996): 425–52; Michelle Haberland, *Striking Beauties: Women Apparel Workers in the U.S. South, 1930–2000* (Athens: University of Georgia Press, 2015). See also Victoria Byerly, *Hard Times Cotton Mill Girls: Personal Histories of Womanhood and Poverty in the South* (Ithaca: Cornell University Press, 1986); Paula McLendon, "Time and Time Again: The Women, the Union, and the Vanity Factory," *Southern Changes* 6 (1984): 8–17, http://southernchanges.digitalscholarship.emory.edu/sc06-5_1204/sc06-5_005/ (accessed 18 January 2019); Mary E. Frederickson, "'I Know Which Side I'm On': Southern Women in the Labor Movement in the Twentieth Century," in *Women, Work, and Protest: A Century of U.S. Women's Labor History*, ed. Ruth Milkman (New York: Routledge, 1985), 156–80; Joey Fink, "The Many Norma Raes: Working-Class Women in the 1970s Campaign to Organize J. P. Stevens" (PhD diss., University of North Carolina, 2015).

gender-based organizing. Nancy A. Hewitt's *Southern Discomfort* (2001) further complicated analyses of gender and race in industrial settings, as she included Florida's Italian- and Cuban-dominated cigar industry. The socialist leanings of the cigar union were apparent as they included members without regard to race, gender, or ethnicity in the first decade of the twentieth century.[13]

Works by Mary Martha Thomas, Megan Taylor Shockley, and others examined the changes brought about by World War II. Thomas found that in Alabama, industries remained closed to African American women even as white women flocked to better-paying heavy industrial jobs. Shockley argued that black women made inroads in positions in the federal government, as well as in taking service jobs vacated by white women. Authors of these studies found economic racism a constant and powerful force. Even after desegregation, African American women struggled to enter better-paying industries. And they still dominated low-wage jobs with terrible conditions, as LaGuana Gray explained in *We Just Keep Running the Line* (2014), an exploration of black women's work and resistance to oppression in chicken- processing plants. More studies of women in the late twentieth-century industrial world are needed to better understand how the landscape changed for working-class southern women.[14]

Although some black women found work in factories, the majority of southern African American women worked in the service industry prior to the 1960s, underpaid and generally without the possibility of union protection. Elizabeth Clark-Lewis's *Living In, Living Out* (1994) focused on domestic workers in Washington, DC. She explained the factors that drew women to the city for work as well as the terrible conditions they faced as on-call servants with no privacy or free time. Clark-Lewis noted how women often became laundresses or performed service beyond their employers' homes when they could find such work, affording them more autonomy. Tera W. Hunter's *To 'Joy My Freedom* (1997) was a groundbreaking study of domestic workers' activism and cultural influence. Her

13. Dolores E. Janiewski, *Sisterhood Denied: Race, Gender, and Class in a New South Community* (Philadelphia: Temple University Press, 1985); Nancy A. Hewitt, *Southern Discomfort: Women's Activism in Tampa, Florida, 1880s–1920s* (Urbana: University of Illinois Press, 2001).

14. Mary Martha Thomas, *Riveting and Rationing in Dixie: Alabama Women and the Second World War* (Tuscaloosa: University of Alabama Press, 1987); Megan Taylor Shockley, *"We, Too, Are Americans": African American Women in Detroit and Richmond, 1940–1954* (Urbana: University of Illinois Press, 2004); LaGuana Gray, *We Just Keep Running the Line: Black Southern Women and the Poultry Processing Industry* (Baton Rouge: Louisiana State University Press, 2014).

book examined ways in which women fought to retain homes of their own, enjoy their autonomy in places of recreation, and work together to fight for better wages in early twentieth-century Atlanta. Rebecca Sharpless's *Cooking in Other Women's Kitchens* (2010) argued that African American women tried to assert autonomy over their recipes and skills as cooks for hire but often quit their positions as a way to claim power. Sharpless, Shockley, and others pointed out that leaving an exploitative job often represented domestic workers' only opportunity to exercise autonomy.[15]

Other scholars explored women in the coal mining industry. Historians of the nineteenth century analyzed how women fashioned community in far-flung company towns, led activist efforts on behalf of male miners, and worked to support the men in the mines. Some scholars emphasized how women took the lead in labor activism, despite their roles as mothers or their employment outside of the mines. Karaleah S. Reichart found that women fully understood what strikes meant to their families' bottom lines. Nevertheless, when company decisions adversely affected their families, they often involved themselves in violent protests. Jessica Wilkerson moved a step further, arguing that women who supported miners during the Brookside Strike of 1974 publicly criticized the poverty and conditions that affected them as family caregivers, thus defining the issues in the coal town as feminist ones.[16] Scholars (notably, sociologists) also examined ways in which women fought for access to, and then respect in, southern mining jobs in the 1970s. They documented women's uphill battles, from fighting through

15. Elizabeth Clark-Lewis, *Living In, Living Out: African American Domestics in Washington, D.C., 1910–1940* (Washington: Smithsonian Institution Press, 1994); Tera W. Hunter, *To 'Joy My Freedom: Southern Black Women's Lives and Labors After the Civil War* (Cambridge: Harvard University Press, 1997); Rebecca Sharpless, *Cooking in Other Women's Kitchens: Domestic Workers in the South, 1865–1960* (Chapel Hill: University of North Carolina Press, 2010); Thomas, *Riveting and Rationing in Dixie;* Shockley, *"We, Too, Are Americans."*

16. Janet Greene, "Strategies for Survival: Women's Work in the Southern West Virginia Coal Camps," *West Virginia History* 49 (March 1990): 37–54, discussed the ways in which women's work enabled families to survive in mining towns. Dealing with inadequate housing, often spotty water supplies, ever-present coal dust, and labor upheavals, women worked to maintain secret gardens to support families during strikes, formed networks of support, and claimed power in the house. See also Karaleah S. Reichart, "Narrating Conflict: Women and Coal in Southern West Virginia," *Journal of Appalachian Studies* 7 (Spring 2001): 6–18; Jessica Wilkerson, "The Company Owns the Mine but They Don't Own Us: Feminist Critiques of Capitalism in the Coalfields of Kentucky in the 1970s," *Gender and History* 28 (April 2016): 199–220. See also Jessica Wilkerson, *To Live Here, You Have to Fight: How Women Led Appalachian Movements for Social Justice* (Urbana: University of Illinois Press, 2018).

the Coal Employment Project to get hired, to navigating sexual harassment from supervisors in a heavily male-dominated field, to support of unions that often failed to take their concerns seriously.[17]

One area of particularly fertile ground for women's historians is the history of women active in social movements. As Hall and Scott explained in their 1987 essay, both they and other scholars had explored the role of women in movements like suffrage, antilynching, and other Progressive-era reform efforts. Much of this work focused on women of privilege, often white women, although Elsa Barkley Brown, Jacqueline Jones, and others examined the roles of African American women in uplift activities. Black women worked in parallel but separate movements, sometimes serving as racial ambassadors reaching out to white women leaders to cooperate on projects, as Glenda Elizabeth Gilmore explained. Hall and Scott also noted that several works had examined the role of women in the Equal Rights Amendment (ERA) battle, which ended with the amendment's expiration in 1982. In the ensuing decades, historians advanced the field tremendously, examining women's role in multiple social movements, including Progressive-era reform efforts, civil rights, labor rights, feminism, and environmentalism. Scholars also worked to unearth the stories of women in conservative movements, analyzing their motives and concerns as they sought to hold back change in the South, as discussed below.[18]

Since the 1980s, historians explored ways in which women of privilege, in both black and white communities, worked to advance progressive goals in a South defined by segregation and white patriarchy. While white women had to negotiate these hazards, their race insulated them from the problems faced by black women, and often their own racism prevented the success of large-scale

17. Carletta Savage, "Re-gendering Coal: Female Miners and Male Supervisors," *Appalachian Journal* 27 (Spring 2000): 232–48; Suzanne E. Tallichet, *Daughters of the Mountain: Women Coal Miners in Central Appalachia* (College Park: Pennsylvania State University Press, 2006).

18. Hall and Scott, "Women in the South"; Jones, *Labor of Love, Labor of Sorrow;* Anne Firor Scott, *The Southern Lady: From Pedestal to Politics, 1830–1930* (Chicago: University of Chicago Press, 1970); Gilmore, *Gender and Jim Crow;* Jacquelyn Dowd Hall, *Revolt against Chivalry: Jesse Daniel Ames and the Women's Campaign against Lynching* (New York: Columbia University Press, 1979); Elsa Barkley Brown, "Womanist Consciousness: Maggie Lena Walker and the Independent Order of Saint Luke," *Signs* 14 (Spring 1989): 610–33. See Hewitt, *Southern Discomfort,* for an exploration of how white, Latina, and African American club women worked to advance change in Tampa, Florida, in the Progressive era. Her work was pathbreaking in the way she interwove white ethnic, Latina, and African American histories together.

reform efforts. Marjorie Spruill Wheeler's *New Women of the New South* (1993), for example, argued that the leaders of the southern suffrage movement wanted the vote to achieve equality and to advance Progressive-era reforms for women and children. Yet their invocation of states' rights ideology and their desire to use their votes to negate black women's political power undermined the movement in the South. Suffrage leaders belonged to a national network of prominent suffragists, many of whom also used racist arguments to promote the vote. Building on this work, Elna C. Green looked at the broader southern suffragist and anti-suffragist movement in *Southern Strategies* (1997). Analyzing the crusade from the ground up, she argued that the complexities of race and gender in the South caused the movement to splinter well beyond the leadership of organizations. Wheeler and Green provided insight into the broader suffrage question in the region, and both built on the works of previous historians. What happened after women gained the vote? Lorraine Gates Schuyler argued that African American and white women used their newly gained political power to influence local and state politics in the 1920s.[19]

Southern white women also looked to reform society in the Progressive era, often by refashioning it according to middle-class standards. In examining how women reshaped society, whether in health movements, urban welfare relief, or education, historians noted the patriarchal restrictions of the South that forced white women to become "stealth feminists," in the words of Sarah Wilkerson Freeman, who studied Arkansas Progressive-era women. To achieve reforms, white women needed to work within the bounds of prescribed gender and racialized norms, which often hampered the effectiveness of their work. Their own

19. See Hall and Scott for citations of early studies of southern suffrage. Newer works include Marjorie Spruill Wheeler, *New Women of the New South: The Leaders of the Woman Suffrage Movement in the Southern States* (New York: Oxford University Press, 1993); Elna C. Green, *Southern Strategies: Southern Women and the Woman Suffrage Question* (Chapel Hill: University of North Carolina Press, 1997); Rosalyn Terborg-Penn, *African American Women and the Struggle for the Vote, 1850–1920* (Bloomington: Indiana University Press, 1998). For studies of what women did in the post-suffrage movement, see Lorraine Gates Schuyler, *The Weight of Their Votes: Southern Women and Political Leverage in the 1920s* (Chapel Hill: University of North Carolina Press, 2006). In addition, Anita Shafer Goodstein found that black women strategically allied with white reformers for two years to secure urban reforms and social welfare programming in "A Rare Alliance: African American and White Women in the Tennessee Elections of 1919 and 1920," *Journal of Southern History* 64 (May 1998): 219–46. Pamela Tyler explored white women's activism from suffrage through the 1960s in *Silk Stockings and Ballot Boxes: Women and Politics in New Orleans, 1920–1963* (Athens: University of Georgia Press, 1996).

biases also blinded them to systemic poverty and educational inequities. Still, white women did help to create Visiting Nurse Programs and supported the opening of colleges for women, among other significant reforms in the urban and rural South.[20]

African American women faced the double burden of race and gender discrimination, and since the 1980s, historians thoroughly examined many ways in which they fought to uplift communities and claim autonomy in the Progressive-era South. As Stephanie J. Shaw explained, many women imbibed the sense of responsibility for the community as college undergraduates. Historians noted the networks and services that black professional women created for their communities. Historians studied the women who led these movements, including Lugenia Burns Hope, Maggie Lena Walker, Mary Church Terrell, and Charlotte Hawkins Brown, as well as the countless women who participated in challenging white supremacy and claiming a place in the New South. Glenda Elizabeth Gilmore's work highlighted how black women worked as "race diplomats," partnering with white women on projects that benefited both communities, but also recognizing the limits of racial cooperation in the segregated South. Other historians noted the "parallel paths" of reforming women, examining how racism constrained the work of white women and complicated the work of black women.[21]

20. Scott, *From Pedestal to Politics;* Hall, *Revolt Against Chivalry;* Elna C. Green, *This Business of Relief: Confronting Poverty in a Southern City, 1740–1940* (Athens: University of Georgia Press, 2003); Gilmore, *Gender and Jim Crow;* Melanie Beals Goan, *Mary Breckenridge: The Frontier Nursing Service and Rural Health in Appalachia* (Chapel Hill: University of North Carolina Press, 2008); Sarah Wilkerson-Freeman, "Stealth in the Political Arsenal of Southern Women: A Retrospective for the Millennium," in *Southern Women at the Millennium: A Historical Perspective,* ed. Melissa Walker, Jeanette R. Dunn, and Joe P. Dunn (Columbia: University of Missouri Press, 2003), 42–82. Kierner, Loux, and Shockley, *Changing History,* explores ways in which women advanced educational, welfare, and other reform in Virginia. Michele Gillespie traced the philanthropy and Progressive reform activism of Katharine Smith Reynolds in *Katharine and R. J. Reynolds: Partners of Fortune in the Making of the South* (Athens: University of Georgia Press, 2016). John Thomas McGuire extended the study of Progressivism through the 1930s, arguing that although key southern Democratic leaders embraced concepts of social justice, eliding race issues meant they failed to connect with African American women, so their work was limited; see "The Boundaries of Democratic Reform: Social Justice Feminism and Race in the South, 1931–1939," *Journal of Southern History* 78 (November 2012): 887–912.

21. Stephanie J. Shaw, *What a Woman Ought to Be and to Do: Black Professional Women Workers during the Jim Crow Era* (Chicago: University of Chicago, 1996); Jacqueline Anne Rouse, *Lugenia Burns Hope: Black Southern Reformer* (Athens: University of Georgia Press, 1989); Brown, "Womanist Consciousness"; Gertrude Woodruff Marlowe, *A Right Worthy Grand Mission: Maggie Lena Walker and the Quest for*

African American women, however, refused to let white women's reluctance deter their efforts. As Crystal N. Feimster, Patricia A. Schechter, Deborah Gray White, Brittney C. Cooper, and others showed, African American women's fights against lynching and for equality positioned them as early civil rights leaders. Historians illustrated the importance of women such as Ida B. Wells, Anna Julia Cooper, and Mary Church Terrell, as well as institutions such as the National Association of Colored Women, in the early fight for civil rights.[22] As many women's historians pointed out, women remained an integral part of the community of civil rights activists thereafter. From Rosalind Rosenberg's biography of Pauli Murray to Patricia Bell-Scott's study of Murray and Eleanor Roosevelt to scholarship on Mary McLeod Bethune by Audrey Thomas McCluskey, Elaine M. Smith, and Rebecca Tuuri, historians demonstrated women's critical role in civil rights organizing throughout the twentieth century. Much of this scholarship—such as Turri's analysis of Bethune's establishment of the National Council of Negro Women—explored the networks women used to achieve their goals. As Tiffany M. Gill demonstrated in her work on African American beauty shops

---

Black Economic Empowerment (Washington: Howard University Press, 2003). As Sarah H. Case noted in *Leaders of Their Race: Educating Black and White Women in the New South* (Urbana: University of Illinois Press, 2017), both black and white women were trained in their colleges for work as reformers and leaders, but for segregated schools. In both black and white schools, concerns about women's respectability and place dominated discourse and activities. Gilmore's *Gender and Jim Crow* is a standard in examining the parallel paths of black and white progressive women, as well as how black women negotiated the oppressive racial and gender structures of North Carolina. See also Mary S. Hoffschwelle, "A Black Woman 'In Orthority': Claiming Professional Status in Jim Crow Alabama," *Journal of Southern History* 81 (November 2015): 843–86; Audrey Thomas McCluskey, *A Forgotten Sisterhood: Pioneering Black Women Educators in the Jim Crow South* (Lanham, MD: Rowman & Littlefield, 2014).

22. Crystal N. Feimster, *Southern Horrors: Women and the Politics of Rape and Lynching* (Cambridge: Harvard University Press, 2009); Patricia A. Schechter, *Ida B. Wells-Barnett and American Reform, 1880–1930* (Chapel Hill: University of North Carolina Press, 2001). Brittney C. Cooper's *Beyond Respectability: The Intellectual Thought of Race Women* (Urbana: University of Illinois Press, 2017) examined black women intellectuals from the late nineteenth through the late twentieth century, and while her book is national in scope, she explored the leadership of many southern women. Deborah Gray White, *Too Heavy A Load: Black Women in Defense of Themselves, 1894–1994* (New York: W. W. Norton, 1999) provided a national study of African American women in the twentieth century. Her work on the women's club movement is essential reading for understanding why African American women stood at the center of the civil rights movements in the early twentieth century. See also Treva B. Lindsey, *Colored No More: Reinventing Black Womanhood in Washington, D.C.* (Urbana: University of Illinois Press, 2017), which posited that club women, beauty culturalists, and intellectuals helped to shape a "New Negro" movement in the Progressive era.

from the 1900s through the 1960s, and Megan Taylor Shockley explained in her work on African American women in Richmond during World War II, women built institutions and networks to support each other, calling upon all available support systems in the battle for equality. Moreover, Cherisse Jones-Branch found that black and white women often came together in organizations such as Church Women United, the National Association for the Advancement of Colored People, and the Young Women's Christian Association to support the burgeoning militant movement.[23]

In the 1950s and 1960s, women continued to play significant roles in the civil rights movement as it exploded in public sit-ins, marches, and other demonstrations. Biographies such as Chana Kai Lee's study of Fannie Lou Hamer, Barbara Ransby's exploration of the life of Ella Baker, and Katherine Mellen Charron's work on Septima Clark centered women as leaders, in particular as "bridge leaders" between the local communities and national organizations, a concept that Belinda Robnett explained in her work on black women in the movement. Scholars also uncovered varied ways in which African American women's networks sustained the long fight for justice. Shannon Frystak and the contributors to *Women in the Civil Rights Movement* (1990) examined how women organized to fight for civil rights, while Danielle L. McGuire uncovered how systemic sexual violence against women motivated activists.[24]

23. Scholars who study women and civil rights before the militancy exhibited in the 1960s include Rosalind Rosenberg, *Jane Crow: The Life of Pauli Murray* (New York: Oxford University Press, 2017); Patricia Bell-Scott, *The Firebrand and the First Lady: Portrait of a Friendship, Pauli Murray, Eleanor Roosevelt, and the Struggle for Social Justice* (New York: Alfred A. Knopf, 2016); Audrey Thomas McCluskey and Elaine M. Smith, eds., *Mary McLeod Bethune: Building a Better World, Essays and Selected Documents* (Bloomington: Indiana University Press, 1999); Rebecca Tuuri, *Strategic Sisterhood: The National Council of Negro Women in the Black Freedom Struggle* (Chapel Hill: University of North Carolina Press, 2018); Tiffany M. Gill, *Beauty Shop Politics: African American Women's Activism in the Beauty Industry* (Urbana: University of Illinois Press, 2010); Shockley, *"We, Too, Are Americans"*; Julia Kirk Blackwelder, *Styling Jim Crow: African-American Beauty Training during Segregation* (College Station: Texas A&M University Press, 2003); Cherisse Jones-Branch, *Crossing the Line: Women's Interracial Activism in South Carolina During and After World War II* (Gainesville: University Press of Florida, 2014).

24. Chana Kai Lee, *For Freedom's Sake: The Life of Fannie Lou Hamer* (Urbana: University of Illinois Press, 1999); Barbara Ransby, *Ella Baker and the Black Freedom Movement: A Radical Democratic Vision* (Chapel Hill: University of North Carolina Press, 2003); Katherine Mellen Charron, *Freedom's Teacher: The Life of Septima Clark* (Chapel Hill: University of North Carolina Press, 2009); Shannon Frystak, *Our Minds on Freedom: Women and the Struggle for Black Equality in Louisiana, 1924–1967* (Baton Rouge: Louisiana State University Press, 2009); Vicki L. Crawford, Jacqueline Anne Rouse, and Barbara Woods, eds.,

Although historians deeply analyzed the role of women and issues of gender in civil rights, more remains to be done in other areas of gender and activism in the late twentieth century. Historians have begun to take feminism in the region seriously. Scholarship in the 1980s focused on ERA ratification in several states, often exploring both pro- and anti-ERA forces. In the 1990s, scholars began to argue for the significance of late twentieth-century feminist activity in the South, countering the prevailing narrative of feminism as a northern and even urban-centered movement. Still, comparatively few studies focused on the women's movement in the South. Carol Giardina looked at the relationship between civil rights activists and feminists in the early women's movement in Florida, and Janet Allured's study of Louisiana located feminism's deep roots in labor, religious, women's, and civil rights organizations. Megan Taylor Shockley's exploration of feminism in Virginia, and chapters in books by Melissa Estes Blair and Stephanie Gilmore, examined the interplay between southern stereotypes and feminist actions, the limits of southern feminism, and ways in which women navigated a more conservative region after the 1970s. We need more studies that examine feminism beyond the white middle class, as Jessica Wilkerson suggested in "The Company Owns the Mine but They Don't Own Us" (2016). In a 2017 essay, Meg Devlin O'Sullivan challenged scholars of southern feminism to look beyond white and African American women's activism. She found that Indigenous southern women fought for a place in the feminist movement as they worked for women's rights.[25] Moreover, historians are beginning to explore the critical role

---

Women in the Civil Rights Movement: Trailblazers and Torchbearers, 1961–1965 (New York: Carlson, 1990); Belinda Robnett, *How Long? How Long? African-American Women in the Struggle for Civil Rights* (New York: Oxford University Press, 2000); Danielle L. McGuire, *At the Dark End of the Street: Black Women, Rape, and Resistance—A New History of the Civil Rights Movement from Rosa Parks to the Rise of Black Power* (New York: Alfred A. Knopf, 2011). See also Anne Stefani, *Unlikely Dissenters: White Southern Women in the Fight for Racial Justice, 1920–1970* (Gainesville: University Press of Florida, 2015); Tiyi M. Morris, *Womanpower Unlimited and the Black Freedom Struggle in Mississippi* (Athens: University of Georgia Press, 2015).

25. Studies of late twentieth-century southern feminism include Joan S. Carver, "The Equal Rights Amendment and the Florida Legislature," *Florida Historical Quarterly* 60 (April 1982): 455–81; Janet Allured, "Arkansas Baptists and Methodists and the Equal Rights Amendment," *Arkansas Historical Quarterly* 43 (Spring 1984): 55–66; Donald G. Mathews and Jane Sherron De Hart, *Sex, Gender, and the Politics of the ERA: A State and the Nation* (New York: Oxford University Press, 1992); Carol Giardina, *Freedom for Women: Forging the Women's Liberation Movement, 1953-1970* (Gainesville: University Press of Florida, 2010). Works that have southern cities in their analysis include Stephanie Gilmore, *Groundswell: Grassroots Feminist Activism in Postwar America* (New York: Routledge, 2012); Melissa Estes Blair,

played by women in the environmental movement. Several scholars explained the value of women's grassroots efforts to effect change in their communities and on the national stage as they worked to restore fragile southern ecosystems. We need more studies illustrating the important work done by women activists.[26]

The exploration of gender in the twentieth-century South has hardly been limited to histories of political activism and social movements, nor to histories of women. Focus on the social construction of gender led, for example, to growing

---

Revolutionizing Expectations: Women's Organizations, Feminism, and American Politics, 1965–1980 (Athens: University of Georgia Press, 2014). Other scholars studying the feminist movement in the South include Janet Allured, *Remapping Second-Wave Feminism: The Long Women's Rights Movement in Louisiana, 1950–1997* (Athens: University of Georgia Press, 2016); Carol E. Jordan, *Violence against Women in Kentucky: A History of U.S. and State Legislative Reform* (Lexington: University Press of Kentucky, 2014); Nancy E. Baker, "Hermine Tobolowsky: A Feminist's Fight for Equal Rights," in *Texas Women: Their Histories, Their Lives,* ed. Elizabeth Hayes Turner, Stephanie Cole, and Rebecca Sharpless (Athens: University of Georgia Press, 2015), 434–56; Marjorie J. Spruill, "Victoria Eslinger, Keller Bumgardner Barron, Mary Heriot, Tootsie Holland, and Pat Callair: Champions of Women's Rights in South Carolina," in *South Carolina Women: Their Lives and Times—Volume 3,* ed. Joan Marie Johnson, Valinda W. Littlefield, and Marjorie J. Spruill (Athens: University of Georgia Press, 2012), 373–408; Nancy E. Baker, "Integrating Women into Modern Kentucky History: The Equal Rights Debate (1972–1978) as a Case Study," *Register of the Kentucky Historical Society* 113 (Summer 2015): 477–508; Harold Smith, "Casey Hayden: Gender and the Origins of SNCC, SDS, and the Women's Liberation Movement," in Turner, Cole, and Sharpless, eds., *Texas Women,* 296–318; Kimberly Wilmot Voss, "The Florida Fight for Equality: The Equal Rights Amendment, Senator Lori Wilson, and Mediated Catfights in the 1970s," *Florida Historical Quarterly* 88 (Fall 2009): 173–208; Katarina Keane, "Second-Wave Feminism in the American South, 1965–1980" (PhD diss., University of Maryland, 2009); Anne M. Valk, *Radical Sisters: Second-Wave Feminism and Black Liberation in Washington, D.C.* (Urbana: University of Illinois Press, 2008); Wilkerson, "The Company Owns the Mine but They Don't Own Us"; Megan Taylor Shockley, *Creating a Progressive Commonwealth: Women Activists, Feminism, and the Politics of Social Change in Virginia, 1970s-2000s* (Baton Rouge: Louisiana State University Press, 2018); Meg Devlin O'Sullivan, "'Engaged in the Struggle for Liberation as They See It': Indigenous Southern Women and International Women's Year," in *The Native South: New Histories and Enduring Legacies,* ed. Tim Alan Garrison and Greg O'Brien (Lincoln: University of Nebraska Press, 2017), 220–37. Sarah Deer noted that Choctaw women in Mississippi and their supporters filed an amicus curiae brief in a case that successfully won the right to file a civil suit in tribal court against a white store manager who had allegedly molested a child on their reservation. This overturned a previous decision that protected whites from tribal law; see "Native People and Violent Crime: Gendered Violence and Tribal Jurisdiction," *Du Bois Review* 15 (Spring 2018): 89–106.

26. Studies include Shannon Elizabeth Bell, *Our Roots Run Deep as Ironweed: Appalachian Women and the Fight for Environmental Justice* (Urbana: University of Illinois Press, 2013); Peggy Macdonald, *Marjorie Harris Carr, Defender of Florida's Environment* (Gainesville: University Press of Florida, 2014); Leslie Kemp Poole, *Saving Florida: Women's Fight for the Environment in the Twentieth Century* (Gainesville: University Press of Florida, 2015).

interest in the history of southern manhood and masculinity. LeeAnn Whites cautioned in her gendered analysis of the Civil War in 1995 that until "we recognize that . . . men, too, have gender . . . gender studies will remain incomplete." Although it would be an overstatement to claim that previous historians failed to recognize that men have gender—earlier works on both honor and lynching in the South, for example, presented them as gendered subjects—southern historiography before the 1990s tended to conflate gender with women and vice versa. Beginning in the 1990s, a proliferation of histories that focused specifically on manhood ended that trend.[27]

Responding to scholars of American masculinity who largely excluded the South from their field of historical vision, Craig Thompson Friend provided the most comprehensive examination of late nineteenth- and twentieth-century southern manhood in his edited collection *Southern Masculinity* (2009). Friend and his contributors pushed back against the notion that there was a uniquely southern ideal of manhood at any point during the late nineteenth or twentieth centuries. Instead, their research collectively revealed a multiplicity of understandings determined by race, time, class, age, religion, and sexuality. Contributors to the collection uncovered, for example, competing ideals of white manhood—the masculine martial ideal, the Christian gentlemen, the self-made man—as well as a radical notion of black masculinity deployed by Black Power activists and a Cherokee construction of masculinity that represented a partial critique of northern manhood.[28]

Other works that explored white manhood in the late nineteenth- and twentieth-century South, specifically, supported *Southern Masculinity*'s insistence on complexity. In contrast to Gail Bederman, E. Anthony Rotundo, and

27. Whites, *The Civil War as a Crisis in Gender*, 7. Bertram Wyatt-Brown, for example, drew on gender as an analytical tool in his 1982 book on white southern men and honor, a fact that Hall and Scott acknowledged in their 1987 essay. Bertram Wyatt-Brown, *Southern Honor: Ethics and Behavior in the Old South* (New York: Oxford University Press, 1982); Hall and Scott, "Women in the South," 468. Pre-1987 histories that addressed gender, manhood, and lynching include George M. Fredrickson, *The Black Image in the White Mind: The Debate on Afro-American Character and Destiny, 1817–1914* (New York: Harper & Row, 1971); Joel Williamson, *The Crucible of Race: Black-White Relations in the American South since Emancipation* (New York: Oxford University Press, 1984); Hall, *Revolt Against Chivalry.*

28. Craig Thompson Friend, ed., *Southern Masculinity: Perspectives on Manhood in the South since Reconstruction* (Athens: University of Georgia Press, 2009). This was the follow-up volume to Craig Thompson Friend and Lorri Glover, eds., *Southern Manhood: Perspectives on Masculinity in the Old South* (Athens: University of Georgia Press, 2004).

others who argued that white manhood in the United States was defined by a new physicality and aggressiveness starting in the late 1800s, Ted Ownby, with a nod to Bertram Wyatt-Brown, insisted that in the South this "masculine ideal was nothing new." Ownby uncovered a variety of rough-and-tumble leisure pursuits popular from the late 1860s through the 1910s, implicitly raising questions about how much the Civil War was, in fact, a gender watershed for white men. In his work on the Spanish-American War, David C. Turpie found that white southern men were not itching for a fight and, instead, largely opted to stay home to protect their homes and families. These and other works grappled with the question of the regional distinctiveness of white southern manhood. In his introduction to a collection of eclectic essays on white southern masculinity, Trent Watts argued that although antebellum notions of racial mastery and independence undergirded a regional ideal of white manhood well into the twentieth century, white southern men were "no more homogenous than any other group historians might consider." According to Alexander Macaulay, white masculinity in the South was not uniquely southern, as demonstrated by Citadel administrators, cadets, and alumni who conflated a tough yet obedient manliness with a national ideal of American citizenship in the decades after World War II.[29]

29. Ted Ownby, *Subduing Satan: Religion, Recreation, and Manhood in the Rural South, 1865–1920* (Chapel Hill: University of North Carolina Press, 1990), 16; E. Anthony Rotundo, *American Manhood: Transformations in Masculinity from the Revolution to the Modern Era* (New York: Basic Books, 1993); Gail Bederman, *Manliness and Civilization: A Cultural History of Gender and Race in the United States, 1880–1917* (Chicago: University of Chicago Press, 1995); James C. Klotter, *Kentucky Justice, Southern Honor, and American Manhood: Understanding the Life and Death of Richard Reid* (Baton Rouge: Louisiana State University Press, 2003); David C. Turpie, "A Voluntary War: The Spanish-American War, White Southern Manhood, and the Struggles to Recruit Volunteers in the South," *Journal of Southern History* 80 (November 2014): 859–92; Trent Watts, "Introduction: Telling White Men's Stories," in *White Masculinity in the Recent South*, ed. Trent Watts (Baton Rouge: Louisiana State University Press, 2008), 7; Alexander Macaulay, *Marching in Step: Masculinity, Citizenship, and The Citadel in Post–World War II America* (Athens: University of Georgia Press, 2009). Historians have also examined male leisure activities such as hunting, fishing, and watching NASCAR, though they have not always shed light on how such activities served as vehicles for shaping notions of masculinity. See Ben A. Shackleford, "Masculinity, Hierarchy, and the Auto Racing Fraternity: The Pit Stop as a Celebration of Social Roles," *Men and Masculinities* 2 (October 1999): 180–96; Daniel S. Pierce, *Real NASCAR: White Lightning, Red Clay, and Big Bill France* (Chapel Hill: University of North Carolina Press, 2010); Stuart A. Marks, *Southern Hunting in Black and White: Nature, History, and Ritual in a Carolina Community* (Princeton: Princeton University Press, 1991); Scott E. Giltner, *Hunting and Fishing in the New South: Black Labor and White Leisure after the Civil War* (Baltimore: Johns Hopkins University Press, 2008).

Analyses that focused on black southern manhood and masculinity also painted a complicated picture. The relationship between region and nation informed these works as well. In *Manliness and Its Discontents* (2004), Martin Summers argued that the transition to a modern, more physically assertive notion of masculinity applied to black men just as it did to white. Summers explored this change at Fisk University in Nashville and Howard University in Washington, DC, where male students rebelled against an older model of bodily control in favor of the new "exuberant body" that relished unfettered consumption and unsupervised fraternizing. Riché Richardson found evidence of a belief in the deficiency of southern black masculinity in her examination of cultural representations of masculinity in twentieth-century novels, movies, and music. Black masculinity in the South was the referent against which "real" black masculinity—read northern, urban, and political—became defined.[30]

By contrast, Steve Estes, who grounded his examination of discourse in the lived experiences of black men during the civil rights movement, argued that southern African American men did, in fact, rely on a militantly masculinist rhetoric to assert manhood and demand citizenship rights. And yet Estes was careful to show that the use of "masculinism," as he called it, was not without problems. Not only did segregationists employ masculinism to demonize black men's sexuality and stymie desegregation, but its use also reinforced heterosexual patriarchy within the black community. Michele Mitchell's *Righteous Propagation* (2004), meanwhile, revealed the close links between international developments—such as post-Reconstruction black colonization in Liberia and turn-of-the-century America—and efforts to fortify black manhood. Angela Hornsby-Gutting, Stephanie J. Shaw, and Elsa Barkley Brown insisted that African American manhood in the turn-of-the-century-South could not be understood outside of the specific spaces where men and women collectively, rather than in opposition or independently, engaged in community-building. According to Hornsby-Gutting, characterizing black manhood in the early Jim Crow South is therefore impossible, since it was dynamic, changing according to contexts.[31]

30. Martin Summers, *Manliness and Its Discontents: The Black Middle Class and the Transformation of Masculinity, 1900–1930* (Chapel Hill: University of North Carolina Press, 2004), 244. See also Riché Richardson, *Black Masculinity and the U.S. South: From Uncle Tom to Gangsta* (Athens: University of Georgia Press, 2007).

31. Steve Estes, *I Am a Man! Race, Manhood, and the Civil Rights Movement* (Chapel Hill: University of North Carolina Press, 2005); Matthew Mace Barbee, *Race and Masculinity in Southern Memory: History*

Histories of sexual violence and lynching published in the 1990s and 2000s illuminated particularly well the connections between ideas about southern manhood, womanhood, race, and sexuality. As Hannah Rosen argued in her analysis of vigilante violence during Reconstruction, violence committed by white men, especially their rape of black women, was intended to prove white mastery as well as black men's inability to protect their homes. In portraying black men as unmanly, white men signaled their unworthiness to exercise political rights. While not all historians agreed with earlier analyses of lynching that insisted on the relevance of gender, such as those of Jacquelyn Dowd Hall and Joel Williamson, others did. According to Martha Hodes, for example, by the 1890s, white men, their masculine authority threatened by black male political power, cast black men as sexually uncontrollable rapists to justify lynching. Indeed, feeling their position under assault on multiple fronts, white men used the trope of the black beast rapist and its companion—the sexually pure white woman—to rein in increasingly assertive white women as well.[32]

---

of Richmond, Virginia's Monument Avenue, 1948–1996 (Lanham, MD: Lexington Books, 2014); Peter J. Ling and Sharon Monteith, eds., *Gender and the Civil Rights Movement* (New York: Garland Publishing, 1999); Michele Mitchell, *Righteous Propagation: African Americans and the Politics of Racial Destiny after Reconstruction* (Chapel Hill: University of North Carolina Press, 2004); Angela Hornsby-Gutting, *Black Manhood and Community Building in North Carolina, 1900–1930* (Gainesville: University Press of Florida, 2009); Hornsby-Gutting, "Manning the Region: New Approaches to Gender in the South," *Journal of Southern History* 75 (August 2009): 664–76; Stephanie J. Shaw, "Black Club Women and the Creation of the National Association of Colored Women," *Journal of Women's History* 3 (Fall 1991): 10–25; Shaw, *What a Woman Ought to Be and to Do;* Elsa Barkley Brown, "Uncle Ned's Children: Negotiating Community and Freedom in Postemancipation Richmond, Virginia" (PhD diss., Kent State University, 1994); Brown, "Negotiating and Transforming the Public Sphere: African American Political Life in the Transition from Slavery to Freedom," *Public Culture* 7 (Fall 1994): 107–46. Hornbsy-Gutting argued that the scholarly focus on black women's turn-of-the-century activism has obscured the history of men and manhood during this period; see "Manning the Region," 673–74.

32. Hannah Rosen, *Terror in the Heart of Freedom: Citizenship, Sexual Violence, and the Meaning of Race in the Postemancipation South* (Chapel Hill: University of North Carolina Press, 2009); Hall, *Revolt Against Chivalry;* Williamson, *Crucible of Race;* Martha Hodes, "The Sexualization of Reconstruction Politics: White Women and Black Men in the South after the Civil War," *Journal of the History of Sexuality* 3 (January 1993): 402–17; Hodes, *White Women, Black Men: Illicit Sex in the Nineteenth-Century South* (New Haven: Yale University Press, 1997); Gilmore, *Gender and Jim Crow;* Kristina DuRocher, *Raising Racists: The Socialization of White Children in the Jim Crow South* (Lexington: University Press of Kentucky, 2011). Works not as concerned with gender as a context for explaining lynching include Stewart E. Tolnay and E. M. Beck, *A Festival of Violence: An Analysis of Southern Lynchings, 1882–1930* (Urbana: University of Illinois Press, 1995); Bruce E. Baker, *This Mob Will Surely Take My Life: Lynchings in the*

Newer works on sexual violence and lynching did not altogether remove the agency of women, white or black. Danielle L. McGuire placed black women's resistance of white male sexual violence at the center of the civil rights movement, revealing a critical, gendered component of movement activism that historians long overlooked. In *Southern Horrors* (2009), Crystal N. Feimster argued that white reformer Rebecca Latimer Felton and black reformer Ida B. Wells harnessed the connections between rape, lynching, and the divergent understandings of white and black manhood for their own political empowerment. Yet the gendered logic of lynching sometimes meant that women who challenged the authority of white men became the victims. Complicating our view of lynching in a different way, Diane Miller Sommerville and Lisa Lindquist Dorr argued that pernicious views of black masculinity did not always mean that African American men accused of rape met death at the hands of white mobs. Still, on the whole, work on sexual violence and lynching bolstered the case for the centrality of gender and sexuality in shoring up white supremacy and white patriarchy, especially as the nineteenth century gave way to the twentieth.[33]

At the same time, a number of historians—including Michele Mitchell, Evelyn Brooks Higginbotham, Deborah Gray White, Hazel V. Carby, and Tera W. Hunter—stressed the importance of gender and sexuality to black politics as Jim Crow hardened. Policing everything from premarital sex to juke-joint dancing to women's clothing, elite and middle-class black women forged a "politics of respectability" that positioned female sexual modesty as key to racial uplift. Reformers viewed the control of women's bodies as a critical component of the larger effort to fight racism and to compensate for black male disfranchisement.

Carolinas, 1871–1947 (New York: Continuum, 2008); Amy Kate Bailey and Stewart E. Tolnay, *Lynched: The Victims of Southern Mob Violence* (Chapel Hill: University of North Carolina Press, 2015). Two good summaries of the historiography of lynching include W. Fitzhugh Brundage, "Introduction," in *Under Sentence of Death: Lynching in the South,* ed. W. Fitzhugh Brundage (Chapel Hill: University of North Carolina Press, 1997), 1–20; Diane Miller Sommerville, "Appendix—Rape, Race, and Rhetoric: The Rape Myth in Historiographical Perspective," in *Rape and Race in the Nineteenth-Century South* (Chapel Hill: University of North Carolina Press, 2004), 223–59.

33. McGuire, *At the Dark End of the Street;* Feimster, *Southern Horrors;* Sommerville, *Rape and Race in the Nineteenth-Century South;* Lisa Lindquist Dorr, *White Women, Rape, and the Power of Race in Virginia, 1900–1960* (Chapel Hill: University of North Carolina Press, 2004). Jeffrey S. Adler argued that the successful prosecution of a white man who sexually assaulted and murdered a black woman could actually reinforce Jim Crow; see "'A Low Caste White Man with Lust in His Heart': Race, Deviance, and Criminal Justice in Jim Crow New Orleans," *Journal of Southern History* 84 (May 2018): 245–76.

Historians carefully highlighted the contradictory results. On the one hand, African American reformers who were heavily indebted to white sexual norms pathologized poorer blacks and reinforced white supremacy. On the other hand, those same sexual norms, discourses, and practices were put to more subversive uses. For example, some African Americans saw in the eugenics movement a chance to combat widespread beliefs in racial degeneracy.[34]

Early twentieth-century concerns about female sexuality (and the white and black masculinities to which it was so intimately bound) continued to shape the contours of southern society for decades thereafter. Susan K. Cahn and Blain Roberts demonstrated that anxiety over adolescent female sexuality and female bodies remained a defining feature of southern culture into the 1960s. This unease stemmed from the region's reluctant accommodation with economic and cultural change and from the difficult work of maintaining white male supremacy. Sexual anxiety, especially among whites, peaked as black southerners took aim at Jim Crow during the civil rights movement, which threatened white male power and white female purity. As many historians argued, anxiety over intersections of sexuality, race, and gender also mobilized proponents of massive resistance.[35]

Works on queer southerners, meanwhile, moved the conversation beyond questions about gender, heterosexuality, modernity, and race. The literature supported the claim of theorists and historians that "queer" as a category of analysis must be understood in expansive terms, as a way of disrupting the traditional heterosexual-homosexual binary too often used in examining sexuality in the

34. Mitchell, *Righteous Propagation;* Evelyn Brooks Higginbotham, *Righteous Discontent: The Women's Movement in the Black Baptist Church, 1880–1920* (Cambridge: Harvard University Press, 1993); Hunter, *To 'Joy My Freedom;* White, *Too Heavy a Load;* Hazel V. Carby, "Policing the Black Woman's Body in an Urban Context," *Critical Inquiry* 18 (Summer 1992): 738–55; Shaw, *What a Woman Ought to Be and to Do.* For an analysis of working-class black women that challenges this literature, see Brandi C. Brimmer, "Black Women's Politics, Narratives of Sexual Immorality, and Pension Bureaucracy in Mary Lee's North Carolina Neighborhood," *Journal of Southern History* 80 (November 2014): 827–58.

35. Susan K. Cahn, *Sexual Reckonings: Southern Girls in a Troubling Age* (Cambridge: Harvard University Press, 2007); Blain Roberts, *Pageants, Parlors, and Pretty Women: Race and Beauty in the Twentieth-Century South* (Chapel Hill: University of North Carolina Press, 2014); Jane Dailey, "Sex, Segregation, and the Sacred after *Brown,*" *Journal of American History* 91 (June 2004): 119–44; Elizabeth Jacoway, *Turn Away Thy Son: Little Rock, The Crisis That Shocked the Nation* (New York: Free Press, 2007); Karen Anderson, *Little Rock: Race and Resistance at Central High School* (Princeton: Princeton University Press, 2010); Phoebe Godfrey, "Bayonets, Brainwashing, and Bathrooms: The Discourse of Race, Gender, and Sexuality in the Desegregation of Little Rock's Central High," *Arkansas Historical Quarterly* 62 (Spring 2003): 42–67.

past. In *Welcome to Fairyland* (2017), for example, Julio Capó Jr. argued that Miami was marketed and consumed as a place where migrants and tourists could engage in any number of transgressive sexual and social acts, all of which were queer. Contributing to hegemonic understandings of both sexual deviancy and normalcy, many queer southerners also created a vibrant and fluid LGBTQ space that complicates views of the South as a conservative bastion.[36]

As a number of historians noted—including John Howard in *Men Like That* (1999) and the contributors to Howard's *Carryin' On in the Gay and Lesbian South* (1997)—the conservatism of the region failed to thwart the growth of LGBTQ communities and activism. Following Howard's lead, most scholars explored LGBTQ community-building and activism in the rural South. Their studies positioned the LGBTQ community in the South as a progressive organizing force that battled an often-hostile society seeking to restrict the rights of those outside of heteronormative sexual orientations. Some scholars focused specifically on how LGBTQ southerners were persecuted in the mid-twentieth century. In *And They Were Wonderful Teachers* (2009), Karen L. Graves examined how LGBTQ teachers negotiated dangerous social and political climates. Stacy Braukman studied the anticommunist Johns Committee in Florida, describing how government investigations reflected mid-century social and political anxieties. In reaction to such oppression and danger, as the contributors to *Southern Perspectives on the Queer Movement* (2017) noted about their home state of South Carolina, activists emerged everywhere in the region. Still, scholars also sought to create more complex arguments about the nature of LGBTQ lives and activism in the conservative South of the 1980s and 1990s. Wesley G. Phelps argued that neoliberalism limited ways by which activists could fight for nondiscrimination policies in local governments. Robert Hunt Ferguson illustrated how mothers in North Carolina claimed to be the arbiters of "family values" as they fought against

36. Julio Capó Jr., *Welcome to Fairyland: Queer Miami before 1940* (Chapel Hill: University of North Carolina Press, 2017). See also Michael P. Bibler, *Cotton's Queer Relations: Same-Sex Intimacy and the Literature of the Southern Plantation, 1936–1968* (Charlottesville: University of Virginia Press, 2009); Benjamin E. Wise, *William Alexander Percy: The Curious Life of a Mississippi Planter and Sexual Freethinker* (Chapel Hill: University of North Carolina Press, 2012); E. Patrick Johnson, "Southern (Dis)Comfort: Creating and Crafting Homosex in the Black South," in *Creating and Consuming the American South*, ed. Martyn Bone, Brian Ward, and William A. Link (Gainesville: University Press of Florida, 2015), 97–116. For a good survey of the field as of 2017, see Jerry Watkins, "Keep On Carryin' On: Recent Research on the LGBTQ History of the American South," *History Compass* 15 (November 2017), https://doi.org/10.1111/hic3.12428 (accessed 18 January 2019).

conservative Senator Jesse Helms while demanding acceptance for their gay and lesbian children and funding for AIDS research.[37]

The greatest impediment to southern LGBTQ history has been the lack of archival resources. In fact, from trailblazers such as James T. Sears to John Howard to E. Patrick Johnson, historians relied heavily on interviews. Not surprisingly, the major LGBTQ archives in the United States are located in cities outside the South: the Archives at the Lesbian, Gay, Bisexual and Transgender Community Center in New York; the Gerber/Hart Library and Archives in Chicago; and the ONE National Gay & Lesbian Archives in Los Angeles. In the South, university archives including Georgia State University, the University of South Florida, and Virginia Commonwealth University committed to expanding archival collections that document regional LGBTQ culture, politics, community relations, and public health, and the University of North Texas took a major role in documenting the history and culture of LGBTQ peoples in the Southwest. At the College of Charleston, an expansive project began in 2018 to collect oral histories as well as

37. John Howard, *Men Like That: A Southern Queer History* (Chicago: University of Chicago Press, 1999); Howard, ed., *Carryin' On in the Lesbian and Gay South* (New York: New York University Press, 1997); Sheila R. Morris, ed., *Southern Perspectives on the Queer Movement: Committed to Home* (Columbia: University of South Carolina Press, 2017); Stacy Braukman, *Communists and Perverts under the Palms: The Johns Committee in Florida, 1956–1965* (Gainesville: University Press of Florida, 2012); Karen L. Graves, *And They Were Wonderful Teachers: Florida's Purge of Gay and Lesbian Teachers* (Urbana: University of Illinois Press, 2009); Wesley G. Phelps, "The Politics of Queer Disidentification and the Limits of Neoliberalism in the Struggle for Gay and Lesbian Equality in Houston," *Journal of Southern History* 84 (May 2018): 311–48; Robert Hunt Ferguson, "Mothers Against Jesse in Congress: Grassroots Maternalism and the Cultural Politics of the AIDS Crisis in North Carolina," *Journal of Southern History* 83 (February 2017): 107–40. See also James T. Sears, *Growing Up Gay in the South: Race, Gender, and Journeys of the Spirit* (New York: Routledge, 1991); Sears, *Lonely Hunters: An Oral History of Lesbian and Gay Southern Life, 1948–1968* (New York: HarperCollins, 1997); Sears, *Rebels, Rubyfruit, and Rhinestones: Queering Space in the Stonewall South* (New Brunswick: Rutgers University Press, 2001); Brock Thompson, *The Un-Natural State: Arkansas and the Queer South* (Little Rock: University of Arkansas Press, 2010); E. Patrick Johnson, *Sweet Tea: Black Gay Men of the South* (Chapel Hill: University of North Carolina Press, 2008); Johnson, *Black. Queer. Southern. Women.: An Oral History* (Chapel Hill: University of North Carolina Press, 2018); Robert J. Corber, "Queer Regionalism," *American Literary History* 11 (Summer 1999): 391–402; Carlos L. Dews and Carolyn Leste Law, eds., *Out in the South* (Philadelphia: Temple University Press, 2001); Jim Downs, *Stand by Me: The Forgotten History of Gay Liberation* (New York: Basic Books, 2016); Megan Taylor Shockley, "Sharon Bottoms and Linda Kaufman: Legal Rights and Lesbian Mothers," in *Virginia Women: Their Lives and Times—Volume 2*, ed. Cynthia A. Kierner and Sandra Gioia Treadway (Athens: University of Georgia Press, 2016), 354–76; Jerry T. Watkins III, *Queering the Redneck Riviera: Sexuality and the Rise of Florida Tourism* (Gainesville: University Press of Florida, 2018).

archival sources about LGBTQ life in the Lowcountry. Born digital collections such as NC HB2: A Citizens' History, on North Carolina's 2016 anti-transgender legislation, and the Invisible Histories Project, which preserves the history of LGBTQ life throughout the South, have also provided new scholarly resources. As archives across the South continue to collect the historical traces of LGBTQ lives, the field will garner more attention.[38]

The history of government regulation of sexuality in the twentieth-century South has proliferated since the 1980s. Many histories of the control of sexuality revealed the inextricable connection between the expansion of state power in the twentieth-century South—through programs and institutions established by political conservatives ostensibly dedicated to small government—and the control of women's bodies. Edward J. Larson argued that although white southerners were slower to embrace eugenics than their contemporaries in other parts of the country, at the urging of medical professionals and, critically, middle-class club women, southern state legislatures slowly established mental institutions after World War I to sterilize "feeble-minded" poor white girls and women. In separate studies on Samarcand Manor, a state juvenile detention center in North Carolina, Karin L. Zipf and Susan K. Cahn showed how eugenic sterilization of sexually delinquent girls was often a whites-only enterprise in early decades, undertaken to ensure unfit white women did not "pollute" the race through reproduction.[39]

38. "LGBTQ+ Studies: LGBTQ+ Studies," Special Collections, Georgia State University, http://research.library.gsu.edu/lgbtqiq (accessed 18 January 2019); LGBT Collections, Special Collections, University of South Florida, https://www.lib.usf.edu/special-collections/lgbt-collections/ (accessed 18 January 2019); "Manuscripts," Special Collections and Archives, James Branch Cabell Library, Virginia Commonwealth University, https://www.library.vcu.edu/research/special-collections/cabell/manuscripts/ (accessed 18 January 2019); Lesbian, Gay, Bisexual and Transgender Archive, Special Collections, University of North Texas, https://library.unt.edu/special-collections/collections/lgbt-archive/ (accessed 18 January 2019); Being LGBTQ in the Lowcountry, Special Collections, College of Charleston, http://speccoll.cofc.edu/lgbtq/ (accessed 18 January 2019); NC HB2: A Citizens' History, North Carolina State University, https://nchb2history.omeka.chass.ncsu.edu/ (accessed 18 January 2019); IHP: The Invisible Histories Project, https://www.invisiblehistory.org/ (accessed 6 June 2019).

39. Edward J. Larson, *Sex, Race, and Science: Eugenics in the Deep South* (Baltimore: Johns Hopkins University Press, 1995); Karin L. Zipf, *Bad Girls at Samarcand: Sexuality and Sterilization in a Southern Juvenile Reformatory* (Baton Rouge: Louisiana State University Press, 2016); Cahn, *Sexual Reckonings;* Steven Noll, "'A Far Greater Menace': Feebleminded Families in the South, 1900–1940," in *Hidden Histories of Women in the New South,* ed. Virginia Bernhard et al. (Columbia: University of Missouri Press, 1994), 31–51; Gregory Michael Dorr, *Segregation's Science: Eugenics and Society in Virginia* (Charlottesville: University of Virginia Press, 2008).

Southern state governments did not ignore the sexual practices of girls and women of color, however. Pippa Holloway argued that Virginia's 1924 sterilization law—as well as state regulations designed to prevent miscegenation, censor obscene movies, and eliminate venereal disease—targeted both poor white and black women. This undifferentiating approach was intended to fortify elite white social and political control and to promote business progressives' pro-growth agenda. Many historians of forced sterilization highlighted the significant role of southern states' financial concerns in changing the racial profile of sterilization victims over time. Johanna Schoen found that the number of black women in North Carolina subjected to forced sterilization increased in the 1960s as legislators sought to rein in state spending on welfare programs. Several studies documented the remarkable longevity of state-sponsored sterilization, which extended, for example, in Alabama well into the 1970s, long after states outside the South abandoned the practice.[40]

The history of southern Indians during Jim Crow, which scholars began to uncover in the 2000s and 2010s, revealed a similar concern with Native American sexuality. Eugenics informed state and federal policies toward Native southerners, too. A number of works focused on the insidious legacies of the Virginia antimiscegenation statute known as the Racial Integrity Act of 1924. Alarmed by the possibility that mixed-race Native Americans might pass for white, state officials used the act to eliminate the racial designation of "Indian" and categorize all Native Americans as black. The prohibition of interracial sex contributed to Native displacement and detribalization, constituting, as some scholars argued, a new era of removal. Historians such as Malinda Maynor Lowery, Rose Stremlau, and Mikaëla M. Adams explored the deep connections between sexuality, domestic arrangements, and federal Indian policy. Created by the United States Congress in the late nineteenth century to divide communal Native lands into individual

40. Pippa Holloway, *Sexuality, Politics, and Social Control in Virginia, 1920–1945* (Chapel Hill: University of North Carolina Press, 2006); Johanna Schoen, "Reassessing Eugenic Sterilization: The Case of North Carolina," in *A Century of Eugenics in America: From the Indiana Experiment to the Human Genome Era,* ed. Paul A. Lombardo (Bloomington: Indiana University Press, 2011), 141–60; Schoen, *Choice and Coercion: Birth Control, Sterilization, and Abortion in Public Health and Welfare* (Chapel Hill: University of North Carolina Press, 2005); Larson, *Sex, Race, and Science;* Cahn, *Sexual Reckonings;* Gregory Michael Dorr, "Protection or Control? Women's Health, Sterilization Abuse, and *Relf v. Weinberger,*" in Lombardo, ed., *A Century of Eugenics in America,* 161–90; Katherine Castles, "Quiet Eugenics: Sterilization in North Carolina's Institutions for the Mentally Retarded, 1945–1965," *Journal of Southern History* 68 (November 2002): 849–78.

allotments, the Dawes Commission frowned on southern Native sexual practices and domestic arrangements, tying allotment to nuclear, patriarchal family structures. The United States government's control of Native bodies and sexuality, in other words, determined who got property, making allotment a profoundly gendered project, according to Stremlau. The politics of recognition—the fraught negotiations over who counted as Indian by proving genealogical connections or blood quantum—hinged on policing marriage and sexuality, as well. In administering the Indian Reorganization Act (1934), for example, the Office of Indian Affairs used such biological concepts, rather than Natives' own understandings of their identity, which were rooted in kin relationships. At times, however, Native southerners manipulated these biological standards and discouraged racial intermarriage, in attempts to defend tribal resources or guard against false claimants.[41]

Notably, few historians explored the state regulation of reproductive rights in the twentieth-century South, especially contraceptive and abortion access. Given that the most contentious battles over abortion access in the 2000s and 2010s transpired in southern states, this lacuna will no doubt be redressed by future southern women's historians. In many cases, conservative women held back progress, not only on abortion access but on progressive social movements as well. From Karen L. Cox's exploration of how the United Daughters of the Confederacy crafted pro-Confederate narratives of the Civil War in the late 1800s and early 1900s, to Elizabeth Gillespie McRae's analysis of white women in the

41. Arica L. Coleman, *That the Blood Stay Pure: African Americans, Native Americans, and the Predicament of Race and Identity in Virginia* (Bloomington: Indiana University Press, 2013); Mika Endo, "'The Word "Mixed" Without the "Indian" Would Be Better': Virginia's Racial Integrity Act and the Destruction of Indian Race in the Early Twentieth Century," *Native South* 7 (2014): 92–107; Angela Gonzales, Judy Kertész, and Gabrielle Tayac, "Eugenics as Indian Removal: Sociohistorical Processes and the De-(con)struction of American Indians in the Southeast," *Public Historian* 29 (Summer 2007): 53–67; Theda Perdue, "Southern Indians and Jim Crow," in *The Folly of Jim Crow: Rethinking the Segregated South,* ed. Stephanie Cole and Natalie J. Ring (College Station: Texas A&M University Press, 2012), 54–90; Rose Stremlau, *Sustaining the Cherokee Family: Kinship and the Allotment of an Indigenous Nation* (Chapel Hill: University of North Carolina Press, 2011), 18; Stremlau, "Allotment, Jim Crow, and the State: Reconceptualizing the Privatization of Land, the Segregation of Bodies, and the Politicization of Sexuality in the Native South," *Native South* 10 (2017): 60–75; Malinda Maynor Lowery, *Lumbee Indians in the Jim Crow South: Race, Identity, and the Making of a Nation* (Chapel Hill: University of North Carolina Press, 2010); Mikaëla M. Adams, *Who Belongs? Race, Resources, and Tribal Citizenship in the Native South* (New York: Oxford University Press, 2016); Adams, "Race, Kinship, and Belonging among the Florida Seminoles," in Garrison and O'Brien, eds., *The Native South,* 144–61; Katherine M. B. Osburn, "Mississippi Choctaws and Racial Politics," *Southern Cultures* 14 (Winter 2008): 32–54.

massive resistance movement against civil rights, historians made it clear that not all women of the South supported change. In their efforts, scholars reminded us that women are not, and never have been, a unified force.[42]

In the 2010s, works illuminating the history of mass incarceration greatly expanded our understanding of gender and state surveillance in the South. Several historians shined a light on imprisoned black women in the post-Emancipation South. Mary Ellen Curtin's work on black prisoners in Alabama uncovered female convicts in prisons and mining camps engaged in daily acts of resistance to protest the physical and sexual abuse they suffered even as they provided domestic labor essential to the penal system's operation. Examining Georgia's penal system from the postbellum years through the 1920s and 1930s, Talitha L. LeFlouria and Sarah Haley found evidence of resistance among incarcerated women. Yet their analyses went further, providing insights into the complicated interplay between the carceral state and gender. In several essays and in her 2015 book, *Chained in Silence,* LeFlouria revealed the problems with black women's reproductive capacity in an incarceration system that prioritized productive labor, the surprising way female convicts contributed to New South modernity by bucking gender conventions and performing traditionally male jobs, and the unique ways women coped with the physical and sexual violence inflicted on them in the penal system.[43]

In her 2016 book, Haley examined how the incarceration of black women informed an entire system of "gendered racial capitalism." Incarcerated black women not only contributed to southern state coffers; they also solidified the

42. Karen L. Cox, *Dixie's Daughters: The United Daughters of the Confederacy and the Preservation of Confederate Culture* (Gainesville: University Press of Florida, 2003); Elizabeth Gillespie McRae, *Mothers of Massive Resistance: White Women and the Politics of White Supremacy* (New York: Oxford University Press, 2018). Other works include Mathews and De Hart, *Sex, Gender, and the Politics of ERA;* Robin Morris, "Organizing Breadmakers: Kathryn Dunaway and the Georgia STOP ERA Campaign" in *Entering the Fray: Gender, Politics, and Culture in the New South,* ed. Jonathan Daniel Wells and Sheila R. Phipps (Columbia: University of Missouri Press, 2009), 161–83; Dailey, "Sex, Segregation, and the Sacred after *Brown.*" Works that explore the history of southern state regulation of contraceptive and abortion access include Schoen, *Choice and Coercion;* Marianne Leung, "'Better Babies': Birth Control in Arkansas during the 1930s," in Bernhard et al., eds., *Hidden Histories of Women in the New South,* 52–68. For an analysis of southern women who championed birth control access before the women's movement, see Leung, "Making the Radical Respectable: Little Rock Clubwomen and the Cause of Birth Control during the 1930s," *Arkansas Historical Quarterly* 57 (Spring 1998): 17–32.

43. Mary Ellen Curtin, *Black Prisoners and Their World, Alabama, 1865–1900* (Charlottesville: University Press of Virginia, 2000); Curtin, "The 'Human World' of Black Women in Alabama Prisons, 1870–1900," in Bernhard et al., eds., *Hidden Histories of Women in the New South,* 11–30; Talitha L. LeFlouria, "'The Hand that Rocks the Cradle Cuts Cordwood': Exploring Black Women's Lives and Labor

position of white women, even those who, if they ended up in the system themselves, were spared from demanding physical labor. In this way, the penal regime both reflected and produced gender in the Jim Crow South. According to Seth Kotch, similarly gendered and racialized dynamics determined the disparate sentencing of white and black women in North Carolina capital cases and suffused state execution protocols. By eliminating public hangings in favor of private, state-controlled electrocutions after 1910, North Carolina officials deliberately deprived African Americans of a space in which to honor victims (mostly black and male) and to critique the criminal justice system. Many historians of gender and the southern carceral state focused on the Jim Crow era, though a few pushed into the civil rights and post–civil rights eras, examining, for example, the famous trial of Joan Little in North Carolina in 1975. Regardless of their chronological framing, historians collectively made the case that twenty-first-century mass incarceration has deep roots in the South—and the nation—that long predated the feverous "War on Drugs."[44]

Works on gender and the southern carceral state, in other words, pointed to a question raised by many works discussed here: how separate was the history of

---

in Georgia's Convict Camps, 1865–1917," *Labor: Studies in Working-Class History of the Americas* 8 (Fall 2011): 47–63; LeFlouria, "Sewing and Spinning for the State: Incarcerated Black Female Garment Workers in the Jim Crow South," in *Crime and Punishment in the Jim Crow South,* ed. Amy Louise Wood and Natalie J. Ring (Urbana: University of Illinois Press, 2019), 130–46; LeFlouria, "'Under the Sting of the Lash': Gendered Violence, Terror, and Resistance in the South's Convict Camps," *Journal of African American History* 100 (Summer 2015): 366–84; LeFlouria, *Chained in Silence: Black Women and Convict Labor in the New South* (Chapel Hill: University of North Carolina Press, 2015); Sarah Haley, "'Like I was a Man': Chain Gangs, Gender, and the Domestic Carceral Sphere in Jim Crow Georgia," *Signs* 39 (Autumn 2013): 53–77; Haley, *No Mercy Here: Gender, Punishment, and the Making of Jim Crow Modernity* (Chapel Hill: University of North Carolina Press, 2016).

44. Haley, *No Mercy Here,* 4; Seth Kotch, "The Making of the Modern Death Penalty in Jim Crow North Carolina," in Wood and Ring, eds., *Crime and Punishment in the Jim Crow South,* 192–214; Kotch, *Lethal State: A History of the Death Penalty in North Carolina* (Chapel Hill: University of North Carolina Press, 2019); Christina Greene, "'She Ain't No Rosa Parks': The Joan Little Rape-Murder Case and Jim Crow Justice in the Post–Civil Rights South," *Journal of African-American History* 100 (Summer 2015): 428–47; Genna Rae McNeil, "The Body, Sexuality, and Self-Defense in *State vs. Joan Little,* 1974–1975," *Journal of African American History* 93 (Spring 2008): 235–61; McGuire, *At the Dark End of the Street;* Kali N. Gross and Cheryl D. Hicks, "Introduction—Gendering the Carceral State: African American Women, History, and the Criminal Justice System," *Journal of African American History* 100 (Summer 2015): 357–65; Michelle Alexander, *The New Jim Crow: Mass Incarceration in the Age of Colorblindness* (New York: New Press, 2010); "Historians and the Carceral State," Special Issue, *Journal of American History* 102 (June 2015): 18–184.

gender and sexuality in the twentieth-century South from the history of gender and sexuality in the nation as a whole? From the history of southern masculinity to southern women's wage labor to southern LGBTQ sexuality to southern women's Progressive-era activities, a distinctive, regional storyline often appears less obvious or pronounced than casual observers imagine. Still, we can hardly conclude that historians documented a total convergence of region and nation when it came to the history of gender and sexuality in the twentieth century. As Jacquelyn Dowd Hall and Anne Firor Scott noted at the end of their 1987 essay, a "peculiar tangle of sex and race" shaped women's place in the South. While various reform movements of the twentieth century mitigated that tangle's worst and most oppressive consequences, it was never completely undone, creating challenges for people in the South who step outside of prescribed norms of gender and sexuality.

Among the greatest contributions of southern historical writing since the 1980s has been the recovery of stories of resistance to these norms, often through the subversive use of the very dynamics embraced by individuals in power. Constructions of gender, race, and sexuality could be used both to reinforce and to contest existing hierarchies precisely because they were so malleable. More generally, historians demonstrated that in a region still struggling to break free from white patriarchy, women acted as important economic and political agents. In the coming years, scholars will no doubt do more to highlight the diversity and complexity of the region's activist movements by focusing on its American Indian and LGBTQ communities, as well as on its newer Latinx, Asian, Caribbean, and African immigrant populations, and by exploring the histories of the growing campaigns for environmental protections, development restrictions, affordable medical and childcare, and paid family leave, as well as against sexual and domestic violence. Much of the work discussed here focused on southerners advocating for progressive change for women and people suffering from gender and sexual inequities. But a number of scholars examined those who fought to maintain existing inequalities. Looking into the future, we anticipate that the next iteration of this essay will engage with a new generation of scholars who explain how and why the cultural battle intensified as a reinvigorated conservative movement pushed back against the progressive transformations of the twentieth century.

FROM THE GREAT DEPRESSION TO THE "END OF SOUTHERN HISTORY"?

Jennifer Ritterhouse and Jason Morgan Ward

When Franklin D. Roosevelt declared the South "the nation's No. 1 economic problem" in 1938, he emphasized that it was "the Nation's problem, not merely the South's." His words highlighted a new commitment not only to increasing the role of the federal government in the region but also to ending the South's isolation from the rest of the country. In the mid-twentieth century, the South appeared isolated in multiple senses of the word. It was poorer, more rural, less technologically advanced, and further removed from the centers of publishing, advertising, and other forms of cultural production than any other section of the United States. It was also held in isolation—one could almost say quarantined—as a place apart: "American with a difference," as Ulrich B. Phillips once wrote of the southern banks of the Ohio River. Southern distinctiveness was not merely the proud claim of white southerners nor the lament of African Americans subjected to a Jim Crow system frequently described by historians as "American apartheid." For non-southerners, it provided a way to remove Americanness from the American apartheid equation—to isolate a variable, in the mathematical sense. Among historians' most important tasks has been to review the cultural construction of distinctive "southern" and "American" identities over time, challenging the political and emotional calculus of earlier eras.[1]

1. Ulrich B. Phillips, "The Central Theme of Southern History," *American Historical Review* 34 (October 1928): 30–43, quote on 30. For Roosevelt's statement and its context, see David L. Carlton and Peter A. Coclanis, eds., *Confronting Southern Poverty in the Great Depression: The Report on Economic Conditions of the South with Related Documents* (Boston: Bedford, 1996), 42. On southern identity, see especially James C. Cobb, *Away Down South: A History of Southern Identity* (New York: Oxford University

From the 1980s to the 2010s, scholarship on the period since the Great Depression grew as quickly as a Sunbelt suburb. Historians interested in southern topics found common ground with scholars of African American history and the "non-South" to examine key questions about the New Deal, World War II, the Cold War, and globalization. In addition to exploring the origins and outcomes of the civil rights movement, a growing number of scholars traced the history of conservatism and debated top-down "Southern Strategy" explanations versus multivariant bottom-up and business-oriented accounts. By the early 2000s, a Sunbelt synthesis that emphasized similarities and convergences across regions emerged, leading a younger generation of scholars to ask whether they had, in fact, reached the "end of southern history." "Certainly by the second half of the twentieth century, if not before as well," Matthew D. Lassiter and Joseph Crespino argued, "focusing on the South's aberrant qualities compared to the rest of the United States obscures much more than it reveals about the fundamental questions of modern American history."[2] If they were correct, then the provocative next question seemed to be whether historians should continue "reinterpreting *southern* histories" at all.

As famous photographs by Dorothea Lange, Margaret Bourke-White, and Walker Evans convey better than any words can, the global economic crisis of the 1930s hit the South with devastating force. Dependent on industries already "sick" during the previous decade such as farming, textiles, and coal, many southerners were poor long before the stock market crash of 1929. The subsequent collapse of businesses and banks, the low prices for farm products, and the added ecological disaster of the Dust Bowl left millions destitute. Beginning with the Agricultural Adjustment Act (AAA) of 1933, New Deal farm policies exacerbated the problems of many southerners by initiating a full-scale transformation of the South's largest and most important economic sector. Written largely by planters for planters, AAA cotton codes that paid landowners to reduce their acreage also gave them

Press, 2005). Relevant discussions of the cultural construction of "American" identity take the form of dismantling "the myth of the liberal consensus." See Matthew D. Lassiter and Joseph Crespino's "Introduction: The End of Southern History," in *The Myth of Southern Exceptionalism*, ed. Matthew D. Lassiter and Joseph Crespino (New York: Oxford University Press, 2010), esp. 8–11 and 17n5; Gary Gerstle, "Race and the Myth of the Liberal Consensus," *Journal of American History* 82 (September 1995): 579–86. Laura F. Edwards addressed the dynamic between southern and American identities and exceptionalisms in "Southern History as U.S. History," *Journal of Southern History* 75 (August 2009): 533–64.

2. Lassiter and Crespino, "Introduction: The End of Southern History," 12.

the capital they needed to buy tractors and other farm equipment while reducing their labor needs. Thus the New Deal fostered mechanization and the growth of agribusiness while eliminating small producers, especially sharecroppers and tenants. Starting with books such as William Stott's *Documentary Expression and Thirties America* (1973), the dozens of contemporary writers and photographers who captured haunting images of the Depression's human toll became the subjects of biographies and cultural histories. Meanwhile, some of the first powerful works by scholars on this period amplified the voices of hard-pressed, dissenting southerners such as Ned Cobb, who joined the Alabama Sharecroppers Union in 1931, and H. L. Mitchell, who helped organize the Southern Tenant Farmers Union in the Arkansas-Mississippi Delta in 1934.[3]

3. Useful overviews include Anthony J. Badger, *The New Deal: The Depression Years, 1933–1940* (New York: Hill and Wang, 1989); Jordan A. Schwarz, *The New Dealers: Power Politics in the Age of Roosevelt* (New York: Alfred A. Knopf, 1993); Roger Biles, *The South and the New Deal* (Lexington: University Press of Kentucky, 1994); William E. Leuchtenburg, *The White House Looks South: Franklin D. Roosevelt, Harry S. Truman, Lyndon B. Johnson* (Baton Rouge: Louisiana State University Press, 2005). See also several valuable essay collections, including James C. Cobb and Michael V. Namorato, eds., *The New Deal and the South* (Jackson: University Press of Mississippi, 1984); Elna C. Green, ed., *The New Deal and Beyond: Social Welfare in the South since 1930* (Athens: University of Georgia Press, 2003); Anthony J. Badger, ed., *New Deal/New South* (Fayetteville: University of Arkansas Press, 2007). On the documentary impulse, see William Stott, *Documentary Expression and Thirties America* (New York: Oxford University Press, 1973); Carl Fleischhauer and Beverly W. Brannan, eds., *Documenting America, 1935–1943* (Berkeley: University of California Press, 1988); Jerrold Hirsch, *Portrait of America: A Cultural History of the Federal Writers Project* (Chapel Hill: University of North Carolina Press, 2003); Richard Godden and Martin Crawford, eds., *Reading Southern Poverty Between the Wars, 1918–1939* (Athens: University of Georgia Press, 2006). A few biographical works that double as cultural histories include Dan B. Miller, *Erskine Caldwell: The Journey from Tobacco Road* (New York: Alfred A. Knopf, 1995); Louis Mazzari, *Southern Modernist: Arthur Raper from the New Deal to the Cold War* (Baton Rouge: Louisiana State University Press, 2006); Linda Gordon, *Dorothea Lange: A Life Beyond Limits* (New York: W. W. Norton, 2009). On Ned Cobb and the Alabama Sharecroppers Union, see Theodore Rosengarten, *All God's Dangers: The Life of Nate Shaw* (New York: Alfred A. Knopf, 1974); Robin D. G. Kelley, *Hammer and Hoe: Alabama Communists during the Great Depression* (Chapel Hill: University of North Carolina Press, 1990). On H. L. Mitchell and the STFU, see Mitchell's autobiography, *Mean Things Happening in This Land: The Life and Times of H. L. Mitchell, Co-founder of the Southern Tenant Farmers Union* (Montclair, NJ: Allanheld, Osmun, 1979); Donald H. Grubbs, *Cry from the Cotton: The Southern Tenant Farmers' Union and the New Deal* (Chapel Hill: University of North Carolina Press, 1971). Discussions of the STFU include Jeannie M. Whayne, *A New Plantation South: Land, Labor, and Federal Favor in Twentieth-Century Arkansas* (Charlottesville: University Press of Virginia, 1996); Mark Fannin, *Labor's Promised Land: Radical Visions of Gender, Race, and Religion in the South* (Knoxville: University of Tennessee Press, 2003); Eric S. Gellman and Jarod Roll, *The Gospel of the Working Class: Labor's Southern Prophets in New Deal America*

During the Depression, the American public learned to feel a great deal of sympathy for displaced sharecroppers, and southern intellectuals—including both the Chapel Hill Regionalists and the Nashville Agrarians—wrote extensively about social and economic aspects of agricultural reform.[4] After the start of World War II, however, interest in the problems of rural southerners waned as former farm workers joined the booming industrial economy and as school desegregation, massive resistance, and the "classical phase" of the civil rights movement captivated the nation's attention. A few scholarly works kept the story of the "southern enclosure movement" alive but, as Numan V. Bartley explained in 1987, a significant revival of interest in these "seismic developments" awaited the 1980s. Authors such as Gilbert C. Fite, Pete Daniel, and Jack Temple Kirby agreed that the South followed what Kirby called "the federal road to rural development," but they disagreed in some of their assessments of federal agencies and bureaucrats. They also split on the question of how much to lament the passing of the agrarian communities and culture that, in Daniel's view, "gave a deeper meaning to life in the rural South." Kirby's evaluation of rural southern culture differed greatly from Daniel's, highlighting racism, greed, abusiveness toward women, and the "brutalization of the poor by men of the same or very similar origins and class." Subsequent scholarship on the rural South frequently emphasized these same characteristics while adding new dimensions. Rebecca Sharpless, Melissa Walker, and others contributed studies of women's work and family life. Mark Schultz examined the "rural face of white supremacy." Alison Collis Greene argued that religious southerners embraced many of the New Deal state's interventions, though white religious leaders worried that it undermined Jim Crow.[5]

(Urbana: University of Illinois Press, 2011); Jason Manthorne, "A View from the Cotton: Reconsidering the Southern Tenant Farmers' Union," *Agricultural History* 84 (Winter 2010): 20–45.

4. For an introduction to the debates between and the substantial scholarship on the Regionalists and the Agrarians, see Carlton and Coclanis, eds., *Confronting Southern Poverty;* Emily S. Bingham and Thomas A. Underwood, eds., *The Southern Agrarians and the New Deal: Essays after* I'll Take My Stand (Charlottesville: University Press of Virginia, 2001); Paul V. Murphy, *The Rebuke of History: Southern Agrarians and American Conservative Thought* (Chapel Hill: University of North Carolina Press, 2001); Bob Holladay, "The Gods That Failed: Agrarianism, Regionalism, and the Nashville–Chapel Hill Highway," *Tennessee Historical Quarterly* 64 (December 2005): 284–307.

5. Pete Daniel, *Breaking the Land: The Transformation of Cotton, Tobacco, and Rice Cultures since 1880* (Urbana: University of Illinois Press, 1985), 296; Jack Temple Kirby, *Rural Worlds Lost: The American South, 1920–1960* (Baton Rouge: Louisiana State University Press, 1987), 222; Numan V. Bartley, "The Southern Enclosure Movement," *Georgia Historical Quarterly* 71 (Fall 1987): 438–50; Gilbert C. Fite,

The significance of the New Deal–initiated transformation of southern agriculture cannot be overstated. Reviewing the state of the field in 2001, Nancy MacLean put cotton plantation sharecropping at the very center of the story of the twentieth-century South. She argued that an interpretation focused on the entrenchment of the plantation system after the Civil War, its shake-up in response to the New Deal, and its ultimate demise after World War II connected with most major themes in twentieth-century southern history. It also "helps to clear up a central paradox: how it was that the South incubated both the most democratic movement of twentieth-century American life, the Civil Rights Movement, and some of the most conservative, even authoritarian organizations from the Ku Klux Klan to the . . . Citizens' Council."[6]

Historians examining southern industrial development pointed out how low wages and poor conditions of farm workers hurt factory workers, too. As Jacquelyn Dowd Hall, Robert Korstad, and James Leloudis wrote in 1986, "textile mills built the New South" and "small-town boosterism supplied the rhetoric of the mill-building campaign," but "the impoverishment of farmers was industrialization's driving force." Important studies by James C. Cobb and Gavin Wright have been particularly influential in highlighting the key component of the South's economic distinctiveness: the isolation of southern labor markets from national and international labor flows that drove industrialization throughout the rest of the United States. As MacLean summarized, this separate regional labor market "helps explain other features of the southern economy commonly taken as signs of backwardness: its low wages, its limited-skill industry, its importation of

---

Cotton Fields No More: Southern Agriculture, 1865–1980 (Lexington: University Press of Kentucky, 1984); R. Douglas Hurt, ed., *The Rural South since World War II* (Baton Rouge: Louisiana State University Press, 1998); Rebecca Sharpless, *Fertile Ground, Narrow Choices: Women on Texas Cotton Farms, 1900–1940* (Chapel Hill: University of North Carolina Press, 1999); Melissa Walker, *All We Knew Was to Farm: Rural Women in the Upcountry South, 1919–1941* (Baltimore: Johns Hopkins University Press, 2000); Lu Ann Jones, *Mama Learned Us to Work: Farm Women in the New South* (Chapel Hill: University of North Carolina Press, 2002); Mark Schultz, *The Rural Face of White Supremacy: Beyond Jim Crow* (Urbana: University of Illinois Press, 2005); Alison Collis Greene, *No Depression in Heaven: The Great Depression, the New Deal, and the Transformation of Religion in the Delta* (New York: Oxford University Press, 2016). Bayard Rustin named the "classical phase" of the civil rights movement in "From Politics to Protest: The Future of the Civil Rights Movement," *Commentary* 39 (February 1965): 25.

6. Nancy MacLean, "From the Benighted South to the Sunbelt: The South in the Twentieth Century," in *Perspectives on Modern America: Making Sense of the Twentieth Century*, ed. Harvard Sitkoff (New York: Oxford University Press, 2001), 202–26, quote on 204.

technology and machinery, its shortage of capital, and its failure to invest in education." Indeed, much of the twentieth-century South's political economy grew from the shared interests in low wages and low taxes of southern industrialists and large landowners, who maintained their power in government through the disfranchisement of blacks and poor whites.[7]

As much as it disrupted southern agriculture, the New Deal had an equally significant and arguably more decisive impact on the South by bringing industrial wages and working conditions closer to national norms. Indeed, the longstanding conventional wisdom that World War II was the pivot for southern economic change seems to be giving way to an interpretation that starts earlier but finishes later. As Robert Lewis observed, "New Deal programs were critical to the making of the postwar South," but "not until the mid-1950s at the earliest can we identify the first significant signs of an independent and modern, albeit heavily militarist, manufacturing economy."[8]

The factors that made the New Deal so important, if not instant or by any means single-handed in its economic effects, came from both top down and bottom up. In addition to establishing standards for wages and hours that, though still regionally differentiated, substantively improved the lives of southern workers, New Deal legislation such as the National Industrial Recovery Act and the National Labor Relations Act invigorated the labor movement nationwide. The shelf of books in southern labor history has grown steadily since the 1980s. Building on the foundation laid by Jacquelyn Dowd Hall et al.'s poignant *Like A Family* (1987), a majority of studies focused on workers in the rigorously segregated textile industry. Bryant Simon, G. C. Waldrep III, Michelle Brattain, and others wrote about textile workers in particular communities and states,

7. Jacquelyn Dowd Hall, Robert Korstad, and James Leloudis, "Cotton Mill People: Work, Community, and Protest in the Textile South, 1880–1940," *American Historical Review* 91 (April 1986): 245–86, quote on 245; MacLean, "From the Benighted South to the Sunbelt," 207; Gavin Wright, *Sharing the Prize: The Economics of the Civil Rights Revolution in the American South* (Cambridge: Harvard University Press, 2013), 44. On industrialization, see James C. Cobb, *The Selling of the South: The Southern Crusade for Industrial Development, 1936–1980* (Baton Rouge: Louisiana State University Press, 1982); Cobb, *Industrialization and Southern Society, 1877–1984* (Lexington: University Press of Kentucky, 1984). In addition to *Sharing the Prize,* Gavin Wright's *Old South, New South: Revolutions in the Southern Economy since the Civil War* (New York: Basic Books, 1986) is indispensable.

8. Robert Lewis, "World War II Manufacturing and the Postwar Southern Economy," *Journal of Southern History* 73 (November 2007): 837–66, quote on 840. See also Gavin Wright, "The New Deal and the Modernization of the South," *Federal History* 2 (January 2010): 58–73.

while John Salmond and Janet Irons analyzed pivotal confrontations—from the bloody Gastonia, North Carolina, strike of 1929 to the general textile strike of 1934. Meanwhile, scholars interested in the challenges of interracial unionism turned to other industries to chronicle the rise of the Congress of Industrial Organizations (CIO) with its explicitly antidiscriminatory policies. Robert Korstad and Michael K. Honey emphasized connections between CIO efforts and blacks' long struggle for civil rights, while Glenda Elizabeth Gilmore made a similar case for the Depression-era race and labor activism of the Communist Party. Building on the pioneering scholarship of Nell Irvin Painter, Robin D. G. Kelley, and others who had recovered the histories of black southerners who joined the Communist Party, Gilmore argued that a vibrant left stretching, at least initially, from Birmingham to Moscow provided the "radical roots" of the civil rights revolution of later years.[9]

Gilmore's take on the Communist Party, and Honey and Korstad's assessment of the "civil rights unionism" of the CIO, dovetailed with other historians' evaluation of the late 1930s and early 1940s as the origins of the postwar civil rights movement. Especially after Jacquelyn Dowd Hall published her groundbreaking essay "The Long Civil Rights Movement and the Political Uses of the Past" in 2005, a growing number of scholars argued for significant continuity between the era's struggles, especially for workers' rights, and the more familiar history of the 1954 *Brown v. Board of Education* decision and the dramatic mass movement of 1955–1968. Cognizant of the fact that not only journalists and documentary filmmakers but also a new generation of conservatives were advancing a short, ideologically narrow, and shallow version of civil rights history, Hall outlined

9. Jacquelyn Dowd Hall et al., *Like a Family: The Making of a Southern Cotton Mill World* (Chapel Hill: University of North Carolina Press, 1987); Bryant Simon, *A Fabric of Defeat: The Politics of South Carolina Millhands, 1910–1948* (Chapel Hill: University of North Carolina Press, 1998); G. C. Waldrep III, *Southern Workers and the Search for Community: Spartanburg County, South Carolina* (Urbana: University of Illinois Press, 2000); Michelle Brattain, *The Politics of Whiteness: Race, Workers, and Culture in the Modern South* (Princeton: Princeton University Press, 2001); John Salmond, *Gastonia 1929: The Story of the Loray Mill Strike* (Chapel Hill: University of North Carolina Press, 1995); Janet Irons, *Testing the New Deal: The General Textile Strike of 1934 in the American South* (Urbana: University of Illinois Press, 2000); Robert Korstad, *Civil Rights Unionism: Tobacco Workers and the Struggle for Democracy in the Mid-Twentieth-Century South* (Chapel Hill: University of North Carolina Press, 2003); Michael K. Honey, *Southern Labor and Black Civil Rights: Organizing Memphis Workers* (Urbana: University of Illinois Press, 1993); Glenda Elizabeth Gilmore, *Defying Dixie: The Radical Roots of Civil Rights, 1919–1950* (New York: W. W. Norton, 2008); Nell Irvin Painter, *The Narrative of Hosea Hudson, His Life as a Negro Communist in the South* (Cambridge: Harvard University Press, 1979); Kelley, *Hammer and Hoe.*

a longer, broader, and deeper framework. In their most succinct form, her key interpretive points are that "the civil rights movement took root in the structural changes and political possibilities of the late 1930s, accelerated during World War II, stretched far beyond the South, was reshaped by the Cold War, and was continuously and ferociously contested. Indeed, from the New Deal onward, it has faced a 'long conservative movement,' and neither of these movements can be understood without the other."[10]

Although much of the scholarly debate over the long civil rights movement framework focused on the definition of "the movement," Hall's most important contribution was to draw attention to the larger, decades-long contest between conservative and progressive forces both within and beyond the South. This regional and national battlefield approach provides a structure for synthesizing scholarship on black activism outside as well as within the South, and white southerners' and non-southerners' recalcitrance. In addition, the long civil rights movement paradigm encouraged reexamination against a national backdrop of white southerners who, in Gilmore's terms, "defied Dixie" as radicals, liberals, or moderates. Like real-life versions of the Atticus Finch who seems, disturbingly, to change between Harper Lee's *To Kill a Mockingbird* (1960) and *Go Set a Watchman* (2015), white southerners who refused to conform to the conventional racism of their time and place both fascinated and confounded historians. Early works tended to be laudatory while underappreciating black agency and perspectives. New treatments seek to provide a richer context for understanding white southerners' departures from the racial status quo, which could be large or small, sustained or abbreviated, but were always race conscious. Only non-southern, white, "American" liberals could be as oblivious or indifferent to racism as Carol

10. Jacquelyn Dowd Hall, "Longer, Broader, Deeper: Rethinking the Civil Rights Movement and the Resistance to It," N. Jack Stallworth Lecture, 9 November 2011, University of South Alabama, Mobile, in possession of authors, 6; Hall, "The Long Civil Rights Movement and the Political Uses of the Past," *Journal of American History* 91 (March 2005): 1233–63. Although many subsequent works adopted or incorporated elements of the long civil rights movement framework, it has also had a number of critics. See Eric Arnesen, "Reconsidering the 'Long Civil Rights Movement,'" *Historically Speaking* 10 (April 2009): 31–34; Alex Lichtenstein, "The Other Civil Rights Movement and the Problem of Southern Exceptionalism," *Journal of the Historical Society* 11 (September 2011): 351–76; Sundiata Keita Cha-Jua and Clarence Lang, "The 'Long Movement' as Vampire: Temporal and Spatial Fallacies in Recent Black Freedom Studies," *Journal of African American History* 92 (Spring 2007): 265–88; Steven F. Lawson, "Long Origins of the Short Civil Rights Movement, 1954–1968," in *Freedom Rights: New Perspectives on the Civil Rights Movement,* ed. Danielle L. McGuire and John Dittmer (Lexington: University Press of Kentucky, 2011), 9–37.

Polsgrove, for example, found many northern intellectuals even in the 1950s and 1960s to have been.[11]

A substantial body of scholarship exposed the discriminatory nature and impact of liberal policies, as well as African Americans' efforts to challenge these practices by using new political leverage gained largely as a result of the Great Migration. Ira Katznelson's *When Affirmative Action Was White* (2005) detailed the long-term effects of New Deal decisions that allowed whites to pull even further ahead of nonwhites—and not merely in the South. His subsequent book, *Fear Itself* (2013), highlighted conservative white southerners' efforts to achieve this outcome by constraining Roosevelt and the more liberal elements of the New Deal coalition. For decades, historians explained the New Deal's limitations by emphasizing discrimination on the part of local administrators and the outsized power of conservative southern congressmen. Katznelson consolidated these interpretations into the image of a "southern cage" that, along with fears of foreign dictatorships and the destructiveness of modern warfare, hemmed in America's democracy. As their party rose to power with Roosevelt's election in 1933, southern Democrats in Congress became "the most important 'veto players' in American politics." They and the shrunken southern electorate that kept returning them to office set the terms "not just for their constituencies but for the country" during the global crises of the Depression and World War II.[12]

11. Major works on white southern liberals, radicals, and moderates include Morton Sosna, *In Search of the Silent South: Southern Liberals and the Race Issue* (New York: Columbia University Press, 1977); Jacquelyn Dowd Hall, *Revolt Against Chivalry: Jessie Daniel Ames and the Women's Campaign against Lynching* (New York: Columbia University Press, 1979); Anthony P. Dunbar, *Against the Grain: Southern Radicals and Prophets, 1929–1959* (Charlottesville: University Press of Virginia, 1981); Charles W. Eagles, *Jonathan Daniels and Race Relations: The Evolution of a Southern Liberal* (Knoxville: University of Tennessee Press, 1982); John T. Kneebone, *Southern Liberal Journalists and the Issue of Race, 1920–1944* (Chapel Hill: University of North Carolina Press, 1985); John A. Salmond, *Miss Lucy of the CIO: The Life and Times of Lucy Randolph Mason, 1882–1959* (Athens: University of Georgia Press, 1988). Two important overviews that appeared in the 1990s are John Egerton, *Speak Now Against the Day: The Generation Before the Civil Rights Movement in the South* (New York: Alfred A. Knopf, 1994); Patricia Sullivan, *Days of Hope: Race and Democracy in the New Deal Era* (Chapel Hill: University of North Carolina Press, 1996). In addition to Gilmore's *Defying Dixie,* efforts to reevaluate white southern liberalism include Jennifer Ritterhouse, *Discovering the South: One Man's Travels Through a Changing America in the 1930s* (Chapel Hill: University of North Carolina Press, 2017); Joseph Crespino, *Atticus Finch: The Biography: Harper Lee, Her Father, and the Making of an American Icon* (New York: Basic Books, 2018). See also Carol Polsgrove, *Divided Minds: Intellectuals and the Civil Rights Movement* (New York: W. W. Norton, 2001).

12. Ira Katznelson, *When Affirmative Action Was White: An Untold History of Racial Inequality in Twentieth-Century America* (New York: W. W. Norton, 2005); Ira Katznelson, *Fear Itself: The New Deal*

Most whites outside the South accepted the terms of the southern cage with few qualms about racial injustice. The southern white supremacist bloc, however, did have to contend with another component of the New Deal coalition: politically mobilized African Americans. An outgrowth of the race and labor activism of the previous decade, the March on Washington movement forced President Roosevelt to issue a 1941 executive order on fair employment practices that electrified wartime politics in the region. This and other efforts on Roosevelt's part to pry open the bars of the southern cage even minimally (and even on the basis of wartime necessity) combined with mounting racial conflicts to make southern modernizers feel trapped between two imperatives: economic development and white supremacy. As federal dollars poured into the region's disproportionate share of military installations, defense plants, and shipyards, southern politicians simultaneously decried the accompanying antidiscriminatory policies and lobbied for as much federally subsidized prosperity as possible. By the end of the war, as Cobb has noted, "a southern governor's obligation to recruit new industry was second only to his obligation to defend segregation."[13]

Because of southern leaders' determination to maintain white supremacy—a continuation and expansion of their response to New Deal–era tensions between regional modernization and racial conservatism—historians disagree about the significance of World War II for civil rights. Some argue the war wrought massive social change while others emphasize the white backlash on the southern home front and mounting opposition to reform initiatives in Washington, DC. And while a postwar spree of white supremacist violence, much of it aimed at

---

and the Origins of Our Time (New York: W. W. Norton, 2013), 15–16. For an overview of scholarship on race and civil rights in the New Deal era, see John Brueggemann, "Racial Considerations and Social Policy in the 1930s," *Social Science History* 26 (Spring 2002): 139–77. On conservatives in the United States Congress and southern state legislatures, see James T. Patterson, *Congressional Conservatism and the New Deal: The Growth of the Conservative Coalition in Congress, 1933–1939* (Lexington: University of Kentucky Press, 1967); Douglas Carl Abrams, *Conservative Constraints: North Carolina and the New Deal* (Jackson: University Press of Mississippi, 1992); Jack Irby Hayes Jr., *South Carolina and the New Deal* (Columbia: University of South Carolina Press, 2001); Ronald L. Heinemann, *Depression and New Deal in Virginia: The Enduring Dominion* (Charlottesville: University Press of Virginia, 1983).

13. James C. Cobb, "World War II and the Mind of the Modern South," in *Remaking Dixie: The Impact of World War II on the American South*, ed. Neil R. McMillen (Jackson: University Press of Mississippi, 1997), 3–21, quote on 5. On World War II and regional transformation, see Pete Daniel, "Going Among Strangers: Southern Reactions to World War II," *Journal of American History* 77 (December 1990): 886–911.

returning black veterans and voters, compelled President Harry S. Truman to unprecedented action on civil rights, the explosive racial politics of the immediate postwar era spawned a revolt among southern Democrats. The standard bearer of this "Dixiecrat" movement, South Carolina governor and States' Rights Democratic Party presidential nominee J. Strom Thurmond, personified the disturbing compatibility between regional modernization and white supremacy. Thurmond ran for governor in 1946 on a platform of economic development and state governmental reform, even as counterparts in Georgia and Mississippi advocated racial terrorism from the stump. Yet his subsequent Dixiecrat campaign, in privileging anti–civil rights animus above all else, demonstrated the limits of region-based politics, capturing the electoral votes of only four Deep South states in 1948. Meanwhile, southern Democrats who remained loyal to Truman in the election of 1948 did so in large part because of their confidence that they could stymie racial reform and facilitate regional development from their perches of power in the federal government. Among historians studying these debates, Kari Frederickson especially underscored the continuity between racial retrenchment and regional transformation by following her authoritative 2001 account of the Dixiecrat movement with a 2013 examination of Cold War modernization in rural South Carolina. The 1948 Dixiecrat revolt ended the national Democratic Party's unquestioned dominance in the South, yet the Cold War deepened ties to the federal government that would be strained in future decades.[14]

The Cold War gave added firepower to anticommunism, an already potent weapon that anti–civil rights forces in the South had used since the start of the New Deal. Although the wartime alliance with the Soviet Union temporarily reduced the red-baiting of labor organizers and civil rights advocates, postwar

14. Morton Sosna, for example, described World War II as a "regional watershed"; see "Introduction," in McMillen, ed., *Remaking Dixie*, xiv. On postwar politics and violence, see Gail Williams O'Brien, *The Color of the Law: Race, Violence, and Justice in the Post–World War II South* (Chapel Hill: University of North Carolina Press, 1999); Jennifer E. Brooks, *Defining the Peace: World War II Veterans, Race, and the Remaking of Southern Political Tradition* (Chapel Hill: University of North Carolina Press, 2004). Arguments for the compatibility of regional development and racial retrenchment can be found in multiple sources, but see especially Bruce J. Schulman, *From Cotton Belt to Sunbelt: Federal Policy, Economic Development, and the Transformation of the South, 1938–1980* (New York: Oxford University Press, 1991); Wright, "The New Deal and the Modernization of the South." On the Dixiecrats and federally subsidized postwar regional development, see Kari Frederickson, *The Dixiecrat Revolt and the End of the Solid South, 1932–1968* (Chapel Hill: University of North Carolina Press, 2001); Frederickson, *Cold War Dixie: Militarization and Modernization in the American South* (Athens: University of Georgia Press, 2013).

anticommunists quickly reloaded to face off against the ideology that historian Mary L. Dudziak called *Cold War Civil Rights* (2000). Just as they had done during World War II, racial reformers linked a global crusade against totalitarianism to a domestic struggle for justice, arguably with greater success. As Truman's Committee on Civil Rights warned in its 1947 report *To Secure These Rights,* "We cannot escape the fact that our civil rights record has been an issue in world politics. The world's press and radio are full of it." The mounting pressure to curb white supremacist abuses in the South and avoid embarrassing international headlines spurred national leaders of both parties to unprecedented steps. Yet, historians of the Cold War–era South are cautious in their assessment of this postwar window of opportunity, and for good reason. Anticommunism not only fueled a racial backlash but also constrained the options of reform-minded southerners. Thus scholars often end studies of New Deal liberalism and the southern left in 1946 or 1948 because of the failures of the CIO's Operation Dixie, the passage of the anticommunist and antilabor Taft-Hartley Act, and the dispiriting denouement of Henry Wallace's Progressive Party campaign. As Patricia Sullivan observed at the end of *Days of Hope* (1996), the optimism "born at the high tide of the New Deal could not survive the repression and political sterility of the cold war era." Instead, opportunities for a labor-based civil rights movement had been "found and lost," as Robert Korstad and Nelson Lichtenstein argued, even as activists laid groundwork for the future.[15]

The immediate postwar years also provided a window of opportunity for southern conservatives to prepare themselves for the coming battle over school desegregation. Responding to earlier studies of segregationists that paid scant attention to anticommunism, historians such as George Lewis and Jeff Woods provided a counterpoint to "Cold War Civil Rights" with their studies of anti–

15. Mary L. Dudziak, *Cold War Civil Rights: Race and the Image of American Democracy* (Princeton: Princeton University Press, 2000); Steven F. Lawson, ed., *To Secure These Rights: The Report of President Harry S Truman's Committee on Civil Rights* (Boston: Bedford/St. Martin's, 2003), 166; Sullivan, *Days of Hope,* 274; Robert Korstad and Nelson Lichtenstein, "Opportunities Found and Lost: Labor, Radicals, and the Early Civil Rights Movement," *Journal of American History* 75 (December 1988): 787–811. See also Barbara S. Griffith, *The Crisis of American Labor: Operation Dixie and the Defeat of the CIO* (Philadelphia: Temple University Press, 1988); Honey, *Southern Labor and Black Civil Rights;* Korstad, *Civil Rights Unionism;* Pete Daniel, *Lost Revolutions: The South in the 1950s* (Chapel Hill: University of North Carolina Press, 2000); Risa L. Goluboff, *The Lost Promise of Civil Rights* (Cambridge: Harvard University Press, 2007); Ken Fones-Wolf and Elizabeth A. Fones-Wolf, *Struggle for the Soul of the Postwar South: White Evangelical Protestants and Operation Dixie* (Urbana: University of Illinois Press, 2015).

civil rights Cold Warriors. In addition to rooting the segregationist movement more firmly in earlier postwar conflicts, these historians emphasized the white South's distinctive twist on a national anticommunist crusade while still depicting a region overshadowed by the looming clouds of massive resistance.[16]

The white South's response to the 1954 Supreme Court decision in *Brown v. Board of Education* and the confrontations that followed subsequent civil rights milestones began to dominate the scholarship on southern politics and society even as the struggle raged. For decades, the civil rights movement attracted more scholarly attention than any other topic in the South's post-Reconstruction history. Yet parallel to a point that Nancy MacLean made about the value of seeing beyond the "Second Wave" to understand postwar women's history in more economic and structural terms, historians of the South benefited from taking a step back from the 1960s battleground. The transformations wrought by the movement and those who resisted it spurred broader debates about southern politics, society, and culture. Building on the foundation established by Numan V. Bartley's *The Rise of Massive Resistance* (1969) and Neil R. McMillen's pioneering 1971 study of the Citizens' Council, subsequent scholars situated white resistance to civil rights in a broader context and chronology. By looking beyond the immediate backlash to *Brown v. Board of Education* and other movement victories, as well as weaving together the stories of those who fought for and against racial change, historians produced more thorough and nuanced accounts of how southerners adapted to the South's "Second Reconstruction."[17]

16. Jeff Woods, *Black Struggle, Red Scare: Segregation and Anti-Communism in the South, 1948–1968* (Baton Rouge: Louisiana State University Press, 2004); George Lewis, *The White South and the Red Menace: Segregationists, Anticommunism, and Massive Resistance, 1945–1965* (Gainesville: University Press of Florida, 2004).

17. Nancy MacLean, "Postwar Women's History: The 'Second Wave' or the End of the Family Wage?" in *A Companion to Post-1945 America,* ed. Jean Christophe Agnew and Roy Rosenzweig (Malden, MA: Blackwell, 2002), 235–55; Numan V. Bartley, *The Rise of Massive Resistance: Race and Politics in the South during the 1950's* (Baton Rouge: Louisiana State University Press, 1969); Neil R. McMillen, *The Citizens' Council: Organized Resistance to the Second Reconstruction, 1954–64* (Urbana: University of Illinois Press, 1971). For examples of works that broaden beyond movement history, see Michael J. Klarman, "How *Brown* Changed Race Relations: The Backlash Thesis," *Journal of American History* 81 (June 1994): 81–118; Charles W. Eagles, "Towards New Histories of the Civil Rights Era," *Journal of Southern History* 66 (November 2000): 815–48; David L. Chappell, *A Stone of Hope: Prophetic Religion and the Death of Jim Crow* (Chapel Hill: University of North Carolina Press, 2004); Jane Dailey, "Sex, Segregation, and the Sacred after *Brown,*" *Journal of American History* 91 (June 2004): 119–44; Jason Sokol, *There Goes My Everything: White Southerners in the Age of Civil Rights, 1945–1975* (New York: Alfred A. Knopf, 2006); Chris

White resistance varied from state to state, and public officials from Capitol Hill to city hall devised a variety of means to delay or derail civil rights campaigns. In an early example of a local history that took seriously regional and strategic variations in white southern politics, William H. Chafe argued that Greensboro's politics of "civility" and moderation, bolstered by North Carolina's "progressive mystique," frustrated black activists in the birthplace of the student sit-in movement. Since that classic 1980 case study, historians demonstrated how the tension between "strategic" and diehard resistance infused regional politics from the Senate floor to Deep South communities. In *Delaying the Dream* (2008), Keith M. Finley traced southern senators' tactic of "strategic delay" from World War II through the mid-1960s. Even as the scheme failed to stop the Civil Rights Act of 1964 and the Voting Rights Act of 1965, southern moderates pursued a variety of similar tactics to stall and limit racial change. The clash between moderation and massive resistance started well before these congressional showdowns, as white residents of Virginia revolted against segregationist attempts to shutter public schools and adopt as state policy the obscure constitutional argument of interposition as a means of nullifying federal court rulings on desegregation. From the Upper and Outer to the Deep South, Anders Walker compared moderate resistance in North Carolina, Florida, and Mississippi in *The Ghost of Jim Crow* (2009). Despite all that separated the Magnolia State from its northern neighbors, Joseph Crespino similarly recognized a strain of "strategic accommodation" in Mississippi that outlasted the bloody summer of 1964.[18]

Myers Asch, *The Senator and the Sharecropper: The Freedom Struggles of James O. Eastland and Fannie Lou Hamer* (New York: New Press, 2008); Timothy J. Minchin and John A. Salmond, *After the Dream: Black and White Southerners since 1965* (Lexington: University Press of Kentucky, 2011); Jason Morgan Ward, *Defending White Democracy: The Making of a Segregationist Movement and the Remaking of Racial Politics, 1936–1965* (Chapel Hill: University of North Carolina Press, 2011). For an interesting cultural history approach to the period, see Stephen A. Berrey, *The Jim Crow Routine: Everyday Performances of Race, Civil Rights, and Segregation in Mississippi* (Chapel Hill: University of North Carolina Press, 2015).

18. William H. Chafe, *Civilities and Civil Rights: Greensboro, North Carolina and the Black Struggle for Freedom* (New York: Oxford University Press, 1980); Keith M. Finley, *Delaying the Dream: Southern Senators and the Fight Against Civil Rights, 1938–1965* (Baton Rouge: Louisiana State University Press, 2008); Anders Walker, *The Ghost of Jim Crow: How Moderates Used* Brown v. Board of Education *to Stall Civil Rights* (New York: Oxford University Press, 2009); Joseph Crespino, *In Search of Another Country: Mississippi and the Conservative Counterrevolution* (Princeton: Princeton University Press, 2007). See also Matthew D. Lassiter and Andrew B. Lewis, eds., *The Moderates' Dilemma: Massive Resistance to School Desegregation in Virginia* (Charlottesville: University Press of Virginia, 1998).

Although segregationist politics, "strategic" or not, seemed at the time to isolate the South from the national mainstream, some historians situated the region at the center of broader postwar transformations. Studies of segregationists and their connection to a burgeoning national conservative movement proliferated in the 1990s and early 2000s. Scholars wrote biographies of prominent officials and case studies of civil rights skirmishes across the region—none more consequential than Dan T. Carter's biography of George Wallace, *The Politics of Rage* (1995). A hardline segregationist governor most famous for his 1963 "Stand in the Schoolhouse Door," Wallace, who ran for president as a Democratic primary challenger in 1964 and 1972 and a third-party candidate in 1968, embodied for Carter the national reach of a racially charged, populist conservatism that Republican strategists increasingly embraced. Following up his Wallace biography with a published lecture series that traced the role of "race in the conservative counterrevolution" from Wallace to then-Speaker of the House Newt Gingrich, Carter rooted the rise of the New Right in the southern backlash to civil rights. Echoing Wallace's apocryphal claim that "The Whole United States is southern," journalists and scholars alike seized upon the "southernization" thesis to explain America's rightward turn.[19]

This "Southern Strategy" argument, which privileged top-down accounts driven by party strategists and presidential election cycles, reflected a broader effort to explain the defection of white southerners from Democratic to Republican ranks. A number of political historians and political scientists, most notably Earl and Merle Black, published exhaustive studies of Republican realignment in the final two decades of the twentieth century. They traced a series of reactions to civil rights gains, from GOP nominee Barry Goldwater's Deep South incursions in 1964 to Richard Nixon's landslide in 1972, extrapolating from high-profile national developments to account for Republican success at the state and local levels. Civil rights opponents who defected to GOP ranks relatively early in this

19. Dan T. Carter, *The Politics of Rage: George Wallace, the Origins of the New Conservatism, and the Transformation of American Politics* (New York: Simon & Schuster, 1995); Carter, *From George Wallace to Newt Gingrich: Race in the Conservative Counterrevolution, 1963–1994* (Baton Rouge: Louisiana State University Press, 1996); Charles M. Payne, "'The Whole United States Is Southern!' *Brown v. Board* and the Mystification of Race," *Journal of American History* 91 (June 2004): 83–91; Peter Applebome, *Dixie Rising: How the South Is Shaping American Values, Politics, and Culture* (New York: Times Books, 1996). A classic work in this vein is John Egerton, *The Americanization of Dixie: The Southernization of America* (New York: Harper's Magazine Press, 1974).

process—most notably Strom Thurmond and Jesse Helms—figured prominently in the wave of scholarship on race and conservatism.[20]

The problem with the "Southern Strategy" argument, historian Matthew D. Lassiter argued in *The Silent Majority* (2006), was that it failed to consider grassroots politics in the emerging center of modern political and economic power: the suburban Sunbelt. Rather than offering a narrative centered around Deep South–driven electoral disasters—from the Dixiecrats' failed attempt to deadlock the 1948 election to Barry Goldwater's landslide loss in 1964 and George Wallace's third-party, third-place finish in 1968—Lassiter shifted the focus to booming metropolitan areas that, he argued, "converged with the class-based voting patterns in the rest of the nation." Along with economic self-interest, ambivalence towards civil rights reforms animated the ostensibly "color-blind" politics of property and prosperity. Yet Lassiter argued that the "trope of southern exceptionalism . . . misses the broader story of the grassroots mobilization of the Silent Majority that reframed racial discourse and subsumed regional differences." Kevin M. Kruse's *White Flight* (2005) and Joseph Crespino's *In Search of Another Country* (2007) similarly concluded that southern conservatism—from the region's major metropolis, Atlanta, to its most rural state, Mississippi—converged with a national rightward turn in the post–civil rights era.[21]

Some scholars bridled at Sunbelt historians' repudiation of prior studies of southern racial politics and reduced their arguments about "color-blind" conservatism to an outright dismissal of the enduring role of race in southern history. But the focus on the suburban Sunbelt pushed historians to reconsider assumptions about the conservative drift of regional and national politics since World War II. Rather than a retreat to "Bourbon" conservatism, as Numan V. Bartley argued in his 1995 synthesis of the post–World War II South, perhaps the most significant shift was the continued migration of political and economic power

20. Joseph A. Aistrup, *The Southern Strategy Revisited: Republican Top-Down Advancement in the South* (Lexington: University Press of Kentucky, 1996); Earl Black and Merle Black, *Politics and Society in the South* (Cambridge: Harvard University Press, 1987); Black and Black, *The Rise of Southern Republicans* (Cambridge: Harvard University Press, 2002).

21. Matthew D. Lassiter, *The Silent Majority: Suburban Politics in the Sunbelt South* (Princeton: Princeton University Press, 2006), quotes on 6; Kevin M. Kruse, *White Flight: Atlanta and the Making of Modern Conservatism* (Princeton: Princeton University Press, 2005); Crespino, *In Search of Another Country.* Political scientists Byron E. Shafer and Richard Johnston also emphasized the convergence of regional and national politics in *The End of Southern Exceptionalism: Class, Race, and Partisan Change in the Postwar South* (Cambridge: Harvard University Press, 2006).

"from Cotton Belt to Sunbelt," as Bruce J. Schulman contended. The Sunbelt synthesis was more compatible with other work on the grassroots right, such as Lisa McGirr's important book on Orange County, California. The synthesis also cohered with scholarship on American, not merely southern, businessmen's crusades against the New Deal and the regulatory state. Books by Katherine Rye Jewell, Darren Grem, and others rigorously traced the connections between southern, business, and Christian conservatism. Meanwhile, by looking beyond the racial politics of the Deep South, the Sunbelt perspective encouraged historians to see more of the region's political spectrum. In addition to prompting a realignment of white southerners, the civil rights movement registered and mobilized tens of thousands of black southerners. Although studies of southern conservatism in various "belts"—Bible, Sun-, and so on—continued to predominate, historians increasingly examined black politics and the emergent interracial coalitions. Such studies, including Tim S. R. Boyd's 2012 history of Georgia Democrats from the end of World War II to Jimmy Carter's presidency, help to explain why Republican dominance in the late twentieth century was neither preordained nor permanent.[22]

By following the story into the 1970s and beyond, Sunbelt historians joined a new generation of scholars filling in a timeline sketched over the previous two decades by historians of regional modernization. In the early 1990s, both Bartley's

22. Numan V. Bartley, *The New South, 1945–1980: The Story of the South's Modernization* (Baton Rouge: Louisiana State University Press, 1995), 104; Schulman, *From Cotton Belt to Sunbelt*; Lisa McGirr, *Suburban Warriors: The Origins of the New American Right* (Princeton: Princeton University Press, 2001); Kim Phillips-Fein, *Invisible Hands: The Businessmen's Crusade against the New Deal* (New York: W. W. Norton, 2009); Katherine Rye Jewell, *Dollars for Dixie: Business and the Transformation of Conservatism in the Twentieth Century* (New York: Cambridge University Press, 2017); Darren Grem, *The Blessings of Business: How Corporations Shaped Conservative Christianity* (New York: Oxford University Press, 2016). See also Darren Dochuk, *From Bible Belt to Sunbelt: Plain-Folk Religion, Grassroots Politics, and the Rise of Evangelical Conservatism* (New York: W. W. Norton, 2011); Kevin M. Kruse, *One Nation Under God: How Corporate America Invented Christian America* (New York: Basic Books, 2015). For studies that emphasize Democratic politics in the post–civil rights era South, see Tim S. R. Boyd, *Georgia Democrats, the Civil Rights Movement, and the Shaping of the New South* (Gainesville: University Press of Florida, 2012); Chris Danielson, *After Freedom Summer: How Race Realigned Mississippi Politics, 1965–1986* (Gainesville: University Press of Florida, 2011). For studies that challenge the Sunbelt narrative of regional/national convergence and continue to stress the "southern" origins of modern conservatism, see Joseph E. Lowndes, *From the New Deal to the New Right: Race and the Southern Origins of Modern Conservatism* (New Haven: Yale University Press, 2008); also multiple works edited or written by Glenn Feldman, including *The Great Melding: War, the Dixiecrat Rebellion, and the Southern Model for America's New Conservatism* (Tuscaloosa: University of Alabama Press, 2015).

synthesis of the post-1945 South and Schulman's sweeping history of regional transformation since the New Deal concluded with discussions of the Sunbelt in the post–civil rights era. Indeed, Schulman followed *From Cotton Belt to Sunbelt* (1991) with an assessment of America in the 1970s, in which he expanded his arguments about the rise of regional power. Like Bartley, Schulman saw evidence of the Sunbelt's eclipse of the deindustrializing Rust Belt not only in congressional reapportionment but also in cultural phenomena. Country music, with a seemingly endless stream of hits about the South rising again, went national in the 1970s and, as Charles L. Hughes demonstrated in *Country Soul* (2015), reflected regional transformations wrought by two decades of civil rights, Black Power, and white backlash. James N. Gregory's explanation for postwar cultural convergence differed, pointing to the massive *Southern Diaspora* (2005) that spanned the twentieth century. Anthropologist Carol Stack described the turning of the migratory tide as African Americans reclaimed the rural South in the 1970s by answering a *Call to Home* (1996). Thus, from the proliferation of air conditioning and regional research parks to the southward migration of people, capital, and professional sports teams, the rise of the Sunbelt presented a vast array of topics for historians of the modern South. Meanwhile, narratives of a convergence between regional and national politics and culture remain in harmonious tension with studies that emphasize enduring regional distinctiveness.[23]

Perhaps one measure of declining southern exceptionalism (as opposed to distinctiveness) is the degree to which scholars wove the region's history into ambitious national historiographical trends. In *Texas Tough* (2010), Robert Perkinson centered the South and its legacy of plantation-based imprisonment in what, by the mid-2010s, became the hottest topic among historians of modern America: mass incarceration. "Crime and punishment in the South has long been the subject of public fascination," Heather Ann Thompson pointed out in a 2010 essay, but popular and scholarly interpretations that emphasized southern exception-

23. Bartley, *The New South*; Schulman, *From Cotton Belt to Sunbelt*; Schulman, *The Seventies: The Great Shift in American Culture, Society, and Politics* (New York: Free Press, 2001); Charles L. Hughes, *Country Soul: Making Music and Making Race in the American South* (Chapel Hill: University of North Carolina Press, 2015); James N. Gregory, *The Southern Diaspora: How the Great Migrations of Black and White Southerners Transformed America* (Chapel Hill: University of North Carolina Press, 2005); Carol Stack, *Call to Home: African Americans Reclaim the Rural South* (New York: Basic Books, 1996). Focusing on race and culture rather than political economy, David R. Goldfield offered an ambitious synthesis stretching from the New Deal to the rise of Ronald Reagan in *Black, White, and Southern: Race Relations and Southern Culture, 1940 to the Present* (Baton Rouge: Louisiana State University Press, 1990).

alism obscured "the extent to which historical penal practices in northern and western states also have been inhumane and deeply racialized." More scholarship that compares and connects regional and national penal histories remains to be done to ensure policymakers can no longer be "blinded by a 'barbaric' South."[24]

Looking outward from the South allowed a number of historians to contribute fresh insights on other political and social developments. In *A Nation of Outsiders* (2011), Grace Elizabeth Hale emphasized the prominent role of the South and southerners—black and white—in a national culture of "rebellion" in postwar America. Conversely, Nancy MacLean's *Democracy in Chains* (2017) argued that the intellectual influence of James McGill Buchanan, a Nobel Prize-winning economist with segregationist roots, gave a reactionary southern accent to the libertarian movement funded by billionaires Charles and David Koch. In *Divided We Stand* (2017), Marjorie J. Spruill demonstrated the decisive role of southern women in the late-1970s battle over the Equal Rights Amendment. Moving into the final two decades of the twentieth century and beyond, Shane Hamilton and Bethany Moreton centered the South in narratives of national economic transformation. The "Walmart economy"—a shift from Rust Belt manufacturing to Sunbelt-centered service and distribution industries—not only takes its name from a southern family business turned transnational corporation but also underscores the profound political, social, and economic consequences of regional modernization.[25]

24. Robert Perkinson, *Texas Tough: The Rise of America's Prison Empire* (New York: Metropolitan Books, 2010); Heather Ann Thompson, "Blinded by a 'Barbaric' South: Prison Horrors, Inmate Abuse, and the Ironic History of American Penal Reform," in Lassiter and Crespino, eds., *Myth of Southern Exceptionalism*, 74–75. On the South's criminal justice system, see David M. Oshinsky, *"Worse Than Slavery": Parchman Farm and the Ordeal of Jim Crow Justice* (New York: Free Press, 1996); Alex Lichtenstein, *Twice the Work of Free Labor: The Political Economy of Convict Labor in the New South* (New York: Verso, 1996); Douglas A. Blackmon, *Slavery by Another Name: The Re-Enslavement of Black Americans from the Civil War to World War II* (New York: Doubleday, 2008). For a broader national context, see the June 2015 special issue of the *Journal of American History* on "Constructing the Carceral State"; and Heather Ann Thompson's *Blood in the Water: The Attica Prison Uprising of 1971 and Its Legacy* (New York: Pantheon Books, 2016).

25. Grace Elizabeth Hale, *A Nation of Outsiders: How the White Middle Class Fell in Love with Rebellion in Postwar America* (New York: Oxford University Press, 2011); Nancy MacLean, *Democracy in Chains: The Deep History of the Radical Right's Stealth Plan for America* (New York: Viking, 2017); Marjorie J. Spruill, *Divided We Stand: The Battle Over Women's Rights and Family Values That Polarized American Politics* (New York: Bloomsbury Press, 2017); Bethany Moreton, *To Serve God and Wal-Mart: The Making of Christian Free Enterprise* (Cambridge: Harvard University Press, 2009); Shane Hamilton, *Trucking Country: The Road to America's Wal-Mart Economy* (Princeton: Princeton University Press, 2008).

The migration and globalization of capital came with human costs, and studies of the South at the end of the twentieth century emphasize socioeconomic continuities as well as demographic changes. As industrialists moved operations south in search of low-wage, nonunion labor, they capitalized on a workforce shaped by generations of exploitation (one that was, not coincidentally, disproportionately black and female). In *The Hamlet Fire* (2017), Bryant Simon told the story of a deadly 1991 fire at a poultry processing plant in southeastern North Carolina to demonstrate how the quest for "cheap" in public policy, private enterprise, and consumer culture reshaped a southern community as well as the global economy in the waning years of the twentieth century. By the dawn of the new millennium, these forces radically altered the South's demographic and cultural landscape. Southern industries, particularly agriculture and food processing, once reliant on cheap black labor, increasingly recruited migrants from Latin America. From labor historian Leon Fink's *Maya of Morganton* (2001) to Julie M. Weise's *Corazón de Dixie* (2015), studies of Central American and Mexican life in the "Nuevo New South" stretched the periodization and pushed past the black-white binary of southern history. These works joined a robust scholarship on twentieth-century Texas that has long rubbed against frameworks that better fit southeastern than southwestern experiences. In tandem with Cindy Hahamovitch's research on migrant farmworkers, which rooted their plight in agricultural practice and policy changes stretching back to the New Deal, both Texas and Nuevo New South historians challenged depictions of an isolated and homogenous region with transnational New South narratives. Furthermore, literature on the globalized South—as evidenced by a 2005 collection edited by James L. Peacock, Harry L. Watson, and Carrie R. Matthews—underscored how research centers and hi-tech industries attracted professionals from around the world and created new immigrant enclaves.[26]

26. Bryant Simon, *The Hamlet Fire: A Tragic Story of Cheap Food, Cheap Government, and Cheap Lives* (New York: New Press, 2017); Leon Fink, *The Maya of Morganton: Work and Community in the Nuevo New South* (Chapel Hill: University of North Carolina Press, 2001); Julie M. Weise, *Corazón De Dixie: Mexicanos in the U.S. South since 1910* (Chapel Hill: University of North Carolina Press, 2015); Raymond Mohl, "Globalization, Latinization, and the Nuevo New South," *Journal of American Ethnic History* 22 (Summer 2003): 31–66; Mohl, "Latinization in the Heart of Dixie: Hispanics in Late-Twentieth-Century Alabama," *Alabama Review* 55 (October 2002): 243–74; Julia Kirk Blackwelder, *Women of the Depression: Caste and Culture in San Antonio, 1929–1939* (College Station: Texas A&M University Press, 1984); Emilio Zamora, *The World of the Mexican Worker in Texas* (College Station: Texas A&M University Press, 1993); Zamora, *Claiming Rights and Righting Wrongs in Texas: Mexican Workers and Job Politics during World*

The political consequences of economic and demographic change, from the unabated growth of the region's metropolitan suburbs to its increasingly global population, spurred interest in new political coalitions and another era of realignment. In *Blue Texas* (2016), Max Krochmal recovered the progressive interracial coalition of African Americans, Mexican Americans, labor activists, and white liberals that shaped politics from the New Deal to the post–civil rights era. He also contended that Texas history suggested a new way of looking at grassroots coalition politics in the twenty-first century. As states of the Upper and Outer Souths turn "purple" and a swath of Deep South states remain deeply red, historians must account for the persistence of conservatism and the prospects for liberalism in a changing region.[27]

As historians debate the South's exceptional or, indeed, nationally representative characteristics in the twenty-first century, scholars of historical memory have demonstrated that struggles over a distinctive past play out in a global and highly volatile present. W. Fitzhugh Brundage's *The Southern Past* (2005) traced the persistence of the "clash over race and memory" into the twenty-first century. "How southerners choose to grapple with their disputed past will have enduring consequences for the region's civic culture and public institutions," he predicted. Renee C. Romano pointed out that battles over the past extend beyond slavery and Confederate memorials to the meaning and memorialization of the civil rights movement. From controversies over historical markers to high-profile prosecutions of civil rights era murders, memory remains a telling barometer of southern history's long reach and contemporary relevance. History haunts the South and, as James C. Cobb contended in his 2005 study of southern identity, southerners remain "divided by a common past." Sunbelt sprawl and demographic change obscure, but cannot erase, a distinctive past nor silence its

War II (College Station: Texas A&M University Press, 2009); Neil Foley, *The White Scourge: Mexicans, Blacks, and Poor Whites in Texas Cotton Culture* (Berkeley: University of California Press, 1997); Brian D. Behnken, *Fighting Their Own Battles: Mexican Americans, African Americans, and the Struggle for Civil Rights in Texas* (Chapel Hill: University of North Carolina Press, 2011); Cindy Hahamovitch, *The Fruits of Their Labor: Atlantic Coast Farmworkers and the Making of Migrant Poverty, 1870–1945* (Chapel Hill: University of North Carolina Press, 1997); Hahamovitch, *No Man's Land: Jamaican Guestworkers in America and the Global History of Deportable Labor* (Princeton: Princeton University Press, 2011); James L. Peacock, Harry L. Watson, and Carrie R. Matthews, *The American South in a Global World* (Chapel Hill: University of North Carolina Press, 2005).

27. Max Krochmal, *Blue Texas: The Making of a Multiracial Democratic Coalition in the Civil Rights Era* (Chapel Hill: University of North Carolina Press, 2016).

echoes in the present. As the deadly 2017 clash over Confederate monuments in Charlottesville, Virginia, demonstrated, conflicts over southern memory collide with national politics in explosive and unpredictable ways.[28]

In the eighty years since Franklin Roosevelt declared the South's problems the nation's top priority, historians increasingly demonstrated the region's steady integration into the mainstream of American life. They continue to debate what, if anything, remains distinctively southern. Yet the best histories of southern people and places, from precolonial times to the present, emphasize interaction with forces that extend far beyond Dixie. Modernization and globalization since the 1930s may have accelerated and deepened these connections, but the globalized South is not solely a modern creation, nor are isolation and obstinacy sufficient explanations for the region's distinctiveness, past or present. What historians of the South offer, in addition to their diverse insights and innovations, is a reminder that the best stories about the past are rooted in place yet imbued with themes that transcend regional boundaries. In an era when the South matters as much as ever in national politics and global economics, reports of southern history's demise seem premature, if not greatly exaggerated.

28. W. Fitzhugh Brundage, *The Southern Past: A Clash of Race and Memory* (Cambridge: Harvard University Press, 2005), 318; Renee C. Romano, *Racial Reckoning: Prosecuting America's Civil Rights Murders* (Cambridge: Harvard University Press, 2014); Cobb, *Away Down South,* 288. On the historical memory of the twentieth-century southern past, see Renee C. Romano and Leigh Raiford, eds., *The Civil Rights Movement in American Memory* (Athens: University of Georgia Press, 2006); Matthew Mace Barbee, *Race and Masculinity in Southern Memory: History of Richmond, Virginia's Monument Avenue, 1948–1996* (Lanham, MD: Lexington Books, 2014). See also Hawes Spencer, *Summer of Hate: Charlottesville, USA* (Charlottesville: University of Virginia Press, 2018); Louis P. Nelson and Claudrena N. Harold, eds., *Charlottesville 2017: The Legacy of Race and Inequity* (Charlottesville: University of Virginia Press, 2018).

THE SOUTH IN GLOBAL AND TRANSNATIONAL CONTEXTS

Don H. Doyle and Marko Maunula

The turn toward Atlantic World and global perspectives on the American South has been uneven in its speed and coverage. Historians of the American South met this trend by turns of cool indifference and enthusiastic acclamation. When John B. Boles and Evelyn Thomas Nolen assessed the state of southern historical scholarship in 1987, several authors in their volume noted key pioneering works connecting the South to the wider world, usually through cross-cultural comparative studies of slavery and race in Latin America or South Africa.[1] But enthusiasm for internationalizing American and southern history awaited the end of the Cold War, the surge of globalization and immigration in the twenty-first century, and not least, deliberate efforts within the profession to transcend parochial boundaries confining historical scholarship. The turn toward transnational history threatened to submerge southern history at the same time it promised exciting new possibilities for revitalizing the field.

The makings of an Atlantic World approach to early America took hold first among historians of the colonial era where the yet undefined boundaries of rival European empires and Indigenous peoples, the global flow of plantation commodities, and the introduction of African slavery across multiple empires demanded a broader framework. In the late 1960s, the idea of Atlantic history took on a self-conscious identity and purposeful institutional thrust. Johns Hopkins

1. John B. Boles and Evelyn Thomas Nolen, eds., *Interpreting Southern History: Historiographical Essays in Honor of Sanford W. Higginbotham* (Baton Rouge: Louisiana State University Press, 1987). See, for example, the essays by George C. Rogers, "The South before 1800" (6–47); Charles B. Dew, "The Slavery Experience" (120–61); and LaWanda Cox, "From Emancipation to Segregation: National Policy and Southern Blacks" (199–253) for several references to comparative and transatlantic studies.

University established its Program in Atlantic History and Culture, a deliberate effort to foster research and bring historians of British North America into collaboration with counterparts working on Latin America and the Caribbean, Africa, and Europe. Despite its great success in directing a whole new current of historical scholarship, the program remained alone throughout the 1980s. In the 1990s, other leading research universities incorporated Atlantic history as a focus of graduate training and collaborative research. In 1993, Daniel Walker Howe announced that American history in its Atlantic context would be the future focus of the Oxford Institute of American Studies. Two years later, Bernard Bailyn launched the Harvard International Seminar on the History of the Atlantic World, 1500–1800. Over the next fifteen years, Bailyn's seminar drew no less than 366 historians from the United States and abroad, and they in turn helped spread interest in Atlantic history as a field of research and teaching.[2]

These pioneering initiatives tended to spawn new scholarship on the colonial South, a subject more fully treated by Noeleen McIlvenna and Justin Roberts's essay in this volume. Our essay, therefore, gives more attention to the nineteenth and twentieth centuries, especially those topics that seem to have compelled an international approach: the Civil War era and economic development, for example.

The impulse to internationalize American history arose as a reaction to Cold War–era parochialism and nationalistic exceptionalism that had been associated with the school of consensus history led by such historians as Louis Hartz, Daniel J. Boorstin, David M. Potter, and Richard Hofstadter. Consensus history often bolstered the central premise of American exceptionalism: America's national character, including its liberal democracy, entrepreneurial spirit, and history of social consensus derived from unique historical circumstances that could not be replicated elsewhere. As the term implies, consensus history also minimized fundamental social and ideological conflicts. For historians of the South, where deep and abiding divisions of race, class, and region defined the past, notions of pervasive national consensus based on fundamental liberal principles of democracy

2. Jack P. Greene and Philip D. Morgan, eds., *Atlantic History: A Critical Appraisal* (New York: Oxford University Press, 2009), 25; Ian K. Steele, "Bernard Bailyn's American Atlantic," *History and Theory* 46 (February 2007): 48–58; Daniel Walker Howe, *American History in an Atlantic Context: An Inaugural Lecture Delivered before the University of Oxford on 3 June 1993* (New York: Oxford University Press, 1993); Bernard Bailyn, *Atlantic History: Concept and Contours* (Cambridge: Harvard University Press, 2005); International Seminar on the History of the Atlantic World, 1500–1825, https://atlantic.fas.harvard.edu/home (accessed 18 January 2019).

rang hollow. It was no wonder that historians, beginning in the 1960s, grew impatient with consensus history and American exceptionalism and gravitated toward southern history topics that evidenced more dissension and conflict in the American past, such as slavery, race relations, the Civil War, and Reconstruction.[3]

Logically, reaction against notions of American exceptionalism ought to have compelled more attention to cross-cultural comparative studies, but the new social history ascending in the late 1960s trended in an opposite direction toward intensely empirical micro-level studies that typically focused on slavery, race relations, non-elite whites, the working class, or women, gender, and the family. Coinciding with the wave of new social history studies was the underlying notion that a distinctive South served as an "American counterpoint," a contradiction to the supposed homogeneous liberal nation. The enthusiasm for empirical historical studies modeled on the social sciences ebbed by the late 1970s. As one of its champions, Charles Tilly, wryly observed, "what looked like the wave of the future in the late 1960s began to resemble spent foam on a littered beach a decade later."[4]

The rash of micro-level studies that had multiplied in the interlude seemed in the eyes of critics never to arrive at any significant conclusions. Bernard Bailyn lamented that "large areas of history, including some of the most intensively cultivated, have become shapeless, and scholarship is heavily concentrated on unconnected technical problems." Thomas Bender became a leading voice criticizing the fragmentation of historical research and setting forth practical plans for internationalizing American history. The Organization of American Historians (OAH) proactively advanced the cause of internationalizing United States history through the *Journal of American History*, which, beginning with editor

3. Louis Hartz, *The Liberal Tradition in America: An Interpretation of American Political Thought since the Revolution* (New York: Harcourt, Brace, 1955); Daniel J. Boorstin, *The Americans: The Colonial Experience* (New York: Random House, 1958); Boorstin, *The Americans: The National Experience* (New York: Random House, 1965); David M. Potter, *People of Plenty: Economic Abundance and the American Character* (Chicago: University of Chicago Press, 1954); Richard Hofstadter, *The American Political Tradition and the Men Who Made It* (New York: Alfred A. Knopf, 1948). For an early critique of consensus history, see John Higham, "Beyond Consensus: The Historian as Moral Critic," *American Historical Review* 67 (April 1962): 609–25.

4. C. Vann Woodward, *American Counterpoint: Slavery and Racism in the North-South Dialogue* (Boston: Little, Brown, 1971); Larry J. Griffin and Don H. Doyle, eds., *The South as an American Problem* (Athens: University of Georgia Press, 1995); Charles Tilly, *Explaining Social Processes* (2008; repr., New York: Routledge, 2016), 163.

David P. Thelen, launched special issues, roundtable discussions, and collaborative "interchanges" on topics situating America in the world.[5] The OAH cosponsored a 1997 conference that Bender organized in Italy, after which he authored "The LaPietra Report," a clarion call to train historians and teach students for the global age. Bender's *Rethinking American History in a Global Age* (2002) served as a guidebook for historians seeking to move beyond national frameworks, and his *A Nation Among Nations* (2006), demonstrated how to internationalize the American past.[6]

The historiographical questions driving history research also seemed isolated and nation-bound. In 2009 Bailyn wrote of early American historiography: "though voluminous, exhaustively researched, and in many ways original and sophisticated, [the field] seems over the years to have been self-enclosed, a world of creative scholarship with surprisingly little resonance in or influence on the major strains of Western historiography, British or continental European." He worried that, as "transnational structures and large-scale patterns" are identified, "clarity and comprehension are difficult to achieve, especially in those subtler realms of experience that are close to the inner lives of people involved."[7] Atlantic and global history seemed to confront historians with a very different problem from that of the micro-historical studies that occupied an earlier generation. Although the new social history sometimes lost sight of the forest for the trees, the global turn risked losing the familiar touchstones of place and people that traditionally drew students and readers to history.

5. Bernard Bailyn, "The Challenge of Modern Historiography," *American Historical Review* 87 (February 1982): 1–24; Thomas Bender, "Wholes and Parts: The Need for Synthesis in American History," *Journal of American History* 73 (June 1986): 120–36. For examples of interchange discussions, see David Armitage et al., "Interchange: Nationalism and Internationalism in the Era of the Civil War," *Journal of American History* 98 (September 2011): 455–89; Richard Carwardine et al., "Interchange: The Global Lincoln," *Journal of American History* 96 (September 2009): 462–99. For an example of a special issue, see David P. Thelen, "Rethinking History and the Nation-State: Mexico and the United States as a Case Study," *Journal of American History* 86 (September 1999): 439–697, esp. David P. Thelen, "Rethinking History and the Nation-State: Mexico and the United States" (439–52).

6. Organization of American Historians, "The LaPietra Report: A Report to the Profession," http://www.oah.org/about/reports/reports-statements/the-lapietra-report-a-report-to-the-profession/ (accessed 18 January 2019); Thomas Bender, ed., *Rethinking American History in a Global Age* (Berkeley: University of California Press, 2002); Bender, *A Nation Among Nations: America's Place in World History* (New York: Hill and Wang, 2006).

7. Bernard Bailyn and Patricia L. Denault, eds., *Soundings in Atlantic History: Latent Structures and Intellectual Currents, 1500–1830* (Cambridge: Harvard University Press, 2009), 2.

If, for example, the new boundaries of transnational history made older lines of inquiry about enduring southern distinctiveness vis-à-vis the North or the peculiar origins of slavery in the Chesapeake seem passé, the American South was far from lost in the panoramic view of global history. By the turn of the twenty-first century, many historians of the South welcomed the new challenges and opportunities of international history. The University of South Carolina Press, in cooperation with the College of Charleston's Carolina Lowcountry and the Atlantic World program (CLAW), launched a new book series on the Carolina Lowcountry and the Atlantic World. Louisiana State University Press initiated a similar project: "Antislavery, Abolition, and the Atlantic World." The University of Alabama Press sponsored another book series on Atlantic Crossings.[8] Scholars routinely included in the titles of books, articles, and conference papers such terms as "Atlantic World," "global," or "transnational." In contrast, the Southern Historical Association issued fewer signs of enthusiasm. Between 1986 and 2018, *The Journal of Southern History* published only twenty-four articles (of 488 total) dealing with the Atlantic World, global history, or other distinctly international subjects. Nor have SHA conference programs sufficiently reflected the growing interest of scholars in the global history of the American South.[9]

Since the 1980s, some economic historians broke free from their focus on cliometrics to play a leading role in mapping the contours of the Atlantic World. Bailyn credited them with providing the "grout lines" for a "pan-Atlantic mosaic." The various imperial strategies for economic development of the American colonies, different modes of exploitation and enslavement of Indigenous American and African peoples, the evolution of plantation production, and the commerce in commodities such as tobacco, rice, sugar, and cotton demanded comparative and transnational analysis, inviting connections between the American South and the wider world.

8. CLAW: Carolina Lowcountry and the Atlantic World, http://claw.cofc.edu/ (accessed 18 January 2019); "The Carolina Lowcountry and the Atlantic World," https://www.sc.edu/uscpress/claw.html (accessed 18 January 2019); "Books by Series—Antislavery, Abolition, and the Atlantic World," Louisiana State University Press, https://lsupress.org/books/by-series/antislavery-abolition-and-the-atlantic-world/ (accessed 18 January 2019); "University of Alabama Press: 'Atlantic Crossings," http://www.uapress.ua.edu/ (accessed 18 January 2019).

9. We identified articles involving international topics in *The Journal of Southern History,* volumes 52 through 84, by evaluating titles. A less rigorous examination of Southern Historical Association conference programs from the 2010s revealed that international history topics were rare in the southern history section of the annual conference.

The coherent and distinctive eighteenth-century Atlantic economy gave way to a broader global economy in the 1820s. The American South came to play an important role in global commerce, coinciding with the advent of what Dale W. Tomich coined the "Second Slavery." This modern phase of slavery involved far more efficient (and more brutal) exploitation of enslaved labor. One result, according to this view, was enhanced productivity of the cotton economy in the South, sugar in Cuba, and coffee in Brazil, all of which served vast world markets. Rather than viewing slavery and slaveholding elites as obstacles to economic modernization, many historians, their work informed by the global turn, came to view slavery as the foundation for modern capitalism.[10] Enrico Dal Lago's *American Slavery, Atlantic Slavery, and Beyond* (2012) effectively connected the new global history of the Second Slavery to the American South.[11] One of the most successful methods of linking globalization to the American South became focused studies of specific plantation commodities to which Richard Follett's collaborative book, *Plantation Kingdom* (2016), provided an important overview. The authors demonstrated connections between plantation economies and mass agricultural production for world markets: Barbara Hahn on tobacco, Peter A. Coclanis on rice, Follett on sugar, and Sven Beckert on cotton.[12]

The global turn was slow in coming to antebellum, Civil War, and Reconstruc-

10. Bailyn and Denault, *Soundings in Atlantic History*, 4; Dale W. Tomich, *Through the Prism of Slavery: Labor, Capital, and World Economy* (Lanham, MD: Rowman & Littlefield, 2004); Tomich, ed., *New Frontiers of Slavery* (Albany: State University of New York Press, 2016); Tomich, *Slavery and Historical Capitalism during the Nineteenth Century* (Lanham, MD: Lexington Books, 2017); Tomich and Michael Zeuske, "Introduction, the Second Slavery: Mass Slavery, World-Economy, and Comparative Microhistories," *Review (Fernand Braudel Center)* 31 (2008): 91–100.

11. Enrico Dal Lago, *American Slavery, Atlantic Slavery, and Beyond: The U.S. "Peculiar Institution" in International Perspective* (Boulder: Paradigm, 2012); Dal Lago, "The End of the 'Second Slavery' in the Confederate South and the Great Brigandage in Southern Italy: Some Comparative Suggestions," *Almanack* 4 (July/December 2012): 63–74.

12. Richard Follett et al., *Plantation Kingdom: The American South and Its Global Commodities* (Baltimore: Johns Hopkins University Press, 2016). See also Barbara M. Hahn, *Making Tobacco Bright: Creating an American Commodity, 1617–1937* (Baltimore: Johns Hopkins University Press, 2011); Peter A. Coclanis, *The Shadow of a Dream: Economic Life and Death in the South Carolina Low Country, 1670–1920* (New York: Oxford University Press, 1989); Coclanis, "Distant Thunder: The Creation of a World Market in Rice and the Transformations It Wrought," *American Historical Review* 98 (October 1993): 1050–78; Richard Follett, *The Sugar Masters: Planters and Slaves in Louisiana's Cane World, 1820–1860* (Baton Rouge: Louisiana State University Press, 2007); Sven Beckert, "Emancipation and Empire: Reconstructing the Worldwide Web of Cotton Production in the Age of the American Civil War," *American Historical Review* 109 (December 2004): 1405–38; Beckert, *Empire of Cotton: A Global History* (New York: Alfred A. Knopf, 2014).

tion historiography, despite determined efforts by some scholars to excite interest. During the 1960s, David M. Potter suggested how the South and the Civil War could be better understood within international contexts of nineteenth-century nationalism, separatism, and nation-building. C. Vann Woodward similarly advocated comparative international studies of the South, arguing plausibly that the region's history of defeat and poverty had shared more in common with the rest of the world than did the North.[13]

Beginning in the 1960s, Eugene D. Genovese stirred stimulating debate over the nature of the South's slaveholding elite and its relation to the bourgeois capitalist ethos of the North. In their last major work, *The Mind of the Master Class* (2005), he and Elizabeth Fox-Genovese amplified his interpretations by situating southern slaveholders within the transatlantic debate over slavery and free labor society. Similarly, Michael O'Brien's magnum opus, *Conjectures of Order* (2004), followed southern intellectuals at home and abroad as they contemplated their society's place in the world. Beginning with *Unfree Labor* (1987), which compared Russian serfdom with American slavery, Peter Kolchin demonstrated the value of comparative history in several notable works on the American South.[14]

The South's imperial design for mastery also contributed to transnational contexts for the region's history. Robert E. May led off with *The Southern Dream of a Caribbean Empire* (2002) and published several other influential works revealing southern ambitions to create a tropical empire in the Caribbean. May also edited *The Union, the Confederacy, and the Atlantic Rim* (1995), a volume that included

13. David M. Potter, "The Historian's Use of Nationalism and Vice Versa," *American Historical Review* 67 (July 1962): 924–50; Potter, "The Civil War in the History of the Modern World: A Comparative View," in *The South and the Sectional Conflict* (Baton Rouge: Louisiana State University Press, 1968), 287–300; C. Vann Woodward, ed., *The Comparative Approach to American History* (New York: Oxford University Press, 1967); Woodward, *The Old World's New World* (New York: Oxford University Press, 1991).

14. Elizabeth Fox-Genovese and Eugene D. Genovese, *The Mind of the Master Class: History and Faith in the Southern Slaveholders' Worldview* (New York: Cambridge University Press, 2005); Michael O'Brien, *Conjectures of Order: Intellectual Life and the American South, 1810–1860*, 2 vols. (Chapel Hill: University of North Carolina Press, 2004); Peter Kolchin, *Unfree Labor: American Slavery and Russian Serfdom* (Cambridge: Harvard University Press, 1987); Kolchin, "Some Thoughts on Emancipation in Comparative Perspective: Russia and the United States South," *Slavery & Abolition* 11 (June 1990): 351–67; Kolchin, "The Big Picture: A Comment on David Brion Davis's 'Looking at Slavery from Broader Perspectives,'" *American Historical Review* 105 (April 2000): 467–71; Kolchin, "Variations of Slavery in the Atlantic World," *William and Mary Quarterly* 59 (July 2002): 551–54; Kolchin, *A Sphinx on the American Land: The Nineteenth-Century South in Comparative Perspective* (Baton Rouge: Louisiana State University Press, 2003); Kolchin, "The South and the World," *Journal of Southern History* 75 (August 2009): 565–80.

essays by Howard Jones, R. J. M. Blackett, Thomas Schoonover, and James M. McPherson that expanded the international history of the Civil War. In *Mastering America* (2009), Robert E. Bonner depicted the southern elite not as a beleaguered separatist minority but as a confident governing class accustomed to ruling America and prepared to extend its dominance overseas. Matthew Karp's *This Vast Southern Empire* (2016) focused on the commanding role southern slaveholders took in directing antebellum foreign policy and argued one major goal of secession was to free planter-politicians to pursue ambitions for an empire of slavery southward.[15]

While imperial ambitions offered a framework for historians to envision how southerners sought to interact with the world, other historians explored how the world shaped southern nationalism and separatism. Interest in these subjects took place after World War II as historians witnessed two major flurries of separatist movements: the first was driven by the postwar disintegration of European colonial empires in Asia, the Middle East, and Africa; the second followed the collapse of the Soviet Union after 1989. The South's abortive bid to break away from an established nation provided an ideal case for comparative historical study. In *The Creation of Confederate Nationalism* (1998), Drew Gilpin Faust described some international ingredients that went into the making of the South's sense of separate nationhood and argued that the lack of an authentic, firmly rooted popular nationalism was a fatal flaw in the South's struggle to secede. Paul Quigley's *Shifting Grounds* (2012) went deeper into the origins and changing nature of southern nationalism between 1848 and the end of the Civil War. Southern nationalists, Quigley showed, looked abroad to Hungary and Ireland for models and borrowed from foreign ideas about nationhood. In *Confederate Visions* (2013), Ian Binnington offered a thoughtful examination of the symbols and material culture underlying Confederate nationalism. Timothy Mason Roberts's *Distant Revolutions* (2009) showed how antislavery partisans in the United States viewed the Slave Power through the lens of the European revolutions of 1848. Patrick J. Kelly's 2014 article, "The European Revolutions of 1848 and the Transnational Turn in Civil War History," provided a perceptive

15. Robert E. May, *The Southern Dream of a Caribbean Empire, 1854–1861* (Gainesville: University of Florida Press, 2002); May, ed., *The Union, the Confederacy, and the Atlantic Rim* (West Lafayette, IN: Purdue University Press, 1995); Robert E. Bonner, *Mastering America: Southern Slaveholders and the Crisis of American Nationhood* (New York: Cambridge University Press, 2009); Matthew Karp, *This Vast Southern Empire: Slaveholders at the Helm of American Foreign Policy* (Cambridge: Harvard University Press, 2016).

review of transnational scholarship. In *The Revolution of 1861* (2012), Andre M. Fleche followed southern separatists as they situated their bid for independence in company with the multitude of nationalist revolutions erupting throughout the Atlantic World. Ann L. Tucker's *Newest Born of Nations* (2019) revealed how southern nationalism borrowed from European ideas of nationhood, dating from the Greek revolution of the 1820s through the Italian *Risorgimento*.[16]

Finally, scholars began to examine the place of immigrant soldiers in the Civil War, although they were far less numerous in the Confederacy compared to the Union. David T. Gleeson's *Green and Gray* (2013) considered Irish soldiers who fought for the South. Dean B. Mahin's overview of Europeans in the Civil War illuminated the long-neglected role of immigrant soldiers on both sides of the conflict.[17]

Nationalist ideology often serves to unite and inspire a people at war; it also explains to the world the purpose of their struggle. In the nineteenth century, as Quigley showed, the main currents of nationalism in Europe and the Americas drew on liberal principles of human rights to live free and govern themselves. Southern secessionists faced a dilemma, addressed in several ways in the studies: appealing to whites by defending white supremacy against northern abolitionists at home, while fashioning liberal arguments abroad for the right to self-rule.

In reexamining old questions by comparing the South with other parts of the world, historians interrogated the nature of the South's planter class with refreshing results. Shearer Davis Bowman, comparing Prussian Junkers with southern planters as landed ruling classes, illuminated shared conservative allegiances. In his study of Italy and its *Mezzogiorno* (a popular name for the Italian South), En-

16. Drew Gilpin Faust, *The Creation of Confederate Nationalism: Ideology and Identity in the Civil War South* (Baton Rouge: Louisiana State University Press, 1988); Paul Quigley, *Shifting Grounds: Nationalism and the American South, 1848–1865* (New York: Oxford University Press, 2012); Ian Binnington, *Confederate Visions: Nationalism, Symbolism, and the Imagined South in the Civil War* (Charlottesville: University of Virginia Press, 2013); Timothy Mason Roberts, *Distant Revolutions: 1848 and the Challenge to American Exceptionalism* (Charlottesville: University of Virginia Press, 2009); Patrick J. Kelly, "The European Revolutions of 1848 and the Transnational Turn in Civil War History," *Journal of the Civil War Era* 4 (September 2014): 431–43; Andre M. Fleche, *The Revolution of 1861: The American Civil War in the Age of Nationalist Conflict* (Chapel Hill: University of North Carolina Press, 2012); Ann L. Tucker, *Newest Born of Nations* (Charlottesville: University of Virginia Press, 2019).

17. David T. Gleeson, *The Green and the Gray: The Irish in the Confederate States of America* (Chapel Hill: University of North Carolina Press, 2013); Dean B. Mahin, *The Blessed Place of Freedom: Europeans in Civil War America* (Washington: Brassey's, 2002).

rico Dal Lago contrasted the masters of Italian *latifundia* with southern planters.[18] Susanna Delfino compared the American and Italian Souths as economically backward regions. Don H. Doyle's *Nations Divided* (2002) interpreted the oppositional roles played by the Italian and American Souths in defining nationalistic ideals. Paul D. Escott compared the popular memory and commemoration of civil wars in the United States and Spain in *Uncommonly Savage* (2014), a timely reminder that the South is not alone in suffering the deep scars of fratricidal war. In their collection of essays on *Reconciliation after Civil Wars* (2018), editors Paul Quigley and James Hawdon offered a panoramic view of the effects of civil war on nations around the world.[19]

Comparative or cross-cultural analyses involving case studies of behavior or institutions occurring in two or more cultures have helped clarify the discussion of southern distinctiveness and introduced new ways of understanding the American South's contentious relation to the nation. The newer trend toward global and transnational history tended to subordinate subnational distinctions among regions or intra-national conflicts in favor of larger patterns and categories of historical analysis.

One of the most striking features of the international turn was the large number of historians coming from outside the United States. Whether working at American universities or abroad, international scholars bring the cosmopolitan perspective of the foreign eye to America's history. Their influence was most evident in 2014 when several historians who view the American past from abroad contributed to an engaging collection of essays, *Historians across Borders,* and to a

18. Shearer Davis Bowman, *Masters & Lords: Mid-19th-Century U.S. Planters and Prussian Junkers* (New York: Oxford University Press, 1993); Enrico Dal Lago, *Agrarian Elites: American Slaveholders and Southern Italian Landowners 1815–1861* (Baton Rouge: Louisiana State University Press, 2005). Dal Lago continued this comparative approach in a brilliant collection, coedited with Rick Halpern, comparing the history of the two nations and their Souths: *The American South and the Italian* Mezzogiorno: *Essays in Comparative History* (New York: Palgrave Macmillan, 2002). See also Dal Lago, "The End of the 'Second Slavery' in the Confederate South and the Great Brigandage in Southern Italy."

19. Susanna Delfino, "The Idea of Southern Economic Backwardness," in *Global Perspectives on Industrial Transformation in the American South,* ed. Susanna Delfino and Michele Gillespie (Columbia: University of Missouri Press, 2005), 105–30; Don H. Doyle, *Nations Divided: America, Italy, and the Southern Question* (Athens: University of Georgia Press, 2002); Paul D. Escott, *Uncommonly Savage: Civil War and Remembrance in Spain and the United States* (Gainesville: University Press of Florida, 2014); Paul Quigley and James Hawdon, eds., *Reconciliation after Civil Wars: Global Perspectives* (New York: Routledge, 2018).

stimulating roundtable in the *American Historical Review* on "Europeans Writing American History," which featured contributions by Susanna Delfino, an Italian historian of the South.[20]

In 1968, David M. Potter lamented the "parochialism of American historians" generally, noting that "some of our worst navel-gazing has occurred in connection with the Civil War," which most historians view as "a conflict all our own, as American as apple pie." Twenty years later, Joel Gray Taylor's essay on Civil War historiography in *Interpreting Southern History* (1987) lauded Harold M. Hyman's *Heard Round the World* (1969), an outstanding collection of essays by experts on France, Central Europe, Russia, Canada, and Latin America. But by 1987, there was little to suggest much response to Potter's reproach when it came to writing about the Civil War era.[21]

Since the 1980s, global historians paid attention to America's internecine war and its impact on the world. C. A. Bayly's *The Birth of the Modern World* (2012) included a stimulating section on "The American Civil War as a Global Event," which emphasized the repercussions of the conflict on world commerce with some attention to European imperialist aggression in the Americas. In Jürgen Osterhammel's massive history of the nineteenth century, the author situated the violent destruction of slavery in America's Civil War within the wider history of world abolition and compared it to Brazil's slow peaceful path to abolition.[22]

In his *Transnational Nation* (2007), Ian Tyrrell included a chapter on "America's Civil War and its World Historical Implications" that neatly summarized foreign views of the war at the time and took a fresh look at some of the actual and potential geopolitical outcomes of the war. Tyrrell, an Australian scholar, was especially adroit at showing how parochial views of American history limit the questions posed and answers sought. Thomas Bender's *A Nation among Nations* (2006) framed the Civil War within the ascent of liberal nationalism and argued

20. Nicolas Barreyre et al., eds., *Historians across Borders: Writing American History in a Global Age* (Berkeley: University of California Press, 2014); Susanna Delfino et al., "Europeans Writing American History: The Comparative Trope," *American Historical Review* 119 (June 2014): 791–99.

21. David M. Potter, *The South and the Sectional Conflict* (Baton Rouge: Louisiana State University Press, 1968), 287; Joel Gray Taylor, "The White South from Secession to Redemption," in Boles and Nolen, eds., *Interpreting Southern History*, 169–70; Harold M. Hyman, ed., *Heard Round the World: The Impact Abroad of the Civil War* (New York: Alfred A. Knopf, 1969).

22. C. A. Bayly, *The Birth of the Modern World, 1780–1914: Global Connections and Comparisons* (Malden, MA: Blackwell, 2004), 361–65; Jürgen Osterhammel, *The Transformation of the World: A Global History of the Nineteenth Century* (Princeton: Princeton University Press, 2014), 448–50, 845–48.

that the Union embraced liberal ideals of emancipation and equality during the war only to abandon them later. Steven Hahn's *A Nation without Borders* (2016), part of a five-volume series devoted to reinterpreting American history within a global context, positioned the Civil War and Reconstruction as a crucial turning point between the consolidation of the American nation and the expansion of an American empire.[23]

Another outstanding feature of the turn toward global history in Civil War–era scholarship was the proliferation of conferences and collaborative publications that brought together experts on different parts of the world. A pathbreaking example of this genre was Stig Förster and Jörg Nagler's edited volume, *On the Road to Total War* (1997), which includes essays by an impressive cast of American and European scholars. International experts who gathered for a 2011 conference marking the sesquicentennial of the war contributed to a thought-provoking collection, *The Civil War as a Global Conflict* (2014), edited by David T. Gleeson and Simon Lewis of the CLAW program. Jörg Nagler, Don H. Doyle, and Marcus Grässer edited *The Transnational Significance of the American Civil War* (2016), a collection of original essays by American and European historians that grew out of conferences in Jena, Germany, and the German Historical Institute in Washington, DC. Doyle also edited *Secession as an International Phenomenon* (2010), an interdisciplinary collection of essays, several of which bear on the role of the American South as an important precedent for separatism in the modern world. In another edited volume, *American Civil Wars* (2017), Doyle brought together prominent historians of Europe, Latin America, and the United States to address the interconnected histories of nations and empires involved in the transatlantic "crisis of the 1860s." From abroad, Italian scholars Tiziano Bonazzi and Carlo Galli edited a collection of annotated documents that illuminated European views of the war. Cornelis van Minnen and Manfred Berg brought historians from the United States and Europe to the Roosevelt Study Center in Holland for a conference that led to the publication of *The U.S. South and Europe* (2013).[24] These anthologies demonstrate the value of collaboration among historians coming from different specialties in an academic discipline

23. Ian Tyrrell, *Transnational Nation: United States History in Global Perspective since 1789* (New York: Palgrave Macmillan, 2007), 84–93; Bender, *A Nation among Nations;* Steven Hahn, *A Nation without Borders: The United States and Its World in an Age of Civil Wars, 1830–1910* (New York: Viking, 2016).

24. Stig Förster and Jörg Nagler, *On the Road to Total War: The American Civil War and the German Wars of Unification, 1861–1871* (New York: Cambridge University Press, 1997); David T. Gleeson and

that remains fragmented along national and linguistic boundaries. Among the conclusions one can draw from these multifaceted views of the American conflict is that the world watched events in America's war with itself closely and with the understanding that the outcome of that distant war would affect the future.

Historians of diplomacy and international law brought their expertise to new studies of the Civil War. Stephen C. Neff engaged the legal history of the Civil War in *Justice in Blue and Gray* (2010), a penetrating examination of the multitude of vexing legal problems the Civil War posed for each side and for the world of nations. John Fabian Witt situated Francis Lieber's *Code for the Government of Armies in the Field,* drafted for the Union army in 1863, within the larger history of the laws of war as practiced by the United States and the world, recognizing Lieber's code as precedent for the Geneva Conventions. In *The Burden of Confederate Diplomacy* (1998), Charles M. Hubbard agreed with Frank Owsley that inept diplomats, rather than slavery per se, became the main obstacle to Confederate diplomatic success. Howard Jones reexamined the Union's troubled relationship with Britain in two incisive books, *Union in Peril* (1992), which dealt with the intervention crisis in 1862, and *Abraham Lincoln and a New Birth of Freedom* (1999), which explored the impact of the Emancipation Proclamation abroad. Jones followed in 2010 with *Blue and Gray Diplomacy,* the first full treatment of Union and Confederate diplomacy under one cover. He shed new light on Europeans' views that the Union could never reconcile with the South and that the conflict proved democracy was a failure. He also attended to European interests in the Americas, including France's effort to bring Mexico under European control.[25]

In *Debtor Diplomacy* (2005), Jay Sexton went beyond formal government-

Simon Lewis, eds., *The Civil War as Global Conflict: Transnational Meanings of the American Civil War* (Columbia: University of South Carolina Press, 2014); Nicholas Guyatt, "Tocqueville's Prophecy: The United States and the Caribbean, 1850–1871," in *The Transnational Significance of the American Civil War,* ed. Jörg Nagler, Don H. Doyle, and Marcus Gräser (New York: Palgrave Macmillan, 2016), 205–30; Doyle, ed., *Secession as an International Phenomenon: From America's Civil War to Contemporary Separatist Movements* (Athens: University of Georgia Press, 2010); Doyle, ed., *American Civil Wars: The United States, Latin America, Europe, and the Crisis of the 1860s* (Chapel Hill: University of North Carolina Press, 2017); Tiziano Bonazzi and Carlo Galli, eds., *La guerra civile americana vista dall'Europa* (Bologna, Italy: Mulino, 2004); Cornelis A. van Minnen and Manfred Berg, eds., *The U.S. South and Europe Transatlantic Relations in the Nineteenth and Twentieth Centuries* (Lexington: University Press of Kentucky, 2013).

25. Stephen C. Neff, *Justice in Blue and Gray: A Legal History of the Civil War* (Cambridge: Harvard University Press, 2010); Neff, *War and the Law of Nations: A General History* (New York: Cambridge University Press, 2005); John Fabian Witt, *Lincoln's Code: The Laws of War in American History* (New

to-government diplomatic relations to illuminate the neglected subject of international finance and how it affected foreign relations. Sexton's *The Monroe Doctrine* (2011) provided a sweeping review of the subject, culminating in European violations of the doctrine during the Civil War. In a notable 2017 article in the *Journal of Southern History,* Robert E. May focused on the failed Confederate dreams for expansion. Don H. Doyle's *The Cause of All Nations* (2015) followed Union and Confederate agents overseas as they sought to win public support in what foreign spectators came to see as an epic battle between aristocracy and republicanism, slavery and free labor. Few historians demonstrated the value of a global perspective so impressively as Sven Beckert, particularly in *Empire of Cotton* (2014). By Beckert's account, America's Civil War set off a crisis in cotton production that led to its rapid global dispersion and helped lay the foundation for the rise of modern capitalism.[26]

Foreign relations with Britain became a favorite subject among historians looking at the international dimensions of the Civil War. British politicians and public opinion divided over the American rebellion, and the government's policy was often duplicitous. Historians sought to clarify British foreign policy and public sentiment. Martin Crawford's contributions focused on *The Times* of London and its special correspondent in America, William Howard Russell. Russell's fascinating reports from the South and from the Union front at Bull Run gave Britain and much of Europe its first indelible impression of southern rebels prepared to fight to the last man, and Union soldiers and political leaders wholly unprepared for the struggle ahead. In two important works, *English Public*

York: Free Press, 2012); Charles M. Hubbard, *The Burden of Confederate Diplomacy* (Knoxville: University of Tennessee Press, 1998); Howard Jones, *Union in Peril: The Crisis over British Intervention in the Civil War* (Chapel Hill: University of North Carolina Press, 1992); Jones, *Abraham Lincoln and a New Birth of Freedom: The Union and Slavery in the Diplomacy of the Civil War* (Lincoln: University of Nebraska Press, 1999); Jones, *Blue and Gray Diplomacy: A History of Union and Confederate Foreign Relations* (Chapel Hill: University of North Carolina Press, 2010).

26. Jay Sexton, *Debtor Diplomacy: Finance and American Foreign Relations in the Civil War Era, 1837–1873* (New York: Oxford University Press, 2005); Sexton, "International Finance in the Civil War Era," in Nagler, Doyle, and Gräser, eds., *The Transnational Significance of the Civil War,* 91–106; Sexton, *The Monroe Doctrine: Empire and Nation in Nineteenth-Century America* (New York: Hill and Wang, 2011); Robert E. May, "The Irony of Confederate Diplomacy: Visions of Empire, the Monroe Doctrine, and the Quest for Nationhood," *Journal of Southern History* 83 (February 2017): 69–106; Don H. Doyle, *The Cause of All Nations: An International History of the American Civil War* (New York: Basic Books, 2015); Beckert, *Empire of Cotton.* See also Beckert, "Emancipation and Empire"; Beckert, "Cotton and the Global Origins of Capitalism," *Journal of World History* 28 (March 2017): 107–20.

Opinion and the American Civil War (2003) and *Unlikely Allies* (2007), Duncan Andrew Campbell sustained the idea of a "special relationship" binding the two countries, though few Union leaders recognized British intentions as friendly at the time. Phillip E. Myers also supported the argument for Britain's benign intentions toward the Union in *Conflict and Cooperation* (2008), as did Amanda Foreman's *A World on Fire* (2010), an exciting, panoramic treatment of wartime Anglo-American relations. R. J. M. Blackett's *Divided Hearts* (2001) addressed a long-simmering dispute over British working-class support for the Union and highlighted the important role of black abolitionists in clarifying the moral issues at stake. Hugh DuBrulle's 2018 book, *Ambivalent Nation,* showed how Britain projected domestic anxieties over democratic reform onto the American war. In *Persuading John Bull* (2014), Thomas E. Sebrell shed light on Confederate and Union propaganda in Britain. Robert E. Bonner examined Confederate efforts to link their cause to emerging ideas about scientific racism. Christopher Dickey provided a rare portrait of British diplomacy at the consular level, featuring Robert Bunch as *Our Man in Charleston* (2015) who secretly warned Britain against Confederate designs to expand slavery and reopen the slave trade.[27]

Nimrod Tal's study of the war's meaning to Britain offered a fascinating story of the war's lasting imprint abroad and how the "special relationship" between the United States and Britain was invented long after the war. *The Global Lincoln* (2011), edited by Richard Carwardine and Jay Sexton, constituted an unusually

27. Martin Crawford, *The Anglo-American Crisis of the Mid-Nineteenth Century: The Times and America, 1850–1862* (Athens: University of Georgia Press, 1987); Crawford, ed., *William Howard Russell's Civil War: Private Diary and Letters, 1861–1862* (Athens: University of Georgia Press, 1992); Duncan Andrew Campbell, *English Public Opinion and the American Civil War* (New York: The Boydell Press for the Royal Historical Society, 2003); Campbell, *Unlikely Allies: Britain, America and the Victorian Origins of the Special Relationship* (London: Continuum, 2007); Phillip E. Myers, *Caution and Cooperation: The American Civil War in British-American Relations* (Kent: Kent State University Press, 2008); Amanda Foreman, *A World on Fire: Britain's Crucial Role in the American Civil War* (New York: Random House, 2010); R. J. M. Blackett, *Divided Hearts: Britain and the American Civil War* (Baton Rouge: Louisiana State University Press, 2001); Hugh Dubrulle, "'We Are Threatened with . . . Anarchy and Ruin': Fear of Americanization and the Emergence of an Anglo-Saxon Confederacy in England during the American Civil War," *Albion* 33 (December 2001): 583–613; Dubrulle, *Ambivalent Nation: How Britain Imagined the American Civil War* (Baton Rouge: Louisiana State University Press, 2018); Thomas E. Sebrell, *Persuading John Bull: Union and Confederate Propaganda in Britain, 1860–1865* (Lanham, MD: Lexington Books, 2014); Robert E. Bonner, "Roundheaded Cavaliers? The Context and Limits of a Confederate Racial Project," *Civil War History* 48 (March 2002): 34–59; Bonner, "Slavery, Confederate Diplomacy, and the Racialist Mission of Henry Hotze," *Civil War History* 51 (September 2005): 288–316; Christopher Dickey, *Our Man in Charleston: Britain's Secret Agent in the Civil War South* (New York: Crown, 2015).

strong collection of essays on the meaning of America's war to the wider world.[28] Long after the war, admirers revered Lincoln as the Great Emancipator but even more as the personification of government by the people, an idea that had frightened conservative leaders in Europe and Latin America but gradually came to be accepted as inevitable and positive.

When Confederate emissaries in Europe became disheartened by Britain's unwillingness to aid its cause, they turned to France, but few historians followed their path. The impressive body of scholarship on France and the Civil War produced by an earlier generation of historians may have dissuaded many.[29] Stève Sainlaude's work in French and English broke new ground by examining influential dispatches out of consulates inside the Confederacy, notably Alfred Paul in Richmond, who warned the French government about the dangers of allying with the Confederacy.[30]

The important connections of Mexico and other parts of Latin America to America's Civil War attracted only a few intrepid historians. Edward B. Rugemer's *The Problem of Emancipation* (2008) examined how slave revolts in the Caribbean fueled southern secessionism. In Doyle's edited collection, *American Civil Wars,* essays by Erika Pani on the collaboration of Mexican monarchists with the French, Anne Eller on Spain's attempted takeover of Santo Domingo, Matt Childs on Cuba, Rafael Marquese on Brazil, and Patrick Kelly on Confederate policy toward Mexico untangled the interconnected histories of Latin America,

28. Nimrod Tal, *The American Civil War in British Culture: Representations and Responses, 1870 to the Present* (New York: Palgrave Macmillan, 2015); Richard Carwardine and Jay Sexton, eds., *The Global Lincoln* (New York: Oxford University Press, 2011).

29. Lynn Marshall Case and Warren F. Spencer, *The United States and France: Civil War Diplomacy* (Philadelphia: University of Pennsylvania Press, 1970); Henry Blumenthal, *France and the United States: Their Diplomatic Relation, 1789–1914* (Chapel Hill: University of North Carolina Press, 1970); David H. Pinkney, "France and the Civil War," in Hyman, ed., *Heard Round the World,* 97–144; Serge Gavronsky, *The French Liberal Opposition and the American Civil War* (New York: Humanities Press, 1968); Alfred Jackson Hanna and Kathryn Abbey Hanna, *Napoleon III and Mexico: American Triumph over Monarchy* (Chapel Hill: University of North Carolina Press, 1971); Kathryn Abbey Hanna, "The Roles of the South in the French Intervention in Mexico," *Journal of Southern History* 20 (February 1954): 3–21.

30. Stève Sainlaude, *Le gouvernement impérial et la guerre de sécession (1861–1865), l'action diplomatique* (Paris: L'Harmattan, 2011); Sainlaude, *La France et la Confédération sudiste, 1861–1865: la question de la reconnaissance diplomatique pendant la guerre de Sécession* (Paris: L'Harmattan, 2011); Sainlaude, *France and the American Civil War: A Diplomatic History* (Chapel Hill: University of North Carolina Press, 2019); Sainlaude, "France's Grand Design and the Confederacy," in Doyle, ed., *American Civil Wars,* 107–24.

Europe, the Confederacy, and the Union.[31] Kelly's "The North American Crisis of the 1860s" (2012) advanced understanding of Mexico's relationship with the Confederacy. Marjorie Locke Mahoney and Harry Thayer Mahoney coauthored *Mexico and the Confederacy* (1996), which took the story up to the fall of Maximilian's empire in 1867. In an essay on fugitive slaves from the Deep South seeking freedom in Mexico, Sarah E. Cornell examined how blacks viewed their experiences in the two countries. Two studies followed the self-exiled Confederados in Brazil: a book by Laura Jarnigan and a collection of essays coedited by Cyrus B. Dawsey and James M. Dawsey. Todd W. Wahlstrom's *The Southern Exodus to Mexico* (2015) examined ex-Confederates' efforts to colonize south of the border. Donald C. Simmons Jr. explored similar efforts, albeit in a different location, in *Confederate Settlements in British Honduras* (2001).[32]

Unlike the Civil War, the history of Reconstruction remained firmly ensconced within a nation-bound narrative, with a few notable exceptions. Richard White's sweeping interpretation of Reconstruction for the Oxford History of the United States, for example, took little notice of the world beyond the nation. Only a handful of scholars embraced the challenge. Mark M. Smith's perceptive review of comparative and transnational treatments of Reconstruction acknowledged several excellent comparative studies of emancipation and race relations but lamented the curious lack of interest in foreign affairs. Eric Foner's *Nothing but Freedom* (2007) briefly compared emancipation in the United States with that

31. Edward Bartlett Rugemer, *The Problem of Emancipation: The Caribbean Roots of the American Civil War* (Baton Rouge: Louisiana State University Press, 2008); Doyle, ed., *American Civil Wars*, esp. Erika Pani, "Juárez vs. Maximiliano: Mexico's Experiment with Monarchy" (167–84); Anne Eller, "Dominican Civil War, Slavery, and Spanish Annexation, 1844–1865" (147–66); Matt D. Childs, "Cuba, the Atlantic Crisis of the 1860s, and the Road to Abolition" (204–21); Rafael Marquese, "The Civil War in the United States and the Crisis of Slavery in Brazil" (222–46); and Patrick J. Kelly, "The Cat's-Paw: Confederate Ambitions in Latin America" (58–81).

32. Patrick J. Kelly, "The North American Crisis of the 1860s," *Journal of the Civil War Era* 2 (September 2012): 337–68; Harry Thayer Mahoney and Marjorie Locke Mahoney, *Mexico and the Confederacy: 1860–1867* (San Francisco: Austin & Winfield, 1996); Cyrus B. Dawsey and James M. Dawsey, eds., *The Confederados: Old South Immigrants in Brazil* (Tuscaloosa: University of Alabama Press, 1995); Sarah E. Cornell, "Citizens of Nowhere: Fugitive Slaves and Free African Americans in Mexico, 1833–1857," *Journal of American History* 100 (September 2013): 351–74; Laura Jarnagin, *A Confluence of Transatlantic Networks: Elites, Capitalism, and Confederate Migration to Brazil* (Tuscaloosa: University of Alabama Press, 2008); Todd W. Wahlstrom, *The Southern Exodus to Mexico: Migration across the Borderlands after the American Civil War* (Lincoln: University of Nebraska Press, 2015); Donald C. Simmons Jr., *Confederate Settlements in British Honduras* (Jefferson, NC: McFarland, 2001).

in Haiti and Jamaica. In his monumental *Reconstruction* (2003), Foner included only a few pages on Caribbean annexation controversies.[33]

Nor have diplomatic historians attended much to the immediate postwar period. Walter LaFeber, the leading historian of late nineteenth-century foreign policy, viewed the Civil War and Reconstruction era as an undifferentiated part of the "years of preparation" for imperialist expansion in the 1890s. In *Race over Empire* (2004), Eric T. L. Love argued convincingly that America's aversion to amalgamating nonwhites thwarted imperialist impulses to acquire Caribbean territories. Jay Sexton noted that the main thrust of United States foreign policy since the Seward-Lyon treaty of 1862 was decidedly antislavery and aimed at building an informal commercial empire rather than acquiring a colonial empire.[34] Stephen McCullough, *The Caribbean Policy of the Ulysses S. Grant Administration* (2018), one of the few concentrated studies of United States foreign policy for the era, showed how southern filibustering expeditions before the war presented the Grant administration with the prospect of annexation in Cuba and San Domingo. Phillip E. Myers's *Dissolving Tensions* (2015) dealt with postwar foreign affairs, focusing on Anglo-American relations relating to the confederation of Canada and the *Alabama* Claims, the legacy of the Confederate raider the British allowed to be constructed in violation of their own neutrality vows. Mitchell Snay's *Fenians, Freedmen, and Southern Whites* (2010) also illuminated Anglo-American affairs insofar as the raids of Irish American Fenians, many of them Union veterans, helped prompt Britain to create a self-governing dominion among its disparate North American possessions.[35]

33. Richard White, *The Republic for Which It Stands: The United States during Reconstruction and the Gilded Age, 1865–1896* (New York: Oxford University Press, 2017); Mark M. Smith, "The Past as a Foreign Country: Reconstruction, Inside and Out," in *Reconstructions: New Perspectives on the Postbellum United States*, ed. Thomas J. Brown (New York: Oxford University Press, 2006), 117–40; Eric Foner, *Nothing but Freedom: Emancipation and Its Legacy* (Baton Rouge: Louisiana State University Press, 1983); Foner, *Reconstruction: America's Unfinished Revolution, 1863–1877* (New York: Harper & Row, 1988), 494–97.

34. Walter LaFeber, *The New Cambridge History of American Foreign Relations.* Vol. 2, *The American Search for Opportunity, 1865–1913* (New York: Cambridge University Press, 2013); LaFeber, *The New Empire: An Interpretation of American Expansion, 1860–1898* (Ithaca: Cornell University Press, 1963); Eric T. L. Love, *Race over Empire: Racism and U.S. Imperialism, 1865–1900* (Chapel Hill: University of North Carolina Press, 2004); Jay Sexton, "The Civil War and U.S. World Power," in Doyle, ed., *American Civil Wars*, 15–33; Sexton, "William H. Seward in the World," *Journal of the Civil War Era* 4 (August 2014): 398–430; Sexton, "Steam Transport, Sovereignty, and Empire in North America, circa 1850–1885," *Journal of the Civil War Era* 7 (December 2017): 620–47; Sexton, *Debtor Diplomacy;* Sexton, *The Monroe Doctrine.*

35. Stephen McCullough, *The Caribbean Policy of the Ulysses S. Grant Administration: Foreshadowing an Informal Empire* (Lanham, MD: Lexington Books, 2017); Phillip E. Myers, *Dissolving Tensions: Rap-*

The advent of Reconstruction's sesquicentennial witnessed a flurry of essays, conferences, and other initiatives to broaden the frame surrounding the history of the era. Several collections of essays illuminated the global history of Reconstruction. Kate Masur and Gregory P. Downs's edited compilation of essays, *The World the Civil War Made* (2015), dealt mostly with the United States in isolation but included pieces by Andrew Zimmerman and Steven Hahn that took the conversation beyond the nation. *Reconstruction in a Globalizing World* (2018), edited by David Prior, made a determined effort to break Reconstruction history out of its nation-bound confines. In a similar effort to internationalize the history of Reconstruction in relation to Latin America, William A. Link edited essays by Edward B. Rugemer, Rafael Marquese, and Don H. Doyle.[36] All of these collections demonstrate the international importance of the events of Reconstruction to the wider world and suggest promising avenues for future research on international abolitionism, the transition to free labor, and postwar United States foreign policy.

The question about the survival of a distinctive southern identity has a long history. As the economic, cultural, and demographic impacts of the post–World War II globalization on the South grew stronger during the decades surrounding the new millennium, the question gained added gravitas. In *Grounded Globalism* (2007), anthropologist James L. Peacock observed that the very character of the early twenty-first-century South was undergoing a radical transformation: "I argue that the South is shifting its frame of reference from nation to world, causing its oppositional identity to diminish."[37]

---

prochement and Resolution in British-American-Canadian Relations in the Treaty of Washington Era, 1865–1914 (Kent: Kent State University Press, 2015); Mitchell Snay, *Fenians, Freedmen, and Southern Whites: Race and Nationality in the Era of Reconstruction* (Baton Rouge: Louisiana State University Press, 2007).

36. Kate Masur and Gregory P. Downs, eds., *The World the Civil War Made* (Chapel Hill: University of North Carolina Press, 2015), specifically Andrew Zimmerman, "From the Second American Revolution to the First International and Back Again: Marxism, the Popular Front, and the American Civil War" (304–36), and Steven Hahn, "Afterword: What Sort of World Did the Civil War Make?" (337–56); David Prior, ed., *Reconstruction in a Globalizing World* (New York: Fordham University Press, 2018); William A. Link, ed., *United States Reconstruction across the Americas* (Gainesville: University Press of Florida, 2019), esp. Rafael Marquese, "The Legacies of the Second Slavery: The Cotton and Coffee Economies of United States and Brazil during the Reconstruction Era, 1865–1904" (11–46); Don H. Doyle, "Reconstruction and Anti-imperialism: The United States and Mexico" (47–80); and Edward B. Rugemer, "Jamaica's Morant Bay Rebellion and the Making of Radical Reconstruction" (81–112).

37. James L. Peacock, *Grounded Globalism: How the U.S. South Embraces the World* (Athens: University of Georgia Press, 2007), 17.

The juxtapositional character of southern culture is rooted in our very understanding of the region. From C. Vann Woodward's classic characterization of the South as a place easier for foreigners to understand, due to its history of defeat and occupation, to Sheldon Hackney's 1973 essay about the South as a counterculture, to James L. Peacock's discussion of the South's "oppositional identity," scholars have thoroughly dissected the region's deviation from the triumphalist narrative of the United States writ large.[38] But globalization forces us to continue our rethinking of southern history, evaluation that began with substantial new works in the fields of immigration, the economy, culture, and diplomacy.[39]

Inspired by the New Left and history from the bottom up, scholars focused on narratives of immigrants and other marginalized groups, introducing them as new parties in old southern battles over race, gender, and the economy. Often moralistic and participatory in tone, some studies blurred the line between scholarship and advocacy. James L. Peacock, Harry L. Watson, and Carrie R. Matthews edited *The American South in a Global World* (2005) with a section discussing "Activist Approaches to the Transnational South."[40]

Scholarly focus on immigration to the South emerged soon after World War II. The new role of the United States as leader of the western alliance invited reevaluations of America's relationship with the world, and scholars of the South joined the movement. Rowland T. Berthoff's classic 1951 article, "Southern Attitudes toward Immigration, 1865–1914," aptly summarized the motives and failures of southern planters, land speculators, railroad companies, and industrialists in their recruitment efforts. To the planters' dismay, the plan to replace freedmen with

38. C. Vann Woodward, "The Irony of Southern History," in *The Burden of Southern History* (Baton Rouge: Louisiana State University Press, 1960); Sheldon Hackney, "The South as a Counterculture," *American Scholar* 42 (Spring 1973): 283–93; Peacock, *Grounded Globalism,* 17. See also Dewey W. Grantham, *The South in Modern America: A Region at Odds* (New York: HarperCollins, 1994). For a revisionist take, arguing against the very distinctiveness of southern history, see Laura F. Edwards, "Southern History as U.S. History," *Journal of Southern History* 75 (August 2009): 533–64.

39. For some early successful attempts to tackle the topic, see James L. Peacock, "The South in a Global World," *Virginia Quarterly Review* 78 (Autumn 2002): 581–94; David R. Goldfield, "The Impact of Globalization on the American South: Culture, Ecology, and Economy," in *Which "Global Village"? Societies, Cultures, and Political-Economic Systems in a Euro-Atlantic Perspective,* ed. Valeria Gennardo Lerda (Westport: Praeger, 2002), 145–54. *Southern Cultures,* a quarterly journal published by the Center for the Study of the American South, has commendably introduced global themes and viewpoints into studies of the South, including thematic volumes such as "The Global South," *Southern Cultures* 13 (Winter 2007).

40. James L. Peacock, Harry L. Watson, and Carrie R. Matthews, eds., *The American South in a Global World* (Chapel Hill: University of North Carolina Press, 2005).

white Europeans largely failed, as Europeans were not interested in subjugating themselves to the socioeconomic position that freedmen had sought to escape.[41]

Berthoff's article pointed to themes that characterized southern attitudes toward immigrant labor, as well as scholarship covering the topic. Since the 1940s, studies of Chinese in Mississippi, Mexicans in Texas, Italians in Louisiana and elsewhere, and Cubans and others in Florida documented the southern desire for labor, marred by white southerners' disdain for people not like themselves.[42] Partial assimilation often required adapting local whites' prevailing views on race and African Americans, as the literature on Mississippi Chinese demonstrated. Stephanie Hinnershitz, *A Different Shade of Justice* (2017) expanded the field to cover other Asian immigrants' assertions to their equal rights.[43]

Gary R. Mormino and George E. Pozzetta demonstrated in *The Immigrant World of Ybor City* (1987) that immigrants became increasingly willing to form alliances across ethnic lines. *Shades of the Sunbelt* (1988), edited by Randall M. Miller and George E. Pozzetta, offered pioneering discussions of the long history and diversity of immigrant experiences in the South.[44] As white southerners reacted to changing demographics with a mix of often conflicting emotions, newcomers worked to build the New South more to their liking.

41. Rowland T. Berthoff, "Southern Attitudes toward Immigration, 1865–1914," *Journal of Southern History* 17 (August 1951): 328–60.

42. For Italian experiences in Louisiana, see J. Vincenza Scarpaci, "Labor for Louisiana's Sugar Cane Fields: An Experiment in Immigrant Recruitment," *Italian Americana* 7 (September 1981): 19–41; Barbara Botein, "The Hennessy Case: An Episode in Anti-Italian Nativism," *Louisiana History* 20 (Summer 1979): 261–79. For examples of state-level studies, see Frank E. Dykema, "An Effort to Attract Dutch Colonists to Alabama, 1869," *Journal of Southern History* 14 (May 1948): 247–61; George E. Pozzetta, "Foreigners in Florida: A Study of Immigration Promotion, 1865–1910," *Florida Historical Quarterly* 53 (October 1974): 164–80; Barbara J. Rozek, *Come to Texas: Attracting Immigrants, 1865–1915* (College Station: Texas A&M University Press, 2003).

43. James W. Loewen, *The Mississippi Chinese: Between Black and White* (Cambridge: Harvard University Press, 1971); Robert Seto Quan, *Lotus among the Magnolias: The Mississippi Chinese* (Jackson: University Press of Mississippi, 1982). For more studies on Chinese in the South, see Lucy Cohen, *Chinese in the Post–Civil War South: A People without a History* (Baton Rouge: Louisiana State University Press, 1984); Edward J. M. Rhoads, "The Chinese in Texas," *Southwestern Historical Quarterly* 81 (July 1977): 1–36; Stephanie Hinnershitz, *A Different Shade of Justice: Asian American Civil Rights in the South* (Chapel Hill: University of North Carolina Press, 2017).

44. Gary R. Mormino and George E. Pozzetta, *The Immigrant World of Ybor City: Italians and Their Latin Neighbors in Tampa, 1885–1985* (Urbana: University of Illinois Press, 1987); Randall M. Miller and George E. Pozzetta, eds., *Shades of the Sunbelt: Essays on Ethnicity, Race, and the Urban South* (New York: Greenwood Press, 1988).

Since the 1980s, the South witnessed a rapidly growing immigration of Latinx. The size and impact of the movement necessitated scholarly attention. Geographers, cultural anthropologists, sociologists, legal scholars, and others focused on various aspects of social changes have done their share of the heavy lifting.[45] Historians occasionally entered the fray, utilizing their methodologies and knowledge to situate these changes into a historical framework. Leon Fink's *The Maya of Morganton* (2003) combined southern labor history with a discussion of globalization and questions of cultural transformation and preservation among migrants and native-born North Carolinians alike. Essays in Mary E. Odem and Elaine Cantrell Lacy's *Latino Immigrants and the Transformation of the U.S. South* (2009), revealed disruptions in local economies, gender and racial hierarchies, and native-born and immigrant communities, often resulting in strong negative counterreactions from native-born populations.[46] Perla M. Guerrero's *Nuevo South* (2017) also explored the conflicted and often negative perceptions surrounding immigrants. By keeping the book's focus on Northeast Arkansas, Guerrero ably combined the impact of newcomers on southern traditional ideas of

45. See Fran Ansley and Jon Shefner, eds., *Global Connections & Local Receptions: New Latino Immigration to the Southeastern United States* (Knoxville: University of Tennessee Press, 2009); Carole E. Hill and Patricia D. Beaver, eds., *Cultural Diversity in the U.S. South: Anthropological Contributions to a Region in Transition* (Athens: University of Georgia Press, 1998); Arthur D. Murphy, Colleen Blanchard, and Jennifer A. Hill, eds., *Latino Workers in the Contemporary South* (Athens: University of Georgia Press, 2001). See also essays in William Graves and Heather A. Smith, eds., *Charlotte, NC: The Global Evolution of a New South City* (Athens: University of Georgia Press, 2010), esp. David R. Goldfield, "A Place to Come To" (10–23); and José L. S. Gámez, "*Mi Reina:* Latino Landscapes in the Queen City (Charlotte, NC)" (263–83).

46. Leon Fink, *The Maya of Morganton: Work and Community in the Nuevo New South* (Chapel Hill: University of North Carolina Press, 2003). See also Fink, "New People of the Newest South: Prospects for the Post-1980 Immigrants," *Journal of Southern History* 75 (August 2009): 739–50; Mary E. Odem and Elaine Cantrell Lacy, eds., *Latino Immigrants and the Transformation of the U.S. South* (Athens: University of Georgia Press, 2009). See also Raymond A. Mohl, "Globalization, Latinization, and the Nuevo New South," *Journal of American Ethnic History* 22 (Summer 2003): 31–66, as well as his similarly named essay in *Other Souths: Diversity and Difference in the U.S. South, Reconstruction to Present,* ed. Pippa Holloway (Athens: University of Georgia Press, 2008), 408–42. See also José Maria Mantero, *Latinos and the U.S. South* (New York: Praeger, 2008); Heather A. Smith and Owen J. Furuseth, eds., *Latinos in the New South: Transformations of Place* (Burlington, VT: Ashgate Publishing, 2006); Robert Cassanello and Colin J. Davis, eds., *Migration and the Transformation of the Southern Workplace since 1945* (Gainesville: University Press of Florida, 2009); David R. Goldfield, "Unmelting the Ethnic South: Changing Boundaries of Race and Ethnicity in the Modern South," in *The American South in the Twentieth Century,* ed. Craig S. Pascoe, Karen Traham Leathem, and Andy Ambrose (Athens: University of Georgia Press, 2005), 19–38.

community. In *Agrarian Crossings* (2017), Tore C. Olsson showed larger political and economic similarities that straddle the border of the two countries—and the lessons that both United States and Mexican governments drew from each other as they attempted to revitalize economically downtrodden regions.[47]

In many ways, post–World War II globalization of the South represented the internationalization of the Sunbelt boom, which in large part grew out of recruitment of northern and, later, foreign corporations. James C. Cobb's formative *The Selling of the South* (1993) documented systematic efforts of southern states to recruit northern companies with the lures of cheap, unorganized, and docile labor. Cobb also portrayed South Carolina's pioneering efforts in pursuing foreign corporations, a theme later expanded by Marko Maunula in *Guten Tag, Y'All* (2009).[48] Maunula saw the recruitment of foreign corporations in Spartanburg, South Carolina, as a classic revolution from above, a carefully managed economic transformation to supplement and partially replace the declining textile industry—a transition that included the local embrace of arriving foreigners, bringing jobs and investments in their wake.[49] Monica Laney's *German Rocketeers in the Heart of Dixie* (2015) focused on the occasionally perplexing intersections of

47. Perla Guerrero, *Nuevo South: Asians, Latinas/os, and the Remaking of Place* (Austin: University of Texas Press, 2017). See also Julie M. Weise, *Corazón de Dixie: Mexicanos in the U.S. South since 1910* (Chapel Hill: University of North Carolina Press, 2015); Tore C. Olsson, *Agrarian Crossings: Reformers and the Remaking of U.S. and the Mexican Countryside* (Princeton: Princeton University Press, 2017). See also Natalie J. Ring, *The Problem South: Region, Empire, and the New Liberal State, 1880–1930* (Athens: University of Georgia Press, 2012).

48. James C. Cobb, *The Selling of the South: The Southern Crusade for Industrial Development, 1936–1990*, 2nd ed. (Urbana: University of Illinois Press, 1993); Marko Maunula, *Guten Tag, Y'All: Globalization and the South Carolina Piedmont, 1950–2000* (Athens: University of Georgia Press, 2009). For the uneven distribution of the Sunbelt boom's economic blessings, see Thomas A. Lyson, *Two Sides to the Sunbelt: The Growing Divergence between the Rural and Urban South* (New York: Praeger, 1989).

49. For courting and local reception of foreign businessmen in the South, see Sayuri Guthrie-Shimizu, "From Southeast Asia to the American Southeast: Japanese Business Meets the Sun Belt South," in *Globalization and the American South,* ed. James C. Cobb and William Stueck (Athens: University of Georgia Press, 2005), 135–63. See also essays in Peacock, Watson, and Matthews, eds., *The American South in a Global World,* specifically Sawa Kurotani, "The South Meets the East: Japanese Professionals in North Carolina's Research Triangle" (175–91); and Ajantha Subramanian, "North Carolina's Indians: Erasing Race to Make the Citizen" (192–201). See also Timothy J. Minchin, "When Kia Came to Georgia: Southern Transplants and the Growth of America's 'Other' Automakers," *Journal of Southern History* 83 (November 2017): 889–930; Becky Gillette, "Southern Auto Corridor: 'The Rage' for U.S., World Automakers," *Mississippi Business Journal,* 31 May 2004, https://msbusiness.com/2004/05/southern-auto-corridor-8216the-rage8217-for-us-world-automakers/ (accessed 19 January 2019).

race, the Cold War, boosterism, and cultural transformations in Huntsville, Alabama: an exceptional but important southern community known for its partially German-powered rocket program.[50] Both Maunula and Laney used case studies to show southern communities' eager embrace of white foreign newcomers who arrived with financial and cultural capital. The pattern repeated in most southern communities interested in foreign recruitment.

Scholars also tracked the effects of the global shift on the southern economy and southern distinctiveness. With the end of slavery and the growing role of federal government programs in the twentieth century, the uniqueness of the southern economy eroded. By the twenty-first century, the South's distinctive job markets and economy had disappeared, as Gavin Wright argued in *Old South, New South* (1986). Specifically, the region's role as a domestic colonial economy ended, as Wright concluded: "The South is not a colony to any other geographic entity, but to placeless global organizations and markets."[51]

Globalization is but one front in a larger economic transformation that has stirred the South and the nation since the 1970s. Labor historians noted how globalization and expatriation of southern industries followed the same logic that brought the factories to the South in the first place: cheap labor, low unionization, low taxes, and compliant political machines. In these analyses, labor and workers' rights become the losers in the globalization game. In *Capital Moves* (1999), Jefferson Cowie followed the path of one company as its search for cheap labor led it from New Jersey to Indiana, Tennessee, and eventually Ciudad Juarez, Mexico. Cowie argued that the investors' "command of spatial relations . . . becomes a crucial weapon in management's arsenal."[52] Corporations used relocations to erode labor's power, domestically and internationally.

In *Looking South* (2011), Mary E. Frederickson posited that the New South model of industrialization through cheap labor, antiunionization, and occupational segregation by race and gender "has been transformed again and taken worldwide."[53] When compared alongside Guerrero's *Nuevo South* and Olsson's

50. Monique Laney, *German Rocketeers in the Heart of Dixie: Making Sense of the Nazi Past during the Civil Rights Era* (New Haven: Yale University Press, 2015).

51. Gavin Wright, *Old South, New South: Revolutions in the Southern Economy since the Civil War* (New York: Basic Books, 1986), 269–74, quote on 273.

52. Jefferson Cowie, *Capital Moves: RCA's Seventy-Year Quest for Cheap Labor* (Ithaca: Cornell University Press, 1999), 185.

53. Mary E. Frederickson, *Looking South: Race, Gender, and the Transformation of Labor from Reconstruction to Globalization* (Gainesville: University Press of Florida, 2011). For background information on

Agrarian Crossings, Frederickson's study advanced John Egerton's old "Southernization of America" thesis in a more global manner. Michael Dennis, in *The New Economy and the Modern South* (2009), argued that globalization provided an important tool in the monetarist-libertarian attack on the rights of labor and the welfare state. Dennis concluded that, "the globalization trope distracts attention from the most significant development of the era: the rise of an ideology that placed the unfettered marketplace at the center of American life."[54]

Executives of multinational businesses became increasingly skilled in reading foreign economic landscapes, thus weakening any home-court advantage of local corporations. In his 2001 essay "Greenfields in the Heart of Dixie," Karsten Hülsemann, studying Nissan's arrival in Tennessee in 1980 and the ensuing entry of other automakers to the South, argued that Nissan's example actually helped American carmakers to expand their operations into the region. In *Japanese Industry in the American South* (1995), anthropologist Choong Soon Kim maintained that managerial ideology, along with geographical proximity to suppliers, played an important role in location decisions. The key factor, Kim concluded, was southern state and municipal governments' cooperative attitudes toward businesses.[55]

David L. Carlton and Peter A. Coclanis, together and separately, illuminated the region's economic bonds with the world throughout much of their careers. *The South, the Nation, and the World* (2003) gathered their essays, some published previously, into an argument against simplistic cultural explanations for the South's

---

one particularly important and mobile southern industry, see Beth English, *Common Thread: Labor, Politics, and Capital Mobility in the Textile Industry* (Athens: University of Georgia Press, 2006). For an analysis of protectionist mindset in the South, focused on textiles, see Timothy Minchin, *Empty Mills: The Fight Against Imports and the Decline of the U.S. Textile Industry* (Lanham, MD: Rowman & Littlefield, 2013).

54. John Egerton, *The Americanization of Dixie: The Southernization of America* (New York: Harper's Magazine Press, 1974); Michael Dennis, *The New Economy and the Modern South* (Gainesville: University Press of Florida, 2009), 1.

55. Karsten Hülsemann, "Greenfields in the Heart of Dixie: How the American Auto Industry Discovered the South," in *The Second Wave: Southern Industrialization from the 1940s to the 1970s*, ed. Philip Scranton (Athens: University of Georgia Press, 2001), 219–54. See also Robert Perrucci, *Japanese Auto Transplants in the Heartland: Corporatism and Community* (New York: Aldine de Gruyter, 1994); Michele M. Hoyman, *Power Steering: Global Automakers and the Transformation of Rural* Communities (Lawrence: University Press of Kansas, 1997); David M. Anderson and Andrew C. McKevitt, "From 'the Chosen' to the Precariat: Southern Workers in Foreign-Owned Factories since the 1980s," in *Reconsidering Southern Labor History: Race, Class, and Power*, ed. Matthew Hild and Keri Leigh Merritt (Gainesville: University Press of Florida, 2018), 255–70; Choong Soon Kim, *Japanese Industry in the American South* (New York: Routledge, 1995), 166.

historically poor economic performance in comparison to the North.[56] The South's underdevelopment was structural and institutional, they concluded, and the people operating in the economy acted rationally within this framework. The South's dependency on the vagaries of foreign markets contributed to its economic weakness, making it particularly vulnerable to global events and disruptions.

Although the South's economic sensitivity to global trends is obvious, many of the region's corporations proved skilled in reacting to international trends in production and consumption. The South was birthplace to some of the most iconic global brands, from Coca-Cola and CNN to Walmart and even the Tennessee Valley Authority (TVA). David Ekbladh's 2010 article, "Meeting the Challenge from Totalitarianism," offered fascinating insight into how the TVA inspired some western liberals as they faced existential threats from seemingly more dynamic fascist and communist societies.[57] Bartow J. Elmore's *Citizen Coke* (2015) discussed the company's often pioneering skills in securing global supplies, marketing, and working with wildly divergent regulatory environments. Nelson Lichtenstein edited *Wal-Mart* in 2006, and it remains the best work on this revolutionary southern company. Lichtenstein viewed Walmart as a global leader in attempts to eradicate remaining New Deal labor protections and squeeze labor.[58]

Culturally, the South appeals to foreigners in ways that the rest of the nation does not, save perhaps the mythos of the western frontier. The Japanese and European fascination with southern history, jazz and rock and roll, and southern

56. David L. Carlton and Peter A. Coclanis, *The South, the Nation, and the World: Perspectives on Southern Economic Development* (Charlottesville: University of Virginia Press, 2003). See also Michael L. Walden, *North Carolina in the Connected Age: Challenges and Opportunities in a Globalizing Economy* (Chapel Hill: University of North Carolina Press, 2008). An economist, Walden thoughtfully discussed the state's massive economic transformation since the 1970s.

57. David Ekbladh, "Meeting the Challenge from Totalitarianism: The Tennessee Valley Authority as a Global Model for Liberal Development, 1933–1945," *International History Review* 32 (March 2010): 47–67. See also Ekbladh, "Mr. TVA: 'Grass Roots' Development, David Lilienthal, and the Rise and Fall of the Tennessee Valley Authority as a Symbol for U.S. Overseas Development, 1933–1973," *Diplomatic History* 26 (Summer 2002): 335–74.

58. Bartow J. Elmore, *Citizen Coke: The Making of Coca-Cola Capitalism* (New York: W. W. Norton, 2015); Nelson Lichtenstein, ed., *Wal-Mart: The Face of Twenty-First-Century Capitalism* (New York: New Press, 2006); Lichtenstein, "Wal-Mart: A Template for Twenty-First-Century Capitalism," in Lichtenstein, ed., *Wal-Mart,* 4–5. See also Sandra S. Vance and Roy V. Scott, "Sam Walton and Wal-Mart Stores, Inc.: A Study in Modern Southern Entrepreneurship," *Journal of Southern History* 58 (May 1992): 231–52; Bethany Moreton, *To Serve God and Wal-Mart: The Making of Christian Free Enterprise* (Cambridge: Harvard University Press, 2009).

writers is common knowledge. In his 2003 essay, "'By Elvis and All the Saints,'" Brian Ward discussed the impact of southern rock music on British youth, including its sensuous and rebellious nature.[59] Penny M. Von Eschen's *Satchmo Blows Up the World* (2006) described how the United States used southern music to win hearts and minds of Europeans and newly independent Asian and African nations alike. Karen L. Cox, in *Dreaming of Dixie* (2011), explored the creation of the South in national and, by extension, global popular culture and consciousness. Suzanne W. Jones and Sharon Monteith's edited collection, *South to a New Place* (2002), contains important works that put the South in a comparative cultural framework, contrasting and analyzing its writers and even punk musicians, discussing how outsiders shaped the region and its global image.[60]

The South's economic globalization occurred alongside changes in its diplomatic motivations. Some historians, such as Joseph A. Fry, argued for regional self-interest, while others, like Tennant S. McWilliams, more sensitively approached the idea of culture and tradition as motivators.[61] The role of race in southern diplomatic thought remains an important topic, especially considering how America's territorial imperialism coincided with the end of Reconstruction, restoration of white supremacy, and growing southern political influence.[62]

Some of the most interesting diplomatic and/or transnational history has focused on black southerners' ideas and interactions with the world—especially Africa. Mary G. Rolinson, in *Grassroots Garveyism* (2007), pointed out the wide-

59. Brian Ward, "'By Elvis and All the Saints': Images of the American South in the World of 1950s British Popular Music," in *Britain and the American South: From Colonialism to Rock and Roll*, ed. Joseph P. Ward (Jackson: University Press of Mississippi, 2003): 187–213. See also Glenn Eskew, *Johnny Mercer: Southern Songwriter for the World* (Athens: University of Georgia Press, 2013).

60. Richard Pells, *Not Like Us: How Europeans Have Loved, Hated, and Transformed American Culture since World War II* (New York: Basic Books, 1997); Penny M. Von Eschen, *Satchmo Blows Up the World: Jazz Ambassadors Play the Cold War* (Cambridge: Harvard University Press, 2006); Karen L. Cox, *Dreaming of Dixie: How the South Was Created in American Popular Culture* (Chapel Hill: University of North Carolina Press, 2011); Suzanne W. Jones and Sharon Monteith, eds., *South to a New Place: Region, Literature, Culture* (Baton Rouge: Louisiana State University Press, 2002).

61. Joseph A. Fry, *Dixie Looks Abroad: The South and U.S. Foreign Relations, 1789–1973* (Baton Rouge: Louisiana State University Press, 2002); Tennant S. McWilliams, *The New South Faces the World: Foreign Affairs and the Southern Sense of Self, 1877–1950* (Baton Rouge: Louisiana State University Press, 1988).

62. For a good biography depicting the internal contradictions and rapid shifts in southern imperial thinking, see Daniel S. Margolies, *Henry Watterson and the New South: The Politics of Empire, Free Trade, and Globalization* (Lexington: University Press of Kentucky, 2006). See also Erin Elizabeth Clune, "From Light Copper to the Blackest and Lowest Type: Daniel Tompkins and the Racial Order of the Global

spread popularity of the Universal Negro Improvement Association among African Americans in the rural South. Many southern Garveyites found the idea of migrating to Africa more attractive than remaining in the South or moving to northern cities. In *Alabama in Africa* (2010), Andrew Zimmerman showed how Germans sought the help of Booker T. Washington and Tuskegee experts to start cotton cultivation in Togo. Tuskegee leaders' interest in black uplift and unity created uncomfortable alliances with German imperialists interested in perpetuating the American South's model of racial separation and cotton economy in their African empire.[63]

African Americans also deeply connected their struggle for civil rights with African independence movements. Danny Duncan Collum's edited collection, *African Americans in the Spanish Civil War* (1992), revealed how African Americans saw the worrying connections between the global rise of fascism and their struggles against racism at home. Thomas Borstelmann argued, in *The Cold War and the Color Line* (2001), that after World War II American race relations became intertwined with Cold War foreign policy, and black Americans understood that their status and that of black people everywhere were connected.[64]

New South," *Journal of Southern History* 76 (May 2010): 275–314. Willard B. Gatewood Jr., "Black Americans and the Quest for Empire, 1898–1903," *Journal of Southern History* 38 (November 1972): 545–66, pointed out the African American anger toward the hypocrisy of talking liberation abroad while cementing white supremacy at home. David Turpie, "'Howling upon the Scent of another Victim': Senator Edward W. Carmack, the Philippine Issue, and Southern Opposition to Imperialism," *Tennessee Historical Quarterly* 68 (Winter 2009): 411–32, offers an example of southern anti-imperialist thought of the era. Christopher Lasch argued that northern anti-imperialists had to walk the fine line creating alliances with southern anti-imperialists. Eventually the erosion of idealism, enforced by Darwinist notions about race, gained at least tacit national acceptance, hindering American colonialism. The views of southern racists largely carried the day; see "The Anti-Imperialists, the Philippines, and the Inequality of Man," *Journal of Southern History* 24 (August 1958): 319–31.

63. Mary G. Rolinson, *Grassroots Garveyism: The Universal Negro Improvement Association in the Rural South, 1920–1927* (Chapel Hill: University of North Carolina Press, 2007), 154. See also Michael W. Fitzgerald, "'We Have Found a Moses': Theodore Bilbo, Black Nationalism, and the Greater Liberia Bill of 1939," *Journal of Southern History* 63 (May 1997): 293–320; Andrew Zimmerman, *Alabama in Africa: Booker T. Washington, the German Empire, and the Globalization of the New South* (Princeton: Princeton University Press, 2010). See also Sven Beckert, "From Tuskegee to Togo: The Problem of Freedom in the Empire of Cotton," *Journal of American History* 92 (September 2005): 498–526.

64. Danny Duncan Collum, ed., *African Americans in the Spanish Civil War: "This Ain't Ethiopia, But It'll Do"* (New York: G. K. Hall, 1992); Thomas Borstelmann, *The Cold War and the Color Line: American Race Relations in the Global Arena* (Cambridge: Harvard University Press, 2001), 41, 45. For an informative individual-centered story capturing the impact of the southern civil rights movement in European

Mid-twentieth-century African American interest in Ghana, with its pan-African ideals, United States–educated charismatic leader, and position at the forefront of the anticolonial wave, received particular attention. In *African Americans in Ghana* (2006), Kevin K. Gaines put the civil rights movement into the global context of anticolonialism, African American intellectual traditions, and Kwame Nkrumah–inspired pan-African ideology. The connections between African anticolonial movements, African Americans, and American ideology became strong and obvious. "From early on, institutions such as Tuskegee Institute, Fisk University, Wilberforce University, Lincoln, and Howard had global profiles and a foreign presence," Jason C. Parker pointed out, demonstrating the role of historically black colleges and universities in shaping African independence movements and intellectual atmosphere during the twentieth century.[65]

As the Cold War escalated and the United States saw shaking dominoes in Southeast Asia, the South became one of the staunchest supporters of Lyndon B. Johnson's war efforts. Literature on the South and Vietnam portrays a region where a substantial section of its population expressed strong support for its militaristic traditions. Simultaneously, underneath the surface, some activists hammered cracks into the old myth of the solid South, demonstrating the emerging diversity of the region's foreign policy attitudes and widening the old chasms in its political makeup.[66] The South moved toward a more heterogeneous view

---

liberal consciousness, see Michael O. West, "Little Rock as America: Hoyt Fuller, Europe, and the Little Rock Racial Crisis of 1957," *Journal of Southern History* 78 (November 2012): 913–42.

65. Kevin K. Gaines, *African Americans in Ghana: Black Expatriates and the Civil Rights Era* (Chapel Hill: University of North Carolina Press, 2006); Jason C. Parker, "Made-in-America Revolutions? The 'Black University' and the American Role in the Decolonization of the Black Atlantic," *Journal of American History* 96 (December 2009): 729. See also Frank Andre Guridy, *Forging Diaspora: Afro-Cubans and African Americans in a World of Empire and Jim Crow* (Chapel Hill: University of North Carolina Press, 2010); Kenneth James King, *Pan-Africanism and Education: A Study of Race Philanthropy and Education in the Southern States of America and East Africa* (Oxford, UK: Clarendon Press, 1971). Kevin E. Grimm, "Gazing toward Ghana: African American Agency in the Eisenhower Administration's Relations with Africa," *Journal of Contemporary History* 48 (July 2013): 578–96, discussed African American efforts to shape American foreign policy toward African countries moving toward independence and attempts to push America to occupy the middle ground between European intransigency and African aspirations.

66. Joseph A. Fry, *The American South and the Vietnam War: Belligerence, Protest, and Agony in Dixie* (Lexington: University Press of Kentucky, 2015); Adrienne Caughfield, "Fighting the Cold War at Southern Methodist University," *Journal of Southern History* 81 (August 2015): 647–74; Randall Bennet Woods, "Dixie's Dove: J. William Fulbright, the Vietnam War, and the American South," *Journal of Southern History* 60 (August 1994): 533–52.

of the world, triggered in large part by the demographic, economic, and cultural changes discussed above.

Much work remains to be done on globalization of the South and the South's impact on the world. Southern music's full impact upon the world deserves more historical attention, from country to rock and roll, jazz to southern hip-hop. While we have plenty of effective, if often emotive studies surrounding the rapid demographic change in the South, further interrogations will put immigration to the South into larger global economic and political contexts. In political history, further research of the connections between twentieth-century southern white nativism and worldwide anti-immigration and antiglobalization movements will create new and valuable knowledge.

The South's new residents created new global networks between the South and their points of origin. How has immigration connected southern communities to international networks of people in diaspora, today as well as a century ago? How has the relationship between southern cities and their surrounding areas evolved during the long globalization? To what degree does globalization impact the South's relationship with the rest of the nation? As shifts in political and spatial understandings of regions, nations, and transnational networks evolve, areas of necessary and relevant research will multiply. Without doubt, however, historical scholarship on the global South in the twenty-first century demonstrated that a dense web of connections between the South and the wider world shaped the region from its beginnings.

THE NATIVE SOUTH

Christina Snyder and Theda Perdue

Neither predecessor to this volume—Arthur S. Link and Rembert W. Patrick's *Writing Southern History* (1965), or John B. Boles and Evelyn Thomas Nolen's *Interpreting Southern History* (1987)—included a chapter on Native southerners. Indeed, Indians barely received a mention.[1] Until the 1970s, the perceived cultural, racial, and historical "otherness" of Indians relegated them to bit parts in dramas that starred Europeans. Nevertheless, Indians did appear in the historical record—trade records and legislative journals, for example—and amateur natural historians and archaeologists, not the least of whom was Thomas Jefferson, took serious interest in their physical appearances, histories, and cultures.[2]

But Indians were curiosities at best and impediments at worst. Since then, historians have gradually acknowledged Indians not only as historical actors with their own legitimate worldviews, economic interests, and political objectives, but also as intrinsic players in the history of the region.

Research by academic historians on Indians in southern history is almost as old as the field itself. Before going to Columbia University for his doctoral work,

1. Arthur S. Link and Rembert W. Patrick, eds., *Writing Southern History: Essays in Historiography in Honor of Fletcher M. Green* (Baton Rouge: Louisiana State University Press, 1965); John B. Boles and Evelyn Thomas Nolen, *Interpreting Southern History: Historiographical Essays in Honor of Sanford W. Higginbotham* (Baton Rouge: Louisiana State University Press, 1987). The earlier volume has five entries for Indians in the index; the second has seven.

2. Thomas Jefferson, *Notes on the State of Virginia* (Paris: privately published, 1785). Other examples include William Bartram, *Travels Through North & South Carolina, Georgia, East & West Florida, the Cherokee Country, the Extensive Territories of the Muscogulges, or Creek Confederacy, and the Country of the Chactaws* (Philadelphia: James & Johnson, 1791); Charles Colcock Jones Jr., *Antiquities of the Southern Indians, Particularly of the Georgia Tribes* (New York: D. Appleton, 1873).

pioneer southern historian Ulrich B. Phillips studied at the University of Chicago with frontier historian Frederick Jackson Turner. Turner's influence lingered and, although Phillips wrote his dissertation with William A. Dunning, he focused on Indian affairs. His acknowledgements in his published dissertation, *Georgia and States Rights* (1902), opened with a paean to Turner.[3] Nearly half of that work directly addressed the removal of the Creeks and Cherokees, which Phillips argued gave birth to the state's resistance to an increasingly centralized national government. True to Turner's "frontier thesis," Indians served only as an obstacle to Georgia's development and a catalyst for a new political culture. Phillips also made removal the pivotal event in the history of southern Indians, and there it remains. If most southerners know one thing about Indians, it is the "Trail of Tears," a fascination that many historians have exploited.[4]

Phillips's work was imperialistic history—the triumph of Euro-Americans over Indians—but such an approach was not limited to him. The colonial period, in particular, attracted southern historians who emphasized colonists instead of Indians, whose role was merely reactive. The interests, views, and actions of colonists drove the narrative, and the denouement was the same: Indians lost. Despite the Indians' lack of agency in most of these works, some, such as Verner W. Crane's *The Southern Frontier* (1928), remain useful for their research if not their interpretations of Native behavior.[5]

Cultural imperialism in the form of exalting southern Indians as the "civilized tribes" also became a theme. In *Cherokees of the Old South* (1956), for example, Henry Thompson Malone placed Indians at the center of his narrative, but he focused on highly acculturated, mission-educated Cherokee men who seemed to replicate white southern society. A racial analysis, particularly of economic and

3. Frederick Jackson Turner, "The Significance of the Frontier in American History," *Annual Report of the American Historical Association for the Year 1893* (Washington: Government Printing Office, 1894), 197–228; Ulrich B. Phillips, *Georgia and State Rights: A Study of the Political History of Georgia from the Revolution to the Civil War, with Particular Regard to Federal Relations* (Washington, DC: Government Printing Office, 1902), 199–227. On the application of the "frontier thesis" to southern Native peoples, see, for example, Verner W. Crane, *The Southern Frontier, 1670–1732* (Durham: Duke University Press, 1928).

4. Among them are Grant Foreman, *Indian Removal: The Emigration of the Five Civilized Tribes of Indians* (Norman: University of Oklahoma Press, 1953); Arthur H. DeRosier Jr., *The Removal of the Choctaw Indians* (Knoxville: University of Tennessee Press, 1970); Theda Perdue and Michael D. Green, *The Cherokee Nation and the Trail of Tears* (New York: Viking, 2007). On the continued role of removal as *the* pivotal event, see, for example, Gregory D. Smithers, *Native Southerners: Indigenous History from Origins to Removal* (Norman: University of Oklahoma Press, 2019).

5. Crane, *The Southern Frontier.*

political factionalism, dominated many interpretations such as that of Arrell M. Gibson who, in *The Chickasaws* (1971), titled his chapter on late eighteenth- and early nineteenth-century political realignment "Twilight of the Fullbloods."[6] What made southern Indians "civilized," such works often implied, was intermarriage with whites.

Colonial histories of the subjugation of Indians and scholars' fascination with the travails of "civilized" Indians ultimately fell victim to a major shift in perspective as well as methodology. That transformation emerged from the work of anthropologists, historians, and legal scholars employed by the Indian Claims Commission between 1946 and 1978. Established by Congress, the commission sought to resolve outstanding claims of Native nations against the United States. Resolution of these claims forced researchers to take Indian perspectives seriously, leading to the development of ethnohistory, a methodology that broadened the sources used in writing about the Indian past, and brought an anthropological understanding of culture to historical scholarship. The American Society for Ethnohistory, established in 1953, began publishing its journal *Ethnohistory* the following year.[7] Instead of passive victims, Indians became active participants in their own pasts.

Ethnohistory reached southern history through anthropology and other disciplines. Legal scholar John Phillip Reid drew on ethnographic research to write culturally informed studies of eighteenth-century Cherokee legal culture. Anthropologist Raymond Fogelson combined his own ethnographic fieldwork with linguistic and documentary records to explore Cherokee kinship, spirituality, art, and more. Sociologist Duane Champagne used theoretical models as well as historical sources to understand Native political and cultural change in the nineteenth century, especially the development of constitutional democracies among Native southerners. Anthropologist Helen Rountree, the foremost scholar of Indigenous Virginians, drew on a broad range of interdisciplinary data to examine familiar historical figures like Powhatan and Pocahontas and elucidate the lesser known histories of contemporary Indian communities.[8]

6. Henry Thompson Malone, *Cherokees of the Old South, A People in Transition* (Athens: University of Georgia Press, 1956); Arrell M. Gibson, *The Chickasaws* (Norman: University of Oklahoma Press, 1971), chap. 4.

7. For a methodological essay, see James Axtell, "Ethnohistory: An Historian's Viewpoint," *Ethnohistory* 26 (Winter 1979): 1–13.

8. John Phillip Reid, *A Law of Blood: The Primitive Law of the Cherokee Nation* (New York: New York University Press, 1970); Duane Champagne, *Social Order and Political Change: Constitutional Government*

The most influential work in the transition of southern historians to ethnohistory has been Charles Hudson's *The Southeastern Indians* (1976).[9] Trained as a cultural anthropologist, Hudson first wrote an ethnography of mid-twentieth-century Catawba society. Over time, he incorporated perspectives from archaeology, folklore, geography, linguistics, and history into his analysis, a skill set fully on display in *The Southeastern Indians.* Hudson later critiqued that book as too synchronic—that is, failing to effectively capture change over time. To remedy this, he increasingly turned to the discipline of history, especially social history and the works of Fernand Braudel, the influence of which is apparent in several of Hudson's later works, including *Knights of Spain, Warriors of the Sun* (1997) and the edited volumes *The Forgotten Centuries* (1994) and *The Transformation of the Southeastern Indians* (2002). As these titles suggest, Hudson strove to understand how and why the Native South transformed from dozens of Mississippian chiefdoms that dominated the region from roughly 1000 to 1600 CE to a handful of powerful Indian nations in the colonial era.[10] Hudson's work motivated scholars to analyze the violent forces of colonialism as well as Indigenous adaptations and persistence.

Colonialism

A growing number of scholars foregrounded Indigenous experiences in what Hudson called the "older South" by illuminating the central role Native peoples

---

among the Cherokee, the Choctaw, the Chickasaw, and the Creek (Stanford: Stanford University Press, 1992); Helen Rountree, *Pocahontas, Powhatan, Opechancanough: Three Indian Lives Changed by Jamestown* (Charlottesville: University of Virginia Press, 2005); Rountree, *Pocahontas's People: The Powhatan Indians of Virginia Through Four Centuries* (Norman: University of Oklahoma Press, 1990). Raymond Fogelson authored dozens of important articles; for example, "The Cherokee Ballgame Cycle: An Ethnologist's View," *Ethnomusicology* 15 (1971): 327–38; and "The Ethnohistory of Events and Nonevents," *Ethnohistory* 36 (Spring 1989): 133–47.

9. Charles Hudson, *The Southeastern Indians* (Knoxville: University of Tennessee Press, 1976). Hudson's use of "southeastern" reflected his training as an anthropologist. Beginning in the late nineteenth century, museum curators organized exhibits by dividing continents into culture areas (e.g. "the Southeast"), geographic regions with shared culture. Though many anthropologists critique the culture area concept, it is still widely used in the discipline. Because the authors of this essay are historians, we use another regional abstraction that is similarly flawed but still useful—"the South."

10. Charles Hudson, *Knights of Spain, Warriors of the Sun: Hernando de Soto and the South's Ancient Chiefdoms* (Athens: University of Georgia Press, 1997); Hudson and Carmen Chaves Tesser, eds., *The Forgotten Centuries: Indians and Europeans in the American South, 1521–1704* (Athens: University of Georgia

played in trade, diplomacy, warfare, and slavery. Influenced by postcolonial studies as well as ethnohistory, these works positioned the devastation of colonialism in tension with Indigenous efforts to adapt and survive.

Several important works explored the process by which Indigenous peoples created new polities in the colonial era. James H. Merrell argued that European arrival created a "New World" for colonists and Indians alike. Focusing on the Carolina Piedmont, Merrell explored the ethnic and political diversity that persisted until the eighteenth century. Siouan-speaking peoples of that region responded creatively to European threats like disease, violence, and land encroachment. By cultivating an alliance with South Carolina and repeatedly reinventing their economy, the Catawba Nation persisted and today remains on a portion of its homeland. Scholars in the field dubbed the process of creating a new group identity "ethnogenesis." In her book on the subject, Patricia Galloway highlighted the early colonial forces, especially disease, that toppled the region's chiefdoms. Focusing on what is now Mississippi, she explained how survivors gathered in forty to fifty autonomous towns, which by the late seventeenth century had banded together to create the Choctaw Nation. The new polity emerged through an alliance built on novel religious ceremonies and political institutions.[11]

Scholarship on Indian enslavement provided startling insights into slavery's birth, development, and legacy. Theda Perdue located the origins of African American slavery among the Cherokees in war captives who had no kin ties and therefore no rights, a social construction that they adapted to plantation slavery. In her more broadly conceived work, Christina Snyder demonstrated that slavery came to the South before race. Indeed, slavery was widespread across North America, though it differed from one region to the next and changed over time. Among Native southerners, warfare produced captives whom Indians killed, enslaved, held for ransom, or adopted without regard to race. Fluidity characterized captivity, but within Native societies, only adoption transformed it into freedom. Unlike adoptees, slaves were not incorporated into kinship networks and were

Press, 1994); Hudson and Robbie Ethridge, eds., *The Transformation of the Southeastern Indians, 1540–1760* (Jackson: University Press of Mississippi, 2002). Among those influenced by Hudson's methods for bridging the divide between pre- and post-contact is Daniel K. Richter, *Before the Revolution: America's Ancient Pasts* (Cambridge: Harvard University Press, 2011).

11. James H. Merrell, *The Indians' New World: Catawbas and Their Neighbors from European Contact through the Era of Removal* (Chapel Hill: University of North Carolina Press, 1989); Patricia Galloway, *Choctaw Genesis, 1500–1700* (Lincoln: University of Nebraska Press, 1995).

subject to menial labor, sale, or trade. Early European colonists did not bring to America a robust system of slavery or a clear racial schema, but they did have an insatiable demand for labor and insinuated themselves into Indigenous trade networks, amplifying the Indian slave trade to unprecedented levels.[12] Kristalyn Marie Shefveland revealed that many prominent Virginia families built their fortunes on this trade, relying on Indian middlemen to penetrate trade networks of the southern interior. By the late seventeenth century, South Carolina eclipsed Virginia as the hub of this terrible traffic. Alan Gallay estimated that at the trade's height—1670 to 1715—between 24,000 and 51,000 Indian slaves were exported from Charleston.[13] The Indigenous slave trade transformed the entire region, booming before Africans came to North America in large numbers, and, until the 1720s (even later in some areas), it coexisted with the Atlantic slave trade.

Robbie Ethridge is prominent among scholars who explored how the Indian slave trade contributed to the colonial South's transformation from a realm of dozens of chiefdoms to a handful of powerful nations. Drawing on Immanuel Wallerstein's version of world-systems theory, Ethridge traced the impact of burgeoning capitalism.[14] She focused on how European centers drew on resources, namely furs and Indigenous slaves, from their southern colonies. Also influenced by Marxist anthropologist Eric Wolf, Ethridge argued that the American South had "shatter zones," which she described as "large regions of instability from which shock waves radiate out for sometimes hundreds and hundreds of miles."[15] Because of Europeans' insatiable demand for slaves, power in the southern inte-

12. Theda Perdue, *Slavery and the Evolution of Cherokee Society, 1540–1866* (Knoxville: University of Tennessee Press, 1979); Christina Snyder, *Slavery in Indian Country: The Changing Face of Captivity in Early America* (Cambridge: Harvard University Press, 2010); Matthew Jennings, *New Worlds of Violence: Cultures and Conquests in the Early American Southeast* (Knoxville: University of Tennessee Press, 2011). For Indigenous slavery elsewhere in North America, see, for example, James F. Brooks, *Captives and Cousins: Slavery, Kinship, and Community in the Southwest Borderlands* (Chapel Hill: University of North Carolina Press, 2002); Brett Rushforth, *Bonds of Alliance: Indigenous and Atlantic Slaveries in New France* (Chapel Hill: University of North Carolina Press, 2012).

13. Kristalyn Marie Shefveland, *Anglo-Native Virginia: Trade, Conversion, and Indian Slavery in the Old Dominion, 1646–1722* (Athens: University of Georgia Press, 2016); Alan Gallay, *The Indian Slave Trade: The Rise of the English Empire in the American South, 1670–1717* (New Haven: Yale University Press, 2002).

14. Robbie Ethridge, "Introduction," in *Mapping the Mississippian Shatter Zone: The Colonial Indian Slave Trade and Regional Instability in the American South,* ed. Robbie Ethridge and Sheri M. Shuck-Hall (Lincoln: University of Nebraska Press, 2009), 16–26.

15. Eric R. Wolf, *Europe and the People Without History* (Berkeley: University of California Press, 1982), 33, 230.

rior became concentrated in "a handful of militaristic Indian slaving societies that held control of the trade and that, through their slave raiding, caused widespread dislocation, migration, amalgamation, and, in some cases, extinction of Native peoples."[16]

Like Ethridge, Paul Kelton's approach to southern Indian history is multiscalar, exploring how global forces impacted Indigenous communities. Kelton critiqued Alfred W. Crosby's influential "virgin soil thesis," which argued that European diseases brought by unwitting colonizers resulted in Indigenous demographic disaster over the century following first contact. Returning the focus to human agents, Kelton contended that "the disease component of the Columbian Exchange was a mediated process in which the larger aspects of colonialism heightened Native vulnerability to infection and mortality." Specifically, he blamed European warfare and slave raiding for amplifying epidemic mortality and impeding recovery. But Kelton also demonstrated that Native people had agency even during the darkest days of colonial invasion. Overturning Crosby's assumption that incompetent Native healers worsened the effects of disease, Kelton analyzed Cherokee medical practices and concluded that they were at least as effective as contemporaneous European ones.[17]

James Taylor Carson and Greg O'Brien explored how Choctaws attempted to preserve power in the face of colonial invasion. Carson argued that Choctaws embraced foreign practices that they found empowering—adding animal husbandry

16. Ethridge first applied the "shatter zone" concept to the region with "Creating the Shatter Zone: Indian Slave Traders and the Collapse of the Southeastern Chiefdoms," in *Light on the Path: The Anthropology and History of the Southeastern Indians,* ed. Thomas J. Pluckham and Robbie Ethridge (Tuscaloosa: University of Alabama Press, 2006), 207–18, quotes on 208. She further developed this idea in *From Chicaza to Chickasaw: The European Invasion and the Transformation of the Mississippian World, 1540–1715* (Chapel Hill: University of North Carolina Press, 2010).

17. Alfred W. Crosby, "Virgin Soil Epidemics as a Factor in the Aboriginal Depopulation in America," *William and Mary Quarterly* 33 (April 1976): 289–99; Paul Kelton, *Epidemics and Enslavement: Biological Catastrophe in the Native Southeast, 1492–1715* (Lincoln: University of Nebraska Press, 2007), xvii. Among Kelton's major critiques of Crosby, and the many historians and journalists who adapted Crosby's theory, is that they homogenized "the varied experiences Natives had with colonialism" (23). To remedy this, Kelton's second monograph explored how one Native nation dealt with the deadliest of colonial pathogens; see *Cherokee Medicine, Colonial Germs: An Indigenous Nation's Fight against Smallpox, 1518–1824* (Norman: University of Oklahoma Press, 2015). Kelton also coedited an important volume that reassessed the relationship between disease and human agency through North America. See Catherine M. Cameron, Paul Kelton, and Alan C. Swedlund, eds., *Beyond Germs: Native Depopulation in North America* (Tucson: University of Arizona Press, 2015).

to their economic activities, for example—but also preserved "deep structures" fundamental to their identity, including chiefly political organization, matrilineal kinship, a gendered division of labor, and a cosmology focused on balance and reciprocity. O'Brien examined how Choctaw elites attempted to harness the power of colonial trade. Just as they had in the pre-contact era, Native chiefs forged trade alliances with foreigners by redistributing rare goods as evidence of their political and even spiritual power. French traders cooperated with these protocols, but the British did not. Still, Native chiefs sought to control trade, so they encouraged—sometimes demanded—that traders marry into their families, thereby preserving privileged access.[18]

Most who study colonialism in the South have focused on relations between southern Indians and Anglo-Americans, but an increasing number are delving into French and Spanish archives.[19] Kathleen DuVal pointed out that many historians ignored the South's deep and complex colonialism as well as its longstanding diversity and instead depicted the story of non-Anglo empires and Indian nations alike as one of declension. Power dynamics in the southern interior, she asserted, differed from the "middle ground" that Richard White observed in the Great Lakes region. DuVal offered a new model of colonial-Indigenous interaction: she argued that "only relatively weak people desired the kinds of compromises inherent in a middle ground." Powerful Native nations "wanted to set the terms of engagement with neighboring peoples," and therefore took the lead in shaping trade and diplomacy. In her study of the Gulf South during the Revolutionary era, DuVal explained how European empires and Indian nations strove for "advantageous interdependency," securing a favorable position in a broader web of protective ties that bound them to other polities. Indian nations of the southern interior weathered Spanish, French, and British intrusions—some even thrived through colonial trade—and continued to dominate their regions until the 1810s or later.[20]

18. James Taylor Carson, *Searching for the Bright Path: The Mississippi Choctaws from Prehistory to Removal* (Lincoln: University of Nebraska Press, 1999); Greg O'Brien, *Choctaws in a Revolutionary Age, 1750–1830* (Lincoln: University of Nebraska Press, 2002).

19. Moravian missionaries also left rich records in German script. See Rowena McClinton, ed. and trans., *The Moravian Springplace Mission to the Cherokees*, 2 vols. (Lincoln: University of Nebraska Press, 2007).

20. Kathleen DuVal, *The Native Ground: Indians and Colonists in the Heart of the Continent* (Philadelphia: University of Pennsylvania Press, 2006), 5; DuVal, *Independence Lost: Lives on the Edge of the American Revolution* (New York: Random House, 2015), xxi; Richard White, *The Middle Ground: Indians, Empires, and Republics in the Great Lakes Region, 1650–1815* (New York: Cambridge University Press, 1991).

Foregrounding Native-Spanish relations, Alejandra Dubcovsky demonstrated that placing understudied historical actors at the center of southern history can transform our picture of the region. Previously, most works on communication in early America focused on the Northeast, which had regular mail service and printing presses, instead of the presumably uninformed South. Through deep archival research and innovative methodology, Dubcovsky uncovered a vast information network created and maintained by Indians that shaped the South well into the colonial period. She revealed the power and reach of early Native southern communications while analyzing ways in which colonialism increasingly transformed that world.[21]

Economics

In the late 1940s, scholars of global economics developed dependency theory as a means to explore how wealthy nations exploited the resources of "underdeveloped" countries. Drawing on earlier studies of imperialism, scholars of dependency theory offered a new vantage point on colonialism. For example, Richard White applied dependency theory to the colonial South by exploring Choctaws' engagement with global markets from the sixteenth to the nineteenth century. White argued that the lure of European manufactured goods and alcohol drove Choctaws to overhunt deer, alter their ecosystem, and strain domestic and foreign relations. By the 1770s, he claimed, Choctaws had become entirely dependent on European trade partners, a situation that precipitated economic crisis, undermined their political autonomy, and eventually led to removal.[22]

Critics of dependency theory contend that it leaves "far too undeveloped the ways generations of southeastern Indians resisted, undermined, and countered the forces, trends, and practices that produce economic dependency." Joel W. Martin, for example, posited that "since we are greatly influenced by a historiography that depicts (to far too great a degree) an antebellum South without Native Americans, we are inclined to think that the southeastern Native Americans and

For an exploration of similar themes farther west, see Juliana Barr, *Peace Came in the Form of a Woman: Indians and Spaniards in the Texas Borderlands* (Chapel Hill: University of North Carolina Press, 2007).

21. Alejandra Dubcovsky, *Informed Power: Communication in the Early American South* (Cambridge: Harvard University Press, 2016).

22. Richard White, *The Roots of Dependency: Subsistence, Environment, and Social Change among the Choctaws, Pawnees, and Navajos* (Lincoln: University of Nebraska Press, 1983).

the Cotton Kingdom were absolutely incompatible, that . . . Native Americans really had no future in the South and must have felt completely desperate." In *Indians, Settlers, and Slaves in a Frontier Exchange Economy* (1992), Daniel H. Usner argued that instead of seeing the "frontier" as a racial or cultural boundary, scholars should understand it as a regional zone "of cross-cultural interaction through which native and colonial groups circulated goods and services." Usner provided a model to explain how Native Americans adapted to the economic changes wrought by colonialism.[23]

In the wake of the Yamasee War (1715–1717), a multinational Indigenous uprising against British colonialism, southern Indian nations seized on the deerskin trade as a way to reestablish relationships with European traders without relying on slavery. At the same time, a bovine plague forced English ports to ban European cattle hides for which deerskins proved an excellent substitute. In *Deerskins and Duffels* (1993), Kathryn E. Holland Braund explained the shift in the Creek Nation: "Far from being hapless cogs in the British wheel of expansion and exploitation, the Creeks embraced the role that opportunity thrust before them." While providing Creeks with a ready supply of firearms, clothing, and other important manufactures, the deerskin trade also created problems, including debt and a growing class divide.[24]

In the late eighteenth century, Britain and France exited the South and Spain retreated from Indian alliances, a situation that deprived Native nations of valuable trade and military support. Furthermore, tensions mounted as United States citizens, previously prohibited by the British Proclamation of 1763 from moving west of the Appalachians, began to encroach on Native lands. Indian leaders and federal officials wanted to avoid hostilities, so they seized on trade as a means to develop peaceful ties. As Robbie Ethridge detailed in *Creek Country* (2003), the United States created trade "factories" throughout Indian country, hoping to extend its influence and, ultimately, its sovereignty in the West. Indian leaders, like United States officials, saw these factories as more political than economic and

23. Joel W. Martin, "Southeastern Indians and the English Trade in Skins and Slaves," in Hudson and Tesser, eds., *The Forgotten Centuries*, 304–5; Martin, *Sacred Revolt: The Muskogees' Struggle for a New World* (Boston: Beacon Press, 1991), 173; Daniel H. Usner Jr., *Indians, Settlers, and Slaves in a Frontier Exchange Economy: The Lower Mississippi Valley Before 1783* (Chapel Hill: University of North Carolina Press, 1992), 6.

24. Kathryn E. Holland Braund, *Deerskins and Duffels: The Creek Indian Trade with Anglo-America, 1685–1815* (Lincoln: University of Nebraska Press, 1993), 31. For more on the relationship between the fur trade and the Yamasee War, see William L. Ramsey, *The Yamasee War: A Study of Culture, Economy, and Conflict in the Colonial South* (Lincoln: University of Nebraska Press, 2008).

sought to cultivate peace while retaining their own sovereignty. David Andrew Nichols aptly called these Indian trading factories "engines of diplomacy." Still, federal presence in Indian nations proved increasingly intrusive. Claudio Saunt argued that such trade heightened wealth disparities in Indian country, enriching some and ruining others. Moreover, the new federal government encouraged Indian consumers to run up debts and then pressured for cessions of land to satisfy those debts. The United States built roads through Indian nations, creating flashpoints of conflict. In her study of the Creek Nation, Angela Pulley Hudson noted how some Indian elites profited by operating inns, taverns, and ferries while most Creeks suffered. Ultimately, Hudson argued, such economic disparity led to the Red Stick War (1813–1814), a civil war in which Red Stick Creeks rejected economic alliance with the United States as a viable path forward. After the War of 1812, United States leaders, too, decided to move away from trade as a front line of Indian diplomacy. With a stronger presence in the West, the United States aggressively demanded land and used violence or the threat of violence as a cudgel.[25]

Even as Alabama Fever ravaged the Deep South, Native Americans blended old and new ways and adapted to life in a changing region. When the deerskin trade failed, Native Americans reshaped and diversified their economies: they became planters, ranchers, tavern-keepers, guides, craftspeople, and more. The United States encouraged this economic transformation in its first fully articulated Indian policy, the "Civilization Program." Implemented in 1796 by Benjamin Hawkins, General Superintendent of Indian Affairs for the lands south of the Ohio River, the policy funded federal agents to reside among Indians, establish model farms, and hire blacksmiths, millers, and other artisans to model "civilized" life. As Native peoples appropriated white ways, however superficially, white southerners increasingly considered the five large southern Indian nations

25. Robbie Ethridge, *Creek Country: The Creek Indians and Their World* (Chapel Hill: University of North Carolina Press, 2003); David Andrew Nichols, *Engines of Diplomacy: Indian Trading Factories and the Negotiation of American Empire* (Chapel Hill: University of North Carolina Press, 2016); Claudio Saunt, *A New Order of Things: Power, Property, and the Transformation of the Creek Indians, 1733–1816* (New York: Cambridge University Press, 1999); Angela Pulley Hudson, *Creek Paths and Federal Roads: Indians, Settlers, and Slaves and the Making of the American South* (Chapel Hill: University of North Carolina Press, 2010). For more on the Red Stick War, see Kathryn E. Holland Braund, ed., *Tohopeka: Rethinking the Creek War and the War of 1812* (Tuscaloosa: University of Alabama Press, 2012); Gregory A. Waselkov, *A Conquering Spirit: Fort Mims and the Redstick War of 1813–1814* (Tuscaloosa: University of Alabama Press, 2009).

to be "civilized tribes," a term that scholars once used particularly in reference to the postremoval period but now consider ethnocentric.[26]

African American enslavement played an increasing role in the transformation of Native societies. After the Yamasee War slowed the Indian slave trade, Indian slavery gave way to African slavery throughout the South, including among the Cherokees, Chickasaws, Choctaws, and Creeks. By the end of the eighteenth century, drawing on a growing collective identity as Indians, these groups rarely captured or enslaved fellow Natives in warfare. Instead they increasingly targeted African Americans for capture, and when warfare did not meet demand, they purchased them from whites. Using enslaved African American labor, Indian elites and a rising middle class built new commercial enterprises that came to dominate Native politics, and they developed increasingly elaborate laws designed to ensure the transgenerational enslavement of African Americans. By 1830, slaves composed about 20 percent of the Chickasaw Nation, roughly the same as the neighboring state of Tennessee. During the era of removal, masters forced their enslaved peoples to accompany them westward to Indian Territory, where slavery persisted until 1866. Even thereafter, the status of the formerly enslaved remained ill-defined among southern Indians who, like white southerners, often resisted extending the rights of citizenship to African Americans.[27]

Gender

Before the 1990s, histories of the Native South always had been about gender—the male gender. They focused on relations between men, and the trade, wars, and treaties that defined men's public lives. Women remained invisible until European men wanted food, shelter, or sex, but such interactions did not seem

26. Daniel H. Usner Jr., "American Indians on the Cotton Frontier: Changing Economic Relations with Citizens and Slaves in the Mississippi Territory," *Journal of American History* 72 (September 1985): 297–317; Michael D. Green, "The Five Tribes of the Southeastern United States," in *The Historical Atlas of Oklahoma,* ed. Charles Robert Goins, Danney Goble, and James H. Anderson (Norman: University of Oklahoma Press, 2006), 52; Theda Perdue, *Nations Remembered: An Oral History of the Cherokees, Chickasaws, Choctaws, Creeks, and Seminoles, 1865–1907,* pbk. ed. (Norman: University of Oklahoma Press, 1993), ix–x.

27. Snyder, *Slavery in Indian Country;* Barbara Krauthamer, *Black Slaves, Indian Masters: Slavery, Emancipation, and Citizenship in the Native American South* (Chapel Hill: University of North Carolina Press, 2013); Alaina E. Roberts, "Chickasaw Freedpeople at the Crossroads of Reconstruction" (PhD diss., Indiana University, 2017); Melanie Benson Taylor, *Reconstructing the Native South: American Indian Literature and the Lost Cause* (Athens: University of Georgia Press, 2011).

momentous enough for historians to explore. Furthermore, assumptions of male dominance in societies perceived as savage shaped both primary and secondary sources about southern Indians. Disciplines other than history, in contrast, did not ignore southern Indian women, largely because matrilineal kinship systems organized southern Indian societies. When legal scholar John Phillip Reid wrote *A Law of Blood* (1970), he revealed a world in which children inherited their mothers' clan affiliations, and their clan kin became their teachers, protectors, and avengers.[28] Fathers were almost tangential. Instead, mothers' brothers assumed the responsibilities that Europeans delegated to fathers. The chapter on kinship in Charles Hudson's *The Southeastern Indians* (1976)—based largely on John Swanton's early twentieth-century ethnography of the Creeks that Hudson read through the lens of a cultural anthropologist—opened the door for historians of Indigenous women.

Inspired by social history and second-wave feminism, women's history initially focused on women's contributions to the standard narrative. By the time American Indian historians began to write about women in the 1990s and 2000s, however, the field had moved beyond that phase. Scholars addressed Native women's history more analytically and explored how centering on women changed the narrative. As Indian historians read the work of anthropologists, they left behind the portrayal of degraded Indian women that early sources (and the historians who relied on them) had created. In reevaluating the South, historians found that matrilineal kinship, agricultural production by women, and a prominent female presence in religious beliefs and ceremonies gave women an arena of power that balanced that of men. Contrasting Europeans' very different gender norms, scholars discovered opportunities to write historically, rather than merely ethnographically, about Native women. With the exception of religious studies scholar Michelene E. Pesantubbee, who adopted a declension model in *Choctaw Women in a Chaotic World* (2005), most scholars have focused on continuity and adaptation in Native women's lives.[29]

In *Cherokee Women* (1998), Theda Perdue described gender roles of women and men as dynamic but not synchronous. In the eighteenth century, warfare and diplomacy dominated the political lives of Cherokee men, and male economic contributions centered on the deerskin trade. By the end of the century, wars

28. Reid, *A Law of Blood.*

29. Michelene E. Pesantubbee, *Choctaw Women in a Chaotic World: The Clash of Cultures in the Colonial Southeast* (Albuquerque: University of New Mexico Press, 2005).

with Europeans ceased, the deerskin trade dwindled, and traditional sources of male economic and political power shifted. Women, however, continued to operate largely within their traditional arena of power, retaining considerable political authority through their matrilineal kinship system at least until removal. They became a major source of cultural continuity in the face of profound change. Similarly, in *Weaving New Worlds* (1997), Sarah H. Hill used baskets as evidence and metaphor for change among the Eastern Band of Cherokees. Women adopted new materials and styles as their own needs, available materials, and market demands changed, but they remained basket makers as surely as they remained Cherokees.[30]

As Cherokee society became more culturally diverse in Indian Territory, generalizing about gender constructions becomes more difficult. Sources increasingly focused on elite women. Devon A. Mihesuah confronted this problem in *Cultivating the Rosebuds* (1993), a study of the Cherokee Female Seminary, whose students were mostly economically privileged young women. For Mihesuah, the seminary reflected an emerging social, cultural, and economic hierarchy in Cherokee society that, following common usage at the time her book was written, she linked to European ancestry or "blood." In *Cherokee Women in Crisis* (2003), Carolyn Ross Johnston examined women during removal, the Civil War, and the allotment period. As time passed, Johnson found fewer sources that described a more traditional and empowering role for women. Measured against works that focused on an earlier period, Johnston more often found decline than a gendered balance of power. Unlike Mihesuah, she attributed the imbalance in sources to cultural diversity and political inequity.[31]

No work dealt better with the centrality of Native women in twentieth-century southern Indian history than Daniel H. Usner's *Weaving Alliances with Other Women* (2015).[32] Usner explored the relationships that developed between

30. Theda Perdue, *Cherokee Women: Gender and Culture Change, 1700–1835* (Lincoln: University of Nebraska Press, 1998); Sarah H. Hill, *Weaving New Worlds: Southeastern Cherokee Indian Women and Their Basketry* (Chapel Hill: University of North Carolina Press, 1997). See also Virginia Moore Carney, *Eastern Band Cherokee Women: Cultural Persistence in Their Letters and Speeches* (Knoxville: University of Tennessee Press, 2005).

31. Devon A. Mihesuah, *Cultivating the Rosebuds: The Education of Women at the Cherokee Female Seminary, 1851–1909* (Urbana: University of Illinois Press, 1993); Carolyn Ross Johnston, *Cherokee Women in Crisis: Trail of Tears, Civil War, and Allotment, 1838–1907* (Tuscaloosa: University of Alabama Press, 2003).

32. Daniel H. Usner, *Weaving Alliances with Other Women: Chitimacha Indian Work in the New South* (Athens: University of Georgia Press, 2015).

a Chitimacha woman and two elite white women, each of whom represented defining aspects of gender. Victorian philanthropy motivated the first of the white women. The second was a "new woman" engaged in scientific inquiry. And the Chitimacha woman was a basket weaver whose skills formed the basis of relationships with the two white women. These relationships enabled the Chitimachas to secure their land, gain the attention of the Bureau of Indian Affairs, and survive as a people. Women retained power even among a small impoverished tribe in which they did not openly play political roles. Usner provided a rare look not merely at the interstices between Indian and non-Indian women but at the possibilities for bridging those gaps.

Challenges and opportunities remain for historians of Native women in the South. First, most of the scholarship on gender among southern Indians focuses on Cherokees. Other nations in the South—those that removed, remnants that remained, and tribes never targeted for removal—demand attention. Then there is the challenge that confronts all historians: how do we get beyond the histories of elites and reveal the lives of non-elites? The most successful effort to do this is Rose Stremlau's *Sustaining the Cherokee Family* (2011).[33] Although this work is not specifically about women, they are at the heart of Stremlau's study, which she grounded in late nineteenth- and early twentieth-century allotment records. Decades after Perdue's study ended, women's arena of power—subsistence, shelter, kinship—persisted, and women marshalled its strength to cope with radical change.

Religion

Charles Hudson explored Indians' complex explanations for how the world came to be as well as religious beliefs, ceremonies, and codes of behavior, but most scholars of Native southerners have focused on Christianity. This scholarly interest is not necessarily commensurate with that of the historical actors involved: throughout the colonial era and well into the nineteenth century, southern Indians showed far less interest in Christianity than in other aspects of European culture. Efforts to convert Indigenous people to Christianity began with the Spanish, who built missions in Florida and up the Atlantic coast that succeeded mostly as targets for English invasion. Pocahontas became the first English convert, a feat

33. Rose Stremlau, *Sustaining the Cherokee Family: Kinship and the Allotment of an Indigenous Nation* (Chapel Hill: University of North Carolina Press, 2011).

accomplished while, and perhaps because, she was in captivity. In the eighteenth century, the College of William & Mary admitted a few Indians with the intent to convert as well as educate them but met with limited success. Throughout the coastal plains, ministers occasionally preached to Indian communities and even ventured into the Piedmont to spread the Word. Still, Native peoples showed little interest.[34]

In the early nineteenth century, missionaries joined traders and government agents in the interior South as instigators of change. Early efforts seldom succeeded. It took thirteen years for Moravians, who established a mission in the Cherokee Nation in 1800, to acquire their first convert. The Second Great Awakening aroused an overt evangelicalism in other Protestant denominations, and Baptists, Methodists, and the American Board of Commissioners for Foreign Missions (Congregationalists and Presbyterians) began to focus their attention on southern Indian nations. The Civilization Program, which provided funding for mission schools beginning in 1819, offered financial incentive to minister to Indians.[35]

Cherokee, Chickasaw, Choctaw, and Creek nations all admitted missionaries, and tribal leaders enrolled relatives in mission schools.[36] It was a symbiotic relationship: headmen understood the advantages of an English education for their families and fortunes as well as their nations, and missionaries tended to curry favor with prominent families whose hospitality, protection, and influence they enjoyed. It also inspired competition among headmen. Among the Cherokees, the site chosen for the school operated by the American Board of Commissioners for Foreign Missions appeased chiefs jealous of the proximity of the Moravian mission to another chief. Political controversy in the Choctaw Nation led to the establishment of Choctaw Academy in Kentucky, which ultimately attracted students from seventeen different southern and midwestern nations.

Christian missions did not sound the death knell for Indigenous religions. Their survival manifested during times of stress. One such moment was the Creeks' cession of land in Georgia and the construction of the Federal Road

34. Hudson, *Southeastern Indians*, chap. 3; Rountree, *Pocahontas, Powhatan, Opechancanough.*

35. William G. McLoughlin, *Cherokees and Missionaries, 1789–1839* (New Haven: Yale University Press, 1984). Rowena McClinton's volumes are an incredibly rich source on early missions as well as Cherokee life; see *Moravian Springplace Mission to the Cherokees.*

36. Clara Sue Kidwell, *Choctaws and Missionaries in Mississippi, 1818–1918* (Norman: University of Oklahoma Press, 1995).

through their nation, both of which, Angela Pulley Hudson argued, aroused considerable anger. When the Shawnee Tecumseh arrived, his message of renewal and resistance, as Joel W. Martin pointed out in *Sacred Revolt* (1991), became the catalyst for a religious revival among the Creeks and set the stage for the outbreak of the Creek War in 1813.[37] About the same time but unaided by Tecumseh, Cherokees also experienced a religious revival ignited by land cessions. Again, in the 1820s, dances and ceremonies that marked southern Native religions reappeared as pressure for removal increased.

Similarly, reservation and allotment policies of the 1880s and 1890s sparked religious revivals across Indian country, but these revivals were not of the evangelical Christian kind. Although tribes from other regions turned to peyotism and prophets, the Yuchis, a small tribe living under the umbrella of the Creek Nation, inspired southern Indians to meet at ceremonial grounds, make medicine, and perform a sacred dance called, in English, a stomp dance.[38] Their ceremony did not exactly replicate religious rites that early ethnographers recorded or Charles Hudson described in *The Southeastern Indians,* but Indians, after all, are also entitled to change, even in spiritual expressions. The stomp dance, with individual tribal modifications, endured. Native peoples danced as their nations began to reorganize themselves and reemerge in the mid-twentieth century. By the twenty-first century, Oklahoma stomp grounds no longer stood in opposition to Christian churches, if they ever had. Such ceremonies became central to ethnic identity and Native spirituality, often in harmony with Christianity.[39]

Similarly, among Native peoples like the Cherokees, Choctaws, and Seminoles who remained in their traditional homelands, beliefs and practices with long histories persisted. One of the public expressions of ancient culture was stickball. In his work on the Choctaws, anthropologist Kendall Blanchard regarded

37. Martin, *Sacred Revolt.*

38. For Yuchi ceremonial life, see anthropologist Jason Baird Jackson, *Yuchi Ceremonial Life: Performance, Meaning, and Tradition in a Contemporary American Indian Community* (Lincoln: University of Nebraska Press, 2003); Jackson, *Yuchi Folklore: Cultural Expression in a Southeastern Native American Community* (Norman: University of Oklahoma Press, 2013).

39. The following contain mostly primary materials: James H. Howard, *Oklahoma Seminoles: Medicine, Magic, and Religion* (Norman: University of Oklahoma Press, 1984); Alan Kilpatrick, *The Night Has a Naked Soul: Witchcraft and Sorcery Among the Western Cherokee* (Syracuse: Syracuse University Press, 1997); David Lewis Jr. and Ann T. Jordan, *Creek Indian Medicine Ways: The Enduring Power of Mvskoke Religion* (Albuquerque: University of New Mexico Press, 2002). More analytical is Tom Mould, *Choctaw Prophecy: A Legacy of the Future* (Tuscaloosa: University of Alabama Press, 2003).

stickball largely as "play," but Michael J. Zogry's 2014 book on Cherokee stickball demonstrated its deep spiritual significance. Today, stickball coexists comfortably with Christianity in most Native communities.[40]

Race

Race has been a central theme ever since southern history emerged as a distinct field.[41] Throughout early southern history, racial lines were fluid, not just within Native societies but among Americans more generally. In his study of cross-cultural relations along the southern frontier, Andrew K. Frank argued, "most eighteenth-century Creeks and Americans relied on traits that could be learned, practiced, altered, contested, and concealed to determine who was who." Such racial fluidity persisted until Indian removal, as Christina Snyder demonstrated in *Great Crossings* (2017). Snyder's study explored a multiracial community that coalesced in 1825, when Senator Richard M. Johnson founded the first federal Indian school on his Kentucky plantation as a way to foster Indian "civilization," advance his fortunes, and covertly educate some African Americans, including Johnson's biracial daughters. Many Americans shared Johnson's faith that education and opportunity could erase racial distinctions. The vision that Great Crossings encapsulated faded as new views on race, rooted in "science," discredited the idea that Indians could be civilized or African Americans free. The school at Great Crossings closed in 1848, and instead of "collaboration and alliance," the American empire "coalesced around principles of intolerance, exclusion, and racial injustice."[42]

Despite this fluidity, Native Americans developed notions of race. In a groundbreaking 1997 article, "How Indians Got to be Red," Nancy Shoemaker demon-

40. Kendall Blanchard, *Mississippi Choctaws at Play: The Serious Side of Leisure* (Urbana: University of Illinois Press, 1981); Michael J. Zogry, *Anetso, the Cherokee Ball Game: At the Center of Ceremony and Identity* (Chapel Hill: University of North Carolina Press, 2010).

41. Ulrich B. Phillips, "The Central Theme of Southern History," *American Historical Review* 34 (October 1928): 30–43. Historians have denounced his interpretation of white racial superiority. They also have expanded white supremacy as a central theme in analyzing all US history.

42. Andrew K. Frank, *Creeks and Southerners: Biculturalism on the Early American Frontier* (Lincoln: University of Nebraska Press, 2005), 47; Christina Snyder, *Great Crossings: Indians, Settlers, and Slaves in the Age of Jackson* (New York: Oxford University Press, 2017), 315, 317. For more on intellectual and cultural exchange, see Nancy Shoemaker, *A Strange Likeness: Becoming Red and White in Eighteenth-Century North America* (New York: Oxford University Press, 2004).

strated that Native southerners discussed race at least as far back as the early eighteenth century. Native peoples, not Europeans, first called themselves "red." They did so not because of phenotype, but rather for symbolic reasons: in Native southern cultures, red was the opposite of white, the descriptor favored by colonists. Over the eighteenth and early nineteenth centuries, southern Indians developed more elaborate theories of race, influenced by both Euro-Americans and Indian prophets who formulated a nativist, anticolonial ideology.[43]

By the turn of the nineteenth century, the Atlantic model of racial slavery gained currency among Cherokees, Creeks, Choctaws, and Chickasaws, contributing to anti-black racism. Historians long have recognized the existence of chattel slavery among these nations, but racial assumptions about Indians often tainted their perspective. For example, Annie Heloise Abel, who authored a trilogy on the five southern nations in Indian Territory, wrote that Indians became slaveholders because they had "an aversion to work." Influenced by studies in comparative slavery, Theda Perdue traced the transformation of slavery from an ethnohistorical perspective in *Slavery and the Evolution of Cherokee Society, 1540–1866* (1979).[44] She concluded that the nature of slaveholding tended to vary with the cultural orientation of masters, even on the eve of the Civil War.

Many Indians retained familial ties to people of African descent. In *Black, White, and Indian* (2005), Claudio Saunt described the disintegration of the Creek Grayson family in which one sibling abandoned her African American husband and children, remarried a Creek, and became a slaveholder while her brother remained with and emancipated his African American wife and children. Tiya Miles traced generations of the biracial Shoeboots family since the early nineteenth century in *Ties That Bind* (2005). The marriage of a Cherokee man and an enslaved African American woman led to generations of contested identity and legal status. Celia E. Naylor presented a different view, one in which Cherokees and "African Cherokees" shared a cultural and social life, in *African Cherokees in Indian Territory* (2008).[45]

43. Nancy Shoemaker, "How Indians Got to be Red," *American Historical Review* 102 (June 1997): 625–44.

44. Annie Heloise Abel, *The Slaveholding Indians,* 3 vols. (Cleveland: A. C. Clark, 1915–1925), 1:46; Perdue, *Slavery and the Evolution of Cherokee Society.*

45. Claudio Saunt, *Black, White, and Indian: Race and the Unmaking of an American Family* (New York: Oxford University Press, 2005); Tiya Miles, *Ties That Bind: The Story of an Afro-Cherokee Family in Slavery and Freedom* (Berkeley: University of California Press, 2005); Celia E. Naylor, *African Cherokees in Indian Territory: From Chattels to Citizens* (Chapel Hill: University North Carolina Press, 2008). Miles

Growing opposition to marriage with African Americans did not carry over to intermarriage with whites. In the colonial period, most interracial marriages united white men and Native women. Under the matrilineal kinship system of southern Indians, the children of these unions belonged to the family and nation of their mother. In the nineteenth century, Native men, especially elite men, occasionally married white women. In *The Heathen School* (2014), John Demos contrasted the reactions of whites and Cherokees when two Cherokee students at a New England school married local white women. Locals forced the school to close, and the Cherokees took their brides back to their nation.[46]

In response to the episode in New England, the Cherokee National Council extended citizenship to intermarried white women. Such laws did not apply to intermarried African Americans and became part of a systematic effort by southern Indians to use sovereignty to create a racial divide. In *Race and the Cherokee Nation* (2008), Fay A. Yarbrough skillfully demonstrated how laws regulating interracial marriage shaped racial ideology among the Cherokees, one that has endured into the twenty-first century.[47]

In *Blood Politics* (2002), Circe Sturm pointed out that "for white Cherokees, having a little Indian blood has proven to be a valuable commodity, ensuring them a political identity and access to economic resources in the Cherokee Nation. The Cherokee freedmen have not fared so well, oppressed as they are by the logic of hypodescent that denies their Cherokee blood while it emphasizes their social and political blackness."[48] She suggested as well that Cherokees conflated culture and race, so that the greater the Cherokee ancestry, the more traditional culture a person was thought to maintain. That is, the full-blood/mixed blood dichotomy is alive and well in the Cherokee Nation and much of Indian country.

Historical distinctions between white and Indian exerted almost as much power in the South as that between white and black. Often obscured by land

---

examined the household dynamics and legacy of the Cherokee Nation's largest slaveholder in *The House on Diamond Hill: A Cherokee Plantation Story* (Chapel Hill: University of North Carolina Press, 2010).

46. John Demos, *The Heathen School: A Story of Hope and Betrayal in the Age of the Early Republic* (New York: Alfred A. Knopf, 2014). See also Ann McGrath, *Illicit Love: Interracial Sex and Marriage in the United States and Australia* (Lincoln: University of Nebraska Press, 2015).

47. Fay A. Yarbrough, *Race and the Cherokee Nation: Sovereignty in the Nineteenth Century* (Philadelphia: University of Pennsylvania Press, 2008).

48. Circe Sturm, *Blood Politics: Race, Culture, and Identity in the Cherokee Nation of Oklahoma* (Berkeley: University of California Press, 2002), 203–4.

hunger, political ambitions, and factionalism, the movement to expel Indians from the South also was riddled by racism. In *The Legal Ideology of Indian Removal* (2002), Tim Alan Garrison demonstrated how the rise of racial determinism in the early nineteenth century induced whites to dismiss the achievements of individual Indians as superficial and declare the prognosis for the race as dismal. Court cases arising from removal "forced southern judges to think about race in a context beyond the master-slave relationship."[49] These cases and Indian removal itself became foundations for racial segregation.

Southern Indians in Oklahoma became legally white with Oklahoma statehood in 1907 (although informal discrimination persisted), but Indians remaining in the South struggled with black/white segregation. Most southern states classified Indians alongside African Americans as "colored," but by the late nineteenth century, some states developed a three-tiered system of Jim Crow. The three remnants of removed tribes—Cherokees, Choctaws, and Seminoles—had no difficulty defining themselves racially since they spoke their Native languages and publicly performed their "Indianness." That did not obliterate the racism directed toward them or the exploitation they endured, as Katherine M. B. Osburn demonstrated in *Choctaw Resurgence in Mississippi* (2014).[50] But no one seriously questioned their identity as Indians. The fact that they were not white was enough for those who stole their land, forced them into sharecropping, enslaved them through peonage, denied them the vote, and subjected them to violence and intimidation.

In both Oklahoma and the South, the Ku Klux Klan and other white terrorists targeted Indians as well as African Americans. In *Seminole Burning* (1996), Daniel F. Littlefield Jr. raised compelling questions about the guilt of two Seminole teenagers lynched in 1898 for the murder of a white woman. The Klan touched Indians in many ways. In the 1920s, for example, the Klan targeted a Catholic church that served a Mississippi Choctaw community. Somewhat later, a Klansman served as a Choctaw Agency farmer, and in 1964, a Choctaw man discovered the bodies of three murdered civil rights workers. In North Carolina, the Grand Dragon of the North Carolina KKK spearheaded a 1958 rally to intimidate Lum-

49. Tim Alan Garrison, *The Legal Ideology of Removal: The Southern Judiciary and the Sovereignty of Native American Nations* (Athens: University of Georgia Press, 2002), 8.

50. Katherine M. B. Osburn, *Choctaw Resurgence in Mississippi: Race, Class, and Nation Building in the Jim Crow South, 1830–1977* (Lincoln: University of Nebraska Press, 2014).

bees, but the tribe fought back and routed the Klan in what became known as the Battle of Hayes Pond.[51]

Whites found it simpler to discriminate against and menace Native peoples who had no association with the removed nations, often by denying that they were Indians. As Helen Rountree pointed out in *Pocahontas's People* (1990), Virginia's Racial Integrity Law of 1924 made it almost impossible legally to claim an Indian identity despite the presence of thousands of Indians in the state. Classified as "colored," they went to African American public schools (or their own church schools), sat in the balconies of movie theaters, and used "colored" restrooms and water fountains. They could not legally marry "whites" until Mildred Jeter, who self-identified as a Rappahannock Indian, and Richard Loving, a white man, challenged the law and, in 1967, won their case in the United States Supreme Court.[52]

Unlike Virginia, North Carolina politicians recognized the state's Indian tribes in the 1880s and set up a separate school system for their children. But when federal officials considered extending recognition to Lumbees in the 1930s, a problem emerged. Lumbees spoke English and shared many of the customs of their white and black neighbors. Furthermore, their physical appearance fit no single phenotype. In her study of Lumbee Indians and Jim Crow, Malinda Maynor Lowery recounted how officials from Washington, DC, tried to determine whether or not Lumbees were Indians by probing, scratching, and measuring a small group of Lumbees.[53] The study produced inconsistent results with even siblings exhibiting different racial features. Could people who did not "look" like Indians really be Indians?

51. Daniel F. Littlefield Jr., *Seminole Burning: A Story of Racial Vengeance* (Jackson: University Press of Mississippi, 1996); Osburn, *Choctaw Resurgence in Mississippi;* Malinda Maynor Lowery, *Lumbee Indians in the Jim Crow South: Race, Identity, and the Making of a Nation* (Chapel Hill: University of North Carolina Press, 2010).

52. Christopher Arris Oakley, *Keeping the Circle: American Indian Identity in Eastern North Carolina, 1885–2004* (Lincoln: University of Nebraska Press, 2005); Rountree, *Pocahontas's People.* See also Samuel R. Cook, *Monacans and Miners: Native Americans and Coal Mining Communities in Appalachia* (Lincoln: University of Nebraska Press, 2000), 124–34. Peter Wallenstein puts this case in a broader context of marital discrimination in *Race, Sex, and the Freedom to Marry:* Loving v. Virginia (Lawrence: University Press of Kansas, 2014). For the case as part of Virginia's racial history, see Arica L. Coleman, *That the Blood Stay Pure: African Americans, Native Americans, and the Predicament of Race and Identity in Virginia* (Bloomington: Indiana University Press, 2013), 153–75. For another study of white efforts to marginalize and erase Indians from the Jim Crow South, see Theda Perdue, *Race and the Atlanta Cotton States Exposition of 1895* (Athens: University of Georgia Press, 2010).

53. Lowery, *Lumbee Indians in the Jim Crow South.*

Given the weight placed on "authorities," how historians label people can shape their perceived and even legal identity. An earlier generation of scholars placed Indian communities who had no formal relationship with the United States in the category of "tri-racial isolate."[54] Scholars have begun to set the record straight. Christopher Arris Oakley analyzed the impact of segregation on North Carolina tribes that did not have federal recognition and how they managed to sustain or reclaim their Native identity. Anthropologist Brian Klopotek's study of the struggles of three Louisiana tribes to achieve recognition argued that segregation actually strengthened the racial identity of three small Louisiana tribes and helped them lay claim to their political sovereignty.[55]

Like Rountree, Lowery, Oakley, and Klopotek, scholars tend to follow the racial/ethnic designation that communities themselves use, but that, too, raises problems. What about groups with no historical and cultural experience as Indians and whose members have little or no Native ancestry? What about people who simply lay claim to an Indian identity just because family lore includes an Indian great-great-grandmother for whom corroboration is lacking? In *Real Indians* (2003), Eva Marie Garroutte examined the problems that such claims, as well as the acceleration of intermarriage of Indians and non-Indians, posed for Indians. What does it mean if ultimately everyone is an Indian? Somewhat more optimistically, in *Becoming Indian* (2011), Circe Sturm suggested that the increase in claims of Indian identity points to growing acceptance of Indians and declining racism.[56]

Becoming a citizen of an Indian nation involved—and continues to involve—far more than claiming ancestry. Under the principle of tribal sovereignty, each Indigenous nation holds the legal right to establish citizenship criteria. Many factors entered into such decisions, but one of the most powerful was what colloquially (and offensively) is referred to as "blood quantum." In the late nineteenth century, the United States began defining Indian people by racial fractions, and many Indian nations subsequently adopted the practice. In *Who Belongs?* (2016),

54. For example, Brewton Berry, *Almost White* (New York: Macmillan, 1963); Virginia Easley DeMarce, "Looking at Legends—Lumbee and Melungeon: Applied Genealogy and the Origins of Tri-racial Isolate Settlements," *National Genealogical Society Quarterly* 81 (March 1993): 240–45.

55. Oakley, *Keeping the Circle;* Brian Klopotek, *Recognition Odysseys: Indigeneity, Race, and Federal Tribal Recognition Policy in Three Louisiana Indian Communities* (Durham: Duke University Press, 2011).

56. Eva Marie Garroutte, *Real Indians: Identity and the Survival of Native America* (Berkeley: University of California Press, 2003); Circe Sturm, *Becoming Indian: The Struggle over Cherokee Identity in the Twenty-first Century* (Santa Fe: School for Advanced Research Press, 2011).

Mikaëla M. Adams explored how six southern tribes resolved the issue of tribal citizenship. Long before the era of casino gaming, Indian nations sought to restrict citizenship so that they could protect resources. One of Adams's most novel contributions was her argument that, despite grossly unequal power relations, Indian nations tried to adapt or, in some cases, challenge racialist state and federal Indian policies. Even those who instituted a minimum blood quantum interpreted it in their own way: while United States officials believed (erroneously) that it measured biological Indianness, for Native people "blood became an index for how connected an individual was to the tribal community." Ultimately, each tribe adopted differing criteria, which might have included residency, cultural affiliation, and gendered notions of kinship as well as ancestry.[57]

Race also shapes the politics of citizenship in present-day Oklahoma. In the late twentieth century, the Cherokee Nation took steps to deny citizenship to Cherokee freedmen, who had been citizens since 1866. In 2017 the freedmen won their suit for Cherokee citizenship in United States federal court, a decision that both challenged tribal sovereignty and brought racial justice. Tribal sovereignty, recognized and embodied in treaties, has been the holy grail for most historians of Native America, but the concept raised troubling issues when Native nations used their sovereignty to exclude people based on race. How Indian nations arrived at this point is likely to be one of the most challenging future topics for historians.

Politics and Sovereignty

Despite relentless assaults, southern nations sought to retain their sovereignty, and scholarly interest in how Native peoples articulated, defended, and reimagined their polities is longstanding. Classic works such as Henry Thompson Malone's *Cherokees of the Old South* (1956) explored the Cherokees' transformation from an eighteenth-century group bound by culture, language, and kinship to a nineteenth-century nation-state that championed education, literacy, and economic development as keys to retaining self-government. The transformation was, at times, hampered by factional disputes which Malone described as a battle between "progressives" (those who favored adopting or adapting aspects of Western culture) and "traditionalists" (those who resisted outside influences).

57. Mikaëla M. Adams, *Who Belongs? Race, Resources, and Tribal Citizenship in the New South* (New York: Oxford University Press, 2016), 213.

Many scholars agreed with Malone, highlighting factionalism as central to Native polities and even adopting his terminology.[58]

With the publication of *The Politics of Indian Removal* (1982), Michael D. Green became the first ethnohistorian to write a political history of a southern Indian nation. Green offered a new view of factionalism. Although many scholars associated "full-bloods" with traditionalism and "mixed-bloods" with progressivism, Green critiqued this approach, demonstrating that culture (especially the strength or weakness of one's ties to a Creek town) was more important in determining political positions. Previous scholarship portrayed factionalism as detrimental, but Green argued that it benefited Creeks throughout the colonial period. Because factions developed alliances with different imperial powers, Creek leaders readily engaged in play-off diplomacy. As the United States rose to power, Chief Alexander McGillivray reorganized and centralized Creek government, usurping authority that formerly rested with clans or towns. For Green, the pivotal moment in Creek political history came in the aftermath of the Red Stick War as Creeks struggled to reconcile and rebuild. Despite lingering anxiety about centralized government, the Creek National Council executed William McIntosh for the capital crime of selling land. Then Creeks protested the resulting Treaty of Indian Springs (1825), forcing the abrogation of the treaty in favor of the more favorable Treaty of Washington, a unique feat in Native political history. In Green's words, "No native nation had ever before persuaded the United States to tear up a ratified treaty, and none would ever succeed again."[59]

William G. McLoughlin studied Cherokee history as means to understand nationalism, politics, and race continentally, even globally. In his masterful *Cherokee Renascence in the New Republic* (1986), McLoughlin placed Cherokee nation-building at the vanguard of the Romantic nationalist movement of the nineteenth century by arguing that they, like their European contemporaries, "concluded that national identity rested upon a cultural heritage imbedded in history, language, culture, and a distinct and identifiable 'homeland.'" In the early 1800s, as Cherokees faced an aggressively expansionist United States empire, they relied on "traditional" elements such as kinship but also layered new "tests of Cherokee identity," namely residence within specific boundaries and allegiance to the Cherokee state. In a centralizing process that outpaced that

58. Malone, *Cherokees of the Old South.*

59. Michael D. Green, *The Politics of Indian Removal: Creek Government and Society in Crisis* (Lincoln: University of Nebraska Press, 1982), 125.

of the Creek Nation, Cherokees revolutionized their government in the 1820s, establishing a three-branch central government modeled on the United States. Like Malone and Green, McLoughlin noted the internal strife generated by this transformation, but he ultimately concluded that this "renascence" triumphed because most Cherokee leaders believed that "economic self-sufficiency and political self-determination" would preserve their nation.[60]

Building on McLoughlin's work, Steven C. Hahn and Julie L. Reed explored how Indian nationalists drew on pre-existing webs of kinship and culture. In *The Invention of the Creek Nation* (2004), Hahn analyzed the dual origins of the Creek Nation. In what he called "aboriginal nationhood," Creeks stressed their widespread (though not universal) Muscogee language as well as cultural and religious traditions. Hahn argued that ambitious chiefs built on this foundation to forge "legal nationhood," a process by which Creek leaders legitimized their own authority and formalized the territorial bounds of their country in a way intelligible to European powers. According to Julie L. Reed, such reinvention also occurred in the Cherokee Nation. Traditionally, Cherokee clans took charge of social welfare, but in the early nineteenth century, as part of the United States' Civilization Program, missionaries entered the nation and replicated or replaced some of these social services. In the wake of removal, however, the Cherokee national government expanded its mission and assumed authority over education, poor relief, orphan care, and healthcare. Adapting traditional kinship responsibilities, the Cherokee state took a leading role in administering social welfare in order to strengthen tribal sovereignty and transmit Cherokee culture.[61]

Izumi Ishii explored another aspect of Cherokee state-building by examining how the Cherokee Nation tried to regulate alcohol. Like Paul Kelton, Ishii strenuously critiqued biological determinism by arguing that Cherokee struggles with alcohol emanated from colonialism. Alcohol, in the form of an inexpensive rum called *taffia*, became a major trade good in the seventeenth century. Hard liquor was novel, and chiefs soon realized that excessive consumption and alcohol dependency threated their communities. At the same time, these problems, accord-

60. William G. McLoughlin, *Cherokee Renascence in the New Republic* (Princeton: Princeton University Press, 1986), xvii, 277.

61. Steven C. Hahn, *The Invention of the Creek Nation, 1670–1763* (Lincoln: University of Nebraska Press, 2004); Julie L. Reed, *Serving the Nation: Cherokee Sovereignty and Social Welfare, 1800–1907* (Norman: University of Oklahoma Press, 2016).

ing to Ishii, presented leaders with an opportunity to exercise tribal sovereignty. Beginning in the eighteenth century, several southern Indian nations began to regulate and tax alcohol, and in the early 1800s, many Native communities started temperance societies. Indian removal, however, exacerbated alcohol-related problems in two ways: before removal, southern states, which did not regulate alcohol, extended their laws over Indian nations; and the trauma of removal coupled with the ready availability of alcohol led to violence and addiction. Ishii carried her story to Indian Territory and explored how Cherokees, especially women, rebuilt the temperance movement by joining with the Women's Christian Temperance Union.[62]

Andrew Denson also bridged the divide between pre- and postremoval in his exploration of nineteenth-century Cherokee political thought. During the removal crisis, Cherokee political leaders developed a corpus of arguments to defend sovereignty: a nation-to-nation relationship with the United States based upon treaty making; a shared culture of republican virtue; and, to counter the myth that Indians were a primitive people doomed to extinction, their achievements in progress and "civilization." Marshalling legal and moral arguments for the survival of Indian nations in a federalist system of divided sovereignty, Cherokees repeatedly pushed back against aggressive colonial demands for Indian land and resources. Although United States leaders argued that "development and progress necessitated the end of tribal autonomy," Cherokees argued that Indian nations were the vehicle for change, "the *key* to modernity for Native people."[63]

The minority of southern Indians who managed to avoid removal and remain in their homelands faced tremendous challenges to their political autonomy. Under the United States government's allotment policy (1887–1934), southern Indian nations lost at least ninety million acres of land. However, the Eastern Band of Cherokees took advantage of the Progressive era's strong protection of corporations, winning title to their land and then securing it by incorporating under state law. Still, the Eastern Band of Cherokees realized that they needed economic self-sufficiency to retain their communities, and they exploited opportunities that ranged from logging to tourism. How they achieved such economic

62. Izumi Ishii, *Bad Fruits of the Civilized Tree: Alcohol & the Sovereignty of the Cherokee Nation* (Lincoln: University of Nebraska Press, 2008).

63. Andrew Denson, *Demanding the Cherokee Nation: Indian Autonomy and American Culture, 1830–1900* (Lincoln: University of Nebraska Press, 2004), 6.

accomplishments is the subject of Christopher Arris Oakley's *New South Indians* (2018), which explained the tribal council's decision in the 1990s to embark on casino gaming.[64]

Indians in the postremoval South also looked for ways to bolster political power. Until the 1930s, federal recognition was a liability that made Indian land and other resources vulnerable to oversight and confiscation. But the New Deal brought change. For Native people, the most important legislation was the Indian Reorganization Act (1934), which provided a path for communities to reconstitute tribal governments and reassemble a land base. Though many in Indian country critiqued the rigidity of the policy, Indians who remained in the South found it particularly useful because, after removal, southern states had outlawed their governments and taken control of much of their land. Harry A. Kersey Jr.'s study of the Seminoles and Miccosukees demonstrated how those peoples used the Indian New Deal to facilitate self-determination by building reservation communities, unifying under tribal governments, and developing a cattle ranching industry.[65]

The rise of casino gaming in the 1990s also reconfigured Native political and economic power. Today, the majority of federally recognized tribes in the lower forty-eight states have developed gaming enterprises, grossing $31.2 billion in fiscal year 2016, for example. However, that revenue is unevenly distributed; most Indian nations realize a modest profit that is used to fund tribal services like healthcare and education. In both Oklahoma and the postremoval South, however, Native nations capitalized on their proximity to large population centers to develop especially successful gaming operations. The achievement confounds non-Indian expectations, as Jessica R. Cattelino observed: "In both American popular culture and classic Western social theory, money and capitalism are often identified with an essentialized modernity, and as such are understood to erode or dissolve cultural and individual distinctiveness." Seminoles disagree and use their gaming wealth to protect their distinctive identity through language revitalization, cultural preservation programs, eldercare, and more. Scholars such as

64. John R. Finger, *The Eastern Band of Cherokees, 1819–1900* (Knoxville: University of Tennessee Press, 1984); Finger, *Cherokee Americans: The Eastern Band of Cherokees in the Twentieth Century* (Lincoln: University of Nebraska Press, 1991); Christopher Arris Oakley, *New South Indians: Tribal Economics and the Eastern Band of Cherokee in the Twentieth Century* (Knoxville: University of Tennessee Press, 2018).

65. Finger, *Cherokee Americans;* Harry A. Kersey Jr., *The Florida Seminoles and the New Deal, 1933–1942* (Boca Raton: Florida Atlantic University Press, 1989).

Cattelino, by critiquing Western constructions of modernity, demonstrated that varied aspects of capitalism—wage labor, industry, and entrepreneurship—are central to modern Indigenous history.[66]

Cattelino is among a group of scholars expanding notions of sovereignty. She demonstrated that Florida Seminoles consider sovereignty not just "a politico-legal status" but also "cultural, moral, and material." That is, true sovereignty allows a nation greater autonomy over nonpolitical aspects of life—more opportunities to speak one's native tongue, or the means for cultural insiders to build their own tribal museum. Even in the political realm, sovereignty should not be "measured along a singular axis of autonomy and dependency," according to Cattelino. Instead, all nations, including Indian nations, are embedded in a network of obligations. Florida Seminoles have engaged with outside polities on four levels: tribe-to-tribe diplomacy; participation in regional communities through the states, educational institutions, and philanthropy; as domestic nations in the United States federal system; and, with the purchase of the Hard Rock hotel and casino empire in 2006, through a tribally owned corporation with a presence in dozens of countries around the world.[67]

There are many tribal histories left to write. The vast majority of historical scholarship has focused on the five removed tribes, especially the Cherokee and Creek nations. Scholars who expanded beyond these nations explored the diversity of the Native South, where each group's culture, history, and goals shaped politics. Mikaëla M. Adams demonstrated that, even when confronted with the same Jim Crow policies, tribal governments responded quite differently, drawing on their own experiences to navigate separate courses to the future. Rejecting a static or monolithic view of Indigenous groups, Malinda Maynor Lowery argued that "geographic movement (rather than attachment to one specific place) and expansive attitudes about adoption and cultural exchange (resulting in racial mixing and cultural adaptation) more accurately describe Indian groups historically."[68]

66. Jessica R. Cattelino, *High Stakes: Florida Seminole Gaming and Sovereignty* (Durham: Duke University Press, 2008), 12.

67. Cattelino, *High Stakes*, 139–40, 162. See also Daniel H. Usner Jr., *Indian Work: Language and Livelihood in Native American History* (Cambridge: Harvard University Press, 2009); Alexandra Harmon, *Rich Indians: Native People and the Problem of Wealth in American History* (Chapel Hill: University of North Carolina Press, 2013).

68. Adams, *Who Belongs?*; Lowery, *Lumbee Indians in the Jim Crow South*, xii.

Among the region's understudied groups are the Petit Nations, lower Mississippi Valley groups who weathered a series of invasions, wars, and epidemics but survived because of interdependency, namely their alliances with external Indian nations and European empires. Elizabeth Ellis, who pieced together the eighteenth-century history of the Petit Nations, contrasted their experiences with those of the five removed tribes that coalesced after the fall of Mississippian chiefdoms as disparate towns weaved political alliances to forge new nations. But coalescence, as Ellis explained, was "neither the obvious nor logical response to dealing with enemy Indians . . . or colonialism." Because of their small size and histories of interdependence, federal officials overlooked Petit Nations during Indian removal, and most of them managed to remain in or near their homelands. As Ellis and other scholars continue to explore little-studied corners of the Native South, we will gain new perspectives on sovereignty, colonialism, and citizenship.[69]

Research on the Native South has been at the forefront of one of the most powerful historiographical trends: the quest to overcome the parochial bounds of region and nation-state in favor of transnational stories that speak to global history. Native American history encourages scholars to expand the scope of their analysis in a different way, not just geographically and culturally, but also temporally by placing the European invasion of the Americas in the context of a complex Indigenous history stretching back thousands of years. As Theda Perdue argued in her 2011 Southern Historical Association presidential address, "Indians provide us with an opportunity to examine different experiences and perspectives in the history of the South, ones that do not follow the standard narrative but instead promise both to challenge and to enrich it."[70]

69. Elizabeth Ellis, "The Many Ties of the Petites Nations: Relationships, Power, and Diplomacy in the Lower Mississippi Valley, 1685–1785" (PhD diss., University of North Carolina at Chapel Hill, 2015), 13.

70. Theda Perdue, "The Legacy of Indian Removal," *Journal of Southern History* 78 (February 2012): 3–36, quote on 36.

SOUTHERN RELIGIOUS HISTORY

John M. Giggie and Paul Harvey

The modern epoch of scholarship on southern religious history arrived with Samuel Hill's *Southern Churches in Crisis* (1967) and John Lee Eighmy's *Churches in Cultural Captivity* (1972), and since then, studies of Christianity in the South moved in two basic directions: the first is a more traditional line of scholarly inquiry focused on the "cultural captivity" of whites. These studies, mostly by white men from the civil rights era, grappled with the all-too-evident moral failings of white southern churches, particularly seeking explanations for the often violent resistance to the civil rights movement. In *Religion in the Old South* (1977), for example, Donald G. Mathews centered white theologians and evangelical believers as the major actors; other historical subjects surround them but are acted upon rather than acting themselves.[1]

Another line of inquiry moved beyond the reigning paradigm of the culturally captive, white evangelical South to more expansive readings into concerns about religion, politics, culture, gender, sexuality, and identity. Scholarship traced a long narrative arc of the South originating as a polyglot region that moved gradually toward religious homogeneity dominated by white and black evangelical Protestants, and by the late twentieth century, was beginning to return to a more multireligious and multiracial society. Southern religious history increasingly incorporated diverse stories, ranging from the Powhatan Confederacy in early Virginia to Moravians in North Carolina, Spiritualists in New Orleans, and Jews and Catholics.[2] So too did immigrants become historical subjects as they trans-

1. Donald G. Mathews, *Religion in the Old South* (Chicago: University of Chicago Press, 1977); Samuel S. Hill, *Southern Churches in Crisis* (New York: Holt, Rinehart & Winston, 1967); John Lee Eighmy, *Churches in Cultural Captivity* (Knoxville: University of Tennessee Press, 1972).

2. For Catholics, see Emily Clark, *Masterless Mistresses: The New Orleans Ursulines and the Development of a New World Society, 1727–1834* (Chapel Hill: University of North Carolina Press, 2007); Emily Suzanne

formed Sunbelt cities such as Atlanta and Charlotte (and even smaller southern regional centers such as Dalton, Georgia) into places where Hindus, Buddhists, Muslims, and Latinx Catholics established their own places of worship alongside more traditional white evangelical churches such as the Southern Baptists and Methodists.[3] The new narrative situated the era of evangelical dominance in its proper context: the *longue durée* of a region constantly changing and beset by turmoil and internal frictions.[4]

Attention to immigrants, in particular, addresses one of the basic tensions within southern historiography: the South's central role in fashioning a globalized world economy (including a circulation of people and ideas as well as goods) versus a regional provincialism marked by hostility to outside ideas. For much of the nineteenth and twentieth centuries, the South's dominant evangelical establishment was internally focused and often repressive. The consequences of this cultural tension produced art and music that reached world audiences.[5]

Since the 1980s, historians relocated the South out of its regional ghetto and into dialogue with scholarship on the Atlantic World (for early America), the global world of nineteenth-century capitalism and religion, and international movements for civil and human rights and decolonization across the twentieth century. And although evangelical Protestantism ostensibly centers on doctrine,

---

Clark, *A Luminous Brotherhood: Afro-Creole Spiritualism in Nineteenth-Century New Orleans* (Chapel Hill: University of North Carolina Press, 2016); Michael Pasquier, *Fathers on the Frontier: French Missionaries and the Roman Catholic Priesthood in the United States, 1789–1870* (New York: Oxford University Press, 2010).

3. See, for example, Khyati Y. Joshi and Jigna Desai, eds., *Asian Americans in Dixie: Race and Migration in the South* (Urbana: University of Illinois Press, 2013); Corrie E. Norman and Don S. Armentrout, eds., *Religion in the Contemporary South: Changes, Continuities, and Contexts* (Knoxville: University of Tennessee Press, 2005).

4. For syntheses of the early religious history of the South, see Jon Sensbach, "Before the Bible Belt: Indians, Africans, and the New Synthesis of Eighteenth-Century Southern Religious History," in *Religion in the South: Protestants and Others in History and Culture,* ed. Beth Barton Schweiger and Donald G. Mathews (Chapel Hill: University of North Carolina Press, 2004), 5–30; Rebecca Goetz, ed., "Religion in the Early South: A Roundtable Edited by Rebecca Goetz," *Journal of Southern Religion* 14 (2012), http://jsr.fsu.edu/issues/vo114/ (accessed 18 January 2019).

5. Paul Harvey, *Christianity and Race in the American South: A History* (Chicago: University of Chicago Press, 2016); Randall J. Stephens, *The Devil's Music: How Christians Inspired, Condemned, and Embraced Rock 'n' Roll* (Cambridge: Harvard University Press, 2018); John M. Giggie, *After Redemption: Jim Crow and the Transformation of African American Religion in the Delta, 1875–1915* (New York: Oxford University Press, 2008); John Hayes, *Hard, Hard Religion: Interracial Faith in the Poor South* (Chapel Hill: University of North Carolina Press, 2017).

scholars increasingly emphasized religious practices expressed through art, music, folklore, and products of material culture, expanding the field of the sacred and breaking the bounds of what typically has been regarded as "southern religion."[6]

The Colonial South

Historians of religion, race, and culture in the early South revealed a region dramatically different from the South as popularly conceived. Before the South was partly evangelical, it was largely not Christian. Before it was dominated by a white master class and populated by black slaves in an expansive United States, it was a multicultural and multipolar region. English Protestants and Catholics, French Catholics and Huguenots, German Anabaptists, and African Muslims and Catholics inhabited localized worlds linked to international patterns of expansion, trade, and proselytization.[7]

Competition between the Spanish in Florida and the English in South Carolina, and the immense slave trade in Indian bodies, shaped the religious and social history of the early Southeast. That struggle, as scholars have made clear, became part of an apocalyptic vision of English-Protestant versus Catholic-Spanish conflict. Florida was, for Spanish Catholics, the outpost for the spread of the one true faith; Virginia served that purpose for Protestants; and in between the two Carolinas became an important battleground for both political and religious reasons.[8]

Seventeenth-century English entrepreneurs had a diverse set of reasons for colonization, "from the most devout hope of spreading God's holy word to the basest search for booty," wrote historian Edward L. Bond. As Bond argued in *Damned Souls in a Tobacco Colony* (2000), the conventional designation of Virginia as the mercantilist colony and New England as the religious settlement understates the importance of religion to the architects of the Virginia colony. The English who conceived of Virginia's settlement employed the supernatural

6. Carol Crown, ed., *Coming Home! Self-Taught Artists, the Bible, and the American South* (Jackson: University Press of Mississippi, 2004).

7. Goetz, ed., "Religion in the Early South."

8. Amy Turner Bushnell, "The Sacramental Imperative: Catholic Ritual and Indian Sedentism in the Provinces of Florida," in *Columbian Consequences: Archaeological and Historical Perspectives on the Spanish Borderlands East,* ed. David Hurst Thomas, 2 vols. (Washington, DC: Smithsonian Institution Press, 1989), 2: 475–90; Jerald T. Milanich, *Laboring in the Fields of the Lord: Spanish Missions and Southeastern Indians* (Washington, DC: Smithsonian Institution Press, 1999); David S. Williams, *From Mounds to Megachurches: Georgia's Religious Heritage* (Athens: University of Georgia Press, 2008).

world to explain their mission, justify wars and conquests, and comprehend how God would have them govern the world. Frequent violent conflicts with Native peoples quickly soured the English Virginians' providential thinking, transforming their earlier visions of a city on a hill into a settlement set upon a swamp. Declining social conditions forced the "damned souls" of the Virginia tobacco colony eventually (if unintentionally) to put into place a religious culture that presaged a degree of religious toleration (for other Christian groups but not for Native or African traditions). Virginia's Protestants and Maryland's Catholics, for example, coexisted peaceably.[9]

Moreover, Anglican polity and theology itself was in flux. Besides some commonly held sentiments in the *Book of Common Prayer,* few specific theological precepts bound English Atlantic worshippers. Behavior mattered far more than belief, for Anglicans understood right conduct as the path to salvation. By the early eighteenth century, Anglicanism took hold less by its institutional presence than by its ritual practice in white households, a feature of colonial Virginia explored expertly in Rhys Isaac's *The Transformation of Virginia* (1982) and in Lauren F. Winner's *A Cheerful and Comfortable Faith* (2010).[10]

Anglican emphasis on right conduct, however, had difficulty reconciling with the emergence of racialized slavery. As some slaves converted to Christianity, white colonists questioned whether baptism required freedom. Historians have been intent on documenting white southerners' answers to that question. As a result, Christianity and enslavement became competing categories in colonial law as colonists attempted to resolve the ambiguous status of black slaves and the tradition that slavery was for "heathen" others, not fellow Christians. By the early eighteenth century, white Virginians legally defined slavery as a status for non-Christians. Twenty-first-century historians expanded on the work of an older generation of scholars, notably Winthrop D. Jordan, who traced the evolution of ideas of racial hierarchy. Katharine Gerbner demonstrated how religious divisions drawn by Europeans became part of defining race. "European" or "English" meant "Christian."[11]

9. Edward L. Bond, *Damned Souls in a Tobacco Colony: Religion in Seventeenth-Century Virginia* (Macon: Mercer University Press, 2000).

10. Rhys Isaac, *The Transformation of Virginia, 1740–1790* (Chapel Hill: University of North Carolina Press, 1982); Lauren F. Winner, *A Cheerful and Comfortable Faith: Anglican Religious Practice in the Elite Households of Eighteenth-Century Virginia* (New Haven: Yale University Press, 2010).

11. Harvey, *Christianity and Race in the American South,* 19–25; Winthrop D. Jordan, *The White Man's Burden: Historical Origins of Racism in the United States* (New York: Oxford University Press, 1974);

In *The Baptism of Early Virginia* (2012), Rebecca Anne Goetz explained the process whereby religion created race and race thereafter shaped religion. In 1705, Virginians enumerated the status of free and unfree people: "all servants imported and brought into this country . . . who were not Christians in their native country . . . before they were shipped . . . shall be accounted and be slaves, and as such be here bought and sold notwithstanding a conversion to Christianity afterwards."[12] Conversion in the form of baptism, then, did not affect a person's status as enslaved or free. The 1705 laws defined white and Christian privilege by separating it from black or Indian—and therefore heathen—submission. Thereby, as Goetz concluded, "Race trumped religion as the most important category in an ordered society."[13]

Slavery for Africans in the Americas became specifically a form of *racial* bondage. Any religious justification for slavery needed to clarify God's providence in having one race of people enslave another. As a result, European colonists and later Euro-Americans developed meanings of "race"—of what constituted whiteness and blackness—that codified and transcended slavery. Those categories were, at least initially, fundamentally religious ones.[14]

Since the 1990s, scholars of early African American history including Goetz, Jason R. Young, and Michael A. Gomez interrogated the religious lives of enslaved peoples to uncover how their beliefs shaped American slave societies, particularly those in the Caribbean and Lowcountry. During the years of the international slave trade to North America (1619 to 1808), approximately 400,000 enslaved people came from societies that already had been Christianized or "Islamicized." In *Rituals of Resistance* (2007), Young demonstrated that, by the

---

Katharine Gerbner, *Christian Slavery: Conversion and Race in the Protestant Atlantic World* (Philadelphia: University of Pennsylvania Press, 2018).

12. "An Act concerning Servants and Slaves," in *The Statutes at Large: Being a Collection of All the Laws of Virginia from the First Session of the Legislature, in the Year 1619*, ed. William Waller Hening, 13 vols. (Philadelphia: R. & W. & G. Bartow, 1823), 3:447–63. See also Thomas J. Little, *The Origins of Southern Evangelicalism: Religious Revivalism in the South Carolina Lowcountry, 1670–1760* (Columbia: University of South Carolina Press, 2013), 84–85; Edward E. Andrews, *Native Apostles: Black and Indian Missionaries in the British Atlantic World* (Cambridge: Harvard University Press, 2013).

13. Rebecca Anne Goetz, *The Baptism of Early Virginia: How Christianity Created Race* (Baltimore: Johns Hopkins University Press, 2012), 137.

14. Jordan, *The White Man's Burden;* Gerbner, *Christian Slavery.* For a different perspective, emphasizing the history of Christian universalism vis-à-vis race, see Colin Kidd, *The Forging of the Races: Race and Scripture in the Protestant Atlantic World, 1600–2000* (New York: Cambridge University Press, 2006).

eighteenth century, enslaved people showed that their religious beliefs not only survived the tortuous middle passage, but that faith empowered resistance. Followers of *Orisha* religions, practicing Muslims, and Catholic Kongolese were all part of this mix.[15]

By the 1730s, despite decades of efforts by early missionaries, few planters evinced any interest in promoting Christianity to the people they enslaved. English colonists rightly feared the possible effects of slave Christianization. Some of the enslaved already practiced Christianity, although in a form quite different from European Protestantism. As John Thornton pointed out in *Africa and Africans in the Making of the Atlantic World* (1992), the Afro-Catholicism of slaves who had come from the Christianized region of current-day Angola, for example, inspired rebellion along South Carolina's Stono River in 1739. The rebels evidently attributed a right to be free to their Catholicism, and some of them may have had military experience with militia orders in the Kongo kingdom.[16]

From the Revolution to the Civil War

Since the 1980s, scholars have characterized southern religious history from the evangelical awakenings of the eighteenth century through the American Revolutionary era as the age of revolutionaries and revivalists. They parsed Revolutionary-era documents to understand the coincidence of the rise of religious freedom alongside the determination to defend slavery. The definition of revolutionaries thus expanded beyond those who inspired the revolt against England and the establishment of the American Republic. Scholars examined early

15. Goetz, *The Baptism of Early Virginia*; Jason R. Young, *Rituals of Resistance: African Atlantic Religion in Kongo and the Lowcountry South in the Era of Slavery* (Baton Rouge: Louisiana State University Press, 2007); Michael A. Gomez, *Exchanging Our Country Marks: The Transformation of African Identities in the Colonial and Antebellum South* (Chapel Hill: University of North Carolina Press, 1998).

16. John Thornton, *Africa and Africans in the Making of the Atlantic World, 1400–1800* (New York: Cambridge University Press, 1992); Thornton, "African Dimensions of the Stono Rebellion," *American Historical Review* 96 (October 1991): 1101–13; Mark M. Smith, "Remembering Mary, Shaping Revolt: Reconsidering the Stono Rebellion," *Journal of Southern History* 67 (August 2001): 513–34; Annette Laing, "'Heathens and Infidels'? African Christianization and Anglicanism in the South Carolina Low Country, 1700–1750," *Religion and American Culture* 12 (Summer 2002): 197–228. See also Fred E. Witzig, *Sanctifying Slavery and Politics in South Carolina: The Life of Reverend Alexander Garden, 1685–1756* (Columbia: University of South Carolina Press, 2018).

evangelicals who attacked the system of slavery that supported the republic, and revivalists who slowly and incompletely led the South from a polyglot pluralism to a provincial Protestantism. For many white southerners, the disturbing implications of political and religious revolutions compelled the intellectual birth of southern conservatism (with its theological emphasis on order and obedience). Well into the nineteenth century, a nascent theology of egalitarianism inspired more radical evangelicals to question slavery's suppression of human rights. Revolutionaries and revivalists fueled the simultaneous explosions of democratic politics, evangelical religion, and chattel slavery.[17]

Although they appeared to be theologically opposed, the revolutionaries and the revivalists became unlikely allies. The former moved towards enlightened "theistic rationalism," a term from scholar Gregg L. Frazer, and the latter towards a supernatural millennialism. But on issues of religious liberty, their interests converged. Their alliance, as detailed in numerous scholarly works, forged some of the epic documents of the era, including the Virginia Statute for Religious Freedom, James Madison's *Memorial and Remonstrance* against religious assessments, and the "disestablishment" and "free exercise" clauses of the First Amendment.[18] The rhetoric of the revolutionaries promised universal freedom but delivered a republic that became, in practice, racially exclusivist and white supremacist. In *Southern Cross* (1997), Christine Leigh Heyrman showed how religious freedom, democracy, and republicanism fostered religiously sanctioned repression in the guise of paternalist benevolence.[19]

Beginning with the formation of the new nation, evangelicalism and slavery simultaneously expanded across the South. As detailed in works by John B. Boles and Janet Duitsman Cornelius, the Christianization of the planter class, the intro-

17. Sam Haselby, *The Origins of American Religious Nationalism* (New York: Oxford University Press, 2015).

18. Gregg L. Frazer, *The Religious Beliefs of America's Founders: Reason, Revelation, and Revolution* (Lawrence: University Press of Kansas, 2012). See also Sarah Barringer Gordon, "The First Wall of Separation between Church and State: Slavery and Disestablishment in Late-Eighteenth-Century Virginia," *Journal of Southern History* 85 (February 2019): 61–104. For contrasting views on the meaning of religious freedom from the Revolutionary era, see Thomas Kidd, *God of Liberty: A Religious History of the American Revolution* (New York: Basic Books, 2012); David Sehat, *The Myth of American Religious Freedom* (New York: Oxford University Press, 2011).

19. Christine Leigh Heyrman, *Southern Cross: The Beginnings of the Bible Belt* (New York: Alfred A. Knopf, 1997).

duction of slavery westward, and the adoption of an ideal of the planter patriarch as "Christian steward" fed planter support for missionary work among enslaved people.[20] And the original evangelical antislavery impulse waned as a result. Over the course of the early nineteenth century, the ministerial establishment and the master class found common cause in discouraging black independent religious expression. In order to inspire "good order," they promoted white-supervised religious instruction. Evangelical doctrine taught spiritual brotherhood and equality, but evangelicals increasingly patterned their churches and institutions on the planter hierarchy of white authority and black subordination. As explained by scholars such as Gregory A. Wills and Robert Elder, evangelical churches monitored congregants' propensity to sin, and in doing so kept social order in an unruly society full of migrating peoples, legal contests over land, drinking, and fighting.[21]

Spread of Christian churches provided enslaved African Americans places of communal gathering and fellowship, even as it assured whites that slaves were being taught biblical notions of a proper social order. "Southern religion," as a white evangelical formation with a suppressed but adaptively creative number of black participants, began to assume its modern shape. Southern conservative thought came into full flower. As Eugene D. Genovese and Elizabeth Fox-Genovese explained in *The Mind of the Master Class* (2005), Christianity underlay the ideology of the master class. Planters feared the implications of political and social revolutions that rocked the nineteenth-century world. The rise of the religious proslavery argument centered white southerners' worldview on principles of hierarchy, order, and orthodoxy. Sermons that defended slavery, the origins of which can be seen in Larry E. Tise's groundbreaking *Proslavery* (1987), became religious rituals of self-defense. These exegeses drew deeply from the republican-evangelical synthesis created in the late eighteenth century while sustaining his-

20. John B. Boles, ed., *Masters & Slaves in the House of the Lord: Race and Religion in the American South, 1740–1870* (Lexington: University Press of Kentucky, 1988); Janet Duitsman Cornelius, *Slave Missions and the Black Church in the Antebellum South* (Columbia: University of South Carolina Press, 1999). See also Charles F. Irons, *The Origins of Proslavery Christianity: White and Black Evangelicals in Colonial and Antebellum Virginia* (Chapel Hill: University of North Carolina Press, 2008); Erskine Clarke, *Dwelling Place: A Plantation Epic* (New Haven: Yale University Press, 2005).

21. For the fullest examination of the nature and meaning of Baptist church discipline, see Gregory A. Wills, *Democratic Religion: Freedom, Authority, and Church Discipline in the Baptist South, 1785–1900* (New York: Oxford University Press, 1996); Robert Elder, *The Sacred Mirror: Evangelicalism, Honor, and Identity in the Deep South, 1790–1860* (Chapel Hill: University of North Carolina Press, 2016).

torically conservative views of hierarchy that the evangelical-planter alliance reinforced in the nineteenth century.[22]

As evangelicalism spread throughout the South, white slave-owners often brought slaves to church with them. Over 150 black churches also formed in the first half of the nineteenth century, many in separate buildings from white congregations and with their own pastors and deacons. Congregating mostly in the major southern antebellum urban centers, black churches became particularly prominent in the Upper South, as explained in Luke E. Harlow's *Religion, Race, and the Making of Confederate Kentucky* (2014).[23]

The culture of slave religion exploded on the scholarly landscape in the 1970s with landmark works by Albert J. Raboteau and Mechal Sobel and continued as a prominent historiographical theme into the twenty-first century. Raboteau and Sobel investigated how subversive readings of the Bible and Christianity spread through slave communities, periodically frightening white authorities enough to monitor or prohibit black religious meetings. The tunes and lyrics of spirituals emerged as the communal voice of enslaved believers, articulating their need for consolation and community, and their aspirations for freedom and justice. The call-and-response pattern of the spirituals and their rhythmically complex and antiphonal structure clearly evidenced the influence of African music. Beyond music, African Americans both enslaved and free incorporated Christian theology into their worldviews. Religion and magic, the subject of excellent works by Yvonne P. Chireau and Jeffery E. Anderson, provided complementary strategies to deal with the most philosophical and long-range challenges (through religion) as well as the most immediate and practical needs of their spiritual lives (through magic).[24] As Stephen Ward Angell demonstrated in *Bishop Henry McNeal Turner*

22. Eugene D. Genovese and Elizabeth Fox-Genovese, *The Mind of the Master Class: History and Faith in the Southern Slaveholders' Worldview* (New York: Cambridge University Press, 2005); Larry E. Tise, *Proslavery: A History of the Defense of Slavery in America, 1701–1840* (Athens: University of Georgia Press, 1987).

23. Luke E. Harlow, *Religion, Race, and the Making of Confederate Kentucky, 1830–1880* (New York: Cambridge University Press, 2014).

24. Albert Raboteau, *Slave Religion: The "Invisible Institution" in the Antebellum South* (New York: Oxford University Press, 1978); Mechal Sobel, *Trabelin' On: The Slave Journey to an Afro-Baptist Faith* (1978; repr., Princeton: Princeton University Press, 1988); Lawrence W. Levine, *Black Culture and Black Consciousness: Afro-American Folk Thought from Slavery to Freedom* (New York: Oxford University Press, 1977); Allen Dwight Callahan, *The Talking Book: African Americans and the Bible* (New Haven: Yale University Press, 2006), 236; Yvonne P. Chireau, *Black Magic: Religion and the African American*

and African American Religion in the South (1992), by the 1850s many black Christians applied this theology lens to the political world around them, understanding the coming of the Civil War as providentially related to the end of slavery.[25]

Civil War, Reconstruction, and the Lost Cause

The irony of white southern Christianity during the Civil War was how much it might have done to undermine the Confederate cause in the name of bolstering it, a central theme of George C. Rable's deeply researched history of religion in the war. "I think as much of religion as any man," a Confederate soldier said while tippling some apple brandy, "but there's such a thing as having too damn much of it."[26] Religious faith was omnipresent during the Civil War and certainly steeled soldiers preparing for battle. But at the same time, religious faith probably lengthened and worsened the war. Preachers, congregants, soldiers, and slaves searched for the providential meaning of the great conflict. There was, in that sense, too much of it.

Meanwhile, the war turned into a cataclysm of material, social, and environmental destruction. Drew Gilpin Faust's *This Republic of Suffering* (2008), a work made into a moving two-hour documentary for public television, showed how religion cleared the road for a coming generation of intellectuals who relied on skepticism, irony, and parody more than piety.[27] Yet to the end of the war and after, ordinary Americans placed their lives, and the broader story of the war, within an interpretive framework of God's purposes. To fulfill God's will, they had to pursue their divine ends with more fervor. Religion thus sacralized distrust and hatred.

Many scholars in the 1990s and early 2000s took as their themes the interaction of blacks and whites, the intersection of religious identity and politics, and the diversity of sacred expressions and beliefs after the war. The end of the

---

Conjuring Tradition (Berkeley: University of California Press, 2003); Jeffrey E. Anderson, *Conjure in African American Society* (Baton Rouge: Louisiana State University Press, 2005).

25. Stephen Ward Angell, *Bishop Henry McNeal Turner and African American Religion in the South* (Knoxville: University of Tennessee Press, 1992).

26. George C. Rable, *God's Almost Chosen Peoples: A Religious History of the American Civil War* (Chapel Hill: University of North Carolina Press, 2010), 100.

27. Drew Gilpin Faust, *This Republic of Suffering: Death and the American Civil War* (New York: Alfred A. Knopf, 2008); *American Experience,* season 24, episode 8: "Death and the Civil War," directed by Ric Burns, aired 18 September 2012 (WGBH, 2012).

Civil War forced white and black southern Christians to come to terms with the meaning of the conflict and make sense of a scale of death and destruction unprecedented in US history. Digging deeply into archival sources and denominational publications, historians uncovered how white Baptists, Methodists, Episcopalians, and Presbyterians cast aside olive branches extended by their northern counterparts, whose missionaries they regarded as sly emissaries of the victorious Union army intent on winning converts to a new faith that promoted racial and social egalitarianism. They preferred to go about the project of rebuilding faith communities on their own. Chief among the issues to be resolved was the place of newly freed blacks in the church body. White southern religious leaders generally scuttled requests from black members seeking to be received on equal terms and instead extended a limited hand of fellowship. Every denomination continued the antebellum practices, though to varying degrees, of restricting the ability of blacks to become pastors, deacons, and prayer leaders, and even to worship alongside whites. The Methodist Episcopal Church, South, authorized the creation of black-only conferences within local jurisdictions but made sure they operated under the strict rule of a white bishop.[28]

Not surprisingly, most black southern Christians cut ties with white churches after the Civil War. Some initially hoped to stay, but only if they were received as full-fledged members. When white clergy refused, they left in droves for independent black churches, including the African Methodist Episcopal Church and the African Methodist Episcopal Zion Church, which flooded the eastern seaboard with missionaries.[29] Black Methodists formed the Colored (later Chris-

28. Daniel W. Stowell, *Rebuilding Zion: The Religious Reconstruction of the South, 1863–1877* (New York: Oxford University Press, 1998). For Baptists, see Rufus B. Spain, *At Ease in Zion: A Social History of Southern Baptists, 1865–1900* (Nashville: Vanderbilt University Press, 1967); Gregory A. Wills, *Democratic Religion: Freedom, Authority, and Church Discipline in the Baptist South, 1785–1900* (New York: Oxford University Press, 1997). For Methodists, see Christopher H. Owen, *The Sacred Flame of Love: Methodism and Society in Nineteenth-Century Georgia* (Athens: University of Georgia Press, 1998); Grant S. Shockley, ed., *Heritage and Hope: The African American Presence in United Methodism* (Nashville: Abingdon Press, 1991). For Episcopalians, see Gardiner H. Shattuck Jr., *Episcopalians and Race: Civil War to Civil Rights* (Lexington: University Press of Kentucky, 2000). For Presbyterians, see Walter H. Conser Jr. and Robert J. Cain, *Presbyterians in North Carolina: Race, Politics, and Religious Identity in Historical Perspective* (Knoxville: University of Tennessee Press, 2012).

29. William E. Montgomery, *Under Their Own Vine and Fig Tree: The African American Church in the South, 1865–1900* (Baton Rouge: Louisiana State University Press, 1993). For a more concise summary, see Albert J. Raboteau, *Canaan Land: A Religious History of African Americans* (New York: Oxford University Press, 2001), chap. 5; Paul Harvey, *Through the Storm, Through the Night: A History of African American*

tian) Methodist Episcopal Church in Jackson, Tennessee, in 1873, which received some financial backing from the Methodist Episcopal Church, South, as part of an attempt at interracial fellowship.[30] Baptists, by far the most numerous black religious body, founded hundreds of local churches and important black religious organizations, a story pioneered in the work of James M. Washington.[31]

Regardless of denomination, black clergy emerged as powerful leaders in the reconstruction of the South. Some served as elected officials, such as Reverend Hiram Revels of Mississippi, a minister with the African Methodist Episcopal Church and a United States Senator, and Reverend Richard Cain of South Carolina, a missionary with the African Methodist Episcopal Church and a United States Congressman.[32] More commonly, they campaigned for Republican causes and led public calls for the protection and extension of black liberties. They also spearheaded local drives to build churches and schools and promote literacy.

Although black religious leaders developed communities and politics distinct from—and often in conflict with—their white evangelical peers, the two groups shared broad similarities in dogma. Both preached the inerrancy of the Bible, a strict morality, the innate sinfulness of humankind, and the necessity for all seeking to enter heaven to be "born again" in the Holy Spirit. They nurtured a common religious vocabulary and set of beliefs that, during the civil rights movement, black religious leaders marshalled to convince whites of the injustice of segregation.

Whatever their theological parallels, however, critical differences remained in black and white religious visions for the New South. Tracing how those different visions played out became a key historiographical theme beginning in the 1980s. Political historians showed that Reconstruction did not just "die"; rather, white southerners killed it. By the late 1870s, new Democratic leaders proclaimed that the South had been "redeemed" from the clutches of carpetbaggers and scalawags,

---

Christianity (New York: Rowman & Littlefield, 2011), chap. 4; Angell, *Bishop Henry McNeal Turner and African American Religion in the South;* Sandy Dwayne Martin, *For God and Race: The Religious and Political Leadership of AMEZ Bishop James Walker Hood* (Columbia: University of South Carolina Press, 1999).

30. Raymond R. Sommerville, *An Ex-Colored Church: Social Activism in the CME Church, 1870–1970* (Macon: Mercer University Press, 2004).

31. The foundational work is James M. Washington, *Frustrated Fellowship: The Black Baptist Quest for Social Power* (Macon: Mercer University Press, 1986). See also Wilson Fallin Jr., *Uplifting the People: Three Centuries of Black Baptists in Alabama* (Tuscaloosa: University of Alabama Press, 2007).

32. Philip Dray, *Capitol Men: The Epic Story of Reconstruction Through the Lives of the First Black Congressmen* (New York: Houghton Mifflin, 2008).

an overbearing national government, and a black populace unfit to discharge the duties of citizenship.[33] This notion of cultural redemption—of the South being returned to its rightful guardians—figured prominently in the emergence of a civil religion that developed among southern white Christians: the Lost Cause, which continued to haunt the region into the twenty-first century. Detailed memorably in Charles Reagan Wilson's *Baptized in Blood* (1980), the religion of the Lost Cause framed the Civil War and Confederate defeat as part of God's plan to purify white southern culture and elevate it to sanctified status. Confederate military leaders Robert E. Lee and Stonewall Jackson acquired the status of saintly heroes while rank-and-file Johnny Rebs became holy foot soldiers. White southerners interpreted slavery as a positive force that provided badly needed discipline and purpose to grateful black Americans.[34]

By the early 1900s, the Lost Cause exerted a powerful hold over most southern whites, including not only Protestants but also, as seen in the scholarship of Arthur Remillard, Jews and Catholics.[35] State and local governments invested heavily in the religion of the Lost Cause, honoring fallen heroes by building cemeteries and setting aside Confederate Memorial Days. The United Daughters of the Confederacy and the Sons of Confederate Veterans raised funds for their civil religion as well, a story told skillfully by Gaines M. Foster, Karen L. Cox, and Caroline E. Janney.[36] These organizations collectively created a rich public

33. Paul Harvey, *Redeeming the South: Religious Cultures and Racial Identities Among Southern Baptists, 1865–1925* (Chapel Hill: University of North Carolina Press, 1997); Harvey, *Freedom's Coming: Religious Culture and the Shaping of the South from the Civil War through the Civil Rights Era* (Chapel Hill: University of North Carolina Press, 2005).

34. The classic exploration of the Lost Cause is Charles Reagan Wilson, *Baptized in Blood: The Religion of the Lost Cause, 1865–1920* (Athens: University of Georgia Press, 1980). See also David W. Blight, *Race and Reunion: The Civil War in American Memory* (Cambridge: Harvard University Press, 2001); William A. Blair, *Cities of the Dead: Contesting the Memory of the Civil War in the South, 1865–1914* (Chapel Hill: University of North Carolina Press, 2004); John R. Neff, *Honoring the Civil War Dead: Commemoration and the Problem of Reconciliation* (Lawrence: University Press of Kansas, 2005); Caroline E. Janney, *Remembering the Civil War: Reunion and the Limits of Reconciliation* (Chapel Hill: University of North Carolina Press, 2013); W. Fitzhugh Brundage, *The Southern Past: A Clash of Race and Memory* (Cambridge: Harvard University Press, 2005).

35. Arthur Remillard, *Southern Civil Religions: Imagining the Good Society in the Post-Reconstruction Era* (Athens: University of Georgia Press, 2011).

36. Gaines M. Foster, *Ghosts of the Confederacy: Defeat, the Lost Cause, and the Emergence of the New South, 1865–1913* (New York: Oxford University Press, 1987); Karen L. Cox, *Dixie's Daughters: The United Daughters of the Confederacy and the Preservation of Confederate Culture* (Gainesville: University Press of

culture of parades, parties, portraits, and monuments that celebrated the white race and explicitly excluded blacks or represented them as satisfied servants and workers. Most devastatingly, the religion of the Lost Cause corroded appreciation for black liberty and dignity, providing ideological cover for the sharp rise in racial violence that included lynchings. Donald G. Mathews's book, *At the Altar of Lynching* (2017), theologically connected the rituals of lynching to the white southern emphasis on "atonement." In this theology, the burned black body served as a communal sacrifice, an offering, to restore order to the community. To be sure, many white churches eventually opposed the most despicable and public acts of racial violence, but they still lent their blessing to the hardening culture of white supremacy.[37]

Numerous studies demonstrated how blacks also attributed the Civil War to providence, although they concluded that the war was divinely appointed retribution heaped upon the nation and especially the South for the sin of human bondage. They testified that God used the war to emancipate faithful Christians from slavery. As a freed people, however, blacks were guardedly optimistic about the lasting significance of the conflict. Many openly worried that racism's poison would limit their newly won rights as citizenship.[38]

Partly in response to the expansion of the Lost Cause as a civil religion and to the steady deterioration of their rights, some black church leaders encouraged an exodus to the North or even Africa.[39] But most met the crisis and their congre-

---

Florida, 2003); Caroline E. Janney, *Burying the Dead but Not the Past: Ladies' Memorial Associations and the Lost Cause* (Chapel Hill: University of North Carolina Press, 2008).

37. Donald G. Mathews, *At the Altar of Lynching: Burning Sam Hose in the American South* (New York: Cambridge University Press, 2017); Amy Louise Wood, *Lynching and Spectacle: Witnessing Racial Violence in America, 1890–1940* (Chapel Hill: University of North Carolina Press, 2009); Philip Dray, *At the Hands of Persons Unknown: The Lynching of Black America* (New York: Random House, 2002). For the relationship between lynching and white and black religion, see especially James H. Cone, *The Cross and the Lynching Tree* (Maryknoll, NY: Orbis Books, 2011).

38. Raboteau, *Slave Religion*, 319–22; C. Eric Lincoln and Lawrence H. Mamiya, *The Black Church in the African American Experience* (Durham: Duke University Press, 1990); Montgomery, *Under Their Own Vine and Fig Tree.*

39. Kenneth C. Barnes, *Journey of Hope: The Back-to-Africa Movement in Arkansas in the Late 1800s* (Chapel Hill: University of North Carolina Press, 2004); Claude A. Clegg III, *The Price of Liberty: African Americans and the Making of Liberia* (Chapel Hill: University of North Carolina Press, 2004); Marie Tyler-McGraw, *An African Republic: Black and White Virginians in the Making of Liberia* (Chapel Hill: University of North Carolina Press, 2007).

gants' ambitions for a richer spiritual life by rapidly expanding the breadth and scope of their institutions. Beginning in the late 1800s, black ministers doubled efforts to found local presses and build schools and seminaries. They openly supported black fraternal orders to provide personal loans, mutual aid societies, illness and funeral insurance, and a dense ritual life that celebrated black achievement.[40]

Evelyn Brooks Higginbotham and Glenda Elizabeth Gilmore led in efforts to unlock the role of black women in the evolution of black churches in the late 1800s. These scholars illuminated how black women encouraged churches to become more overtly political, including frequently converting houses of worship into forums to debate matters of sexism within black culture and demanding greater opportunities for leadership and authority.[41] Women organized antilynching and antidiscrimination campaigns as well, occasionally uniting with elite white women to push these causes. Although their changes failed to fully counter the impact of white civil religion on black political fortune, they minimized its ill effects and integrated black religion and calls for racial justice ever more tightly, setting the stage for the emergence of the civil rights movement in the next generation.

Movements of the Spirit

As the religion of the Lost Cause developed in the late nineteenth century, a series of other religious movements focused on experiencing the Holy Spirit in new ways took root. Most important was Pentecostalism, which traced its origins to John Wesley's early nineteenth-century teachings on moral perfectionism and holiness. Born partly out of widespread dissatisfaction with the popular turn in denominational churches toward more elaborate decoration, highly educated ministers, and restrained liturgy and song, Pentecostals testified that the truly saved were those Christians who underwent the life-altering experience of sanctification, through which the Holy Spirit infused the saved with God's grace, which

40. Giggie, *After Redemption;* Mathew Harper, *The End of Days: African American Religion and the Politics in the Age of Emancipation* (Chapel Hill: University of North Carolina Press, 2016).

41. Evelyn Brooks Higginbotham, *Righteous Discontent: The Women's Movement in the Black Baptist Church, 1880–1920* (Cambridge: Harvard University Press, 1994); Glenda Elizabeth Gilmore, *Gender and Jim Crow: Women and the Politics of White Supremacy in North Carolina, 1896–1920* (Chapel Hill: University of North Carolina Press, 1996).

in turn triggered bouts of speaking in tongues or "glossolalia." They practiced a fresh worship style that suited the physical experience of being seized by the Holy Spirit: men and women often jumped, spun around, danced, sang lustily, and clutched at the heavens with outstretched arms. And Pentecostals testified that those newly sanctified frequently enjoyed special spiritual powers, such as abilities to heal bodily ills, cast out evil spirits, and prophesy. Outside of church, Pentecostals strove to lead visibly "holy lives," placing faith in the Holy Spirit to provide for their needs and avoiding worldly temptations.[42]

Like other southern churches in the twentieth century, Pentecostals typically divided along lines of race. The predominantly white Church of God (Cleveland, Tennessee) began as a series of camp meetings along the Tennessee and North Carolina border in 1886. Eleven years later, Charles H. Mason founded the mostly African American Church of God in Christ in Memphis and served as its senior bishop for fifty years. It grew rapidly in large part because of the strong leadership of black women who, as seen in the work of Anthea D. Butler, exercised a degree of authority unmatched in denominational churches.[43] In 1914, white ministers founded the Assemblies of God in Hot Springs, Arkansas, for white Pentecostals.[44]

Pentecostal churches pioneered new forms of song and praise: they formed bands that featured drums, fiddles, tambourines, and guitars; they performed pieces that freely mixed field hollers, blues, spirituals, and dance tunes. Musicians were not shy about performing on the radio and cutting records, either, helping to spread the Pentecostal message and sound but also promoting the radio as a source of modern entertainment. Black and white Pentecostals influ-

42. Randall J. Stephens, *The Fire Spreads: Holiness and Pentecostalism in the American South* (Cambridge: Harvard University Press, 2008); Arlene Sanchez Walsh, *Pentecostals in America* (New York: Columbia University Press, 2018).

43. Anthea D. Butler, *Women in the Church of God in Christ: Making a Sanctified World* (Chapel Hill: University of North Carolina Press, 2007). See also Estrelda Y. Alexander, *Black Fire: One Hundred Years of African American Pentecostalism* (Downers Grove, IL: Inter-Varsity Press, 2011); Calvin White Jr., *The Rise to Respectability: Race, Religion, and the Church of God in Christ* (Fayetteville: University of Arkansas Press, 2012).

44. Edith L. Blumhofer, *Restoring the Faith: The Assemblies of God, Pentecostalism, and American Culture* (Urbana: University of Illinois Press, 1993). See also Margaret M. Poloma, *The Assemblies of God at the Crossroads: Charisma and Institutional Dilemmas* (Knoxville: University of Tennessee Press, 1989); Margaret M. Poloma and John C. Green, *The Assemblies of God: Godly Love and the Revitalization of American Pentecostalism* (New York: New York University Press, 2010).

enced each other musically and shaped the emergence of gospel in the 1910s and 1920s. Historians—including James R. Goff, Peter Guralnick, Gayle F. Wald, and Randall J. Stephens—explored how the interactions between popular music and charismatic faith created a musical genealogy that included Elvis Presley and Sister Rosetta Tharpe.[45]

While most southern churches happily employed the region's developing communication and transportation infrastructures to proselytize more effectively, conservative churches questioned the concurrent growth of academic disciplines like biblical criticism, geology, paleontology, and especially evolutionary biology that cast doubts on their view of scripture as the literal and unchanging word of God. Their beliefs seemed under attack, most notably during the 1925 Scopes Trial in Dayton, Tennessee, a story movingly told by Edward J. Larson in *Summer for the Gods* (1997). In 1925, John Scopes, a Tennessee high school teacher, broke a state law prohibiting the teaching of human evolution in public schools. Covered extensively by the media and broadcast over the radio, the trial pitted Modernists, who claimed evolution was compatible with religion, against Fundamentalists, who believed in creationism and that the Bible superseded science as a source of unimpeachable truth. Scopes lost the case but southern churches, as Charles A. Israel demonstrated in *Before Scopes* (2004), gained a reputation (which was somewhat inflated) of being illiberal and antimodern.[46]

The Scopes trial accelerated the growth of southern Fundamentalism. Led by George M. Marsden, historians of Fundamentalism documented its northern origins and relatively slower spread in the South, but also its growing importance in the region by the late twentieth century. As the name suggests, Fundamentalism called on Christians to adhere strictly to the "fundamental" tenets of their faith, including core principles of the infallibility of scripture, the virgin birth of Jesus, the reality of his miracles, the death of Jesus as atonement for the sins of mankind, and his resurrection. Within southern denominations, Fundamentalists squared off against Modernists, forcing bishops and church leaders to clarify core

45. Peter Guralnick, *Last Train to Memphis: The Rise of Elvis Presley* (New York: Little, Brown, 1994); James R. Goff, *Close Harmony: A History of Southern Gospel* (Chapel Hill: University of North Carolina Press, 2002); Gayle F. Wald, *Shout, Sister, Shout! The Untold Story of Rock-and-Roll Trailblazer Sister Rosetta Tharpe* (Boston: Beacon Press, 2007); Stephens, *The Devil's Music.*

46. Edward J. Larson, *Summer for the Gods: The Scopes Trial and America's Continuing Debate over Science and Religion* (New York: Basic Books, 1997); Charles A. Israel, *Before Scopes: Evangelicalism, Education, and Evolution in Tennessee 1870–1925* (Athens: University of Georgia Press, 2004).

dogma. These tensions split some houses of worship but more importantly laid the groundwork for the development of conservative theological wings within denominations during the 1960s and 1970s.[47]

Civil Rights, the Religious Right, and Pluralism

The language of evangelical Christianity and biblically based ideas of community and justice occasionally produced genuine moments of interracial fellowship that also cut across class lines. As historians Erik S. Gellman and Jarod Roll vividly detailed in *The Gospel of the Working Class* (2011), during the New Deal, Claude Williams, a white Presbyterian minister from Tennessee, and Owen Whitfield, a black farmer and preacher from Mississippi, formed the People's Institute for Applied Religion. The institute proposed to integrate Jesus's call for a just society with contemporary struggles for improved wages, working conditions, housing, and federal aid. The two leaders drew recruits from local unions and won concessions from employers. Although the Institute struggled to survive amidst the swell of political conservatism after World War II, it stood as an example of black-white cooperation that prefigured the mid-twentieth century's civil rights movement.[48]

The great attack on segregation in southern churches and society, of course, occurred during the civil rights movement. Led by black church leaders such as Martin Luther King Jr., C. T. Vivian, and Ralph Abernathy, the movement transformed the long-running African American battle to end racial discrimination into a national crusade to live out Jesus's call for justice and to fulfill the promise of American democracy. Drawing from the nonviolent teachings of Dorothy Day's Catholic Worker movement, Mahatmas Gandhi, and the historical witness of a long line of black leaders including Ida B. Wells and A. Phillip Randolph, the movement challenged the South to end the color line.[49] King, in particular,

47. The classic is still George M. Marsden, *Fundamentalism and American Culture* (New York: Oxford University Press, 1980). See also Molly Worthen, *Apostles of Reason: The Crisis of Authority in American Evangelicalism* (New York: Oxford University Press, 2014); Andrew Christopher Smith, *Fundamentalism, Fundraising, and the Transformation of the Southern Baptist Convention, 1919–1925* (Knoxville: University of Tennessee Press, 2016).

48. Erik S. Gellman and Jarod Roll, *The Gospel of the Working Class: Labor's Southern Prophets in New Deal America* (Urbana: University of Illinois Press, 2011).

49. The best summary of the civil rights movement is still Taylor Branch's trilogy: *Parting the Waters: America in the King Years, 1954–1963* (New York: Simon & Schuster, 1988); *Pillar of Fire: America in the*

offered a religious vision of redeeming the South from the sin of racial oppression that slowly attracted important white southern Protestants, Catholics, and Jews.[50] Most notable was the leading white evangelist of the day, Billy Graham, who famously invited King to join him at his New York Crusade in Madison Square Garden in 1957, and afterwards began to refuse to address whites-only audiences. Graham also paid King's bail money during the Albany Movement in the summer of 1962. But as Grant Wacker explained in *America's Pastor* (2014), Graham grew increasingly suspicious of the movement in the mid-1960s, urging King to "put the brakes on a little bit."[51]

King has long been the most studied figure in the field of religion and civil rights, and twenty-first-century historiographical trends showed no signs of that changing. Scholars probed King's relationship to the black social gospel, his concepts of social justice and poverty relief, and the evolution of his notion of faith and politics.[52] Others draw attention to the work of black women, showing how

---

King Years, 1963–1965 (New York: Simon & Schuster, 1998); *At Canaan's Edge: American in the King Years, 1965–1968* (New York: Simon & Schuster, 2006). On King's life specifically, see the magisterial work by David J. Garrow, *Bearing the Cross: Martin Luther King Jr. and the Southern Christian Leadership Conference* (New York: William Marrow, 1986). See also Clayborne Carson, ed., *The Autobiography of Martin Luther King Jr.* (New York: Warner Books, 1998).

50. On Jews, see Mark K. Bauman and Berkley Kalin, eds., *The Quiet Voices: Southern Rabbis and Black Civil Rights, 1880s to 1990s* (Tuscaloosa: University of Alabama Press, 1997); Debra L. Schultz, *Going South: Jewish Women in the Civil Rights Movement* (New York: New York University Press, 2001); Clive Webb, *Fight Against Fear: Southern Jews and Black Civil Rights* (Athens: University of Georgia Press, 2001); P. Allen Krause, *To Stand Aside or Stand Alone: Southern Reform Rabbis and the Civil Rights Movement*, ed. Mark K. Bauman and Stephen Krause (Tuscaloosa: University of Alabama Press, 2016). On Catholics, see R. Bentley Anderson, *Black, White and Catholic: New Orleans Interracialism, 1947–1956* (Nashville: Vanderbilt University Press, 2005); Danny Duncan Collum, *Black and Catholic in the Jim Crow South: The Stuff That Makes Community* (New York: Paulist Press, 2006); Amy L. Koehlinger, *The New Nuns: Racial Justice and Religious Reform in the 1960s* (Cambridge: Harvard University Press, 2007).

51. Grant Wacker, *America's Pastor: Billy Graham and the Shaping of a Nation* (Cambridge: Harvard University Press, 2014), 127.

52. On the place of the civil rights movement within the larger tradition of the black social gospel, see Gary J. Dorrien, *Breaking White Supremacy: Martin Luther King Jr. and the Black Social Gospel* (New Haven: Yale University Press, 2018). On King's vision of social justice and poverty relief, see Michael K. Honey, *To the Promised Land: Martin Luther King and the Fight for Economic Justice* (New York: W. W. Norton, 2018). On the development of King's politics and faith, see Jonathan Rieder, *Gospel of Freedom: Martin Luther King Jr.'s Letters from Birmingham Jail and the Struggle that Changed a Nation* (New York: Bloomsbury Press, 2013); Patrick Parr, *The Seminarian: Martin Luther King Jr. Comes of Age* (Chicago: Lawrence Hill Books, 2018); Tommie Shelby and Brandon Terry, eds., *To Shape a New World: Essays on*

they influenced King's philosophy and his path of resistance to segregation.[53] Some of the most important studies set King's leadership and vision into international contexts. As illuminated by Mary L. Dudziak, Timothy B. Tyson, and Sarah Azaransky, King inspired leaders to look beyond the borders of the United States and carry the fight for religious and civil liberty to far-flung corners of the globe.[54]

The civil rights movement laid bare the strong current of white supremacy coursing through the heart of much of white southern religion, a subject which has been a rich source of scholarship. To be sure, a few white religious leaders readily joined King, but they often paid a steep price. Ed King, a Methodist minister from Jackson, Mississippi, served as a chaplain at all-black Tougaloo College, joined black students at sit-ins in Woolworth's department stores, served in the Student Nonviolent Coordinating Committee, and was a leader in the Mississippi Freedom Democratic Party. He was also regularly beaten by white toughs and shunned by most of his peers.[55]

A much more common response to the civil rights movement by white southern ministers was to simply ignore it. As seen in works by Carolyn Renée DuPont, Carter Dalton Lyon, and Elaine Allen Lechtreck, most claimed that their leadership did not extend beyond the doors of their sanctuary, that the Bible actually endorsed segregation, and that changing people's attitudes about race was simply not their job—they were in the business of saving souls. Others ducked the issues entirely and remained quiet for fear of upsetting conservative

---

the Political Philosophy of Martin Luther King Jr. (Cambridge: Harvard University Press, 2018); James M. Washington, ed., *A Testament of Hope: The Essential Writings and Speeches of Martin Luther King Jr.* (New York: HarperCollins, 1996).

53. Belinda Robnett, *How Long? How Long? African American Women in the Struggle for Civil Rights* (New York: Oxford University Press, 1997); Bettye Collier-Thomas and V. P. Franklin, eds., *Sisters in the Struggle: African American Women in the Civil Rights–Black Power Movement* (New York: New York University Press, 2001); Janet Dewart Bell, *Lighting the Fires of Freedom: African American Women in the Civil Rights Movement* (New York: New Press, 2018).

54. Mary L. Dudziak, *Cold War Civil Rights: Race and the Image of American Democracy* (Princeton: Princeton University Press, 2000); Timothy B. Tyson, *Radio Free Dixie: Robert F. Williams and the Roots of Black Power* (Chapel Hill: University of North Carolina Press, 1999); Sarah Azaransky, *This Worldwide Struggle: Religion and the International Roots of the Civil Rights Movement* (New York: Oxford University Press, 2017).

55. Ed King and Trent Watts, *Ed King's Mississippi: Behind the Scenes of Freedom Summer* (Jackson: University Press of Mississippi, 2014); Joseph T. Reiff, *Born of Conviction: White Methodists and Mississippi's Closed Society* (New York: Oxford University Press, 2015).

congregations.[56] Most laymen, as seen in the pathbreaking work of Jane Dailey, adopted a folk theology of segregation that championed the social and sexual purity of white southern women. They vigorously supported segregation because it protected white women from the invented threat of sexual violation by black men (who supposedly lusted after them). The most radical of white southern segregationists simply understood integration as an utter abomination of God's will.[57]

Ultimately, these white southern churchgoers failed to halt the movement, hampered by their own failure to organize effective and durable anti-integration campaigns, outsmarted by black leaders, and compelled by federal law. By the 1970s, some white southerners slowly began to come to terms with their denominations' histories of slavery and segregation. They openly admitted the wrongness of their ways, distanced themselves from the racist actions of their forebears, and renounced biblically sanctioned arguments that favored the color line.[58]

In the midst of the social movements of the 1960s and the 1970s, gender also challenged traditional theologies in southern churches. Black women seeking to be ordained in black churches generally struggled, with most Baptist churches very slow to accept them.[59] Although the United Methodist Church accepted women as clergy in 1956 and the Episcopal Church in 1974, the South's largest

56. Carolyn Renée DuPont, *Mississippi Praying: Southern White Evangelicals and the Civil Rights Movement, 1945–1975* (New York: New York University Press, 2013); Carter Dalton Lyon, *Sanctuaries of Segregation: The Story of the Jackson Church Visit Campaign* (Jackson: University Press of Mississippi, 2017); Elaine Allen Lechtreck, *Southern White Ministers and the Civil Rights Movement* (Jackson: University Press of Mississippi, 2018). For a broad survey of race and evangelicals, see Michael O. Emerson and Christian Smith, *Divided by Faith: Evangelical Religion and the Problem of Race in America* (New York: Oxford University Press, 2000).

57. Jane Dailey, "Sex, Segregation, and the Sacred after *Brown*," *Journal of American History* 91 (June 2004): 119–44; Charles Marsh, *God's Long Summer: Stories of Faith and Civil Rights* (Princeton: Princeton University Press, 1997).

58. David L. Chappell, *A Stone of Hope: Prophetic Religion and the Death of Jim Crow* (Chapel Hill: University of North Carolina Press, 2004); Donald Collins, *When the Church Bell Rang Racist: The Methodist Church and the Civil Rights Movement in Alabama* (Macon: Mercer University Press, 1998); William G. McAtee, *Transformed: A White Mississippi Pastor's Journey into Civil Rights and Beyond* (Jackson: University Press of Mississippi, 2011); Phil Noble, *Beyond the Burning Bus: The Civil Rights Revolution in a Southern Town* (Montgomery: New South Books, 2003).

59. Bettye Collier-Thomas, *Daughters of Thunder: Black Women Preachers and Their Sermons, 1850–1979* (San Francisco: Jossey-Bass Books, 1988); Collier-Thomas, *Jesus, Jobs, and Justice: African American Women and Religion* (New York: Alfred A. Knopf, 2010).

Protestant denomination, the Southern Baptist Convention, restricted leadership roles for women as part of a larger belief in "traditional" family and social values that placed men at the head of the family and the church.[60] Faced with greater pastoral and liturgical roles for women, conservatives in the Presbyterian church broke away in 1973 and founded the Presbyterian Church of America.[61]

The conservative turn taken by some evangelicals initiated a broader campaign to carry their values directly into politics at local, state, and national levels. Although white southern clergy always sought to influence and elect politicians sympathetic to their beliefs, a new and more aggressive cohort came to power in the late twentieth century, intent on combatting what they feared was an attack on America's "Christian heritage" in order to win a "culture war" that threatened their values. Led by Jerry Falwell, Pat Robertson, Phyllis Schlafly, and Oral Roberts, they formed the Moral Majority and later, under the leadership of Ralph Reed, the Christian Coalition. Collectively, they became known as the Religious Right.[62]

The Religious Right strove to make politics conform to a moral outlook based on a strict interpretation of the Bible. Specifically, leaders demanded protection of school prayer, the definition of marriage as exclusively between a man and a woman, unstinting financial and military support for the state of Israel, and an end to abortion, pornography, and contraception. Their ranks quickly grew to include hundreds of thousands of enthusiasts, mostly southern whites, who formed a powerful conservative voting bloc.[63] Savvy users of technology, they

60. Bill J. Leonard, *God's Last and Only Hope: The Fragmentation of the Southern Baptist Convention* (Grand Rapids: William B. Eerdmans, 1990); David T. Morgan, *The New Crusades, The New Holy Land: Conflict in Southern Baptist Convention, 1969–1991* (Tuscaloosa: University of Alabama Press, 1996); Barry Hankins, *Uneasy in Babylon: Southern Baptist Conservatives and American Culture* (Tuscaloosa: University of Alabama Press, 2002).

61. Joel L. Alvis Jr., *Religion and Race: Southern Presbyterians, 1946–1983* (Tuscaloosa: University of Alabama Press, 1994); Sean Michael Lucas, *For a Continuing Church: The Roots of the Presbyterian Church in America* (Phillipsburg, NJ: P & R Publishing, 2015).

62. James Davison Hunter, *Culture Wars: The Struggle to Define America* (New York: Basic Books, 1991); Andrew Hartman, *A War for the Soul of America: A History of the Culture Wars* (Chicago: University of Chicago Press, 2015).

63. Donald T. Critchlow, *Phyllis Schlafly and Grassroots Conservatism: A Women's Crusade* (Princeton: Princeton University Press, 2005); Daniel K. Williams, *God's Own Party: The Making of the Christian Right* (New York: Oxford University Press, 2010); J. Brooks Flippen, *Jimmy Carter, the Politics of Family, and the Rise of the Religious Right* (Athens: University of Georgia Press, 2013).

founded their own radio stations, television networks, and websites to broadcast messages and raise money. In their studies of the Religious Right, Bethany Morton, Darren Dochuk, and Darren E. Grem expanded understanding of how evangelicals secured political power and business success by constructing networks in high schools and colleges as well as business associations across the South and beyond.[64]

The rise of southern evangelical political power in the late nineteenth and early twentieth centuries occurred simultaneous to an unprecedented growth in religious pluralism. When President Lyndon B. Johnson signed the Hart-Cellar Immigration Bill in October 1965, he eliminated the national origin quota system put in place more than forty years earlier. It opened the doors for millions of immigrants to relocate to the United States, many of whom moved to the South to build new lives. Buddhism grew in Sunbelt cities such as Houston, where Chinese and Vietnamese immigrants built temples. By the late 2010s Houston housed more than forty different Buddhist communities. Muslims from the Middle East settled in smaller numbers in major southern cities, building mosques and running stores that catered to their religious needs and preferences.[65] Much more numerously, Latinx Catholics from Mexico and South America made the United States their home. By 2015, approximately 37 percent of them, or more than twenty million, lived in the South, with Texas and Florida being the most densely populated states. Seeking to understand how Latinx migration impacted southern religion, Gastón Espinosa and Juan Francisco Martinez studied Catholic, Pentecostal, and evangelical reactions to immigrants. At times, new arrivals sparked new forms of worship and political activism; at other moments, they triggered painful debates over how to incorporate newcomers into standing congregations. The future growth of traditional southern religious groups depends

64. Bethany Moreton, *To Serve God and Wal-Mart: The Making of Christian Free Enterprise* (Cambridge: Harvard University Press, 2009); Darren Dochuk, *From Bible Belt to Sunbelt: Plain-Folk Religion, Grassroots Politics, and the Rise of Evangelical Conservatism* (New York: W. W. Norton, 2011); Darren E. Grem, *The Blessings of Business: How Corporations Shaped Conservative Christianity* (New York: Oxford University Press, 2016).

65. Jeff Wilson, *Dixie Dharma: Inside a Buddhist Temple in the American South* (Chapel Hill: University of North Carolina Press, 2012); Edward E. Curtis IV, *Muslims in America: A Short History* (New York: Oxford University Press, 2009); Curtis, *The Call of Bilal: Islam in the African Diaspora* (Chapel Hill: University of North Carolina Press, 2014); Harold D. Morales, *Latino and Muslim in America: Race, Religion, and the Making of a New Minority* (New York: Oxford University Press, 2018).

in large part on how they respond to the growing numbers and power of Latinx immigrants.[66]

Conclusion

Religion in the South, like so many fields in modern southern historiography, has undergone a revolution. The cultural captivity thesis, which argued that southerners chose culture over Christ, strongly shaped earlier interpretations of southern religion. Beginning in the 1980s, it expanded to include different voices—focusing on black southerners, women, Catholics, and Jews, to take just a few examples—to produce fresh appreciations of the range of faiths and their historical intersections.[67]

Just as they established the South's religious diversity as one of its central features, scholars also drew attention to new paths of inquiry into the region. Older articles and books tended to focus on matters of Christian dogma, theology, male leadership, and institutional growth—all important objects of study, to be sure. Later analyses, incorporating race, gender, sexuality, and immigration, introduced pressing questions of how religion inspired campaigns of social justice or resistance to it, how it led to community cohesion or fragmentation, and how religion confirmed individual dignity or denied it.

By the late 2010s, the next generation of scholarship on religion and the South began to take shape. Scholars cast light on how southern sacred beliefs and institutions intersected with the evolution of contemporary politics, as in the case of evangelicals participating in the conservative movement in the era of Donald Trump. They also illuminated how waves of new immigrants and new technolo-

66. "Facts on U.S. Latinos, 2015: Statistical Portrait of Hispanics in the United States," *Hispanic Trends,* Pew Research Center, http://www.pewhispanic.org/2017/09/18/facts-on-u-s-latinos-current-data/ (accessed 18 January 2019); Gastón Espinosa, *Latino Pentecostals in America: Faith and Politics in Action* (Cambridge: Harvard University Press, 2014); Juan Francisco Martinez, *The Story of Latino Protestants in the United States* (Grand Rapids, MI: William B. Eerdmans, 2018). See also Gastón Espinosa, Virgilio Elizondo, and Jesse Miranda, eds., *Latino Religion and Civic Activism in the United States* (New York: Oxford University Press, 2005); Gary Laderman, *Religions of Atlanta: Religious Diversity in the Centennial Olympic City* (New York: Oxford University Press, 1996).

67. See "Religious Landscape Study: Adults in the South," *Religion and Public Life,* Pew Research Center, http://www.pewforum.org/religious-landscape-study/region/south/ (accessed 18 January 2019); Paul Harvey, "Race, Religion and Culture in the US South," *Oxford Online Research Encyclopedia,* http://religion.oxfordre.com/view/10.1093/acrefore/9780199340378.001.0001/acrefore-9780199340378-e-7 (accessed 18 January 2019).

gies constantly reinvented and enlarged southern faiths.[68] The best scholarship, however, continues to probe the fundamental issues that have long animated the field—namely, how southerners relied on religion to answer questions about the meaning of human worth and dignity in their lives.

68. Kenneth L. Woodward, "How Religion Got Trump: Faith in the 2016 Election," *Commonweal*, 7 May 2018, https://www.commonwealmagazine.org/how-religion-got-trump (accessed 18 January 2019); Charles Reagan Wilson, "Religion and the US South," *Southern Spaces* (16 March 2004): https://southernspaces.org/2004/overview-religion-and-us-south (accessed 18 January 2019); Wilson, *Flashes of a Southern Spirit: Meanings of the Spirit in the U.S. South* (Athens: University of Georgia Press, 2011); Patricia Ehrkamp and Caroline Nagel, "'Under the Radar': Undocumented Immigrants, Christian Faith Communities, and the Precarious Spaces of Welcome in the U.S. South," *Annals of the Association of American Geographers* 104 (March 2014): 319–28.

RACE, POWER, AND THE LAW
Southern Legal and Constitutional History

Sally E. Hadden and Charles L. Zelden

Legal and constitutional matters have always been part of southern history and historiography. From the imposition of Spanish or French law in the Southeast soon after European contact with Native Americans to debates about the nature of the American union (antebellum or modern), legal and constitutional issues permeate southern history. Yet, the concept of southern legal and constitutional history as a *separate* field of study is a phenomenon of the late twentieth century.[1] Only in the 1970s did historians conceptualize southern law and constitutional thought as a unique field of study, and only in the 1980s

1. Thanks to Richard B. Bernstein for editorial assistance. A noteworthy exception to this trend was Fletcher M. Green's *Constitutional Development in the South Atlantic States, 1776–1860* (Chapel Hill: University of North Carolina Press, 1930). See also Don E. Fehrenbacher, *Sectional Crisis and Southern Constitutionalism* (Baton Rouge: Louisiana State University Press, 1995), combining two earlier books by Fehrenbacher, *The South and Three Sectional Crises* (Baton Rouge: Louisiana State University Press, 1980) and *Constitutions and Constitutionalism in the Slaveholding South* (Athens: University of Georgia Press, 1989). The many works touching upon the ratification of the US Constitution likewise explored southern elements in Antifederalist critiques, but few suggested that the South deserved study as a distinct legal region. Later works contained scattered references to legal history in the South: Ernest M. Lander, "The 'Critical Period,' the Constitution, and the New Nation," in *Writing Southern History: Essays in Historiography in Honor of Fletcher M. Green,* ed. Arthur S. Link and Rembert W. Patrick (Baton Rouge: Louisiana State University Press, 1965), 65–90, blended constitutional with political analysis; and select pages in John B. Boles and Evelyn Thomas Nolen, eds., *Interpreting Southern History: Historiographical Essays in Honor of Sanford W. Higginbotham* (Baton Rouge: Louisiana State University Press, 1987), especially Drew Gilpin Faust, "The Peculiar South Revisited: White Society, Culture, and Politics in the Antebellum South, 1800–1860" (95–99), Charles R. Dew, "The Slavery Experience" (155–56), and LaWanda Cox, "From Emancipation to Segregation: National Policy and Southern Blacks" (215–18). Neither collection had a full article specifically addressing legal history.

did scholars begin explicitly to craft full-length monographs describing how law shaped southern history and how southern historical experience shaped law.[2]

Two books symbolize the effort at historical synthesis: *Ambivalent Legacy* (1984) by David J. Bodenhamer and James W. Ely Jr., and *An Uncertain Tradition* (1989) by Kermit L. Hall and James W. Ely Jr.[3] Each contained essays arguing for southern legal and constitutional history as a distinct topic of study. As reviews noted, both books fell short of their goals to provide a coherent "conceptual framework for an interpretation of southern legal history."[4] Still, the volumes marked the beginning of sustained attention to the subject.[5] The 1990s and the new millennium saw the publication of more books, dissertations, and articles focusing on the South's legal heritage.[6]

The 2013 publication of *Signposts: New Directions in Southern Legal History,* edited by Sally E. Hadden and Patricia Minter, confirmed that two key subjects have come to dominate the region's legal history: race and power. Still, contributors to *Signposts* broadened their inquiries, revealing interpretive trends that remain strong, embracing issues of gender and ethnicity, alcoholism, regional indebtedness, and the intellectual development of a distinct southern legal culture. The result was a multifaceted, nuanced, and expansive assessment of law

2. See Paul Finkelman, "Exploring Southern Legal History," *North Carolina Law Review* 64 (November 1985): 77–116.

3. David J. Bodenhamer and James W. Ely Jr., eds., *Ambivalent Legacy: A Legal History of the South* (Jackson: University Press of Mississippi, 1984); Kermit L. Hall and James W. Ely Jr., eds., *An Uncertain Tradition: Constitutionalism in the History of the South* (Athens: University of Georgia Press, 1989).

4. Paul Finkelman, review of *Ambivalent Legacy* edited by David J. Bodenhamer and James W. Ely Jr., *Journal of American History* 72 (September 1985): 381–82, quote on 381; J. Morgan Kousser, review of *An Uncertain Tradition* edited by Kermit C. Hall and James W. Ely Jr., *Georgia Historical Quarterly* 73 (Winter 1989): 843–44.

5. See, for example, Edward L. Ayers, *Vengeance and Justice: Crime and Punishment in the 19th-Century South* (New York: Oxford University Press, 1984); Tony Freyer, *The Little Rock Crisis: A Constitutional Interpretation* (Westport: Greenwood Press, 1984); Donald G. Nieman, *To Set the Law in Motion: The Freedmen's Bureau and the Legal Rights of Blacks, 1865–1868* (Millwood, NY: KTO Press, 1979).

6. Thomas D. Morris, *Southern Slavery and the Law, 1619–1860* (Chapel Hill: University of North Carolina Press, 1996); Timothy S. Huebner, *The Southern Judicial Tradition: State Judges and Sectional Distinctiveness 1790–1890* (Athens: University of Georgia Press, 1999); William G. Thomas, *Lawyering for the Railroad: Business, Law, and Power in the New South* (Baton Rouge: Louisiana State University Press, 1999); James W. Ely Jr. and Bradley G. Bond, eds., *The New Encyclopedia of Southern Culture.* Vol. 10, *Law and Politics* (Chapel Hill: University of North Carolina Press, 2008); Sally E. Hadden and Patricia Hagler Minter, eds., *Signposts: New Directions in Southern Legal History* (Athens: University of Georgia Press, 2013), 5.

and constitutionalism in southern history. Hadden and Minter's introduction surveyed southern legal history scholarship from the 1980s to 2010. This essay focuses primarily on books, dissertations, and selected articles published since 2010.[7] Using 2010 as a beginning does not and should not minimize the importance of earlier works. Rather, we simply recognize the rapid expansion of southern legal historical scholarship and historiographic analyses.

Any survey of southern legal and constitutional history must commence with twin discussions of "legal and constitutional history" and "southern history." When *Ambivalent Legacy* (1984) and *An Uncertain Tradition* (1989) were published, scholars viewed legal history and constitutional history as distinct topics. Over time, however, the lines between these two topics blurred, making it increasingly difficult to separate the legal from the constitutional, as both have common origins and an almost dialectical effect on each other. Tellingly, a leading textbook on constitutional history, Melvin I. Urofsky and Paul Finkelman's *A March of Liberty* (2011), spends nearly as much time on private legal change as it does on public constitutional developments.[8] Much of the newest scholarship combines legal with constitutional history, private with public law.[9] As a result, scholars increasingly leave out "and constitutional" when discussing southern legal history.[10]

Similarly, in its formative years, the emerging field of "southern" legal history focused on a geographically narrow range of places. Seeking to avoid New England's gravitational pull, many essays in *Ambivalent Legacy* found a new southern touchstone: Virginia. Other essays in the volume broadened this focus to examine macro-level pan-southern topics, such as the legal strategy pursued by the National Association for the Advancement of Colored People (NAACP),

7. Hadden and Minter, eds., *Signposts,* 4–15.

8. Melvin I. Urofsky and Paul Finkelman, *A March of Liberty: A Constitutional History of the United States,* 3rd ed. (New York: Oxford University Press, 2011).

9. For examples of this trend, see the essays in Hadden and Minter, eds., *Signposts;* Christopher Waldrep and Donald G. Nieman, eds., *Local Matters: Race, Crime, and Justice in the Nineteenth-Century South* (Athens: University of Georgia Press, 2001).

10. See, for example, Ely and Bond, eds., *Law and Politics,* which merges topics of public and private legal matters under the categorization of "law."

judicial elections, and the antebellum economy. Even so, the emphasis remained on the periphery: the Upper South.[11] As Hadden and Minter later explained, "Southern state debt, slave codes, and criminal justice all had their moments in the sun—but only a Commonwealth sun."[12]

Beginning around 2010, detailed research into southern legal history expanded to cover the full breadth of the region, raising important questions about just what constitutes the South's legal boundaries, both intellectually and geographically.[13] Like other southern historians, legal historians grapple with defining their subject area as well as determining its relationship to national and international scholarship.[14] Edward L. Ayers, Peter Kolchin, and Laura F. Edwards stepped forward to assess what makes southern history "southern," stressing a less-than-exceptionalist view that nonetheless acknowledged something different about the South that makes it appear distinctive, both to self-identified southerners and outsiders.[15] But for the southern legal historian, this legacy of not-quite-exceptionalism is problematic; given the law's tendency to affect topics beyond the legal, historians face definitional problems that refuse to go away. Where are the region's boundaries and by what definition—geographic, cultural, or legal—do we establish them? When discussing the South, do we mean only the Confederate South, only the slave-owning South, or perhaps only the predominantly English-speaking common-law South?

Legal historians working in different periods offer divergent answers. Colonial and early national legal historians describe a South hardly coterminous (legally or geographically) with the future Confederacy. The Spanish, French, and British empires created legal regimes that operated in the geographic South

11. Bodenhamer and Ely, *Ambivalent Legacy.*

12. Hadden and Minter, eds., *Signposts,* 2.

13. Alabama is indicative of this fertile territory, for example. See Paul M. Pruitt Jr., "Alabama Legal History as a Field of Study," in *New Field, New Corn: Essays in Alabama Legal History,* ed. Paul M. Pruitt Jr. (New Orleans: Quid Pro Books, 2015), 1–12. See also Joseph A. Ranney, *A Legal History of Mississippi: Race, Class, and the Struggle for Opportunity* (Jackson: University Press of Mississippi, 2019).

14. For example, Paul Quigley, "Civil War Conscription and the International Boundaries of Citizenship," *Journal of the Civil War Era* 4 (September 2014): 373–97.

15. Edward L. Ayers, "What We Talk About When We Talk About the South," in *All over the Map: Rethinking American Regions,* ed. Edward L. Ayers et al. (Baltimore: Johns Hopkins University Press, 1995), 62–82; Peter Kolchin, *A Sphinx on the American Land: The Nineteenth-Century South in Comparative Perspective* (Baton Rouge: Louisiana State University Press, 2003); Kolchin, "The South and the World," *Journal of Southern History* 75 (August 2009): 565–80; Laura F. Edwards, "Southern History as U.S. History," *Journal of Southern History* 75 (August 2009): 533–64.

for decades—in each case, for much longer than the Confederacy. Laws in three European languages crafted the labor regimes and property rules that dominated the region before 1861, covering territories well beyond the future boundaries of the Confederacy. Matthew C. Mirow's scholarship on Spanish Florida demonstrated the impact that Roman law had upon what became "the Sunshine State." Others considered customary law and French law in Louisiana.[16] Atlantic World history affected southern legal history, too: historians integrated southern legal material into their considerations of the Atlantic or Caribbean or the maritime specifically.[17] This focus upon the oceanic "front door" of the South followed

16. M. C. Mirow, *Florida's First Constitution: The Constitution of Cádiz* (Durham: Carolina Academic Press, 2012); Mirow, "Law in East Florida 1783–1821," *American Journal of Legal History* 55 (January 2015): 89–118; Mirow, "Testamentary Proceedings in Spanish East Florida, 1783–1821," in *Studies in Canon Law and Common Law in Honor of R. H. Helmholz*, ed. Troy L. Harris (Berkeley: Robbins Collection Publications, 2015), 281–301; Mirow, "The Cádiz Constitution in Cuba and Florida," in *The Rise of Constitutional Government in the Iberian Atlantic World: The Impact of the Cádiz Constitution of 1812*, ed. Scott Eastman and Natalia Sobrevilla Perea (Tuscaloosa: University of Alabama Press, 2015), 194–211; Mirow, "The Supreme Court, Florida Land Claims, and Spanish Colonial Law," *Tulane European and Civil Law Forum* 31/32 (2017): 181–218. See also Robert M. Jarvis, ed., *Florida's Other Courts: Unconventional Justice in the Sunshine State* (Gainesville: University Press of Florida, 2018) on the Spanish and American territorial periods; Ronald A. Fonseca, "The Supreme Court of Louisiana's 1840 'Course of Studies for Lawyers': Was It a Reflection of Common Law Influence on Louisiana's Civilian Legal System?" *Louisiana History* 53 (Spring 2012): 182–226; Gail S. Stephenson, "Custom as a Source of Law in Louisiana," *Louisiana Law Review* 79 (Summer 2019), *SSRN*, 6 March 2018, https://dx.doi.org/10.2139/ssrn.3130198 (accessed 18 January 2019).

17. See the collected articles of "Law, Slavery, and Justice: A Special Issue," *Law and History Review* 29 (November 2011), particularly Rebecca Scott, "Slavery and the Law in Atlantic Perspective: Jurisdiction, Jurisprudence, and Justice" (915–25). See also Robert J. Cottroll, *The Long, Lingering Shadow: Slavery, Race, and Law in the American Hemisphere* (Athens: University of Georgia Press, 2013); Emily Blanck, *Tyrannicide: Forging an American Law of Slavery in Revolutionary South Carolina and Massachusetts* (Athens: University of Georgia Press, 2014); Lee B. Wilson, "Masters of Law: English Legal Culture and the Law of Slavery in Colonial South Carolina and the British Atlantic World, 1669-1783" (PhD diss., University of Virginia, 2014); Andrew T. Fede, *Homicide Justified: The Legality of Killing Slaves in the United States and the Atlantic World* (Athens: University of Georgia Press, 2017). On maritime law, see Michael Schoeppner, "Peculiar Quarantines: The Seamen Acts and Regulatory Authority in the Antebellum South," *Law and History Review* 31 (August 2013): 559–86; and Schoeppner, *Moral Contagion: Black Atlantic Sailors, Citizenship, and Diplomacy in Antebellum America* (New York: Cambridge University Press, 2019). Other works discuss southern seaports in larger contexts: David Head, "Sailing for Spanish America: The Atlantic Geopolitics of Foreign Privateering from the United States in the Early Republic" (PhD diss., SUNY–Buffalo, 2010); Kevin Arlyck, "Plaintiffs v. Privateers: Litigation and Foreign Affairs in the Federal Courts, 1816–1822," *Law and History Review* 30 (Autumn 2012): 245–78; Arlyck, "Forged By War: The Federal Courts and Foreign Affairs in the Age of Revolution" (PhD diss., New York University, 2014); Hannah Atlee Farber, "Underwritten States: Marine Insurance and the Making of Bodies Politic in

strong currents in history generally, emphasizing global or world history. Similarly, the increasingly western-facing nature of United States history placed a premium upon continent-wide explorations.[18] Since 2010, the geographic expansion of southern legal history increased focus upon the trans-Appalachian West, territories abutting the Mississippi River, as well as Texas, Arkansas, and Missouri—places that might be considered West, Midwest, or mid-America, yet which have manifest ties to the South.[19] The Mississippi and Ohio valleys proved most fertile for slavery scholars investigating legal ways enslaved people challenged their bondage, although Loren Schweninger's *Appealing for Liberty*

America, 1622–1815" (PhD diss., University of California, Berkeley, 2014); Gautham Rao, *National Duties: Customs Houses and the Making of the American State* (Chicago: University of Chicago Press, 2016).

18. On the refocusing of geographical perspective in the American narrative, see Daniel K. Richter, *Facing East from Indian Country: A Native History of Early America* (Cambridge: Harvard University Press, 2001); Paul W. Mapp, *The Elusive West and the Contest for Empire, 1713–1716* (Chapel Hill: University of North Carolina Press, 2011); Alan Taylor, *American Revolutions: A Continental History, 1750–1804* (New York: W. W. Norton, 2016). See Sara Nell Chatfield, "Multiple Orders in Multiple Venues: The Reform of Married Women's Property Rights, 1839–1920" (PhD diss., University of California, Berkeley, 2014) for a comparison of regional legal regimes in and beyond the South.

19. For the trans-Appalachian West, see David J. Langum and Howard P. Walthall, *From Maverick to Mainstream: Cumberland School of Law, 1847–1997* (Athens: University of Georgia Press, 1997); Turk McCleskey, *The Road to Black Ned's Forge: A Story of Race, Sex, and Trade on the Colonial American Frontier* (Charlottesville: University of Virginia Press, 2014); Greg Ablavsky, "The Adjudicatory State: Sovereignty, Property, and Law in the U.S. Territories, 1783–1802" (PhD diss., University of Pennsylvania, 2016). For the Mississippi Valley, see Mark Arvid Warburton, "'For the Purposes of Example and Justice': Native American Incarceration in the Upper Mississippi Valley, 1803–1849" (PhD diss., University of Iowa, 2011); Kristin D. Morgan, "Establishing the Order: Forming an American Common Law in Louisiana, Missouri, and New Mexico Territories" (PhD diss., Oklahoma State University, 2013); Muriel Ann Everton, "Libel in Mississippi, 1798–1832" (PhD diss., University of Southern Mississippi, 2010). On Texas, see Jean Stuntz, *Hers, His, and Theirs: Community Property Law in Spain and Early Texas* (Lubbock: Texas Tech University Press, 2005); Jason A. Gillmer, *Slavery and Freedom in Texas: Stories from the Courtroom, 1821–1871* (Athens: University of Georgia Press, 2017); Eric Miller, "From Frontier Paradigm to Modern Public Policy: The Development of Homestead and Property Exemption Law in Texas, Florida, and Alaska" (MA thesis, Florida State University, 2012). On Arkansas, see Jerry W. Looney, "'A Stronghold of Southern Legal Puritanism': The Arkansas Supreme Court and the Development of Criminal Law and Procedure, 1836–1874" (MA thesis, University of Arkansas, 2010). On Missouri, see Sharon Romeo, *Gender and the Jubilee: Black Freedom and the Reconstruction of Citizenship in Civil War Missouri* (Athens: University of Georgia Press, 2016); Bonnie Aileen Speck, "Minor Courts and Communities at the Frontier: The Justice of the Peace in Early Missouri" (PhD diss., Wayne State University, 2010); Lucas P. Volkman, "Houses Divided: Evangelical Schisms, Society, and Law and the Crisis of the Union in Missouri, 1837–1876" (PhD diss., University of Missouri–Columbia, 2012).

(2018) demonstrated that such freedom suits appeared in every state from the American Revolution to the Civil War.[20]

By contrast, nineteenth- and twentieth-century legal historians largely stuck to a South shaped geographically and conceptually by slavery, race, and the Civil War. Most followed the traditional narrative progression of slavery to emancipation, Reconstruction to Redemption, Jim Crow segregation to the civil rights era and beyond. Taken together, these works made clear the importance of law and legal action in shaping the contours of southern race relations; they also stressed ways that questions of race and power shaped the law's evolution. Still, even within the realm of race and power, in the 2000s and 2010s, the focus shifted from mostly top-down analyses of racial oppression and redemption to bottom-up narratives of self-determination in trying circumstances.[21]

Legal biography continued to draw scholarly attention, but studies of "great men" declined in the late twentieth century. Important contributions in the 2010s clustered around the Constitutional Convention: Jared McClain's study of Charles Pinckney (South Carolina), Karen E. Robbins's analysis of James McHenry (Maryland), and Mary Sarah Bilder's book about post-convention revisions made to James Madison's notes. Creating in essence a biography of Madison's convention notes, Bilder revealed how Madison's political experiences later in life shaped his ultimate revisions. However, leaving aside men of the founding generation or justices on the Supreme Court, the planter elite became more likely to be put on trial in southern legal history, as Jessica K. Lowe did, than venerated.[22]

20. Mark Salafia, *Slavery's Borderland: Freedom and Bondage along the Ohio River* (Philadelphia: University of Pennsylvania Press, 2013); Anne Twitty, *Before* Dred Scott: *Slavery and Legal Culture in the American Confluence, 1787–1857* (New York: Cambridge University Press, 2016); Kelly M. Kennington, *In the Shadow of* Dred Scott: *St. Louis Freedom Suits and the Legal Culture of Slavery in Antebellum America* (Athens: University of Georgia Press, 2017); Jesse Nasta, "Making Slavery's Borders: Legal Culture and the Transformation of Slavery's Northwestern Frontier, 1787–1860" (PhD diss., Northwestern University, 2017); Loren Schweninger, *Appealing for Liberty: Freedom Suits in the South* (New York: Oxford University Press, 2018).

21. For an exceptional example of this bottom-up trend, see Tomiko Brown-Nagin, *Courage to Dissent: Atlanta and the Long History of the Civil Rights Movement* (New York: Oxford University Press, 2012). For a more top-down approach, see Michael J. Klarman, *From Jim Crow to Civil Rights: The Supreme Court and the Struggle for Racial Equality* (New York: Oxford University Press, 2006).

22. Jared McClain, "An Analysis of Charles Pinckney's Contributions at the Constitutional Convention of 1787," *Journal of Southern Legal History* 24 (2016): 1–68; Karen E. Robbins, *James McHenry, Forgotten Federalist* (Athens: University of Georgia Press, 2013); Mary Sarah Bilder, *Madison's Hand: Revising the Constitutional Convention* (Cambridge: Harvard University Press, 2015). On Supreme Court

Bottom-up narratives inspired more scholarly investigations. Christopher Tomlins's magisterial history of unfree labor, *Freedom Bound* (2010), undermined received wisdom about indentured servitude, the household economy, and the immigration and colonization project in early America. Perhaps Tomlins's greatest contribution was rejecting the American Revolution as a boundary between presumptions of freedom and slavery (which often resulted in southern slave law seeming like a nineteenth-century exception).[23] His close textual analysis of slavery and indentured servitude laws showed that unfree labor dominated all aspects of pre-1865 America, North and South. Tomlins reconceived unfree labor as not uniquely "southern" and identified the introduction of unfree labor in the seventeenth century as the pivotal moment in labor and immigration history.[24]

Tomlins's work served as a harbinger for what scholars sometimes described as the new history of capitalism in the South. Edward E. Baptist's *The Half Has Never Been Told* (2014), contributors to Sven Beckert and Seth Rockman's anthology *Slavery's Capitalism* (2016), and Beckert's sweeping *Empire of Cotton* (2014) well documented how the global and Industrial-Revolution-driving cotton economy was reliant upon slavery.[25] The legal structures undergirding cotton's

---

justices, see Joel McMahon, *Our Good and Faithful Servant: James Moore Wayne and Georgia Unionism* (Macon: Mercer University Press, 2017); Thomas Edward Reidy, "Objects of Confidence and Choice: Professional Communities in Alabama, 1804–1861" (PhD diss., University of Alabama, 2014); William S. Belko, *Philip Pendleton Barbour in Jacksonian America: An Old Republican in King Andrew's Court* (Tuscaloosa: University of Alabama Press, 2016); Alexander Wohl, *Father, Son, and Constitution: How Justice Tom Clark and Attorney General Ramsey Clark Shaped American Democracy* (Lawrence: University Press of Kansas, 2013). On trials of the planter elite, see Jessica K. Lowe, *Murder in the Shenandoah: Making Law Sovereign in Revolutionary Virginia* (New York: Cambridge University Press, 2018). Elite control over courts remained the norm; see Aaron J. Palmer, *A Rule of Law: Elite Political Authority and the Coming of the Revolution in the South Carolina Lowcountry, 1763–1776* (Leiden: Brill, 2014). On the training of southern legal elites, see Justin Simard, "Slavery's Legalism: Lawyers and the Commercial Route of Slavery," *Law and History Review* 37 (May 2019): 571–603.

23. Christopher Tomlins, *Freedom Bound: Law, Labor, and Civic Identity in Colonizing English America, 1580–1865* (New York: Cambridge University Press, 2010), 65, 504.

24. Connecting property ownership to slavery and citizenship is central to Christopher Michael Curtis, *Jefferson's Freeholders and the Politics of Ownership in the Old Dominion* (New York: Cambridge University Press, 2012). Indentured labor continues to be a rich scholarly field. See Allison Noelle Madar, "'A People Between': Servitude in Colonial Virginia, 1700–1783" (PhD diss., Rice University, 2013).

25. Edward E. Baptist, *The Half Has Never Been Told: Slavery and the Making of American Capitalism* (New York: Basic Books, 2014); Sven Beckert and Seth Rockman, eds., *Slavery's Capitalism: A New History of American Economic Development* (Philadelphia: University of Pennsylvania Press, 2016); Sven Beckert, *Empire of Cotton: A Global History* (New York: Alfred A. Knopf, 2014).

commercial trade remain less well understood but are slowly coming into focus. That commercial law might have contained within it the potential to unravel slavery (as well as sustain it) lay at the core of research by Matthew A. Axtell, who investigated riverfront law practitioners and how their private law activism disrupted slavery economically.[26] Findings in his riverine, border-based study paralleled publications that emphasized the fluidity of legal status along the Ohio and Mississippi rivers.[27]

The implications of southern law on the economy, broadly conceived, as well as economic effects upon the law, gained increased visibility as scholars investigated indebtedness, both private and public. Exciting studies explored how pre-Revolutionary Virginia debtors understood debt and how international tribunals resolved southern indebtedness during the tumultuous 1790s.[28] Brent Tarter showed how Virginia's public debt spiraled into a post–Civil War legal nightmare.[29] The interplay of law and plantation economics garnered more attention in South Carolina, either through slaves engaged in selling goods or when white slave-owning families overextended themselves financially and veered towards insolvency.[30] Slave mortgaging, marine insurance for slave-trading vessels, and financial speculation likewise attracted scholarly attention.[31] Beyond debt, the protection or seizure of assets emerged as a topic of interest, possibly due to the intense economic fluctuations of 2008.[32]

26. Matthew A. Axtell, "Toward a New Legal History of Capitalism and Unfree Labor: Law, Slavery, and Emancipation in the American Marketplace," *Law & Social Inquiry* 40 (Winter 2015): 270–300; Axtell, "American Steamboat Gothic: Disruptive Commerce and Slavery's Liquidation, 1832–1865" (PhD diss., Princeton University, 2016).

27. See also Salafia, *Slavery's Borderland;* Twitty, *Before* Dred Scott; Kennington, *In the Shadow of* Dred Scott.

28. Jackson N. Sasser, "Poor and Dead and Much Involved: The Afterlife of Private Debt in Post-Revolutionary Virginia" (PhD diss., College of William & Mary, 2015).

29. Brent Tarter, *A Saga of the New South: Race, Law, and Public Debt in Virginia* (Charlottesville: University of Virginia Press, 2016); Chad Holmes, "The Role of Debt and Dependency in Shaping West Virginia's Political Economy, 1820–1920" (MA thesis, West Virginia University, 2016).

30. Justene Hill, "Felonious Transactions: Legal Culture and Business Practices of Slave Economies in South Carolina, 1787–1860" (PhD diss., Princeton University, 2015); Ivy Farr McIntyre, "Families in Extremis: South Carolina in the Early Republic" (PhD diss., Saint Louis University, 2015).

31. Peter Depuydt, "The Mortgaging of Souls: Sugar, Slaves, and Speculation," *Louisiana History* 54 (Fall 2013): 448–64; Anita Rupprecht, "'Inherent Vice': Marine Insurance, Slave Ship Rebellion and Law," *Race and Class* 57 (January 2016): 31–44.

32. Farber, "Underwritten States"; Rachel Katlyn Deale, "Acts of War: The Southern Seizure of Federal Property, 1860–1861" (PhD diss., University of Alabama, 2017).

Family struggles could have intense economic ramifications, particularly for those disinherited by their richer (deceased) relatives.[33] Scholars examined the multiple roles that women played in early southern courts as defendants, plaintiffs, witnesses, and attorneys—generally stressing their agency as actors maneuvering within legal processes that tended to disadvantage women systematically.[34] Scholars debate whether the post-Revolution generation of women gained or lost legal power over property.[35]

Native American legal history also experienced a rapid upsurge in the decade beginning in 2010. Two exceptional studies stand out: Andrés Reséndez's *The Other Slavery* (2016) and Deborah A. Rosen's *Border Law* (2015). Well written and deeply researched, both books analyzed rich veins of materials on law and Indigenous peoples. Reséndez utilized Spanish legal materials to explain the sixteenth-century New Laws that barred using Native slave labor—laws largely ignored in the Americas.[36] The long-term impact of this system upon parts of northern

33. Yvonne Pitts, *Family, Law, and Inheritance in America: A Social and Legal History of Nineteenth-Century Kentucky* (New York: Cambridge University Press, 2013); Catherine Wisnosky, "The Will of the Master: Testamentary Manumission and Will Contests in Virginia, 1800–1858" (MA thesis, University of Nevada, Las Vegas, 2015).

34. Loren Schweninger, "'To the Honourable': Divorce, Alimony, Slavery, and the Law in Antebellum North Carolina," *North Carolina Historical Review* 86 (April 2009): 127–79; Monica Witkowski, "'Justice without Partiality': Women and the Law in Colonial Maryland, 1648–1715" (PhD diss., Marquette University, 2010); Christine Powers, "Tyrants of the 'Peace': Intimate Violence and the Local Legal Environment of Late Antebellum Baltimore" (MA thesis, University of Maryland, Baltimore County, 2010); Amanda Lea Miracle, "Intimate Connections: Violence, Patriarchy, and the Law in Seventeenth-Century Maryland Infanticide Cases," *Maryland Historical Magazine* 105 (Spring 2010): 6–16; Daphne A. Fruchtman, "'They Acted Pretty Much as Man and Wife': Race, Slavery, and the Borders of Marriage and Family in the Antebellum South" (MA thesis, University of North Carolina, Chapel Hill, 2013); Miracle, "Negotiating the Legal Tradition: Juries of Matrons in Seventeenth-Century Maryland," *Maryland Historical Magazine* 108 (Fall 2013): 321–43; Schweninger, "Freedom Suits, African American Women, and the Genealogy of Slavery," *William and Mary Quarterly* 71 (January 2014): 35–62.

35. For debates, see, for example, Jacqueline Beatty, "In Dependence: Women's Protection and Subordination as Power in Early America, 1750–1820" (PhD diss., George Mason University, 2016); Emily Hope Margolis, "Propertied White Women, Family Property, and Governance in the Post-Revolutionary South" (PhD diss., Duke University, 2017), who argued that women lost power; and Angela Boswell, "Married Women's Property Acts and the Challenge to Patriarchal Order: Colorado County, Texas," in *Negotiating Boundaries of Southern Womanhood: Dealing with the Powers That Be*, ed. Janet L. Coryell et al. (Columbia: University of Missouri Press, 2000), 93–98, who concluded that married women's property acts offered greater power or respect.

36. Andrés Reséndez, *The Other Slavery: The Uncovered Story of Indian Enslavement in America* (New York: Houghton Mifflin, 2016). See also Kristofer Ray, "'The Indians of Every Denomination Were Free,

New Spain (which included modern-day Texas, Florida, and the Gulf Coast) was dramatic. Reséndez's study explained how legal structures enabled Native American slavery to persist, within as well as beyond the South. In a more focused work, Rosen explored how the First Seminole War in Florida led to wartime tribunals, Indigenous military prisoners, debates on the nature of sovereignty, and the allocation of rights along racial lines.[37] Although Creek and Choctaw law and identity have been explored, Cherokee legal issues like sovereignty continue to predominate, in no small part because the United States Supreme Court's rulings are implicated.[38] The liminal legal space occupied by individuals of African and Native descent was admirably considered by Honor Sachs, who traced more than forty years of freedom suit litigation by an Afro-Indian family in Virginia.[39]

Although Native Americans garnered heightened visibility in southern legal history in the 2000s and 2010s, enslaved men and women attracted the lion's share of scholarship.[40] Proslavery thought and its connections to southern courtrooms as well as universities occupied Alfred L. Brophy in his sweeping study of southern legal intellectuals.[41] Abolitionism's connection to international

and Independent of Us': Anglo-Virginian Explorations of Indigenous Slavery, Freedom, and Society, 1772–1830," *American Nineteenth Century History* 17 (June 2016): 139–59.

37. Deborah A. Rosen, *Border Law: The First Seminole War and American Nationhood* (Cambridge: Harvard University Press, 2015). For elsewhere in the South, see Warburton, "'For the Purposes of Example and Justice.'"

38. Kelly N. Fayard, "'We've Always Known Who We Are': Belonging in the Poarch Band of Creek Indians" (PhD diss., University of Michigan, 2011); Katherine M. B. Osborn, "Tribal 'Remnants' or State Citizens: Mississippi Choctaws in the Post-Removal South," *American Nineteenth Century History* 17 (August 2016): 199–214; Nancy Morgan, "'Fraught with Disastrous Consequences for Our Country': Cherokee Sovereignty, Nullification, and the Sectional Crisis" (PhD diss., Temple University, 2015); Stefan Bullock, "'Respecting the Original Justice of the Claim': Reality and Legality in John Marshall's Myth of Indian Divestiture, *Johnson v. M'Intosh*" (MA thesis, McGill University, 2010).

39. Honor Sachs, "'Freedom by a Judgment': The Legal History of an Afro-Indian Family," *Law and History Review* 30 (February 2012): 173–203.

40. See, for example, Terri L. Snyder, "Marriage on the Margins: Free Wives, Enslaved Husbands, and the Law in Early Virginia," *Law and History Review* 30 (February 2012): 141–71.

41. Alfred L. Brophy, *University, Court, and Slave: Pro-Slavery Thought in Southern Colleges and Courts and the Coming of the Civil War* (New York: Oxford University Press, 2016). See also Farah Peterson, "Statutory Interpretation and Judicial Authority, 1776–1860" (PhD diss., Princeton University, 2015) regarding intellectuals and the rise of jurisprudential formalism in the Jacksonian era. Chad Vanderford, *The Legacy of St. George Tucker: College Professors in Virginia Confront Slavery and Rights of States, 1771–1897* (Knoxville: University of Tennessee Press, 2015), analyzed natural law arguments used by intellectuals.

law has received renewed attention as well.[42] How enslaved peoples endured the prison workhouse or the penitentiary system has been explored broadly in South Carolina, Virginia, Louisiana, and the South Atlantic rim.[43] Paradoxical legal situations, as when an enslaved person might have owned and controlled property or free African Americans might have petitioned to be re-enslaved, complicate long-held "absolutes" associated with antebellum slave law. The latitude that enslaved men and women experienced in Louisiana, with its hybrid French-Spanish-English legal system, continues to be plumbed through studies of slave-initiated litigation, typically investigating the degree to which bondsmen and women utilized the legal system to their own advantage.[44] Accusations of kidnapping brought against former enslavers during the Civil War reveal how the South's changing legal landscape turned those formerly protected by the law into the accused.[45]

Legal historians found the transition from slavery to freedom and subse-

42. Marco Perry Basile, "The Slave Trade and the Foundations of U.S. International Legal Thought, 1808–1870" (PhD diss., Harvard University, 2016).

43. Jeff Forret, "Before Angola: Enslaved Prisoners in the Louisiana State Penitentiary," *Louisiana History* 54 (Spring 2013): 133–71; Taja-Nia Henderson, "Crucibles of Discontent: Penal Practice in the Shadow of Slavery, Virginia, 1796–1865" (PhD diss., New York University, 2013); Samanthis Smalls, "Behind Workhouse Walls: The Public Regulation of Slavery in Charleston, 1730–1850" (PhD diss., Duke University, 2015); Christina Pruett Hermann, "Specters of Freedom: Forced Labor, Social Struggle, and the Louisiana State Penitentiary System, 1835–1935" (PhD diss., Michigan State University, 2015); Hilary Louise Coulson, "The Penitentiary at Richmond: Slavery, State Building, and Labor in the South's First State Prison" (PhD diss., University of California, San Diego, 2016); Max Mishler, "The Atlantic Origins of Mass Incarceration Punishment, Abolition, and Racial Inequality" (PhD diss., New York University, 2016).

44. Erica Bruchko, "'Slave Traffick': The Informal Economy, the Law, and the Social Order of South Carolina Cotton Country, 1793–1860" (PhD diss., Emory University, 2016); Ted Maris-Wolf, *Family Bonds: Free Blacks and Re-Enslavement Law in Antebellum Virginia* (Chapel Hill: University of North Carolina Press, 2015); Kenneth R. Aslakson, *Making Race in the Courtroom: The Legal Construction of Three Races in Early New Orleans* (New York: New York University Press, 2014); Steve Peraza, "Suing the Master: Slave Litigation as Resistance in Eighteenth-Century Louisiana" (PhD diss., SUNY–Buffalo, 2015); Jessica Marie Johnson, "Death Rites as Birthrights in Atlantic New Orleans: Kinship and Race in the Case of *María Teresa v. Perine Dauphine,*" *Slavery & Abolition* 36 (September 2015): 233–56. See also M. J. Morgan, "Indians on Trial: Crime and Punishment in French Louisiana on the Eve of the Seven Years' War," *Louisiana History* 50 (Summer 2009): 293–319.

45. Adam Rothman, *Beyond Freedom's Reach: A Kidnapping in the Twilight of Slavery* (Cambridge: Harvard University Press, 2015); Michael A. Ross, *The Great New Orleans Kidnapping Case: Race, Law, and Justice in the Reconstruction Era* (New York: Oxford University Press, 2015).

quently to subjugation an equally fruitful topic. Two field-defining books explored the evolving meanings of freedom under law during the turbulent years of the Civil War era: Laura F. Edwards's *A Legal History of the Civil War and Reconstruction* (2015) and Timothy S. Huebner's *Liberty and Union* (2016).[46] Edwards's book stressed the war's transformative effects on the nation's legal order. The challenge of legally dismantling slavery—and the necessary reconstruction of almost every aspect of southern life that this task entailed—changed the very nature of law and constitutional rights, and consequently, Americans' relationship with and to the law. Redefining the legal nature of freedom, Edwards argued, expanded the categories of people making claims on the government for protection of newly enhanced civil and political rights. Unfortunately, in the decades following the Civil War, expansion of both rights and the range of claimants to these rights proved more aspirational than actual. In fact, an additional century passed before the issues once again took center stage.

Building on similar insights, Huebner emphasized the constitutional origins of debates about the proper scope of individual rights under the Constitution. The legal and constitutional transformations of the Civil War era had roots in the constitutional challenges and compromises of the founding, Huebner demonstrated. War came in large part as a result of the differing interpretations that individuals North and South gave to the founding concepts of liberty and union. These conceptual differences, in turn, shaped the nature of Reconstruction, both its revolutionary nature and its ambivalent legacy.

Huebner and Edwards both highlighted an emerging theme in southern legal history: the transition from slavery to freedom to segregation and then back to (mostly) freedom was neither a fixed nor inevitable process. Reading southern legal history as simply the road to and then from *Brown v. Board of Education* misses the complexities of the historical reality. Such a simplistic interpretation also understates the roles played by individual actors both inside and outside of the courtroom.

Take, for example, the deliberate use of courts and the legal system by minority groups to achieve desired policy ends. Traditional narratives largely paint (with good reason) courts and legal institutions as agents of oppression—places

46. Laura F. Edwards, *A Legal History of the Civil War and Reconstruction: A Nation of Rights* (New York: Cambridge University Press, 2015); Timothy S. Huebner, *Liberty and Union: The Civil War Era and American Constitutionalism* (Lawrence: University Press of Kansas, 2016).

where the disadvantaged in southern society were helpless and subjugated.[47] But some scholars questioned the extent of this powerlessness. Exploring the dynamics of interracial rape, Lisa Lindquist Dorr found that whereas rape trials often were "grand public spectacles" of race oppression, cracks in white solidarity across class and gender lines sometimes provided black men with opportunities to challenge white racial power and avoid the "ultimate sanction" of legal or extralegal execution.[48] In comparable fashion, Melissa Milewski argued in *Litigating across the Color Line* (2017) that newly freed African Americans in the post-Reconstruction South made explicit use of state civil courts to defend their economic interests. They did not always win, Milewski noted, but in a surprising number of cases (in fact, roughly half of the four thousand or so cases she studied), African American plaintiffs negotiated a white-dominated legal system to victory.[49] Brandon Jett offered a similar perspective on African American strategic interactions with white police in twentieth-century Memphis. Despite ongoing tensions between white police and Memphis's black residents as a consequence of Jim Crow segregation, the high rate of black-on-black violence led black Memphians to choose cooperation with the police as a means of removing unwanted murderers from their midst. Largely turning Jim Crow against itself,

47. David M. Oshinsky, *"Worse Than Slavery": Parchman Farm and the Ordeal of Jim Crow Justice* (New York: Free Press, 1996); Douglas A. Blackmon, *Slavery by Another Name: The Re-Enslavement of Black Americans from the Civil War to World War II* (New York: Doubleday, 2008); Michelle Alexander, *The New Jim Crow: Mass Incarceration in the Age of Colorblindness,* rev. ed. (New York: New Press, 2010).

48. Lisa Lindquist Dorr, *White Women, Rape, and the Power of Race in Virginia, 1900–1960* (Chapel Hill: University of North Carolina Press, 2004). See also Radley Balko, *The Cadaver King and the County Dentist: A True Story of Injustice in the American South* (New York: PublicAffairs, 2018). For a similar take on gender and alcohol convictions, see Dorr, "A Place for Themselves in the Modern World: Southern Women and Alcohol in the Age of Prohibition, 1912–1933," in Hadden and Minter, eds., *Signposts,* 317–44.

49. Melissa Milewski, *Litigating across the Color Line: Civil Cases Between Black and White Southerners from the End of Slavery to Civil Rights* (New York: Oxford University Press, 2017). For a comparable study in an earlier era, see Kimberly M. Welch, *Black Litigants in the Antebellum American South* (Chapel Hill: University of North Carolina Press, 2018). Whites also used the uneven terrain of Reconstruction justice for their own ends. See Helen H. LaCroix, "In the Absence of Reconstruction: Race, Politics, and State Power in Kentucky, 1850–1872" (PhD diss., University of Wisconsin, 2011). For a penetrating analysis examining Milewski, Welch, and others, see Pippa Holloway, "Race and Law from the Bottom Up in the Nineteenth-Century South: A Review Essay," *Journal of Southern History* 85 (May 2019): 393–408. Holloway highlights Milewski's insight about the "relevance of a kind of political irrelevance," specifically how African American litigants gain greater legal protections when the overall challenge to white supremacy is relatively small (405).

this strategy of cooperation served the interests of the African American community, while allowing white police to combat what was nationally recognized as a murder epidemic.[50]

Even when minority groups did not triumph by working within the legal system, themes of resistance and organization (legal and political) run through the scholarship on Jim Crow segregation. In *No Mercy Here* (2016), Sarah Haley explored resistance and even outright sabotage by black female prisoners in southern prisons.[51] In *Beyond the Rope* (2016), Karlos K. Hill took up the issue of lynching from a black perspective, exposing the growth of a multifaceted legal (and extralegal) culture of resistance within the African American community.[52] Meanwhile, Robert Cassanello's *To Render Invisible* (2013) described African American resistance to Jim Crow in Jacksonville, Florida, arguing that the black space legally created by segregation and adapted by local community

50. Brandon Jett, "'Many People "Colored" Have Come to the Homicide Office': Police Investigations of African American Homicides in Memphis, 1920–1945," in *Crime and Punishment in the Jim Crow South,* ed. Amy Louise Wood and Natalie J. Ring (Urbana: University of Illinois Press, 2019), 32–57. For more on African Americans using the police, despite hostile attitudes toward them, to combat crime in their communities, see Elijah Anderson, *Street Wise: Race, Class, and Change in an Urban Community* (Chicago: University of Chicago Press, 1990), 203–4. See also Michele Grigsby Coffey, "*The State of Louisiana v. Charles Guerand:* Interracial Sexual Mores, Rape Rhetoric, and Respectability in 1930s New Orleans," *Louisiana History* 54 (Winter 2013): 47–93, for a role reversal in which a white policeman was convicted of killing a black woman who refused his demands for sex. In "Less Crime, More Punishment: Violence, Race, and Criminal Justice in Early Twentieth-Century America," *Journal of American History* 102 (June 2015): 34–46, Jeffrey S. Adler noted how in 1920s New Orleans, "Southern law enforcers (disingenuously) insisted that jurors—still all-white—would not convict African Americans charged with intraracial violence. According to a New Orleans official, 'it is almost impossible to get a jury who will convict a negro for killing another negro.' During the early 1920s jurors acquitted roughly half of all felony defendants, yet this accounted for less than one-tenth of the cases that ended without a conviction." See "Less Crime, More Punishment," 38. Ironically, as crime rates plummeted in the late 1920s, punishments for criminals, in particular African Americans, skyrocketed. See also Adler, "'The Greatest Thrill I Get Is When I Hear a Criminal Say, 'Yes I Did It': Race and the Third Degree in New Orleans, 1920–1945," *Law and History Review* 34 (February 2016): 1–44.

51. Sarah Haley, *No Mercy Here: Gender, Punishment, and the Making of Jim Crow Modernity* (Chapel Hill: University of North Carolina Press, 2016).

52. Karlos K. Hill, *Beyond the Rope: The Impact of Lynching on Black Culture and Memory* (New York: Cambridge University Press, 2016). See also Donald G. Mathews, *At the Altar of Lynching: Burning Sam Hose in the American South* (New York: Cambridge University Press, 2017); Tameka Bradley Hobbs, *Democracy Abroad, Lynching at Home: Racial Violence in Florida* (Gainesville: University Press of Florida, 2015). A similar pattern existed for Mexican Americans in Texas. See Nicholas Villanueva Jr., *The Lynching of Mexicans in the Texas Borderlands* (Albuquerque: University of New Mexico Press, 2017).

leaders served the community's needs and not those of the dominant white social order.[53]

The theme of resistance through legal and extralegal means did not end with the Jim Crow era. In fact, legal historical scholarship challenged the traditional civil rights timeline of Jim Crow segregation (roughly 1880s–1940s) leading to the civil rights era (1950s through the mid-1960s) and followed by the post–civil rights era (late 1960s to the present). In common with other genres of southern history, many legal historians adopted the concept of the long civil rights movement to describe the mobilization efforts and ideas that underlay the black freedom struggle. In this view, resistance to Jim Crow segregation served as the seed stock of an emerging civil rights struggle, a fight that carried on past the heroic Montgomery-to-Selma phase and into the late twentieth and early twenty-first centuries.[54]

For instance, Risa Goluboff noted the existence in the 1940s of a "lost" civil rights fight by elements of the NAACP and US Justice Department lawyers to combat discrimination by attacking economic inequalities in the workplace rather than through desegregation litigation. She called this episode a "lost" fight not only because historians mostly ignored these efforts but also because civil rights leaders ultimately abandoned the plan for defeating Jim Crow through economic reforms in favor of an all-out fight for desegregation.[55] In her 2011 study of the long civil rights movement in Atlanta, Tomiko Brown-Nagin explained how the African American community used an underappreciated "pragmatic" approach to civil rights reform, supporting the direct fight against Jim Crow segregation through litigation but also through direct action, lobbying for legislation,

53. Robert Cassanello, *To Render Invisible: Jim Crow and Public Life in New South Jacksonville* (Gainesville: University Press of Florida, 2013). See also Chris Bray, "'Every Right to be Where She Was': The Legal Reconstruction of Black Self-Defense in Jim Crow Florida," *Florida Historical Quarterly* 87 (Winter 2009): 352–77; Jonathan Harrison, "The Rise of Jim Crow in Fort Myers, 1885–1930," *Florida Historical Quarterly* 94 (Summer 2015): 40–67.

54. Much of our discussion here draws on the superb review essays of Christopher W. Schmidt, "Legal History and the Problem of the Long Civil Rights Movement," *Law & Social Inquiry* 41 (Fall 2016): 1081–107; Risa Goluboff, "Lawyers, Law, and the New Civil Rights History," *Harvard Law Review* 126 (June 2013): 2312–35.

55. Risa Goluboff, *The Lost Promise of Civil Rights* (Cambridge: Harvard University Press, 2007). See also David Freeman Engstrom, "The Lost Origins of American Fair Employment Law: Regulatory Choice and the Making of Modern Civil Rights, 1943–1972," *Stanford Law Review* 63 (May 2011): 1071–143; Glenda Elizabeth Gilmore, *Defying Dixie: The Radical Roots of Civil Rights, 1919–1950* (New York: W. W. Norton, 2008).

and creating private forms of social and political negotiation.[56] Meanwhile, Christopher W. Schmidt took a standard part of the traditional civil rights narrative, the sit-in protests, and recast them to emphasize not the courts but Congress's role (via the Civil Rights Act of 1964) in reshaping the Constitution in response to direct action by student protesters.[57] In turn, Mary L. Dudziak expanded the scope of the civil rights fight by placing the legal struggle against Jim Crow in an international context.[58] And Anders Walker recrafted the legal narrative of resisting Jim Crow by exploring views of southern moderate whites on issues of civil rights reform and equality.[59]

As informative as the long civil rights movement narrative has been, many southern legal historians continued to concentrate on traditional narratives of court-based civil rights. Between 2008 and 2013, eight separate biographies of Thurgood Marshall appeared, examining all aspects of his life and career.[60] Other books told the life stories of Marshall's fellow civil rights lawyers, broke down landmark civil rights court cases, chronicled ongoing legal efforts of the NAACP, and analyzed legal, political, and practical fallout from the United States Supreme Court's ruling in *Brown v. Board of Education.*[61] Other productive threads fo-

56. Brown-Nagin, *Courage to Dissent.*

57. Christopher W. Schmidt, *The Sit-ins: Protest and Legal Change in the Civil Rights Era* (Chicago: University of Chicago Press, 2018).

58. Mary L. Dudziak, *Cold War Civil Rights: Race and the Image of American Democracy,* rev. ed. (Princeton: Princeton University Press, 2011).

59. Anders Walker, *The Ghost of Jim Crow: How Southern Moderates Used* Brown v. Board of Education *to Stall Civil Rights* (New York: Oxford University Press, 2009); Walker, *The Burning House: Jim Crow and the Making of Modern America* (New Haven: Yale University Press, 2018). For a view of more extreme segregationists, see Elizabeth Gillespie McRae, *Mothers of Massive Resistance: White Women and the Politics of White Supremacy* (New York: Oxford University Press, 2018).

60. Mary L. Dudziak, *Exporting American Dreams: Thurgood Marshall's African Journey* (New York: Oxford University Press, 2008); Howard Ball, *A Defiant Life: Thurgood Marshall and the Persistence of Racism in America* (New York: Crown Publishers, 1998); James Rawn Jr., *Root and Branch: Charles Hamilton Houston, Thurgood Marshall, and the Struggle to End Segregation* (New York: Bloomsbury Press, 2010); Juan Williams, *Thurgood Marshall: American Revolutionary* (New York: Times Books, 1998); Larry S. Gibson, *Young Thurgood: The Making of a Supreme Court Justice* (New York: Prometheus Books, 2012); Gilbert King, *Devil in the Grove: Thurgood Marshall, The Groveland Boys, and the Dawn of a New America* (New York: HarperCollins, 2012); Wil Haygood, *Showdown: Thurgood Marshall and the Supreme Court Nomination That Changed America* (New York: Alfred A. Knopf, 2015); Charles L. Zelden, *Thurgood Marshall: Race, Rights, and the Struggle for a More Perfect Union* (New York: Routledge, 2013).

61. On lawyers, see Kenneth W. Mack, *Representing the Race: The Creation of the Civil Rights Lawyer* (Cambridge: Harvard University Press, 2012); Maurice C. Daniels, *Saving the Soul of Georgia* (Athens:

cused on the evolving nature of white opposition to civil rights.[62] A parallel trend focused on the civil rights struggles of Mexican Americans in Texas, reformist whites fighting for legislative reapportionment, as well as legal and constitutional histories for Native Americans, prisoners, vagrants, and women in the South.[63]

University of Georgia Press, 2013); Gordon Andrews, *Undoing* Plessy: *Charles Hamilton Houston, Race, Labor, and the Law, 1895–1950* (Newcastle upon Tyne: Cambridge Scholars Publishing, 2014); W. Lewis Burke, *All for Civil Rights: African American Lawyers in South Carolina, 1868–1968* (Athens: University of Georgia Press, 2017); Gary L. Ford Jr., *Constance Baker Motley: One Woman's Fight for Civil Rights and Equal Justice under Law* (Tuscaloosa: University of Alabama Press, 2017); Margaret Edds, *We Face the Dawn: Oliver Hill, Spottswood Robinson, and the Legal Team That Dismantled Jim Crow* (Charlottesville: University of Virginia Press, 2018). On civil rights cases, see Gary M. Lavergne, *Before* Brown: *Heman Marion Sweatt, Thurgood Marshall, and the Long Road to Justice* (Austin: University of Texas Press, 2010); Jeffrey D. Gonda, *Unjust Deeds: The Restrictive Covenant Cases and the Making of the Civil Rights Movement* (Chapel Hill: University of North Carolina Press, 2015); James W. Endersby and William T. Horner, *Lloyd Gaines and the Fight to End Segregation* (Columbia: University of Missouri Press, 2016); Cheryl Elizabeth Brown Wattley, *A Step toward* Brown v. Board of Education: *Ada Louis Sipuel Fisher and Her Fight to End Segregation* (Norman: University of Oklahoma Press, 2018). On the NAACP, see Eric W. Rise, "Crime, Comity and Civil Rights: The NAACP and the Extradition of Southern Black Fugitives," *American Journal of Legal History* 55 (January 2015): 119–47; W. Lewis Burke, "*Pink Franklin v. South Carolina:* The NAACP's First Case," *American Journal of Legal History* 54 (July 2014): 265–302. On *Brown v. Board of Education,* see Herbert Lovelace, "King Making: *Brown v. Board* and the Rise of a Racial Savior," *American Journal of Legal History* 57 (December 2017): 393–446; Ben Keppel, Brown v. Board *and the Transformation of American Culture: Education and the South in the Age of Desegregation* (Baton Rouge: Louisiana State University Press, 2016).

62. Stacy Braukman, *Communists and Perverts under the Palms: The Johns Committee in Florida, 1956–1965* (Gainesville: University Press of Florida, 2012); McRae, *Mothers of Massive Resistance;* John Kyle Day, *The Southern Manifesto: Massive Resistance and the Fight to Preserve Segregation* (Jackson: University Press of Mississippi, 2014).

63. On Mexican American civil rights, see Philippa Strum, Mendez v. Westminster: *School Desegregation and Mexican-American Rights* (Lawrence: University Press of Kansas, 2010); Brian D. Behnken, *Fighting Their Own Battles: Mexican Americans, African Americans, and the Struggle for Civil Rights in Texas* (Chapel Hill: University of North Carolina Press, 2011); Julian Lim, *Porous Borders: Multiracial Migrations and the Law in U.S.-Mexico Borderlands* (Chapel Hill: University of North Carolina Press, 2017). On reapportionment, see Charles L. Zelden, "The Southern Roots of the Reapportionment Revolution," in Hadden and Minter, eds., *Signposts,* 393–416. On Native American civil rights, see Brian Klopotek, *Recognition Odyssey: Indigeneity, Race, and Federal Tribal Recognition Policy in Three Louisiana Indian Communities* (Durham: Duke University Press, 2011); Joanne Barker, *Native Acts: Law, Recognition, and Cultural Authenticity* (Durham: Duke University Press, 2011). On prisoners, vagrants, and women, see Gregory L. Richard, "The Rule of Three: Federal Courts and Prison Farms in the Post-Segregation South" (PhD diss., University of Mississippi, 2013); Risa Goluboff, *Vagrant Nation: Police Power, Constitutional Change, and the Making of the 1960s* (New York: Oxford University Press, 2017); Rosalind Rosenberg,

Aside from civil rights jurisprudence, scholars scrutinized the South's state and federal courts through a mix of institutional histories and biographies of notable courts, judges, and lawyers, and the effects of each on judicial process and the history of the South.[64] One especially interesting analysis of southern lawyers came from Cynthia Nicoletti, who investigated how white southern lawyers crafted negative legal responses to the Civil War, Reconstruction, and the freedoms promised to African Americans by the Civil Rights Amendments. In "Strategic Litigation and the Death of Reconstruction" (2013), Nicoletti showed how a network of southern lawyers successfully created and applied "cause lawyering" in opposition to Reconstruction and civil rights long before Thurgood Marshall and the NAACP used the concept in defense of minority rights in the 1930s. Her book, *Secession on Trial* (2017), narrated the interactions between lawyers who worked on both sides of the never held, post–Civil War treason prose-

---

Jane Crow: The Life of Pauli Murray (New York: Oxford University Press, 2017); Laura E. Free, *Suffrage Reconstructed: Gender, Race, and Voting Rights in the Civil War Era* (Ithaca: Cornell University Press, 2015); Brown Wattley, *A Step toward* Brown v. Board of Education, 53; Janet Allured, "Louisiana, the American South, and the Birth of Second-Wave Feminism," *Louisiana History* 54 (Fall 2013): 380–423.

64. On courts, see James L. Haley, *The Texas Supreme Court: A Narrative History, 1836–1986* (Austin: University of Texas Press, 2013); Frances Mitchell Ross, ed., *United States District Courts and Judges of Arkansas, 1836–1960* (Fayetteville: University of Arkansas Press, 2016); James M. Denham, *Fifty Years of Justice: A History of the U.S. District Court for the Middle District of Florida* (Gainesville: University Press of Florida, 2015); Peter Graham Fish, *Federal Justice in the Mid-Atlantic South: United States Courts from Maryland to the Carolinas, 1836–1861* (Durham: Carolina Academic Press, 2015); Burton A. Boxerman, *And Justice for All: A History of the Federal District Court of Eastern Missouri* (Cape Girardeau: Southeast Missouri State University Press, 2014); John O. Peters, *From Marshall to Moussaoui: Federal Justice in the Eastern District of Virginia* (Petersburg, VA: Dietz Press, 2013). On judges, see Timothy S. Huebner, "Emory Speer and Federal Enforcement of the Rights of African Americans, 1880–1910," *American Journal of Legal History* 55 (January 2015): 34–63; Anne Emanuel, *Elbert Parr Tuttle: Chief Jurist of the Civil Rights Revolution* (Athens: University of Georgia Press, 2011); Joel William Friedman, *Champion of Civil Rights: Judge John Minor Wisdom* (Baton Rouge: Louisiana State University Press, 2009); Brent J. Aucoin, *Thomas Goode Jones: Race, Politics, and Justice in the New South* (Tuscaloosa: University of Alabama Press, 2016); Howard E. Covington Jr., *Henry Frye: North Carolina's First African American Chief Justice* (Jefferson, NC: McFarland, 2013); Frank R. Kemerer, *William Wayne Justice: A Judicial Biography* (Austin: University of Texas Press, 1991). On lawyers, see Dorothy S. Shawhan and Martha H. Swain, *Lucy Somerville Howorth: New Deal Lawyer, Politician, and Feminist from the South* (Baton Rouge: Louisiana State University Press, 2006); Kenneth T. Andrews and Kay Jowers, "Lawyers and Embedded Legal Activity in the Southern Civil Rights Movement," *Law & Policy* 40 (January 2018): 10–32; Kent Spriggs, ed., *Voices of Civil Rights Lawyers: Reflections from the Deep South, 1964–1980* (Gainesville: University Press of Florida, 2017).

cution of Confederate President Jefferson Davis. Lawyers recognized the case had the potential to disrupt the verdict of the battlefield against the Confederacy's constitutional vision that supported secession and states' rights.[65]

Civil rights and legal or judicial biographies are not the only areas of twentieth-century southern life subjected to scrutiny. Legal historians also studied the impact of law on urban, economic, and (nonracial) political history.[66] Still, as southern legal historians took on topics later in the region's chronology, the quantity (though not quality) of nonracial southern legal history declined sharply.

As productive as southern legal historians have been in the twenty-first century, much work remains to be done. Beyond Maryland, the acceptance or disdain for English law in the colonial period needs attention.[67] Use of religious tribunals to deliver justice within spiritual communities, colonial, antebellum,

65. Cynthia Nicoletti, "Strategic Litigation and the Death of Reconstruction," in Hadden and Minter, eds., *Signposts*, 265–88; Nicoletti, *Secession on Trial: The Treason Prosecution of Jefferson Davis* (New York: Cambridge University Press, 2017). For the similar focus on southern state judges, see Adam M. Carrington, "Running the Robed Gauntlet: Southern State Courts' Interpretation of the Emancipation Proclamation," *American Journal of Legal History* 57 (December 2017): 556–84; David C. Willard, "Criminal Amnesty, State Courts, and the Reach of Reconstruction," *Journal of Southern History* 85 (February 2019): 105–36. See also Peter Charles Hoffer, *Uncivil Warriors: The Lawyers' Civil War* (New York: Oxford University Press, 2018).

66. On urban connections, see Daniel Farbman, "Reconstructing Local Government," *Vanderbilt Law Review* 70 (March 2017): 413–97; Frederick M. Wirt, *Politics of Southern Equality: Law and Social Change in a Mississippi County* (Chicago: Aldine, 1970); Ross, *The Great New Orleans Kidnapping Case*. On economic links, see Rafael I. Pardo, "Documenting Bankrupted Slaves," *Vanderbilt Law Review* 71 (May 2018): 73–116; Adam Woolkoff, "Every Man His Own Avenger: Landlord Remedies and the Antebellum Roots of the Crop Lien and Chattel Mortgage in the United States," *Law and History Review* 35 (February 2017): 131–54; Sean M. Kammer, "Railroad Land Grants in an Incongruous Legal System: Corporate Subsidies, Bureaucratic Governance, and Legal Conflict in the United States, 1850–1903," *Law and History Review* 35 (May 2017): 391–432; Alicia M. Dewey, *Pesos and Dollars: Entrepreneurs in the Texas-Mexico Borderlands, 1880–1940* (College Station: Texas A&M University Press, 2014). On political ties, see Charles L. Zelden, Bush v. Gore: *Exposing the Hidden Crisis of American Democracy* (Lawrence: University Press of Kansas, 2008); Laura Kalman, *The Long Reach of the Sixties: LBJ, Nixon, and the Making of the Contemporary Supreme Court* (New York: Oxford University Press, 2017); Kalman, *Right Star Rising: A New Politics, 1974–1980* (New York: W. W. Norton, 2010).

67. Albert Martinez, "The Palatinate Court of the Maryland Charter 1632–1776: From Independent Jurisdiction to Independence," *American Journal of Legal History* 50 (July 2008): 305–25; Jeffrey Sawyer, "The Rhetoric and Reality of English Law in Colonial Maryland, Part I: 1632–1689," *Maryland Historical Magazine* 108 (Winter 2013): 393–410; Sawyer, "The Rhetoric and Reality of English Law in Colonial Maryland, Part II: 1689–1732," *Maryland Historical Magazine* 109 (Spring 2014): 81–95.

or modern, awaits further investigation.[68] The spread of legal knowledge via law texts, the development of law libraries, and widening access to law through print or media demands consideration.[69] Digital tools exist to aid scholars who study the influence of specific texts.[70] Regulation of sexual practices through law before the twentieth century requires more examination.[71] The spreading codification movement across numerous states in the nineteenth century calls for additional studies.[72] Legal conflicts between military and common law, aside from a few Civil War studies, remain undissected.[73] Beyond civil rights, legal history across much of the twentieth-century South lacks depth. Legal historians working on other regions published exciting new studies on social welfare, legal aid, disability rights, and the administrative state, but there is little or no comparable work in the South.[74]

68. Early forays in this area include Layne Carpenter, "'Live by the Spirit': Institutional Discipline for Crimes against Order and Morals, Mecklenburg County, North Carolina, 1767–1839" (MA thesis, University of North Carolina, Charlotte, 2015); Jeffrey Thomas Perry, "'Courts of Conscience': Local Law, the Baptists, and Church Schism in Kentucky, 1780–1840," *Church History* 84 (March 2015): 124–58. See also Volkman, "Houses Divided."

69. W. Hamilton Bryson, "Virginia Law Reports," *American Journal of Legal History* 54 (April 2014): 107–20; Warren M. Billings and Brent Tarter, eds., *"Esteemed Bookes of Lawe" and the Legal Culture of Early Virginia* (Charlottesville: University of Virginia Press, 2017).

70. Kellen Funk and Lincoln A. Mullen, "The Spine of American Law: Digital Text Analysis and U.S. Legal Practice," *American Historical Review* 123 (February 2018): 132–64. On using Google N-Grams, the Legal Language Explorer, and Viral Texts, see Eric C. Nystrom and David S. Tanenhaus, "The Future of Digital Legal History: No Magic, No Silver Bullets," *American Journal of Legal History* 56 (March 2016): 150–67.

71. See, for example, Terri L. Snyder, *Brabbling Women: Disorderly Speech and the Law in Early Virginia* (Ithaca: Cornell University Press, 2003); Diane Miller Sommerville, *Rape and Race in the Nineteenth-Century South* (Chapel Hill: University of North Carolina Press, 2004); James Cusick, "Slanders and Sodomy: Studying the Past through Colonial Investigation," *Florida Historical Quarterly* 93 (Winter 2015): 415–45.

72. Scholars could possibly utilize ideas found in Christopher Curtis, "Codification in Virginia: Conway Robinson, John Mercer Patton, and the Politics of Law Reform," *Virginia Magazine of History and Biography* 117 (2009): 140–80.

73. Victoria Stewart, "Conscripting Billy Yank and Johnny Reb: The Plight and Consequence of Conscription Dodgers, Disruptors, and Resisters" (PhD diss., Northern Illinois University, 2017), offered a model. David A. Collins, "Absentee Soldier Voting in Civil War Law and Politics" (PhD diss., Wayne State University, 2014), examined changes triggered in state law during military conflicts.

74. Karen M. Tani, *States of Dependency: Welfare, Rights and American Governance, 1935–1972* (New York: Cambridge University Press, 2016); Felice Batlan, *Women and Justice for the Poor: A History of Legal Aid, 1863–1945* (New York: Cambridge University Press, 2015); Rabia Shahin Belt, "Mental Disability and the Right to Vote" (PhD diss., University of Michigan, 2015); Daniel R. Ernst, *Tocqueville's Nightmare: The*

That much remains to be done in southern legal history does not lessen our gratitude for the studies completed thus far but reflects the relatively short moment in which southern legal history has stood apart as a unique subject of study. Given the vitality and range of works published since 2010, the future of southern legal and constitutional history appears strong and vibrant.

Administrative State Emerges in America, 1900–1940 (New York: Oxford University Press, 2014); Sophia Z. Lee, *The Workplace Constitution from the New Deal to the New Right* (New York: Cambridge University Press, 2014); Joanna L. Grisinger, *The Unwieldy American State: Administrative Politics since the New Deal* (New York: Cambridge University Press, 2012). An exception to this trend is Sara Mayeux, "*Poor Defenses: The American Legal Profession and the Problem of the 'Indigent Accused' in the Twentieth Century*" (PhD diss., Stanford University, 2016), which documented the rise of public defenders in Atlanta.

SOUTHERN ENVIRONMENTAL HISTORY

Kathryn Newfont and William Thomas Okie

You may not be able to judge a book by its cover, but you can tell a lot by its opening page. Consider early lines of a few leading books in southern history.[1]

"Let us begin by discussing the weather, for that has been the chief agency in making the South distinctive."[2]

"The destructive character of agricultural methods in the old tobacco regions of Virginia and Maryland has been commented on by almost every writer who has dealt with that section."[3]

"I had forgotten, or perhaps never even bothered to consider, that the gentry of prerevolutionary Virginia spent most of their waking hours thinking about crops and livestock."[4]

"On a ridge high above the Savannah River stands Redcliffe, presiding over carefully planned avenues of magnolias and groves of hickory and pine that slope down towards Augusta, visible more than five miles away."[5]

1. We borrow this "first line" method from Aaron Sachs, who used it to different effect in "Letters to a Tenured Historian: Imagining History as Creative Nonfiction—or Maybe Even Poetry," *Rethinking History* 14 (March 2010): 5–38.

2. Ulrich Bonnell Phillips, *Life and Labor in the Old South* (1929; repr., Columbia: University of South Carolina Press, 2007), 3.

3. Avery O. Craven, *Soil Exhaustion as a Factor in the Agricultural History of Virginia and Maryland, 1606–1860* (1926; repr., Columbia: University of South Carolina Press, 2006), 11.

4. T. H. Breen, *Tobacco Culture: The Mentality of the Great Tidewater Planters on the Eve of Revolution* (Princeton: Princeton University Press, 1985), 3.

5. Drew Gilpin Faust, *James Henry Hammond and the Old South: A Design for Mastery* (Baton Rouge: Louisiana State University Press, 1982), 1.

"It is pretty scenery, to be sure, if you have come in the spring before the heat dulls the vernal prism."[6]

"Water and trees—trees and water."[7]

"O water, voice of my heart, crying in the sand."[8]

Environmental history is not new to the South. True, there was no comparable essay in *Interpreting Southern History* (1987) or *Writing Southern History* (1965), but southern history that incorporates what we have come to call "the environment" has a distinguished tradition.[9] Environmental history may be a relative newcomer to southern *historiography*, yet for nearly a century it has been accumulating, like the soils beneath the region's staple-crop agriculture, in the bottoms and bays of southern history.

Environmental history, simply put, is history that takes seriously what we

6. David R. Goldfield, *Cotton Fields and Skyscrapers: Southern City and Region, 1607–1980* (Baton Rouge: Louisiana State University Press, 1982), 1.

7. Rhys Isaac, *The Transformation of Virginia, 1740–1790* (Chapel Hill: University of North Carolina Press, 1982), 11.

8. W. E. B. Du Bois, *The Souls of Black Folk* (Chicago: A. C. McClurg, 1903), 1.

9. We are not the first to point this out. For surveys of southern environmental historiography, in chronological order, see Jack Temple Kirby and Barbara J. Fields, "Bioregionalism: Landscape and Culture in the South Atlantic," in *The New Regionalism: Essays and Commentaries,* ed. Robert L. Dorman and Charles Reagan Wilson (Jackson: University Press of Mississippi, 1998), 19–43; Otis L. Graham, "Again the Backward Region? Environmental History in and of the American South," *Southern Cultures* 6 (Summer 2000): 50–72; Mart A. Stewart, "Southern Environmental History," in *A Companion to the American South,* ed. John B. Boles (Hoboken: Blackwell, 2002), 405–23; Stewart, "If John Muir Had Been an Agrarian: American Environmental History West and South," *Environment and History* 11 (May 2005): 139–62; Christopher Morris, "A More Southern Environmental History," *Journal of Southern History* 75 (August 2009): 581–98; Paul S. Sutter, "Introduction: No More the Backward Region: Environmental History Comes of Age," in *Environmental History and the American South: A Reader,* ed. Paul S. Sutter and Christopher J. Manganiello (Athens: University of Georgia Press, 2009), 1–24; Ellen G. Spears, "Landscapes and Ecologies of the U.S. South: Essays in Eco-Cultural History," *Southern Spaces,* 18 February 2013, http://www.southernspaces.org/2013/landscapes-and-ecologies-us-south-essays-eco-cultural-history (accessed 18 January 2019); Paul S. Sutter, "Waving the Muddy Shirt," in *The Blue, the Gray, and the Green: Toward an Environmental History of the Civil War,* ed. Brian Allen Drake (Athens: University of Georgia Press, 2015), 225–36; Brian Allen Drake, "New Fields of Battle: Nature, Environmental History, and the Civil War," in Drake, ed., *The Blue, the Gray, and the Green: Toward an Environmental History of the Civil War,* 1–15; Mark D. Hersey, "The Lay of the Land: Environmental History, the South, and Kentucky," *Register of the Kentucky Historical Society* 115 (March 2017): 129–53; Hersey, "Environmental History in the Heart of Dixie," *Alabama Review* 70 (April 2017): 99–111.

would casually call "nature," that is, animals, plants, fungi, microbes, waters, soils, climates, and the interrelationships of all those things.[10] The current field is incredibly vibrant. It boasts an annual conference of several hundred attendees, a journal with an acceptance rate of less than 15 percent, and the fastest proportional expansion of any topical field in history.[11] But environmental history is also fractured. From the 1970s through the 1990s, the field was animated by both moral and analytical imperatives: as Paul S. Sutter described it in his state-of-the-field essay, extending "moral consideration to the natural world" on one hand and bringing "environmental causation into historical narration" on the other.[12] Since the 1980s, scholars took pains to complicate both imperatives, questioning the heroes-and-villains narratives of environmental innocence, human sin leading to environmental destruction, and, occasionally, redemption courtesy of the environmental regulatory state. Conservation, we learned, had a "hidden history" of exploitation and dispossession; environmentalism, we saw, had often been a movement of the upper class seeking to secure for themselves amenities of clean air, clean water, and recreational space, the lives of the poor be damned.[13] Meanwhile, the stories of "nature fighting back" or "nature's agency" that made early environmental histories so satisfying began to seem too simple, for had

10. For a primer on environmental history, start with Richard White, "American Environmental History: The Development of a New Historical Field," *Pacific Historical Review* 54 (August 1985): 297–335; Donald Worster, "Transformations of the Earth: Toward an Agroecological Perspective in History," *Journal of American History* 76 (March 1990): 1087–106; Paul S. Sutter, "The World with Us: The State of American Environmental History," *Journal of American History* 100 (June 2013): 94–119.

11. In 1975, only 5 percent of history departments employed an environmental historian; in 2015, almost half did. See Robert B. Townsend, "The Rise and Decline of History Specializations over the Past 40 Years," *Perspectives on History*, 1 December 2015, https://www.historians.org/publications-and-directories/perspectives-on-history/december-2015/the-rise-and-decline-of-history-specializations-over-the-past-40-years (accessed 18 January 2019).

12. Sutter, "The World with Us," 97, 94.

13. For examples of this literature, see Mark David Spence, *Dispossessing the Wilderness: Indian Removal and the Making of the National Parks* (New York: Oxford University Press, 1999); Karl Jacoby, *Crimes Against Nature: Squatters, Poachers, Thieves, and the Hidden History of American Conservation* (Berkeley: University of California Press, 2001); Louis S. Warren, *The Hunter's Game: Poachers and Conservationists in Twentieth-Century America* (New Haven: Yale University Press, 1997); Andrew Hurley, *Environmental Inequalities: Class, Race, and Industrial Pollution in Gary, Indiana, 1945–1980* (Chapel Hill: University of North Carolina Press, 1995); Adam Rome, *The Bulldozer in the Countryside: Suburban Sprawl and the Rise of American Environmentalism* (New York: Cambridge University Press, 2001). For environmental activism beyond the upper class, see Chad Montrie, *A People's History of Environmentalism in the United States* (New York: Continuum, 2011).

not their authors assumed that "nature" was something out there, separate from humans, to be destroyed or preserved at human discretion? Nor did agency, with its connotations of premeditated thought and action, seem quite right. Hybridity—mixtures of the human and the nonhuman, with messy, complicated stories that had neither villains nor heroes—became the order of the day.[14]

Self-consciously environmental history of the South emerged somewhat later than the rest of the field, but it found itself in step with these trends. Southern environmental history, as Mart A. Stewart noted, never had to "trouble" the concept of wilderness, because the concept never had as much currency in southern history as it did in western history. The South was not bifurcated into uninhabited wilds and densely populated cities. It instead comprised simply the cultivated and uncultivated, and even uncultivated places had their human purposes.[15] And because enslaved blacks powered the most prominent early economic regimens, much of the southern landscape seemed racialized and obviously so. Environmental historians of the West and North have had to repent of their "holism," of ignoring "conflict and difference *within* groups of people" in the name of tracing human-environment interaction. Southern environmental historians, as Stewart observed, did not need to "discover" the importance of race, endemic disease, or the environmental ravages of modern war and a colonial economy.[16]

Because of its background, southern environmental history is strong and getting stronger, even as the broader field of environmental history frets about fragmentation and the perils associated with being, as Harriet Ritvo memorably put it in a 2005 forum, "an unevenly spreading blob."[17] Even as southern history received little recognition from the American Society for Environmental His-

14. For examples of environmental histories that emphasize hybridity, see William Cronon, ed., *Uncommon Ground: Toward Reinventing Nature* (New York: W. W. Norton, 1995); Jennifer Price, *Flight Maps: Adventures with Nature in Modern America* (New York: Basic Books, 1999); Mark Fiege, *Irrigated Eden: The Making of an Agricultural Landscape in the American West* (Seattle: University of Washington Press, 1999); Matthew Klingle, *Emerald City: An Environmental History of Seattle* (New Haven: Yale University Press, 2007).

15. Mart A. Stewart, "If John Muir Had Been an Agrarian," 143.

16. William Cronon, "Modes of Prophecy and Production: Placing Nature in History," *Journal of American History* 76 (March 1990): 1128. For another critique of holism, see Karl Jacoby, "Class and Environmental History: Lessons from 'The War in the Adirondacks,'" *Environmental History* 2 (July 1997): 324–26.

17. Harriet Ritvo, "What's Next for Environmental History?" *Environmental History* 10 (January 2005): 75. See also Douglas R. Weiner, "A Death-Defying Attempt to Articulate a Coherent Definition of Environmental History," *Environmental History* 10 (July 2005): 404–20.

tory—no work in southern history has won the ASEH book prize since it was created in 1989, and only one dissertation on southern history has won the best dissertation award—southern environmental history gained national recognition.[18] Jack Temple Kirby won a 2007 Bancroft Prize for *Mockingbird Song;* Jack E. Davis received the 2018 Pulitzer Prize for History for *The Gulf.*[19] There was a time when lamenting the sorry state of southern environmental history was a sort of cottage industry. That time is past.

Key to both the longer southern tradition of environmental awareness and the newer self-consciously southern environmental history is an emphasis on place. Instead of a chronological, topical, or subregional approach, we decided to orient our essay around four kinds of places—waters, woods, farms, and towns—that compose much of the South. This organizational approach is not meant to be exhaustive. Rather than providing an overview, we sit down in a locale and ask what we can see from that particular vantage point. Like Appalachian coal deposits, each of these places has been at least scratched out by scholars, some since the earliest days of the profession, but our understanding of each is better for having the questions and methods of environmental history applied to them. Environmental history has made each vein richer.

"O water, voice of my heart, crying in the sand."[20]

The South is richly watered. The continent's largest river system courses through it and scores of other streams do too, some pouring their waters into the Mississippi and others emptying into the Atlantic directly or by way of the Gulf of Mexico. Together fresh and salt waters create over 33,000 miles of coast and an array of estuarine waters, including the Chesapeake Bay, one of the world's largest estuary systems. The Chesapeake shoreline alone stretches longer than the entire

18. The one American Society for Environmental History award winner that might be considered southern is Conevery Bolton Valençius, *The Health of the Country: How American Settlers Understood Themselves and Their Land* (New York: Basic Books, 2002). The dissertation was Christopher J. Manganiello, "Dam Crazy with Wild Consequences: Artificial Lakes and Natural Rivers in the America South, 1845–1990" (PhD diss., University of Georgia, 2010).

19. Jack Temple Kirby, *Mockingbird Song: Ecological Landscapes of the South* (Chapel Hill: University of North Carolina Press, 2006); Jack E. Davis, *The Gulf: The Making of An American Sea* (New York: Liveright, 2017).

20. Du Bois, *The Souls of Black Folk,* 1.

Pacific coast of the United States.[21] Wetland forests, from Louisiana's Atchafalaya Basin to the Great Dismal Swamp on the North Carolina–Virginia border, dot the region. Florida's famed Everglades and a host of other fresh- and brackish-water marshes spread across the southlands. For millennia, the South's many waters supported human communities not only as sources of drinking water but also as fisheries, cleansers, transportation routes, irrigation sources, recreation avenues, and spiritual sites. Water events, most dramatically hurricanes but also thunderstorms, neap tides, torrential rains, snowstorms, and river floods, have always been a regional fact of life.

While studies of the arid West dominated early environmental history, southern environmental history made water abundance a central object of study. Water scholarship consequently emerged as an arena where scholars of the South not only contributed but also led.[22] In *This Land, This South* (1983), the first monograph to claim the southern environmental history label, medical historian Albert E. Cowdrey described the South as "an old, warm, and wet region." He considered disease and flood control before ending the work with a discussion of the then-recent 1980 Ixtoc I oil spill in the Gulf of Mexico. Like the BP Deepwater Horizon failure three decades later, Ixtoc I proved a major disaster, polluting saltwater habitats and delicate estuarine ecosystems along the southern coast and threatening important fisheries.[23]

Since Cowdrey's opening gambit, the region's environmental historians have explored water in a host of ways. Some have studied waters alongside woods,

21. Coastline totals calculated from National Oceanic and Atmospheric Administration data for states from Maryland to Texas; see "Shoreline Mileage for the United States," https://coast.noaa.gov/data/docs/states/shorelines.pdf (accessed 18 January 2019). For the Chesapeake, see Virginia Institute of Marine Science, "How Big is the Bay?" http://www.vims.edu/bayinfo/faqs/estuary_size.php (accessed 18 January 2019). See also Chris J. Magoc, "In Search of a Useable—and Hopeful—Environmental Narrative in the Mid-Atlantic," *Pennsylvania History* 82 (Summer 2015): 314–28.

22. Examples of such leadership include Christopher J. Manganiello's Rachel Carson Award for the best dissertation in environmental history for the work that would become his *Southern Water, Southern Power: How the Politics of Cheap Energy and Water Scarcity Shaped a Region* (Chapel Hill: University of North Carolina Press, 2015); and Jack E. Davis's Pulitzer Prize for *The Gulf*. For early studies of water in the West, see Donald Worster, *Rivers of Empire: Water, Aridity, and the Growth of the American West* (New York: Pantheon Books, 1985); Marc Reisner, *Cadillac Desert: The American West and Its Disappearing Water* (New York: Viking Press, 1986).

23. Albert E. Cowdrey, *This Land, This South: An Environmental History* (Lexington: University Press of Kentucky, 1983). For further discussion of oil spills, including BP Deepwater Horizon, see Davis, *The Gulf*.

soils, and climates, as well as the remarkably rich and varied plant and animal communities these supported. Such communities have always been dynamic, constantly responding to fluctuations caused by weather events, climate changes, diseases, migrations, human technologies, and a host of other factors. *Longue durée* histories usefully remind us of this pattern. Timothy Silver and Jack E. Davis each started their southern studies with the ancient supercontinent Pangaea, for instance. In *Mount Mitchell and the Black Mountains* (2003), Silver pointed out how tectonic plate collisions raised the Appalachians to greater-than-Himalayan heights while water, wind, and ice—in a still-ongoing process—scoured them down. In *The Gulf* (2017), Davis described how the Gulf of Mexico shapeshifted for 150 million years and noted that its shores at one point extended into present-day Illinois. These works troubled simplistic notions of waterways and mountains as somehow stable, and they linked history to geologic time. They also highlighted the diversity of living nonhuman actors: mammoths, ground sloths, mosses, fir trees, oysters, egrets, tarpon.[24]

Yet each historian left out far more than she or he could possibly include. "Nature" is never static, and it long predates and far exceeds its human elements. Although "agency" may be a problematic term for describing this reality, environmental dynamism could hardly be clearer. Tracing the environmental history of any one southern landmark—Mount Mitchell for Silver, the tallest peak in eastern North America; and the Gulf of Mexico for Davis, the largest gulf on earth—is a remarkably complex task requiring attention to diversity and dynamism long before introducing humans. Human entrances and actions create additional layers of dynamism, diversity, and complexity.

In his bioregional history of the Potomac River watershed, James D. Rice attended to just such dynamism, diversity, and complexity among prehistoric North Americans.[25] Turning his attention to the rarely studied period between

24. Timothy Silver, *Mount Mitchell and the Black Mountains: An Environmental History of the Highest Peaks in Eastern America* (Chapel Hill: University of North Carolina Press, 2003); Davis, *The Gulf*. Valuable coast-focused works include Paul S. Sutter and Paul M. Pressly, eds., *Coastal Nature, Coastal Culture: Environmental Histories of the Georgia Coast* (Athens: University of Georgia Press, 2018); David Cecelski, *The Waterman's Song: Slavery and Freedom in Maritime North Carolina* (Chapel Hill: University of North Carolina Press, 2001).

25. For "bioregion," see Dan Flores, "Place: An Argument for Bioregional History," *Environmental History Review* 18 (Winter 1994): 1–18.

700 and 1700 CE, Rice found cultural and diplomatic "faultlines" among Indigenous peoples that mirrored faultlines of climate and topography. He showed ancient Potomac peoples changing economies and settlement patterns in response to environmental shifts such as the "Little Ice Age." Europeans arriving in the watershed had to adapt not only to environmental but also existing cultural conditions, so choices made centuries before affected their decisions. "Indians in effect governed the timing, extent, and character of colonization," Rice concluded.[26] In fact, he argued, the long arm of ancient creativity in response to environmental factors continues to influence even the present day. *Nature and History in the Potomac Country* (2009) offered a more nuanced account of Indian-European encounters than appeared in cutting-edge earlier works by some of the field's founding scholars, including Carolyn Merchant and William Cronon, and questioned how quickly, completely, and unilaterally "ecological revolutions" and "changes in the land" took place.[27]

Other scholars of the ancient South, including Robbie Ethridge and Robin Beck, uncovered similarly complex and dynamic histories. Ethridge traced elaborate environmentally inflected migration patterns among Mississippian peoples in the post-contact "shatter zone," which was itself shaped by environmental factors. Such scholarship counters ethnocentric notions of ancient peoples as static rather than inventive. These and other ethnohistorical pieces also remind us that the early South is a rich field for environmental history, much of it still waiting to be explored. Timothy Silver, Mart A. Stewart, Craig E. Colten, and others made contributions. In *Plantation Enterprise in Colonial South Carolina* (2006), S. Max Edelson effectively combined environmental and cultural approaches to trace the roots of Lowcountry rice plantation agriculture, demonstrating the promise of environmental approaches to the colonial era. James Taylor Carson centered *Making an Atlantic World* (2007) on environment as a social construct, tracing the ideas and experiences of "founding peoples"—Indigenous residents, African captives, and European newcomers—who created the Creole South. Despite these beginnings, there is as yet no outpouring of French and Indian

26. James D. Rice, *Nature and History in the Potomac Country: From Hunter-Gatherers to the Age of Jefferson* (Baltimore: Johns Hopkins University Press, 2009), 255.

27. Carolyn Merchant, *Ecological Revolutions: Nature, Gender, and Science in New England* (Chapel Hill: University of North Carolina Press, 1989); William Cronon, *Changes in the Land: Indians, Colonists, and the Ecology of New England* (New York: Hill and Wang, 1983).

War or American Revolution environmental history, for example, comparable to that for the Civil War.[28]

In another *longue durée* river-based history, Christopher Morris complicated our understanding by arguing that his subject was neither land nor water. The Mississippi River and its expansive floodplain (especially the lower Mississippi Valley), Morris noted in *The Big Muddy* (2012), are best understood as "a liquid earth" ranging from "wet dirt" in the plain to "dirty water" in the river. Pre-Columbian peoples generally chose to adapt to these vast muddy wetlands, while European colonizers and especially cotton-growing Americans preferred to think of water as distinct from land and set about constructing the separation. Morris called the result "a pathological landscape" marked by human-engineered drought, disease, and other ailments.[29]

Although western dams—on the Columbia, the Colorado, the Tuolumne—drew earlier environmental inquiries, scholars turned their attention to the histo-

28. Robbie Ethridge, *From Chicaza to Chickasaw: The European Invasion and the Transformation of the Mississippian World, 1540–1715* (Chapel Hill: University of North Carolina Press, 2010); Robin Beck, *Chiefdoms, Collapse, and Coalescence in the Early American South* (New York: Cambridge University Press, 2013); Timothy Silver, *A New Face on the Countryside: Indians, Colonists, and Slaves in South Atlantic Forests, 1500–1800* (New York: Cambridge University Press, 1990); Silver, "Learning to Live with Nature: Colonial Historians and the Southern Environment," *Journal of Southern History* 73 (August 2007): 539–52; Mart A. Stewart, "From King Cane to King Cotton: Razing Cane in the Old South," *Environmental History* 12 (January 2007): 59–79; Craig E. Colten, "Meaning of Water in the American South: Transatlantic Encounters," *Atlantic Studies* 5 (August 2008): 203–22; S. Max Edelson, *Plantation Enterprise in Colonial South Carolina* (Cambridge: Harvard University Press, 2006); James Taylor Carson, *Making an Atlantic World: Circles, Paths, and Stories from the Colonial South* (Knoxville: University of Tennessee Press, 2007). See also David Hurst Thomas, ed., *Columbian Consequences.* Vol. 1, *Archaeological and Historical Perspectives on the Spanish Borderlands West* (Washington, DC: Smithsonian Institution Press, 1989); Thomas, *Columbian Consequences.* Vol. 2, *Archaeological and Historical Perspectives on the Spanish Borderlands East* (Washington, DC: Smithsonian, 1990); Thomas, *Columbian Consequences.* Vol. 3, *The Spanish Borderlands in Pan-American Perspective* (Washington, DC: Smithsonian, 1991); Daniel H. Usner Jr., *Indians, Settlers, and Slaves in a Frontier Exchange Economy: The Lower Mississippi Valley Before 1783* (Chapel Hill: University of North Carolina Press, 1992); Kathryn E. Holland Braund, *Deerskins and Duffels: The Creek Indian Trade with Anglo-America, 1685–1815* (Lincoln: University of Nebraska Press, 1993); Theda Perdue, *Cherokee Women: Gender and Culture Change, 1700–1835* (Lincoln: University of Nebraska Press, 1998); James Taylor Carson, *Searching for the Bright Path: The Mississippi Choctaws from Prehistory to Removal* (Lincoln: University of Nebraska Press, 1999). See also Shepard Krech, *The Ecological Indian: Myth and History* (New York: Norton, 2000).

29. Christopher Morris, *The Big Muddy: An Environmental History of the Mississippi and Its Peoples from Hernando de Soto to Hurricane Katrina* (New York: Oxford University Press, 2012), 10, 169.

ries of massive waterworks in the South, built over a longer period and on an even larger scale. In *Southern Water, Southern Power* (2015), Christopher J. Manganiello used the term "hydraulic waterscape" to describe the region's reengineered environment.[30] The scope of these southern works is staggering. The Mississippi may be the most heavily engineered water system in the United States; or perhaps that honor goes to the Florida peninsula. Massive drainage projects and other water control measures transformed Florida's complicated hydrology, separating earth from water where previously the two were mixed. Morris's "liquid earth" offers a useful way to think about this region's vast pre-engineering wetlands, and his "pathological landscape" has resonance for a peninsula ripped by hurricanes that those once-immense wetlands formerly helped quiet. Nearly all the South's great wetlands have been similarly drained and otherwise dramatically reengineered. Then there is the enormous Tennessee Valley Authority (TVA) system, which includes twenty-nine dams spread over seven states. Many Atlantic-side river projects joined these, including Manganiello's Savannah River dams. And the list goes on. The Tennessee-Tombigbee Waterway is the largest inland water project ever undertaken by the Army Corps of Engineers. A series of harbor-deepening projects—Charleston, Wilmington, and others—reshaped those ports and their surroundings. Yet even this is just a partial tally.[31]

The mighty Chesapeake Bay, which once boasted the nation's largest inland fishery, offers yet another "hydraulic waterscape" example, again with sobering "pathological landscape" resonance. More than ten thousand streams and rivers feed into the Bay. As John R. Wennersten demonstrated in *The Chesapeake* (2001), this complicated Bay hydrology has been heavily reengineered, both pur-

30. Manganiello, *Southern Water, Southern Power.* For examples of western dam and water issues, see Richard White, *The Organic Machine: The Remaking of the Columbia River* (New York: Hill and Wang, 1996); Donald Worster, *Rivers of Empire: Water, Aridity, and the Growth of the American West* (New York: Pantheon Books, 1985); Reisner, *Cadillac Desert;* Robert W. Righter, *The Battle over Hetch Hetchy: America's Most Controversial Dam and the Birth of Modern Environmentalism* (New York: Oxford University Press, 2005).

31. For Florida and Atchafalaya, see Craig E. Colten, *Southern Waters: The Limits to Abundance* (Baton Rouge: Louisiana State University Press, 2014). For the Great Dismal Swamp, see Jack Temple Kirby, *Poquosin: A Study of Rural Landscape and Society* (Chapel Hill: University of North Carolina Press, 1995). For Tennessee-Tombigbee, see Jeffrey K. Stine, *Mixing the Waters: Environment, Politics, and the Building of the Tennessee-Tombigbee Waterway* (Akron: University of Akron Press, 1993). On harbor deepening, see Christopher J. Manganiello, "Fish Tales and the Conservation State," *Southern Cultures* 20 (Fall 2014): 43–62.

posely and inadvertently. Drainage, canal, and other water management projects deliberately reshaped the system. So did many additional factors, including everything from inland timber harvests—which released silt, clouded Chesapeake waters, and reduced overall estuarine productivity and mollusk populations in particular—to nuclear power development, which left similarly broad ecological footprints by heating the Bay. Add suburban growth, agricultural erosion and runoff, industrial pollution, human waste disposal, highway development, and factory-scale poultry production into this mix, and the scale of Bay reengineering becomes clear: it was powerful both where it was deliberate and where unintentional.[32]

Christopher Morris and other southern water scholars, notably Christopher J. Manganiello and Craig E. Colten, demonstrated how projects designed to control flooding and aid navigation actually created drought conditions and water shortages, and even contributed to flood damages. "Billions of dollars and immeasurable quantities of human energies" poured into Mississippi flood control, Morris wrote, but failed to prevent—and in fact exacerbated—disasters such as the 1927 flood and Hurricane Katrina in 2005. In *Southern Waters* (2014), Colten discussed efforts to drain the Atchafalaya Basin and the Everglades and to move water from places of "excess" (Louisiana) to places of "shortage" (Texas). Manganiello and Colten pointed out how contentious water management issues, far from being limited to the arid West, proved a hallmark of the drenched South.[33]

Through at least the first decades of the twentieth century, nearly all the "immeasurable quantities of human energies" dedicated to southern hydraulic reengineering came from forcibly held African American laborers, enslaved and free. The Mississippi River itself built levees in the form of alluvial ridges, but scholars traced how black workers performed the backbreaking human labor of additional levee-building while reaping few of the benefits. In fact, as John M. Barry explained in *Rising Tide* (1997), black families were often at greater risk after levee-building, since levees protect some landed assets at the expense of others, often those of the poor and people of color. The most infamous incident occurred with the deliberate destruction of levees during the 1927 Mississippi flood, which

32. John R. Wennersten, *The Chesapeake: An Environmental Biography* (Baltimore: Maryland Historical Society, 2001). See also John R. Wennersten, *The Oyster Wars of Chesapeake Bay* (Centreville, MD: Tidewater Publishers, 1981); Christine Keiner, *The Oyster Question: Scientists, Watermen, and the Maryland Chesapeake Bay since 1880* (Athens: University of Georgia Press, 2009).

33. Morris, *The Big Muddy*, 206; Colten, *Southern Waters.*

directed floodwaters into heavily African American communities—a deadly example of environmental white supremacy. Though ostensibly free, black laborers were forced at gunpoint to fortify and rebuild levees, just as enslaved laborers of an earlier era had performed the immense hydraulic engineering work necessary for tidal rice agriculture under the immediate threat of violence.[34]

An echo of guns on the levees sounds through a number of works documenting the grim power of environmental racism. Mart A. Stewart found that money could not compel post-Emancipation laborers to do the enormous labors they had previously performed as slaves to maintain canals, sluices, and banks required for wet-rice agriculture, much less entice them to create the elaborate infrastructure. Violence built those systems, as palpably as human bodies moving earth. A chilling precursor to levee destruction in 1927 and Hurricane Katrina's racialized devastations in 2005 occurred during the Civil War, as Amy Murrell Taylor demonstrated in *Embattled Freedom* (2018). African American freedom-seekers found themselves relegated to low-lying flood-prone areas of United States Army camps while troops bivouacked on higher ground. Similarly, in Tyler Priest's "Shrimp and Petroleum" (2016), Louisianan Bob Long recalled the long offshore reach of Jim Crow violence. "Shrimping, they'd shoot at us," Long remembered, explaining how black harvesters were driven from the industry. These examples evidence the centuries-deep history of southern environmental injustice. They also suggest how much work yet remains to be done in this vital area.[35]

The power of Bob Long's remembrance underscores the importance of scholarship such as Richard M. Mizelle Jr.'s innovative work in *Backwater Blues* (2014). Mizelle used blues lyrics, oral histories, and other black cultural creations to excavate African Americans' racialized experiences of the 1927 Mississippi River flood and to counter assumptions of "black environmental illiteracy." The region's "engineered environmental ecology of vulnerability" increased the burden of

34. John M. Barry, *Rising Tide: The Great Mississippi Flood of 1927 and How it Changed America* (New York: Simon & Schuster,1997). See also Pete Daniel, *Deep'n As It Come: The 1927 Mississippi Flood* (New York: Oxford University Press, 1977); Robyn Spencer, "Contested Terrain: The Mississippi Flood of 1927 and the Struggle to Control Black Labor," *Journal of Negro History* 79 (Spring 1994): 170–82. For tidal rice agriculture, see Mart A. Stewart, *"What Nature Suffers to Groe": Life, Labor, and Landscape on the Georgia Coast, 1680–1920* (Athens: University of Georgia Press, 1996).

35. Stewart, *"What Nature Suffers to Groe,"* 237; Amy Murrell Taylor, *Embattled Freedom: Journeys through the Civil War's Slave Refugee Camps* (Chapel Hill: University of North Carolina Press, 2018); Tyler Priest, "Shrimp and Petroleum: The Social Ecology of Louisiana's Offshore Industries," *Environmental History* 21 (July 2016): 488–515, quote on 493.

suffering for black southerners. Black cultural creations recorded race and "nature" as interrelated burdens, and emphasized the environmental disaster as a racialized political moment.[36]

Mizelle's book exemplifies the importance of oral history to southern environmental history. "The written record is not absolute," L. Rain Cranford-Gomez noted in an essay reflecting on Louisiana's creole communities and Hurricane Katrina. "It does not account for the histories of complex silenced peoples." She emphasized the importance of material culture as well as oral narratives to documenting such histories.[37] Carolyn Finney, exploring past and present questions of race and environment, similarly "went beneath" the archival record. Like Mizelle, Finney drew on oral histories and music—to which she added art, poetry, and media sources—to understand black environmental experiences and uncover buried narratives. Though national in scope, Finney's work grew from research on Florida's Amelia Island, where MahVynee Betsch worked for decades to protect the American Beach community her great-grandfather founded. A long history of racialization and erasure, combined with habits of thought and image coding the "environment" as "white," obscured such environmental activism, Finney argued.[38]

In addition to recovery of stories obscured by racism, oral historians helped to document environmental knowledge, including dispossessed and endangered knowledge systems. To restore complexity to lost landscapes and erased communities, Robert P. Shapard interviewed South Carolinians displaced by Savannah River damming. The peopled and productive landscapes and waterscapes that his narrators remembered stood in stark contrast to archival documents' descriptions of those same places as impoverished and nearly abandoned. Working in the Appalachians, folklorist Mary Hufford demonstrated how environmental knowledges, including experiential forest knowledge and commons practices such as ginseng harvest, are embedded in oral cultures. Kathryn Newfont and Debbie Lee drew on insights from oral histories and research in animal and plant com-

36. Richard M. Mizelle Jr., *Backwater Blues: The Mississippi Flood of 1927 in the African American Imagination* (Minneapolis: University of Minnesota Press, 2014), 12, 15.

37. L. Rain Cranford-Gomez, "Brackish Bayou Blood: Weaving Mixed-Blood Indian-Creole Identity Outside the Written Record," *American Indian Culture and Research Journal* 32 (2008): 93–108, quote on 95.

38. Carolyn Finney, *Black Faces, White Spaces: Reimagining the Relationship of African Americans to the Great Outdoors* (Chapel Hill: University of North Carolina Press, 2014). For more on MaVynee Betsch, see Russ Rymer, *American Beach: A Saga of Race, Wealth, and Memory* (New York: HarperCollins, 1998).

munication to suggest that long years of practiced attention could enable people to understand and discuss communications from animals, trees, and insects. A range of scholarship thus points to rich strands of environmental thought and experience not captured in traditional archives.[39] Oral history interviews, along with song lyrics, material culture, and other artworks, allow scholars to study these strands.[40]

"Water and trees—trees and water."[41]

Trees are living water columns. They are built for water; their lives depend on a gravity-defying ability to pull it skyward. It may come as no surprise, then, that the well-watered South supports some of the continent's richest native forests. Words like "swamp" invoke this close tree-and-water relationship. Swamps, which once constituted much of the region, are water-forests. Even where waters do not lap trunks, however, woods and waters intertwine. Southern waters have supported forest types too numerous and diverse to catalog here, but their broad outlines include mangroves, maritime forests of live oak, cypress-gum swamps, extensive bottomland hardwoods, pine flatwoods and sandhill "piney woods," upland hardwoods, mixed mesophytic forests, and mountaintop spruce-fir forests. Again, early southern environmental historians took note; works by Albert E. Cowdrey, Timothy Silver, Mart A. Stewart, and Jack Temple Kirby, among others, made forests—and swampy water-forests—a focus.[42]

39. Robert P. Shapard, "Sending the Flood Upriver: Impersonal Change and Personal Stories in the Savannah River Valley," in *The Land Speaks: New Voices at the Intersection of Oral and Environmental History,* ed. Debbie Lee and Kathryn Newfont (New York: Oxford University Press, 2017), 137–54; Manganiello, "Fish Tales"; Mary Hufford, "Forest Talk on Coal River," *American Forests* 101 (Autumn 1995): 16–24; Kathryn Newfont with Debbie Lee, "Introduction: Listening to the Land through Oral History," in Lee and Newfont, eds., *The Land Speaks,* 1–34. See also Anne Secord, "Science in the Pub: Artisan Botanists in Early Nineteenth-Century Lancashire," *History of Science* 32 (September 1994): 269–315.

40. Southern environmental scholars can draw on excellent regional oral history resources, including the Southern Oral History Program at the University of North Carolina at Chapel Hill, the Louie B. Nunn Center for Oral History at the University of Kentucky, the Samuel Proctor Oral History Program at the University of Florida, the Institute for Oral History at Baylor University, the Center for Oral History and Cultural Heritage at the University of Southern Mississippi, the Citadel Oral History Program, and the Foxfire Project in Georgia.

41. Isaac, *The Transformation of Virginia,* 11.

42. Cowdrey, *This Land This South;* Silver, *A New Face on the Countryside;* Stewart, *"What Nature Suffers to Groe";* Kirby, *Mockingbird Song.*

Through much of southern history both woods and waters functioned, even when privately owned, as common property—also known as "commons." The field of commons studies is immense, interdisciplinary, and global in scope, dedicated to unearthing the contours of various commons systems past and present. Like the private property regimes with which they contrast, commons systems are complex and dynamic. Unlike private property systems and their accompanying thickets of law, however, commons systems are often invisible, or nearly so, in the written record. They have nonetheless proved powerful and important in the present as well as in the past. The study of commons and "commoning"—meaning practices for regulating, exchanging knowledge about, and harvesting common resources—is a central project in environmental history, so much so, in fact, that it is difficult to overstate its importance. Commons resources and commoning practices enabled countless people to earn livings, acquire knowledge, and connect to human and beyond-human communities. Privatization of once-common resources foreclosed untold livelihoods and left immense numbers dispossessed, denying access to basic sustenance, valuable income sources, and cherished landscapes. Like farming, mining, seafaring, wilderness recreation, and other more widely familiar activities, commoning has been a formative means of human interaction with environment, and profoundly shaped human understandings of "nature."[43]

Scholars of the South made vital contributions to US and global commons history. This is, in fact, another area of regional leadership. Though few southern

43. The global literature on commons is immense, but useful starting places include Donald M. Nonini, ed., *The Global Idea of "The Commons"* (New York: Bergahn Books, 2008); John A. Baden and Douglas S. Noonan, eds., *Managing the Commons* (Bloomington: Indiana University Press, 1998); Elinor Ostrom, *Governing the Commons: The Evolution of Institutions for Collective Action* (New York: Cambridge University Press, 1990); David Feeny et al., "The Tragedy of the Commons: Twenty-two Years Later," *Human Ecology* 18 (March 1990): 1–19; Bonnie J. McCay and James M. Acheson, *The Question of the Commons: The Culture and Ecology of Communal Resources* (Tucson: University of Arizona Press, 1987). United States commons history is also large; examples include Richard W. Judd, *Common Lands, Common People: The Origins of Conservation in Northern New England* (Cambridge: Harvard University Press, 1997); Brian Donahue, *The Great Meadow: Farmers and the Land in Colonial Concord* (New Haven: Yale University Press, 2004); Daniel W. Schneider, "Enclosing the Floodplain: Resource Conflict on the Illinois River," *Environmental History* 1 (April 1996): 70–96; Benjamin Heber Johnson, "Conservation, Subsistence, and Class at the Birth of Superior National Forest," *Environmental History* 4 (January 1999): 80–99; Karen R. Merrill, *Public Lands and Political Meaning: Ranchers, the Government, and the Property Between Them* (Berkeley: University of California Press, 2002); Jake Kosek, *Understories: The Political Life of Forests in Northern New Mexico* (Durham: Duke University Press, 2006).

historians announced commons as a central theme in book titles, as did New England scholars Richard W. Judd and Brian Donahue in now classic works, some used the term extensively in their texts while others employed alternate terms to describe commons subjects, including "use rights," "open range," and "public access."[44] Whatever their semantic framing, collectively these works reveal a robust and dynamic southern history of commons, what scholar Mary Hufford usefully called "a vernacular cultural domain that transcends state boundaries."[45] At its most basic, this domain identifies and grants legitimacy to shared use rights. The "state boundaries" transcended by commons regimes often include law. Because commoning is vernacular, it can remain invisible until thrown into relief at moments of sharply contested power. At such moments, commons users typically defy with determination any effort to privatize, or "enclose," traditional rights, whether legal or extralegal.[46]

Jack Temple Kirby made the vernacular domain of commons—both wooded and watered—a central theme in two major works of environmental history, *Poquosin* (1995) and *Mockingbird Song* (2006). The former, set in wetland forests along the eastern North Carolina–Virginia border, explored the long vibrancy and eventual demise of commoning communities. Open-range animal husbandry, together with agricultural plots and small-scale forest production such as shingling, supported these neighborhoods. They evolved and persisted well into the twentieth century, eventually displaced as larger industries and federal water projects—followed by suburban sprawl and reworked hydrologies—multiplied claims on forests and waters. In *Mockingbird Song,* Kirby reiterated these themes but traced them across a broader landscape, framing the South's environmental history writ large as a story of wooded and watery commons supporting livelihoods for southerners black and white, poor and middling. Commons weakened

44. Judd, *Common Lands, Common People;* Brian Donahue, *Reclaiming the Commons: Community Farms and Forests in a New England Town* (New Haven: Yale University Press, 1999). For commons in a southern context, see Kathryn Newfont, *Blue Ridge Commons: Environmental Activism and Forest History in Western North Carolina* (Athens: University of Georgia Press, 2012).

45. Mary Hufford, "Reclaiming the Commons: Narratives of Progress, Preservation, and Ginseng," in *Culture, Environment, and Conservation in the Appalachian South,* ed. Benita J. Howell (Urbana: University of Illinois Press, 2002), 101. See also Hufford's work at "Tending the Commons," Library of Congress, https://www.loc.gov/collections/folklife-and-landscape-in-southern-west-virginia/about-this-collection/ (accessed 18 January 2019).

46. For commons legal history, see Peter Linebaugh, *The Magna Carta Manifesto: Liberties and Commons for All* (Berkeley: University of California Press, 2008).

under repeated large-scale enclosures. Plantation development, industrial extraction, and suburban sprawl topped Kirby's enclosure list.[47]

Kirby's insights drew on earlier southern scholarship as well as his own experience growing up among "commoners," but he was not alone in recognizing the centrality of commons to southern history. Political historian Steven Hahn, though he did not use the term in his groundbreaking *The Roots of Southern Populism* (1983), emphasized the centrality of disputes over "the grid of use-rights in the land," including stock and game laws, to the construction of new labor systems after Emancipation. Planters saw access to unenclosed lands as a threat to their ability to control labor. Seeking to prevent black men's economic independence, white landholders turned to game restrictions and ended the open range. Newly free black laborers, as well as white smallholders and landless white farmers, recognized the importance of forest access, wild animals, and open range to independent livelihoods and vehemently opposed stock laws. In Hahn's study, planters sought to enclose, and the emerging Populists determined to defend, existing wildlife and livestock commoning grounds. Scott E. Giltner expanded Hahn's analysis in *Hunting and Fishing in the New South* (2008).[48]

Striking parallels appeared in Christopher Morris's discussion of Mississippi levees and Christine Keiner's history of Maryland oyster fisheries. Morris described how increased levee-building after the Civil War carried additional burdens for the black laborers who did the work. First, swamp, forest, and field-edge "ecotones" diminished. These zones had served as de facto commons and helped sustain African American families who hunted, fished, and gathered there. Second, the availability of additional dry land enabled planters to expand commercial agriculture and further coerce black labor. Keiner's Chesapeake history began in 1880, when oyster fishery privatization found serious advocates. Like

47. Jack Temple Kirby, *Rural Worlds Lost: The American South: 1920–1960* (Baton Rouge: Louisiana State University Press, 1986); Kirby, *The Countercultural South* (Athens: University of Georgia Press, 1995); Kirby, *Poquosin.* Kirby, *Mockingbird Song* (2006) won the Bancroft Prize. For similar works on other wetland communities, see Megan Kate Nelson, *Trembling Earth: A Cultural History of the Okefenokee Swamp* (Athens: University of Georgia Press, 2005); Laura A. Ogden, *Swamplife: People, Gators, and Mangroves Entangled in the Everglades* (Minneapolis: University of Minnesota Press, 2011).

48. Steven Hahn, *The Roots of Southern Populism: Yeoman Farmers and the Transformation of the Georgia Upcountry, 1850–1890* (New York: Oxford University Press, 1983); Scott E. Giltner, *Hunting and Fishing in the New South: Black Labor and White Leisure after the Civil War* (Baltimore: Johns Hopkins University Press, 2008). See also Stuart A. Marks, *Southern Hunting in Black and White: Nature, History, and Ritual in a Carolina Community* (Princeton: Princeton University Press, 1991).

Morris's "ecotones," Chesapeake oyster bed commons had supported small-scale livelihoods, while privatization benefited larger commercial enterprises. These four cases—illuminated by Hahn, Giltner, Morris, and Keiner—suggest momentum on behalf of commons enclosure, couched as "improvement," in the late nineteenth- and early twentieth-century South.[49]

But commons disputes extended both backward in time and into urban spaces in the region. Harry L. Watson investigated a series of disputes over mill dams and shad-fishing rights that erupted in many riverside communities in the late eighteenth and early nineteenth centuries. Like Hahn's stock-law opponents in a later era, Watson's early republican white yeomen opposed dams as threats to livelihood and independence—what they called "the common rights of mankind." Dam disputes roiled Georgia, North Carolina, South Carolina, and Virginia, an early example of vernacular commons rising to visibility when faced with enclosure threats.[50] An urban case of this enclosure-resistance pattern emerged in Ari Kelman's fine riverfront-focused study of New Orleans. Early nineteenth-century residents organized a commons-defense campaign against a court-approved effort to privatize one portion of their city's Mississippi waterfront. They implemented a watch system, appointing guards to bang drums and draw a defensive crowd each time the would-be privatizer's hired canal diggers approached. In this way, New Orleans residents successfully defended the "batture" in question, which they valued as a soil harvest-ground, a storage area, and a promenade. Their actions defied judiciary "state boundaries" in support of a "vernacular cultural domain" centered on the batture.[51]

Scholars revealed similarly determined commons defense efforts at work in the highland South, which proved something of a hotbed for commons studies. Though neither used the term, Appalachian history groundbreakers Ronald D. Eller and Durwood Dunn demonstrated the importance of commoning to nineteenth-century rural highland residents. John C. Inscoe's pioneering work on mountain slaveholders underscored the importance of the region's woods-based open-range livestock trade and its ties to the cotton economy. In a nuanced West Virginia study, Ronald L. Lewis traced the devastations wrought on

49. Morris, *The Big Muddy*; Keiner, *The Oyster Question.*

50. Harry L. Watson, "'The Common Rights of Mankind': Subsistence, Shad, and Commerce in the Early Republican South," *Journal of American History* 83 (June 1996): 13–43.

51. Ari Kelman, *A River and Its City: The Nature of Landscape in New Orleans* (Berkeley: University of California Press, 2003), 19–49.

forest farming communities by massive turn-of-the-twentieth-century timber harvests. Donald Edward Davis documented patterns of commons harvest from the Mississippian era to the early twentieth century, and also recounted instances from his own post–World War II upland Georgia upbringing. Ralph H. Lutts explored the "chestnut commons" through southwestern Virginia's lively early twentieth-century trade in the native nut. Kathryn Newfont demonstrated how western North Carolina's woods-based commons traditions played a central role in its hotly contested late twentieth-century national forest politics. Luke Manget unearthed a vibrant nineteenth-century trade in medicinal plants that linked mountain diggers to Chinese markets and the developing pharmaceutical industry. Each of these works detailed how southern highlands forest commons tied mountain residents to national and global markets, ecologies, and political developments.[52]

Examples from the highland South underscore how central commons traditions have been to what Karl Jacoby called "the hidden history" of conservation. Conservationist federal and state land acquisition and water engineering projects often dispossessed commons users and criminalized traditional harvest. Jacoby, Mark David Spence, and Louis S. Warren explored this previously hidden history in a series of mostly western cases. Indigenous peoples bore the brunt of conservationist dispossessions, which also affected other subsistence hunters—now redefined as "poachers" and "trespassers." Southern scholarship reveals what might be called a "long hidden history" of conservation, as similar commons-

52. Ronald D. Eller, *Miners, Millhands, and Mountaineers: Industrialization of the Appalachian South, 1880–1930* (Knoxville: University of Tennessee Press, 1982); Durwood Dunn, *Cades Cove: The Life and Death of a Southern Appalachian Community, 1818–1937* (Knoxville: University of Tennessee Press, 1988); John C. Inscoe, *Mountain Masters: Slavery and the Sectional Crisis in Western North Carolina* (Knoxville: University of Tennessee Press, 1989); Ronald L. Lewis, *Transforming the Appalachian Countryside: Railroads, Deforestation, and Social Change in West Virginia, 1880–1920* (Chapel Hill: University of North Carolina Press, 1998); Donald Edward Davis, *Where There Are Mountains: An Environmental History of the Southern Appalachians* (Athens: University of Georgia Press, 2000); Davis, *Homeplace Geography: Essays for Appalachia* (Macon: Mercer University Press, 2006); Ralph H. Lutts, "Like Manna from God: The American Chestnut Trade in Southwestern Virginia," *Environmental History* 9 (July 2004): 497–525; Newfont, *Blue Ridge Commons;* Luke Manget, "Nature's Emporium: The Botanical Drug Trade and the Commons Tradition in Southern Appalachia, 1847–1917," *Environmental History* 21 (October 2016): 660–87. Steven Stoll also emphasized commons in *Ramp Hollow: The Ordeal of Appalachia* (New York: Hill and Wang, 2017). Social scientists Herbert Reid and Betsy Taylor featured Appalachian commons in *Recovering the Commons: Democracy, Place, and Global Justice* (Urbana: University of Illinois Press, 2010).

dispossession patterns played out in the Appalachians, the Okefenokee Swamp, and other locales over a longer time frame.[53]

Margaret Lynn Brown's history of the Great Smoky Mountains National Park addresses these themes in what might be called a "second dispossession" context, where most Indigenous people had earlier been killed or violently evicted. Brown's study, *The Wild East* (2001), followed the enforced removal of largely non-Indigenous local communities to make way for park development, pushing the "hidden history" timeline into the New Deal era. Anne Mitchell Whisnant's deeply researched history of the Blue Ridge Parkway treated a different type of federal park but told a similar mid-twentieth-century dispossession story. The TVA, an even more far-reaching conservation and economic development project, dramatically expanded the scale of southern rural dispossessions. The TVA has been the subject of too many histories to list here, but Matthew L. Downs's nuanced work on Muscle Shoals, Alabama, is a good place to start. Downs's title, *Transforming the South* (2014), aptly captured both the TVA's ambitions and its eventual results, though the two diverged sharply.[54]

Sara M. Gregg's *Managing the Mountains* (2010) offered new insight into these kinds of "hidden histories" with an innovative comparative case study. Juxtaposing highland Virginia with Vermont, she emphasized the important roles local governments played in shaping outcomes. What Gregg called "a federalized landscape" developed in each state but on very different scales despite initial similarities in federal programs and local receptions. The Shenandoah National Park and Skyline Drive forcibly evicted Virginians, but Vermonters met no such

53. Jacoby, *Crimes Against Nature;* Spence, *Dispossessing the Wilderness;* Warren, *The Hunter's Game;* Nelson, *Trembling Earth.*

54. Margaret Lynn Brown, *The Wild East: A Biography of the Great Smoky Mountains* (Gainesville: University Press of Florida, 2001); Daniel S. Pierce, *The Great Smokies: From Natural Habitat to National Park* (Knoxville: University of Tennessee Press, 2000); Anne Mitchell Whisnant, *Super-Scenic Motorway: A Blue Ridge Parkway History* (Chapel Hill: University of North Carolina Press, 2006); Matthew L. Downs, *Transforming the South: Federal Development in the Tennessee Valley, 1915–1960* (Baton Rouge: Louisiana State University Press, 2014). See also Michael J. McDonald and John Muldowny, *TVA and the Dispossessed: The Resettlement of Population in the Norris Dam Area* (Knoxville: University of Tennessee Press, 1982); William Bruce Wheeler and Michael J. McDonald, *TVA and the Tellico Dam: A Bureaucratic Crisis in Post-Industrial America* (Knoxville: University of Tennessee Press, 1986). For public-private initiative, see Sarah Mittlefehldt, *Tangled Roots: The Appalachian Trail and American Environmental Politics* (Seattle: University of Washington Press, 2014).

fate. Gregg argued that local governments—more democratic in Vermont's townships, more elite-controlled in Virginia's counties—made the difference. In a parallel to Christine Keiner's oyster research, Gregg found communities facing conservation initiatives that threatened livelihoods. In both studies, some local governments successfully fended off these threats. These communities avoided becoming "poachers" and "trespassers" partly by engaging and reshaping conservationist efforts, an interesting twist on the "hidden history" model.[55]

Christine Keiner also suggested that local commons-based oysterbed management built an impressive if imperfect conservationist track record. This finding parallels a trend in commons studies away from the "tragedy of the commons" model made famous in Garrett Hardin's 1968 essay. Hardin argued that commons inevitably fail due to overharvest. Scholarship such as Elinor Ostrom's work on commons governance documented longevity and conservationist success in well-governed commons systems worldwide. Keiner's oyster communities offer a compelling historical example of effective commons governance, as well as a more inclusive brand of conservation.[56]

Much work also remains to be done on the South's many federal landscapes—which, in theory anyway, are managed *by* the state *for* the people. Here the South lags behind western environmental history, though excellent works appeared in the 2010s. Again, the scale is large. Land reforms sought by formerly enslaved African Americans never took place, but immense land transfers did occur in the twentieth-century South. Between 1911 and the 1970s, the federal government purchased millions of southern acres for national forests and parks, hydroelectric and flood control projects, military bases, nuclear weapons plants, NASA facilities, installations along the United States–Mexico border, and other endeavors. The stories of these southern lands differ in important ways from those of the West, though both are part of a larger narrative of federal landholding. T. Robert Hart found the New Deal Santee-Cooper project, for instance, pivotal in transforming the South Carolina Lowcountry from an Old South to a Sunbelt landscape.[57]

Some federal lands, especially well-known parks such as the Great Smoky

55. Sara M. Gregg, *Managing the Mountains: Land Use Planning, the New Deal, and the Creation of a Federal Landscape in Appalachia* (New Haven: Yale University Press, 2010); Keiner, *The Oyster Question.*

56. Ostrom Garrett Hardin, "The Tragedy of the Commons," *Science* 162 (13 December 1968): 1243–48; Ostrom, *Governing the Commons.*

57. T. Robert Hart, "The Lowcountry Landscape: Politics, Preservation, and the Santee-Cooper Project," *Environmental History* 18 (January 2013): 127–56. For other southern examples, see Downs, *Transforming the South;* Gregg, *Managing the Mountains;* Manganiello, *Southern Water;* Newfont, *Blue Ridge Commons.*

Mountains and the Everglades, attracted chroniclers. A few histories of the sweeping southern national forest units have appeared, with Will Sarvis's fine book on the Jefferson National Forest providing a particularly strong model. A handful of less iconic federal parks such as South Carolina's Congaree National Park and the Santa Ana National Wildlife Refuge in South Texas received attention. In *Beyond the Mountains* (2018), Drew A. Swanson discussed the development of federal facilities at Oak Ridge, Tennessee. But far more federal southern lands await historians.[58]

Among southern forests, the pine woods have received particular attention. Thomas D. Clark argued in his 1984 book *The Greening of the South* that historians, "cotton-blinded" in their focus on plantation economies, had for too long ignored the centrality of naval stores to the southern economy. Twenty years later, two important pine-centered histories appeared. In *Tapping the Pines* (2004), Robert B. Outland III examined the multicentury and multistate history of the naval stores industry from an economic perspective, with attention to both social and environmental factors. Outland traced the spread of turpentining and its heavy reliance on black laborers, enslaved before the Civil War and exploited by the convict leasing system after. In *Looking for Longleaf* (2004), Lawrence S. Earley also considered turpentine and naval stores, but provided a broader and more conservation-focused history of longleaf pineries that emphasized the vast scale of past harvests and considered present management issues. In 2011, Albert G. Way built on Earley's approach with *Conserving Southern Longleaf*, which traced twentieth-century shifts in conservation approaches and paid close attention especially to quail and pine ecologies.[59]

58. Brown, *The Wild East*; Pierce, *The Great Smokies*; Jack E. Davis, *An Everglades Providence: Marjory Stoneman Douglas and the American Environmental Century* (Athens: University of Georgia Press, 2009); Will Sarvis, *The Jefferson National Forest: An Appalachian Environmental History* (Knoxville: University of Tennessee Press, 2011); Mark Kinzer, *Nature's Return: An Environmental History of Congaree National Park* (Columbia: University of South Carolina Press, 2017); M. J. Morgan, *Border Sanctuary: The Conservation Legacy of the Santa Ana Land Grant* (College Station: Texas A&M University Press, 2015); Drew A. Swanson, *Beyond the Mountains: Commodifying Appalachian Environments* (Athens: University of Georgia Press, 2018).

59. Thomas D. Clark, *The Greening of the South: The Recovery of Land and Forest* (Lexington: University Press of Kentucky, 1984); Robert B. Outland III, *Tapping the Pines: The Naval Stores Industry in the American South* (Baton Rouge: Louisiana State University Press, 2004); Lawrence S. Earley, *Looking for Longleaf: The Fall and Rise of an American Forest* (Chapel Hill: University of North Carolina Press, 2004); Albert G. Way, *Conserving Southern Longleaf: Herbert Stoddard and the Rise of Ecological Land Management* (Athens: University of Georgia Press, 2011).

Important studies of the lumber and paper industries contributed to the history of southern forests. Mikko Saikku's bioregional history of the Yazoo-Mississippi Delta, *This Delta, This Land* (2005), took a *longue durée* approach and, in an echo of Clark, found timber even more important than cotton. In *The Slain Wood* (2015), William Boyd considered the paper industry's sweeping role in southern history, noting how shifts to monoculture pine plantations caused significant wildlife habitat loss and how paper production poisoned southern waters. Boyd demonstrated how Jim Crow structures kept black workers in the woods as poorly paid loggers and restricted their entry into safer, better-paying jobs as paper millhands. Labor historian William P. Jones's *The Tribe of Black Ulysses* (2005) focused on the lumber industry's black working class, arguing that many African American men embraced industrial work in woods' products as a way to build robust families and communities.[60]

Jones's attention to masculinity and forest work serves as a reminder that despite Carolyn Merchant's decades of pathbreaking work, the gendered dimensions of environmental history remain only partially unearthed in and beyond the South.[61] This area is ripe for deeper exploration. While further studies of masculinity are needed, we know far more about men's experiences in woods, waters, and fields than about women's experiences. A few important works addressed this imbalance. Lu Ann Jones's innovative *Mama Learned Us to Work* (2002), though not framed as environmental history, demonstrated complex gendered relationships that twentieth-century southern farm women had with agricultural landscapes. Sarah H. Hill's nuanced study of Cherokee women's basketry, *Weaving New Worlds* (1997), revealed shifts in crafters' material and aesthetic preferences over the course of three centuries. Indigenous women developed rivercane

60. Mikko Saikku, *This Delta This Land: An Environmental History of the Yazoo-Mississippi Floodplain* (Athens: University of Georgia Press, 2005); William Boyd, *The Slain Wood: Papermaking and its Environmental Consequences in the American South* (Baltimore: Johns Hopkins University Press, 2015); William P. Jones, *The Tribe of Black Ulysses: African American Lumber Workers in the Jim Crow South* (Urbana: University of Illinois Press, 2005).

61. Carolyn Merchant, *The Death of Nature: Women, Ecology, and the Scientific Revolution* (San Francisco: Harper & Row, 1980); Merchant, *Ecological Revolutions;* Merchant, "Gender and Environmental History," *Journal of American History* 76 (March 1990): 1117–21; Merchant, *Earthcare: Women and the Environment* (New York: Routledge, 1996); Merchant, "George Bird Grinnell's Audubon Society: Bridging the Gender Divide in Conservation," *Environmental History* 15 (January 2010): 3–30. For Merchant's influence, see Kenneth Worthy, Elizabeth Allison, and Whitney A. Bauman, eds., *After the Death of Nature: Carolyn Merchant and the Future of Human-Nature Relations* (New York: Routledge, 2018).

basketry into an art form so sophisticated it drew admiration on both sides of the Atlantic. When Euro-American newcomers introduced oak-split traditions to the southern mountains, Cherokee craftswomen incorporated this medium, eventually making native white oak their preferred material. Twentieth-century weavers innovated further, adding introduced plants such as Japanese honeysuckle to their basketry palettes. Hill demonstrated how female artisans' choices not only reflected but also created changes in local ecologies and cultures. Elizabeth D. Blum's pioneering exploration of enslaved women's experiences of "wilderness" in her 2002 essay, "Power, Danger, and Control," offered another important model. Blum described swamps and forests as a kind of gendered double-edged sword for captive laborers. On the one hand, these were sites of racialized danger, preferred by white rapists as well as venomous snakes. On the other hand, they could also be sites of women's power, places to escape enslavers' brutality and develop useful skills and knowledge. Medicinal plant knowledge proved especially valuable, and Blum found evidence that some enslaved women successfully parlayed this expertise into greater power within the institution of slavery.[62]

By asking questions about women's worlds on farms, in forests, and in swamps, these historians joined Carolyn Merchant, Nancy Unger, and others in demonstrating the rich potential in gendered lines of environmental inquiry. Not only women's gendered experiences of "nature," but also specific nonhuman species played leading roles in these studies. Tomatoes, for example, emerged as an especially important plant for the farming women whom Jones studied, just as rivercane, white oak, and honeysuckle did for Hill's subjects, and medicinal plant species did for Blum's. The presence of chickens profoundly shaped women's daily lives in Jones's study, while the presence of water moccasins challenged swamp-goers in Blum's work. These studies also demonstrated how much women's lives took place outdoors. Jones's farmers tended and harvested gardens and

62. Lu Ann Jones, *Mama Learned Us to Work: Farm Women in the New South* (Chapel Hill: University of North Carolina Press, 2002); Sarah H. Hill, *Weaving New Worlds: Southeastern Cherokee Women and Their Basketry* (Chapel Hill: University of North Carolina Press, 1997); Elizabeth D. Blum, "Power, Danger and Control: Slave Women's Perceptions of Wilderness in the Nineteenth Century," *Women's Studies* 31 (March/April 2002): 247–67. For an introduction to women in US environmental history, see Nancy C. Unger, *Beyond Nature's Housekeepers: American Women in Environmental History* (New York: Oxford University Press, 2012). See also Daniel H. Usner, *Weaving Alliances with Other Women: Chitimacha Indian Work in the New South* (Athens: University of Georgia Press, 2015); Usner, "From Bayou Teche to Fifth Avenue: Crafting a New Market for Chitimacha Indian Baskets," *Journal of Southern History* 79 (May 2013): 339–74.

flocks, while Hill's and Blum's women used forests as key harvest sites. Hill's and Blum's studies also underscored the importance of wooded common lands to southern women, and of women to these lands.[63]

"The destructive character of agricultural methods in the old tobacco regions of Virginia and Maryland has been commented on by almost every writer who has dealt with that section."[64]

Southern woodlands are not always what they seem. Driving around the rural South today, you might come upon one of thousands of groves of pine trees, in perfect rows, with a sign out front announcing: "Trees are a crop." The signs attest to the fact that these are not the native forests of generations past, and that timber has replaced traditional crop farming for many landowners throughout the Southeast. They also speak to the long shadow of the agricultural South, both in the southern landscape and in southern historiography.[65] Since the 1980s, though, historians called their histories of southern agriculture "environmental" with increasing self-consciousness, giving rise to what Christopher Morris dubbed "the new agricultural history."[66]

The new agricultural histories of the South provided more satisfying and intricate accounts of traditional agricultural topics. Albert E. Cowdrey and Timothy Silver both addressed agriculture in their early treatments of southern environmental history, but it was Mart A. Stewart's *"What Nature Suffers to Groe"* (1996) that pioneered the "agroecological" approach in southern history.[67] Stewart's three-

63. Jones, *Mama Learned Us to Work;* Hill, *Weaving New Worlds;* Blum, "Power, Danger and Control"; Merchant, *Ecological Revolutions;* Unger, *Beyond Nature's Housekeepers.*

64. Craven, *Soil Exhaustion as a Factor in the Agricultural History of Virginia and Maryland,* 11.

65. See, for example, Craven, *Soil Exhaustion as a Factor in the Agricultural History of Virginia and Maryland;* Phillips, *Life and Labor in the Old South;* Lewis C. Gray and Esther Katherine Thompson, *History of Agriculture in the Southern United States to 1860* (Washington: Carnegie Institution, 1933); Willard Range, *A Century of Georgia Agriculture, 1850–1950* (Athens: University of Georgia Press, 1954); James C. Bonner, *A History of Georgia Agriculture, 1732–1860* (Athens: University of Georgia Press, 1964); Faust, *James Henry Hammond and the Old South;* Gilbert Courtland Fite, *Cotton Fields No More: Southern Agriculture, 1865–1980* (Lexington: University Press of Kentucky, 1984); Breen, *Tobacco Culture;* Pete Daniel, *Breaking the Land: The Transformation of Cotton, Tobacco, and Rice Cultures Since 1880* (Urbana: University of Illinois Press, 1985); Kirby, *Rural Worlds Lost.*

66. Morris, "A More Southern Environmental History," 592.

67. Donald Worster was the first to promote "agroecological" history under that title; see "Transformations of the Earth: Toward an Agroecological Perspective in History," *Journal of American History* 76 (March 1990): 1087–106.

century history of the Georgia Lowcountry considered rice not just as a profitable commodity but as a member of an ecological community that included humans, animals, waters, and weather. Stewart also meticulously untangled ways in which environmental knowledge and practice were socially differentiated in a slave society. Planters operated "hydraulic machines," otherwise known as rice plantations, with the muscle of enslaved African Americans who carved out a "counterlandscape" of their own in the swamps and interstices of the plantation regime.[68]

Although southern historians long considered crops and soils to be significant features of southern history, the agroecological perspective is reshaping our understanding of the South's agricultural past. Contrast, for instance, T. H. Breen's extended meditation on how pre-Revolutionary Virginia gentry spent most of their waking hours thinking about crops and livestock in *Tobacco Culture* (1985) with Drew A. Swanson's insistence in *A Golden Weed* (2016) that, because the tobacco plant provided "a medium through which people understood and interacted with the environment" in the North Carolina–Virginia Piedmont, farmers not only pursued profit but developed an "intimate knowledge of local environments."[69] Or, compare what is often cited as the progenitor of southern environmental history, Avery O. Craven's *Soil Exhaustion as a Factor in the Agricultural History of Virginia and Maryland, 1606–1860* (1926), with Paul S. Sutter's *Let Us Now Praise Famous Gullies* (2015). Both investigated the history of soil erosion in particular locales. Craven applied a Frederick Jackson Turner frontier analysis to southern history to show how southern farmers wasted soil fertility. Sutter found a much more locally idiosyncratic and therefore less regionally exceptionalist story. Although the spectacular gullies of Lumpkin County, Georgia, derived in part from the abuses of staple-crop agriculture, they also reflected the particularities of the local environment—in this case the mix of clay and sand that made it possible for a small amount of washing to metastasize into what become known as the "Little Grand Canyon."[70]

Along with Swanson, a number of other historians reconsidered southern staple crops. Alan L. Olmstead and Paul W. Rhode's *Creating Abundance* (2008),

68. Stewart, *"What Nature Suffers to Groe,"* 111–13, 250.

69. Breen, *Tobacco Culture,* 3; Drew A. Swanson, *A Golden Weed: Tobacco and Environment in the Piedmont South* (New Haven: Yale University Press, 2014), 8, x.

70. Craven, *Soil Exhaustion as a Factor in the Agricultural History of Virginia and Maryland;* Paul S. Sutter, *Let Us Now Praise Famous Gullies: Providence Canyon and the Soils of the South* (Athens: University of Georgia Press, 2015). See also Sutter, "What Gullies Mean: Georgia's 'Little Grand Canyon' and Southern Environmental History," *Journal of Southern History* 76 (August 2010): 579–616.

though not self-consciously environmental history, offered a more complete understanding of the cotton South by attending to biological innovation. For too long, Olmstead and Rhode argued, historians overplayed the role of Eli Whitney's cotton gin, when the breeding of Mexican hybrid cottons was just as important.[71] In *Boll Weevil Blues* (2011), meanwhile, James C. Giesen took on another venerable myth of the cotton South: that the boll weevil dramatically diversified southern agriculture. Giesen revealed that, in fact, the changes wrought by the boll weevil depended on local environmental conditions and human power relations. Government agencies and planters emerged as the clear winners in the wake of the weevil crisis—while southern farmers grew just as much cotton as before. Giesen provided a model cultural history of the weevil, and his fine-grained analyses of different crop-pest interactions across different ecosystems also offered the best environmental history of cotton to date.[72] Similarly, William Thomas Okie's *The Georgia Peach* (2016) took seriously *Prunus persica* as an organism, and also showed how environmental aesthetics underlay the outsized cultural footprint of Georgia's most famous crop.[73]

Paul S. Sutter's work on southern soils, likewise, joined a series of reconsiderations of how soil erosion and soil conservation shaped southern history. Jack Temple Kirby was the first to recover Edmund Ruffin as an innovative soil scientist—not just a fire-breathing secessionist who famously shot himself as federal troops approached. Ruffin's discovery of the fertility-releasing effects of fossilized seashells promised to reverse the degradation of eastern seaboard plantations and stem the tide of westward migration.[74] Steven Stoll's *Larding the Lean Earth* (2002) built on Kirby's work, placing the southern experience with agricultural conservation in the context of a broader history of nineteenth-century agricultural reform.[75] Lynn A. Nelson's *Pharsalia* (2007), meanwhile,

71. Alan L. Olmstead and Paul W. Rhode, *Creating Abundance: Biological Innovation and American Agricultural Development* (New York: Cambridge University Press, 2008). Edmund Russell expanded on the importance of cotton evolution in *Evolutionary History: Uniting History and Biology to Understand Life on Earth* (New York: Cambridge University Press, 2011).

72. James C. Giesen, *Boll Weevil Blues: Cotton, Myth, and Power in the American South* (Chicago: University of Chicago Press, 2011).

73. William Thomas Okie, *The Georgia Peach: Culture, Agriculture, and Environment in the American South* (New York: Cambridge University Press, 2016).

74. Kirby, *Poquosin;* Edmund Ruffin, *Nature's Management: Writings on Landscape and Reform, 1822–1859,* ed. Jack Temple Kirby (Athens: University of Georgia Press, 2000).

75. Steven Stoll, *Larding the Lean Earth: Soil and Society in Nineteenth-Century America* (New York: Hill and Wang, 2002).

zoomed in on a single plantation to consider that world of southern agricultural reform, demonstrating how difficult it was to enact the recommendations of agricultural reformers such as Ruffin and John Taylor of Caroline while enjoying the leisurely lifestyle assumed to be the planter's birthright.[76] In a similar vein, Joyce E. Chaplin's *An Anxious Pursuit* (1993) presented elite southern planters in the eighteenth century as modern and conversant with broader currents in political economy and philosophy. For Chaplin, planters' reading and worldview shaped their farming, as they scientifically studied their surroundings and tinkered with their agricultural practices.[77] Benjamin R. Cohen's *Notes from the Ground* (2009) reversed the current of this flow of knowledge, showing how nineteenth-century farmers and planters allowed their agricultural experiences to shape their worldview. Cohen imported from Virgil the useful concept of "the georgic ethic" to help explain the kind of experience-based, labor-oriented agricultural science that was typical of farming in the Early Republic.[78]

Soil fertility continued to be a central southern concern even in the era of manufactured fertilizer, as suggested by Timothy Johnson's work on the fertilizer industry and Randal S. Beeman and James A. Pritchard's *A Green and Permanent Land* (2001).[79] Nor was it only elite white reformers who fretted over soils. Mark D. Hersey's *My Work Is That of Conservation* (2011) showed how George Washington Carver came to understand the problem of soil fertility in the Black Belt as both economic and ecological. In so doing, Hersey restored Carver to his place not just as a peanut scientist but as an agroecological advocate of poor farmers.[80]

76. Lynn A. Nelson, *Pharsalia: An Environmental Biography of a Southern Plantation, 1780–1880* (Athens: University of Georgia Press, 2007). On John Taylor of Caroline as an agricultural reformer, see *Arator: Being a Series of Agricultural Essays, Practical and Political—in Sixty-Four Numbers*, ed. M. E. Bradford (Indianapolis: Liberty Fund, 2012).

77. Joyce E. Chaplin, *An Anxious Pursuit: Agricultural Innovation and Modernity in the Lower South, 1730–1815* (Chapel Hill: University of North Carolina Press, 1993).

78. Benjamin R. Cohen, *Notes from the Ground: Science, Soil, and Society in the American Countryside* (New Haven: Yale University Press, 2009).

79. Timothy Johnson, "Reconstructing the Soil: Emancipation and the Roots of Chemical-Dependent Agriculture in America," in Drake, ed., *The Blue, the Gray, and the Green*, 191–208; Johnson, "Nitrogen Nation: The Legacy of World War I and the Politics of Chemical Agriculture in the United States, 1916–1933," *Agricultural History* 90 (Spring 2016): 209; Randal S. Beeman and James A. Pritchard, *A Green and Permanent Land: Ecology and Agriculture in the Twentieth Century* (Lawrence: University Press of Kansas, 2001).

80. Mark D. Hersey, *My Work Is That of Conservation: An Environmental Biography of George Washington Carver* (Athens: University of Georgia Press, 2011).

The quest for manufactured fertilizer brought new developments to long-established southern extractive industries as well. In *Mountains on the Market* (2012), Randal L. Hall revealed how lead mining developed in Virginia's New River valley during the colonial era, followed eventually by iron, salt, copper, zinc, limestone, and calcium carbide extraction. Across the border in Tennessee, Duncan Maysilles's *Ducktown Smoke* (2011) traced copper mining's antebellum origins as well as the multistate legal battles that its air pollution eventually provoked. Both authors demonstrated how extractive industries relied on enslaved as well as free laborers, engaged regional, national, and global markets, and brought intense environmental destruction—not only air, but also water and soil pollution, and large-scale deforestation. Ducktown and New River ore facilities produced sulfuric acid for the commercial fertilizer market while themselves causing massive soil erosion—creating, for instance, a large barren area known as the "Ducktown desert." In the twentieth century, these operations met sulfuric acid demands from the munitions industry while continuing to degrade soils and waters. In addition to landmark legal precedents, Superfund designations and ongoing pollution are among their present-day legacies.[81]

Like mining enterprises, petroleum extraction remade southern land and waterscapes while engaging global markets. In *American Energy, Imperiled Coast* (2014), for example, Jason P. Theriot demonstrated how a century of petroleum development had sweeping effects in Louisiana. Canals, pipelines, and other industry infrastructure reworked wetland hydrologies and contributed to erosion that has decreased the state's land base by an astonishing two thousand square miles—an area that, as Jack E. Davis pointed out, is the size of Delaware. The industry remade Louisiana's sociopolitical landscape in similarly dramatic fashion, Theriot revealed, reshaping economies, politics, and cultural values.[82]

Southern extraction also yielded other riches. Gold-mining enjoyed nineteenth-century heydays in North Carolina and Georgia, as Jason Hauser and Drew A.

81. Randal L. Hall, *Mountains on the Market: Industry, the Environment, and the South* (Lexington: University Press of Kentucky, 2012); Duncan Maysilles, *Ducktown Smoke: The Fight over One of the South's Greatest Environmental Disasters* (Chapel Hill: University of North Carolina Press, 2011). For salt, see also John E. Stealey, *The Antebellum Kanawha Salt Business and Western Markets* (Lexington: University Press of Kentucky, 1993); Swanson, *Beyond the Mountains.*

82. Jason P. Theriot, *American Energy, Imperiled Coast: Oil and Gas Development in Louisiana's Wetlands* (Baton Rouge: Louisiana State University Press, 2014); Davis, *The Gulf.* See also Tyler Priest, *The Offshore Imperative: Shell Oil's Search for Petroleum in Postwar America* (College Station: Texas A&M University Press, 2007).

Swanson argued, respectively. From the late nineteenth century well into the early twenty-first century, the presence of coal deposits shaped large sections of the South, in and beyond the highlands. Coal mining drew a great deal of scholarly attention, particularly from labor historians who attended to the tolls mining took on human bodies—lungs, limbs, lives—and communities, and addressed issues such as water quality as well. Ronald L. Lewis discussed industrial slavery in an early work, *Coal, Iron, and Slaves* (1979). Several studies, including Chad Montrie's *To Save the Land and People* (2003), considered anti-strip-mining activism. Few histories of coal mining, however, approached the topic from a deliberately environmental perspective. We need more work on the environmental history of southern minerals and mining: coal, iron, phosphates, kaolin, mica, and beyond.[83]

Agroecological history tends to be messy. Scholars sought not only to assign agency to nature but, as Paul S. Sutter put it, to point out "how entangled human actions have been with nonhuman entities and forces," and therefore offer "a

83. Jason Hauser, "'A Golden Harvest': Gold Mining and Agricultural Reform in North Carolina, 1799–1842," *Agricultural History* 91 (Fall 2017): 469–87; Drew A. Swanson, "From Georgia to California and Back: The Rise, Fall, and Rebirth of Southern Gold Mining," *Georgia Historical Quarterly* 100 (Summer 2016): 160; Swanson, *Beyond the Mountains;* Sean Patrick Adams, *Old Dominion, Industrial Commonwealth: Coal, Politics, and Economy in Antebellum America* (Baltimore: Johns Hopkins University Press, 2004); Ronald L. Lewis, *Coal, Iron, and Slaves: Industrial Slavery in Maryland and Virginia, 1715–1865* (Westport: Greenwood Press, 1979); Chad Montrie, *To Save the Land and People: A History of Opposition to Surface Coal Mining in Appalachia* (Chapel Hill: University of North Carolina Press, 2003); Jinny A. Turman, "Green Civic Republicanism and Environmental Action against Surface Mining in Lincoln County, West Virginia, 1974–1990," *Journal of Southern History* 82 (November 2016): 855–900; Eileen Michelle Hagerman, "Water, Workers, and Wealth: How 'Mr. Peabody's' Coal Barge Stripped Kentucky's Green River Valley," *Register of the Kentucky Historical Society* 115 (Spring 2017): 183–221. See also Joe William Trotter Jr., *Coal, Class, and Color: Blacks in Southern West Virginia, 1915–32* (Urbana: University of Illinois Press, 1990); Chad Montrie, "Continuity in the Midst of Change: Work and Environment for West Virginia Mountaineers," *West Virginia History* 1 (March 2007): 1–22; Richard J. Callahan Jr., *Work and Faith in the Kentucky Coal Fields: Subject to Dust* (Bloomington: Indiana University Press, 2009); James Sanders Day, *Diamonds in the Rough: A History of Alabama's Cahaba Coal Field* (Tuscaloosa: University of Alabama Press, 2013). On black lung, see Barbara Ellen Smith, "History and Politics of the Black Lung Movement," *Radical America* 17 (March/June 1983): 89–109. On kaolin, see Paul A. Schroeder, "Kaolin," *New Georgia Encyclopedia,* 12 December 2003, http://www.georgiaencyclopedia.org/articles/business-economy/kaolin (accessed 18 January 2019). On phosphate mining, see Scott H. Dewey, "The Fickle Finger of Phosphate: Central Florida Air Pollution and the Failure of Environmental Policy, 1957–1970," *Journal of Southern History* 65 (August 1999): 565–603; Shepherd W. McKinley, *Stinking Stones and Rocks of Gold: Phosphate, Fertilizer, and Industrialization in Postbellum South Carolina* (Gainesville: University Press of Florida, 2014).

fundamental challenge to still-dominant notions of *human* agency."[84] This "entangled history" is exemplified in the vigorous new subfield of southern animal studies. For instance, Claire Strom's *Making Catfish Bait out of Government Boys* (2009) chronicled the twentieth-century campaign to eradicate cattle ticks, the vector for Texas Fever. The commercial cattle farmers of the South in the early twentieth century favored national economic integration, which meant eradication of Texas Fever, which in turn meant dipping cattle in vats of pesticide. The subsequent eradication campaign earned the ire of yeomen farmers, who had grown accustomed to ranging their cattle in common lands and had little interest in selling the animals beyond the local community. Strom thus told a story of class conflict as well as the entangled lives of organisms: the protozoa that parasitized the tick, the tick that parasitized the cattle, and the cattle that lived in a rough symbiosis with their human counterparts. The behavior of each organism shaped the lives of the others.[85]

As Strom's work demonstrated, animal history has much to offer southern history.[86] Joshua Blu Buhs's *The Fire Ant Wars* (2004) centered on *Solenipsis invicta* and, like other animal histories, drew on the history of science to explain the battle to exterminate fire ants from the mid-twentieth-century Southeast. Native to the wetlands along the Rio Paraguay in Brazil, Paraguay, and Argentina, *S. invicta* arrived in Mobile, Alabama, sometime in the 1930s or 1940s—just before what C. Vann Woodward famously called the southern "Bulldozer Revolution."[87] Since fire ants thrive on disturbed environments, they spread rapidly across the Southeast, occasioning pain, a handful of deaths, and alarm among farmers and entomologists. The United States Department of Agriculture tried to eradicate

84. Sutter, "Waving the Muddy Shirt," 227.

85. Claire Strom, *Making Catfish Bait out of Government Boys: The Fight against Cattle Ticks and the Transformation of the Yeoman South* (Athens: University of Georgia Press, 2009).

86. In addition to Strom, see Virginia DeJohn Anderson, *Creatures of Empire: How Domestic Animals Transformed Early America* (New York: Oxford University Press, 2004); Thomas G. Andrews, "Beasts of the Southern Wild: Slaveholders, Slaves, and Other Animals in Charles Ball's Slavery in the United States," in *Rendering Nature: Animals, Bodies, Places, Politics,* ed. Marguerite S. Shaffer and Phoebe S. K. Young (Philadelphia: University of Pennsylvania Press, 2015): 21–47; Abraham H. Gibson, *Feral Animals in the American South: An Evolutionary History* (New York: Cambridge University Press, 2016); Christopher J. Manganiello, "From a Howling Wilderness to Howling Safaris: Science, Policy and Red Wolves in the American South," *Journal of the History of Biology* 42 (May 2009): 325–59; Kirby, *The Countercultural South.*

87. C. Vann Woodward, *The Burden of Southern History,* 3rd ed. (Baton Rouge: Louisiana State University Press, 1993), 6.

fire ants with insecticides, a campaign that may have actually expanded the ants' range. Here again, the story subverts the very categories of agency and nonagency. An organism that owed its presence to human commerce spread across the South due to human disturbance. Humans in their hubris sought to destroy the organism, using chemicals that had a wide range of unintended consequences. The organism proved much more resilient than expected, even changing reproductive strategies in the midst of the eradication campaign.[88]

Some of the most innovative southern environmental histories subverted the very category of place. The things that make up what we call "the environment"—organisms micro and macro, chemicals and nutrients, weather, radioactive isotopes—are not easily contained. From the colonial era through the middle of the twentieth century, hogs and cattle ran free in swamps and woods, and occasionally cities and towns, too. Sometimes they became feral, which caused observers to lament the sorry state of southern agriculture and created conflict between and among whites and Native Americans.[89] Even something that seems fixed, such as the earth itself, moved across boundaries. Indeed, one of the defining features of southern history is the erosion of the region's soils, as Paul S. Sutter and Drew A. Swanson documented for the Georgia and Virginia–North Carolina Piedmonts, respectively.[90] Malaria and yellow fever microbes spread between mammals and mosquitos in ways that baffled planters, slaves, settlers, and public health officials from the 1600s through the early twentieth century.[91] Conevery Bolton Valençius's *The Health of the Country* (2002) documented ways in which Arkansas and

88. Joshua Blu Buhs, *The Fire Ant Wars: Nature, Science, and Public Policy in Twentieth-Century America* (Chicago: University of Chicago Press, 2004), 166–67; Pete Daniel, *Toxic Drift: Pesticides and Health in the Post–World War II South* (Baton Rouge: Louisiana State University Press, 2005).

89. Anderson, *Creatures of Empire.*

90. Sutter, *Let Us Now Praise Famous Gullies;* Swanson, *A Golden Weed.* For a discussion of large-scale soil erosion due to offshore oil drilling, see Davis, *The Gulf.*

91. Paul S. Sutter, "Nature's Agents or Agents of Empire? Entomological Workers and Environmental Change during the Construction of the Panama Canal," *Isis* 98 (December 2007): 724–54; Timothy Mitchell, *Rule of Experts: Egypt, Techno-Politics, Modernity* (Berkeley: University of California Press, 2002); Margaret Humphreys, *Malaria: Poverty, Race, and Public Health in the United States* (Baltimore: Johns Hopkins University Press, 2001); J. R. McNeill, *Mosquito Empires: Ecology and War in the Greater Caribbean, 1620–1914* (New York: Cambridge University Press, 2010); Andrew McIlwaine Bell, *Mosquito Soldiers: Malaria, Yellow Fever, and the Course of the American Civil War* (Baton Rouge: Louisiana State University Press, 2010); Kirby, *Poquosin;* Urmi Engineer Willoughby, *Yellow Fever, Race, and Ecology in Nineteenth-Century New Orleans* (Baton Rouge: Louisiana State University Press, 2017); Jim Downs, *Sick from Freedom: African American Illness and Suffering during the Civil War and Reconstruction* (New York:

Missouri settlers understood themselves to have an "intricate and intimate set of connections with the surrounding world," connections that surpassed the "seeming boundary of the skin." Their southern landscape was inhabited by airs and waters that were sickening or salubrious. Valençius, in recovering what she called this "surprising holism," took aim at the false notion of human dominance. Antebellum settlers lived in a conscious, "constant interplay between human agency and human lack of control."[92]

With new attention to human bodies and their relationship to the environments that not only surrounded but also interpenetrated, food would seem to be an obvious target for southern environmental history. Foodways are universal points of connection between humans and the environment, and southern cuisine became particularly fashionable in the twenty-first century. In addition to a raft of new books on southern food, there arose hip new restaurants offering "New Southern Cuisine" in revitalized downtowns across the former Confederacy, magazines such as *Garden and Gun* and *The Local Palate,* and southern culinary celebrities such as Paula Deen and Patti LaBelle and Sean Brock.[93] One might at first glance think that such interest, both scholarly and popular, would enrich southern environmental history, but few links emerged. Southern food history addressed how food reveals the contradictions of southern culture, the dynamics of racial and ethnic identity, and the rebooting of a cuisine, but we still need works that frame food as a fundamentally environmental relationship. David S. Shields's history of Lowcountry cuisine in the nineteenth century, *Southern Provi-*

Oxford University Press, 2012); Silver, *A New Face on the Countryside;* Mariola Espinosa, "The Threat from Havana: Southern Public Health, Yellow Fever, and the U.S. Intervention in the Cuban Struggle for Independence, 1878–1898," *Journal of Southern History* 72 (August 2006): 541–68; Albert G. Way, "The Invisible and Indeterminable Value of Ecology: From Malaria Control to Ecological Research in the American South," *Isis* 106 (June 2015): 310–36.

92. Conevery Bolton Valençius, *The Health of the Country: How American Settlers Understood Themselves and Their Land* (New York: Basic Books, 2002), 2, 3, 12.

93. For histories of southern food, see John T. Edge, *The Potlikker Papers: A Food History of the Modern South* (New York: Penguin Press, 2017); Michael W. Twitty, *The Cooking Gene: A Journey through African American Culinary History in the Old South* (New York: Amistad, 2017); Marcie Cohen Ferris, *The Edible South: The Power of Food and the Making of an American Region* (Chapel Hill: University of North Carolina Press, 2014); David S. Shields, *Southern Provisions: The Creation and Revival of a Cuisine* (Chicago: University of Chicago Press, 2015); Jessica B. Harris, *High on the Hog: A Culinary Journey from Africa to America* (New York: Bloomsbury, 2011); Angela Jill Cooley, *To Live and Dine in Dixie: The Evolution of Urban Food Culture in the Jim Crow South* (Athens: University of Georgia Press, 2015).

sions (2015), came the closest to an environmental history of southern food, alluding to the catalyzing effects of "the degradation of soil quality" and the enclosure of the southern free range on the creation of Lowcountry cuisine, but his environmental analysis is more suggestive than definitive.[94] The gap between southern food history and environmental history may be explained partly in that word "environment," which in common parlance is something that surrounds. Food does not surround us; we surround it. "Environmental history" is a poor description of what many in the field actually do, tracing the ways that bodies are porous and are sites of environmental knowledge and practice.[95]

Transnational history did for national boundaries what environmental history did for the boundaries of the human body. Its southern manifestation built on C. Vann Woodward's 1953 insight that the South's experience of "military defeat, occupation, and reconstruction" was distinctly unexceptional in a global context.[96] In early American history, transnational environmental history kept pace with broader trends, with Judith A. Carney's provocative *Black Rice* (2001) and J. R. McNeill's *Mosquito Empires* (2010) leading the way.[97] In Carney's geography of Atlantic World rice production, organisms—the species of rice grown in Africa and the Carolinas—and environmental knowledge alike played central roles in her argument for the significance of African expertise in the creation and maintenance of the southern rice industry. McNeill, meanwhile, put mosquitoes and the diseases they carried at the center of his *longue durée* history of the Caribbean world.

In contrast, pioneering twentieth-century transnational historians of the South did not make much of the insights of environmental history. Tore C. Olsson's excellent *Agrarian Crossings* (2017) convincingly argued for the interconnections between the United States and Mexico in the 1930s and 1940s, and for the centrality of the South to the so-called Green Revolution of the 1950s and 1960s. His suggestion that the South be seen as the "northernmost reach of the Latin American and Caribbean World" had clear environmental implications, but

94. Shields, *Southern Provisions*, 26–27, 19.

95. Drew A. Swanson, for instance, used the rich archives of Wormsloe Plantation near Savannah, Georgia, to chronicle not just what the residents ate over the last two centuries but also the environmental factors that made that diet possible. See Swanson, "Wormsloe's Belly: The History of a Southern Plantation through Food," *Southern Cultures* 15 (Winter 2009): 50–66.

96. C. Vann Woodward, "The Irony of Southern History," in *The Burden of Southern History*, 190.

97. Judith A. Carney, *Black Rice: The African Origins of Rice Cultivation in the Americas* (Cambridge: Harvard University Press, 2001); McNeill, *Mosquito Empires*.

nonhuman actors were not central to his story.[98] Andrew Zimmerman similarly uncovered a surprising story of connections between Germany, its African colony Togo, and Tuskegee agricultural experimentation, but again environmental adaptation played only a small role.[99]

There are exceptions to this rule. Albert G. Way's work on Bermuda grass and coastal longleaf traced connections across national boundaries, while Mart A. Stewart placed the agroecology of the southern plantation system in an international context.[100] And Bartow J. Elmore's *Citizen Coke* (2015) traced the business and environmental history of the Atlanta-based Coca-Cola Company across national boundaries. Elmore's painstaking research revealed the Coca-Cola Company's dependence on the products of nature such as water, caffeine, coca, sugar, glass, metal, and plastic. Especially in the book's second half, the ecological and economic footprint of Coke—the Coke-shed—clearly had transnational dimensions, draining aquifers in remote Indian villages for bottling plants and leaving fungus-infested soil in the highlands of Hawaii from an abandoned coca plant-breeding experiment. Yet these are relatively short-lived scenes in Elmore's story.[101] Much of the promise of transnational, southern environmental history remains untapped.

"It is pretty scenery, to be sure, if you have come in the spring before the heat dulls the vernal prism."[102]

The fact that Coca-Cola, one of the world's largest transnational corporations, was born in Atlanta, one of the South's largest cities, brings us finally to south-

98. Tore C. Olsson, *Agrarian Crossings: Reformers and the Remaking of the U.S. and Mexican Countryside* (Princeton: Princeton University Press, 2017), 5.

99. Andrew Zimmerman, *Alabama in Africa: Booker T. Washington, the German Empire, and the Globalization of the New South* (Princeton: Princeton University Press, 2010).

100. Albert G. Way, "'A Cosmopolitan Weed of the World': Following Bermudagrass," *Agricultural History* 88 (Summer 2014): 354–67; Way, "Longleaf Pine, from Forest to Fiber: Production, Consumption, and the Cutover on Georgia's Coastal Plain, 1865–1900," in Sutter and Pressly, eds., *Coastal Nature, Coastal Culture*, 209–42; Mart A. Stewart, "Plantations, Agroecology, Environmental Thought, and the American South," in *Comparing Apples, Oranges, and Cotton: Environmental Histories of the Global Plantation*, ed. Frank Uekötter (Frankfurt: Campus Verlag, 2014), 27–48; Stewart, "Islands, Edges, and Globe: The Environmental History of the Georgia Coast," in Sutter and Pressly, eds., *Coastal Nature, Coastal Culture*, 23–56.

101. Bartow J. Elmore, *Citizen Coke: The Making of Coca-Cola Capitalism* (New York: W. W. Norton, 2015), 10.

102. Goldfield, *Cotton Fields and Skyscrapers*, 1.

ern urban environmental history. Beyond the South, urban environmental history emphasized cities as hybrid landscapes, simultaneously destructive of and dependent on their environments. William Cronon, for instance, showed how Chicago both shaped and then obscured its connections to the rural hinterland that made its existence possible.[103] Southern cities were different. As David R. Goldfield argued, they were little more than agricultural marketplaces for most of their histories. The countryside, and the southern staple-crop planters who owned great swaths of it, shaped and dominated the southern city. Goldfield's analysis was not explicitly environmental, though as with most southern history that takes materiality seriously, it was environmentally inflected. Nevertheless, it points to two important characteristics of southern environmental history. First, the narrative of a countryside-dominated urban South has left us without much of a distinctly southern urban environmental history. Notable exceptions offer models for future scholarship. Raymond Arsenault's "The End of the Long Hot Summer" (1984), for instance, traced the impact of air-conditioning on the South, starting with factories, movie theaters, hotels, and banks in the 1910s and 1920s, before finally reaching southern homes in the 1950s—and thus creating the climatic conditions for a recognizably urban South.[104]

Among southern cities, New Orleans earned the lion's share of scholarly attention. Environmental histories of the city by Ari Kelman and Craig E. Colten emphasized the role of the Mississippi River in building the city and in creating a context for its environmental inequalities of race and class. Geographers Richard Campanella and Peirce F. Lewis took longer and more encyclopedic views of the city's relationship to its topography, climate, and waters. And Urmi Engineer Willoughby showed how the city did not just belong to a river, but to the Caribbean and Atlantic World—and how that status shaped the nineteenth-century "ecology of disease" for yellow fever.[105] Like New Orleans, Houston, and especially

103. William Cronon, *Nature's Metropolis: Chicago and the Great West* (New York: W. W. Norton, 1991). See also Klingle, *Emerald City.*

104. Goldfield, *Cotton Fields and Skyscrapers;* Raymond Arsenault, "The End of the Long Hot Summer: The Air Conditioner and Southern Culture," *Journal of Southern History* 50 (November 1984): 597–628.

105. Kelman, *A River and Its City;* Craig E. Colten, *An Unnatural Metropolis: Wresting New Orleans from Nature* (Baton Rouge: Louisiana State University Press, 2006); Richard Campanella, *Bienville's Dilemma: A Historical Geography of New Orleans* (Lafayette: University of Louisiana at Lafayette Press, 2008); Peirce F. Lewis, *New Orleans: The Making of an Urban Landscape,* 2nd ed. (Charlottesville: University of Virginia Press, 2003); Willoughby, *Yellow Fever, Race, and Ecology in Nineteenth-Century New Orleans.* See also Scott Frickel, "On Missing New Orleans: Lost Knowledge and Knowledge Gaps in an Ur-

its petroleum industry, benefited from keen historical analysis.[106] For the most part, however, the South's urban environmental history still awaits its chroniclers.

Perhaps the more interesting story of southern urbanization—so different from northern models—is suburbanization. Despite the new interest in southern suburbs, we have little in the way of environmental histories of these places.[107] Andrew C. Baker's *Bulldozer Revolutions* (2018) broke new ground by telling the story of suburban development from the perspective of a countryside that often invited such development, and several scholars pointed out the dispersed and rural character of twentieth-century southern industrialization.[108]

The centrality of the suburbs in southern urban history relates to a second important characteristic of southern environmental history: the different shape of environmental activism in the South. As scholars from Samuel P. Hays to Adam Rome documented, the environmental movement of the 1960s and 1970s was largely one of urban middle-class people trying to protect their access to nature.[109] The South, it has long been assumed, lacked a middle class that would care about

---

ban Hazardscape," *Environmental History* 13 (October 2008): 643–50; Daniel H. Usner, *American Indians in Early New Orleans: From Calumet to Raquette* (Baton Rouge: Louisiana State University Press, 2018).

106. Martin V. Melosi and Joseph A. Pratt, eds., *Energy Metropolis: An Environmental History of Houston and the Gulf Coast* (Pittsburgh: University of Pittsburgh Press, 2007). Houston also featured prominently in Joseph A. Pratt, Martin V. Melosi, and Kathleen A. Brosnan, eds., *Energy Capitals: Local Impact, Global Influence* (Pittsburgh: University of Pittsburgh Press, 2014); Melosi, *The Sanitary City: Environmental Services in Urban America from Colonial Times to the Present,* abridged ed. (Pittsburgh: University of Pittsburgh Press, 2000); Melosi, *Coping with Abundance: Energy and Environment in Industrial America* (New York: Alfred A. Knopf, 1985). On Birmingham, see Jonathan Foster, "The Political Air: Birmingham and the Struggle for Statewide Air Quality Legislation, 1967–1971," *Alabama Review* 65 (January 2012): 40.

107. Kevin M. Kruse, *White Flight: Atlanta and the Making of Modern Conservatism* (Princeton: Princeton University Press, 2005); Matthew D. Lassiter, *The Silent Majority: Suburban Politics in the Sunbelt South* (Princeton: Princeton University Press, 2006); Michelle Nickerson and Darren Dochuk, eds., *Sunbelt Rising: The Politics of Space, Place, and Region* (Philadelphia: University of Pennsylvania Press, 2011).

108. Andrew C. Baker, *Bulldozer Revolutions: A Rural History of the Metropolitan South* (Athens: University of Georgia Press, 2018); James C. Cobb, *The Selling of the South: The Southern Crusade for Industrial Development 1936–1990,* 2nd ed. (Urbana: University of Illinois Press, 1993); Bryant Simon, *The Hamlet Fire: A Tragic Story of Cheap Food, Cheap Government, and Cheap Lives* (New York: New Press, 2017); Tyler Gray Greene, "Farm to Factory: Secondary Road Building and the Rural Industrial Geography of Post–World War II North Carolina," *Journal of Southern History* 84 (May 2018): 277–310.

109. Samuel P. Hays and Barbara D. Hays, *Beauty, Health, and Permanence: Environmental Politics in the United States, 1955–1985* (New York: Cambridge University Press, 1987); Hurley, *Environmental Inequalities;* Rome, *The Bulldozer in the Countryside;* Christopher C. Sellers, *Crabgrass Crucible: Suburban*

environmental amenities. Although it is true that southern politicians generally have had a stereotypically conservative response to environmental regulation, the South has a long tradition of environmental activism. Kathryn Newfont identified what she calls "commons environmentalism" in western North Carolina, and demonstrated how its forest-protection ambitions often outpaced those of national groups.[110] Albert G. Way's *Conserving Southern Longleaf* positioned Georgia-based quail biologist Herbert Stoddard as a pivotal early twentieth-century conservationist, alongside the more well-known midwesterner Aldo Leopold. As Christopher J. Manganiello documented, building on the work of the late Mark Finlay, Georgia became one of the first states to protect coastal areas, with the Georgia Coastal Marshlands Protection Act (1970) predating the federal Coastal Zone Management Act (1972).[111] And William D. Bryan, in *The Price of Permanence* (2018), argued that even the New South—which at least since C. Vann Woodward's *The Origins of the New South* (1951) we have imagined as a particularly rapacious era—was balanced with concern for environmental quality.[112]

Given the region's history of racial injustice and civil rights activism, it is perhaps unsurprising that some of the most important works on southern environmental activism focus on environmental justice. Sociologist Robert D. Bullard's *Dumping in Dixie* (1990) initiated the conversation with spatial analysis of municipal waste disposal in Houston, highlighting a nascent environmental justice movement.[113] Temma Kaplan's *Crazy for Democracy* (1997) included chapters on Dollie and Kim Burwell, leaders in the Warren County, North Carolina, anti-PCB-dump campaigns and among the first to identify "environmental racism." Eileen McGurty's *Transforming Environmentalism* (2007) brought book-length focus to Warren County and demonstrated how profoundly it shaped the larger environ-

---

Nature and the Rise of Environmentalism in Twentieth-Century America (Chapel Hill: University of North Carolina Press, 2012); Adam Rome, *The Genius of Earth Day: How a 1970 Teach-In Unexpectedly Made the First Green Generation* (New York: Hill and Wang, 2013).

110. Newfont, *Blue Ridge Commons.*

111. Way, *Conserving Southern Longleaf;* Christopher J. Manganiello, "The Gold Standard: Sunbelt Environmentalism and Coastal Protection," in Sutter and Pressly, eds., *Coastal Nature, Coastal Culture,* 279–308.

112. William D. Bryan, *The Price of Permanence: Nature and Business in the New South* (Athens: University of Georgia Press, 2018); C. Vann Woodward, *Origins of the New South, 1877–1913* (Baton Rouge: Louisiana State University Press, 1951).

113. Robert D. Bullard, *Dumping in Dixie: Race, Class, and Environmental Quality,* 3rd ed. (Boulder: Westview Press, 1990).

mental justice movement. Ellen Griffith Spears's *Baptized in PCBs* (2014) told the long story of Anniston, Alabama, from 1876 to 2013. She chronicled the town's battles with Monsanto's production of PCBs and the United States Army's stockpiling and destruction of Cold War–era chemical weapons. Although civil rights activism animated Anniston's environmental justice crusade, Spears rejected a regionally exceptionalist interpretation of environmental justice. The particularities of pollution in Anniston had as much to do with global developments—militarization and industrial chemical production—as with southern history.[114]

Women played key roles in many of these stories, and a robust history of southern women's environmental leadership emerged in tandem with the environmental justice scholarship of the late 1990s and early 2000s. In *An Everglades Providence* (2009) Jack E. Davis traced Marjory Stoneman Douglas's central role in Everglades conservation efforts and showed how her work presaged the environmental justice movement. Carolyn Finney's research on MaVynee Betsch documented the activist's work to preserve northeast Florida's American Beach, another example of female-led African American environmental advocacy.[115] Shannon Elizabeth Bell's monograph on women's anti-mountaintop-removal activism, Chad Montrie's work on strip-mining opposition, and Jessica Wilkerson's study of feminist activism documented important examples of southern women's environmental leadership in Appalachia. Environmental justice activism is clearly a fruitful vein for further study.[116]

Military landscapes appear consistently throughout the history of southern environmental activism: chemical weapons in Alabama, suburb-spawning bases in Virginia and Texas, conservation in the wake of the Civil War. Although battles were often fought and bases often built in rural areas, they frequently had an

114. Temma Kaplan, *Crazy for Democracy: Women in Grassroots Movements* (New York: Routledge, 1997); Eileen McGurty, *Transforming Environmentalism: Warren County, PCBs, and the Origins of Environmental Justice* (New Brunswick: Rutgers University Press, 2007); Ellen Griffith Spears, *Baptized in PCBs: Race, Pollution, and Justice in an All-American Town* (Chapel Hill: University of North Carolina Press, 2014).

115. Davis, *An Everglades Providence;* Finney, *Black Faces, White Spaces.*

116. Shannon Elizabeth Bell, *Our Roots Run Deep as Ironweed: Appalachian Women and the Fight for Environmental Justice* (Urbana: University of Illinois Press, 2013); Chad Montrie, *Making a Living: Work and Environment in the United States* (Chapel Hill: University of North Carolina Press, 2008); Montrie, *To Save the Land and People;* Jessica Wilkerson, *To Live Here, You Have to Fight: How Women Led Appalachian Movements for Social Justice* (Urbana: University of Illinois Press, 2019). See also Michele Morrone and Geoffrey L. Buckley, eds., *Mountains of Injustice: Social and Environmental Justice in Appalachia* (Athens: Ohio University Press, 2013); Suzanne Marshall, *Lord, We're Just Trying to Save Your Water: Environmental Activism and Dissent in the Appalachian South* (Gainesville: University Press of Florida, 2002).

effect analogous to urbanization. Improved infrastructure for troop and supply transport, increased population density and internal migration (both coerced and voluntary), more frequent disease outbreaks and corresponding sanitation crusades, pollution, deagriculturalization, economic opportunities—all came along with southern militarization, beginning with the Civil War and continuing through the Cold War. While the post–World War II economic transformation of the South is a touchstone of historical scholarship, the environmental dimensions of that transformation are still just beginning to be understood. David Allen Burke's *Atomic Testing in Mississippi* (2012) and Drew A. Swanson's *Beyond the Mountains* (2018) enriched understanding of the often-overlooked "nuclear South." Caroline Peyton's "Kentucky's 'Atomic Graveyard'" (2017) illuminated the "slow violence" of nuclear waste disposal and the human and environmental costs it exacted from the rural Maxey Flats community. These initial forays make clear there is plenty of work yet to be done.[117]

Although the late twentieth-century military-industrial complex profoundly shaped the South, the Civil War attracted much more attention from scholars and the public alike. In 2001, Jack Temple Kirby urged historians to consider the subject more closely by attending to the war's environmental dynamics.[118] Civil War historians slowly took up Kirby's charge, but the subfield eventually became one of the liveliest areas of military environmental history.[119] Andrew McIlwaine Bell's *Mosquito Soldiers* (2010) reintroduced yellow fever and malaria, and the *Aedes* and *Anopholes* mosquitoes that respectively spread those diseases, into the

117. David Allen Burke, *Atomic Testing in Mississippi: Project Dribble and the Quest for Nuclear Weapons Treaty Verification in the Cold War Era* (Baton Rouge: Louisiana State University Press, 2012); Swanson, *Beyond the Mountains;* Caroline Peyton, "Kentucky's 'Atomic Graveyard': Maxey Flats and Environmental Inequity in Rural America," *Register of the Kentucky Historical Society* 115 (March 2017): 223–63. See also Peyton, "Nuclear Ghosts and the Atomic Landscape of the American South," Environment & Society Portal, *Arcadia* 19 (Autumn 2015), http://www.environmentandsociety.org/arcadia/nuclear-ghosts-and-atomic-landscape-american-south (accessed 18 January 2019). On "slow violence," see Rob Nixon, *Slow Violence and the Environmentalism of the Poor* (Cambridge: Harvard University Press, 2011).

118. Jack Temple Kirby, "The American Civil War: An Environmental View," "Nature Transformed: The Use of the Land," National Humanities Center, http://nationalhumanitiescenter.org/tserve/nattrans/ntuseland/essays/amcwar.htm (accessed 18 January 2019).

119. Examples include "The Blue, The Gray, and the Green," a conference at the University of Georgia in 2011, and the edited volume that proceeded from it: Drake, ed., *The Blue, the Gray, and the Green.* The Cold War became the most common subject of military environmental studies; see David A. Biggs, *Quagmire: Nation-Building and Nature in the Mekong Delta* (Seattle: University of Washington Press, 2010); J. R. McNeill and Corinna R. Unger, eds., *Environmental Histories of the Cold War* (New York: Cambridge University Press, 2010).

causal ecology of the war. Kathryn Shively Meier, in *Nature's Civil War* (2013), chronicled the extent to which environmental diseases such as dysentery, scurvy, and malaria, as well as mental illnesses such as depression and anxiety, shaped the Shenandoah Valley and Peninsula campaigns of 1861–1862. She reinterpreted both seasoning and straggling as fundamentally environmental processes. In *Sick from Freedom* (2012), Jim Downs applied a similar interpretive lens to the plight of freed people, tens of thousands of whom died due to the dislocation of Emancipation and the failure of the federal government or any other group to adequately provide for their health. Lisa M. Brady's *War upon the Land* (2012), meanwhile, proved the most militarily minded of the new environmental histories. Brady demonstrated how important environmental engineering became to war efforts, with canals, mines, and even river diversion as a means of exerting power over nature. Similarly, Union troops' massive foraging raids late in the war, according to Brady, targeted the "Confederacy's agroecological foundations." The region's agroecological transformation begun by the war continued afterward: Erin Stewart Mauldin showed how the Civil War, and Emancipation in particular, quickened the pace of environmental degradation and economic breakdown in the cotton South.[120]

The outpouring of environmental Civil War scholarship is a logical development. The war was "largely fought," as Kenneth W. Noe wryly noted, "outdoors." To experience the war as "ruination," as Megan Kate Nelson put it, was not just apocalyptic rhetoric but an acute physical and emotional experience. The South's landscape and its endemic diseases shaped military strategy and the fate of the emancipated who dwelt there, and the agroecological (plantation) system that powered the South proved central to the conflict and to the Union's eventual victory. The Civil War has long been central to southern history, but the environmental history of the conflict that emerged since the 2000s demonstrated that we still have very much to learn.[121]

120. Bell, *Mosquito Soldier;* Kathryn Shively Meier, *Nature's Civil War: Common Soldiers and the Environment in 1862 Virginia* (Chapel Hill: University of North Carolina Press, 2013); Downs, *Sick from Freedom;* Lisa M. Brady, *War upon the Land: Military Strategy and the Transformation of Southern Landscapes during the American Civil War* (Athens: University of Georgia Press, 2012), 16, 23; Erin Stewart Mauldin, *Unredeemed Land: An Environmental History of Civil War and Emancipation in the Cotton South* (New York: Oxford University Press, 2018).

121. Kenneth W. Noe, "Fateful Lightning: The Significance of Weather and Climate to Civil War History," in Drake, ed., *The Blue, the Gray, and the Green,* 16–33, quote on 17; Megan Kate Nelson, *Ruin Nation: Destruction and the American Civil War* (Athens: University of Georgia Press, 2012).

"Let us begin by discussing the weather, for that has been the chief agency in making the South distinctive."[122]

Southern environmental history is deepening our understanding of the southern past while also sharpening the "Hybridity and Complexity Studies" approach that sometimes threatens to overtake environmental history.[123] There is more work to do, clearly. Like the Appalachian Mountains on a foggy morning, strong contours have emerged but much more remains shrouded. We have identified a few ridges: agroecology, commons, environmental white supremacy, environmental justice movements, hydraulic waterscapes, Civil War environments. Others we glimpse, if somewhat hazily: early America, the "nuclear South," urban landscapes, women's and gendered environmental history, southern conservation and environmental activism, federalized landscapes and waterscapes and even mudscapes. A few are hazier still, their outlines only just emerging: environmental ethnohistory, food studies, and animal history. Beyond those lie largely obscured peaks: mining environments, environmental perspectives of African American and Latinx southerners and other marginalized groups, and more we can only guess. A few tools seem particularly useful for building our capacity to understand this land where mists cloak even the most visible ridges: oral history methods, transnational approaches, and organism-centered perspectives. Certainly, the unfolding views reward.

Ulrich B. Phillips wanted us to "begin by discussing the weather." Instead, we end by observing that the people who populate our histories are organisms, interacting visibly and invisibly with a welter of other organisms both inside and outside their bodies—and yes, wind and rain, and proximity to the sun, and composition of the particular patches of earth on which they stood, built, gathered, and farmed, created and procreated, resisted and oppressed. If all historians remember and attend to the matter and biota of the past, then southern environmental historians might be out of a job, but our historical understanding would be much richer.

122. Phillips, *Life and Labor in the Old South,* 3.

123. Patty Limerick, "Everything and the Kitchen Sink: Enriching the U.S. History Survey Course with Environmental History," *OAH Magazine of History* 25 (October 2011): 9–13.

THE TRANSFORMATION OF SOUTHERN INTELLECTUAL HISTORY

Sarah E. Gardner and David Moltke-Hansen

Long derogated as an impoverished intellectual and cultural domain, the American South emerged as a place of remarkable interest for intellectual historians of the late twentieth and early twenty-first centuries. Newer ways of seeing and engaging the region explain why. Previously, scholars had ignored critical aspects of, and players in, the South's intellectual development. As they began to focus less on how a subset of white southerners nurtured and expressed a hegemonic (or ruling) culture, they radically recast the subject, interrogating racial, gender, and class conflicts and transatlantic influences bubbling up in southerners' texts and interactions. As a result, the intellectual South increasingly mapped as networks of networks.[1]

Although the South took geographic form with the expulsion of most of the remaining Native American groups in the 1830s and the annexation of Texas at the end of 1845, historians (first amateur and then professional) have spent over five hundred years gathering and mining printed texts from the region's first European explorations and (attempted) colonizations. Nevertheless, southern in-

1. Houston A. Baker Jr. and Dana D. Nelson called attention to the need for a "new southern studies" in their "Preface: Violence, the Body, and the 'South,'" *American Literature* 73 (June 2001): 231–43. See also Michael Kreyling, "Toward 'A New Southern Studies,'" *South Central Review* 22 (Spring 2005): 4–18; Jon Smith, *Finding Purple America: The South and the Future of American Cultural Studies* (Athens: University of Georgia Press, 2013); Brian Ward, ed., "Forum: What's New in Southern Studies—And Why Should We Care?" *Journal of American Studies* 48 (August 2014): 691–733; James L. Peacock, *Grounded Globalism: How the U.S. South Embraces the World* (Athens: University of Georgia Press, 2007); Michele Grigsby Coffey and Jodi Skipper, eds., *Navigating Souths: Transdisciplinary Explorations of a U.S. Region* (Athens: University of Georgia Press, 2017).

tellectual historians were Anglocentric, paying little attention to how the South entered Native America's or Africa's consciousness. They asked instead how intellectual production and consumption developed in the southern English colonies and what subsequently constrained, distinguished, and characterized thought there. The pinnacle of this scholarship, Richard Beale Davis's *Intellectual Life in the Colonial South, 1585–1763* (1978), did acknowledge and trace development of a richer, more diverse cultural life than earlier works had.[2]

Since Davis, scholars have increasingly considered transatlantic and intercultural intellectual implications of Western imperial and colonial encounters in the American Southeast. Patricia Galloway argued, in *Choctaw Genesis, 1500–1700* (1996), that Native American groups radically reconfigured themselves, constructing new alliances and identities in the wake of the demographic collapse that followed the spread of European diseases. Joyce E. Chaplin's *Subject Matter* (2001) examined ways the British and Native Americans learned and thought about each other between 1500 and 1676, and how those encounters influenced developments in technology, science, and medicine. Alejandra Dubcovsky's *Informed Power* (2016) considered how Native Americans, Africans, and Europeans used orally based information networks to assert and contest power. In *Central Africans, Atlantic Creoles, and the Foundation of the Americas* (2007), Linda M. Heywood and John K. Thornton contended that Central Africans—often Christians—brought an Atlantic creole culture with them to the Americas.[3]

New World interactions required New World narratives, such as those that Peter Martyr d'Anghiera collected in *De orbe novo decades* (*Decades of the New World*) (issued in parts, starting in 1511, and, then, published together for the first time in 1530). His sources widely informed national and religious policy, according to Michael Brennan. The first published account of Hernando de Soto's expe-

2. Richard Beale Davis, *Intellectual Life in the Colonial South, 1585–1763*, 3 vols. (Knoxville: University of Tennessee Press, 1978); Louis B. Wright, *The First Gentlemen of Virginia: Intellectual Qualities of the Early Colonial Ruling Class* (San Marino, CA: Huntington Library, 1940). See also Jay B. Hubbell, *The South in American Literature, 1607–1900* (Durham: Duke University Press, 1954), which helped launch modern southern literary study.

3. Patricia Galloway, *Choctaw Genesis, 1500–1700* (Lincoln: University of Nebraska Press, 1996); Joyce E. Chaplin, *Subject Matter: Technology, the Body, and Science on the Anglo-American Frontier, 1500–1676* (Cambridge: Harvard University Press, 2001); Alejandra Dubcovsky, *Informed Power: Communication in the Early American South* (Cambridge: Harvard University Press, 2016); Linda M. Heywood and John K. Thornton, *Central Africans, Atlantic Creoles, and the Foundation of the Americas, 1585–1660* (New York: Cambridge University Press, 2007).

dition from the Gulf Coast through the Southeast to Arkansas, by "A Gentleman of Elvas" (1557), appeared in an English translation in 1609, adding further to a new genre identified by Brennan as personal accounts of the "History of the Indies." Other reports, including by missionaries, did not see print but nevertheless informed judgments and actions of the Roman Catholic Church, merchants, and government officials. Colin M. MacLachlan argued that exploration and colonization required "an intellectual reordering of reality," one that injected a future South into Europe's consciousness, as analyzed by Sandra Young in *The Early Modern Global South in Print* (2015).[4] The Spanish not only claimed the region in these ways but also, as Daniela Bleichmar demonstrated, pursued scientific investigations there. In addition, as David J. Weber detailed, the Spanish sought to establish control by spreading religion and culture into Native communities, using networks of mostly Franciscan missions, as surveyed by Jerald T. Milanich.[5]

Seeking to counter Spanish colonial claims while making their own in the 1580s, the English failed to successfully colonize Roanoke Island on the North Carolina coast. Yet as Michiel van Groesen explained in *The Representations of the Overseas World in the De Bry Collection of Voyages* (2008), the Native Americans whom colonists encountered there shaped Europeans' perceptions through engravings of watercolors by John White, a governor of the short-lived enterprise. Peter C. Mancall noted in his biography of White's contemporary, Richard Hakluyt the Younger, that the Anglican minister did more than any other English writer to promote American exploration and colonization, especially in the Southeast. For instance, Hakluyt published the first map to designate a portion of North America as Virginia.[6]

The ongoing English quest to create a godly commonwealth, according to

4. Michael Brennan, "The Texts of Peter Martyr's *De orbe novo decades* (1504–1628), A Response to Andrew Hadfield," *Connotations* 6 (1996/1997): 227–45, quote on 228–29; Colin M. MacLachlan, *Spain's Empire in the New World: The Role of Ideas in Institutional and Social Change* (Berkeley: University of California Press, 1988); Sandra Young, *The Early Modern Global South in Print: Textual Form and the Production of Human Difference as Knowledge* (Burlington, VT: Ashgate Publishing, 2015).

5. Daniela Bleichmar et al., eds., *Science in the Spanish and Portuguese Empires, 1500–1800* (Palo Alto: Stanford University Press, 2009); David J. Weber, *The Spanish Frontier in North America* (New Haven: Yale University Press, 1992), esp. chap. 4; Jerald T. Milanich, *Laboring in the Fields of the Lord: Spanish Missions and Southeastern Indians* (Washington: Smithsonian Institution Press, 1999).

6. Michiel van Groesen, *The Representations of the Overseas World in the De Bry Collection of Voyages (1590–1634)* (Leiden: Brill, 2008); Peter C. Mancall, *Hakluyt's Promise: An Elizabethan's Obsession for an English America* (New Haven: Yale University Press, 2007).

Alexander B. Haskell, motivated framers of the enterprise from the sixteenth century well into the seventeenth. J. A. Leo Lemay explored the writings of John Smith, including *A True Relation of Such Occurrences and Accidents of Note as* Hath *Hapned in Virginia Since the First Planting of that Colony,* which appeared a year after the 1607 settlement of Jamestown.[7] Only after wars with the Tuscarora and the Yamasee between 1712 and 1717, and the 1719 revolt against the Lords Proprietors of Carolina, did the Lowcountry begin to catch up with the Chesapeake colonies. By then, the Carolina governments looked very different than envisioned in the Fundamental Constitutions, drafted for the Lords Proprietors by Anthony Ashley Cooper, later the first Earl of Shaftesbury, and his secretary, the philosopher John Locke. According to David Armitage, the subsequent crafting of constitutional revisions played an important role in Locke's evolving understanding of private property as "the foundation of both liberty and happiness." Holly Brewer subsequently argued that Locke and Ashley Cooper resisted not only the idea of monarchical absolutism but also that of hereditary status, as in slavery and feudalism. They did so despite their inclusion of both in the Fundamental Constitutions.[8]

How much did Locke influence the thinking of British Americans three generations later? T. H. Breen's *Tobacco Culture* (1985), on the "mentality" of the great Virginia tobacco planters of the mid-1700s, sought to explain why the colonial society that these men led became revolutionary. Breen argued that growing debt fed radicalism. Rhys Isaac found part of the reason for *The Transformation of Virginia, 1740–1790* (1982) in the Backcountry, where dissenters disrupted not just the established church, but also the Tidewater-dominated politics and society once described by Louis B. Wright.[9]

Dissenters started claiming scholarly attention among intellectual historians by the late 1980s, but white women and children, Native Americans and blacks

7. Alexander B. Haskell, *For God, King, and People: Forging Commonwealth Bonds in Renaissance Virginia* (Chapel Hill: University of North Carolina Press, 2017); J. A. Leo Lemay, *The American Dream of Captain John Smith* (Charlottesville: University Press of Virginia, 1991).

8. David Armitage, "John Locke, Carolina, and the Two Treatises of Government," *Political Theory* 32 (October 2004): 602–27, quote on 627; Holly Brewer, "Slavery, Sovereignty, and 'Inheritable Blood': Reconsidering John Locke and the Origins of American Slavery," *American Historical Review* 122 (October 2017): 1038–78.

9. T. H. Breen, *Tobacco Culture: The Mentality of the Great Tidewater Planters on the Eve of Revolution* (Princeton: Princeton University Press, 1985); Rhys Isaac, *The Transformation of Virginia, 1740–1790* (Chapel Hill: University of North Carolina Press, 1982); Wright, *The First Gentlemen of Virginia.*

(both Africans and African Americans), and also lower-class white men rarely appeared in the scholarship. Focus on privileged elites and social hierarchy began to change when James Horn's *Adapting to a New World* (1994), David Hackett Fischer's *Albion's Seed* (1989), and Grady McWhiney's *Cracker Culture* (1988) appeared. They all examined cultural transfers from the Old World to the New. Further, Jack P. Greene, Ira Berlin, Fischer, and others conceptualized distinct early colonial cultural and social hearths—in the Chesapeake, the Lowcountry, the lower Mississippi Valley, and the Backcountry. Intellectual life, the argument went, reflected ties to European influences.[10]

In the next decade, the 1990s, and after, social historians produced innovative works on race and class in the southern colonies. Intellectual and cultural historians followed suit. Noeleen McIlvenna studied the early idealism that defined colonial Georgia, and Charles Joyner explored Creole culture on the South Carolina coast. Mechal Sobel considered black and white values in *The World They Made Together* (1987). Michael Mullin examined *Africa in America* (1992) to assess slave resistance and acculturation in the South and the British Caribbean between 1736 and 1831. Daniel H. Usner looked at the dynamics shaping relationships among *Indians, Settlers, and Slaves in a Frontier Exchange Economy* (1992). Philip D. Morgan's *Slave Counterpoint* (1998) juxtaposed different labor regimes, cultures, and enslaved populations in the Chesapeake and the Lowcountry. Ras Michael Brown traced the development and persistence of *African-Atlantic Cultures and the South Carolina Lowcountry* (2012). Sylvia R. Frey and Betty Wood portrayed the conversion of the (mostly) enslaved in *Come Shouting to Zion* (1998). According to Charles F. Irons, the conversion of blacks ironically fostered the emergence of proslavery Christianity among white evangelicals.[11]

10. James Horn, *Adapting to a New World: English Society in the Seventeenth-Century Chesapeake* (Chapel Hill: University of North Carolina Press, 1994); David Hackett Fischer, *Albion's Seed: Four British Folkways in America* (New York: Oxford University Press, 1989); Grady McWhiney, *Cracker Culture: Celtic Ways in the Old South* (Tuscaloosa: University of Alabama Press, 1988); Jack P. Greene, *Pursuits of Happiness: The Social Development of Early Modern British Colonies and the Formation of American Culture* (Chapel Hill: University of North Carolina Press, 1988); Greene, *Creating the British Atlantic: Essays on Transplantation, Adaptation, and Continuity* (Charlottesville: University of Virginia Press, 2013); Ira Berlin, *Many Thousands Gone: The First Two Centuries of Slavery in North America* (Cambridge: Harvard University Press, 1998).

11. Noeleen McIlvenna, *The Short Life of Free Georgia: Class and Slavery in the Colonial South* (Chapel Hill: University of North Carolina Press, 2015); Charles Joyner, *Down by the Riverside: A South Carolina Slave Community* (Urbana: University of Illinois Press, 1984); Mechal Sobel, *The World They Made Together: Black and White Values in Eighteenth-Century Virginia* (Princeton: Princeton University Press,

The new social history encouraged intellectual historians to revise scholarly understanding of how various strains of Enlightenment thought engaged the colonies. Southern encounters continued to prove central both to European thought about North America and to ways colonists experienced that thought. Eric Hinderaker and Peter C. Mancall, for instance, assessed the interplay of colonial and Native cultures and interests *At the Edge of Empire* (2003). Christopher P. Iannini argued that the West Indian sugar colonies and the subtropical Southeast shaped eighteenth-century Americans' perceptions of, and writings on, natural history. Ronald L. Meek considered how the Scots applied their understanding of American colonial development in analyses of the evolution of peoples from savagery to civilization. Knud Haakonssen examined how such stadialists, among them Adam Smith, drew as well on natural law.[12]

Joyce Appleby contended that natural rights thinking by Locke and later writers became central to the liberal ideology of patriot leaders. Two other strains of thought became fundamental as well to British-American worldviews. One, as J. G. A. Pocock argued in *The Machiavellian Moment* (1975), drew on the preoccupation of republican thinkers who wanted to balance government and sustain a republic in the face of tendencies to corruption and self-interest. English common law became another source of political ideology. In a four-volume study of *The Common Law in Colonial America* (2008–2018), William E. Nelson detailed

1987); Michael Mullin, *Africa in America: Slave Acculturation and Resistance in the American South and the British Caribbean, 1736–1831* (Urbana: University of Illinois Press, 1992); Daniel H. Usner Jr., *Indians, Settlers, and Slaves in a Frontier Exchange Economy: The Lower Mississippi Valley Before 1783* (Chapel Hill: University of North Carolina Press, 1992); Philip D. Morgan, *Slave Counterpoint: Black Culture in the Eighteenth-Century Chesapeake and Lowcountry* (Chapel Hill: University of North Carolina Press, 1998); Ras Michael Brown, *African-Atlantic Cultures and the South Carolina Lowcountry* (New York: Cambridge University Press, 2012); Sylvia R. Frey and Betty Wood, *Come Shouting to Zion: African American Protestantism in the American South and British Caribbean to 1830* (Chapel Hill: University of North Carolina Press, 1998); Charles F. Irons, *The Origins of Proslavery Christianity: White and Black Evangelicals in Colonial and Antebellum Virginia* (Chapel Hill: University of North Carolina Press, 2008).

12. Erik Hinderaker and Peter C. Mancall, *At the Edge of Empire: The Backcountry in British North America* (Baltimore: Johns Hopkins University Press, 2003); Christopher P. Iannini, *Fatal Revolutions: Natural History, West Indian Slavery, and the Routes of American Literature* (Chapel Hill: University of North Carolina Press, 2012); Ronald L. Meek, *Social Science and the Ignoble Savage* (New York: Cambridge University Press, 1976); Knud Haakonssen, *Natural Law and Moral Philosophy: From Grotius to the Scottish Enlightenment* (New York: Cambridge University Press, 1996). See also J. G. A. Pocock, "Adam Smith and History," in *The Cambridge Companion to Adam Smith*, ed. Knud Haakonssen (New York: Cambridge University Press, 2006), 270–87; Emma Rothschild, "Adam Smith in the British Empire," in *Empire and Modern Political Thought*, ed. Sankar Muthu (New York: Cambridge University Press, 2012), 184–98.

first how, by 1660, "two regional bodies of law had begun to emerge" in New England and the Chesapeake, then how the colonies developed an increasingly shared legal culture. Liberal, republican, and legal strains of thought informed what Robert E. Shalhope, Lance Banning, and Gordon S. Wood, as well as Appleby eventually labeled "liberal republicanism."[13]

Virginia, the biggest and most influential of the English mainland colonies, proved central in the evolution of republican thought. After the American Revolution, many of the nation's founders from the Old Dominion led in establishing the Democratic-Republican Party, which dominated throughout most of the South. Yet according to Christopher Michael Curtis, Thomas Jefferson soon learned that the agrarian republic he envisioned could not survive the commodification of land that followed elimination of feudal tenure in 1775. Often judged inconsistent on race, the role and limits of government, and the place of nationalism, Jefferson emerged in works by Ari Helo and Brian Steele as remarkably consistent in his moral and political philosophy. Nevertheless, Annette Gordon-Reed and Peter S. Onuf argued subsequently that the logic shaping his thought does not explain why scholars still found tensions rending Jefferson's judgments and feelings.[14]

As potent as Jeffersonianism became, it only served as one element of the emerging white South's intellectual and emotional landscape. After two-and-a-half centuries of missionizing, sermonizing, and Great Awakenings, the new republic also laid the foundations for the Bible Belt. In *Southern Cross* (1997), Christine Leigh Heyrman contended that evangelicals succeeded in becoming a major regional influence only after they overcame theological resistance to southern patriarchy and its racial and gender hierarchies. Anticipating them, the

13. Joyce Appleby, *Liberalism and Republicanism in the Historical Imagination* (Cambridge: Harvard University Press, 1992); J. G. A. Pocock, *The Machiavellian Moment: Florentine Political Thought and the Atlantic Republican Tradition* (Princeton: Princeton University Press, 1975); William E. Nelson, *The Common Law in Colonial America,* 4 vols. (New York: Oxford University Press, 2008–18); Robert E. Shalhope, *The Roots of Democracy: American Thought and Culture, 1760–1800* (Lanham, MD: Rowman & Littlefield, 1990); Lance Banning, *Founding Visions: The Ideas, Individuals, and Intersections That Created America,* ed. Todd Estes (Lexington: University Press of Kentucky, 2015); Gordon S. Wood, *The Radicalism of the American Revolution* (New York: Alfred A. Knopf, 1991).

14. Christopher Michael Curtis, *Jefferson's Freeholders and the Politics of Ownership in the Old Dominion* (New York: Cambridge University Press, 2012); Ari Helo, *Thomas Jefferson's Ethics and the Politics of Human Progress: The Morality of a Slaveholder* (New York: Cambridge University Press, 2014); Brian Steele, *Thomas Jefferson and American Nationhood* (New York: Cambridge University Press, 2012); Annette Gordon-Reed and Peter S. Onuf, *"Most Blessed of the Patriarchs": Thomas Jefferson and the Empire of the Imagination* (New York: W. W. Norton, 2016).

Protestant Salzburger pietists who settled in early Georgia shifted, in James Van Horn Melton's analysis, from rejection to acceptance of slavery.[15]

Methodism became a major force, not only in the Second Great Awakening, but as Richard E. Brantley and others contended, in Anglo-American Romanticism.[16] In 1817, essayist and critic Charles Lamb famously evoked the "natural methodism" of English Romantic William Wordsworth. The poet deployed Methodist-inflected language and ideas about nature and the divine that suffused the work of Anglo-American Romantics. As Mark A. Noll observed, Charles Wesley also used both the language and the ideas of Methodism in his more than six thousand hymns. Sung not just in churches, but also in camp meetings and revivals, Wesley's hymns influenced black and white southerners.[17]

Yet southernists paid little attention to this strain of Romanticism or its sociolinguistic and intellectual consequences. They focused more on the influence of Sir Walter Scott. David Moltke-Hansen argued that such alternate voices from Scotland and Ireland helped nineteenth-century southern writers contest the dominance of English culture while asserting a (proto-)national identity and tradition. They carried forward their ethnoculturalism by fostering, as C. Hugh Holman observed, "a national literature on native subjects."[18]

Paul Quigley contended that the meanings and dictates of nationalism evolved in the 1840s and 1850s, unsettling and challenging white southerners as they decided how to define their allegiances in the face of changing circumstances.

15. Christine Leigh Heyrman, *Southern Cross: The Beginnings of the Bible Belt* (New York: Alfred A. Knopf, 1997); James Van Horn Melton, *Religion, Community, and Slavery on the Colonial Southern Frontier* (New York: Cambridge University Press, 2015). See also Michael A. Lofaro, *Southern Manuscript Sermons before 1800: A Bibliography* (Knoxville: Newfound Press, 2010).

16. Richard E. Brantley, *Transatlantic Trio: Empiricism, Evangelicalism, Romanticism: Essays and Reviews, 1974–2017* (Ames, IA: Culicidae Press, 2017); David Moltke-Hansen, "Natural Methodism and Varieties of Romanticism," *Simms Review* 24 (Summer/Winter 2016): 117–25; Helen Boyles, *Romanticism and Methodism: The Problem of Religious Enthusiasm* (New York: Routledge, 2017); Jasper Albert Cragwell, *Lake Methodism: Polite Literature and Popular Religion in England, 1780–1830* (Columbus: Ohio State University Press, 2013). Cynthia Lynn Lyerly, *Methodism and the Southern Mind, 1770–1810* (New York: Oxford University Press, 1998), contended rather that egalitarianism continued to draw converts. Charity R. Carney, *Ministers and Masters: Methodism, Manhood, and Honor in the Old South* (Baton Rouge: Louisiana State University Press, 2011), saw patriarchy fostering hierarchy.

17. Richard E. Brantley, "Wielding Natural Methodism: Prospect's Retrospection," *Wordsworth Circle* 47 (Winter 2016): 3–16; Mark A. Noll, "Romanticism and the Hymns of Charles Wesley," *Evangelical Quarterly* 46 (October 1974): 195–223.

18. David Duff and Catherine Jones, eds., *Scotland, Ireland, and the Romantic Aesthetic* (Lewisburg, PA: Bucknell University Press, 2007); Murray Pittock, *Scottish and Irish Romanticism* (New York: Oxford

Robert E. Bonner found antebellum southern intellectuals acting as spokesmen for the master class and pursuing proslavery nationalism, first within and then beyond the United States. Steven Hahn and Enrico Dal Lago cast the conflict as between Americans who urged the growing, centripetal claims of the state and those, often southerners, who remained resistant to those claims. Both sides used the language of nationalism and ethnocentrism to justify their actions.[19] In Europe, conflicts between central statism and localism multiplied in the decades leading up to the American Civil War. Southerners watched and considered the implications for themselves and their defense of slavery.

Two erudite, blockbuster studies made clear elements of *how.* First was Michael O'Brien's transformative 2004 work, *Conjectures of Order.* O'Brien considered how southerners' involvement in modernity continued through multiplying cultural institutions and print vehicles which, in turn, enhanced and extended the search for intellectual order. Second, Elizabeth Fox-Genovese and Eugene D. Genovese launched the Mind of the Master Class series. It drew on over forty years of analysis of the ruling culture of antebellum white southerners. Genovese and Fox-Genovese's examination showed, too, how regional writers deeply engaged contemporary transatlantic intellectual debates.[20]

Yet O'Brien, Genovese, and Fox-Genovese conceived their overlapping sub-

---

University Press, 2008); C. Hugh Holman, "Introduction," in William Gilmore Simms, *Views and Reviews in American Literature, History and Fiction,* ed. C. Hugh Holman (Cambridge: Harvard University Press, 1962), xxiv. On Simms and Scott, see David Moltke-Hansen, "Southern Literary Horizons in Young America: Imaginative Development of a Regional Geography," *Studies in the Literary Imagination* 42 (Summer 2009): 1–31; Moltke-Hansen, "The Library of American Books: *Views and Reviews, First & Second Series* and *The Wigwam and the Cabin,*" in *Reading William Gilmore Simms: Essays of Introduction to the Author's Canon,* ed. Todd Hagstette (Columbia: University of South Carolina Press, 2017), 189–99; Moltke-Hansen, "To Civilize King Cotton's Realm: William Gilmore Simms's Chivalric Quest," in *The Field of Honor: Essays on Southern Character and American Identity,* ed. John Mayfield and Todd Hagstette (Columbia: University of South Carolina Press, 2017), 21–39.

19. Paul Quigley, *Shifting Grounds: Nationalism and the American South, 1848–1865* (New York: Oxford University Press, 2012); Robert E. Bonner, *Mastering America: Southern Slaveholders and the Crisis of American Nationhood* (New York: Cambridge University Press, 2009); Steven Hahn, *A Nation Without Borders: The United States and Its World in an Age of Civil Wars, 1830–1910* (New York: Viking, 2016); Enrico Dal Lago, *Civil War and Agrarian Unrest: The Confederate South and Southern Italy* (New York: Cambridge University Press, 2018).

20. Michael O'Brien, *Conjectures of Order: Intellectual Life and the American South, 1810–1860,* 2 vols. (Chapel Hill: University of North Carolina Press, 2004); Elizabeth Fox-Genovese and Eugene D. Genovese, *The Mind of the Master Class: History and Faith in the Southern Slaveholders' Worldview* (New York: Cambridge University Press, 2005).

jects very differently. O'Brien considered over a hundred of the South's intellectual producers in the half century before the Civil War. He asked how they networked and organized themselves, how they institutionalized their interests, how their output grew and changed, what genres they deployed, where, for what audiences, with what foci, and under what influences. Less interested in intellectual production, Genovese and Fox-Genovese studied the planter class's thought within the contexts of members' educations, readings, and preoccupations. Their first volume—*Mind of the Master Class* (2005)—considered development of the patriarchy's historical and religious views. *Slavery in Black and White* (2008) looked at evolving understandings of the relationship between class and race: this "social question" led planters from the sometimes-reluctant defense of slavery to the assertion of the "peculiar institution" as a positive good. *Fatal Self-Deception* (2011) assessed the metaphor of "our family black and white," including ways in which planters used it as a self-serving, self-deceiving description of their relationships with the enslaved.[21]

O'Brien did not subscribe to Genovese and Fox-Genovese's understanding that southern planters shared a ruling culture and class identity. Nevertheless, he, Genovese, and Fox-Genovese privileged many of the same materials and subjects. They drew deeply from intimate writings—letters and diaries—and closely examined formal, intellectual writings: books, essays, sermons, and speeches. Except for the minutes of debating and literary societies and the records of libraries, however, O'Brien, Genovese, and Fox-Genovese all paid scant attention to transactional records, whether of businesses, governments, institutions, or organizations. Southern newspapers, almanacs, and handbills did not figure significantly, either. Yet most literary criticism and much popular literature, such as Davy Crockett tales examined by Michael A. Lofaro, appeared in these more popular media. Other staples of planters' intellectual concerns and consumption—scientific and agricultural literature—also failed to get much attention despite Lester D. Stephens's recovery of the community of naturalists who made Charleston, South Carolina, the most important center of life sciences in the nineteenth-century South.[22]

21. Fox-Genovese and Genovese, *The Mind of the Master Class;* Fox-Genovese and Genovese, *Slavery in White and Black: Class and Race in the Southern Slaveholders' New World Order* (New York: Cambridge University Press, 2008); Genovese and Fox-Genovese, *Fatal Self-Deception: Slaveholding Paternalism in the Old South* (New York: Cambridge University Press, 2011).

22. Scholars organized numerous forums devoted to the impact of O'Brien's, Genovese's, and Fox-Genovese's scholarship. See Sarah E. Gardner, "Michael O'Brien, Intellectual History, and the History

In short, much of what most antebellum southerners read and said did not get substantially considered by O'Brien, Genovese, or Fox-Genovese. Already changing when *Conjectures of Order* and *Mind of the Master Class* appeared, scholarly attention to ways in which more common literature was indicative of the intellectual life of the early South accelerated in the 2000s and 2010s. Andrea Wulf, David S. Shields, James Everett Kibler Jr., and William Thomas Okie recovered early southern horticultural interests.[23] Beth Barton Schweiger found whites acquiring literacy to keep in touch with loved ones during the Civil War, at the same time agreeing with William Gilmore-Lehne that the war "pitted against each other two of the most literate societies on earth." In *I Remain Yours* (2018), Christopher Hager showed how soldiers and their families used letters to sustain bonds during the war. Janet Duitsman Cornelius, Heather Andrea Williams, and Christopher Hager examined how and what, as well as why, African Americans learned to read in the antebellum South and how they used that knowledge after Emancipation. Manisha Sinha considered how African Americans drove public perceptions and debates through abolitionism and the sectional crisis. Keith Cartwright extended the map and chronology of Senegambian cultural influences in American slavery

---

of the American South," introduction to forum on Michael O'Brien, 10 March 2017, Society for U.S. Intellectual History, https://s-usih.org/2017/03/michael-obrien-intellectual-history-and-the-history-of-the-american-south-introduction-by-sarah-gardner/ (accessed 18 January 2019); Steven M. Stowe, ed., "Michael O'Brien and the Endeavor of Southern Intellectual History: A Forum," introduction to forum on Michael O'Brien, *Georgia Historical Quarterly* 101 (Winter 2017): 320–23; David Moltke-Hansen, "Eugene Dominick Genovese: A Forum," introduction to forum on Eugene D. Genovese, *Georgia Historical Quarterly* 98 (Winter 2014): 341–44; Moltke-Hansen, "The Turn to the South: The Influence of Elizabeth Fox-Genovese's Southern Studies," *Mississippi Quarterly* 65 (Fall 2012): 557–76. On Crockett tales, see Michael A. Lofaro, ed., *Davy Crockett's Riproarious Shemales and Sentimental Sisters: Women's Tall Tales from the Crockett Almanacs (1835–1856)* (Mechanicsburg, PA: Stackpole Books, 2001); Lester D. Stephens, *Science, Race, and Religion in the American South: John Bachman and the Charleston Circle of Naturalists, 1815–1895* (Chapel Hill: University of North Carolina Press, 2000).

23. For an earlier discussion of this limitation, see David Moltke-Hansen, "Intellectual and Cultural History of the Old South," in *A Companion to the American South*, ed. John B. Boles (Malden, MA: Blackwell Publishing, 2002), 212–31. On horticulture, see Andrea Wulf, *Founding Gardeners: The Revolutionary Generation, Nature and the Shaping of the American Nation* (New York: Alfred A. Knopf, 2011); David S. Shields, ed., *Pioneering American Wine: Writings of Nicholas Herbemont, Master Viticulturist* (Athens: University of Georgia Press, 2009); James Everett Kibler Jr., ed., *Taking Root: The Nature Writing of William and Adam Summer of Pomaria* (Columbia: University of South Carolina Press, 2017); William Thomas Okie, *The Georgia Peach: Culture, Agriculture, and Environment in the American South* (New York: Cambridge University Press, 2016).

and beyond. Erskine Clarke explored missionary efforts by white Presbyterians among enslaved antebellum African Americans and Africans.[24]

Scholars of journalism, print culture, and religion, such as Beth Barton Schweiger and Jonathan Daniel Wells, turned increasingly to southern periodicals in search of southern intellectual life. As three-quarters of antebellum newspapers and magazines had religious ties, religion's role in daily intellectual discourse claimed new attention from Randall M. Miller, Harry S. Stout, Kurt O. Berends, and others. Richard J. Carwardine and Mitchell Snay found evangelicalism central to mid-nineteenth-century political judgments. Slavery increasingly divided voters and their religious leaders as white southerners insisted on its biblical sanction. Consequently, Protestant denominations split along sectional and theological lines.[25]

The Old South was not monolithic, however, and historians of the Old Southwest argued that studies built on general comparisons between the North and

24. Beth Barton Schweiger, "The Literate South: Reading before Emancipation," *Journal of the Civil War Era* 3 (September 2013): 331–59, quote at 331; Christopher Hager, *I Remain Yours: Common Lives in Civil War Letters* (Cambridge: Harvard University Press, 2018). On literacy and the Civil War, see Drew Gilpin Faust, "The Civil War Soldier and the Art of Dying," *Journal of Southern History* 67 (February 2001): 3–38. On African American literacy, see Janet Duitsman Cornelius, *"When I Can Read My Title Clear": Literacy, Slavery, and Religion in the Antebellum South* (Columbia: University of South Carolina Press, 1991); Heather Andrea Williams, *Self-Taught: African American Education in Slavery and Freedom* (Chapel Hill: University of North Carolina Press, 2005); Christopher Hager, *Word by Word: Emancipation and the Act of Writing* (Cambridge: Harvard University Press, 2013). On the impact of African American writing and the oral culture behind it, see Manisha Sinha, *The Slave's Cause: A History of Abolition* (New Haven: Yale University Press, 2016); Keith Cartwright, *Reading Africa into American Literature: Epics, Fables, and Gothic Tales* (Lexington: University Press of Kentucky, 2002). On planter missionaries, see Erskine Clarke, *Dwelling Places: A Plantation Epic* (New Haven: Yale University Press, 2005); Clarke, *By the Rivers of Water: A Nineteenth-Century Atlantic Odyssey* (New York: Basic Books, 2013).

25. Beth Barton Schweiger, "Alexander Campbell's Passion for Print: Protestant Sectarians and the Press in the Trans-Alleghany West," *Proceedings of the American Antiquarian Society* 118 (April 2008): 117–54; Jonathan Daniel Wells, *Women Writers and Journalists in the Nineteenth-Century South* (New York: Cambridge University Press, 2011); Richard J. Carwardine, *Evangelicals and Politics in Antebellum America* (New Haven: Yale University Press, 1993); Mitchell Snay, *Gospel of Disunion: Religion and Separatism in the Antebellum South* (New York: Cambridge University Press, 1993); Randall M. Miller, Harry S. Stout, and Charles Reagan Wilson, eds., *Religion and the American Civil War* (New York: Oxford University Press, 1998), specifically Kurt O. Berends, "'Wholesome Reading Purifies and Elevates the Man': The Religious Military Press in the Confederacy," (131–66); Randall M. Miller, "Catholic Religion, Irish Ethnicity, and the Civil War" (261–96); and Harry S. Stout and Christopher Grasso, "Civil War, Religion and Communications: The Case of Richmond" (313–59).

South minimize important differences between emergent subregions and the South Atlantic states. Johanna Nicol Shields found that issues of slavery and freedom looked different to white writers in Alabama than they did to their counterparts in Virginia. John Mayfield insisted that gender, humor, class, and honor functioned differently in the Old Southwest than in the Southeast. Contributors to the collection he coedited with Todd Hagstette, *The Field of Honor* (2017), elaborated on this view. They also agreed on the need to reconsider Bertram Wyatt-Brown's thesis that the antebellum South's honor culture reflected transhistorical values and attitudes found across traditional societies. In confronting change, nineteenth-century southerners harnessed the idea of honor. For example, Timothy J. Williams found that students at the University of North Carolina defined *Intellectual Manhood* (2015) as an honorable pursuit; and Robert Elder contended that southern evangelicals implicitly understood honor culture and faith as value systems that mirrored each other and together molded behavior in the face of a rapidly modernizing world.[26]

The nature of class culture and the role of capitalism in the slave South have continued in dispute. Eugene D. Genovese, Elizabeth Fox-Genovese, Scott P. Marler, John Ashworth, and other, often Marxian-influenced scholars insisted that the South fed the development of industrial capitalism in the North and in Britain but did not experience such development itself. Yet a growing number of scholars also found urban, middle-class values embraced in towns and across professions in the slave South, in part through the same books and magazines as the bourgeoisie read in industrial centers. Historians such as Beth Barton Schweiger, Jonathan Daniel Wells, Johanna Nicol Shields, Jennifer R. Green, and Jennifer L. Goloboy argued that the planter class did not have hegemonic sway but shared power and influence with middle-class folks. That said, Walter Johnson and Edward E. Baptist contended that the growth of slavery and the cotton economy in the Old Southwest not only drew the entire South further into the capitalist

26. Johanna Nicol Shields, *Freedom in a Slave Society: Stories from the Antebellum South* (New York: Cambridge University Press, 2012); John Mayfield, *Counterfeit Gentlemen: Manhood and Humor in the Old South* (Gainesville: University Press of Florida, 2009); Mayfield and Hagstette, eds., *The Field of Honor;* Bertram Wyatt-Brown, *Southern Honor: Ethics and Behavior in the Old South* (New York: Oxford University Press, 1982); Timothy J. Williams, *Intellectual Manhood: University, Self, and Society in the Antebellum South* (Chapel Hill: University of North Carolina Press, 2015); Robert Elder, *The Sacred Mirror: Evangelicalism, Honor, and Identity in the Deep South, 1790–1860* (Chapel Hill: University of North Carolina Press, 2016).

nexus, but made the region a central driver in American capitalist development and exploitative inhumanity.[27]

As the South's communications, transportation, and urban networks expanded, they also enhanced the range and reach of intellectual life, physically linking distant parts of the South for the first time. John F. Kvach noted that the spread of cotton capitalism worried some, such as New Orleans magazinist and economist J. D. B. De Bow, who argued for economic diversification. He joined a swelling chorus of proslavery writers. The role and nature of proslavery thought continued to get historiographical attention. Drew Gilpin Faust detailed *The Ideology of Slavery* (1981) that arose as a critical component of the secessionist mind. John Patrick Daly assessed how evangelicals contributed to the emerging ideology, and Alfred L. Brophy examined southern colleges' and courts' complicity.[28]

Scholars such as William W. Freehling, Stephen Berry, Michael E. Woods, and Lawrence T. McDonnell explored how political ambitions and psychological developments colored thought and galvanized action in the late antebellum era. In *Road to Disunion,* Freehling focused on the outsized influence gained by "fire eaters" in a South where only 50 percent of the people ever supported the Confederacy. Berry considered how understandings of gender roles and affective bonds shaped Confederate men's conceptions of duty and honor. Woods extended the

27. Scott P. Marler, *The Merchants' Capital: New Orleans and the Political Economy of the Nineteenth-Century South* (New York: Cambridge University Press, 2013); John Ashworth, *Slavery, Capitalism, and Politics in the Antebellum Republic.* Vol. 2, *The Coming of the Civil War, 1850–1861* (New York: Cambridge University Press, 2007); Beth Barton Schweiger, *The Gospel Working Up: Progress and the Pulpit in Nineteenth-Century Virginia* (New York: Oxford University Press, 2000); Jonathan Daniel Wells, *The Origins of the Southern Middle Class, 1800–1861* (Chapel Hill: University of North Carolina Press, 2004); Shields, *Freedom in a Slave Society;* Jennifer R. Green, *Military Education and the Emerging Middle Class in the Old South* (New York: Cambridge University Press, 2008); Jennifer L. Goloboy, *Charleston and the Emergence of Middle-Class Culture in the Revolutionary Era* (Athens: University of Georgia Press, 2016); Walter Johnson, *River of Dark Dreams: Slavery and Empire in the Cotton Kingdom* (Cambridge: Harvard University Press, 2013); Edward E. Baptist, *The Half Has Never Been Told: Slavery and the Making of American Capitalism* (New York: Basic Books, 2014).

28. John F. Kvach, *"De Bow's Review": The Antebellum Vision of a New South* (Lexington: University Press of Kentucky, 2013); Drew Gilpin Faust, ed., *The Ideology of Slavery: Proslavery Thought in the Antebellum South, 1830–1860* (Baton Rouge: Louisiana State University Press, 1981); John Patrick Daly, *When Slavery Was Called Freedom: Evangelicalism, Proslavery, and the Causes of the Civil War* (Lexington: University Press of Kentucky, 2002); Alfred L. Brophy, *University, Court, and Slave: Pro-Slavery Thought in Southern Colleges and Courts and the Coming of the Civil War* (New York: Oxford University Press, 2016). See also Andrew L. Slap and Frank Towers, eds., *Confederate Cities: The Urban South during the Civil War Era* (Chicago: University of Chicago Press, 2015).

study of emotions in the interpretation and acceleration of the sectional conflict. McDonnell argued that white clerks and artisans, among volunteer militiamen in 1860 Charleston, sought social security and validation but made a revolution when *Performing Disunion* (2018). Clearly, many future Confederates had been intellectually equipping themselves for secession and civil war for a long time before the crisis of disunion, and they redoubled this work in the late 1850s.[29]

Ian Binnington considered how white southerners imagined the Confederacy before and during the war. Michael T. Bernath's *Confederate Minds* (2010) examined how southerners geared up a national and nationalist publication program: the new nation's capital, Richmond, became the center, but periodicals, text books, and religious works issued from railroad hubs across the Confederacy. David B. Sachsman, David W. Bulla, Patricia G. McNeely, and other historians of journalism examined the impact of newspapers on the war and of the war on the media, focusing in part on individual reporters. Coleman Hutchison closely read instances of the artistic deployment—in music, poetry, and fiction—of Confederate aspirations, allegiance, and loss. Alice Fahs's *The Imagined Civil War* (2001), looked at the production and distribution of popular fiction during the war. Steven M. Stowe's *Keep the Days* (2018) asked how the attitudes and judgments of slaveholding women shaped the recording of the experience and impact of the war in their diaries.[30] Other scholars focused on ways southerners, who resisted or lived outside the Confederacy, thought and fought. Following Freehling's over-

29. William W. Freehling, *The Road to Disunion.* Vol. 2, *Secessionists Triumphant, 1854–1861* (New York: Oxford University Press, 2007); Stephen W. Berry II, *All that Makes a Man: Love and Ambition in the Civil War South* (New York: Oxford University Press, 2003); Michael E. Woods, *Emotional and Sectional Conflict in the Antebellum United States* (New York: Cambridge University Press, 2014); Lawrence T. McDonnell, *Performing Disunion: The Coming of the Civil War in Charleston, South Carolina* (New York: Cambridge University Press, 2018).

30. Ian Binnington, *Confederate Visions: Nationalism, Symbolism, and the Imagined South in the Civil War* (Charlottesville: University of Virginia Press, 2013); Michael T. Bernath, *Confederate Minds: The Struggle for Intellectual Independence in the Civil War South* (Chapel Hill: University of North Carolina Press, 2010); David B. Sachsman, S. Kittrell Rushing, and Roy Morris Jr., eds., *Words at War: The Civil War and American Journalism* (West Lafayette: Purdue University Press, 2008); David W. Bulla and Gregory R. Borchard, *Journalism in the Civil War Era* (New York: Peter Lang, 2010); Patricia G. McNeely, Debra Ridden van Tuyll, and Henry H. Schulte, eds., *Knights of the Quill: Confederate Correspondents and Their Civil War Reporting* (West Lafayette: Purdue University Press, 2010); Coleman Hutchison, *Apples and Ashes: Literature, Nationalism, and the Confederate States of America* (Athens: University of Georgia Press, 2012); Alice Fahs, *The Imagined Civil War: Popular Literature of the North and South, 1861–1865* (Chapel Hill: University of North Carolina Press, 2001); Steven M. Stowe, *Keep the Days: Reading the Civil War Diaries of Southern Women* (Chapel Hill: University of North Carolina Press, 2018). See also Coleman

view of *The South vs. the South* (2001), Victoria E. Bynum considered southern dissenters from North Carolina to Texas during the war. In *Mothers of Invention* (1996), Drew Gilpin Faust concluded that elite southern women understood their roles and identities differently in Confederate defeat than did men. In particular, they grappled with the consequences of the failure of men to protect them.[31]

Reconstruction opened possibilities for the expansion of African American intellectual production and activity. Steven Hahn argued that African American communities, often centered on plantations and in churches, drove black politics and extended informational and literacy networks. In *Claiming the Union* (2014), Susanna Michele Lee examined how black and white men who remained loyal to the Union asserted and defined citizenship. In *Rebuilding Zion* (1998), Daniel W. Stowell assessed the postbellum recovery of white Protestant denominations and the emergence of black churches as well as the roles of northern evangelicals across the South. According to Luke E. Harlow, after the war white Protestant religious leaders in Kentucky helped align their state with the former Confederacy because of concerns over social order and racial hierarchy. Charles Reagan Wilson contended that the region's white civic culture became infused with former Confederates' commitment to the validation of their sacrifices and their redemption through service to the men and myths representing their Lost Cause.[32]

Rather than as a civil religion, Gaines M. Foster's *Ghosts of the Confederacy* (1987) presented the Lost Cause as an evolving tradition used by white southerners to maintain their honor while reintegrating themselves into the United States, resisting Reconstruction, and reestablishing social hierarchy. David W. Blight contended that, after the war, northerners and southerners selected memories to

---

Hutchison, ed., *A History of American Civil War Literature* (New York: Cambridge University Press, 2015); Timothy Sweet, ed., *Literary Cultures of the Civil War* (Athens: University of Georgia Press, 2016).

31. William W. Freehling, *The South vs. the South: How Anti-Confederate Southerners Shaped the Course of the Civil War* (New York: Oxford University Press, 2001); Victoria E. Bynum, *The Long Shadow of the Civil War: Southern Dissent and Its Legacies* (Chapel Hill: University of North Carolina Press, 2010); Drew Gilpin Faust, *Mothers of Invention: Women of the Slaveholding South in the American Civil War* (Chapel Hill: University of North Carolina Press, 1996).

32. Steven Hahn, *A Nation under Our Feet: Black Political Struggles in the Rural South from Slavery to the Great Migration* (Cambridge: Harvard University Press, 2003); Susanna Michele Lee, *Claiming the Union: Citizenship in the Post–Civil War South* (New York: Cambridge University Press, 2014); Daniel W. Stowell, *Rebuilding Zion: The Religious Reconstruction of the South, 1863–1877* (New York: Oxford University Press, 1998); Luke E. Harlow, *Religion, Race, and the Making of Confederate Kentucky, 1830–1880* (New York: Cambridge University Press, 2014); Charles Reagan Wilson, *Baptized in Blood: The Religion of the Lost Cause, 1865–1920* (Athens: University of Georgia Press, 1980).

promote national reunion and curtail the political and civil rights of formerly enslaved people. In *Remembering the Civil War* (2013), however, Caroline E. Janney argued that former Confederates sought to assert and honor their memories, not share a reconciliation narrative. In *Blood and Irony* (2004), Sarah E. Gardner considered how southern white women used writing not only to make sense of their experiences in the war and after defeat but also to craft and defend the Confederacy's postbellum claims on them and their society. David Moltke-Hansen contended that Confederate children learned to honor their elders in the war's wake, not only for what some had done but because they were white and continued to defend white women, children, and power. The historic preoccupation with whiteness spawned a subfield of whiteness studies.[33]

Many scholars accepted that defeat cast the South into a cultural wasteland. In the twenty-first century, however, historians began to question the assumption. Brook Thomas's *The Literature of Reconstruction* (2016) persuasively demonstrated ways in which southern authors addressed the central concerns of Reconstruction, including federalism, westward expansion, citizenship, and political violence. Often those concerns centered on race. Edlie L. Wong complicated the black-white binary by exposing the "Afro-Asian analogy." In the war's aftermath, she argued, "the U.S. began to define the meaning of post-emancipation freedoms," not only in relation to free white labor but against "colonial Cuba, where experiments with Chinese labor appeared closely connected to and possibly co-constitutive of—black chattel slavery." And in 2018, Robert J. Cook, along with Ethan J. Kytle and Blain Roberts, demonstrated that the neo-Confederate memory industry was contested as soon as it began. Cook, for example, identified four distinct narrative strands that shaped the ways in which Americans

33. Gaines M. Foster, *Ghosts of the Confederacy: Defeat, the Lost Cause, and the Emergence of the New South, 1865–1913* (New York: Oxford University Press, 1987); David W. Blight, *Race and Reunion: The Civil War in American Memory* (Cambridge: Harvard University Press, 2001); Caroline E. Janney, *Burying the Dead but Not the Past: Ladies' Memorial Associations and the Lost Cause* (Chapel Hill: University of North Carolina Press, 2008); Janney, *Remembering the Civil War: Reunion and the Limits of Reconciliation* (Chapel Hill: University of North Carolina Press, 2013); Barton A. Myers, *Rebels against the Confederacy: North Carolina's Unionists* (New York: Cambridge University Press, 2014); Sarah E. Gardner, *Blood and Irony: Southern White Women's Narratives of the Civil War, 1861–1937* (Chapel Hill: University of North Carolina Press, 2004). A good appraisal of whiteness studies into the twenty-first century is Peter Kolchin, "Whiteness Studies: The New History of Race in America," *Journal of American History* 89 (June 2002): 154–73. See also David Moltke-Hansen, "Honoring Confederate Defeat the Georgia Way," *Georgia Historical Quarterly* 101 (Spring 2017): 1–23.

remembered the Civil War. In a sprawling account that spans 150 years, Kytle and Roberts documented the emergence of a rival memory of slavery that threatened the sanitized version put forward by the sons and daughters of Confederates.[34]

Scholars of African American print culture enlivened the discussion of intellectual life in the postwar South as well. John Ernest's perceptive work on William Wells Brown's 1867 *The Negro in the American Rebellion* and Eric Gardner's masterful *Black Print Unbound* (2015) helped to reshape the scholarly contours of Reconstruction historiography.[35] Indeed, sustained attention to print culture, the literary marketplace, and the history of the book has increasingly shaped Civil War and Reconstruction-era historiography in the twenty-first century.[36] Despite such impressive works, though, much of the intellectual history of Reconstruction in the South remains unwritten.

For a long time, historians portrayed the South at the end of the nineteenth century as similarly intellectually barren. C. Vann Woodward argued in 1951 that "sterility and imitation were the marks of the culture" in the post–Civil War South. That assumption, too, came under challenge by twenty-first-century scholars taking a more sophisticated approach to cultural production. In *Upon Provincialism* (2011), Bill Hardwig argued that tourist literature, travelogues, and especially local-color fiction about the South revealed as much about readers' desires and national magazine editors' predilections for authenticity as it did about the southern mind. The need to "know the South" in the last three decades of the nineteenth century drove publishers "to forward specific versions of the region and specific notions of 'authentic authorship' that generally depended

34. Brook Thomas, *The Literature of Reconstruction: Not in Plain Black and White* (Baltimore: Johns Hopkins University Press, 2017); Edlie L. Wong, *Racial Reconstruction: Black Inclusion, Chinese Exclusion, and the Fictions of Citizenship* (New York: New York University Press, 2015), 18; Robert J. Cook, *Civil War Memories: Contesting the Past in the United States since 1865* (Baltimore: Johns Hopkins University Press, 2017); Ethan J. Kytle and Blain Roberts, *Denmark Vesey's Garden: Slavery and Memory in the Cradle of the Confederacy* (New York: New Press, 2018).

35. John Ernest, "*The Negro in the American Rebellion:* William Wells Brown and the Design of African American History," in Sweet, ed., *Literary Cultures,* 57–76; Eric Gardner, *Black Print Unbound: "The Christian Recorder," African American Literature, and Periodical Culture* (New York: Oxford University Press, 2015). See also Wong, *Racial Reconstruction;* Coleman Hutchison, "Book History," in *Keywords for Southern Studies,* ed. Scott Romine and Jennifer Rae Greeson (Athens: University of Georgia Press, 2016), 239–49; K. Stephen Prince, *Stories of the South: Race and the Reconstruction of Southern Identity, 1865–1915* (Chapel Hill: University of North Carolina Press, 2014).

36. See "Reenvisioning Reconstruction," *American Literary History* 30 (Fall 2018): 403–651.

on the foreignness of the material and authors."[37] To be sure, southern authors responded to market demands. As Hardwig and K. Stephen Prince suggested, however, transactions between writer and publisher were hardly that simple or imitative. The debut of southern literary reviews such as the *Sewanee Review* (1892) and the *South Atlantic Quarterly* (1901), along with the founding of state historical journals such as the *Virginia Magazine of History and Biography* (1893) and the *Georgia Historical Quarterly* (1917), further belied the claim of intellectual sterility. The journals were not yet academically rigorous and had a bent toward elite family history and antiquarianism, but nevertheless they fostered the sharing and analysis of historical records and assessments.[38]

Other writers, previously ignored by scholars, began to receive historiographical attention as well. According to biographer Finnie D. Coleman, Sutton E. Griggs, the Texas-born son of a former slave, produced much but reached few, in part because his writings diverged from the programs espoused by the leaders of Harlem's New Negro movement. Even so, Griggs's works became popular at the time of their publications: *Imperium in Imperio* (1899), his well-known novel about a separate and independent African American state in Texas, and *The Hindered Hand* (1905), a response to Thomas Dixon Jr.'s *The Leopard's Spots* (1902).[39]

Still, historical reevaluations of late nineteenth-century southern literary culture remain vexed. David Moltke-Hansen made clear the popularity of New South booster Henry Grady's Atlanta *Constitution,* Populist Thomas E. Watson's *Tom Watson Magazine,* and the postwar writings of Millie Rutherford, proud member of the United Daughters of the Confederacy.[40] As Kathryn B. McKee ex-

37. C. Vann Woodward, *Origins of the New South, 1877–1913* (Baton Rouge: Louisiana State University Press, 1951), 429; Bill Hardwig, *Upon Provincialism: Southern Literature and National Periodical Culture, 1870–1900* (Charlottesville: University of Virginia Press, 2013), 3.

38. Hardwig, *Upon Provincialism;* Prince, *Stories of the South.* On the founding of state historical journals, see Randall M. Miller, "The Birth (and Life) of a Journal: A 100-Year Retrospective of the *Virginia Magazine of History and Biography,*" *Virginia Magazine of History and Biography* 100 (April 1992): 143–72; Sarah E. Gardner, "'History in the Making': The Early Years of the *Georgia Historical Quarterly,*" *Georgia Historical Quarterly* 101 (Summer 2017): 102–13.

39. Finnie D. Coleman, *Sutton E. Griggs and the Struggle Against White Supremacy* (Knoxville: University of Tennessee Press, 2007). See also John Cullen Gruesser, *The Empire Abroad and the Empire at Home: African American Literature and the Era of Overseas Expansion* (Athens: University of Georgia Press, 2012); Maria Karafilis, "Oratory, Embodiment, and US Citizenship in Sutton E. Griggs's *Imperium in Imperio,*" *African American Review* 40 (Spring 2006): 125–43; Caroline Levander, "Sutton Griggs and the Borderlands of Empire," *American Literary History* 22 (Spring 2010): 57–84.

40. Moltke-Hansen, "Honoring Confederate Defeat the Georgia Way," 1–23.

plained in her 2019 study of Sherwood Bonner, a return to such literature "brings its own hesitations," for it risks "elevating voices we have done well to not hear and giving them space in a critical discussion improved by their absence." McKee argued, however, that in the end, the literature of white supremacy needs to be interrogated: it "forces a reexamination of racist ideology as it was being built."[41]

Just as abolitionist crusaders of the antebellum era had highlighted the South's distinctiveness from the rest of the nation, so too did Progressives of the late nineteenth century insistently cast the South as out of step with a modernizing America. In 1917 journalist H. L. Mencken famously and derisively characterized the South as "The Sahara of the Bozart." Natalie J. Ring demonstrated that long before Mencken launched his salvo, "an array of institutions and people, including northern philanthropists, federal officials, social scientists, national journalists, progressive reformers, clergymen, and academicians, helped fashion an image of the South as a regional, national, and even global problem." Anticipating New Deal reformers and social critics by as much as half a century, this pioneering group of Progressive reformers drew attention to the South's distinctive poverty and backwardness, in essence defining "the Problem South."[42]

Competing discourses to the "Problem South" existed, of course. Henry Grady's New South Creed, for example, worked against an image of a benighted South by touting the possibility of southern industrial development and racial harmony. So, too, did the literature of sectional reconciliation, which muted the call for racial justice in favor of national harmony. Although Ring saw the emergence of these two competing narratives as paradoxical, they are perhaps more appropriately seen as two sides of the same coin. Tara McPherson's term "lenticular logic" applies here: one strain of discourse cannot exist without the other. The "Problem South" coexisted with the "Reconciled South," even if the two could not be seen clearly at the same time.[43]

Certainly, those who promulgated the image of the "Problem South" suggested that political and cultural reunion alone could not bring the region back

41. Kathryn B. McKee, *Reading Reconstruction: Sherwood Bonner and the Literature of the Post–Civil War South* (Baton Rouge: Louisiana State University Press, 2019), 9.

42. H. L. Mencken, "The Sahara of the Bozart," *New York Evening Mail,* 13 November 1917; Natalie J. Ring, *The Problem South: Region, Empire, and the New Liberal State, 1880–1930* (Athens: University of Georgia Press, 2012), 3–4. See also William A. Link, *The Paradox of Southern Progressivism, 1880–1930* (Chapel Hill: University of North Carolina Press, 1992).

43. Tara McPherson, *Reconstructing Dixie: Race, Gender, and Nostalgia in the Imagined South* (Durham: Duke University Press, 2003).

into the American fold. The scope of southern economic, racial, and social problems demanded national involvement and, perforce, the power of the modern liberal state to intervene in southern problems, especially those that contributed to continued rural poverty and disease. In addition, northern philanthropic organizations had an array of causes to choose from: literacy campaigns, antilynching efforts, and health improvements, to name but a few.

Liberal southerners participated in these conversations, and their voices became particularly pronounced during the Great Depression when some, such as New Orleans writer Lyle Saxon and North Carolina publisher William T. Couch, worked for the Works Progress Administration. As director of the University of North Carolina Press, Couch left a particularly heavy imprint with the titles he published, many of which countered perceptions of a materially, intellectually, and spiritually impoverished region.[44] Howard W. Odum, one of Couch's authors, had perhaps the greatest reach, especially with his magnum opus, *Southern Regions of the United States* (1936), a sociological study that responded to national criticisms of the region.[45]

Working against efforts to portray the region as progressive were the horrors of Jim Crow, reported to the world through media coverage of public lynchings. Amy Louise Wood's *Lynching and Spectacle* (2009) and Donald G. Mathews's *At the Altar of Lynching* (2017) noted ways in which white evangelical Protestantism was put in service of lynching's defense, or worse, its imperative.[46] For Wood especially, lynching relied on a number of modern cultural forms, including photography and cinema. Similarly, in *Chained in Silence* (2015), Talitha L. LeFlouria argued that the emergence of black female convict labor in the New South spoke not of continuity with enslaved labor but rather of the rise of modernized business practices. Convict labor was not, in other words, "slavery by another name." By the turn of the twentieth century, Wood and LeFlouria suggested, southern racial violence took on a distinctly modern form.[47]

44. Sarah E. Gardner, *Reviewing the South: The Literary Marketplace and the Southern Renaissance, 1920–1941* (New York: Cambridge University Press, 2017).

45. Howard W. Odum, *Southern Regions of the United States* (Chapel Hill: University of North Carolina Press, 1936); Daniel Joseph Singal, *The War Within: From Victorian to Modernist Thought in the South, 1919–1945* (Chapel Hill: University of North Carolina Press, 1982).

46. Amy Louise Wood, *Lynching and Spectacle: Witnessing Racial Violence in America, 1890–1940* (Chapel Hill: University of North Carolina Press, 2009); Donald G. Mathews, *At the Altar of Lynching: Burning Sam Hose in the American South* (New York: Cambridge University Press, 2017).

47. Talitha L. LeFlouria, *Chained in Silence: Black Women and Convict Labor in the New South* (Chapel Hill: University of North Carolina Press, 2015). See also Douglas A. Blackmon, *Slavery by Another Name:*

Modernity intruded into the South in other ways, not all of them horrific. Louis A. Ferleger and John D. Metz examined how farmers used innovation and investment in Georgia's post-Reconstruction Cotton Belt. David A. Davis argued that World War I precipitated the emergence of southern literary modernism, evinced by writers such as William Faulkner, Zora Neale Hurston, John Crowe Ransom, Elizabeth Madox Roberts, Allen Tate, Jean Toomer, Richard Wright, and others. The war, Davis explained, forced southerners "into contact with more modernized cultures outside the South," while altering the southern economy and challenging gender and racial hierarchies. In the postwar period, southern writers turned to modernist literary techniques to depict southern society, developing a more critical perspective on the region.[48]

Modern did not mean less exotic in the eyes of the nation, as John Shelton Reed suggested in *Dixie Bohemia* (2012), his study of 1920s New Orleans.[49] Moreover, the problems identified in the late nineteenth century persisted, despite the efforts of reformers, bohemians, and literary modernists. Onset of the Great Depression exacerbated what modernizers abhorred most—Jim Crow injustice, racial violence, and systemic poverty with all its attendant ills. The South, so the reasoning went, threatened the nation's survival as capitalist institutions approached collapse and, then, as war clouds gathered overseas.

Scholars found ongoing debates about the intellectual underpinnings of both early twentieth-century problems and their solutions to be fertile ground for understanding the southern mind. *Reassessing the 1930s South* (2018), a collection of essays edited by Karen L. Cox and Sarah E. Gardner, highlighted ways in which cultural critics and scholars pushed back against popular notions of the region as intellectually, morally, and physically stunted, or as romantic and sentimentalized, untouched by national economic woes and out of touch with modernization. Contributors Douglas E. Thompson and Ted Atkinson, for example, each surveyed southerners' positive responses to technological advancement and efforts at modernization. Steven Knepper and Scott L. Matthews chronicled

---

The Re-enslavement of Black Americans from the Civil War to World War II (New York: Doubleday, 2008); David M. Oshinsky, *"Worse than Slavery": Parchman Farm and the Ordeal of Jim Crow Justice* (New York: Free Press, 1996).

48. Louis A. Ferleger and John D. Metz, *Cultivating Success in the South: Farm Households in the Postbellum Era* (New York: Cambridge University Press, 2014); David A. Davis, *World War I and Southern Modernism* (Jackson: University Press of Mississippi, 2018), 4.

49. John Shelton Reed, *Dixie Bohemia: A French Quarter Circle in the 1920s* (Baton Rouge: Louisiana State University Press, 2012).

ways in which southerners, African American and white, countered prevailing myths that glorified the Old South as well as alarmist reports that highlighted the region's economic distress. Emily Senefeld and Robert Hunt Ferguson pointed to strains of radicalism and interracialism often overlooked in discussions of the Depression-era South. And Anthony J. Stanonis, Robert W. Haynes, and Lisa Dorrill examined how drama and federally sponsored public art entered national discussions about the South's place in the nation.[50]

Even as many southerners sought to rescue their region's reputation, other southerners countered its racial violence. In *Set the World on Fire* (2018), Keisha N. Blain studied the networks forged by black nationalist and internationalist women in the Mississippi Delta, Chicago, Harlem, Jamaica, and Great Britain. She revealed how "black nationalist women maintained a global racial consciousness to universal emancipation."[51] Some forms of black resistance proved more circumspect. The Scott newspaper syndicate, which began in 1928 with a four-page weekly, grew into a massive chain based out of Atlanta that, at its peak, had more than 240 affiliated newspapers. Thomas Aiello charted the outsized role the Scott syndicate played in reaching southern African American readers in the decades before the civil rights movement accelerated. The newspapers gave audiences an alternative to northern urban publications, such as *The Crisis, Opportunity,* and *The Chicago Defender.* As Aiello concluded, the Scott newspaper syndicate acted out of two intertwined missions: informing readers and keeping them safe from white violence.[52]

World War II, not the Great Depression, changed ways in which leading intellectuals discussed the South's putative outsider status. Easy assumptions about the region's exceptionalism that fueled so much intellectual and political discourse in the century's early decades seemed no longer warranted. A 1943 editorial by sociologist Howard W. Odum and journalist Virginius Dabney in

50. Karen L. Cox and Sarah E. Gardner, eds., *Reassessing the 1930s South* (Baton Rouge: Louisiana State University Press, 2018).

51. Keisha N. Blain, *Set the World on Fire: Black Nationalist Women and the Global Struggle for Freedom* (Philadelphia: University of Pennsylvania Press, 2018), 8.

52. Thomas Aiello, *The Grapevine of the Black South: The Scott Newspaper Syndicate in the Generation Before the Civil Rights Movement* (Athens: University of Georgia Press, 2018), 3. See also John Egerton, *Speak Now Against the Day: The Generation Before the Civil Rights Movement in the South* (Chapel Hill: University of North Carolina Press, 1995); Tomiko-Brown Nagin, *Courage to Dissent: Atlanta and the Long History of the Civil Rights Movement* (New York: Oxford University Press, 2011).

The Saturday Review of Literature drove home the point that everyone had a part to play in the nation's wartime effort. They hoped the war would mark a turning point for the South and how the rest of the nation viewed the region, and that the "southern question" had been answered.[53]

Not all of the South's spokespeople welcomed the kinds of changes encouraged by Odum and Dabney. In one of the more provocative works on Jim Crow modernism to emerge in the last two decades, Anders Walker's *The Burning House* (2018) engaged a wide range of southern writers, black and white, who questioned the desirability of "liberal, integrationist efforts at reform." Walker, who offered close readings of texts by midcentury authors such as William Faulkner, Flannery O'Connor, Eudora Welty, Harper Lee, Richard Wright, Zora Neale Hurston, and Robert Penn Warren, as well as those who earned their reputations half a generation later, including Alice Walker, demonstrated how southern intellectuals "invoked the values of diversity and pluralism to critique integration." As Anders Walker made clear, such pluralistic views also tolerated inequality. For many of the subjects of his study, including Justice Lewis F. Powell Jr., that was a tradeoff worth making.[54]

In some ways, the flurry of reminiscences by the likes of William Alexander Percy, Hodding Carter, Ralph McGill, Ben Robertson, John Temple Graves, and Harry S. Ashmore that appeared at midcentury offered a similar critique. At the very least, each, to greater or lesser degrees, lamented Dixie's demise, marked most notably by the threats to southern-style segregation.[55] The authors might have framed their works differently, but they nonetheless articulated a worldview that, in Walker's terms, extolled "two cultures—one white and one black—each with its own institutions, traditions, even identities."[56]

Robert H. Brinkmeyer Jr. suggested in *The Fourth Ghost* (2009) that World War II loomed large in southerners' imaginations in other ways. He focused on how southern writers, including Lilian Smith and W. J. Cash, grappled with the

53. Virginius Dabney and Howard W. Odum, "The Upper Old South: An Editorial," *Saturday Review of Literature* 26 (23 January 1943): 3. See also Gardner, *Reviewing the South,* 12, 197.

54. Anders Walker, *The Burning House: Jim Crow and the Making of Modern America* (New Haven: Yale University Press, 2018), 4–5, 179. See also Joseph Crespino, *Atticus Finch: The Biography* (New York: Basic Books, 2018).

55. Gardner, *Reviewing the South,* 300–303.

56. Walker, *The Burning House,* 4.

all-too-apparent connections between authoritarianism in Nazi Germany and the racial politics of the American South, a point further developed by Nina Silber in *This War Ain't Over* (2018).[57]

But the "southern question" that seemed to be answered by the South's participation in World War II resurfaced less than a decade later with the advent of the modern civil rights movement, precipitated by a rethinking of southern institutions and mores in the midst of the Cold War. Borrowing from Derrick Bell's interest convergence theory, which argued that whites support civil rights initiatives only if they see a political or material benefit for themselves, Mary L. Dudziak explained how civil rights became part of the United States' Cold War policy. She opened *Cold War Civil Rights* (2000) by recounting the story of Jimmy Williams, who in 1957 had been sentenced to death in Alabama for stealing less than two dollars. The case garnered the kind of international attention that worried the State Department. "How could American democracy be a beacon during the Cold War, and a model for those struggling against Soviet oppression, if the United States practiced brutal discrimination within its own borders?" Dudziak asked.[58] The answer rested with both substantive and illusory reform. The Little Rock Nine, for example, compelled the federal government to protect the rights of African Americans for the first time since Reconstruction.

One of the more salutary trends in the intellectual historiography of the civil rights movement has been the acknowledgement that ordinary people—activists and foot-soldiers of the movement—led intellectual lives. In *Civil Rights and the Idea of Freedom* (1992), Richard H. King argued that rank-and-file participants defined concepts such as citizenship, rights, equality, and freedom. Since King, scores of biographies of freedom fighters such as Fannie Lou Hamer, Robert F. Williams, Fred Shuttlesworth, Anne Braden, and Ella Baker reoriented conventional thinking about who counted as an intellectual.[59]

57. Robert H. Brinkmeyer Jr., *The Fourth Ghost: White Southern Writers and European Fascism, 1930–1950* (Baton Rouge: Louisiana State University Press, 2009); Nina Silber, *This War Ain't Over: Fighting the Civil War in New Deal America* (Chapel Hill: University of North Carolina Press, 2018).

58. Mary L. Dudziak, *Cold War Civil Rights: Race and the Image of American Democracy* (Princeton: Princeton University Press, 2000), 3.

59. Richard H. King, *Civil Rights and the Idea of Freedom* (New York: Oxford University Press, 1992); Chana Kai Lee, *For Freedom's Sake: The Life of Fannie Lou Hamer* (Urbana: University of Illinois Press, 1999); Timothy B. Tyson, *Radio Free Dixie: Robert F. Williams and the Roots of Black Power* (Chapel Hill: University of North Carolina Press, 1999); Andrew M. Manis, *A Fire You Can't Put Out: The Civil Rights Life of Birmingham's Reverend Fred Shuttlesworth* (Tuscaloosa: University of Alabama Press, 1999);

Since 2014, the African American Intellectual History Society (AAIHS) has been at the forefront of redefining what it means to do intellectual history. Especially important in the scholarship that emerges from AAIHS has been the insistence that ideas cannot be contained by geographic boundaries. They roam freely, as Keisha N. Blain's book on black nationalist and international women demonstrates. And because much of the work in African American intellectual history centers on engagement with ideas—and not merely on formal thought—the scholarship promises to animate new lines of inquiry in related subfields.[60]

The backlash against the civil rights movement prompted scholars to challenge the notion of southern exceptionalism. Dan T. Carter and Joseph Crespino, for example, noted ways in which southern racism and conservatism transformed national politics, giving new life to the Republican Party in the decades following the 1965 Voting Rights Act. Katherine Rye Jewell examined how big business in the South transformed American conservatism, starting in the 1950s.[61] The South did not join the national fold, as many midcentury commentators had hoped, but instead the nation became more "southern," abandoning the Great Society and embracing not only social and racial conservatism but, increasingly, a defiant strain of nationalism.

In the last quarter of the twentieth century, perhaps for that reason, the South found increased purchase in the national imagination. Zachary J. Lechner posited that, after the 1960s, the white South became in the national mind, not a land of problems as it had been at the turn of the twentieth century, but rather a bulwark against social upheaval. Lechner pointed to cultural producers, including filmmakers, journalists, and musicians, who offered an image of the South as timeless, rooted, and tradition-bound.[62] If Lechner looked for the South in the national mind, others continued to focus on the South as a "geographical entity." The

---

Catherine Fosl, *Subversive Southerner: Anne Braden and the Struggle for Racial Justice in the Cold War South* (New York: Palgrave Macmillan, 2002); Barbara Ransby, *Ella Baker and the Black Freedom Movement: A Radical Democratic Vision* (Chapel Hill: University of North Carolina Press, 2003).

60. African American Intellectual History Society, https://www.aaihs.org/ (accessed 18 January 2019).

61. Dan T. Carter, *The Politics of Rage: George Wallace, the Origins of the New Conservatism, and the Transformation of American Politics* (New York: Simon & Schuster, 1995); Joseph Crespino, *In Search of Another Country: Mississippi and the Conservative Counterrevolution* (Princeton: Princeton University Press, 2007); Katherine Rye Jewell, *Dollars for Dixie: Business and the Transformation of Conservatism* (New York: Cambridge University Press, 2017).

62. Zachary J. Lechner, *The South of the Mind: American Imaginings of White Southernness, 1960–1980* (Athens: University of Georgia Press, 2018).

Encyclopedia of Southern Culture, edited by Charles Reagan Wilson and William Ferris (1989), defined the South in cultural terms: "'The South' is found wherever southern culture is found," they wrote, "and that culture is located not only in the Deep South, the Upper South, and the border cities, but also . . . among black Mississippians who migrated to south Chicago, among white Appalachians and black Alabamians who migrated to Detroit, and among former Okies and Arkies who settled around Bakersfield, California." Wilson and Ferris saw the South as a historical fact while acknowledging how regional consciousness and mythologies shaped ideas about the region. They hoped their work would foster interdisciplinary conversations about the American South.[63]

Four years later, historian Harry L. Watson and sociologist John Shelton Reed founded the journal *Southern Cultures.* As the journal's name suggested, a lot had happened in the intervening years. Perhaps too much for some; the journal's name was hotly contested. As Reed recalled, "I'd been assuming that the journal would be called *Southern Culture,*" based on his conviction that "there is such a thing, albeit with racial, social-class, and subregional variations." The journal's original publisher, Duke University Press, insisted (and Watson concurred), that it should be called *Southern Cultures.* "I thought this was a chickenshit concession to fashionable multiculturalism," Reed admitted, "But I was outvoted, and conceded with an ill grace." The journal's editors agreed to adopt an expansive understanding of the South's geographical and metaphysical boundaries. As the journal's website explains: "From Faulkner in Bulgaria to Lebanese in Mississippi, and from teaching *Gone with the Wind* in Vietnam to the international avant-garde at Black Mountain, we recognize that no border can contain our complex region."[64]

In a 2001 essay launching the New Southern Studies series at the University of Georgia Press, Houston A. Baker and Dana Nelson appealed to Malcolm X's summation that Mississippi "is anywhere in the United States south of the Canadian border." The New Southern studies emerged out of an effort to investigate "regions, national formations, speculations, intuitions, and assertions" that either tacitly or explicitly informed scholarly inquiry about the region. But at the heart of the project was the question, "Whose 'South' is it that appears in so many discourses?"[65]

63. Charles Reagan Wilson and William Ferris, eds., *Encyclopedia of Southern Culture* (Chapel Hill: University of North Carolina Press, 1989), xv–xvi, xxii.

64. "About," Southern Cultures, http://www.southerncultures.org/about/ (accessed 18 January 2019).

65. Baker and Nelson, "Preface: Violence, the Body, and the 'South,'" 231–32. See also Patricia Yaeger, *Dirt and Desire: Reconstructing Southern Women's Writing, 1930–1990* (Chicago: University of Chicago

Such an expansive and critical view of "southern" diluted the idea of "the South," and by the early twenty-first century, a growing number of scholars questioned whether there was a South at all. Jon Smith, a prominent figure in New Southern studies, noted the pushback from Americanists and southernists who, he implied, held vested interests in clinging tightly to older, more definitive notions of region and nation. In other words, southernists put up a fight because they did not believe southern history or literary studies could exist in the absence of "the South."[66]

A robust body of literature arose in the early twenty-first century that tackled the questions originally asked by Baker and Nelson, and posed new ones. These works put the South in conversation with other parts of the nation and the world. Historians and literary scholars weighed in on the prospects for this new scholarship. Brian Ward's 2014 forum in the *Journal of American Studies,* "What's New in Southern Studies—And Why Should We Care?" highlighted transnational and interdisciplinary approaches that reflected broader trends in the academy.[67] In this sense, New Southern studies became capacious: scrutinizing the region's past, present, and future.[68] Still, at its heart, New Southern studies interrogates the assumption that a geographical region known as "the South" ever existed. In

---

Press, 1996); Anne Goodwyn Jones and Susan Donaldson, eds., *Haunted Bodies: Gender and Southern Texts* (Charlottesville: University Press of Virginia, 1997); Richard Gray, *Southern Aberrations: Writers of the American South and the Problems of Regionalism* (Baton Rouge: Louisiana State University Press, 2000).

66. Jon Smith, "What the New Southern Studies Does Now," *Journal of American Studies* 49 (November 2015): 861–70. See also Smith's fuller treatment, *Finding Purple America.*

67. Ward, ed., "Forum: What's New in Southern Studies—And Why Should We Care?" See also James L. Peacock, Harry L. Watson, and Carrie W. Matthews, eds., *The American South in a Global World* (Chapel Hill: University of North Carolina Press, 2005); Jon Smith and Deborah Cohn, eds., *Look Away! The U.S. South in New World Studies* (Durham: Duke University Press, 2004); Matthew Pratt Guterl, *American Mediterranean: American Slaveholders in the Age of Emancipation* (Cambridge: Harvard University Press, 2008); John T. Matthews, "Recalling the West Indies: From Yoknapatawpha to Haiti and Back," *American Literary History* 16 (Summer 2004): 238–62; Keith Cartwright, *Sacral Grooves, Limbo Gateways: Travels in Deep South Time, Circum-Caribbean Space, Afro-Creole Authority* (Athens: University of Georgia Press, 2013); Katherine Renee Henninger, "How New? What Place? Southern Studies and the Rest of the World," *Contemporary Literature* 45 (Spring 2004): 177–85; Harilaos Stecopoulos, *Reconstructing the World: Southern Fictions and U.S. Imperialism, 1898–1976* (Ithaca: Cornell University Press, 2008); Philip Joseph, *American Literary Regionalism in a Global Age* (Baton Rouge: Louisiana State University Press, 2007).

68. See Riché Richardson, *Black Masculinity and the U.S. South: From Uncle Tom to Gangsta* (Athens: University of Georgia Press, 2007); Jennifer Rae Greeson, *Our South: Geographic Fantasy and the Rise of National Literature* (Cambridge: Harvard University Press, 2010).

The Real South (2008), Scott Romine argued that reality mattered less than perception. Communities decide what is "real" to fit their needs and desires.[69] The South, then, is not a place or even an idea, but a feeling about what a place needs to be.

The South remains a locus of intellectual historical interest, but why? The region's white culture has lost its putative hegemonic command. After fifty years of out-migration, in-migration grew tremendously, not only from the North but also from around the globe. Ideas and orientations flooded in, too. The old verities no longer held. In fact, they never conveyed truth, just the power of those who embraced them. And the process of rethinking southern intellectual history began anew.

69. Scott Romine, *The Real South: Southern Narrative in the Age of Cultural Reproduction* (Baton Rouge: Louisiana State University Press, 2008).

CONTRIBUTORS

Mikaëla M. Adams is associate professor of Native American history at the University of Mississippi. Her first book, *Who Belongs? Race, Resources, and Tribal Citizenship in the Native South* (2016), explores Indigenous identity, citizenship, and sovereignty in the Jim Crow South. Her current project examines the influenza pandemic of 1918–1920 in Indian country. She has published articles in the *Florida Historical Quarterly* and the *South Carolina Historical Magazine.*

Bruce E. Baker is Reader in American history at Newcastle University. He authored *What Reconstruction Meant: Historical Memory in the American South* (2007) and *This Mob Will Surely Take My Life: Lynchings in the Carolinas, 1871–1947* (2008); coauthored *The Cotton Kings: Capitalism and Corruption in Turn-of-the-Century New York and New Orleans* (2015); and coedited *After Slavery: Race, Labor and Citizenship in the Reconstruction South* (2013) and *Remembering Reconstruction: Struggles Over the Meaning of America's Most Turbulent Era* (2017). He coedited *American Nineteenth Century History* from 2010 to 2018.

Edward E. Baptist is professor of history at Cornell University. He is the author of *Creating an Old South: Middle Florida's Plantation Frontier before the Civil War* (2002), *New Studies in the History of American Slavery* (coedited with Stephanie M. H. Camp, 2005), *American Capitalism* (with Louis Hyman, 2014), and *The Half Has Never Been Told: Slavery and the Making of American Capitalism* (2014).

Stephen Berry is the Gregory Professor of the Civil War Era at the University of Georgia, where he teaches courses on life and death in the long nineteenth century. Berry is the author or editor of six books on the Civil War Era, including *House of Abraham: Lincoln and the Todds, A Family Divided by War* (2007) and *Weirding the War: Tales from the Civil War's Ragged Edges* (2011). He is codirector, with Claudio Saunt, of the Center for Virtual History, and coeditor, with Amy Murrell Taylor, of the UnCivil Wars series at University of Georgia Press.

Katherine Mellen Charron is associate professor of history at North Carolina State University, specializing in African American, southern, and women's history. She earned her BA in literature from UNC–Asheville, her MA in Afro-American studies from UW–Madison, and her PhD in history from Yale University. She is the author of the award-winning *Freedom's Teacher: The Life of Septima Clark* (2009) and coeditor of William Henry Singleton's *Recollections of My Slavery Days* (1999).

Catherine Clinton is the Denman Professor of American History at the University of Texas at San Antonio and professor emerita at Queen's University Belfast. A past president of the Southern Historical Association, Clinton has authored or edited over two dozen books, including *The Plantation Mistress: Woman's World in the Old South* (1982), *Harriet Tubman: The Road to Freedom* (2004), and *Stepdaughters of History: Southern Women and the American Civil War* (2016). She is spearheading the Cassandra Project, a nonprofit dedicated to combating sexual harassment within history departments and organizations.

Don H. Doyle is McCausland Professor of History Emeritus at the University of South Carolina. His works include *The Cause of All Nations: An International History of the American Civil War* (2014), *Nations Divided: America, Italy, and the Southern Question* (2002), *American Civil Wars: The United States, Latin America, Europe and the Crisis of the 1860s* (2017), *Secession as an International Phenomenon* (2010), *Nationalism in the New World* (coedited with Marco Pamplona, 2006).

Alejandra Dubcovsky is associate professor of history at the University of California, Riverside. She is the inaugural fellow for the Huntington Library–UCR Program for the Advancement of the Humanities. Her first book, *Informed Power: Communication in the Early American South* (2016), won the 2016 Michael V. R. Thomason Book Award from the Gulf South Historical Association. Her work has been featured in several journals, including *Ethnohistory,* the *William and Mary Quarterly,* the *Journal of Southern History, Native South,* and *Early American Studies.*

Elaine S. Frantz is professor of history at Kent State University. She is the author of *Ku-Klux: The Birth of the Klan in the Reconstruction Era* (2016) and *Manhood Lost: Drunken Men and Redeeming Women in the Nineteenth Century United States* (2002). She has published articles in the *Journal of American History, Journal of Southern History,* and *Journal of Social History.*

Craig Thompson Friend is professor of history and public history at North Carolina State University. He authored *Kentucke's Frontiers* (2010) and *Along the Maysville Road: The Early American Republic in the Trans-Appalachian West* (2005), coedited *Death and the American South* (2015) and *Southern Manhood: Perspectives on Masculinity in the Old South* (2004) with Lorri Glover, coedited *Family Values in the Old South* (2010) with Anya Jabour, and edited *Southern Masculinity: Perspectives on Manhood in the South since Reconstruction* (2009) and *The Buzzel about Kentuck: Settling the Promised Land* (1999).

Sarah E. Gardner is Distinguished University Professor of History at Mercer University, Macon, Georgia, where she teaches courses on the Civil War era and on the intellectual and cultural history of nineteenth-century America. She is the author of *Blood and Irony: Southern White Women's Narratives of the Civil War, 1861–1937* (2004) and of *Reviewing the South: The Literary Marketplace and the Southern Renaissance, 1920–1941* (2017).

John M. Giggie is associate professor of history and African American studies at the University of Alabama, where he serves as director of the Summersell Center for the Study of the South and as a Distinguished Teaching Fellow. He published *After Redemption: Jim Crow and the Transformation of African American Religion in the Delta, 1875–1917* (2008), coedited *Faith in the Market: Religion and the Rise of Commercial Culture* (2002), edited two documentary readers, and coauthored a college history textbook.

Lorri Glover is the John Francis Bannon Chair in the Department of History at Saint Louis University. Her works include *Southern Sons: Becoming Men in the New Nation* (2007), *The Shipwreck that Saved Jamestown* (2008), coauthored with Daniel Blake Smith, *Founders as Fathers: The Private Lives and Politics of the American Revolutionaries* (2015), and *The Fate of the Revolution: Virginians De-*

bate the Constitution (2016). She and Craig Thompson Friend coedited *Southern Manhood: Perspectives on Masculinity in the Old South* (2004) and *Death and the American South* (2014).

Lesley J. Gordon is the Charles G. Summersell Chair of Southern History at the University of Alabama. Her publications include *General George E. Pickett in Life and Legend* (1998), *Inside the Confederate Nation: Essays in Honor of Emory M. Thomas* (2005), and *A Broken Regiment: The 16th Connecticut's Civil War* (2014). From 2010 to 2015, Gordon was editor of the academic journal *Civil War History.*

Sally Hadden is professor of history at Western Michigan University. Her publications include *Slave Patrols* (2001), *Signposts: New Directions in Southern Legal History* (coedited with Patricia Minter, 2013), *A Companion to American Legal History* (coedited with Alfred Brophy, 2013), and *Traveling the Beaten Trail* (coauthored with Paul Pruitt and David Durham, 2013). Her work has also appeared in the *North Carolina Law Review,* the *Law and History Review,* and the *Cambridge History of Law in America.*

Claudrena N. Harold is professor of history and African American and African studies at the University of Virginia. She has published two monographs: *The Rise and Fall of the Garvey Movement in the Urban South, 1918–1942* and *New Negro Politics in the Jim Crow South,* and coedited two volumes, *The Punitive Turn: New Approaches to Race and Incarceration* (2013) and *Charlottesville 2017: The Legacy of Race and Inequity* (2018).

Paul Harvey is professor of history and Presidential Teaching Scholar at the University of Colorado. He is the author of *Christianity and Race in the American South: A History* (2016), and other books.

Vanessa M. Holden is assistant professor of history and of African American and Africana studies at the University of Kentucky. Her work focuses on the roles that African American women and children, free and enslaved, played in the Southampton Rebellion (Nat Turner's Rebellion). Her work also explores their roles in the enslaved communities' strategies for resistance and survival. Holden is cofounder and co-organizer of the Queering Slavery Working Group (QSWG) with Jessica M. Johnson.

Cherisse Jones-Branch is professor of history and the James and Wanda Lee Vaughn Endowed Professor of History at Arkansas State University–Jonesboro. A graduate of the College of Charleston, she received her PhD in history from Ohio State University. She has authored numerous articles on women's Civil Rights activism and *Crossing the Line: Women and Interracial Activism in South Carolina during and after World War II* (2014) and coedited *Arkansas Women: Their Lives and Times* (2018).

Blair L M Kelley is associate professor of African American history and assistant dean for Interdisciplinary Studies and International Programs in the College of Humanities and Social Sciences at North Carolina State University. She received her BA from the University of Virginia in History and African and African American studies and PhD in History from Duke University. Kelley's book, *Right to Ride: Streetcar Boycotts and African American Citizenship in the Era of Plessy v. Ferguson* (2010), was awarded the Letitia Woods Brown Memorial Prize by the Association of Black Women Historians.

John Majewski is the Michael Douglas Dean of Humanities and Fine Arts and professor of history at the University of California, Santa Barbara. He holds a PhD in history from UCLA, an MA in economic history from the London School of Economics, and a BA in economics from University of Texas, Austin. His research interests focus on the political economy of the nineteenth-century United States. His latest book is *Modernizing a Slave Economy: The Economic Vision of the Confederate Nation* (2009), and he has authored numerous articles and book chapters.

Marko Maunula is professor of history at Clayton State University. He holds a PhD in history from the University of North Carolina at Chapel Hill. His first book, *Guten Tag, Y'All: Globalization and the South Carolina Piedmont, 1950–2000* (2010), focused on southern campaigns to recruit foreign corporations and the ensuing economic and social transformations. In addition, he has published several book reviews, articles, and book chapters about the southern economy and culture in the twentieth century.

Noeleen McIlvenna is professor of history at Wright State University. Her books, *A Very Mutinous People* (2009) and *The Short Life of Free Georgia* (2015), examine poor white southerners who lived through the transition from a labor force of indentured servants to one based on enslavement of Africans. She argued that these colonists understood the world from a perspective of class hierarchy rather than race. Many opposed the shift forced by a few planters in North Carolina and Georgia. She is completing a book on radicals in the seventeenth-century Chesapeake.

David Moltke-Hansen developed collections and programs at the South Carolina Historical Society, the University of North Carolina's Southern Historical Collection and Center for the Study of the American South, and the Historical Society of Pennsylvania before turning to full-time writing and editing. Author of fifty-plus essays and editor of nine volumes, primarily on aspects of southern intellectual and cultural history, he directed the launch of the William Gilmore Simms Initiatives, and the dozens of related publications, at the University of South Carolina, and cofounded Cambridge Studies on the American South.

Kathryn Newfont is associate professor of history at the University of Kentucky and author of *Blue Ridge Commons: Environmental Activism and Forest History in Western North Carolina* (2012), which won the Appalachian Studies Association's Weatherford Award and the Thomas Wolfe Memorial Literary Award. She coedited with Debbie Lee *The Land Speaks: Voices at the Intersection of Oral and Environmental History* (2017). She has held fellowships from the National Endowment for the Humanities and the Mellon Foundation.

William Thomas Okie is associate professor of history and history education at Kennesaw State University and the associate editor of the journal *Agricultural History*. He is the author of *The Georgia Peach: Culture, Agriculture, and Environment in the American South* (2016). His work has won prizes from the Society of American Historians, the Southern Historical Association, the Agricultural History Society, and the Georgia Historical Society.

Peter S. Onuf is Thomas Jefferson Foundation Professor of History Emeritus at the University of Virginia and the author of numerous books, including, with Annette Gordon-Reed, *"Most Blessed of the Patriarchs": Thomas Jefferson and the Empire of the Imagination* (2016). He received his PhD from Johns Hopkins

University, where he studied with Jack P. Greene, and taught at Columbia and Southern Methodist Universities and University College, Dublin, before arriving at Virginia. An elected member of the American Academy of Arts and Sciences, Onuf lives in Portland and Winter Harbor, Maine.

Ted Ownby is William Winter Professor of History and Southern Studies at the University of Mississippi. He authored *Subduing Satan: Religion, Recreation, and Manhood in the Rural South, 1865–1920* (1990), *American Dreams in Mississippi: Consumers, Poverty, and Culture, 1830–1998* (1999), and *Hurtin' Words: Debating Family Problems in the Twentieth-Century South* (2018). His edited works include *The Mississippi Encyclopedia* (2017), with Charles Reagan Wilson, and *The Larder: Methods in Southern Foodways Research* (2013), with John T. Edge and Elizabeth Engelhardt.

Theda Perdue is Atlanta Distinguished Professor Emerita at the University of North Carolina, Chapel Hill, and has published fourteen books, including *Cherokee Women: Gender and Culture Change* (1998), *"Mixed Blood" Indians: Racial Construction in the Early South* (2003), and *Race and the Atlanta Cotton States Exposition of 1895* (2010). She has held fellowships from the Rockefeller Foundation, Newberry Library, National Humanities Center, Wilson Center, and John Simon Guggenheim Foundation. Perdue has served as president of the Southern Association for Women Historians, the American Society for Ethnohistory, and the Southern Historical Association.

Jennifer Ritterhouse is professor of history at George Mason University. She is the author of *Discovering the South: One Man's Travels through a Changing America in the 1930s* (2017) and *Growing Up Jim Crow: How Black and White Southern Children Learned Race* (2006). She edited a reprint edition of Sarah Patton Boyle's autobiography, *The Desegregated Heart: A Virginian's Stand in Time of Transition* (2001) and was one of several coeditors of *Remembering Jim Crow: African Americans Tell About Life in the Segregated South* (2001).

Blain Roberts is professor of history at California State University, Fresno. She is the author of the award-winning *Pageants, Parlors, and Pretty Women: Race and Beauty in the Twentieth-Century South* (2014) and the coauthor of *Denmark*

Vesey's Garden: Slavery and Memory in the Cradle of the Confederacy (2018). Her work has appeared in the *Journal of Southern History, Southern Cultures,* the *New York Times,* and the *Atlantic.*

Justin Roberts is associate professor in the Department of History at Dalhousie University. He is a specialist in slavery and the Atlantic World. His first book, *Slavery and the Enlightenment in the British Atlantic, 1750–1807* (2013), explored plantation slavery in Barbados, Jamaica, and Virginia. His shorter works address aspects of seventeenth- and eighteenth-century plantation slavery and Caribbean history and he has published these in a variety of places, including the *William and Mary Quarterly, Slavery & Abolition* and *Historical Geography.*

Megan Taylor Shockley is a former professor of history at Clemson University and the author of *Creating a Progressive Commonwealth: Women Activists, Feminism, and the Politics of Social Change in Virginia, 1970s–2000s* (2018), *The Captain's Widow of Sandwich: Self-Invention and the Life of Hannah Rebecca Burgess, 1836–1917* (2010), and *"We, Too, Are Americans": African American Women in Detroit and Richmond, 1940–1954* (2003), and the coauthor of *Changing History: Virginia Women Through Four Centuries* (2013).

Christina Snyder is the McCabe Greer Professor of History at Penn State University. She is an historian of colonialism, race, and slavery, with a focus on North America from the pre-contact era through the nineteenth century. Her books include *Great Crossings: Indians, Settlers, and Slaves in the Age of Jackson* (2017) and *Slavery in Indian Country: The Changing Face of Captivity in Early America* (2010). Among Snyder's accolades are the Francis Parkman Prize, the James H. Broussard Prize, and the John C. Ewers Award.

Brian Steele is associate professor of history at the University of Alabama at Birmingham. His book *Thomas Jefferson and American Nationhood* (2012) was a finalist for the George Washington Book Prize. His recent essays have appeared in the *Journal of American Studies, Amerikastudien,* and *Variaciones Borges.*

Daniel H. Usner is the Holland N. McTyeire Professor of History at Vanderbilt University. His publications include *Indians, Settlers, and Slaves in a Frontier Exchange Economy: The Lower Mississippi Valley before 1783* (1992), *American Indians* *in the Lower Mississippi Valley: Social and Economic Histories* (1998), *Indian Work: Language and Livelihood in American History* (2009), *Weaving Alliances with Other Women: Chitimacha Indian Work in the New South* (2015), and *American Indians in Early New Orleans: From Calumet to Raquette* (2018).

Jason Morgan Ward is professor of history at Emory University. He is the author of *Hanging Bridge: Racial Violence and America's Civil Rights Century* (2016) and *Defending White Democracy: The Making of a Segregationist Movement and the Remaking of Racial Politics, 1936–1965* (2011). His work has appeared in the *Journal of Southern History, Journal of Civil and Human Rights, Agricultural History,* and several edited collections.

Harry L. Watson is Atlanta Distinguished Professor in Southern Culture at the University of North Carolina, Chapel Hill. He directed the UNC Center for the Study of the American South from 1999 to 2012. Watson has published seven books, including *Liberty and Power: The Politics of Jacksonian America* (1990) and *Andrew Jackson vs. Henry Clay: Democracy and Development in Antebellum America* (1997). A revised edition of *Liberty and Power* appeared in 2006. With Marcie Cohen Ferris, he edits *Southern Cultures.* His latest work is *Building the American Republic: A Narrative History to 1877* (2018).

Emily West is professor of American history at the University of Reading in the UK. She is the author of *Chains of Love: Slave Couples in Antebellum South Carolina* (2004), *Family or Freedom: The Expulsion and Enslavement of Free People of Color in the Antebellum South* (2012), and *Enslaved Women in America* (2014). She has published in journals including *Slavery & Abolition,* the *Journal of Southern History,* and the *Women's History Review.*

Charles L. Zelden is professor of history and political science at Nova Southeastern University. His publications include *Justice Lies in the District: The U.S. District Court for the Southern District of Texas* (1993), *Voting Rights on Trial* (2002), *The Battle for the Black Ballot* (2004), *Bush v. Gore: Exposing the Hidden Crisis in American Democracy* (2008), *The Supreme Court and Elections* (2009), and *Thurgood Marshall: Race, Rights, and the Struggle for a More Perfect Union* (2013).

INDEX